Bibliography of
International Law

Bibliography of International Law

INGRID DELUPIS

née Detter

D.Phil.(Oxon.), J.D.(Stockholm), Acting Professor of International Law in the University of Stockholm; formerly Talbot Research Fellow of Lady Margaret Hall, Oxford

**BOWKER
LONDON & NEW YORK**

Copyright © 1975 Bowker Publishing Company Ltd.,
Epping, Essex

ISBN 0 85935 004 5

L C Catalog Number 75-7920

All rights reserved. No part of this publication may be reproduced or transmitted in any form or by any means, electronic or mechanical, including photocopy, recording or any information storage retrieval system, without permission in writing from the publisher.

Published in the United Kingdom by the Bowker Publishing Company, and in the United States of America by R.R.Bowker, Inc., New York.

Printed and bound in Great Britain by
Redwood Burn Limited
Trowbridge & Esher

Preface

A vast number of books and articles have been published in many languages on the subject of international law. I have compiled this bibliography to provide a guide to this material for students and teachers of the subject, for practitioners and government advisers, and for those engaged in research.

The material has been classified under 14 main headings, with works that relate to the whole field of international law in Section 1. Each main section is further subdivided with ever-increasing specificity. This detailed classification has been adopted to enable a user to locate the works relevant to a particular problem as rapidly as possible. The contents list provides a full guide to the classification and should always be consulted first. Where it would be useful, cross-references are given in a section to closely related sections where a user may find relevant material. Having consulted a section that deals specifically with the topic under consideration, a user should also look at more general sections in order to find works that will set the specific matter in the context of a more general treatment.

Users who wish to find the works of a particular author should consult the author index at the end.

Important sections usually begin with an introduction in which I have set the topic in its context in the complex framework of international law. I have also mentioned in these introductions which works in each section may be considered to be particularly important, either because they are widely respected 'standard' treatises or because they present one viewpoint in the continuing controversies that are a feature of many areas of the dynamic and evolving subject of international law. In some cases a writer may present a view which diverges from the majority opinion and attracts criticism. However, the originality of such views contributes to the spectrum of international law and I have sometimes felt it useful to point out the attention that controversial opinions have attracted.

In order to keep the bibliography to manageable proportions (both for the user and the compiler) a careful selection has been made from the available material. In choosing works for inclusion I have concentrated on those published in book form and I have sought to include most books published up to 1974 and a few even more recent. In many cases, however, the most useful or even the only available material is in journals and so I have included a considerable number of journal articles.

Because of the dynamic nature of the study of international law I have felt it reasonable to exclude most work published before 1920. Earlier work that has been included falls under three main headings: (1) the 'classics' of international law like those listed in Section 2.1; (2) those 'semi-classics', mostly written at the turn of the century, that have had a profound and continuing influence on modern thought on their topics; (3) works on particularly important cases, treaties or incidents.

Some topics in international law have received a disproportionate amount of attention and for those I have chosen only the leading works.

The language of a work has not influenced its choice for inclusion. There is naturally a predominance of English, French and German in the bibliography because a great many international lawyers have written in those languages. However, there are also many works in Spanish, Italian, Portuguese, Russian and the Scandinavian languages. East European and South American scholarship has not been neglected.

Since this bibliography is intended primarily as a guide to the literature for those whose work involves questions of international law, I have normally given only brief information necessary to locate an item in a library catalogue, though for recently published books I have given the name of the publisher also. However, because it is likely that librarians and other nonspecialists will consult the bibliography I have given information in a little more detail than lawyers will normally need. For example, initials of authors are given or, when they can be ascertained from title pages, full forenames. I have also departed from the style of abbreviation customarily used for legal periodicals. The system adopted here is in accordance with the Anglo-American standard on abbreviations of periodical titles. Users who are familiar with the periodicals cited will, I hope, be able to recognize them from the abbreviations used here but I have also included, in Section 1.6, a full list of periodical titles and abbreviations.

It is my hope and ambition that this bibliography will not merely be a guide to those who teach and study international law but will inspire scholars to fill in the gaps indicated by sections on topical problems that have comparatively few entries.

London, April 1975

Contents

1 GENERAL MATERIAL   1

  1.1 Documents of International Organizations   1
  1.2 Bibliographies on International Law   2
  1.3 Festschrifte   4
  1.4 Cases   4
      1.4.1 General   5
      1.4.2 Cases and Materials   6
      1.4.3 Cases Before Specific Courts   8
            1.4.3.1 Permanent Court of International Justice (PCIJ)   8
            1.4.3.2 International Court of Justice (ICJ)   8
            1.4.3.3 PCIJ and ICJ Unofficial Reports   9
            1.4.3.4 Cases Relating to European Human Rights   10
            1.4.3.5 Cases Before the Court of the European Communities   10
            1.4.3.6 Cases Before Courts of Arbitration   11
  1.5 Collections of Treaties   12
      1.5.1 General   12
      1.5.2 Treaties and Other Source Material of Historical Interest   13

	1.5.3	National Collection of Treaties	15
		1.5.3.1 Great Britain	15
		1.5.3.2 France	15
		1.5.3.3 Germany	16
		1.5.3.4 Italy	16
		1.5.3.5 United States	16
		1.5.3.6 USSR	17
		1.5.3.7 Concordats	17
		1.5.3.8 Other Treaties	17
	1.5.4	Treaties and Texts	18
	1.5.5	Texts and Constitutions of International Organizations	19
1.6	Periodicals		19
1.7	Handbooks, Dictionaries and Encyclopedias		24
1.8	General Textbooks, Manuals and Courses		25

2 NATURE AND ORIGIN OF INTERNATIONAL LAW   49

2.1	The Classics	49
2.2	History of International Law	51
2.3	The Nature of International Law	54
2.4	Jus Cogens	57
2.5	Relationship between International Law and Sociology	59
2.6	Relationship between International Law and Social Sciences	59
2.7	Relationship between International Law and Politics	59
2.8	Dynamic Nature of International Law	60

3 THE RELATIONSHIP BETWEEN INTERNATIONAL AND MUNICIPAL LAW   62

3.1	Regional Approach to International Law		62
	3.1.1	Attitudes of Groups of States or of Different Continents	63
	3.1.2	Europe in General	63

	3.1.3	Different European Countries	63
	3.1.4	USSR and other Socialist States	64
	3.1.5	North America	65
	3.1.6	Canada	65
	3.1.7	Pan America	65
	3.1.8	Asia in General	65
	3.1.9	China	66
	3.1.10	Africa	66
3.2	Relationship and conformity of Constitutions with International Law		66
3.3	The Relationship between International Law and Internal Law		67
	3.3.1	Dualism and Monism	67
	3.3.2	Relationship between International Law and Specific Countries	74
		3.3.2.1 International Law and Several Countries or Groups of Countries	74
		3.3.2.2 Great Britain	75
		3.3.2.3 France	76
		3.3.2.4 Germany and the Reich	76
		3.3.2.5 Netherlands	77
		3.3.2.6 Italy	77
		3.3.2.7 Switzerland	78
		3.3.2.8 Austria	78
		3.3.2.9 Norway	78
		Sweden (see 3.1.1)	79
		3.3.2.10 Greece	79
		3.3.2.11 Spain	79
		3.3.2.12 USSR	79
		3.3.2.13 Yugoslavia	80
		3.3.2.14 Australia	80
		3.3.2.15 Canada	80
		3.3.2.16 United States	80
		3.3.2.17 Latin America	81
		3.3.2.18 India	81
		3.3.2.19 Japan	81

4	CODIFICATION OF INTERNATIONAL LAW		82
5	SOURCES OF INTERNATIONAL LAW		91
	5.1 History of the Sources of International Law		91
	5.2 Sources in General		91
	5.3 Custom and Customary Law		93
	5.4 Treaties		95
	5.5 General Principles		96
	5.5.1 Identification of General Principles		96
	5.5.2 General Principles as Applied in Case Law		98
	5.5.3 Equity		99
	5.6 Unilateral Acts		100
	5.6.1 General		100
	5.6.2 Traditional Unilateral Acts		101
	5.6.2.1 Notification		101
	5.6.2.2 Promise		102
	5.6.2.3 Protest		102
	5.6.2.4 Renunciation		102
	5.6.2.5 Acquiescence		102
	5.6.3 Acts of International Organizations		103
	5.7 Gaps or Lacunas in International Law		103
6	SUBJECTS OF INTERNATIONAL LAW		105
	6.1 Personality		106
	6.2 Subjects in General		106
	6.3 States		107
	6.4 Subjects other than States		107
	6.4.1 International Organizations		107
	6.4.2 Order of Malta		107
	6.4.3 Individuals		107
	6.5 Widening Range of Subjects		109
7	STATES AND SOVEREIGNTY		110

7.1	Sovereignty		110
	7.1.1	Self-Determination	112
	7.1.2	Independence	112
	7.1.3	Equality	112
7.2	Statehood and Characteristics of a State		113
7.3	Rights and Duties of States		114
7.4	Types of States		114
	7.4.1	British Commonwealth	114
	7.4.2	Divided States	115
	7.4.3	Condominia	115
	7.4.4	Dependent States	115
	7.4.5	Protectorates	115
	7.4.6	Holy See	115
	7.4.7	Microstates	116
	7.4.8	Arabian Gulf States	116
	7.4.9	Internationalized Territories	117
7.5	Identity, Continuity and Succession of States		117
	7.5.1	Identity and Continuity in General	117
	7.5.2	Cessation of States	118
	7.5.3	State Succession	118
		7.5.3.1 General	119
		7.5.3.2 Effect of State Succession on Certain Obligations	120
		7.5.3.3 Succession and Nationality	122
	7.5.4	Formation, Extinction and Identity of Particular States	122
	7.5.5	New and/or Developing States	126
	7.5.6	Decolonization	128
	7.5.7	Recognition	129
7.6	Territory of States		135
	7.6.1	Legal Nature	135
	7.6.2	Neighbourhood Relations between States	135
	7.6.3	Boundaries of States	135

	7.6.4	Particular Frontiers	136
	7.6.5	Acquisition of Territory	137
	7.6.6	Loss of Title to Territory	137
	7.6.7	Arctic and Antarctic Territories	138
	7.6.8	Disputed Territories	138
	7.6.9	Servitudes	139
	7.6.10	Right of Transit of Landlocked States	139
7.7.	International Communications		140
7.8	Law of the Sea		140
	7.8.1	General	141
	7.8.2	Territorial Waters	147
		7.8.2.1 Innocent Passages and Freedom of Navigation	151
		7.8.2.2 Hot Pursuit	151
	7.8.3	Contiguous Zone	152
	7.8.4	Special 'Zones'	152
	7.8.5	Submerged Marine Areas	156
		7.8.5.1 General	156
		7.8.5.2 Submarine Boundaries	156
		7.8.5.3 Continental Shelf	157
		7.8.5.4 Seabed and Ocean Floor	159
	7.8.6	The High Seas	160
		7.8.6.1 General	160
		7.8.6.2 Resources of the Sea and the Oceans	161
	7.8.7	International Waterways	163
		7.8.7.1 Rivers and Drainage Basins	163
		7.8.7.2 Interoceanic Canals	165
		7.8.7.3 International Straits	166
		7.8.7.4 Bays and Gulfs	166
		7.8.7.5 Ports and Harbours	167
		7.8.7.6 Lakes	167
7.9	The Law of the Airspace		167
	7.9.1	The Right to Fly	168

7.9.2	Sovereignty and the Extent of National Airspace	168
7.9.3	Air Law and Transport	170
7.9.4	Space Law	171
7.9.5	Satellites	182
	7.9.5.1 General	182
	7.9.5.2 Telecommunications by Satellites	183
7.9.6	Planets	185
7.10	Immunity from Jurisdiction	185
7.10.1	Immunity of States	186
	7.10.1.1 Immunity in General	186
	7.10.1.2 Immunity for State Trading Activities	189
	7.10.1.3 Immunity of Exile Governments	190
7.10.2	Immunity of Diplomats	190
7.10.3	Immunity of Consuls	196
7.10.4	Immunity of Foreign Forces	196
7.10.5	Other Immunity	200
7.11	Law of Diplomats and Consuls	200
7.11.1	Diplomats	201
	7.11.1.1 History	201
	7.11.1.2 Functions of Diplomats and Protection of Nationals	201
	7.11.1.3 Extra-Territorial Asylum	204
	7.11.1.4 Immunity of Diplomats	205
7.11.2	Consuls	
	7.11.2.1 Functions in General	205
	7.11.2.2 Immunity of Consuls	205
7.12	Human Rights	206
7.12.1	History	206
7.12.2	Human Rights in General	207
7.12.3	Special Human Rights and Particular Violations of Such Rights	216

7.12.4	Rights of Minorities	218
7.12.5	Human Rights in Particular Countries	221
7.12.6	Universal and Regional Approach to Human Rights	224
7.12.7	Conventions on Human Rights in General	225
7.12.8	Human Rights and the United Nations	226
	7.12.8.1 General	226
	7.12.8.2 The Universal Declaration on Human Rights	228
	7.12.8.3 The United Nations Covenants	230
	7.12.8.4 The United Nations Convention Against Racial Discrimination	231
7.12.9	The Red Cross Conventions	231
7.12.10	Human Rights and Europe	231
	7.12.10.1 European Human Rights in General	231
	7.12.10.2 Human Rights and the European Community	232
	7.12.10.3 The European Convention on Human Rights	233
	7.12.10.4 Human Rights and the Committee of Ministers of the Council of Europe	238
	7.12.10.5 European Commission on Human Rights	239
	7.12.10.6 European Court for Human Rights	240
7.12.11	Inter-American Commission on Human Rights	243
7.12.12	Human Rights and the International Labour Organization	244

	7.12.13	Treatment of Aliens	244
	7.12.14	Nationality	247
	7.12.15	Passports	249
	7.12.16	Protection of Nationals	249
	7.12.17	Statelessness	250
	7.12.18	Refugees	251
	7.12.19	Asylum	256
	7.12.20	Extradition	260
7.13	Law of Treaties		261
	7.13.1	Law of Treaties: History	262
	7.13.2	Law of Treaties in General	263
	7.13.3	Definition of Treaties	264
	7.13.4	Classification of Treaties	265
	7.13.5	Nature and Function of Treaties	265
		7.13.5.1 General	265
		7.13.5.2 Character of Multilateral Treaties	266
		7.13.5.3 Law-Making Treaties	267
		7.13.5.4 Right of Participation in Collective Treaties	267
		7.13.5.5 Regional Treaties	268
		7.13.5.6 Agreements in Simplified Form	268
		7.13.5.7 Agreements with Other than States	269
		7.13.5.8 Agreements with Private-Law Subjects and State Contracts	269
		7.13.5.9 Concordats	269
	7.13.6	The Time of Creation of Legal Bonds	270
	7.13.7	The Binding Character of Treaties and the Rule Pacta Sunt Servanda	270
	7.13.8	Conclusion of Treaties	
		7.13.8.1 Conclusion of Treaties and Treaty-Making Power in General	272

7.13.8.2	Colonial Clauses	275
7.13.8.3	Federal States and Treaties	275
7.13.8.4	Conclusion of Treaties and the Practice of Particular Countries	276

7.13.8.4.1	Gt. Britain	276
7.13.8.4.2	France	277
7.13.8.4.3	Germany	277
7.13.8.4.3	Belgium	279
7.13.8.4.5	Italy	279
7.13.8.4.6	Netherlands	279
7.13.8.4.7	Switzerland	280
7.13.8.4.8	Sweden	281
7.13.8.4.9	Denmark	281
7.13.8.4.10	USSR	281
7.13.8.4.11	Luxembourg	281
7.13.8.4.12	Greece	282
7.13.8.4.13	Israel	282
7.13.8.4.14	United States	282
7.13.8.4.15	Australia	284
7.13.8.4.16	Canada	284
7.13.8.4.17	Brazil	285
7.13.8.4.18	India & Pakistan	285
7.13.8.4.19	Japan	285
7.13.8.4.20	Vietnam	286

7.13.8.5	Ratification	286
7.13.8.6	Registration of Treaties	289
7.13.8.7	Depositaries of Treaties	291
7.13.9	Effect of Treaties	292
7.13.9.1	Reservations to Treaties	292
7.13.9.2	Interpretation of Treaties	296
7.13.9.2.1	General	296

    7.13.9.2.2 Interpretation
     of Multilingual Texts 297
    7.13.9.2.3 Interpretation
     of Constitutions of
     Organizations 298
    7.13.9.2.4 Other
     Special Questions 298
    7.13.9.2.5 Methods of
     Interpretation 299
    7.13.9.2.6 Role of the
     Preamble 300
    7.13.9.2.7 Role of Travaux
     Preparatoires 301
    7.13.9.2.8 Interpretation
     by Courts in General 301
    7.13.9.2.9 Interpretation
     by PCIJ 301
    7.13.9.2.10 Interpretation
     by ICJ 302
    7.13.9.2.11 Interpretation
     by National Courts 303
    7.13.9.2.12 Interpretation
     by Courts of Arbitra-
     tion 304
    7.13.9.2.13 Interpretation
     by Administrative
     Tribunals 305
    7.13.9.2.14 Interpretation
     by the Court of the 305
     European Communities
 7.13.10 Modification of Treaties 305
   7.13.10.2 Revision of treaties 305
   7.13.10.3 Termination of Treaties 308
   7.13.10.4 Fundamental Changes and
    Clausula Rebus Sic
    Stantibus 310
 7.13.11 Validity of Treaties 312

7.13.11.1	Validity in General	312
7.13.11.2	Breach of Treaties	314
7.13.11.3	Treaties and Coersion	314
7.13.11.4	Unequal Treaties	315
7.13.12	The Effect of War on Treaties	316
7.13.13	Transformation of Treaties into Internal Law	319
7.13.13.1	Transformation in General	319
7.13.13.2	Effect of Treaties in the Municipal Sphere and the question of Hierarchy of Norms	320
7.13.13.3	Self-Executing Treaties	326
7.13.13.4	Compatibility of Treaties with Constitutions	327
7.13.13.5	Compatibility with Other Treaties	328
7.13.14	Treaties and Third Parties	328
7.13.14.1	General	328
7.13.14.2	Most-Favoured-Nation Clauses	330

8 SETTLEMENT OF DISPUTES AND INTERNATIONAL TRIBUNALS 334

8.1	Settlement of Disputes in General	334
8.2	Conciliation	334
8.3	Negotiation	335
8.4	Good Offices	335
8.5	Mediation	335
8.6	Commission of Inquiry	336
8.7	International Adjudication in General	336
8.8	Arbitration and its Procedure	338
8.9	International Tribunals in General: Law and Procedure	341

8.9.1	Special Procedural Aspects and Mechanisms of Litigation	342
8.9.2	Non-Liquet	342
8.9.3	Plea of Domestic Jurisdiction	343
8.9.4	Exhaustion of Local Remedies	343
8.9.5	Interim Measures	344
8.9.6	Judgments ex aequo et bono	344
8.9.7	Forum Prorogatum	346
8.9.8	Excess of Power by Courts	346
8.9.9	Execution of Judgments	346
8.9.10	Courts and Individuals: Rights of Petition	347
8.10	Permanent Court of International Justice (PCIJ)	348
8.10.1	General	348
8.10.2	Advisory Jurisdiction of the PCIJ	350
8.10.3	Optional Clause of the PCIJ	351
8.11	International Court of Justice (ICJ)	351
8.11.1	General	351
8.11.2	Justiciable and non-Justiciable disputes	358
8.11.3	Election of Judges	358
8.11.4	Individual and Dissenting Opinions	359
8.11.5	Forum prorogatum	359
8.11.6	The Optional Clause of the ICJ	359
8.11.7	Reservations to the Optional Clause	360
8.11.8	Preliminary Objections	361
8.11.9	Plea of Domestic Jurisdiction	361
8.11.10	Advisory Jurisdiction of the ICJ	362
8.11.11	Execution of Judgments	363
8.12	Administrative Tribunals	364
8.12.1	Administrative Tribunals in General	364
8.12.2	Administrative Tribunals of the United Nations	365

  8.12.3 Administrative Tribunal of the ILO 366
 8.13 Special Tribunals and Projected Tribunals 368

9 PEACE, INTERNATIONAL SECURITY
  AND SANCTIONS 369
 9.1 History of Peace 369
 9.2 International Security 369
 9.3 Disarmament 375
 9.4 Peaceful Coexistence 375
 9.5 International Control 376
 9.6 Sanctions in General 378
 9.7 Use of Force 378
 9.8 Intervention 380
 9.9 Aggression and its Definition 386
 9.10 Self-Defence 390
 9.11 Self-Help and Necessity 392
 9.12 Reprisals 393
 9.13 Blockade 394

10 WAR AND ARMED CONFLICTS 397

 10.1 General 397
 10.2 Legitimacy of War 404
 10.3 Pacts Against War 407
 10.4 Occupation 411
 10.5 Conquest by Annexation 413
 10.6 Humanitarian Law in War 414
 10.7 Permissibility of Certain Weapons 415
 10.8 Biological Warfare 415
 10.9 Nuclear Weapons 415
 10.10 Civil War and Unconventional Warfare
    by Guerillas 417
 10.11 Humanitarian Law in Civil War 418
 10.12 Neutrality 420
 10.13 Particular Disputes 422

11 RESPONSIBILITY 428

11.1	Responsibility	428
11.2	Abuse of Rights	430
11.3	Responsibility for Nuclear Activity	431
11.4	Responsibility for Pollution	431
11.5	Responsibility for Other Specific Acts	432
11.6	Reparation	434

12 INTERNATIONAL CRIMINAL LAW — 436

12.1	General		436
12.2	Specific Crimes		438
	12.2.1	Air Piracy	438
	12.2.2	Maritime Piracy	440
	12.2.3	Radio Piracy	441
	12.2.4	Terrorism	441
	12.2.5	Other Special Crimes	442
	12.2.6	War Crimes Trials	443

13 INTERNATIONAL ORGANIZATIONS — 450

13.1	International Conferences		450
13.2	History of International Organizations		451
13.3	International Institutes		451
	13.3.1	Institut International de Cooperation Intellectuelle	451
	13.3.2	Institut International d'Agriculture	451
	13.3.3	Office International d'Hygiene Publique	452
13.4	Unions		
13.5	Non-Governmental Organizations		454
13.6	International Organizations in General		455
13.7	Personality of International Organizations		461
13.8	Civil Servants of International Organizations		462
13.9	Rules of Procedure		463
13.10	Voting in Organizations		463

13.11	Budget Questions of Organizations		464
13.12	Headquarter Agreements, Immunities and Privileges		464
13.13	Subsidiary Organs of Organizations		464
13.14	Treaty-Making Power of Organizations		465
13.15	International Relations of Organizations		466
13.16	Law-Making by Organizations		467
13.17	Revision of Constitutions		470
13.18	Exercise of Power of Organizations		470
13.19	Excess of Power of Organizations		471
13.20	Relationship between Organizations and Municipal Law		471
13.21	Membership of Organizations		472
13.22	New States and Organizations		473
13.23	Sanctions of Organizations		473
13.24	Particular Organizations		473
	13.24.1	League of Nations	473
	13.24.2	United Nations	475
		13.24.2.1 History	475
		13.24.2.2 United Nations	476
		13.24.2.3 Charter of the UN	479
		13.24.2.3.1 Interpretation of the Charter	480
		13.24.2.3.1 Revision of the Charter	481
		13.24.2.4 Legal Personality of the UN	481
		13.24.2.5 Implied Powers of the UN	482
		13.24.2.6 Treaty-Making Power of the UN	482
		13.24.2.7 The General Assembly	482
		13.24.2.7.1 Competence and General	483

	13.24.2.7.2 Uniting for Peace Resolution	484
	13.24.2.7.3 Effect of Resolutions of the General Assembly	484
13.24.2.8	Security Council	485
13.24.2.9	Voting in the UN	486
13.24.2.10	UN and Domestic Jurisdiction	487
13.24.2.11	ESOSOC	488
13.24.2.12	Secretariat	488
13.24.2.13	Trusteeship Council, Mandates and Trusteeship Agreements	489
13.24.2.14	Subsidiary Organs of the UN	490
	13.24.2.14.1 TAB and Technical Assistance	490
	13.24.2.14.2 Development Aid	491
	13.24.2.14.3 The Economic Commissions of the UN	491
	13.24.2.14.4 International Law Commission	492
	13.24.2.14.5 UNCTAD	492
13.24.2.15	Internal Law of the UN	492
13.24.2.16	Finances of the UN	493
13.24.2.17	Headquarter Agreements	493
13.24.2.18	Privilages and Immunities of the UN	494

13.24.2.19	Membership of the UN	494
13.24.2.20	UN and Non-Members	495
13.24.2.21	UN Sanctions	495
13.24.2.22	UN Peacekeeping	495
13.24.2.23	UN Forces	497
13.24.2.24	The Specialized Agencies	500
13.24.2.24.1	General	500
13.24.2.24.2	External Relations	501
13.24.2.24.3	Universal Postal Union (UPU)	501
13.24.2.24.4	International Tele-Communications Union (ITU)	502
13.24.2.24.5	International Labour Organization (ILO)	503
13.24.2.24.5.1	General	503
13.24.2.24.5.2	ILO Conventions and Particular States	505
13.24.2.24.5.3	ILO Headquarters	506
13.24.2.24.6	Bretton Woods Negotiations for the World Bank and the IMF	507
13.24.2.24.7	International Bank for Reconstruction and Development (IBRD)	507
13.27.2.24.8	International Finance Corporation (IFC)	508
13.24.2.24.9	International Development Association (IDA)	508
13.24.2.24.10	International Monetary Fund (IMF)	508
13.24.2.24.11	Food and Agriculture Organization (FAO)	509

13.24.2.24.12	United Nations Educational, Scientific and Cultural Organization (UNESCO)	510
13.24.2.24.13	World Health Organization (WHO)	511
13.24.2.24.14	International Civil Aviation Organization (ICAO)	512
13.24.2.24.15	Inter-Governmental Maritime Consultative Organization (IMCO)	513
13.24.2.24.16	International Refugee Organization (IRO)	513
13.24.2.24.17	Other Bodies Associated with the UN	513
	13.24.2.24.17.1 International Atomic Energy Agency (IAEA)	513
	13.24.2.24.17.2 General Agreement for Tariffs and Trade (GATT)	514
13.24.3	Regional Organizations	515
13.24.3.1	General	515
13.24.3.2	European Organizations in General	516
13.24.3.3	Organization for European Economic Cooperation (OEEC) and the Organization for Economic Cooperation and Development (OECD)	516
13.24.3.4	Council for Mutual Economic Aid (COMECON)	517
13.24.3.5	Nordic Council	518

13.24.3.6 European Free Trade
 Association (EFTA) 519
13.24.3.7 Benelux 519
13.24.3.8 Council of Europe 519
13.24.3.9 West European Union (WEU) 520
13.24.3.10 North Atlantic Treaty
 Organization (NATO) 521
13.24.3.12 European Communities
  13.24.3.12.1 General 523
  13.24.3.12.2 The Nature of the
   European Communities 524
  13.24.3.12.3 The European Coal and
   Steel Community (ECSC) 526
  13.24.3.12.4 European Economic
   Community (EEC) 528
  13.24.3.12.5 European Atomic
   Energy Community
   (EURATOM) 529
  13.24.3.12.6 Organs of the
   Communities 530
    13.24.3.12.6.1 Council 530
    13.24.3.12.6.2 Commission 530
    13.24.3.12.6.3 Parliament 531
    13.24.3.12.6.4 Other
     Institutions 531
    13.24.3.12.6.5 Court of Justice 532
     13.24.3.12.6.5.1 Judicial
      Control of the
      Communities 537
     13.24.3.12.6.5.2 Right of
      Petition of
      Individuals 537
     13.24.3.12.6.5.3 Prejudicial
      Questions 538
  13.24.3.12.7 Law-Making in the
   Communities 539
  13.24.3.12.8 Voting in the
   Communities 541

13.24.3.12.9 European Civil
 Servants 541
13.24.3.12.10 Execution of Acts 542
13.24.3.12.11 Acts taken by Member
 States 542
13.24.3.12.12 Common Market
  13.24.3.12.12.1 Circulation of
  Goods, Workers and
  Capital 543
  13.24.3.12.12.2 Right of
  Establishment 543
  13.24.3.12.12.3 Competition 543
  13.24.3.12.12.4 Transport 545
  13.24.3.12.12.5 Harmonization
  of Legislation 545
  13.24.3.12.12.6 EEC Commercial
  Policy 546
13.24.3.12.13 International Relations
 of the Communities 546
13.24.3.12.14 Treaty-Making Power
 of the Communities 548
13.24.3.12.15 The Communities and
 Third States 550
13.24.3.12.16 The Relationship between
 the Communities and GATT 550
13.24.3.12.17 Association of the
 Communities with States 551
13.24.3.12.18 The Relationship between
 the Law of the European Communities and the Law of the
 Member States 553
13.24.3.12.19 Direct Application of
 Community Law 557
13.24.3.13 The Arab League 557
13.24.3.14 East African Community (EAC) 558
13.24.3.15 Organization for African
 Unity (OAU) 558

	13.24.3.16 Central American Common Market (CACM)	558
	13.24.3.17 Latin American Free Trade Association (LAFTA)	559
	13.24.3.18 Organization of American States and the Pan American Movement	559

14 INTERNATIONAL ECONOMIC LAW   563

14.1	Permanent Sovereignty over Resources	563
14.2	International Economic Law in General	563
14.3	Multinational Companies	564
14.4	State Trading in General	564
14.5	Protection of Property and Foreign Investments	565
14.6	Treaties on Trade and Monetary Matters	570
14.7	Treaties for the Protection of Property and Investments	570
14.8	State Contracts	572
14.9	Concessions and Economic Development Agreements	573
14.10	State Loans	575
14.11	Nationalization	576
14.12	Acquired Rights	580
14.13	Particular Investment Disputes	581

1 General Material

1.1 DOCUMENTS OF INTERNATIONAL ORGANIZATIONS

A wealth of information of interest to the study of international law is found in the documentation of international organisations, particularly in the publications of the United Nations. This work does not list such documents, or reports apart from certain case reports, and treaty collections. However, I may here refer to a useful guide to documents of the United Nations and the specialised agencies.

WINTON, Harry N M (ed), Publications of the United Nations System: A Reference Guide. (New York/London: Bowker, 1972)

See also

McCONAUGHY, J B & BLANKS, H J, A Student's Guide to United Nations Documents and their Use (New York: Council on International Relations and United Nations Affairs, 1969). 17 pp.

A useful guide to the important work of the International Law Commission is found in the United Nations publication The Work of the International Law Commission, revised edition, UN Publication E.72.I.17 (New York: United Nations, 1972) which also contains the the text of treaties elaborated by the ILC

GENERAL MATERIAL

A more detailed guide to specific documents and reports of the ILC is International Law Commission - A Guide to the Documents 1949-1969. (United Nations document ST/GENEVA/LIB/SER.B/Ref.2.)

1.2 BIBLIOGRAPHIES ON INTERNATIONAL LAW

There are few bibliographies on international law and those that exist are either obsolete or incomplete. Of the works listed below, the bibliographies by Olivart and Strupp have largely historical interest. The work by Morgenstern does not pretend to be more than an 'introduction' of a mere 47 pages, and is not classified in any way. Some later bibliographies are available on specific parts of international law, as indicated below.

DALMAU Y DE OLIVART, Bibliographie du droit international (Madrid: 1907/Paris: Pédone, 1905-10)

GASCARD, J, Bibliographie des deutschen Schriftums (BRD) zum Völkerrecht, 1965-1971 (Hamburg: Hansischer Gildenverlag, 1972). 414 pp. (Continuation of: RAUSCHING, D, Ibid, 1945-1964, Hamburg: Hansischer Gildenverlag, 1966

MORGENSTERN, P, Einführung in die Bibliographie und das Schriftum zum Völkerrecht (Göttingen, 1963) 47 pp.

ROBINSON J, International Law and Organisation, General Sources and Information (Leiden: Sijthoff, 1967). 560 pp.

STRUPP, K, Bibliographie du droit des gens et des relations internationales (Leiden: Sijthoff, 1972). 521 pp.

See also

BERNES, A, & LEVY, J P, Bibliographie du droit de la mer (Paris, 1973)

Bibliography of the International Court of Justice, nos 1-17, reprinted from the Yearbook 1946/7 -

1962/3 (Den Haag, 1947-63)
DE SCHUTTER, B, & ELIAERTS, C, Bibliography on
  International Criminal Law (Leidon: Sijthoff, 1972).
  li + 423 pp.
HEERE, W Y, International Bibliography of Air Law
  1900-1971 (Leiden: Sijthoff/Dobbs Ferry NY:
  Oceana, 1972). xxxvi + 569 pp.
NEUMANN, Inge S, A Bibliography of the European War
  Crimes Trials (New York, 1951). 113 pp.
Ocean Affairs Bibliography, 1971. A Selected List
  Emphasising International Law, Politics and
  Economics of Ocean Uses. Oceans Series No 302.
  (Washington: Woodrow Wilson International Center
  for Scholars, 1971). 201 pp.
WHITE, I, WILSON, C E, & VOSSBURGH, J, Law and
  Politics in Outer Space: A Bibliography (Tucson,
  Ariz: University of Arizona Press, 1972). 176 pp.
There are some bibliographies on 'European law',
generally understood as the law of the European
Communities. Two out of the three listed below are not
very exhaustive. The third one, Publications
juridiques, is perhaps too detailed to give much guidance
as it lists also unimportant notes. It has been dis-
continued since 1967.
A Brief Bibliography of European Integration (London:
  European Communities Information Office,
  January 1972)
Publications juridiques concernant l'intégration
  Européenne (Luxembourg: Service de Documentation
  de la Cour de Justice des Communautés Européennes,
  1966). A supplement was published in 1967.
Selected Bibliography of European Law (Strasbourg:
  Council of Europe, 1971).
Some readers may find the following work useful:
Where to Find your Community Law, 2nd edition
  (London:British Institute of International and
  Comparative Law, 1973).

GENERAL MATERIAL

1.3   FESTSCHRIFTE

Many important articles and notes are found in volumes published 'en hommage' of some outstanding scholar. Such works, 'hommages', 'mélanges', 'Festschrifte' or however termed, are as far as those of interest to lawyers are concerned, listed in
    ROBERTS, L M, A Bibliography of Legal Festschriften (Den Haag: Nijhoff, 1972)

1.4   CASES

Cases obviously form the backbone of international law and those decided by the International Court of Justice and its predecessor the Permanent Court of International Justice are of particular importance. There are numerous 'casebooks' but perhaps the work by L V GREEN listed below is most useful to the modern scholar.
    Other works, which I have listed under 'cases and materials' contain not only extracts from cases but also other relevant material, such as extracts from treaties, diplomatic correspondence or information on some incident of interest to the study of international law. In this category, Fontes juris gentium may, to readers who have mastered the German language, be of interest although certain volumes treat only German case law. HACKWORTH, HUDSON, MOORE and WHITEMAN are the outstanding American writers providing the reader with a wealth of information on a host of different subjects of international law. The work by H W BRIGGS is used by many as a textbook or manual. Many books of 'cases and materials' are published in the United States and I have selected only those I consider particularly helpful. There are not so many works of this type published in Britain, or in any other country. Lord McNAIR's International Law Opinions

are of obvious merit and the Digest by Clive PARRY and Sir Gerald FITZMAURICE provides much useful and interesting information.

In the third group, I have listed works which report cases before specific tribunals and here I have distinguished between official reports by the relevant court and unofficial collections published by various writers.

1.4.1 GENERAL

Annual Digest of Public International Law Cases. Being a selection from the decisions of international and national courts (from 1946: and tribunals and military courts) given during the years. (London: Butterworths, 1932-). Edited by Sir Hersch Lauterpacht. Since vol 9 (1950) the series has been called International Law Reports.

British International Law Cases. A collection of Decisions of Courts in the British Isles on Points of International Law. Prepared under the auspices of the International Law Fund and the British Institute of International and Comparative Law. Edited by Clive Parry (London: Sweet & Maxwell/Dobbs Ferry, NY: Oceana, 1964-73), 9 vols.

FENWICK, C G, Cases on International Law, 2nd edition (Chicago, 1951).

GREEN, L C, International Law through the Cases, 3rd edition (London: Stevens/Dobbs Ferry, NY: Oceana Publications Inc. 1970. xxii and 855 pp).

MARTENS, Baron Charles de, Nouvelles causes célèbres du droit des gens (Leipzig/Paris, 1843). 2 volumes covering the years 1618-1825.

COBBETT, P H, Cases on International Law, 5th edition by Francis Temple Grey (London: Sweet & Maxwell, 1931). 2 volumes.

GENERAL MATERIAL

1.4.2 CASES AND MATERIALS

BISHOP, W W, International Law: Cases and Materials, 3rd edition (Boston, Mass: Little, Brown & Co, 1971).

BRIGGS, Herbert W, The Law of Nations: Cases, Documents and Notes, 2nd edition (London: Sweet & Maxwell, 1953).

COLLIARD, Claude-Albert, Droit international et histoire diplomatique. Documents choisis (Paris, 1950).

COLLINS, E, International Law in a Changing World: Cases, Documents, Readings (New York: Random House, 1970).

DICKINSON, E D, A Selection of Cases and other Readings on the Law of Nations Chiefly as it is Interpreted and Applied by British and American Courts (New York, 1929).

Fontes juris gentium, Founded by Victor Bruns (Berlin, 1931).

FRIEDMANN, W, LISSITZYN, O J, and PUGH, R C, International Law, Cases and Materials (St Paul, Minn: West Publishing Co, 1969). 1205 pp.

HACKWORTH, G H, Digest of International Law (Washington: Government Printing Office, 1940-4). 8 vols.

HARRIS, D J, Cases and Materials on International Law (London: Sweet & Maxwell, 1970).

HOLDER, W E, & BRENNAN, G A, The International Legal System: Cases and Materials (London: Butterworths, 1972) xl + 1048 pp.

HUDSON, Manley O, International Legislation: A Collection of the Texts of Multipartite International Instruments of General Interest (Washington: Carnegie Endowment for International Peace, 1932-50). 9 volumes covering the years 1919-50.

JAEGER, W & O'BRIEN, W, International Law Cases, Text-notes and other Materials (Washington, 1958).
LE FUR, Louis, and CHKLAVER, Georges, Recueil de textes de droit international public (Paris, 1928)
KISS, A Ch, Répertoire de la pratique française en matière de droit international public (Paris: Editions du Centre national de la recherche scientifique, 1962-5). 5 volumes.
McNAIR, A D, (Lord), International Law Opinions (London: Cambridge University Press, 1956). 3 volumes.
MOORE, J B, Digest of International Law (Washington: Government Printing Office, 1906). 8 volumes.
ORFIELD, Lester D, & RE, Edward D, Materials on International Law, 2nd ed (Indianapolis: Bobbs-Merrill, 1965).
PARRY, Clive, British Digest of International Law (London: Stevens, 1965-) 5 volumes published up to 1974; the work will be complete in about 15 volumes.
ROSS, Alf, Folkeretlig materialesamling. Udgivet af Viking Abel og Alf Ross (København: Munksgaard, 1944).
SCHWARZENBERGER, Georg, International Law as applied by International Courts and Tribunals, vol 1 'General principles', 3rd edition (London: Stevens, 1957); vol 2 'The Law of armed Conflict' (London: Stevens, 1968).
SOHN, L B, Cases and Material on World Law (Brooklyn, 1950).
SOHN, Louis B, Cases on United Nations Law (London: Stevens, 1956). xxv + 1048 pp.
WHITEMAN, Marjorie M, Digest of International Law (Washington: Government Printing Office, 1963-5). 5 volumes.

1.4.3 CASES BEFORE SPECIFIC COURTS

1.4.3.1 PERMANENT COURT OF INTERNATIONAL JUSTICE (PCIJ)

Official reports
Publications de la Cour permanente de justice internationale. Recueil des arrêts/Publications of the Permanent Court of International Justice. Collection of judgments. Série A, B et A/B (Leiden, 1922-40).
Unofficial reports
Institut für Internationales Recht, Entscheidungen des Ständigen Internationalen Gerichtshofs (Leiden: Sijthoff, 1929-39). 13 volumes containing German translations of the decisions of the PCIJ.
Handbuch der Entscheidungen des Ständigen Internationalen Gerichtshofs, vol 1 1922-1930 Berlin 1931. vol 2 1931-1934. Berlin 1935. vol 3 1935-1940. (= Fontes Juris Gentium. Series A. Sectio I. Tomus 1, 3, 4).
HUDSON, M O, World Court Reports. A collection of the judgments, orders and opinions of the Permanent Court of International Justice (Washington: Carnegie Endowment for International Peace, 1934-43). 4 volumes.

1.4.3.2 INTERNATIONAL COURT OF JUSTICE (ICJ)

The official publications of the ICJ are of four categories; it is in the first of these that the final judgments are contained. Among the numerous unofficial reports and concise digests, I may refer to works such as that of L C GREEN, listed in Section 1.4.1. However, for a survey of judgments of the ICJ of moderate size and practical use, I may also recommend

Eisemanns (and others), listed below, a short and compressed survey of judgments written by some enterprising French law students.

Official reports
1 Recueil des arrêts, avis consultatifs et ordonnances/Reports of judgments, advisory opinions and orders (Leiden: Cour internationale de justice/International court of justice, 1947-).
2 Pleadings, oral arguments, documents
3 Acts and documents concerning the organisation of the Court.
4 Yearbook.

Unofficial reports

EISEMANN, P M, COUSSIRAT-COUSTERE, V, & HUR, P, Petit Manuel de la jurisprudence de la Cour Internationale de justice (Paris:Pédone, 1970).

HAMBRO, E, et al. (eds), The Case Law of the International Court/La Jurisprudence de la Cour internationale (Leiden: Sijthoff, 1952-74). 7 vols in 13. Text in English and French.

Handbuch der Entscheidungen des Internationalen Gerichtshofs 1947-1958 (Köln usw, 1961).
(= Fontes Juris Gentium. Series A. Sectio I. Tomus 5).

SYATAUW, J, Decisions of the International Court of Justice, A Digest, 2nd edition (Leiden: Sijthoff, 1969)

1.4.3.3 PCIJ AND ICJ, UNOFFICIAL REPORTS

MAREK, K, FURRER, H P, & MARTIN, A, Répertoire des décisions et des documents de la procedure crite et orale de la CPJI et de la CIJ (Genève, 1967). 2 vols.

VERZIJL, J, The Jurisprudence of the World Court. A Case by Case Commentary (Leiden: Sijthoff, 1965-6). 2 vols.

1.4.3.4 CASES RELATING TO EUROPEAN HUMAN RIGHTS

See also Sections 7.12.10.5 (on the European Commission on Human Rights) and 7.12.10.6 (on the European Court for Human Rights).

Annuaire de la Convention européenne des droits de l'homme. Commission et Cour européennes des droits de l'homme 1955-1961 (Den Haag, 1959-1962).

Digest of Case-Law relating to the European Convention on Human Rights 1955-1967 Répertoire de la jurisprudence relative à la Convention Européenne des Droits de l'Homme 1955-1967 (Heule, Belgium: UGA, 1970). xxix + 523 pp.

European Convention on Human Rights (European Commission and European Court of Human Rights)/ Convention européenne des droits de l'homme (Commission et cour européennes des droits de l'homme). Yearbook/Annuaire (Den Haag: Nijhoff). Vol 1 (1955/7). et seq.

1.4.3.5 CASES BEFORE THE COURT OF THE EUROPEAN COMMUNITIES

Recueil de la jurisprudence de la Cour (Luxembourg: Service des publications des Communautés européennes). Vol 1 (1954/5). et seq.

Cour de justice de la Communauté européenne du charbon et de l'acier and after 1958, Cour de justice des Communautés européennes.

See also

Bibliographie de jurisprudence européenne concernant les décisions judiciaires relatives aux traités instituant les Communautés européennes. 1965 and annual supplements (Luxembourg: Service de

documentation de la Cour de justice des
Communautés européennes).

1.4.3.6 CASES BEFORE COURTS OF ARBITRATION

Reports of International Arbitral Awards/Recueil des sentences arbitrales (New York: United Nations. Vol 1 (1948) et seq.

Recueil des décisions des Tribunaux mixtes institues par les traités de paix (Paris, 1921-30).

Recueil des decisions de la Commission de conciliation franco-italienne instituée en execution de l'article 83 du traite de paix avec l'Italie. 7 vols.

Décisions de la Commission arbitrale sur les biens, droits et intérêts en Allemagne (Koblenz, 1958-67). 9 vols.

FELLER, A, The Mexican Claims Commission, 1923-1934 (New York, 1935).

LA FONTAINE, H, Pasicrisie internationale. Histoire documentaire des arbitrages internationaux. 1794-1900 (Bern, 1902).

LA PRADELLE, A de, & POLITIS, N, Recueil des arbitrages internationaux (Paris 1905-54). 3 vols. Vol 1 '1798-1855'; Vol 2 '1856-1872'; Vol 3 '1872-1875'.

MOORE, J B, History and Digest of the International Arbitrations to which the United States has been a Party (Washington 1898). 6 vols.

MOORE, J B, International Adjudications, Ancient and Modern. History and Documents (New York: Oxford University Press, 1929-36). Ancient Series: vol 1 was never published, vol 2 covers 1491-1504. Modern Series: 6 volumes covering 1798-1817.

SCOTT, James Brown, The Hague Court Reports (New York: Oxford University Press). 1st series (covering 1902-1913) published 1916. 2nd series

(covering 1913-1928) published 1932.
STUYT, A M, Survey of International Arbitrations, 1794-1938 (Den Haag: Nijhoff, 1939).
WITENBERG, J C, Commission mixte des réclamations germano-américaine: décisions rendues de 1923 a 1939 (Paris 1926-40). 3 vols.

1.5 COLLECTIONS OF TREATIES

Treaties constitute another important source of international law and it is important to be able to locate specific texts. On aspects of the law of treaties see below, Section 7.13.

1.5.1 GENERAL

Société des Nations. Recueil des traités et des engagements internationaux enregistrés par le Secrétariat de la Société des Nations/League of Nations. Treaty Series. Publication of treaties and international engagements registered with the Secretariat of the League of Nations. Vol 1 (1920) - 205 (1946).

United Nations. Treaty series. Treaties and international agreements registered or filed and recorded with the Secretariat of the United Nations/ Nations Unies. Recueil des traités. Traités et accords internationaux enregistrés ou classes et inscrits au repértoire au Secrétariat des Nations Unies (New York: United Nations). Vol 1 (1946).

To ascertain whether a particular (multilateral) convention is in force, see:

Status of multilateral conventions in respect of which the Secretary-General acts as depositary (New York: United Nations). Rev. ed. 1959-.

DESCHAMPS, Edouard, & RENAULT, Louis, Recueil international des traites du XIXe siècle (Paris 1914)

Covers 1801-25.

DESCHAMPS, & RENAULT, Recueil international des traités du XXe siècle (1901-1907) 7 vols.

HUDSON, Manley O, International Legislation (Washington, DC: Carnegie Endowment for International Peace, 1931-50). 9 vols.

MARTENS, G F de, Nouveau Recueil général de traités, Ser 1 (Göttingen: Dieterich, 1843-75). 20 vols. Ser 2 (Göttingen/Leipzig: Dieterich, 1876-1908), 35 vols. Ser 3 (Leipzig/Greifswald: Dieterich/ Theodor Weicher/ Hans Buske/Julius Abel, 1915-44), 41 vols.

See also

RUHLAND, Kurt, Systematisches Verzeichnis der völkerrechtlichen Kollektivverträge (Kiel 1929).

BRUNS, Viktor, (ed), Politische Verträge. Eine Sammlung von Urkunden (Berlin 1936-42). 3 vols.

Die Zusammenschlüsse und Pakte der Welt auf politischem, militärischem und wirtschaftlichem Gebiet. Zuzammengestellt von Dr Heinrich von Siegler unter Mitarbeit Hans Wilhelm Haefs 6. Aufl. Stand 1.6.1961 (Bonn/Wien/Zürich 1961).

1.5.2 TREATIES AND OTHER SOURCE MATERIAL OF HISTORICAL INTEREST

Archives diplomatiques. Recueil de diplomatie et d'histoire (Paris/Leipzig 1861-1914).

Das Staatsarchiv. Sammlung der offiziellen Aktenstücke zur Geschichte der Gegenwart, edited by L K Aegidi & A Klauhold, vol 1 (1861) - 86 (1919). New series vol 1 (1928) edited by F Thimme. Leipzig 1928.

DESCHAMPS, Edouard, & RENAULT, Louis, Recueil international des traités du XIXe siècle, contenant l'ensemble du droit conventionnel entre les états et les sentences arbitrales (Paris 1914). Covers

GENERAL MATERIAL

1801-25. Original texts with French translation.
DESCHAMPS, Edouard, & RENAULT, Louis, Recueil international des traités du XXe siècle (Paris 1905-21). Covers 1901-7.
DUMONT, Jean, Corps universel diplomatique (Amsterdam/Den Haag 1726-31). 8 vols.
DUMONT, Jean, & ROUSSET, Supplément (Amsterdam/Den Haag 1739). 5 vols.
FLEISCHMANN, Max, Völkerrechtsquellen. Halle 1905. - Verträge u. diplomatischen Urkunden in Auswahl zur Einfuhrung ins Völkerrecht von 1761-1904.
GHILLANY, F W, Diplomatisches Handbuch. Sammlung der wichtigsten europäischen Friedensschlüsse, Congressacten u. sonstigen Staatsurkunden vom Westfalischen Frieden bis auf die neueste Zeit (Nördlingen 1855-68). 3 vols.
GHILLANY, F G, Manuel diplomatique. Recueil des traités de paix européens les plus importants depuis le Traité de Westphalie jusqu'à ces derniers temps (Nördlingen 1856). 2 vols. Covers 1648-1855.
LEIBNITZ, G G, Codex juris gentium diplomaticus (Hannover 1693). Covers 1096-1593)
MARTENS, Ch de, & CUSSY, Ferd de, Recueil manuel et pratique de traité, conventions et autres actes diplomatiques (Leipzig 1846-57). 7 vols. Covers 1516-1856. 2nd series by F H Geffcken (Leipzig 1875-88). 3 vols. Covers 1857-85.
STRUPP, Karl, Documents pour servir à l'histoire du droit des gens, 2nd edition 'Urkunden zur Geschichte des Völkerrechts'. 5 vols, plus index (Berlin 1923). Covers 406 BC-1922.

1.5.3 NATIONAL COLLECTIONS OF TREATIES

1.5.3.1 GREAT BRITAIN

Treaty Series (London: HMSO). Vol 1 (1892) -
British and Foreign State Papers (London: HMSO).
 Vol 1 (1917) - Continuation of:
HERTSLET, Lewis, (ed), A complete collection of the
 treaties and conventions, and reciprocal
 regulations at present subsisting between Great
 Britain and foreign powers and of the laws, decrees,
 orders in council... (London 1840-1925). 31 vols.
For earlier treaties, see:
CHALMERS, George, A Collection of Treaties between
 Great Britain and other powers (London 1790).
 2 vols. Covers 1555-1787.

1.5.3.2 FRANCE

Journal Officiel de la Republique Française (J O)
 (Paris 1869-) Continuation of:
Moniteur universel (Paris 1789-1868) and Bulletin des
 lois (Paris 1794-1931).
BASDEVANT, J, Recueil des traités et conventions en
 vigueur entre la France et les Puissances
 étrangères (Paris, 1918-22). 4 vols.
DE CLERCQ, A, Recueil des traités, conventions et
 actes diplomatiques conclus par la France avec les
 Puissances étrangères (1713-1906). 23 vols
DUPARC, P, Engagements internationaux en
 vigueur souscrits par la France (liste des traités
 bilatéraux en vigueur au 1er janvier 1958) (Paris 1961)
 (et Revue générale de droit international public,
 1958-1961).

1.5.3.3 GERMANY

Bundesgesetzblatt des Norddeutschen Bundes (BGBl)
  (1867-1870)
Reichsgesetzblatt (RGBl) (1871-1945).
BRD
Bundesgesetzblatt (BGBl) (1949-).
Verträge der Bundesrepublik Deutschland. Serie A:
  Multilaterale Verträge. Hrsg. vom Auswärtingen
  Amt. (Bonn). Vol 1 (1955) - Serie B in preparation.
DDR
Dokumente zur Außenpolitik der Regierung der
  Deutschen Demokratischen Republik (Berlin). Vol 1
  (1954) -

1.5.3.4 ITALY

GIULIANO, M, LANFRANCHI, F, & TREVES, T,
  Corpo-Indice degli accordi bilaterali in vigore tra
  l'Italia e gli stati esteri (1718-1967)(Milano 1968).

1.5.3.5 UNITED STATES

Treaty Series (T S) (Washington: Dept. of State, 1908-
  1946)
Executive Agreements Series (EAS) (Washington: Dept.
  of State, 1929-45).
Treaties and Other International Acts Series (TIAS)
  (Washington: Dept. of State, 1945-)
United States Treaties and Other International Agree-
  ments (UST) (Washington: Dept. of State, 1950-).
United States Statutes at Large (Stat) (Washington 1874-
  1950).
MALLOY, Treaties, Conventions, International Acts,
  Protocols and Agreements between the United States
  of America and other Powers (1776-1923) (Washing-
  ton 1910-23). 3 vols.

See also:
Foreign relations of the United States (US For. Rel.)
   (Washington 1861 -) (Annual).
Documents on American Foreign Relations (Boston
   1941-) (Annual).

1.5.3.6   USSR

Sbornik dejstvujuschich dogovorov, soglasenij i
   konvencij zakljucennych SSSR s inostrannymi
   gosudarstvami (Moscow).
SHAPIRO, Leonard, Soviet Treaty Series. A
   collection of bilateral treaties, agreements and
   conventions etc. concluded between the Soviet
   Union and foreign powers (Washington, DC). Vol 1
   (1950)-
See also
DEGRAS, Jane, (ed), Soviet Documents on Foreign
   Policy (London 1951-).

1,5,3,7   CONCORDATS

Raccolta di concordati su materie ecclesiastiche tra la
   Santa Sede e le autorità civili. A cura di Angelo
   Mercati (Roma 1954). Vol 1 1098-1914. Vol 2 1915-
   1954.

1.5.3.8   OTHER TREATIES

Every state usually has an official collection of current
treaties with other powers, such as the Överenskommelser med Främmande Makter, published in Sweden. Such
official series are usually not difficult to trace even if
there may be some problem in establishing whether a
treaty is in force, or with respect to which parties it is
in force. Sometimes guidance may be found in Status
of Multilateral Conventions, listed in Section 1.5.1, in

the case of instruments which are not merely bilateral.

1.5.4 TREATIES AND TEXTS

The most common treaties relevant to the study of international law can be conveniently found in The Work of the International Law Commission, listed in Section 1.1. However, some writers have compiled certain treaties and other 'texts' which may be convenient for reference particularly for texts adopted outside the UN framework. Some of the earlier works listed below contain texts which are now less readily accessible and are of some historical interest.

BROWNLIE, Ian, (ed), Basic Documents in International Law (Oxford: Clarendon Press, 1967). viii + 244 pp.

BROWNLIE, Ian, (ed), Basic Documents on Human Rights (London: Oxford University Press, 1971). x + 531 pp.

COLLIARD, C A, Droit international et histoire diplomatique (Paris: Montchrestien, 1955-7). 2 vols

LE FUR, L, & CHKLAVER, G, Recueil de textes de droit international public, 2nd edition (Paris 1934).

NIBOYET, J P, & GOULE, P, Recueil de textes usuels de droit international (Paris 1929). 2 vols.

REUTER, P, La Convention de Vienne sur le droit des traités (Paris: Armand Colin, 1970). 96 pp

REUTER, P, & GROS, A, Traités et documents diplomatiques (Paris: Presses universitaires de France, 1960).

SOHN, L B, Basic Documents of the United Nations (1950)

VELLAS, P, Droit international et science politique, Recueil de textes, Paris, 1967.

1.5.5 TEXTS AND CONSTITUTIONS OF INTERNATIONAL ORGANIZATIONS

LAWSON, Ruth C, International Regional Organizations: Constitutional Foundations (New York 1962). 386 pp. (Mainly texts).
PEASLEE, A, Constitutions of International Organizations, 2nd edition (Den Haag 1961).

1.6 PERIODICALS

Many valuable articles on international law appear in periodicals and below I have listed most of these that publish material of interest to the international lawyer. Some periodicals may, perhaps because of the language in which they are published, be of greater interest than others. From the point of view of quality the British Yearbook is of particular interest. The Annuaire français publishes, apart from articles by scholars, a valuable guide to newly published works on international law although this is largely restricted to French books. The American Journal is of outstanding importance, both for its articles and its book reviews. The most important periodicals in German are the Zeitschrift für öffentliches Recht und Völkerrecht and the Archiv des Völkerrechts. The Nordisk Tidsskrift with Acta Scandinavia publishes articles not only in the Scandinavian languages but also in English, German and French.

In this section I have also included the very important collection of lectures at the Hague Academy, the Recueil des Cours, although it is, of course, not comparable to other periodicals. It is, however, usually referred to as such by students, as it contains collections of articles, often quite lengthy and usually of high quality, of a wider range of subjects within international law.

The abbreviations given in parentheses after the names of journals are the abbreviations used in this bibliography.

Académie de droit international. Recueil des cours (Acad. Droit Int. Recl. Cours). Vol 1, 1923. Several volumes each year.

Acta scandinavia juris gentium. Vols 1-20, 1930-50. Then combined with Nordisk Tidsskrift for International Ret

American Journal of Comparative Law (Am. J. Comp. Law). Vol 1, 1952.

American Journal of International Law (Am. J. Int. Law). Vol 1, 1907.

American Society of International Law, Proceedings (Am. Soc. Int. Law Proc.). Annual since 1907.

Annuaire de l'Institut de droit international (Annu. Inst. Droit Int.) Annual since 1877.

Annuaire européen/European Yearbook (Annu. Eur.) Vol 1, 1948-53, then one or two volumes each year.

Annuaire français de droit international (Annu. Fr. Droit Int.). Annual since 1955

Annuaire suisse de droit international (Annu. Suisse Droit Int.). Annual since 1954.

Annuario di diritto internazionale (Annu. Diritto Int.). Annual since 1965.

Archiv des Völkerrechts (Arch. Völkerrechts). Vol 1, 1948/9.

Association des auditeurs et anciens auditeurs de l'Académie de droit international de la Haye. Annuaire (Assoc. Auditeurs & Anc. Auditeurs Acad. Droit Int. La Haye Annu.)

The British Year Book of International Law (Br. Yearb. Int. Law). Vol 1, 1920/1.

Cahiers de droit européen (Cah. Droit Eur.)

The Canadian Yearbook of International Law/Annuaire canadien de droit international (Can. Yearb. Int. Law). Vol 1, 1963.

Chronique de politique étrangère (Chron. Polit. Etrang.)
Common Market Law Review (Common Market Law
   Rev.)
Comunicazioni i studi (Comun. & Stud.). Vol 1, 1948.
Diritto internazionale (Diritto Int.). Vol. 1, 1947.
Europarecht Die Friedens-Warte. Vol 1, 1899.
Die Friedens-Warte. Vol 1, 1899.
Grotius Society Transactions (Grotius Soc. Trans.).
   Vols 1-44, 1915/59.
Indian Journal of International Law (Indian J. Int. Law.).
   Vol 1, 1961.
Indian Year Book of International Affairs (Indian Yearb.
   Int. Aff.). Vol 1, 1952.
International Affairs (Int. Aff. (UK)). Vol 1, 1925.
International and Comparative Law Quarterly (Int. &
   Comp. Law Q.). Vol 1, 1952.
International Conciliation (Int. Conciliation). No 1,
   1907.
International Law Association Reports (Int. Law Assoc.
   Rep.). Vol 1, 1873.
International Law Quarterly (Int. Law Q.). Vols 1-4,
   1947-51.
International Organization (Int. Organ.). Vol 1, 1947.
Internationales Recht und Diplomatie (Int. Recht &
   Dipl.). Vol 1, 1956
Jahrbuch des öffentliches Rechts der Gegenwart
   (Jahrb. Off. Recht Ggw.). Vols 1-25, 1907-38.
   New series, vol 1, 1951.
Jahrbuch des Völkerrechts (Jahrb. Volkerrechts).
   Vol 1, 1913-19, then annually from 1926.
Jahrbuch für Internationales Recht (Jahrb. Int. Recht).
   Vol 1, 1948.
Japanese Annual of International Law (Jap. Annu. Int.
   Law). Vol 1, 1957.
Journal du droit international (J. Droit Int.).
   Continuation of Journal du droit international privé.
   Vol 1, 1874.

GENERAL MATERIAL

Journal of Comparative Legislation and International Law (J. Comp. Legis. & Int. Law) 1919-33.
Journal of Common Market Studies (J. Common Market Stud.)
Jus gentium (Denmark). Vols 1-2, 1949-50/51.
Nederlands Tijdschrift voor International Recht (Ned. Tijdschr. Int. Recht). Vol 1, 1953/4.
Niemeyers Zeitschrift für internationales Recht (Niemeyers Z. Int. Recht). Vols 1-52, 1891-1937/8.
Nordisk Tidsskrift for International Ret (Nord. Tidsskr. Int. Ret). Vol 1, 1930.
Ocean Development and International Law Journal (Ocean Dev. & Int. Law J.) Vol 1, 1973.
Ocean Management (Ocean Manage.). Vol 1, 1973.
Österreichische Zeitschrift für öffentliches Recht (Österr. Z. Öff. Recht), new series. Vol 1, 1946/8. Continuation of Zeitschrift für öffentiches Recht (Z. Öff. Recht). Vols 1-22, 1919/20-1943/4. Continuation of Österreichische Zeitschrift fur offentliches Recht. Vols 1-3, 1914-17.
Rabels Zeitschrift für Ausländisches und Internationales Privatrecht (Rabels Z. Ausl. & Int. Privatrecht).
Revista española de derecho internacional (Rev. Esp. Derecho Int.). Vol 1, 1949.
Revue belge de droit international (Rev. Belg. Droit Int.). Vol 1, 1966.
Revue de droit international (Rev. Droit Int.). 1927-40.
Revue de droit international de sciences diplomatiques, politiques (Rev. Droit Int. Sci. Dipl. & Polit.). Vol 1, 1923.
Revue de droit international et de droit comparé (Rev. Droit Int. & Droit Comp.). Vol 1, 1914.
Revue de droit international et de législation comparée (Rev. Droit Int. & Legis. Comp). Series 1, vols 1-30, 1869-98. Series 2, vols 1-16, 1899-1914. Series 3, vol 1, 1920.

Revue de droit public et de la science politique en France et à l'étranger (Rev. Droit Public & Sci. Polit.).
Revue du Marché Commun (Rev. Marche Commun).
Revue générale de droit international public (Rev. Gen. Droit Int. Public). Vol 1, 1894.
Revue hellénique de droit international (Rev. Hell. Droit Int.). Vol 1, 1948.
Revue internationale de droit comparé (Rev. Int. Droit Comp.). Vol 1, 1949. Continuation of Bulletin de la Société de législation comparée.
Revue internationale français du droit des gens (Rev. Int. Fr. Droit Gens).
Revue trimestrielle de droit européen (Rev. Trimest. Droit Eur.).
Rivista di diritto europeo (Riv. Diritto Eur.).
Rivista di diritto internazionale (Riv. Diritto Int.). Vol 1, 1906.
Scandinavian Studies in Law, vol 1, 1957
Schriftenreihe der Deutschen Gruppe der Association des Auditeurs et Anciens Auditeurs de l'Académie de droit International de la Haye (Schriftenr. Dtsch. Gruppe Assoc. Auditeurs & Anc. Auditeurs Acad. Droit Int. La Haye).
Schweizerisches Jahrbuch für Internationales Recht (Schweiz. Jahrb. Int. Recht). Vol 1, 1944.
Sovetskij yezegodnik mezdunarodnogo prava (Sov. Ezheg. Mezhdunar. Prava). Vol 1, 1958.
Turkish Yearbook of International Relations(Turk. Yearb. Int. Relat.). Vol 1, 1960.
Yearbook of World Affairs (Yearb. World Aff.). Vol 1, 1947.
Yearbook on Human Rights (Yearb. Hum. Rights). Vol 1, 1947.
Zeitschrift für ausländisches öffentliches Recht und Völkerrecht (Z. Ausl. Off. Recht & Volkerrecht). Vol 1, 1929.
Zeitschrift für Völkerrecht (Z. Völkerrecht). Vols 1-26, 1907-42.

1.7 HANDBOOKS, DICTIONARIES AND ENCYCLOPEDIAS

Some 'handbooks', 'dictionaries' and 'encyclopedias' contain definitions of international legal terminology and one can often find compressed and useful articles on various subjects within the field of international law. The most important works are:

CALVO, Charles, Dictionnaire de droit international public et privé (Berlin/Paris 1885). 2 vols.
Dictionnaire diplomatique (Ed) Académie diplomatique internationale. Vols 1 & 2. Paris 1934. Supplements 1937; 1951; 1958.
Dictionnaire de la terminologie du droit international. Published under the auspices of the Union Académique internationale (Paris 1960).
Encyclopédie juridique, Répertoire de droit international Published under the direction of Ph. Francescakis (Paris: Dalloz, 1968-9).
Juris-classeur de droit international, Published under the direction of B Goldman (Paris 1966). 6 vols.
Répertoire de droit international, Published under the direction of A de la Pradelle & J P Niboyet (Paris, 1929-31). 10 vols. A supplement was published in 1934.
Wörterbuch des Völkerrechts und der Diplomatie. Edited by Karl Strupp (Berlin/Leipzig 1924-9). 3 vols.
Wörterbuch des Völkerrechts und der Diplomatie. Founded by Karl Strupp. 2nd edition revised by Hans-Jürgen Schlochauer (Berlin 1960-2). 4 vols.
See also:
RENOUX, Y, & YATES, J, Glossary of International Treaties in French, English, Spanish, Italian, Dutch, German and Russian (Amsterdam/London/New York: Elsevier Publishing Co., 1970). 118 pp.
VICHINSKY, A & LAZOVSKY, S, Diplomatitcheski slovar (Moscow 1948-50). 2 vols.

1.8 GENERAL TEXTBOOKS, MANUALS AND COURSES

There are many general textbooks and manuals on international law and their quality and standard vary greatly. Among the works listed below, some writers are particularly outstanding. The Law of Nations by BRIERLY, now edited by Sir Humphrey Waldock, is, to the English speaking reader, of particular merit as it is a comparatively brief book written with admirable clarity. Other writers, such as KELSEN and VERDROSS have contributed to the very theory of international law by their approach to various issues and are, together with the French writer Georges SCELLE, responsible for much of the modern theory on the nature of international law.

In the section below I have also included what I would call 'semi-classics', such as the works by BLUNTSCHLI, CALVO and LISZT, which have been of great importance to the development of international law and whose theories are of the greatest interest to the modern scholar although their main works were published nearly one hundred years ago. On the other hand, I have excluded several other works written towards the end of the last century and during the first decades of this as international law is a dynamic and expanding subject where the treatment of a particular topic may soon become somewhat obsolete.

The works listed below are largely monographs but I have also included some of the most important courses on general international law given at the Hague Academy and which, in spite of their scope, are, technically, articles.

Academy of Sciences of the USSR Institute of State
 and Law, International Law (Moscow: Foreign
 Languages Publishing House, 1961). 477 pp.

GENERAL MATERIAL

ACCIOLY, Hildebrando Pompo Pinto, Tratado de direito international público, 2nd edition (Rio de Janeiro: Impr. nacional, 1956-7). 3 vols.
ACCIOLY, H P P, Manual de direito international público, 2nd edition (São Paulo: Saraiva, 1953).
AGO, Roberto, Scienza giuridica e diritto internazionale (Milano: Giuffrè, 1950). 108 pp.
AGUILAR NAVARRO, Derecho internacional público (Madrid 1954). 2 vols.
AKEHURST, Michael, A Modern Introduction to International Law, 2nd edition (London: George Allen & Unwin, 1971).
ALVAREZ, Alejandro, Le Droit international de l'avenir (Washington, DC: Institut américaine de droit international, 1916). 154 pp.
ALVAREZ, A, & LA PRADELLE, A de, 'Les données fondamentales et les grands principes du droit international moderne', Rev. Droit Int., vol 10 (1932). pp 82-141.
ALVAREZ, A, Le Droit international nouveau (Paris 1959).
AMERASINGHE, C F, Studies in International Law (Colombo: Lake House Investments Ltd, 1969). 275 pp.
ANDRASSY, Juraj, Medunarodno pravo (Zagreb 1949)
ANZILOTTI, Dionisio, Corso di diritto internazionale, 4th edition (Padova: Cedam, 1955). The 3rd edition (Roma: Athenaeum, 1928) was translated into French as: Cours de droit international, translated by Gilbert Gidel (Paris: Recueil Sirey, 1929); into Spanish as: Curso de derecho internacional, translated by Julio Lopez Olivan (Madrid: Editorial Reus, 1935) and into German as Lehrbuch des Völkerrechts, translated by Cornelia Bruns and Karl Schmid (Berlin/Leipzig: Walter de Gruyter, 1929).

BALLADORE-PALLIERI, Giorgio, Diritto Internazionale pubblico, 8th edition (Milano: Giuffrè, 1962). xx + 688 pp.
BASDEVANT, Jules, 'Règles générales du droit de la paix', Acad. Droit Int. Recl. Cours, vol 58 (1936), pp 471-692.
BASKIN, I I, & FELDMAN, D I, Mezhdunarodnoe pravo (Moscow 1971).
BASTID, Suzanne, Cours de droit international public (Paris 1963-4).
BASTID, Suzanne, Droit des gens (Paris: Cours de droit, 1953). 3 vols.
BATY, Thomas, International Law in Twilight (Tokyo: Maruzen, 1954). 227 pp.
BERBER, F, Lehrbuch des Völkerrechts (München/Berlin: Beck, 1960-4). 3 vols.
BIRKENHEAD, Frederick Edwin Smith, 1st Earl of, International Law, 7th edition by Coleman Phillipson (London: J M Dent, 1927).
BISCOTTINI, Giuseppe, Diritto internazionale pubblico, 2nd edition (1943). 232 pp.
BISHOP, W, 'General course of public international law', Acad. Droit Int. Recl. Cours, vol 115 (1965), pp 151-467.
BLUNTSCHLI, J C, Das moderne Völkerrecht der civilizierten Staten als Rechtsbuch dargestellt, 3rd edition (Nördlingen: C H Beck, 1878).
BLUNTSCHLI, J C, Le Droit international codifié, translated by C Lardy, 5th edition (Paris: Alcan, 1895). xxxii + 602 pp.
BOURQUIN, M, 'Règles générales du droit de la paix', Acad. Droit Int. Recl. Cours, vol 35 (1931), pp 1-232.
BOSCO, G, Lezioni di diritto internazionale (Milano: Giuffrè, 1972). 173 pp.
BÖSE, P O R, Der Einfluß des zwingenden Rechts auf internationale Anleihen (Frankfurt/Berlin 1963).

BRIERLY, James Leslie, 'Règles générales du droit de la paix', Acad. Droit Int. Recl. Cours, vol 58 (1936), pp 5-237.
BRIERLY, J L, The Outlook for International Law (Oxford 1955).
BRIERLY, J L, The Law of Nations: An Introduction to the International Law of Peace, 6th edition by Sir Humphrey Waldock (Oxford: Clarendon Press, 1963). 458 pp.
BROWN, D J Latham, Public International Law (London: Sweet & Maxwell, 1970). xxx + 295 pp.
BROWNLIE, Ian, Principles of Public International Law, 2nd edition (London: Oxford University Press, 1973). xxxvi + 733 pp.
BUSTAMANTE y SIRVEN, Antonio Sanchez de, Derecho Internacional publico (Habana, Carasa y cia, 1933-8). 5 vols. Translated into French as: Droit international public, translated by Paul Goulé (Paris: Recueil Sirey, 1934-9). 5 vols.
BUTLER, Sir Geoffrey, & MACOBY, Simon, The Development of International Law (London/New York/ Toronto: Longmans, Green & Co., 1928). 566 pp.
CALVO, Carlos, Derecho internacional teórico y practico de Europa y América (Paris: Amyot 1868). 2 vols. Le Droit international théorique et pratique, précédé d'un exposé historique des progrès de la science du droit des gens, 5th edition (Paris: A Rousseau, 1896). 6 vols.
CASTANOS, Stelios, Critique de droit international public moderne (Paris: Recueil Sirey, 1953). 109 pp.
CASTBERG, Frede, Folkerett, 2nd edition (Oslo: Universitetets studentkontor, 1948). xiii + 242 pp.
CASTBERG, Frede, Studier i folkerett (Oslo: Akademisk forlag, 1952). 249 pp.
CASTBERG, F, Studies in International Law (Oslo 1952).

CASTBERG, F, 'La méthodologie du droit international public', Acad. Droit Int. Recl. Cours, vol 43 (1933), pp 309-83.

CASTEL, J G, International Law chiefly as Interpreted and Applied in Canada (Toronto: University of Toronto Press, 1965). 1402 pp.

CASTRÉN, E, Suomen kansainvalinen oikeus, Borgå, 1959

CAVAGLIERI, Arrigo, Corso di diritto internazionale, 3rd edition (Napoli: Casa editrice Rondinella Alfredo, 1934). vii + 582 pp.

CAVAGLIERI, Arrigo, 'Règles générales du droit de la paix', Acad. Droit Int. Recl. Cours, vol 26 (1929) pp 311-585.

CAVARE, Louis, Le droit international public positif, 2nd edition (Paris: Pédone, 1961). xii + 716 pp.

CLARK, G, & SOHN, L B, Frieden durch ein neues Weltrecht (Frankfurt a M/Berlin, 1961).

COSENTINI, F Code international de la paix et de la guerre. Essai d'une codification intégrale du droit des gens en 2029 articles. Ouvrage proposé pour le prix Nobel 1937 (La Cibourg, Bern/Paris: Marchal & Billard, 1937). 353 pp.

CORBETT, Percy E, Law and Society in the Relations of States (New York: Harcourt, Brace, 1951). 337 pp.

CSARADA, János, A tételes nemzetközi jog rendszere (Budapest: Politzer és fia, 1901). iv + 615 pp.

DAHM, G, Völkerrecht (Stuttgart: Kohlhammer, 1958-61). 3 vols.

DASCOVICI, N, Curs de drept international public dupa prelegerile (de) - (Note scoase de V Crudu.) Complectat cu bibliografia generală si textele principale utilizate la lucrările de seminar intocmite de I. I Popvici, 1930-31 (Iasi: Cultura romaneasca, 1931). 495 pp.

DELBEZ, Louis, Manuel de droit international public: Droit général et droit particulier des Nations Unies, 2nd edition (Paris: Librairie générale de droit et de jurisprudence, 1951). 442 pp.
DELBEZ, Louis, Les Principes généraux du droit international public, 3rd edition (Paris: Librairie generale de droit et de jurisprudence, 1964).
DELUPIS, Ingrid (née Detter), International Law and the Independent State (London: Gower Press 1974). xii + 252 pp.
DESPAGNET, Frantz Clément, René, Cours de droit international public, 4th edition by Ch. de Boeck (Paris: L Larose & L Tennin, 1910). vi + 1430 pp.
DEUTSCH, Karl W, & HOFFMANN, Stanley, The Relevance of International Law: Essays in Honour of Leo Gross (Cambridge, Mass: Schenkman Publishing Co., 1968). 280 pp.
DEVAUX, J, Traité élémentaire de droit international public (Paris: Recueil Sirey, 1935).
DIENA, G Principi di diritto internazionale, 3rd edition (Roma 1930)
DOURDIENEVSKY, V, GRABAR, V, KOJEVNIKOV, F, KRYLOV, S, et al., Mezhdunarodnoe pravo (Moscow 1947).
DROST, Heinrich, Grundlagen des Völkerrechts (München/Leipzig: Duncker & Humblot, 1936). xii + 144 pp.
DUPUIS, Charles, 'Règles générales du droit de la paix', Acad. Droit Int. Recl. Cours, vol 32 (1930), p 5.
EAGLETON, Clyde, International Government (New York: Ronald Press, 1932). xx + 672 pp.
EDMUNDS, Sterling E, Das Völkerrecht: ein Pseudorecht (Berlin/Leipzig: De Gruter & Co., 1933). vii + 405 pp.
EEK, Folkrätten 2nd ed. (Stockholm: Norstedts, 1975)

ENGEL, Salo, & METALL, Rudolph A, (eds), Law, State and International Legal Order: Essays in Honor of Hans Kelsen (Knoxville, Tenn: University of Tennesee Press, 1964). 365 pp.

FALUHELYI, Ferenc, Allamközi jog/Droit des états ou droit des gens (Pecs: Karl, 1936). xxxii + 357 + xvi pp.

FAUCHILLE, Paul, Traité de droit international public (8th edition of Manuel de droit international public by Henry Bonfils) (Paris: Rousseau & cie, 1921-6). 2 vols in 4. Vol 1 (in 3 parts) 'Paix'; vol 2 'Guerre et neutralite'.

FAWCETT, J E S, The Law of Nations, 2nd edition (Harmondsworth: Penguin, 1971)

FAWCETT, J E S 'General course on public international law', Acad. Droit Int. Recl. Cours, vol 132 (1971), pp 363-558.

FEDOZZI, Prospero, Corso di diritto internazionale (Padova: A Milani, 1930).

FENWICK, Charles Ghequiere, International Law, 4th edition (New York: Appleton-Century-Crofts, 1965).

FIORE, Pasquale, Trattato di diritto internazionale pubblico, 4th edition (Torino: Unione Tipografico Editrice, 1904-5).

FITZMAURICE, Sir Gerald, 'The general principles of international law considered from the standpoint of the rule of law', Acad. Droit Int. Recl. Cours, vol 92 (1957), pp 1-223.

FOIGNET, René, Manuel élémentaire de droit international public, 5th edition by E Dupont (Paris 1932).

FOULCKE, G, A Treatise of International Law (Boston, Mass 1922). 2 vols.

FRANÇOIS, J P A 'Règles générales du droit de la paix', Acad. Droit Int. Recl. Cours, vol 66 (1938), pp 5-294.

FRANÇOIS, Jean Pierre Adrien, Gronlijnen van het volkenrecht (Zwolle: Tjeenk Willink, 1954). xxxii + 947 pp.
FRANÇOIS, J P A, Handboek van het volkenrecht, 2nd edition (Den Haag 1956).
FRIEDMANN, Wolfgang, 'The uses of "general principles" in the development of international law', Am. J. Int. Law, vol 57 (1963), p 279.
FRIEDMANN, Wolfgang, Law in a Changing Society (Harmondsworth: Penguin, 1972).
GARAICOA, J, Principios normativos del derecho internacional publico (Guayaquil 1946).
GARCÍA ÁLVAREZ, M y A García Pérez, Derecho Internacional público, 2nd edition (Toledo: Colegio de María Cristina, 1912). x + 199 + iii pp.
GARCIA AMADOR, F V, Introducción al estudio del derecho internacional contemporaneo (Madrid 1959).
GARNER, J W Studies in Government and International Law (Urbana, Ill: University of Illinois Press, 1943). 574 pp.
GENET, L, Manuel de droit international public (Paris 1944).
GIHL, T, International Legislation, translated from the Swedish by Sydney J Charleston (London: Oxford University Press, 1937). 158 pp)
GIHL, T, Internationell Lagstiftning (Uppsala: Lundequistska Bokh, 1938. v + 158 pp.
(Skrifter utg. av Svenska institutet för internationell rätt, No 5).
GIHL, T, Studier i internationell rätt (Stockholm: Norstedt, 1955).
GIHL, T, Huvuddragen av den allmänna folkrätten (Stockholm: Norstedt, 1956).
GIULIANO, Mario, La Communità internazionale e il diritto (Padova: Cedam, 1950). 366 pp.
GJELSVIK, Nikolaus, Laerebok i folkerett (Oslo, Det Norske Samlaget, 1915). 240 pp.

GLAHN, Gerhard von, Law Among Nations: An Introduction to Public International Law, 2nd edition (New York: Macmillan/London: Collier-Macmillan, 1970). 768 pp.

GOLUBEV, N N, 'New tasks of the contemporary science of international law', Pravo i Zhisn, No 3 (1922).

GOULD, Wesley L, An Introduction to International Law (New York: Harper, 1957). 809 pp.

GREIG, D W International Law (London: Butterworth & Co., 1970). xx + 728 pp.

GUGGENHEIM, Paul, Lehrbuch des Völkerrechts; unter berücksichtigung der internationalen und schweizerischen Praxis (Basel, Verlag für Recht und Gesellschaft, 1947-51). 2 vols.

GUGGENHEIM, Paul, & BINDSCHEDLER-ROBERT, Denise, Traité de droit international public, avec mention de la pratique internationale et suisse (Geneve: Georg, 1953-4). 2 vols.

GUGGENHEIM, Paul, 'Les principes de droit international public', Acad. Droit Int. Recl. Cours, vol 80 (1952).

GURKE, H Grundzüge des Völkerrechts (Berlin 1937).

HACKWORTH, Green, Haywood, Digest of International Law (Washington, GPO, 1940-4). 8 vols.

HAGERUP, Francis, Folkerett i fredstid. Efter författerens ufullendte manuskript fullfört og utgitt av Thorvald Boye (Oslo: Christiansen, 1932). 303 pp.

HALL, William Edward, A Treatise on International Law, 8th edition by A Pearce Higgins (London: Oxford University Press, 1924). xlvii + 952 pp.

HALLECK, H W, International Law, vol 1 (London 1905).

HATSCHEK, J, Völkerrecht als System rechtlich bedeutsamer Staatsakte (Leipzig/Erlangen: Scholl, 1923).

HATSCHEK, Julius, An Outline of International Law (London: G Bell & Sons, 1930). 364 pp.
HEFFTER, A W, Das europäische Völkerrecht der Gegenwart, 8th edition by F H Geffcken (Berlin: Verlag von H W Müller, 1888).
HEGEL, F Grundlinien der Philosophie des Rechts (Leipzig 1911).
HEGGSTAD, Ø, 'The international community,' J Comp Legis. & Int. Law, series 3, vol 17 (1935), p 265.
HEILBORN, P, System des Völkerrechts (Berlin 1896).
HERCZEGH, Géza, General Principles of Law and the International Legal Order (Budapest: Akadémiai Kiadó, 1969). 129 pp.
HERSHEY, Amos S, The Essentials of International Public Law and Organization, 2nd edition (New York: Macmillan, 1927).
HEYDTE, Friedrich August, Freiherr von der, Völkerrecht, ein Lehrbook (Köln: Kiepenheuer & Witsch Verlagsgruppe Politik und Wirtschaft, 1958-60) 2 vols.
HIGGINS, A P, Studies in International Law and Relations (London: Cambridge University Press, 1928). 304 pp.
HOLD-FERNECK, A, Lehrbuch des Völkerrechts (Leipzig 1930-2). 2 vols.
HOLLAND, Sir Thomas Erskine, Studies in International Law (Oxford: Clarendon Press, 1898). viii + 314 pp.
HOLLAND, Thomas Erskine, Lectures on International Law (London: Sweet & Maxwell, 1933). 576 pp.
HOLTZENDORFF, Franz Joachim Wilhelm Philipp von, Handbuch des Völkerrechts. Auf Grundlage europäischer Staatspraxis (Berlin: C Habel, 1885-9). 4 vols.

HOLTZENDORFF, Eléments de droit international public, translated from German by Georges Chr. Zographos (Paris: Rousseau, 1891). 213 pp.

HUBER, Max, Die soziologischen Grundlagen des Völkerrechts (Berlin/Grunewald: W Rothschild, 1928). vii + 101 pp. First issued in 1910 in vol iv of the Jahrbuch des öffentlichen Rechts der Gegenwart, with title: Beiträge zur Kenntnis der soziologischen grundlagen des Völkerrechts und der Staatengesellschaft.

HURST, Sir Cecil, International Law: The collected papers of Sir Cecil Hurst (London: Stevens & Sons, 1950). 302 pp.

HYDE, Charles Cheney, International law chiefly as interpreted and applied by the United States, 2nd edition (Boston: Little, Brown, 1945). 3 vols.

ISAY, H, Völkerrecht (Breslau 1924).

JENNINGS, R Y, 'General course on principles of international law', Acad. Droit Int. Recl. Cours, vol 121 (1967), pp 319-605.

JENKS, Clarence Wilfred, The Common Law of Mankind (London: Stevens/New York: Praeger, 1958). xxvi + 456 pp.

JESSUP, Philip C, A Modern Law of Nations: An Introduction (New York:Macmillan, 1948; reissued 1968 by Shoe String Press, Hamden, Conn). xi + 236 pp.

JESSUP, Philip C, Transnational Law (New Haven, Conn. 1956). 113 pp.

JESSUP, Philip C, The Use of International Law (Ann Arbor, Mich: 1959). 164 pp.

JESSUP, Philip C, 'The Concept of transnational law', The Columbia Journal of Transnational Law, vol 1 (1964).

JIMÉNEZ DE ARÉCHAGA, Curso de derecho internacional público (Montevideo 1959-61) 2 vols.

KAMAROVSKY, L, Osnovnye voprosy nauki mezhdunarodnavo prava (Moscow: Ouniversitetskaia tipografiia, 1892). 201 pp.

KAPLAN, M A & KATZENBACH N de B, The Political Foundations of International Law (New York: Wiley, 1961).

KAPLAN, M A, KATZENBACH, N de B & TUNKIN, G I, Modernes Völkerrecht, Form oder Mittel der Außenpolitik (Berlin 1965).

KAUFMANN, Erich, 'Règles générales du droit de la paix', Acad. Droit Int. Recl. Cours, vol 54 (1935), pp 309-620.

KAZANSKY, P, Vvedenie v kours mezhdunarodnavo prava (Odessa: 'Ekonomitcheskaia' tipografiia, 1901). xii + 386 pp.

KEETON, G W, & SCHWARZENBERGER, G Making International Law Work, 2nd edition (London: Stevens, 1946).

KELSEN, Hans, 'Théorie générale du droit international public', Acad. Droit Int. Recl. Cours, (1932), pp 121-35.

KELSEN, Hans, 'The theory of public international law', Acad. Droit Int. Recl. Cours, vol 84 (1953), pp 1-201.

KELSEN, Hans, & TUCKER, R W, Principles of International Law, 2nd edition (New York: Holt, Rinehart & Winston, 1966).

KLEEN, Richard, Kodificerad framställning: mellanfolklig rätt, offentlig och enskild, enligt den civiliserade världens lagar och seder (Stockholm: Norstedt, 1911-20). 3 vols.

KLÜBER, J L, Europäisches Völkerrecht (Stuttgart: Cotta, 1821). 2 vols. 2nd edition C E Morstadt (Schaffhausen: Hurter, 1851). 482 pp.

KOHLER, J, Grundlagen des Völkerrechts (Stuttgart: Ferdinand Enke, 1918).

KOROVIN, E A, Sovremennoe mezhdunarodnoe publitchnoe pravo (Moscow/Leningrad, Gossoudarstvennoe izdatelstvo, 1926). 176 pp.

KOROVIN, E A, Das Völkerrecht der Übergangszeit. Internationalrechtliche Abhandlungen (Berlin/Grünewald: Verein Dr Walther Rothschild, 1929).

KOROVIN, E A, et al., Mezhdunarodnoe pravo (Moscow: Institute of Law of the Academy of Sciences of the USSR, 1951).

KOROWICZ, M St, Introduction to International Law: Present Conceptions of International Law in Theory and Practice (Den Haag 1959).

KOZHEVNIKOV, F I, (ed) International Law (Moscow 1961).

KRYLOV, Sergei Borsovitch, 'Les notions principales du droit des gens (La doctrine soviétique du droit international)', Acad. Droit Int. Recl. Cours, vol 70 (1947), pp 407-76.

KUNZ, Josef Laurenz, Völkerrechtswissenschaft und reine Rechtslehre (Leipzig/Wien: F Deuticke, 1923). 86 pp.

LAPRADELLE, Paul Geoffre de, Cours de droit international public (license 3ème année), 2nd edition (Aix-en-Provence: La Pensée universitaire, 1955). 241 pp.

LAUTERPACHT, Sir Hersch, The Function of Law in the International Community (Oxford: Clarendon Press, 1933: reissued 1966 by Shoe String Press, Hamden, Conn) x + 469 pp.

LAUTERPACHT, H, 'Règles générales du droit de la paix', Acad. Droit Int. Recl. Cours, vol 62 (1937), pp 99-419.

LAUTERPACHT, Sir Hersch, International Law: Collected Papers, vol 1, edited by E Lauterpacht (London:Cambridge University Press, 1970). 539 pp.

LAUTERPACHT, H, 'The law of nature and the rights of man', Grotius Soc. Trans., vol 29 (1943), p 1.
LAWRENCE, T J, The Principles of International Law, 7th edition revised by Percy H Winfield (London: Macmillan, ? 1923).
LAWRENCE-WINFIELD, A Handbook of International Public Law (New York/London 1938).
LE FUR, Louis, Précis de droit international public, 3rd edition (Paris: Dalloz, 1937). 656 pp.
LE FUR, Louis, 'Règles générales du droit de la paix', Acad. Droit Recl. Cours, vol 54 (1935), pp 5-307.
LEVIN, D B, Osnoynye problemy sovremennogo mezhuna rodnogo prava (Moscow 1958).
L'HUILLIER, Jean, Eléments de droit international public (Paris: Rousseau, 1950). vi + 432 pp.
LIPSKY, George A, Law and Politics in the World Community (Berkeley, Calif: University of California Press, 1953). 372 pp.
LISOVSKIJ, V J, Mezdunarodnoe pravo (Kiev 1955).
LISSITZYN, O J, 'International law in a divided world', Int. Conciliation, no 542 (1963).
LISZT, Franz von, Das Völkerrecht, systematisch dargestellt, 12th edition by Max Fleischmann (Berlin: Springer, 1925). xviii + 764 pp.
LUKASHUK, I I & VASILENKO, V A (eds), Mezhdunarodnoe pravo, (Kiev 1971).
McDOUGAL, M S, 'International law, power and policy: a contemporary conception', Acad. Droit Int. Recl. Cours, vol 82 (1953), pp 137-259.
McDOUGAL, Myres S, et al., Studies in World Public Order (New Haven, Conn: Yale University Press, 1960). 1058 pp.
McNAIR, A D,(Lord McNair) The Expansion of International Law (Jerusalem: The Magnes Press, The Hebrew University, 1962).

McWHINNEY, E, 'Le "nouveau" droit international et la "nouvelle" communauté mondiale', Rev. Gen. Droit Int. Public, vol 72 (1968), p 323.

MALBERG, R Carré de, Théorie générale de l'état (Paris 1920-2). 2 vols

MANN, F A, Studies in International Law (London: Oxford University Press, 1973). xxxii + 717 pp.

MARTENS, Fedor Fedorovich, Sovremennoe mezhdunarodnoe pravo tsivilzovannykh narodov, 4th edition (St Petersburg: Benke, 1904-5). 2 vols. The first edition was translated into German as Völkerrecht: Das internationale Recht der civilizierten Nationen systematisch dargestellt, translated by Carl Bergbohm (Berlin: Wiedmann, 1883-6), 2 vols; and into French as Traité de droit international, translated by Alfred Léo (Paris: Chevalier-Mareseq & cie., 1883-7), 2 vols.

MARTENS, Georg Friedrich von, Précis du droit des gens moderne de l'Europe fondé sur les traités et l'usage, 4th edition by M S Pinheiro Ferreira (Paris: J P Aillaud, 1831). The first edition was translated into English as: Summary of the Law of Nations founded on the Treaties and Customs of the Modern Nations of Europe, translated by William Cobbett (Philadelphia: Bradford, 1795).

MARYAN GREEN, N A, International Law: Law of Peace (London:Macdonald & Evans, 1973). xxxvi + 298 pp.

MATEESCO, Nicolas, Doctrines, écoles et développement du droit des gens (Paris : Pedoné, 1951). 54 pp.

MENZEL, E, Völkerrecht (München/Berlin 1962)

MIAJA DE LA MUELA, A, Introducción al derecho internacional público, 4th edition (Madrid 1968).

MIELE, Mario, Principii di diritto internazionale, 2nd edition (Padova: Ceram, 1960). 313 pp.

GENERAL MATERIAL

MIRKINE-GUETZÉVITCH, B, Droit constitutionnel international (Paris: Sirey, 1933).
MØLLER, Axel, Folkeretten i Fredstid og Krigstid (København: Gad, 1925). Translated into English as: International Law in Peace and War, translated by H M Pratt (London: Stevens & Sons, 1931-5). 2 vols.
MONACO, R, Manuale di diritto internazionale pubblico, 2nd edition (Torino 1971). 731 pp.
MORELLI, Gaetano, Nozioni di diritto internazionale, 7th edition (Padova: Cedam, 1967).
MORELLI, G, 'Cours général de droit international public, Acad. Droit Int. Recl. Cours, vol 89, (1956), pp 437-603.
MORENO QUINTANA, L, Derecho internacional público (Buenos Aires 1950).
MOYE, M, Le Droit des gens moderne, 2nd edition (Paris 1928).
MUKHERJEE, S K, A New Outlook for International Law (Calcutta: World Press, 1968). 472 pp.
NIEMEYER, Theodor, Völkerrecht (Berlin/Leipzig: Walter de Gruyter, 1923).
NIEMEYER, Gerhart, Law without Force: The Function of Politics in International Law (Princeton, NJ: Princeton University Press, 1941). 408 pp.
NIPPOLD, Otfried, The Development of International Law after the World War (Oxford: Clarendon Press, 1923). 241 pp.
NYS, Ernest, Le droit international, les principes, les théories, les faits, 2nd edition (Bruxelles: M Weissenbruch, 1912). 3 vols.
NYS, Ernest, Traité de droit international public, vol 1 (Bruxelles, 1921).
O'CONNELL, D P, International Law, 2nd edition (London: Stevens, 1970). 2 vols.
O'CONNELL, D P, International Law for Students (London: Stevens, 1971).

OPPENHEIM, L F L, International Law, Vol 1 'Peace', 8th edition by H Lauterpacht (London: Longmans Green, 1955); vol 2 'Disputes, war and neutrality', 7th edition by H Lauterpacht (London: Longmans Green, 1952).

OPPENHEIM, L, 'The science of international law: its task and method', Am. J. Int. Law (1908), pp 314-56.

OPPENHEIM, L, The Future of International Law (Oxford: Clarendon Press, 1921). 68 pp.

OTTOLENGHI, G, Corso di diritto internazionale pubblico (Torino: G Giappichelli, 1956). 453 pp.

PAREDES, A M, Manual de derecho internacional público (Buenos Aires 1951).

PATEL, Satyaurata R, A Textbook of International Law (London: Asia Publishing House, 1964). 322 pp.

PERASSI, Tomaso, Lezioni di diritto internazionale, 2nd edition (1947; reissued 1952 by Cedam, Padova).

PEREIRA, André Conçalves, Curso de Direito Internacional Público (Lisbon: Ediçoes Atica, 1970). 509 pp.

PHILLIMORE, Sir Robert Joseph, Commentaries upon International Law, 3rd edition (London: Butterworths, 1879-89). 4 vols.

PHILLIPPS, Eduardo, Direito internacional publico, Versão de Leopoldo de Freitas (Rio de Janeiro: Garnier, 1907). 240 pp.

PHILLIPSON, Coleman, Two Studies in International Law (London: Stevens & Haynes, 1908). 136 pp.

PODESTA COSTA, Luis A, Manual de derecho internacional público, 2nd edition (Buenos Aires: Librería-editorial El Ateneo, 1947). 536 pp.

POLITIS, Nicolas, Les Nouvelles Tendances du droit international (Paris 1927). 249 pp.

POLITIS, Nicolas, The New Aspects of International Law (Washington 1928). 86 pp.

POTTER, Pitman B, A Manual Digest of Common International Law (New York: Harper & Brothers, 1932). 284 pp.

PRADIER-FODERE, P L E, Traité de droit international public européen et américain (Paris 1885-1906). 8 vols.

QUADRI, Rolando, Diritto internazionale pubblico, 3rd edition (Palermo: G Priulla, 1960).

QUADRI, R, 'Cours général de droit international public', Acad. Droit Int. Recl. Cours, vol 113 (1964), pp 237-483.

RASTING, Carl, Folkeretten (Copenhagen: Nyt Nordisk Forlag, 1940). 2 vols.

RAUCHHAUPT, W Von, Völkerrecht (Berlin 1937).

REDLICH, M D, The Law of Nations, 2nd edition (New York 1937).

REDSLOB, R, Les principes du droit des gens modernes (Paris 1937).

REDSLOB, Robert, Traité de droit des gens; l'évolution historique, les institutions positives, les idées de justice, le droit nouveau (Paris: Recueil Sirey, 1950). 473 pp.

RENAULT, L, Introduction à l'étude de droit international (Paris 1869).

REUTER, Paul, 'Principes de droit international public', Acad. Droit Int. Recl. Cours, vol 103 (1961), pp 425-655.

REUTER, Paul, Droit international public, 3rd edition (Paris: Presses universitaires de France, 1968).

REUTERSKIÖLD, C A, Folkrätt. Särskildt såsom svensk publik internationell rätt. Föreläsningar (Uppsala/Stockholm: Almqvist & Wiksell, 1928).

RIVIER, A, Principes du droit des gens (Paris: Librairie nouvelle de droit et de jurisprudence, Arthur Rousseau, éditeur, 1896).

ROLIN, Henri, 'Les principes de droit international public', Acad. Droit Int. Recl. Cours, vol 77 (1950), pp 309-479.
RÖLING, B V A, International Law in an Expanded World (Amsterdam 1960).
ROMANO, Santi, Corso di diritto internazionale, 4th edition (Padova: Cedam, 1939).
ROSS, Alf, Laerebog i Folkeret. Almindelig del 2 udgave (Copenhagen: Munksgaard, 1946). 400 pp.
ROSS, Alf, A Textbook of International Law (London: Longmans, Green & Co., 1947). 313 pp.
ROSS, Alf, Lehrbuch des Völkerrechts (Stuttgart: W Kohlhammer, 1951). 296 pp.
ROSS, Alf, & FOIGHEL, Isi, Studiebog i Folkeret (Copenhagen: Nyt Nordisk Forlag, 1954). xx + 419 pp.
ROUSSEAU, C, Principes généraux du droit international public, vol 1 (Paris: Pédone, 1944). xxxviii + 975 pp.
ROUSSEAU, Charles, Droit international public (Paris: Sirey, 1970).
ROUSSEAU, Charles, Droit international public approfondi, 2nd edition (Paris: Dalloz, 1972).
ROUSSEAU, Charles, 'Principes de droit international public', Acad. Droit Int. Recl. Cours, vol 93 (1958), pp 369-549.
RUCK, Erwin, Grundsätze im Völkerrecht (Zürich: Polygraphischer Verlag, 1947). 59 pp.
RUIZ MORENO, Isidoro, Lecciones de derecho internacional público (Buenos Aires: El Ateneo, 1934-5). 3 vols.
SALVIOLI, Gabriele, 'Les règles générales de la paix', Acad. Droit Int. Recl. Cours, vol 46 (1933), pp 5-164.
SAUER, Ernst, Grundlehre des Völkerrechts, 3rd edition (Köln: Heymann, 1955). xvi + 504 pp.

SAUER, E, System des Völkerrecht, 2nd edition (Bonn 1952).
SCELLE, Georges, Précis de droit des gens, principes et systématique (Paris: Recueil Sirey, 1932-4). 2 vols.
SCELLE, Georges, 'Règles générales du droit de la paix', Acad. Droit Int. Recl. Cours, vol 46 (1933), pp 331-694.
SCELLE, Georges, Manuel de droit international public, 3rd edition (Paris: Montchrestien, 1948).
SCHWARZENBERGER, Georg, Einführung in das Völkerrecht (Tubingen 1951)
SCHWARZENBERGER, Georg, 'The fundamental principles of international law', Acad. Droit Int. Recl. Cours, vol 87 (1955), pp 195-385.
SCHWARZENBERGER, Georg, A Manual of International Law, 5th edition (London: Stevens, 1967). lix + 701 + viii pp.
SCHWARZENBERGER, G, International Law and Order (London: Stevens & Sons, 1971). xxiii + 298 pp.
SEFERIADES, Stelio, 'Principes généraux du droit international de la paix', Acad. Droit Int. Recl. Cours, vol 34 (1930), pp 181-492.
SEIDL-HOHENVELDERN, I, Völkerrecht (Köln 1965).
SEIDL-HOHENVELDERN, I, 'Völkerrecht, Verfassungsrecht und Spaltungstheorie,' Wertpapier-Mitteilungen, vol 21 (1967), p 770.
SELA Y SAMPIL, Aniceto, Derecho internacional, 2nd edition (Madrid: Espasa-Calpe, 1932). 235 pp.
SERENI, Angelo Piero, Diritto internazionale (Milano: Giuffré, 1956-65). 5 vols.
SIBERT, Marcel, Traité de droit international public (Paris: Dalloz, 1951). 2 vols.
SMITH, H A, The Crisis in the Law of Nations (London: Stevens & Sons, 1947). 102 pp.

SOHN, L B, 'The development of international law', American Bar Association Journal, vol 33 (1947), pp 727-30
SØRENSEN, Max, 'Principes de droit international public; cours général', Acad. Droit Int. Recl. Cours, vol 101 (1960), pp 1-254.
SØRENSEN, Max, (ed), Manual of Public International Law (London: Macmillan/New York: St Martin's Press, 1968).
SPIROPOULOS, Jean, Théorie générale du droit international (Paris: Librairie générale de droit & de jurisprudence, 1930). xiii + 220 pp.
SPIROPOULOS, Jean, Traité théorique et pratique du droit international public (Paris: Librairie générale de droit et de jurisprudence, 1933). 465 pp.
STARKE, J G, An Introduction to International Law, 7th edition (London: Butterworths, 1972).
STARKE, J G, Studies in International Law (London: Butterworths, 1965).
STOWELL, Ellery C, International Law: A Restatement of Principles in Conformity with Actual Practice (New York: Henry Holt & Co., 1931). 829 pp.
STRÖMBERG, H, Folkrätt, 2nd edition (Lund 1974).
STRUPP, Karl, Eléments du droit international public, 2nd edition (Paris: Les Editions Internationales, 1930). 3 vols.
STRUPP, Karl, Grundzüge des positiven Völkerrechts, 5th edition (Köln 1932).
STRUPP, Karl, 'Les règles générales du droit de la paix', Acad. Droit Int. Recl. Cours, vol 47 (1934), pp 263-595.
SUNDBERG, Halvar G F, Folkrätt. 2 uppl (Stockholm: Institutet för Öffentlig och internationell ratt, 1950). 398 pp.
SVARLEIN, O, An Introduction to the Law of Nations (New York: McGraw-Hill, 1955). 478 pp.

TANDON, Mahesh Prasad, & TANDON, Rajesh, Public International Law, 12th edition (Allahabad: Allahabad Law Agency, 1969). 677 pp.

TUNKIN, G I, Voprosy mezhdunarodnogo prava (Moscow 1962). Translated into German as: Das Völkerrecht der Gegenwart, Theorie und Praxis (East Berlin 1963).

TUNKIN, G I, Droit international public: Problèmes théoriques, translated by the Centre de Recherche sur l'URSS et les Pays de l'Est, Faculté de Droit et des Sciences Politiques et Economiques de Strasbourg (Paris: Editions A. Pédone, 1965).

TUNKIN, G I, The role of international law in international relations, in Völkerrecht und rechtliches Weltbild, p 295.

TUNKIN, G I, Teoriia Mezhdunarodnogo Pravo (Moscow 1970).

ULLMANN, E von, Völkerrecht (Berlin 1931).

ULLOA, A, Derecho internacional público (Madrid: Ediciones Iberamericanas, 1957). 2 vols.

VÁSQUEZ, M S, Derecho Internacional Público, 3rd edition (Mexico City 1971).

WILLIAMS, J F, Some Aspects of Modern International Law (Oxford 1939).

WILSON, G G, Handbook of International Law (St Paul, Minn 1927).

WILSON, George Grafton, International Law, 9th edition (New York: Silver, Burdett & Co., 1937). 372 pp.

WOLGAST, E, Völkerrecht (Berlin 1934).

WOLGAST, Ernst, Grundriss des Völkerrechts (Hannover: Wissenschaftliche Verlagsansalt, 1948). 127 pp.

VALLAT, Sir Francis, International Law and the Practitioner (Manchester: Manchester University Press/Dobbs Ferry, NY: Oceana, 1966). 159 pp.

VELLAS, Pierre, Droit international public (Paris: Librairie générale de droit et de jurisprudence, 1967). 481 pp.
VERDROSS, A, Die Verfassung der Völkerrechtsgemeinschaft (Wien/Berlin: Verlag von Julius Springer, 1926). 228 pp.
VERDROSS, A, Völkerrecht, 5th edition (Berlin: Springer, 1964). 690 pp. The 3rd edition (1950) was translated into Spanish as: Derecho internacional público, translated by Antonio Truyol y Serra (Madrid: Aguilar, 1957). 505 pp.
VERDROSS, A, 'Règles générales du droit international de la paix', Acad. Droit Int. Recl. Cours, vol 30 (1929), pp 275-517.
VICHINSKY, A & LOZOVSKY, S, Voprosy miejdounarodnovo prava i mezhdunarodnoi olitiki (Moscow 1949).
VISSCHER, Charles de, Théories et réalités en droit international public, 4th edition (Paris: Pedone, 1970). An earlier edition was translated into English as: Theory and Reality in Public International Law, translated by P E Corbett (Princeton, NJ: Princeton University Press, 1968).
WACKERNAGEL, J, 'Über rechtssoziologische Betrachtungsweisen, insbesondere im Völkerrecht', in Festschrift für Gutzwiller (1959), p 119.
WALDKIRCH, E V, Das Völkerrecht in seinen Grundzügen dargestellt, (Basel 1926)
WALDOCK, Sir Humphrey, 'General course on public international law', Acad. Droit Int. Recl. Cours, vol 106 (1962), pp 1-251.
WENGLER, W, Völkerrecht (Berlin 1964). 2 vols.
WESTLAKE, John, International Law (Cambridge: The University Press, 1904-7). 2 vols. Reissued 1910-13.
WHEATON, Henry, Elements of International Law, 7th edition by H Berridale Keith (1944).

WHITAKER, Urban G Jr, Politics and Power: A Text in International Law (New York: Harper & Row. 1964). 646 pp.

ZAKHAROF, N A, Kours obchtchavo mezhdunarodnavo prava (Petrograd: Weisbrot, 1917). x + 464 pp.

ZICCARDI, P, La costituzione del l'ordinamento internazionale (1943).

ZICCARDI, P, Diritto internazionale odierno (Milano 1964).

ZORN, Albert, Grundzüge des Völkerrechts (Leipzig: J J Weber, 1903). 315 pp.

2 Nature and Origin of International Law

2.1 CLASSICS

Although the modern international lawyer is concerned with the international community of today, he may occasionally find it useful to revert to the 'classic' writers on international law for different dimensions of a specific problem. On the question of unequal treaties (see Section 7.13.11.4), for example, much material and discussion may be gathered from the works of GROTIUS and BYNKERSHOEK, and on the question of right of transit of landlocked states (see also Section 7.6.10) it may be noted that Grotius held that there existed such a right in the international community.

BELLI, Pierino, De Re Militari et Bello Tractatus, (The Classics of International Law, no. 18) (London 1936).

BODIN, J, Six livres de la République, (Paris 1577).

BYNKERSHOEK, C Van, De Dominio Maris Dissertatio (1702) (The Classics of International Law, no. 11) (translated by Magoffin) (New York 1923).

BYNKERSHOEK, C Van, Quaestionum Juris Publici Libri Duo (1737) (The Classics of International Law, no. 14, 2) (translated by Frank) (Oxford 1930).

BYNKERSHOEK, Cornelius Van, De Foro Legatorum (1721) (Oxford 1940).
GENTILI, A, De Iure Belli ac Pacis, Libria Tres (1625) 1612) (The Classics of International Law, no. 16, 2). Translated by Rolfe with Introduction by C Phillipson (London 1933).
GROTIUS, H, De Jure Belli ac Pacis, Libri Tres (1625) (The Classics of International Law no. 3, 2), Translated by Kelsey (London 1923/Washington, DC 1925).
GROTIUS, H, Mare Liberum (1608), Translated by Magoffin (Oxford 1916).
LEGANANO, Giovanni da, Tractatus de bello, de represaliis et de duello, edited by Sir Erskine Holland. 2 vols. (text and translation) (The Classics of International Law) (London 1917).
PONTANUS, J I, Discussiones Historicae de Mari Libero (Harderwick, 1637).
PUFENDORF, Samuel, Jure Naturae et Gentium (1672) (The Classics of International Law, no. 17, 2) translated by Oldfather (Oxford 1934).
PUFENDORF, Samuel, Jure Naturae et Gentium (1672) universalis libri duo (1672) (Classics of International Law 15) (Oxford: Clarendon Press, 1931). 2 vols.
PUFENDORF, Samuel, De officio hominis et civis juxta legem naturalem libri duo (1682) (Classics of International Law 10) (Oxford: Clarendon Press, 1927). 2 vols.
SUAREZ, Francisco, De legibus ac deo legislatore 1612 in Selections from the Works of Francisco Suarez, 2 vols. (Text and translation) (The Classics of International Law, no. 20) (London 1944).
TEXTOR, Johann Wolfgang, Synopsis Juris Gentium (Basel 1680) 2 vols, edited by L von Bar (The Classics of International Law) (Washington 1916).

VATTEL, Emer de, Le droit des gens ou principes de la loi naturelle; appliqués à la conduite et aux affaires des Nations et des Souverains (1758) (Washington: Carnegie Institution, 1916). 3 vols.

VITORIA, Francisco de, De Indis et de Iure Belli Relectiones (1557) (The Classics of International Law, no. 7) Translated by Bate (Washington, DC, 1917).

WELWOOD, W, De Dominio Maris Juribusque ad Dominium Praecipue Spectantibus Assertio Brevis ac Methodica (1625).

WOLFF, Christian von, Ius Gentium Methodo Scientifica Pertractatum, 2 vols (text and translation) (The Classics of International Law) (London 1934).

ZOUCHE, Richard, Juris Judicii Fecailis, sive, Inter Gentes et Quaestionum de Eodem Explicatio (1650) 2 vols (text and translation) edited by T E Holland (The Classics of International Law) (Washington 1911).

2.2 HISTORY OF INTERNATIONAL LAW

For the 'founders' of international law a scholar must obviously turn to the classics and relevant source material. However, there are some later, useful commentaries on the evolution of international law including analysis of the 'international law' of Greece and Rome and including examination of contributions of certain philosophers to the theory and study of international law.

Among the books mentioned below the comprehensive work by VERZIJL is worth special note. The basic anthology edited by PILLET is still the basic work for any study of the classics.

ALEXANDROWICZ, C H (ed), Studies in the History of the Law of Nations (Den Haag: Nijhoff, 1970).

BASTID, P 'La révolution de 1848 et le droit international', Acad. Droit Int. Recl. Cours, vol 72 (1948), pp 167-282.

BOURGEOIS, L, Manuel historique de politique étrangère, vol 4 (Paris 1926).

DUPUIS, C, Le Droit des gens et les rapports entre les grandes puissances et les autres états (Paris: Plan-Nourrit & Cie, 1921).

GARDOT, André, 'Jean Bodin. Sa place parmi les fondateurs du droit international', Acad. Droit Int. Recl. Cours, vol 50 (1934), pp 549-743.

FORTUIN, U R H, De Natuurrechtlijke Grundslagen van de Groots Völkenrecht (Den Haag: Nijhoff, 1946). 270 pp.

GUGGENHEIM, P, 'Contribution à l'histoire des sources du droit des gens', Acad Droit Int. Recl. Cours (1958), vol 2, pp 1 et seq.

JONES, J Walter, 'Leibniz as international lawyer', Br Yearb. Int. Law, vol 22 (1945), pp 1-10.

LAUTERPACHT, Sir Hersch 'The Grotian tradition in international law', Br. Yearb. Int. Law, vol 23 (1946), pp 1-53.

LAUTERPACHT, Sir Hersch, 'Spinoza and international law', Br. Yearb. Int. Law, vol 8 (1927), pp 89-107.

NUSSBAUM, Arthur, A Concise History of the Law of Nations (New York : Macmillan, 1947). xi + 361 pp.

NYS, E Les Origines du droit international (Harlem/Brussels/Paris, 1894). 414 pp.

OTTENWALDER, P, Zur Naturrechtslehre des Hugo Grotius (Tübingen 1950).

PHILLIPSON, Coleman, The International Law and Custom of Ancient Greece and Rome (London 1911). 2 vols; 419 & 421 pp.

PILLET, Antoine, (ed) Les Fondateurs du droit international (Paris 1904).

RAEDER, A, L'Arbitrage international chez les Hellènes (Christiania 1912).

REDSLOB, Robert, 'La doctrine idéaliste du droit des gens proclamée par la Révolution française et par le philosophe Emmanuel Kant', Rev. Gén. Droit Int. Public, vol 28 (1921), pp 441-56.

REDSLOB, Robert, Histoire des grands principes du droit des gens depuis l'Antiquité jusqu'à la veille de la Grande Guerre (Paris, 1923). 600 pp.

REIBSTEIN, E v, Die Anfänge des neueren Natur-und Völkerrecht (Bern: Verlag Paul Haupt, 1949) 248 pp.

RENOUVIN (ed), Histoire des relations internationales (Paris 1953-8). 8 vols.

RENOUVIN & DOUROSELLE, J B, L'Introduction à l'histoire des relations internationales (Paris 1964).

SCOTT, James Brown, The Spanish Origin of International Law, Part I, Francisco de Vitoria and His Law of Nations (London 1934). 288 pp. Appendixes contain parts of Vitoria's works in translation.

SIMONS, W, The Evolution of International Public Law in Europe since Grotius (New Haven, Conn: Yale University Press, 1931).

STADTMÜLLER, G, Geschichte des Völkerrechts (Hannover: Hermann Schrodel Verlag, 1951) 219 pp.

STRUPP, K, Documents pour servir à l'histoire du droit des gens (Berlin: Hermann Sack Verlag, 1923). 5 vols and index.

SWIFT, R N, International Law Current and Classic (New York: Wiley, 1969). 558 pp.

TAUBE, M de, 'Etudes sur le développement historique de droit international dans l'Europe orientale', Acad. Droit Int. Recl. Cours, vol 11 (1926), pp 345-533.

TAUBE, M de, 'L'apport de Byzance au développement du droit international occidental', Acad. Droit Int. Recl. Cours (1939), vol 1, p 233.

TRELLES, C Barcia, 'Francisco de Vitoria et l'école moderne du droit international', Acad. Droit Int. Recl. Cours, vol 17 (1927), pp 113-333.

TRELLES, C Barcia, 'Francisco Suarez (1548-1617)', Acad. Droit Int. Recl. Cours, vol 43 (1933), pp 389-531.

VAN DER MOLEN, G H J, Alberico Gentili and the Development of International Law (Amsterdam 1937). 342 pp.

VAN DER VLUGT, W, 'L'oeuvre de Grotius et son influence sur le développement du droit international', Acad. Droit Int. Recl. Cours, vol 7 (1925), pp 399-509.

VERZIJL, J H W, International Law in Historical Perspective (Leiden: Sijthoff, 1968-72). 5 vols.

VINOGRADOFF, P Historical Types of International Law. Bibliotheca Visserana, vol 1 (Leiden 1923)

VISWANATHA, S V, International Law in Ancient India (Madras, 1925). 214 pp.

VOLLENHOVEN, C van, The Three Stages in the Evolution of the Law of Nations (Den Haag 1919). 102 pp.

VOLLENHOVEN, C van, Du droit de paix (Den Haag 1932). Translated as The Law of Peace (London/New York 1936). 261 pp.

WEGNER, Artur, Geschichte des Völkerrechts (Stuttgart 1936). 362 pp.

2.3 NATURE OF INTERNATIONAL LAW

The works listed below describe the nature and binding force of international law and some books discuss the relationship between international law and natural law. For other important works relevant to this subject, I may refer to the general works, especially for the theory of the Grundnorm as advanced by KELSEN, and to other exponents of monism or dualism as listed in

Section 3. 3. 1. On the 'objectivist' theory see the work by L DUGUIT listed below.

BRIERLY, J L The Basis of Obligation in International Law and other Papers, Selected and edited by H Lauterpacht and C H M Waldock (Oxford: Clarendon Press, 1958). 424 pp.

BRUNS, V, 'Völkerrecht als Rechtsordnung', Z. Ausl. Öff. Recht & Völkerrecht (1929), p 1.

CONSTANTOPOULOS, D S, Verbindlichkeit und Konstruktion des positiven Völkerrechts (Hamburg 1948). 230 pp.

CONSTANTOPOULOS, D S, 'La force obligatoire du droit des gens', Assoc. Auditeurs & Anc. Auditeurs Acad. Droit Int. La Haye Annu., vol 25 (1955), pp 21-31.

DJUVARA, M, 'Le fondement de l'ordre juridique positif en droit international', Acad. Droit Int. Recl. Cours, vol 64 (1938), p 479.

DUGUIT, L, Traité de droit constitutionnel, 3rd ed., (Paris 1927).

EPPSTEIN, John, The Catholic Tradition of the Law of Nations (London 1935). 525 pp.

JELLINEK, G, Die rechtliche Natur der Staatenverträge (Wien, 1880).

JITTA, D, Josephus, The Renovation of International Law on the Basis of a Juridical Community of Mankind (Den Haag: Nijhoff, 1919)

KAUFMANN, E, Das Wesen des Völkerrechts und die clausula rebus sic stantibus (Tübingen, 1911).

KELSEN, H, Reine Rechtslehre (Leipzig, 1934).

KELSEN, H, Das Problem der Souveränität und die Theorie des Völkerrechts (Tübingen, 1928).

KELSEN, H, 'Zur Grundlegung der Völkerrecht Lehre', Österr. Z. Öff. Recht (1948), p 20.

LE FUR, L, 'La théorie du droit naturel depuis le XVIIe siècle et la doctrine moderne', Acad. Droit Recl. Cours, vol 18 (1927), pp 259-442.

KUNZ, J L, 'De jure naturàe et gentium', Am.J. Int. Law, vol 56 (1962), pp 748-51.

LIPARTITI, C, 'Il Fondamento del diritto internazionale e la portata delle norme pattizie internazionali', Rev. Droit Int. Sci. Dipl. & Polit., 1940 (4, 18e année) pp 244-55. 1941 (1, 19e année) pp 24-36

PARADISI, B, Norma fondamentale e contratto alle origini della communità internazionale (Siena, 1950), 32 pp. From Studi Senesi vol 62 (1950).

POLITIS, N, 'L'Influence de la doctrine de L Duguit sur le développement du droit international', Archives de philosophie de droit, 1932, pp 69-81.

QUADRI, R, 'Le Fondement du caractère obligatoire du du droit international public', Acad. Droit Int. Recl. cours, vol 80 (1952), p 579.

REDSLOB, R, 'Considérations sur les fondements du droit des gens', Rev. Droit Int. & Légis. Comp, (1933) pp 488-513 & 615-33.

RUBIN, A P, 'De jure naturae et gentium', Am. J. Int. Law, vol 56 (1962), p 514-17.

SCELLE, G, 'La Doctrine de L Duguit et les fondements du droit des gens', Archives de philosophie du droit, 1932, pp 83-119

SPERDUTI, G, La Fonte suprema dell'ordinamento internazionale (1946)

TRUYOL, .A, 'Doctrines contemporaines du droit des gens', Rev. Gén. Droit Int. Public (1950), p 369 & (1951), p 199

VERDROSS, A, 'Die "bona fides" als Grundlage des Völkerrechts', Juristische Blätter, vol 23 (1951), pp 223-4. Also in Gegenwärtige Probleme des internationalen Rechts. Festschrift für Laun (1953), p 20.

VERDROSS, Alfred, 'Le fondement du droit international', Acad. Droit Int. Recl. Cours, vol 16 (1927), p 247.

VERDROSS, A V, 'Zum Problem der völkerrechtlichen Grundnorm', in Festschrift für Wehberg (Frankfurt a M, 1956), p 385
WALZ, G A, Wesen des Völkerrechts und Kritik der Völkerrechtsleugner (Stuttgart, 1930).

2.4 JUS COGENS

The discussion of jus cogens is not new in international law: early works by Verdross, as listed under the general section discuss the problem of peremptory norms of international law from which it is not permissible to derogate by treaty. The problem, which is intimately linked to the discussion of the relationship between international law and natural law, has achieved renewed importance after the inclusion, by the International Law Commission, of an article on jus cogens, in the convention on the law of treaties. In recent years there have also been some arguments between the champion of jus cogens, Professor VERDROSS, and the scholar who is a sceptic on this subject, Professor SCHWARZENBERGER, initiated by an article by Schwarzenberger in the Texas Law Review.
JACOVIDES, A, Treaties Conflicting with Preremptory Norms of International Law and the London-Zürich Agreements (Nicosia, 1966)
JURT, J, Zwingendes Völkerrecht, (Zürich, 1933).
MAREK, K, 'Contribution à l'étude du 'jus cogens' en droit international', in Recueil d'études en hommage à Paul Guggenheim (Genève, 1967), p 426
MORELLI, G, 'A proposito di norme internazionali cogenti', Riv. Diritto Int., (1968), p 108
MOSLER, H, 'Jus Cogens im Völkerrecht', Annu. Suisse Droit Int., (1968), p 9
PAUL, 'The legal consequences of conflict between a treaty and an imperative norm of general inter-

national law (Jus Cogens)', Österr. Z. Öff. Recht, (1971), p 19

RIESENFELD, S A, 'Jus dispositivum and jus cogens in international law: in the light of a recent decision of the German Supreme Constitutional Court', Am. J. Int. Law, vol 60 (1966), pp 511 et seq

SCHEUNER, U, 'Conflict of treaty provisions with a peremptory norm of general international law and its consequences', Z. Ausl. Öff. Recht & Völkerrecht, (1967), p 520

SCHWARZENBERGER, G, 'International law jus cogens?' Texas Law Rev., (1965), p 455

SCHWARZENBERGER, G, 'Jus dispositivum and jus cogens in international law', Am. J. Int. Law, (January, 1966)

SCHWEITZER, M, 'Jus Cogens im Völkerrecht', Arch. Völkerrechts, (1971), p 197.

SCHWELB, E, 'Some aspects of international jus cogens as formulated by the International Law Commission', Am. J. Int. Law, vol 61 (1967), pp 946-75.

SZTUCKI, J, Jus Cogens and the Vienna Convention of the Law of Treaties: A Critical Appraisal. (Vienna: Springer, 1974).

VERDROSS, A von, Jus dispositivum and jus cogens in international law, Am. J. Int. Law, vol 60 (1966), p 55.

The Concept of Jus Cogens in International Law (Geneva, 1967)

VIRALLY, M, 'Réflexions sur le "jus cogens"', Annu. Fr. Droit Int., (1966), pp 5-29.

VISSCHER, C de, 'Positivisme et jus cogens', Rev. Gén. Droit Int. Public (1971), p 5.

ZOTIADES, Georg B, 'Staatsautonomie und die Grenzen der Vertragsfreiheit im Völkerrecht', Österr. Z. Öff. Recht, new ser. vol 17 (1967), pp 90-112.

2.5 RELATIONSHIP BETWEEN INTERNATIONAL LAW AND SOCIOLOGY

On the relationship between international law and sociology I may refer to the works by Professor Georges SCELLE listed in Section 1.8 and:
ARANGIO-RUIZ, G, Sulla dinamica della base
    sociale nel diritto internazionale (Milan: Giuffré,
    1954). 180 pp.

2.6 RELATIONSHIP BETWEEN INTERNATIONAL LAW AND SOCIAL SCIENCES

On this topic see:
GOULD, W L & BARKUN, M, International Law and the
    Social Sciences (London: Oxford University Press/
    Princeton: Princeton University Press, 1972).
    388 pp.

2.7 RELATIONSHIP BETWEEN INTERNATIONAL LAW AND POLITICS

The field of international law often comes close to that of politics, especially in matters relating to peace-keeping and security. Some writers, like GIRAUD and WEHBERG have analysed the importance of political factors in international law. Many American writers, such as Quincy WRIGHT, include the study of 'international relations' and 'international politics' in international law. For works by Quincy Wright see Section 1.8 and compare works in Section 2.8
FALK, R A 'The relevance of political context to the
    nature and functioning of international law', in
    The Relevance of International Law, edited by
    K Deutsch & S Hoffmann (Cambridge, Mass:
    Schenkman, 1969), pp 133-52

GIRAUD, E, 'De la valeur et des rapports des
notions de droit et de politique dans l'ordre
international', Rev. Gén. Droit Int. Public, (1922),
pp 473-514
GIRAUD, E, 'Le droit international public et la
politique', Acad. Droit Int. Recl. Cours, vol 110
(1963), pp 419-809.
WEHBERG, H, 'Völkerrecht und Politik', Freidens-
Warte (1934), p 121.

2.8 DYNAMIC NATURE OF INTERNATIONAL LAW

Some writers, such as ALVAREZ and BRIERLY, have analysed the changing structure of international law in the light of traditional concepts of law. Others such as JESSUP, have taken a more progressive approach. McDOUGAL, (see Section 1.8), like HAAS, WHITING, PADELFORD and LINCOLN, take into account also extra-juridical factors that contribute to the evolution of international law in the modern community. See also Arangio-Ruiz listed in section 2.5.

ALVAREZ, A, Le Droit international nouveau dans
   ses rapports actuelle des peuples (Paris, 1959)
ALVAREZ, A, Le Droit international nouveau, son
   acceptation (Paris, 1960)
FRIEDMANN, W G, 'The changing dimensions of
   international law', Columbia Law Review, vol 62
   (1962), p 1160
HAAS, E, & WHITING, A, Dynamic of Inter-
   national Relations (New York, 1956)
JESSUP, P, Transnational law (New Haven, 1956)
KUNZ, Josef L, The Changing Law of Nations
   (Columbus, Ohio: Ohio State University Press,
   1960)
PADELFORD, N, & LINCOLN, G, International
   Relations: A General Theory (London, 1965).

TUNG, W L, International Law in an Organizing World (New York: Thomas Y Crowell, 1968)

3 *The Relationship between International and Municipal Law*

3.1 REGIONAL APPROACH TO INTERNATIONAL LAW

Some works treat international law from a particular angle and discuss problems as seen from the standpoint of one state or a group of states. I have listed such works below as representative of a 'regional approach'. Such regional attitudes may imply that there should be many 'types' of international law whereas the international legal system is, by definition, universal. However, some of these works are interesting in so far as they analyse the attitude of certain state practice to international law and, particularly, to its implementation in the internal legal order of countries. Perhaps the works on Soviet international law are particularly interesting as they largely describe the difference in certain concepts of international law and the different interpretation or emphasis of the basic issues of international law, such as sovereignty. See also Section 7.13.13 on the implementation of treaties into municipal law, Section 13.20 on the relationship between the law of organizations and particular countries, and Section 13.24.3.12.18 on the relationship between the European Communities and individual member states.

For attitudes of African and Asian states see also Sections 7.5.3 and 7.5.5 on state succession and new states. For works treating international law from a regional standpoint see also, HYDE's and KRYLOV's general textbooks listed in Section 1.8 and section on peaceful co-existance.

3.1.1 ATTITUDES OF GROUPS OF STATES OR OF DIFFERENT CONTINENTS

ANAND, R P, 'Attitude of the Asian-Africa states toward certain problems of international law', Int. & Comp. Law Q., vol 15 (1966), p 55

MAHMASSANI, S, 'The principles of international law in the light of Islamic doctrine', Acad. Droit Int. Recl. Cours, vol 117 (1966), p 205

RECHID, A, 'L'Islam et de droit des gens', Acad. Droit Int. Recl. Cours, vol 60 (1937), p 375

TALAAT, Al Ghunaimi, The Muslim Conception of International Law and the Western Approach (Den Haag, 1968)

VALLADÃO, H, Democratisation et socialisation du droit international: L'Impact latino-américain et afro-asiatique (Paris, 1962)

3.1.2 EUROPE IN GENERAL

HEFFTER, A.W, Das europäische Völkerrecht listed under Section 1.8.

3.1.3 DIFFERENT EUROPEAN COUNTRIES

SCOTT, James Brown, The Spanish Conception of International Law and of Sanctions (Washington, DC: Carnegie Endowment for International Peace, 1934), 131 pp.

SERENI, Angelo Piero, The Italian Conception of International Law (New York, 1943), 402 pp

3.1.4 USSR AND OTHER SOCIALIST STATES

GINSBURG, G, 'A case study in the Soviet use of international law: Eastern Poland in 1939', Am. J. Int. Law, vol 52 (1958), pp 67-84

GRZYBOWSKI, Kazimierz, Soviet Public International Law. Doctrines and Diplomatic Practice (Leiden: A W Sijthoff, 1970). xx + 544 pp.

LAPENNA, Ivo, 'International law viewed through Soviet eyes', Yearb. World Aff. (1961), p 204

MAURACH, R, & MEISSNER, B, Völkerrecht in Ost und West (Stuttgart/Berlin/Köln/Mainz, 1967)

MEISSNER, B, Sowjetunion und Völkerrecht, 1917-1962, (Köln, 1963)

MEISSNER, B, 'Die Sowjetische Bewertung der Völkerrechtsquellen', Osteuropa-Recht (1955), pp 2-8

MEISSNER, B, 'Völkerrechtswissenschaft und Völkerrechtskonzeption der UdSSR', Recht in Ost und West (1961), p 1

SCHWEISFURTH, T, Der internationale Vertrag in der modernen sowjetischer Völkerrechtstheorie (Berlin, 1968)

TARACONZIO, T A, The Soviet Union and International Law (New York, 1935)

TUNKIN, G I, 'Forty years of co-existence and international law', Soviet Yearbook of IL (1958-59)

See also:

FILIPUCCI GIUSTINIANI, G, Il concetto sovietista di diritto internazionale. Con alcuni cenni di diritto internazionale asiatico, il testo della costituzione dell'URSS e i principali trattati e leggi di stati asiatici sulla cittadinanza (Roma: Istituto nazionale di contenzioso diplomatico, 1939). 364 pp

3.1.5 NORTH AMERICA

For United States, see HYDE, listed at p

3.1.6 CANADA

CASTEL, J G, International Law Chiefly as Applied and Interpreted in Canada (Toronto, 1965). pp 851-906

3.1.7 PAN AMERICA

ALVAREZ, A, Le Droit international américain (Paris, 1910).
JACOBINI, H B, A Study of the Philosophy of International Law as seen in works of Latin American writers (Den Haag: Nijhoff, 1954). 158 pp
PUIG, J C, Les Principes du droit international public américain (Paris: Pédone, 1954). 87 pp.
SAVELBERG, M M L, Le problème du droit international américain étudié spécialement à la lumière des conventions panaméricaines de La Havane (Den Haag: Stols, 1946). 361 pp
URRUTIA, Francisco-José, 'La codification du droit international en Amérique', Acad. Droit Int. Recl. Cours, vol 22 (1928), pp 81-236
YEPES, J M, 'Les Problèmes fondamentaux du droit des gens en Amérique', Acad. Droit Int. Recl. Cours, vol 47 (1936), pp 5-143

3.1.8 ASIA IN GENERAL

SHEPHERD, Vincent, (ed), Round Table Conference on International Law Problems in Asia (Hong Kong: Hong Kong University Press, 1969). 643 pp

3.1.9 CHINA

COHEN, J A, (ed), China's Practice of International
Law: Some Case Studies (Cambridge, Mass:
Harvard University Press, 1972)
LENG, Shao-Chuan, & CHIU, Hung Dah, Law in
Chinese Foreign Policy: Communist China and
Selected Problems of International Law (Dobbs Ferry,
NY: Oceana, 1972. 387 pp.

3.1.10 AFRICA

BIPOUN-WOUM, Joseph-Marie, Le Droit international africain (Paris: Librairie générale de
droit et de jurisprudence, 1970). 327 pp
YAKEMTCHOUK, R, L'Afrique en Droit International
(Paris: Librairie générale de droit et de jurisprudence,
1971). 319 pp.

3.2 RELATIONSHIP AND CONFORMITY OF
CONSTITUTIONS WITH INTERNATIONAL LAW

MANGOLDT, H von, 'Das Völkerrecht in den neuen
Staatsverfassungen', Jahrb. Int. & Ausl. Öff. Rect,
vol 3 (1954), pp 11-25
MIRKINE-GUETZEVITCH, B, 'Les Tendances
internationales des nouvelles constitutions', Rev.
Gén. Droit Int. Public, vol 52 (1948), pp 375-86
VISSCHER, P de, 'Les Tendances internationales des
constitutions modernes', Acad. Droit Int. Recl.
Cours, vol 80 (1952), pp 511-78

3.3 THE RELATIONSHIP BETWEEN INTERNATIONAL LAW AND INTERNAL LAW

3.3.1 DUALISM AND MONISM

The problem of the relationship between international law and the internal law of states has been subjected to numerous theoretical and practical studies. The theories evolved by scholars largely fall into two categories: the dualist theory and the monist theory. Principal exponents of dualism are writers such as TRIEPEL and, in more modern times, ANZILOTTI. There are 'extreme' monists, such as SCELLE, claiming supremacy of international law over national law and 'moderate' monists, such as KELSEN and GUGGENHEIM. Apart from the works listed below I may refer to Section 1.8 for the works of the above-mentioned scholars. See also other relevant sections such as 7.13.13.2 (effect of treaties in the municipal sphere), 13.24.3.12.18 (relationship between the law of the European Communities and the internal law of the member states) and Section 7 on sovereignty.

ALVAREZ, A, Le Droit international nouveau dans ses rapports avec la vie actuelle des peuples (Paris, 1959)
ANZILOTTI, D, Il diritto internazionale nei giudizi interni (Bologna, 1905)
BALLADORE PALLIERI, G, 'Le dottrine di Hans Kelsen e il problema dei rapporti fra diritto interno e diritto internazionale', Riv. Diritto Int., vol 17 (1935), pp 24-82
BARILE, G, 'Diritto internazionale e diritto interno', Riv. Diritto Int., vol 39 (1956), pp 449-507 and (1957), p 26
BELAUNDE MOREYRA, A, 'El problema de las relaciones entre el derecho internacional y el

interno, según el Profesor Walz', Revista
peruana de derecho internacional enero-junio de
1959 (19, no 55), pp 62-70

BERILE, G, Diritto internazionale e diritto interno:
Rapporte fra sistemi omogenei ed eterogenei de
norme giuridiche (Milano: Giuffré, 1964). 142 pp

BIDART CAMPOS, G J, 'La incorporación del
derecho internacional al derecho interno', La Ley
(Argentina), 17 May 1965, pp 1-5; 18 May 1965, pp
1-4

DECENCIERE-FERANDIERE, A, Considérations sur
le droit international dans ses rapports avec le droit
de l'état, Rev, Gén. Droit Int. Public, vol 44 (1933),
pp 40-70

DIENA, G, Se e in quale misma il diritto interno
possa portare limitazioni alle obbligazioni
internazionale degli stati (Torino, 1901)

DIENA, G, 'Considerazioni critiche sul concetto dell'
assoluta e completa separazione fra il diritto
internazionale e l'interno', Rivista di diritto
publico (1913), p 321

EEK, Hilding, 'Nationell folkrätt och internationell
rätt', Statsvetenskaplig Tidskrift (1950), pp
298-323

FERRARI BRAVO, L, Diritto internazionale e
diritto interno nella stipulazione dei trattati (1964).
349 pp

GEORGESCO, V A, 'La valeur juridique des
conventions internationales et leur conflict avec
de droit interne', in Mélanges Negulesco (Bucureşti,
1935), p 287

GUGGENHEIM, P, Zum Verhaltnis von Volkerrecht
zum staatlichen Recht, (Karlsruhe, 1935), p 91

GÜGGENHEIM, P, Völkerrechtliche Schranken im
Landesrecht (Karlsruhe: Schrif. der jur. Studienges,
1955)

JIMINEZ DE ARECHAGA, E, 'Introducción al problema de las relaciones entre el derecho internacional y el derecho interno', Revista Juridica de Buenos Aires, Enero-Junio 1962 (no 1-2), pp 167-94

JÄGERSKIÖLD, Stig, Folkrätt och inomstatlig rätt, (Stockholm: Almqvist & Wiksell, 1955). 244 pp

JÄGERSKIÖLD, Stig, Folkrättsliga plikter och inomstatliga avgöranden, SVJT (1961), p 689

KELSEN, H, 'Les Rapports de système entre le droit interne et le droit international', Acad. Droit Int. Recl. Cours, vol 14 (1926), p 231

KELSEN, H, 'Die Einheit von Völkerrecht und staatlichem Recht', Z. Ausl. Öff. Recht & Völkerrecht, vol 19, nos 1-3 (August 1958), pp 234-48

KELSEN, H, 'La Transformation du droit international en droit interne', Rev. Gén. Droit Int. Public (1936), p 47

KUNZ, J L, 'Landesrecht und Völkerrecht', in Wörterbuch des Völkerrechts (Berlin: De Gruyter, 1960), vol 1, p 782

KUNZ, J L, 'Pluralism of legal and value systems and international law', Am. J. Int. Law, vol 49 (1955), p 370

KUNZ, J L, 'La primauté du droit des gens', Rev. Droit Int. & Légis. Comp, (1925), p 558

LA PERGOLA, A, Costituzione e adattamento dell' dell'ordinamento interno al diritto internazionale (Milano, 1961).

LA PERGOLA, A, 'La transformación del derecho internacional en derecho interno y la teoria de Hans Kelsen', Rev. Esp. Derecho Int., (1961)

LIPARTITI, C, 'L'adattamento degli ordinamenti interni al diritto internazionale nelle carte costituzionali', Archivio giuridico 'Filippo Serafini', vol 144 nos 1-2 (January-April 1953), pp 73-138

LIPARTITI, C, 'L'adattamento degli ordinamenti giuridici interni alle norme del diritto internazionale sanctito nelle carte costituzionale degli stati', Rev. Droit Int. Sci. Dipl. & Polit., vol 32 no. 1 (January-March, 1954), pp 38-60

McDOUGAL, M S, 'The impact of international law upon national law: A policy-oriented perspective', South Dakota Law Review, vol 4 (1959), pp 25; 33-4

MAREK, K, 'Les rapports entre le droit international et le droit interne à la lumière de la jurisprudence de la CPJI', Rev. Gén. Droit Int. Public (1962), p 260

MARÍN LÓPEZ, A, 'El problema de las relaciones entre el derecho interno y el derecho internacional en las constituciones', Rev. Esp. Derecho Int., vol 5, no. 2 (1952), pp 529-602

MENZEL, E, 'Neue Tendenzen in der Frage der Zuordnung von Völkerrecht und staatlichem Recht', Schriftenr. Dtsch. Gruppe Assoc. Auditeurs & Anc. Auditeurs Acad. Droit Int. La Haye, vol 3 (1969), p 47

MONACO, R, L'ordinamento internazionale in relazione all'ordinamento statuale (Torino, 1932)

MONACO, R, L'ordinamento internazionale in rapporto all'ordinamento statuale (Torino, 1930)

MONACO, R, 'L'adattamento del diritto interno al diritto internazionale', in Conferenze del II Corso di perfezionamento per uditori giudiziari (Milan, 1959), p 139

MORELLI, G, 'L'adattamento del diritto interno al diritto internazionale in alcune recenti constituzioni', Riv. Diritto Int. (1933), p 3

MORGENSTERN, F, 'Judicial practice and the supremacy of international law', Br. Yearb. Int. Law (1950), p 42

MOSLER, H, 'L'application du droit international par les tribunaux nationaux', Acad. Droit Int. Recl. Cours, vol 91 (1957), p 619

MUNCH, F, 'Droit international et droit interne d'après la Constitution de Bonn', Rev. Int. Fr. Droit Gens, vol 19 (1950), pp 5-20

NAGEL, H, 'Die Begrenzung des internationalen Zivilprozeßrechts durch das Völkerrecht zugleich ein Versuch, einige Wechselwirkungen dieser beiden Zweige des Rechts aufzuzeigen', Zeitschrift für Zivilprozeß (1962), p 408

PARTSCH, J, Die Anwendung des Völkerrechts im innerstaatlichen Recht. Überprüfung der Transformationslehre (Berichte der Deutschen Gesellschaft für Völkerrecht, no 6) (Karlsruhe, 1963). 179 pp.

RAPISARDI, MIRABELLI, A, 'Diritto internazionale e diritto interno in ordine alle loro reciproche influenze', in Scritti in onore di Pietro Rossi (Siena, 1931), p 7

RIZA GULLU, A, 'Les rapports entre le droit interne et le droit international', Rev. Droit Int. Sci. Dipl. & Polit., vol 37 (1959), pp 267-73

SALVIOLI, G, 'Diritto internazionale e diritto interno', Archivio di Studi Corperativi (1930), p 325

SCHEUNER, U, 'L'influence du droit interne sur la formation du droit international', Acad. Droit Int. Recl. Cours, vol 68 (1939), p 95

SCHIFFER, W, Die Lehre vom Primat des Völkerrechts in der neueren Litteratur (Leipzig/ Wien, 1937)

SEIDL-HOHENVELDERN, I, 'Grundgesetz und Völkerrecht', Annales Universitatis Saraviensis, vol 8, nos 1-2 (1960), pp 51-8

SEIDL-HOHENVELDERN, I, 'Transformation or adoption of international law into municipal law', Int. & Comp. Law Q., vol 12 (1963), pp 88-124

SOFRONIE, G, 'Les rapports entre le droit international et le droit intérieur à la lumière du principe de l'unité du droit public', in Mélanges Negulesco (Bucharest, 1935), p 663

SMITH, Carsten, 'Den internasjonale rettens innvirkning på den nasjonale retten', Tidsskrift for Rettsvitenskap (1962), pp 182-204

SPERDUTI, G, 'Diritto internazionale e diritto interno', Rev. Diritto Int., vol 41 (1958), pp 188-98

STARKE, J G, 'Monism and dualism in the theory of international law', Br. Yearb. Int. Law (1936), pp 66-81

STARKE, J G, 'Treaties as a "source of international law" ', Br. Yearb. Int. Law (1946), pp 341-6

TRIEPEL, Heinrich, Völkerrecht und Landesrecht (Leipzig: Hirschfeld, 1899). xii + 452 pp. Reissued by Scientia, Aalen, 1958

TRIEPEL, Heinrich, 'Les rapports entre le droit international et le droit interne', Acad. Droit Int. Recl. Cours, vol 1 (1923), pp 73-121

VALLADAO, H, 'O direito internacional no projeto da constituiçao', Boletim da Sociedade brasil de dir. internacional, vol 2 no 3 (1946), pp 7-17

VANDENBRANDE, L, 'Overzicht der bepalingen aangaande de internationale betrekkingen in de Europese grondwetten en in de grondwet der Verenigde Staten van Amerika' Volkenrechtelijke berichten, 1953, no 2, pp 67-133

VERDROSS, A, 'Die normative Verknüpfung von Völkerrecht und staatlichen Recht', in Festschrift für Adolf Merkl (München, 1970), p 425

VERDROSS, A, Die Verfassung der Völkerrechtsgemeinschaft (Wien, 1926)

VERDROSS, A, Die Einheit des rechtlichen Weltbildes auf Grundlage der Völkerrechtsverfassung (Tübingen/Wien, 1923)

VERDROSS, A, 'Zur Konstruktion des Völkerrechts', Z. Völkerrecht (1914), p 329

VEROSTA, S, 'Der Primat des Völkerrechts und die Vereinten Nationen', in Mélanges Andrassy (Den Haag, 1968), p 351

VEROSTA, S, 'Droit international et droit interne chez Jean Dumont (1666-1727)' in Mélanges offerts à Henri Rolin (Paris, 1964), pp 479-87

VIRALLY, M, 'Sur un pont aux anes: les rapports entre droit international et droits internes', in Mélanges offerts à Henri Rolin (Paris, 1964), pp 488-505

WALZ, G A, Völkerrecht und staatliches Recht (Stuttgart: Kohlhammer, 1933)

WALZ, G A, 'Les rapports du droit international et du droit interne', Acad. Droit Int. Recl. Cours, vol 61 (1937), p 379

WENZEL, I, Juristische Grundprobleme (Wien, 1920) 344 pp

WIEBRINGHAUS, H, 'Beitrag zur Frage des Verhältnisses von Internationalprivat - und Völkerrecht', Juristische Rundschau (1952), p 383

WRIGHT, Q, 'The enforcement of international law through municipal law in the United States', Am. J. Int. Law (1916)

WRIGHT, Q, 'Conflicts of international law with national laws and ordinances', Am. J. Int. Law, vol 11 (1917), pp 1-21

WRIGHT, Q, 'International law in its relation to constitutional law', Am. J. Int. Law (1923), pp 234-44

ZEMANEK, K, 'Über das dualistische Denken in der Völkerrechtswissenschaft', in Festschrift für Verdross, (Wien, 1960), p 321

3.3.2 RELATIONSHIP BETWEEN INTERNATIONAL LAW AND SPECIFIC COUNTRIES

The actual implementation or effect of international law in the municipal law of states is a question which is of increasing importance: when joining the European Communities several member states found that their constitutions did not allow for the delegation of law-making power, or for the immediate effect of certain regulations or decisions by the Communities. Discussion among scholars has dealt with international law and constitutions with progressive constitutions (like the Dutch one, which allows for immediate effect of treaties without transformation) and possible revisions of others. Effects of general rules of international law in states, and with the necessity of transformation. Discussion has, on the whole, been more intense in Europe than in other parts of the world. Among the cross-references mentioned at the beginning of Section 3.1, I may specifically refer to Section 7.13.13.2 on the effect of treaties in particular states.

3.3.2.1 INTERNATIONAL LAW & SEVERAL COUNTRIES OR GROUPS OF COUNTRIES

DICKINSON, E D, 'L'interprétation et application du droit international dans les pays anglo-américains', Acad. Droit Int. Recl. Cours, vol 40 (1932), pp 305-95

DICKINSON, E D, The Interpretation and Application of International Law in Anglo-American Countries (Ann Arbor, 1932)

ERADES, L, & GOULD, W, The Relation Between International Law and Municipal Law in the Netherlands and in the United States (Leiden: Sijthoff, 1961). 510 pp.

MASTERS, R D, International Law in National
Courts: A Study of the Enforcement of International
Law in German, Swiss, French and Belgian Courts
(New York: Columbia University Press/London:
King & Son, 1932). 245 pp.

PAYOT, F, 'Les instructions du gouvernement lors de
l'interprétation judiciaire du droit international.
Etude des pratiques anglaise et américaine', Thesis,
Lausanne. 1950

PICCIOTTO, Cyril H, The Relation of International
Law to the Law of England and of the United States
of America (London: McBride, Nast & Co. Ltd, 1915).
128 pp.

3.3.2.2 GREAT BRITAIN

GRASSETTI, C, Diritto interno e diritto internazionale
nell'ordinamento giuridico anglo-americano
(Pavia, 1934)

LAUTERPACHT, E, 'The contemporary practice of the
United Kingdom in the field of international law -
survey and comment,' Int. & Comp. Law Q., vol 4
(1956-7), p 528

LAUTERPACHT, H, 'Is international law a part of the
law of England?' Grotius Soc. Trans., vol 25
(1939)

LEFEBURE, M, 'The application of international law
in the English courts', Z. Ausl. Öff. Recht &
Völkerrecht, vol 17 (1957), pp 568-612

MENZEL, E, 'Der Wirkungsgrad der Völkerrechts-
normen in englischen Recht', Z. Völkerrecht
(1934), pp 155-80

SMITH, H A, Great Britain and the Law of Nations,
vol 1 (London: P S King & Sons Ltd., 1932)

3.3.2.3 FRANCE

DINH, Nguyen Quoc, 'La constitution de 1958 et le droit international', Rev. Droit Public & Sci. Polit., vol 75 (1959), pp 515-64

DONNEDIEU DE VABRES, H, 'La constitution de 1946 et le droit international', Dalloz Chroniques (1948), pp 439-40

KISS, A C, Répertoire de la pratique française en matière de droit international public (Paris: Editions du Centre National de la Recherche Scientifique, 1962-6). 5 vols.

PFLOESCHNER, F, 'Les dispositions de la Constitution du 27 octobre 1946 sur la primauté du droit international et leur effet sur la situation des étrangèrs en France sous la IVe République' (Thesis. Genève, 1961).

PREUSS, L, 'The relation of international law to internal law in the French constitutional system', Am. J. Int. Law, vol 44 (1950), p 641

PREUSS, L, 'Droit international et droit interne dans la constitution française de 1946', RIHPC, nos 3-4 (July-December 1951), pp 199-224

3.3.2.4 GERMANY AND THE REICH

CONSTANTOPOULOS, D S, 'The relation of the law of nations to constitutional law and the new constitutions of Germany', Rev. Hell. Droit Int., vol 5 (1952), pp 42-62

MIECK, A, Die Anerkennung der Regeln des Völkerrechts im Sinne der art. 4 der Reichsverfassung (Heidelberg, 1929)

MIEHSLER, H, 'Alfred Verdross' Theorie des gemässigten Monismus und das Bundesverfassungsgesetz vom 4 März 1964 (BGB1 nr 59)', Juristische Blätter, vol 87, nos 21-12 (13 November 1965), pp 566-73

MOSLER, H, Das Völkerrecht in der Praxis der deutschen Gerichte (Stuttgart: 1957)

MÜNCH, F, 'Droit international et droit interne d'après la Constitution de Bonn', Rev. Int. Fr. Droit Gens., vol 19 (1950), pp 5-20

PIGORSCH, W, Die Einordnung völkerrechtlicher Normen in das Recht der Bundesrepublik Deutschland (Hamburg, 1959)

RUDOLF, W, Völkerrecht und deutsches Recht - Theoretische und dogmatische Untersuchungen über die Anwendung völkerrechtlicher Normen in der Bundesrepublik Deutschland, (Tübingen, 1967)

See also:

PREUSS, L, 'International law in the constitutions of the Länder in the American zone in Germany', Am. J. Int. Law, vol 41 (1947), pp 888-99

3.3.2.5 NETHERLANDS

See the work by ERADES and GOULD listed in Section 3.3.2.1

PANHUYS, H F van, 'The Netherlands constitution and international law', Am J. Int. Law, vol 47 (1953), pp 537-58

PANHUYS, H F van, 'Pays-Bas. La révision récente des dispositions constitutionnelles relatives aux relations internationales', Rev. Droit Public & Sci. Polit., vol 71 (1955), pp 330-56

PANHUYS, H F, van, 'The Netherlands constitution and international law: A decade of experience', Am. J. Int. Law, vol 58 (1964), pp 88-108

3.3.2.6 ITALY

BISCOTTINI, G, 'L'adeguamento del diritto italiano alle norme internazionali', Jus (1951), p 213

FABOZZI, C, Problemi di diritto internazionale nella giurisprudenza italiana (1954)

FIORE, M, 'The relation of the international to the domestic law and the Italian constitution', Schriftenr. Dtsch. Gruppe Assoc. Auditeurs & Anc. Auditeurs Acad. Droit. Int. La Haye (1957), pp 165-78

MONACO, R, 'L'adattamento del diritto interno al diritto internazionale nell'art 10 della Costituzione', Foro Padano, vol 4 (1949), p 190

MIELE, M, La Costituzione Italiana e il diritto internazionale (Milano, 1951)

MIELE, M, 'L'adattamento del diritto italiano al diritto internazionale secondo la nuova costituzione', Rassegna di Diritto Pubblico, vol 6 (1951), pp 221-37

3.3.2.7 SWITZERLAND

GUGGENHEIM, P, 'Le conflit entre le droit des gens et le droit national dans l'ordre juridique suisse', Scritti di diritto internazionale in onore di Tomaso Perassi (Milano, 1957), vol 1 pp 499-513

3.3.2.8 AUSTRIA

RILL, H P, 'Der Rang der allgemein anerkannten Regeln des Völkerrechts in der österreichischen Rechtsordnung', Österr. Z. Öff. Recht, vol 10 (1960), pp 439-51

SEIDL-HOHENVELDERN, I, 'Relation of international law to internal law in Austria', Am. J. Int. Law, vol 49 (1955), pp 451-76

3.3.2.9 NORWAY

HAMBRO, E, 'Noen bemerkninger om forholdet mellom norsk rett og folkerett', Tidsskrift for Rettsvitenskap (1947), pp 96-110

HAMBRO, E, 'Some remarks about the relations
between municipal law and international law in
Norway', Acta Scandinavica juris gentium, vol 19
(1949), pp 3-27
HAMBRO, E, 'La théorie de la réception du droit
international par le droit interne en droit norvégien
in Law, State and International Legal Order, edited by
S Engel & R A Metall (Knoxville, Tenn: University of
Tennesee Press, 1964)

3.3.2.10 SWEDEN

See JÄGERSKIÖLD, listed under 3.3.1.

3.3.2.11 GREECE

VALTICOS, N, 'Monisme ou dualisme? Les rapports
des traités et de la loi en Grèce (spécialement à
propos des conventions internationales du travail)',
Rev. Hell. Droit Int., vol 11 (1958), pp 203-35
KYRIACOPOULOS, E, 'Le droit international et la
constitution hellénique de 1952. (Contribution à
l'étude des rapports entre le droit international et
le droit interne)', Gegenwartsprobleme des
internationalen Rechts und der Rechtsphilosophie
(1953), pp 201-12

3.3.2.12 SPAIN

PERASSI, T, 'La nuova costituzione spagnola e il
diritto internazionale', Riv. Diritto Int. (1932)
pp 453-6

3.3.2.13 USSR

CALVEZ, J Y, Droit international et souveraineté
en URSS l'évolution de l'idéologie juridique

soviétique depuis la révolution d'octobre (Paris, 1953). 299 pp.

MARGOLIS, E, 'Soviet views on the relationship between national and international law', Int. & Comp. Law Q., vol 4 (1955), pp 116-28

3.3.2.14 YUGOSLAVIA

AVRAMOV, S, 'Application of international law in the Yugoslav law', Jugoslovenska Revija za Medzunarodno Pravo (1956) no 1, pp 192-205. (In English and French).

DORDEVIC, J, 'La constitution de la Yougoslavie et le droit international', Jugoslovenska Revija za Medzunarodno Pravo, vol 3, no 1 (1956), pp 5-11

3.3.2.15 AUSTRALIA

ALEXANDROWICZ, C H, 'International law in the municipal sphere according to Australian decisions', Int. & Comp. Law Q., vol 13 (1964), pp 78-95

O'CONNELL, D P, International Law in Australia (London: Stevens & Sons, 1965). 603 pp.

3.3.2.16 CANADA

MACKENZIE, Norman, & LAING, Lionel H, (eds), Canada and the Law of Nations (Toronto: The Ryerson Press/New Haven, Conn: Yale University Press/London: Oxford University Press/For the Carnegie Endowment for International Peace, 1938). 567 pp.

3.3.2.17 UNITED STATES

See also the work by ERADES and GOULD listed in Section 3.3.2.1 and the general textbook by HYDE, listed in Section 1.8

FAWCETT, J E S, 'Some recent applications of international law by the United States', Br. Yearb. Int. Law, vol 34 (1958), pp 384-91

PERGLER, C, Judicial Interpretation of International Law in the United States (New York, 1928).

3.3.2.18 LATIN AMERICA

FAVILLI, V, 'Aspetti internazionalistici in due recenti costituzioni americane; Nicaragua (1950) e Venezuela (1953)', Annu. Diritto Comp. & Studi. Legis., vol 32 (1957)

GIBSON, W M, 'International law and the Columbian constitution 1942', Am. J. Int. Law, vol 36, p 614

3.3.2.19 INDIA

AGRAWALA, S K, 'Law of nations as interpreted and applied by Indian courts and legislature', Indian J. Int. Law, vol 2 (1962), pp 431-78

SARUP, R K P, 'International law and national law: a fresh approach for mutual development. A case study in Indian law', Nord. Tidsskr. Int. Ret. vol 35 (1965), pp 33-60

SINGH, N, & KAZWAK, M K, 'The contemporary practice of India in the field of international law', International Studies, vol 3 (1962)

3.3.2.20 JAPAN

KOTANI, T S, 'Le Japon et le droit international', Rev. Gén. Droit Int. Public, vol 64 (1960), p 18

4 Codification of International Law

As international law is, or at least has been, a largely uncodified legal system, the process of codification is of special importance in this discipline. The nature of a particular 'source' of international law may also change as such a process takes place; from having been a 'customary rule' or a 'general principle' a norm may, by codification, become incorporated in a general treaty and thus, as codification progresses the written sources, especially treaties, will increase and the body of 'customary law' and 'general principles' will, if not decrease, lose some of their autonomous importance. Any reference to works on codification would be incomplete without mentioning the International Law Commission, see above in Section 1.1. Writers have shown interest in the process of codification, first in the early thirties after the first codification conference of the League of Nations, and second after the work of the ILC started to bear fruit.

AGO, R, 'La codification du droit international et
    les problèmes de sa réalisation', in Etudes à
    Guggenheim (Genève, 1968)
ALVAREZ, A, La Codification du droit international
    (Paris, 1912)

ALVAREZ, A, 'Rapport sur la codification du droit international', Académie diplomatique internationale: séances et travaux, vol 2 (1928), pp 29-33

ALVAREZ, A, 'Rapport général au nom du comité de codification du droit international', Académie diplomatique internationale: séances et travaux (3e année no 2), pp 51-3

ALVAREZ, A, 'La codification du droit à l'International law association', Rev. Droit Int. (July-September 1931), pp 7-55

ALVAREZ, A, 'La codification du droit des gens en Europe et en Amérique: ses difficultés; manière de la réaliser', Congrès (Premier) d'études internationales (1937), 1938, pp 229-65

ALVAREZ, A, Le Continent américain et la codification du droit international: Une nouvelle 'école' du droit des gens (Paris: Les éditions internationales, 1938). 95 pp.

ALVAREZ, A, 'Méthodes de la codification du droit international public', Annu. Inst. Droit Int. (1947), pp 38-71

American Society of International Law, Drafts of Conventions prepared for the Codification of International Law. III. Law of Treaties (Rapporteur: J W Garner) (Washington, DC: American Society of International Law, 1935)

ARMINJON, P, 'La codification du droit international', Revue politique et parlementaire (10 January 1933), pp 111-27

BAAK, J C, 'La codification doit-elle être universelle? Une distinction nécessaire', Rev. Droit Int. & Légis. Comp., vol 11 (1930), p 721

BASTID, S, 'Observations sur une étape dans le développement progressif et la codification des principes du droit international', in Etudes Guggenheim (Genève, 1968), p 132

BAXTER, R R, 'The effects of illconceived codification and development of international law', in Etudes Guggenheim (Genève, 1968), p 146

BEUS, J G de, 'De ontwikkeling en codificatie van het internationale recht door de vereenigde naties', Nederlandse jurisprudentie, no 39 (15 November 1947), pp 649-57

BRIERLY, J L, 'The future of codification', Br. Yearb. Int. Law, vol 12 (1931), pp 1-12

BRIERLY, J L, 'The codification of international law', Michigan Law Review (1948), p 2

BRIGGS, H W, 'Codification of treaties and provisions on reciprocity, non-discrimination or retaliation: Editorial comment', Am. J. Int. Law, vol 56 (1962), p 475

BROWN, P M, 'The codification of international law', Am. J. Int. Law, vol 29 (1935), pp 25-39

CANYES, M S, 'La codificación del derecho internacional en America', Annuario juridico interamericano (1948), pp 40-60

CASTRÉN, E, 'La codification du droit international', in International Law Association Report of the Fifty-Second Conference held at Helsinki August 14th to August 20th, 1966 (London: ILA, 1967), pp 11-25

CHENG, B, 'General principles of law as a subject for international codification', Current Legal Problems (1951), pp 35-53

CONSTANTINOFF, J, La Codification du droit international et l'unification législative suivie d'une liste de conventions internationales et des états qui les appliquent (Paris: Duchemin, 1929). 240 pp.

CROCKER, H G, 'The codification of international law: some preliminary queries', Am. J. Int. Law (1924)

DHOKALIA, R P, The Codification of Public International Law (Manchester: Manchester University Press/Dobbs Ferry, New York: Oceana Publications Inc., 1970). xvi + 367 pp.

DREYER, J P, Essai sur l'évolution de la législation internationale depuis le dix-neuvième siècle jusqu'au projet de traité portant statut de la Communauté politique européenne (Basel, 1955). x + 170 pp.
ERICH, R, 'Quelques aspects généraux de la codification du droit international', Rev. Droit Int. & Légis. Comp. (1921), p 1
FRANÇOIS, J P A, 'De aanstaande conferentie tot codificatie van het internationale recht', De Volkebond, June-July 1929, p 266
GIANNINI, A, 'La codificazione del diritto internazionale', Annu. Diritto Comp. & Studi Legis, vol 25, no 1 (1949), pp 1-26
GUERRERO, J G, La codification du droit international (Paris, 1930)
GUTZWILLER, M, 'Menschenrechte und Kodifikation des Völkerrechts. Glossen zur 42. Konferenz der International Law Association, Prag, 31 August bis 6 September 1947', Die Frieden-Warte, vol 47, nos 4-5, pp 198-305
HACKWORTH, G H, 'The International Court of Justice and the codification of international law', American Bar Association Journal (February 1946), pp 81-6
HAZARD, J N, 'Codifying peaceful co-existence', Am. J. Int. Law, vol 55 (1961), pp 109-20
HONIG, F, 'Progress in the codification of international law', Int. Aff. (UK), vol 36, no 1 (January 1960), pp 62-72
HUDSON, M O, 'The first conference for the codification of international law', Am. J. Int. Law, vol 24 (1930), p 447
HUDSON, M O, 'The progressive codification of international law', Am. J. Int. Law (1926), p 655

HURST, Sir Cecil, 'A plea for codification of international law on new lines', Grotius Soc. Trans., vol 32 (1946)

JENNINGS, R Y, 'Progressive development of international law and its codification', Br. Yearb. Int. Law, vol 24 (1947), p 301

KERNO, I, 'Om folkerettens kodifikation', Nord. Tidsskr. Int. Ret., vol 21 (1951), pp 27-37

KUCERA, B, Konference pro kodifikaci prava mezinárodniho v Haagu a její výskeky (n.p., 1930). 14 pp.

KUCERA, B, 'The problem of the progressive codification of international law III. The organizing committee and the results of its activity', (In Czech.), Zahranicni politika, January 1930, p 72; March 1930, p 327; April 1930, p 432

KUNZ, J L, 'La codificazione del diritto internazionale e la commissione delle N U per il diritto internazionale', La Comunità Internazionale, vol 4, nos 2-3 (April-July 1949), pp 277-83

LAUTERPACHT, H, 'Codification and development of international law', Am. J. Int. Law, vol 49 (1955), pp 16-43

LIAIS, M, 'Considération sur l'oeuvre de la Conférence de codification', Rev. Gen. Droit Int. Public, vol 38 (1931), p 215

LIANG, Y, 'Documents on the development and codification of international law', Am.J. Int. Law, vol 41 (1947), supp. p 29

LIANG, Yuen-Li, 'The progressive development of international law and its codification under the United Nations', (followed by discussion), Proceedings of the American Society of International Law (1947), pp 24-64

LIANG, Yuen-Li, 'De forenede nationer og den internationale rets udvikling og kodifikation', Nord. Tidsskr. Int. Ret, vol 18 (1947/8), pp 229-51

LIANG, Yuen-Li, Codification. Report(s) of the 43rd Conference of the International Law Association (1948), pp 155-67

LIANG, Yuen-Li, 'Methods for the encouragement of the progressive development of international law and its codification', Yearb. World Aff. (1948), pp 237-71

LIANG, Yuen-Li, 'The United Nations and the development and codification of international law. Conference (Second international of the legal profession at The Hague (International bar association) 1948

LIANG, Yuen-Li, 'Le developpement et la codification du droit international', Acad. Droit Int. Recl. Cours, vol 73 (1948), pp 407-532

LIANG, Yuen-Li, 'The General Assembly and the progressive development and codification of international law', Am. J. Int. Law, vol 42 (1948), pp 66-97

LINARES FLEYTAS, A, 'La codificación del derecho internacional y su consideración durante el segundo y tercer periodo de sesiones de la comisión de derecho internacional de la ONU', Revista de Derecho Internacional (1951), pp 5-21; pp 409-41

LISSITZYN, O J, 'Efforts to codify or restate the law of treaties', Columbia Law Review, vol 62, no 7 (November 1962), pp 1166-1205

MANCINI, Vocazione dei nostri tempi per los riformo e la codificazione del diritto delle gente (Milano 1873)

MARESH, A, La Codification du droit international (Paris, 1932)

MARX, R, 'Die vereinten Nationen und die kodifikation des internationalen Rechts', Arch. Völkerrechts (1948), pp 270-302

McNAIR, A D, 'The present position of the codification of international law', Grotius Soc. Trans., vol 13 (1927), pp 129-41

MILLER, H, 'The Hague codification conference', Am. J. Int. Law, vol 24 (1930), p 674

MOVTCHANE, A P, 'O znatchenii kodifikatsii printsipov mezhdounarodnovo prava', Sovetskoye Gosudarstvo i Pravo, vol 35, no 1 (January 1965), pp 46-55

NIBOYET, J P, 'La codification du droit international', B L C (April-June 1931), pp 331-59

NIEMEYER, Th, 'Vom Beruf unserer Zeit für Revision und Kodifikation des internationalen Rechtes', Niemeyers Z. Int. Recht, vol 49 (1934), pp 3-21

PIIP, A, 'Codification of international law', American Academy of Political Science Annals, vol 168 (July 1933), pp 220-5

POT, C W Van Der, LANSCHOT, W Van, & FORTUIN, H, 'De codificatie van het internationale recht en de Vereeniging voor Volkenbond en vrede', De Volkenbond, August-September 1932, supp. pp 1-10

RADOJVIC, 'Codification of the principles of active peaceful co-existence', N Y L, vol 12, nos 1-3 (January-September 1961), pp 65-73

RAUCHBERG, H, 'Die erste Konferenz sur Kodifikation des Völkerrechts', Z. Off. Recht., vol 10 (1931), p 481

RAUCHHAUPT, W Von, 'Le problème de la codification du droit international: comparaison entre les méthodes européennes et américaines', pp 39-46 of Introduction à l'étude du droit comparé, vol 2, translated by S Basdevant-Bastid (Paris 1938)

ROLIN, H A, 'Quelques observations sur la conférence de codification (La Haye, Mars-Avril 1930)', Rev. Droit Int. & Légis. Comp. (1930), pp 581-99

RUHLAND, C, System der völkerrechtlichen Kollektivverträge als Beitrag sur Kodifikation des Völkerrechts (Berlin: Stilke, 1929). 104 pp.
REEVES, J S, 'The Hague conference on the codification of international law', Am. J. Int. Law (1930), p 52
ROSENNE, Shabtai, (ed), League of Nations Committee of Experts for the Progressive Codification of International Law (Dobbs Ferry, NY: Oceana, 1972). 2 vols
SAHOVIC, M, 'La codification du droit international dans le monde moderne', Jugoslovenska Revija za Medjunarodno Pravo no 2 (1960)
SCOTT, J B, 'Gradual and progressive codification of international law', Am. J. Int. Law, vol 21 (1927), p 417
SPIROPOULOS, J, 'La codification du droit international par l'Organisation des Nations Unies (Conférence au IXe Congrès de l'A A A, Athènes 3 mai 1957)', Assoc. Auditeurs & Anc. Auditeurs Acad. Droit Int. La Haye, vol 28 (1958), pp 156-65
STEINIGER, P A, 'The United Nations debate on the codification of the principles of international law', German Foreign Policy, vol 5, no 3 (1966), pp 236-45
STRUPP, K, 'Communication sur la tâche confiée à la commission de l'Académie diplomatique internationale, sur la codification du droit international public', Academie Diplomatique Internationale: Séances et Travaux, vol 1, no 2 (1928), pp 33-45
STRUPP, K, 'Völkerrechtskodifikation', Z. Öff. Recht., vol 7 (1927/8), p 153
STRUPP, K, 'Die sogenannte Haager Völkerrechtskodifikationskonferenz (13. März-12.April 1930)', J W (1/14 June 1930), p 1814

THEILER, E, 'La codification du droit international public', Conference (Second international) of the legal profession at The Hague (International bar association) 1948.

THIRLWAY, H W A, International Customary Law and Codification, listed below under 5.3

UDINA, M, 'La codificazione del diritto internazionale', Politica Sociale, (August-October 1930)

URRUTIA, F J, 'La codification du droit international en Amérique', Acad. Droit Int. Recl. Cours, vol 22 (1928), p 81

VISSCHER, Ch. De, 'La codification du droit international', Acad. Droit Int. Recl. Cours (1929), vol 6

WENGLER, W, Reform, Kodifikation und Revision im Völkerrecht (Bad Homburg, 1958)

5 Sources of International Law

Among the works listed below Sørensen's book (see Section 5.2) is interesting for a general survey of sources of international law and it has become a standard book on the subject. For 'subsidiary' sources such as the writings of publicists, see the work by SØRENSEN. For cases, see above under Section 1.4.

5.1 HISTORY OF THE SOURCES OF INTERNATIONAL LAW

GUGGENHEIM, P, 'Contribution à l'histoire des sources du droit des gens', Acad. Droit Int. Recl. Cours, vol 94 (1958), pp 1-84

See also Section 2.2 on the history of international law.

5.2 SOURCES IN GENERAL

AGO, R, 'Positive law and international law', Am. J. Int. Law, vol 51 (1957), p 691

BORCHARD, E M, 'The theory and sources of international law', in Recueil Gény, vol 3 (Paris, 1934), p 328

CORBETT, P E, 'The constitution of states and sources of the law of nations', Br. Yearb. Int. Law, vol 6 (1925)

FINCH, G A, 'Les sources modernes du droit international', Acad. Droit Int. Recl. Cours, vol 53 (1935), pp 531-629

FINCH, G A, The Sources of Modern International Law (Washington, DC: Carnegie Endowment for International Peace, 1937). ix + 124 pp.

FINCH, G A, 'The sources of modern international law', Cursos monograficos (Havana, 1948), vol 1, pp 453-528

FITZMAURICE, Sir Gerald, 'The general principles of international law considered from the standpoint of the rule of law', Acad. Droit Int. Recl. Cours, vol 92 (1957), pp 1-227

FITZMAURICE, G G, 'Some problems regarding the formal sources of international law', in Symbolae Verzijl. Présentées au Professeur J H W Versijl à l'occasion de son LXX-ième anniversaire (Den Haag: Nijhoff, 1958), pp 153-74

GIHL, T, 'The legal character and sources of international law', Scandinavian Studies in Law, vol 1 (1957), pp 51-92

Grotius Society, 'International law in development. Discussion on the report of the committee on "sources of international law". Introduced by W Friedmann before the Grotius Society on July 2, 1941', Grotius Soc. Trans., vol 27 (1942), pp 214-88

HEILBORN, P, 'Les sources du droit international', Acad. Droit Int. Recl. Cours, vol 11 (1926), p 5

JAENICKE, G, 'Völkerrechtsquellen', in Wörterbuch des Völkerrecht, vol 3, p 766

JENNINGS, R Y, 'Recent developments in the International Law Commission: its relation to the sources of international law', Int. & Comp. Law Q., vol 13 (1964), p 385

KOPELMANAS, L, 'Essai d'une théorie des sources formelles du droit international', Rev. Droit Int. (1938), pp 101-50

MARAK, FURRIER & MARTIN, Les Sources du droit international (Genève, 1967)
MEISSNER, B, 'Die Sowjetische Bewertung der Völkerrechtsquellen', Osteuropa-Recht, (March 1955), pp 2-8
PARRY, C, The Sources and Evidence of International Law (Manchester: Manchester University Press, 1965)
QUADRI, R, 'Cours général du droit international public', Acad. Droit Int. Recl. Cours, vol 113 (1964), p 245. Especially pp 319 et seq.
ROSS, A, Theorie der Rechtsquellen (Leipzig/Wien: Deuticke, 1929). xiv + 458 pp.
RUYSSEN, T, Les Sources doctrinales de l'internationalism (Paris, 1954). 3 vols.
SCELLE, G, 'Essai sur les sources formelles du droit internationale', in Recueil d'études sur les sources du droit en l'honneur de Francois Gény (Paris (?) 1936), vol 3, pp 400-30
SØRENSEN, M, Les Sources du droit international. Etude sur la jurisprudence de la Cour permanente de justice internationale (København: Munksgaard, 1946). 274 pp.
VALINDAS, P G, 'Hierarchy of sources of international law', Fundamental Problems of International law, Festschfift - Jean Spiropoulos-Mélanges (Bonn, 1957)
VISSCHER, C de, 'Contribution à l'étude des sources du droit international', Rev. Droit Int. & Legis. Comp. (1933), p 395
VISSCHER, C de,'Coutume et traité en droit international public', Rev. Gen. Droit Int. Public, vol 59 (1955), pp 353-69

5.3 CUSTOM AND CUSTOMARY LAW

The work by D'Amato is a recent and interesting study

of the development of customary law.
BALLADORE PALLIERI, G, 'La forza obbligatoria della consuetudine internazionale', Riv. Diritto Int. (1928), p 338
BOBBIO, N, 'La consuetudine como fatto normativo (Padova, 1942). 49 pp.
CAVAGLIERE, A, La consuetudine giuridica internazionale (Padova, 1907)
D'AMATO, Anthony A, The concept of Custom in International Law (Ithaca, NY/London: Cornell University Press, 1971). xvi + 286 pp.
GIANNI, G, La Coutume de droit international (Paris, 1931)
GOUET, Ivon, La Coutume en droit constitutionnel interne et en droit international (Paris, 1932)
GUGGENHEIM, P, 'L'origine de la notion de l'opinio juris sive necessitatis comme deux éléments de la coutume dans l'histoire du droit des gens', in Etudes en l'honneur de Georges Scelle (Paris: Librairie général de droit et de jurisprudence, 1950)
HAEMMERLE, A, La Coutume en droit des gens après la jurisprudence de la Cour permanente de justice international (Nancy, 1935)
KELSEN, H, 'Théorie du droit international coutumier', Revue International de la Théorie du Droit (1939), p 253
KOPELMANAS, L, 'Custom as a means of the creation of international law,' Br. Yearb. Int. Law (1937), p 127
KUNZ, J L, 'The nature of customary international law', Am. J. Int. Law, vol 47 (1957), p 662
LIPARTITI, C, La estensione in generalità e in obbligatiorietà delle consuetudini internazionali', Arch. giur (1939), p 87
MATEESCO, C, La Coutume dans les cycles juridiques international (Paris, 1947)

OPPENHEIM, L, 'Zur Lehre vom internationalen
  Gewohnheitsrecht', Z. Int. Recht., vol 25, p 5
RAESTAD, A, ' "Sedvanerett" og "almindelige
  grunnsetninger" i folkeretten', Nord. Tidsskr. Int.
  Ret., vol 4 (1933), pp 179-200
RAESTAD, A, ' "Droit Coutumier" et "droit convention-
  nel" en droit international', Acta scandinavica
  juris gentium, vol 4 (1933), pp 61-84
SEFERIADES, S, 'Aperçu de la coutume juridique
  international et notamment sur son fondement',
  Rev. Gén. Droit Int. Public (1936), p 114
SPERDUTI, G, 'La consuetudine internazionale', in
  Scritti per Gaspare Ambrosini (Milano, 1970), vol
  3, p 1977
THIRLWAY, H W A, International Customary Law and
  Codification (Leiden: A W Sijthoff, 1972). xii +
  158 pp.
TUNKIN, G, 'Remarks on the juridical nature of
  customary norms of international law', California
  Law Review (1961), p 419
VERDROSS, A v, 'Das Völkerrechtliche
  Gewohnheitsrecht', Jap. Annu. Int. Law (1963),
  p 4
VISSCHER, C de, 'Coutume et traité en droit
  international public', Rev. Gén. Droit Int. Public
  (1955), p 353
ZICCARDI, P, 'La consuetudine internazionale
  nella teoria delle fonti giuridiche', Comun. &
  Stud., vol 10 (1960), p 189
ZITELMANN, T, 'Gewohnheitsrecht und Irrtum',
  Archiv für die Civilitische Praxis (1883), p 412

5.4 TREATIES

Treaties, conventions and other international agreements constitute the largest source of international law. For such instruments in detail, see Section 7.13.

In this section I have only listed a few works which deal with treaties specifically as a source of international law.

BERGBOHM, K, Staatsverträge und Gesetze als Quellen des Völkerrechts (1877)

STARKE, J G, 'Treaties as a "source" of international law', Br. Yearb. Int. Law (1946), pp 341-6

TRISKA, J F, & SLUSSER, R M, 'Treaties and other sources of order in international relations: The Soviet view', Am. J. Int. Law, vol 52 (1958), p 699

5.5 GENERAL PRINCIPLES

The sources of international law also include 'general principles' or, as the Statute of the International Court of Justice specifies, such general principles as 'are recognized by civilized nations'. There is obviously a problem in identifying such principles and several writers have attempted to define their character and general nature. Bin Cheng's book, listed in Section 5.5.2 is one of the standard textbooks. See also - apart from general textbooks on international law - Jenks The Prospects of International Adjudication, listed in Section 8.7 and the Répertoire by Marek, Furrer and Martin listed in Section 1,4,3,3.

5.5.1 IDENTIFICATION OF GENERAL PRINCIPLES

AGARWALA, C B, 'General principles of law recognized by civilized nations', World Peace through Law Center Conference Reports (1965), p 547

BALLADORE-PALLIERI, G, I principi generali del diritto riconosciuti dalle nazioni civili nell'art. 38 delle Statuto della Corte Permanente di Giustizia internazionale (Torino, 1931)

BAYER, W F, 'Auslegung und Ergänzung internationaler vereinheitlichte Normen durch die staatlichen Gerichte', Rabels Z. Ausl. & Int. Privatrecht, vol 20 (1955), p 603

FAVRE, A, 'Les principes généraux du droit, fonds commun du droit des gens', in Mélanges Guggenheim (Genève, 1968), pp 366-90

FRIEDMANN, W, 'The use of general principles in the development of international law', Am. J Int. Law (1963), pp 279-99

HAMBRO, Edvard, 'De almindelige rettsgrunnsetninger som folkerrettskilde', Svensk juristtidning (1959) pp 245-56

HÄRLE, E, 'Die allgemeinen Rechtsgrundsätze im Völkerrecht', Z. Ausl. Öff. Recht & Völkerrecht (1931), p 208

HEDEMANN, J W, 'Verwendung von Denkformen des bürgerlichen Rechts in der Politik und im Völkerrecht', Blätter für Rechtspflege in Thüringen und Anhalt, vol 62 (1915)

HERCZEGH, G, General Principles of Law and the International Legal Order, (Budapest, 1969)

McNAIR, A D, 'The general principles of law recognized by civilized nations', Br. Yearb. Int. Law, vol 33 (1957), p 1

RIPERT, G, 'Les règles du droit civil applicables aux rapports internationaux, contribution à l'étude des principes généraux du droit visés au Statut de la Cour permanente de justice internationale', Acad. Droit Int. Recl. Cours, vol 44 (1933), pp 569-664

SCHLESINGER, R B, 'Research on the general principles of law recognized by civilized nations', Am. J. Int. Law, vol 51 (1957), p 734

SCHLESINGER, R B, & GÜNDISCH, H J, 'Allgemeine Rechtsgrundsätze als Sachnormen in Schiedsgerichtsverfahren', Rabels Z Ausl. & Int. Privatrecht, vol 28 (1964), p 4

SEIDL-HOHENVELDERN, I, 'General principles of
  law as applied by the conciliation commissions
  established under the peace treaty with Italy of
  1947', Am. J. Int. Law, vol 53 (1959), pp 853-72
SERENI, A P, Principi generali di diritto e processo
  internazionale (Milan, 1955)
SPIROPOULOS, Jean, Die allgemeinen
  Rechtsgrundsätze im Völkerrecht (Kiel: Universität,
  1928). ix + 71 pp.
TUNKIN, G I, 'General principles of law', Acad.
  Droit Int. Recl. Cours, vol 95 (1958), p 9
VALLINDAS, P, 'General principles of law and the
  hierarchy of the sources of international law',
  in Mélanges Spiropoulos (Bonn, 1957), pp 525-31
VERDROSS, A, 'Les principes généraux de droit,
  considerés comme une source du droit des gens,
  Rev. Droit Int., vol 7 (1931), p 446-56
VERDROSS, Alfred von, 'Les principes généraux du
  droit applicables aux rapports internationaux',
  Rev. Gen. Droit Int. Public (1938), pp 44-52

5.5.2 GENERAL PRINCIPLES
       AS APPLIED IN CASE LAW

BLONDEL, A, Les principes generaux du droit
  devant la CPJI et la CIJ', in Melanges
  Guggenheim (Genève, 1968), pp 201-36
CHENG, Bin, General Principles of Law as
  applied by International Courts and Tribunals
  (London: Stevens, 1953)
DEHOUSSE, F, 'Les principes du droit des gens dans
  la jurisprudence de la Cour permanente de justice
  internationale', Rev. Droit Int. (1936), pp 65-117
HÄRLE, E, Die allgemeinen Entscheidungsgrundlages
  des Ständigen Internationalen Gerichtshofes
  (Berlin, 1933)

REUTER, P, 'Le recours de la Cour de justice des Communautés européennes à des principes généraux du droit', in Mélanges Rolin (Paris, 1964), pp 263-83

SCERNI, M, I principi generali di diritto riconosciuti dalle nazioni civili nella giurisprudenzia della Corte permanente di giustizia internazionale (Padova, 1932)

SEIDL-HOHENVELDERN, I, 'General principles of law as applied by the conciliation commission established in the peace treaty with Italy of 1947', Am. J. Int. Law (1959), pp 853-72

STUYT, A M, The General Principles of Law as Applied by International Tribunals to Disputes on Attribution and Exercise of State Jurisdiction (Den Haag, 1946)

VERDROSS, A von, 'Les principes généraux du droit dans la jurisprudence internationale', Acad. Droit Int. Recl. Cours, vol 52 (1935), pp 195-249

ZWEIGERT, K, 'Les principes généraux du droit des Etats membres,' in Droit des Communautés Européennes (Bruxelles, 1969), pp 441-5

5.5.3 EQUITY

See also Sections 2.4 (on jus cogens) and 8.9.6 (on judgments ex aequo et bono)

BENTWICH, Norman, de BUSTAMANTE, A S, MACLEAN, Donald A, RADBRUCH, Gustav, & SMITH, H A, Justice and Equity in the International Sphere (London, 1936)

CHENG, Bin, 'Justice and equity in international law', Current Legal Problems, vol 8 (1955), pp 185-211

DEGAN, V D, L'Equité et le droit international (Den Haag: Maritinus Nijhoff, 1970). 261 pp.

EKA, B U, 'Decisions ex aequo et bono and General Assembly resolutions as secondary sources of international law', The Nigerian Law Journal, vol 4 (1970), pp 119-35

KRAUS, H, 'Revision of the peace treaties ex aequo et bono', New Commonwealth, vol 1 (1935/6), pp 33-43

MOUSKHELI, M, 'L'équité en droit international moderne', Rev. Gén. Droit Int. Public, vol 40 (1933), pp 347-73

NEWMAN, R A, 'The principles of equity as a source of world law', Israel Law Review, vol 1 (1966), pp 616-31

5.6 UNILATERAL ACTS

The problem whether unilateral acts, of states or of organizations, contribute to the development of international law is a largely neglected subject. Traditional lawyers have often disputed the unilateral character of certain acts, for example regulations by international organizations by claiming that they constitute 'disguised' state agreements. It would appear that such a view is now difficult to sustain in view of consistent state practice allowing organizations to bind their member states by unilateral acts. The literature on this point is still sparse, but see DETTER (in Section 13.16) and MORAND (in Section 13.24.3.12.7). Among the works listed in this section, those by PFLUGER and SUY are of particular interest

5.6.1 GENERAL

BISCOTTINI, G, Le manifestazioni unilaterali di volonta nell'ordinamento internazionale (Roma, 1943)

BISCOTTINI, G, Contributo alla teoria degli atti unilaterale nel diritto internazionale (Milano, 1951)

COUTICOV, A, 'Théorie générale de l'acte juridique unilateral en droit international', Annuaire de l'Université de Sofia Faculté de droit, vol 41 (1945/6)

DEHAUSSY, J, 'Les actes juridiques unilatéraux en droit international public: à propos d'une théorie restrictive', J. Droit Int., vol 92 (1963), p 41

GARNER, J W, 'The international binding force of unilateral oral declarations', Am. J. Int. Law, vol 27 (1933), p 493

JACQUE, J P, Eléments pour une théorie de l'acte juridique en droit international public (Paris: Librairie générale de droit et de jurisprudence, 1972)

KISS, A-Ch, 'Les actes unilatéraux dans la pratique française du droit international', Rev. Gen. Droit Int. Public, vol 65, (1961), p 317

MIAJA DE LA MUELA, A, 'Los actos unilaterales en las relaciones internacionales', Rev. Esp. Derecho Int. (1967), pp 429-64

PFLUGER, H, Die einseitigen Rechtsgeschäfte im Völkerrecht, (Zürich, 1936)

SUY, E, 'Les actes unilatéraux en droit international', Acad. Droit Int. Recl. Cours, vol 112 (1964) pp 367-461

VENTURINI, G, 'La portée et les effets juridiques des attitudes et des actes unilatéraux des états', Acad. Droit Int. Recl. Cours, vol 112 (1964), p 363

5.6.2 TRADITIONAL UNILATERAL ACTS

See also Section 7.5.7 (on recognition)

5.6.2.1 NOTIFICATION

CANSACCHI, G, La notificazione internazionale (Milano, 1943)

5.6.2.2 PROMISE

CARBONE, S M, Promessa e affidamento nel diritto internazionale (Milano, 1967)
QUADRI, R, 'La promessa nel diritto internazionale', Riv. Diritto Int.(1963), pp 91-8

5.6.2.3 PROTEST

BRÜEL, E, 'La protestation en droit international', Nord. Tidsskr. Int. Ret (1932), p 75
McGIBBON, I C, 'Some observations on the part of protest in international law', Br. Yearb. Int. Law (1953), p 293
ROTHMANN, G, Der völkerrechtliche Protest (Halle, 1923)

5.6.2.4 RENUNCIATION

CAVAGLIERI, A, 'Alcune osservazioni sul concetto di rinuncia nel diritto internazionale', Riv. Diritto Int. (1918), pp 3-33
OLIVI, G, 'Della rinuncia nel diritto internazionale', Archivio giuridico Filippo Serafini (1943), pp 3-46
TOMMASI DI VIGNANO, A, La rinuncia in diritto internazionale (Padova, 1960)

5.6.2.5 ACQUIESCENCE

BENTZ, J, 'Le silence comme manifestation de volonté en droit international public', Rev. Gen. Droit Int. Public (1963), pp 44-91
CAVAGLIERI, A, 'Il decorseo del tempo ed i suci effetti sui rapporti giuridici internazionale', Rivista di diritto internazionale (1926), pp 184-204
McGIBBON, I C, Customary International law and acquiescence, Br. Yearb. Int. Law (1957), pp 115-145

WAELDOECK, M, 'L'acquiescement en droit des gens',
   Riv. Diritto Int, (1961), pp 38-53
See also (on estoppel)
BOWETT, D W, 'Estoppel before international
   tribunals and its relations to acquiescence',
   Br. Yearb. Int. Law (1957), p 176
McGIBBON, I C, 'Estoppel in international law',
   Int. & Comp. Law Q., vol 7 (1958), pp 468-513

5.6.3 ACTS OF
       INTERNATIONAL ORGANIZATIONS

Decisions, resolutions and regulations of international organizations consitute an ever increasing important source of international law. Below I have merely listed two works which treat such acts as a source of international law. For further detail, see Section 13.16 on law making by international organizations, Section 13.24.2.7.3 on effects of resolutions of the United Nations, and Section 13.24.3.12 on law making by the European Communities.
SCHACHTER, O, 'The development of international
   law through the legal opinion of the United Nations
   Secretariat', Br. Yearb. Int. Law, vol 25 (1948)
TAMMES, A J P, 'Decisions of international organs
   as a source of international law', Acad. Droit Int.
   Recl. Cours, vol 94 (1958), pp 261-364

5.7 GAPS OR LACUNAS IN
     INTERNATIONAL LAW

When the traditional sources do not clearly provide guiding rules we face the problem of a 'gap' in the legal system. As this may largely be a problem of interpretation, some would claim the problem is merely apparent. However, for the technique of overcoming such gaps see the works listed below and see also under international tribunals (Section 8.9) as the problem is largely one which presents itself to the international judge with respect to the law he is to apply to a particular dispute.

DONATI, A, Il problema delle lacuni dell'ordinamento giuridico (Milano: 1910)

LAUTERPACHT, H, Private Law Sources and Analogies of International Law with Special Reference to International Arbitration (London: Longmans Green, 1927, reissued by Archon Books, London, 1970). xvi + 326 pp.

MÜLLER, A, 'Les lacunes du droit international public', Rev. Droit Int. & Légis. Comp. (1926), pp 555-76

SIORAT, L, Le problème des lacunes en droit international (Paris, 1959)

TASHIN, H, 'No Man's Land' en droit international (Paris, 1936)

6 Subjects of International Law

The international legal system applies between its subjects. The traditional subjects are states but the circle is being widened by the increasing number of international organizations which are also held to enjoy international 'personality'. International law is not sufficiently developed to distinguish between 'subjectivity' and 'personality' and, to some, the problem is purely academic: the 'personality' of an organization is put to the test when it concludes a treaty, but there is a vicious circle: personality is necessary to conclude a treaty and, on the other hand, to conclude a treaty indicates that the organization enjoys personality. Whatever may be the merit of the academic discussions on this point the works listed below give some guidance but should be supplemented by works on the treaty-making power of organizations.

Whether or not individuals are 'subjects' of international law may depend on the basic concept of international law: some would hold that the individual does enjoy international personality however restrained, whereas others, perhaps the majority, deny this. The two groups to some extent follow the division between monists and dualists, see Section 3.3.1. On the general position of individuals in international law see also below under human rights (Section 7.12), and treatment of aliens (Section 7.12.13).

6.1 PERSONALITY

See also Section 13.7 on personality of organisations.
AUFRICHT, H, 'Personality in international law', American Political Science Review, vol 37 (April, 1943), pp 217-43
GUTZWILLER, M, 'Die sog. Internationalen Juristischen Personen', Mitteiligungen der deutschen Gesellschaft für Völkerrecht, vol 12 (1933), p 116
HEYDTE, F A von der, 'Rechtssubjekt und Rechtsperson im Völkerrecht. Grundprobleme des int. Recht', in Festschrift für J Spiropoulos (Bonn, 1957), pp 237-55
O'CONNELL, D P, 'La personnalité en droit international', Rev. Gén.Droit Int. Public, vol 67 (1963), pp 6-43

6.2 SUBJECTS IN GENERAL

CAVAGLIERI, A, 'I soggetti del diritto internazionale', Riv. Diritto Int., vol 17 (1925), pp 18-32; pp 169-87
LAUTERPACHT, H, 'The subjects of the law of nations', Law Quarterly Review, vol 63 (1947), pp 438-60; vol 64 (1948), pp 97-119
MODŽORJAN, L A, Subjekte des Völkerrechts (Göttingen: Institut für Völkerrecht der Universität Göttingen, 1963). 182 pp.
WENGLER, W, 'Der Begriff des Völkerrechtssubjektes im Lichte der politischen Gegenwart', Die Friedens-Warte, vol 51 (1951/3), pp 113-42

6.3 STATES

See Section 7

6.4 SUBJECTS OTHER THAN STATES

BEREZOWSKI, G, 'Les sujets non souverains du droit international', Acad. Droit Int. Recl. Cours, vol 65 (1938), pp 1-85
SIOTTO PINTOR, M, 'Les sujets du droit international autres que les états', Acad. Droit Int. Recl. Cours, vol 41 (1932), pp 246-360
See also
LISSITZYN, O J, 'Territorial entities other than independent states in the law of treaties', Acad. Droit Int. Recl. Cours, vol 125 (1968), pp 5-87

6.4.1 INTERNATIONAL ORGANIZATIONS

On international organizations as subjects of international law see Section 13.7

6.4.2 ORDER OF MALTA

FARRAN, C D'O, 'The Sovereign Order of Malta in international law', Int. & Comp. Law Q., vol 3 (1954), pp 217-34
FARRAN, C D'O, 'The Sovereign Order of Malta. Note', Int. & Comp. Law Q., vol 4 (1955), pp 308-9

6.4.3 INDIVIDUALS

See also Sections 7.12 on human rights.
DAHM, G, Die Stellung des Menschen im Völkerrecht unserer Zeit (Tübingen, 1961)
ECKERT, H, 'Der Einzelmensch als Völkerrechtssubjekt', Dissertation. (Marburg, 1951)

GRASSI, M, Die Rechtsstellung des Individuums im Völkerrecht (Winterthur, 1955)

GREEN, L C, 'The individual and his status in international law', Indian J. Int. Law, vol 1 (1961) pp 415-28

HAAKE, E, 'Einzelpersonen als Völkerrechtssubjekte', Dissertation. (Tübingen, 1949)

HOFFMANN, G, 'Die Völkerrechtssubjektivität des Individuums im gegenwärtigen Völkerrecht'. Dissertation. (Erlangen, 1952)

KOROWICZ, M, 'The problems of the international personality of individuals', Am. J. Int. Law, vol 51 (1956), p 533

LAPRADELLE, Albert Geouffre de, 'La place de l'homme dans la construction du droit international', Current Legal Problems, vol 1 (1948), pp 140-51

NØRGAARD, Carl Aage, The Position of the Individual in International Law (Copenhagen, Munksgaard, 1962)

REMEC, P P, The Position of the Individual in International Law according to Grotius and Vattel (Den Haag: Nijhoff, 1960)

ROCHETTE, J, L'Individu devant le droit international (Paris, 1960)

SALVIOLI, G, 'L'individuo in diritto internazionale', Riv. Diritto Int., vol 39 (1956), pp 5-11

SPERDUTI, Giuseppe: 'L'individu et le droit international', Acad. Droit Int. Recl. Cours, vol 90 (1956), pp 727-849

SPIROPOULOS, J, L'Individu en droit international (Paris: Librairie générale de droit & de jurisprudence, 1928). xii + 66 pp.

TORNARITIS, Criton G, The Individual as a subject of International Law (Nicosia: Public Information Office, 1971). 58 pp.

WEGNER, A, 'Die Stellung der Einzelperson im gegenwärtigen Völkerrecht', in Gegenwartsprobleme des

Internationalen Rechts und der Rechtsphilosophie
Festschrift für Rudolf Laun (Hamburg, 1953), p 341

WOOD, H McKinnon, 'Legal relations between
individuals and a world organization of states',
Grotius Soc. Trans., vol 30 (1945), pp 141-64

6.5 WIDENING RANGE OF SUBJECTS

MOSLER, H, 'Die Erweiterung des Kreises der
Völkerrechtssubjekte', Z. Ausl. Öff. Recht &
Völkerrecht, vol 22 (1962), p 1

7 States and Sovereignty

The main subjects of international law are, indisputably, states, and there are many works on their nature, formation, and operations in the international sphere. One basic issue to the concept of a state is that of sovereignty. However, on this somewhat theoretical problem I have only included what I considered to be the most important works. I have excluded certain books on the nature of the state when such works treat the state from the point of view of constitutional law, rather than as a subject of public international law.

7.1 SOVEREIGNTY

On the subject of sovereignty, see, above all, the works by KELSEN, listed below.
BOURQUIN, M, L'Etat souverain et l'organisation internationale (New York, 1959)
CARRILLO SALCEDO, Juan Antonio, Soberania del Estado y Derecho Internacional (Madrid, 1969)
DUPUY, R J, (Ed), La Souveraineté au XXe siècle (Paris: Armand Colin, 1971). 288 pp.
ERMACORA, F, 'Über die Souveränität', Österr. Z. Öff. Recht, (1953), p 10

GIRAUD, E, 'La rejet de l'idée de souveranité: L'aspect juridique et politique de la question, les techniques et les principes du droit public', in Etudes en l'honneur de Georges Scelle (Paris, 1950)
RAESTAD, A, 'Souveraineté et droit international', Rev. Droit Int. & Légis. Comp., vol 17 (1936), pp 27-84
KELSEN, H, Das Problem der Souveränität und die Theorie des Völkerrechts (Tübingen: Verlag JCB Mohr, 1920)
KELSEN, H, 'Aperçu d'une théorie générale de l'état', Rev. Droit Public & Sci. Polit. (1926)
KELSEN, Hans, General Theory of Law and the State, translated by Anders Wedberg (Cambridge, Mass, 1949/Reissued 1961 by Russell & Russell New York)
LARSON, Arthur, et al., Sovereignty within the law (London: Stevens & Sons/Dobbs Ferry NY: Oceana, 1966)
LAUTERPACHT, H, 'Règles générales du droit de la paix', Acad. Droit Int. Recl. Cours, vol 62 (1937) pp 95-522. Esp. Sec. 92 'La souveraineté et l'exercice de la souveraineté: Baux et concessions à perpétuité' (pp 325-6)
LOEWENSTEIN, K, 'Souveränität und zwischenstaatliche Zusammenarbeit', Archiv des Öffentlichen Rechts, vol 80 (1955/6), p 1
McNAIR, Sir Arnold, 'Aspects of state sovereignty', Br. Yearb. Int. Law (1949), p 8
MATTERN, J, Concepts of State, Sovereignty and International Law (Baltimore, Md: John Hopkins Press, 1928)
QUARITSCH, H, Staat und Souveränität (Frankfurt: Athenäum, 1970). 585 pp.
SAUER, E, Souveränität und Solidarität (Göttingen: Musterschmidt, 1954). 174 pp (Göttinger Beiträge für Gegenwartsfragen, vol 9)

SOUNTAUSTA, 'La souveraineté des états',
Dissertation. (Helsinki, 1955)

7.1.1 SELF-DETERMINATION

Sovereignty is traditionally thought to consist of
three conceptual subdivisions: self-determination,
independence and equality. On the relationship
between these concepts, especially as formulated by
state practice, see DELUPIS, I, International Law
and the Independent State, as listed in Section 1.8.
Other monographs and articles on self-determination
are:
ARZINGER, R, Das Selbsbestimmungsrecht im
    allgemeinen Völkerrecht der Gegenwart (Berlin:
    Staatsverlag der DDR, 1966). 466 pp.
COBBAN, A, National Self-Determination (London,
    1945)
EAGLETON, C, 'Self-determination in the United
    Nations', Am. J. Int. Law, vol 43 (1953), p 53
RABL, K, Das Selbsbetimmungsrecht der Völker
    (München: Korn, 1972). 276 pp.
SUREDA, A R, The Evolution of the Right of Self-
    Determination: A Study of the United Nations
    Practice (Leiden: Sijthoff, 1973). 397 pp

7.1.2 INDEPENDENCE

ROUSSEAU, C, 'L'indépendance de l'état dans
    l'ordre international', Acad. Droit Int. Recl.
    Cours, vol 73 (1948), pp 171-233

7.1.3 EQUALITY

See also Section 7.13.11.4 on unequal treaties.
BROMS, B, 'The Doctrine of Equality of States as
    Applied in International Organizations', Dissertation.
    (Helsinki, 1960)

DICKINSON, E d W, The Equality of States in
    International Law (Cambridge, Mass, 1920)
FELDER, J F, Das Problem der Staatengleichheit in
    der Organisation der Völkergemeinschaft
    (Schüpfheim, 1950)
GOEBEL, Julius, The Equality of States: A Study in
    the History of Law (New York: Columbia University
    Press, 1923). 89 pp.
HUBER, Max, 'Die Gleichheit der Staaten', in
    Festschift für Kohler (Stuttgart, 1909)
KOOIJMANS, P H, The Doctrine of the Legal Equality
    of States (Leiden: Sijthoff, 1964)
PADIRAC, Raoul, L'Egalité des états et l'organisation
    internationale (Paris: Librairie générale de droit
    et de jurisprudence, 1953). 246 pp.
SCHAUMANN, Wilfred, Die Gleichheit der Staaten:
    Ein Beitrag zu den Grundprinzipien des
    Völkerrechts (Wien: Springer-Verlag, 1957). 160 pp.
SCOTT, J B, 'Le principe de l'égalité juridique dans
    les rapports internationaux', Acad. Droit Int. Recl.
    Cours, vol 42 (1932), pp 467-630
WEINSCHEL, Herbert, 'The doctrine of equality of
    states and its recent modifications', Am. J. Int.
    Law, vol 45 (1951), p 417

7.2 STATEHOOD AND CHARACTERISTICS OF A STATE

On the requirements for an entity to develop into a
state, see:
BLUNTSCHLI, J C, The Theory of the State (Oxford,
    1895). Translated from the 6th German edition
CARRE DE MALBERG, R, Contribution à la théorie
    générale de l'état (Paris: R Tenin, 1920-2)
GUGGENHEIM, P, 'Les principes de droit inter-
    national public', Acad. Droit Int. Recl. Cours,
    vol 80 (1952), pp 1-189. Especially ch. 5 'Les états
    comme sujets du droit des gens' (pp 80-96)

JELLINEK, G, Allgemeine Staatslehre, 2nd edition (Berlin: Verlag von O Hazing, 1905)
KELSEN, H, Allgemeine Staatslehre (Berlin: Verlag von Julius Springer, 1925)
KELSEN, H, 'La naissance de l'état et la formation de sa nationalité', Rev. Droit Int. (1929), p 613
KOROWICZ, M S, 'Some present aspects of sovereignty law', Acad. Droit Int. Recl. Cours, vol 102 (1961), pp 7-16, 86-103
MOUSKHELY, M, 'La naissance des états en droit international public', Rev. Gén. Droit Int. Public, vol 66 (1962), pp 469-85

7.3 RIGHTS AND DUTIES OF STATES

ALFARO, R J, 'The rights and duties of states', Acad. Droit Int. Recl. Cours, vol 97 (1959), pp 95-103
GIDEL, G, 'Droits et devoirs des nations', Acad. Droit Int. Recl. Cours, vol 10, p 25
PHILLIMORE, W G F, (Lord Phillimore), 'Droits et devoirs fondamentaux des états', Acad. Droit Int. Recl. Cours, vol 1 (1923), pp 25-71

7 4 TYPES OF STATES

7.4.1 BRITISH COMMONWEALTH

BAKER, P J Noel, The Present Juridical Status of the British Dominions in International Law (London/ New York/Toronto: Longmans, Green & Co., 1929). 421 pp.
DAWTON, Robert MacGregor, (ed), The Development of Dominion Status (1900-1936) (London/New York/ Toronto: Oxford University Press, 1937). 466 pp.
FAWCETT, J E S, The British Commonwealth in International Law (London: Stevens & Sons, 1963). 243 pp.

7.4.2 DIVIDED STATES

CATY, Gilbert, Le Statut juridique des états divisés (Paris: Pédone, 1969). 261 pp.

7.4.3 CONDOMINIA

CORET, Alain, Le Condominium (Paris: Librairie générale de droit et de jurisprudence, 1960). 333 pp.
See also
O'CONNELL, D P, 'The condominium of the New Hebrides', Br. Yearb. Int. Law, vol 43 (1968/9), pp 71-145

7.4.4 DEPENDENT STATES

See also Section 13.24.2.13 on trust territories.
VEICOPOULOS, Nicolas, Traité des Territoires Dépendants (Athens: Veicopoulos, 1971). 2 vols.
See also
POULOUSE, T T, 'India as an anomalous international person (1919-1947),' Br. Yearb. Int. Law, vol 44 (1970), pp 201-12

7.4.5 PROTECTORATES

Cf. works on Bohemia and Moravia under 7.5.4.
GREWE, W G, 'Protektorat und Schutzfreundschatt', Monatshefte (1939), p 341.
VENTURINI, G, Il protettorato internazionale (Milano: 1939)

7.4.6 HOLY SEE

See also Sections 1.5.3.7 and 7.13.5.9 on concordats.

FALCO, Mario, The Legal Position of the Holy See Before and After the Lateran Agreements (London: Oxford University Press, 1935). 46 pp.

KUNZ, J L, 'The status of the Holy See in international law', Am. J. Int. Law, vol 46 (1952), pp 308-14

7.4.7 MICROSTATES

BLAIR, P W, The Ministate Dilemma, revised edition (New York: Carnegie Endowment for International Peace, 1968)

DE SMITH, S, Microstates and Micronesia: Problems of America's Pacific Islands and other Minute Territories (New York: New York University Press/ London: University of London Press, 1970). ix + 193 pp.

EHRHARDT, D, Der Begriff des Mikrostaats im Völkerrecht und in der Internationalen Ordnung (Aalen, 1970)

HARRIS, D, 'Microstates in the United Nations: A broader purpose', Columbia Journal of Transnational Law (1970), pp 23-53

SAINT-GIRONS, B, 'Les organisations des Nations Unies et les microstates', Rev. Gén. Droit Int. Public, vol 76 (1972), pp 445-74

7.4.8 ARABIAN GULF STATES

AL-BAHARNA, H, The Legal Status of the Arabian Gulf States. A Study of their Treaty Relations and their International Problems (Manchester: Manchester University Press, 1968)

7.4.9 INTERNATIONALIZED TERRITORIES

STUART, Graham H, The International City of Tangier, 2nd edition (Stanford, Calif: Stanford University Press, 1955). 270 pp.
YDIT, M, Internationalized Territories from the 'Free City of Cracow' to the 'Free City of Berlin' (Leiden: Sijthoff, 1961). 323 pp.
See also
J. L. 'Le statut international de la Palestine', J. Droit Int. (1963), pp 964-85

7.5 IDENTITY, CONTINUITY AND SUCCESSION OF STATES

On the subject of identity, continuity of state and the problem of state succession I may refer to the champion on this subject, Professor O'CONNELL, and his general works listed in Section 7.5.3 on state succession.

7.5.1 IDENTITY AND CONTINUITY IN GENERAL

BERNHARDT, R, 'Kontinuität,' in Wörterbuch des Völkerrechts, vol 2 (Berlin: Verlag Walter de Gruyter, 1961), pp 295-7
CANSACCHI, G, 'Realita e funzione nell'identita degli stati', Commun. & Stud., vol 4 (1952), pp 23-97
CANSACCHI, G,'Identité et continuité des sujets internationaux', Acad. Droit Int. Recl. Cours, vol 130 (1970), pp 1-94
FIEDOROWICZ, G, 'Continuité de l'état', Rev. Droit Int. (1939), pp 129
HERZ, H, 'Beiträge zum Problem der Identität des Staates', Z. Öff. Recht., vol 15 (1935), p 241
KUNZ, J L, 'Identity of states under international law', Am. J. Int. Law, vol 49 (1955), pp 68-76

MANN, F A, 'Germany's present legal status revisited', Int. & Comp. Law Q., vol 16, pp 760-99
MAREK, Krystyna, Identity and Continuity of States in Public International Law, 2nd edition (Genève: Librairie E Droz, 1968)
MERKL, A, 'Das Problem der Rechtskontinuität und die Förderung des einheitlichen rechtlichen Weltbildes', Z. Öff. Recht., vol 5 (1926), p 497
PINTO, R, 'The international status of the German Democratic Republic', J. Droit Int., vol 86 (1959), pp 321-425. In English and French
PLISCHKE, E, 'Reactivation of prewar German treaties', Am. J. Int. Law, vol 48 (1954), pp 245-64
REUT-NICOLUSSI, E, 'Um die Rechtskontinuität Osterreichs', Wissenschaft und Weltbild, vol 3, no 6 (June 1950), p 241
SANDER, F, 'Das Faktum der Revolution und die Kontinuität der Rechtsordnung', Z. Off. Recht, vol 1 (1919), p 132
VERDROSS, A, 'Die völkerrechtliche Identität von Staaten', in Festschrift Heinrich Klang (Wien: Springer-Verlag)

7.5.2 CESSATION OF STATES

RAESTAD, A, 'La cessation des états d'après le droit des gens', Rev. Droit Int. & Légis. Comp. (1939), p 441
SEN, B, 'The partition of British India and succession in international law', The Indian Law Review, vol 1 (1947)

7.5.3 STATE SUCCESSION

In the field, the works by Professor O'CONNELL are, as I have mentioned, particularly comprehensive. For

a different view on the duty of succeeding states to
take over obligations, however, see also, DELUPIS,
International Law and the Independent State, listed in
Section 11.8.

7.5.3.1 GENERAL

BEDJAOUI, M, 'Problèmes récents de succession
   d'états dans les états nouveaux', Acad. Droit Int.
   Recl. Cours, vol 130 (1970), pp 455-586
CAFLISCH, L, 'The law of state succession: theoretical
   observations', Ned. Tijdschr. Int. Recht, vol 10
   (1963), pp 337-66
CASTREN, Erik J S, 'Aspects récents de la
   succession d'états', Acad. Droit Int. Recl. Cours,
   vol 78 (1951), p 385
FLORY, M, ETIENNE, B, FOUILLOUX G, &
   SANTUCCI, J C, La Succession d'états en
   Afrique du nord (Paris, 1968)
GUGGENHEIM, P, Beiträge zur völkerrechtlichen
   Lehre vom Staatenwechsel (Berlin: F Vahlen, 1925)
HERBIG, G, Staatensukzession und
   Staatenintegration: Ein Beitrag zur Frage der
   Kontinuität völkerrechtlicher Verträge bei
   Staatenzusammenschlüssen (Mainz, 1968)
HUBER, M, Die Staatensukzession (Leipzig: Verlag
   von Duncker & Humblot, 1898)
KIRSTEN, J, Einige Probleme der Staatennachfolge
   (Berlin (Ost), 1962)
O'CONNELL, D P, 'State succession in the British
   Commonwealth since the Second World War',
   Br. Yearb. Int. Law, vol 26 (1949)
O'CONNELL, D P, The Law of State Succession
   (London: Cambridge University Press 1956). 425 pp
O'CONNELL, D P, State Succession in Municipal
   Law and International Law (London: Cambridge
   University Press, 1967). 2 vols

O'CONNELL, D P, 'Recent problems of state succession in relation to new states', Acad. Droit Int. Recl. Cours, vol 130 (1970), pp 95-206

RONZITTI, Natalino, La Successione Internazionale tra Stati (Milan: Dott. A Giuffré, 1970). ix + 225 pp.

SCHÖNBORN, W, 'Staatensukzessionen', Handbuch des Völkerrechts, edited by Stier-Somlo, vol 2, sec 5 (Berlin/Stuttgart/Leipzig: Verlag von W Kohlhammer, 1913)

WILKINSON, The American Doctrine of State Succession (Baltimore, Md: Johns Hopkins Press, 1934)

ZEMANEK, K, 'La succession d'état après décolonisation', Acad. Droit Int. Recl. Cours, vol 116 (1965), p 187

7.5.3.2 EFFECT OF STATE SUCCESSION ON CERTAIN OBLIGATIONS

See the comments at the beginning of Section 7.5.3 and Sections 7.6.9 on servitudes and 14.9 on economic development agreements.

BATY, T, 'Division of states: its effects on obligations', Grotius Soc. Trans., vol 9 (1923), p 119

BATY, T, 'The obligations of extinct states', Yale Law Journal, vol 35 (1926)

CAHN, H J, 'The responsibility of the successor state for war debts', Am. J. Int. Law, vol 44 (1950), pp 477-87

Committee on State Succession to Treaties and other Governmental Obligations, The Effect of Independence on Treaties (London: Stevens & Sons/ South Hackensack, NJ: Fred B Rothman, 1965). 389 pp.

DROST, H, 'Le problème de la succession en matière d'obligations juridiques des états', Rev. Droit Int. & Légis Comp., ser 3, vol 20 (1939), pp 700-7

DURIEUX, A, Le Problème juridique des dettes du
  Congo belge et l'état du Congo (Bruxelles, 1961)
EDWARDS, J L J, The Effect of Independence on
  Treaties (London: Stevens & Sons, 1965)
FEILCHENFELD, E H, Public Debts and State
  Succession (New York: Mcmillan, 1931)
GIDEL, G, Des Effets de l'annexion sur les
  concessions (Paris: 1904)
GOERDELER, R, Die Staatensukzession in
  Multilateralen Verträgen (Berlin: Duncker and
  Humblot, 1930)
HERBST, L, Staatensukzession und Staatsservituden
  (Berlin, 1962)
JENKS, C W, 'State succession in respect of law-
  making treaties', Br. Yearb. Int. Law (1952),
  pp 105-44
JONES, Mervyn, 'State succession in the matter of
  treaties', Br. Yearb. Int. Law, vol 24 (1947),
  p 360
KEITH, K J, Succession to bilateral treaties by
  seceding states', Am. J. Int. Law, vol 61 (1967),
  p 521
MOCHI ONORY, A G, La Succession d'états aux
  traités (Mailand, 1968)
MURALT, R W G de, The Problem of State
  Succession with regard to Treaties (Den Haag: W P
  van Stockum & Zoon, 1954)
O'CONNELL, D P, 'Economic concessions in the law
  of state succession', Br. Yearb. Int. Law, vol 27
  (1950)
O'CONNELL, D P, 'Secured and unsecured debts in
  the law of state succession', Br Yearb. Int. Law,
  vol 28 (1951)
O'CONNELL, D P, ' Independence and succession to
  treaties', Br. Yearb. Int. Law, vol 38 (1962), p 84
SACK, A N, Les Effets des transformations des
  états sur leurs dettes publiques et autres
  obligations financières (Paris, 1927)

SACK, A N, Partage des dettes de l'état (1923)
SACK, A N, 'La succession aux dettes publiques d'état', Acad. Droit Int. Recl. Cours, vol 23 (1928), p 149
UDINA, M, 'La succession des états quant aux obligations internationales autres que les dettes publiques', Acad. Droit Int. Recl. Cours, vol 44 (1933), p 665
UDOKANG, Okon, Succession of New States to International Treaties (Dobbs Ferry, NY: Oceana, 1972, 525 pp.
VERDROSS, A, 'Gelten die zwischen Osterreich-Ungarn und dem Deutschen Reiche abgeschlossenen Staatsverträge weiter im Verhältnis zwischen Deutschland und der Republik Osterreich?'Deutsche' Juristen-Zeitung (1920)

7.5.3.3 SUCCESSION AND NATIONALITY

On nationality in general, see Section 7.12.14. On the effect of state succession on nationality see, above all, O'CONNELL's general work on state succession, listed in Section 7.5.3.1.
GRAUPNER, R, 'Nationality and state succession', Grotius Soc. Trans., vol 32 (1946), p 87
GRAUPNER, R, 'British nationality and state succession', The Law Quarterly Review, vol 61 (1942), p 161
MANN, F A, 'The effects of changes of sovereignty upon nationality', The Modern Law Review, vol 5 (1942), p 218

7.5.4 FORMATION, EXTINCTION AND IDENTITY OF PARTICULAR STATES

In the section below I have gathered certain works which treat individual questions relating to specific states and their formation, continuity or extinction and the problems of state succession caused by changes of identity. For problems on formation, see also Section 7.5.7 on recognition.

ANZILOTTI, D, 'La formazione del Regno d'Italia nei riguardi del diritto internazionale', Riv. Diritto Int. (1912), p 1

BAADE, H, 'Baltische Staaten', in Wörterbuch des Völkerrechts, vol 1 (Berlin: Verlag Walter de Gruyter, 1960), pp 143-50

BASDEVANT, Jean, La Condition internationale de l'Autriche (Paris: Librairie du recueil Sirey, 1935)

BISCOTTINI, G, 'Sulla condizione giuridica del Protettorato di Boemia e Moravia', Riv. Diritto Int. (1941), p 379

BÜNGER, K, 'Dokumente zur Entstehung der Vereinigten Staaten von Indonesien', Z. Ausl. Öff. Recht & Völkerrecht, vol 13 (1950/1), p 431

CAFLISCH, L, 'Die Gründung Italiens in schweizerischer Sicht', Annu. Suisse Droit Int., vol 19 (1962), pp 103-20

CLUTE, R E, The International Legal Status of Austria, 1938-1955 (Den Haag: Nijhoff, 1962)

DESPAGNET, F, 'Grande Bretagne, République Sud-Africaine ou du Transvaal et Etat Libre d'Orange', Rev. Gén. Droit Int. Public (1900), pp 84, 276, 655, 764; (1901), pp 157, 608; (1902), pp 129, 629

DOERING, W, 'Ist Jugoslawien (SHS-Staat) im Sinne des Versailler Vertrages, insbesondere im Sinne des Art 297 h letzter Absatz, ein "Neuer Staat"?' Juristische Wochenschrift (1922), p 352

FEDOZZI, P, 'La situation juridique et internationale du Montenegro', J. Droit Int. (1922), p 540

FISCHER, A, Un cas de décolonisation: les USA et les Philippines (Paris: Bibliothèque de Droit international, 1960)

FROWEIN, J I, 'Die Abmachungen von Evian und die Entstehung des algerischen Staates', Z. Ausl. Öff. Recht & Völkerrecht, vol 23 (1963), p 21

GINTHER, K, 'War die Slowakei ein souveräner Staat?' Österr. Z. Öff. Recht, vol 17 (1967), pp 142-72

GRAYSON, C T, Austria's International Position 1938-1953 (Genève: Droz, 1953)

HAMMERBACHER, G, Die völkerrechtliche Stellung Vietnams (Vaduz/Augsburg: Hormann-Druck, 1960). x + 109 pp. (Schriftenreihe der Fürst Franz Josef von Liechtenstein Stiftung, Fridtjof Nansen Institut, no. 1)

HOLZER, E, 'Die Entstehung des jugoslawischen staates', Dissertation. Berlin, 1929

HUGELMAN, K G, 'Das Reichsprotektorat Böhmen und Mähren', Monatshefte (1939), p 399

KAECKENBEECK, G, The International Experiment of Upper Silesia (London, 1942)

KAUFMANN, E, 'Der serbisch-kroatisch-slowenische Staat: ein neuer Staat', Niemeyers Z. Int. Recht, vol 31, p 211

KELSEN, H, 'The international legal status of Germany to be established immediately upon termination of the war', Am. J. Int. Law (1944), p 689

KLINGHOFFER, H, 'Die Moskauer Erklärung über Österreich', Österr. Z. Öff. Recht, vol 6 (1955), pp 461-89

KLEIN, F, 'Die staats- und völkerrechtliche Stellung des Protektorats Böhmen und Mähren', Archiv des öffentlichen Rechts (new series), vol 31, no 3, p 255

KUNZ, J L, 'Österreichischer Staatsvertrag vom 15.5.1955', in Wörterbuch des Völkerrechts, vol 2 (Berlin: Walter de Gruyter, 1961), pp 699-701

KUNZ, J L, 'The state treaty with Austria', Am. J. Int. Law, vol 49 (1955), pp 535-42

MAKAROV, 'Die Eingliederung der baltischen Staaten in die Sowjet-Union', Z. Ausl. Öff. Recht & Völkerrecht (1940/1), p 682

MEGERLE, K, 'Deutchland und das Ende der
   Tchecho-Slowakei', Monatshefte (1939), p 763
MEISSNER, B, Die Sowjetunion, die baltischen Staaten
   und das Völkerrecht (Köln: Verlag für Politik und
   Wirtschaft, 1956)
NAWAZ, M K, 'Bangla Desh and international law',
   Indian J. Int. Law, vol 11 (1971), p 251
NGUYEN-HUU-TRY, Quelques Problèmes de succession
   d'états concernant le Viet-Nam (Bruxelles:
   Etablissement Emile Bruylant, 1970), 323 pp.
RABL, K O, 'Zur jüngsten Entwicklung der
   slowakischen Frage', Z. Ausl. Öff. Recht &
   Völkerrecht (1939/40), p 284
RAGGI, C G, 'Il Protettorato di Boemia e Moravia',
   Riv. Diritto Int. (1940), p 194
ROMANO, S, 'I caratteri giuridici della formazione
   del Regno d'Italia', Riv. Diritto Int. (1912), p 345
ROTH, P, Die Entstehung des polnischen Staates
   (Berlin: O Liebmann, 1926)
RÖPER, Erich, Geteiltes China: Ein Völkerrechtliche
   Studie (Mainz: v Hase & Koehler Verlag, 1967).
   320 pp.
PFEIFER, H, 'Der österreichische Staatsvertrag',
   Arch. Völkerrechts, vol 5, no 3, pp 296-307
SCELLE, G, 'La situation juridique de Vilna et de
   son territoire', Rev. Gén. Droit Int. Public
   (1928), p 730
SCHILLING, K, 'Ist das Königreich Jugoslawien mit
   dem früheren Königreich Serbien völkerrechtlich
   identisch?' Dissertation. Berlin, 1939
SEIDL-HOHENVELDERN, I, 'Die österreichische
   Staatsbürgerschaft von 1938 bis heute', Österr.
   Z. Öff. Recht, vol 6 (1953), pp 21-39
TABORSKY, E, The Czechoslovak Cause: An Account
   of the Problems of International Law in relation to
   Czechoslovakia (London: H F & S Witherby Ltd.,
   1944)

TAYLOR, Alastair M, Indonesian Independence and the United Nations (Ithaca, NY: Cornell University Press, 1960)

TENEKIDES, G, 'La nature juridique des gouvernements institués par l'occupant en Grèce suivant la jurisprudence hellénique', Rev. Gén. Droit Int. Public (1947), p 113

TRAMPLER, K, Deutschösterreich, 1918/19: Ein Kampf um Selbstbestimmung (Berlin: Carl Heymanns Verlag, 1935)

UDINA, M, L'estinzione dell'Impero austro-ungarico nel diritto internazionale, 2nd ed (Padova CEDAM, Casa Editrice Dott. Antonio Milani Già Litotipo, 1933)

VENTURINI, G C, 'La nuova situazione giuridica dei territori della Cecoslovacchia', Diritto Internazionale (1938), p 74

VEROSTA, S, Die internationale Stellung Osterreichs: Eine Sammlung von Erklärungen und Verträgen aus den Jahren 1938 bis 1947 (Wien: Manzsche Verlagsbuchhandlung, 1947)

VIRALLY, Michel, 'La condition internationale de la République fédérale d'Allemagne après les Accords de Paris', Annu. Fr. Droit Int. (1955), p 31

WODIE, F, 'La sécession du Biafra et le droit international public', Rev. Gén. Droit Int. Public, vol 73 (1969), pp 1018-60

WRIGHT, H, 'The legality of the annexation of Austria by Germany', Am. J. Int. Law (1944), p 621

7.5.5 NEW AND/OR DEVELOPING STATES

The formation of new states in the international community does not merely give rise to questions of state succession, but also certain problems about the position of such new states with respect to the international legal order as a whole. There is a

question whether such states 'accept' all, or the
majority, of international legal rules, or whether they,
by becoming 'states' ipso facto are bound by
international law in all its parts. Thus, there is a
question bearing on the very nature of international
law (see Section 2). Second, certain issues are of
particular concern to new states for example, the
problem of unequal treaties (Section 7.13.11.4). In
the section below I have listed some works which deal
with the position of new states in international law as
a general problem. I have also included similar
problems relating to developing countries in this
section although, in a few cases, such developing
nations are not 'new' states.

ABI-SAAB, G M, 'The new independent state and the
 rules of international law: an outline', Howard Law
 Journal, vol 8 (1962)
ANAND, R P, New States and International Law (Delhi:
 Vikas Publishing House, 1972). 119 pp.
ARZINGER, R, & BREHME, G, Völkerrechtliche
 Probleme der jungen Nationalstaaten, Beiträge von
 einem Kollektiv beim Institut für Völkerrecht an
 der Karl-Marx-Universität Leipzig (Berlin, Ost,
 1965)
BOKOR-SZEGÖ, Hanna, New States and International
 Law (Budapest: Akadémiai Kiadó, 1970). 116 pp.
BUCHMANN, J, L'Afrique noire indépendante (Paris,
 1962)
CASTANEDA, J, 'The underdeveloped nations and the
 development of international law', Int. Organ.,
 vol 15 (1961), p 38
DUROSELLE, J B, & MEYRIAT, J, (eds), Les
 Nouveaux Etats dans les relations internationales
 (Paris, 1962)
DUGARD, C, 'The Organization of African Unity and
 colonialism', Int. & Comp. Law Q., vol 16 (1967),
 p 157

GRAHAM, M W, New Governments in Central Europe (New York: Henry Holt and Company, 1926)
HYDE, O N, 'Law and developing countries', Am. J. Int. Law, vol 61 (1967), p 571
LONDON, K, (ed), New Nations in a Divided World: The International Relations of the Afro-Asian States (New York/London, 1963)
McWHINNEY, E, 'The "new" countries and the "new" international law: the United Nations specia¹ conference on friendly relations and cooperation among states', Am. J. Int. Law, vol 60 (1966), p 1
MERILLAT, H C L, 'Law and developing countries', Am. J. Int. Law, vol 60 (1966), p 71
O'BRIEN, William, The New Nations in International Law and Diplomacy (London: Stevens & Sons, 1965). 323 pp.
OKOYE, F C, International Law and the New African States (London: Sweet & Maxwell, 1972). xv + 225 pp.
SINHA, S Prakash, 'Perspective of the newly independent states', Int. & Comp. Law Q., vol 14 (1965), p 121
SERENI, A P, 'Les nouveaux états et le droit international', Rev. Gen. Droit Int. Public (1968), p 305
SYATAUW, J J G, Some Newly Established Asian States and the Development of International Law (Den Haag: Nijhoff, 1961). 249 pp.

7.5.6 DECOLONIZATION

A problem interrelated with that of state succession and 'new or developing states' is that concerned with 'decolonization'. Some of the works below, for example the article by VIRALLY, analyse this problem particularly as discussed in the United Nations. See also Section 7.4.4 on dependent states, certain works on the dominions in Section 7.4.1 on the British Commonwealth and the works listed in Section 13.24.2.13 on mandates and trusteeship agreements.

ALBERTINI, R von, Dekolonisation: Die Diskussion über Verwaltung und Zukunft der Kolonien 1919-1960 (Köln/Opladen, 1966)

DÖLLE, H, REICHERT-FACILIDES, F, & ZWEIGERT, K, Internationalrechtliche Betrachtungen zur Dekolonisierung (Tübingen, 1964)

EL-AYOUTY, Y, The United Nations and decolonisation. The Role of Afro-Asia (Den Haag: Nijhoff, 1971)

GRIMAL, H, La Décolonisation 1919-1963 (Paris, 1965)

SEIDL-HOHENFELDEN, I, 'Dekolonisierung, Politik und Positives Recht', Juristenzeitung (1964), p 489

VIRALLY, M, 'Droit international et décolonisation devant les Nations Unies', Annu. Fr. Droit Int. (1963), p 508

WENGLER, W, 'Kolonien: II. Kolonialrecht', HdSW, vol 6 (1959), p 69

7.5.7 RECOGNITION

There are two theories on the relevance of recognition of a new state: the theory that claims that such an act is necessary for the creation of a state (the constitutive theory favoured, for example, by LAUTERPACHT and GUGGENHEIM) and the theory that suggests that such an act is not necessary for the formation but is a mere formality (the declaratory theory adopted, for example, by BRIERLY and WALDOCK). The basic works on recognition in general are those by CHEN and LAUTERPACHT listed below. For other general aspects on recognition see the Hague course by JENNINGS and works by GUGGENHEIM, KUNZ, VERDROSS and WALDOCK listed in Section 1.8. For recognition and civil war

see the Hague course by WEHBERG listed in Section
10.10. For recognition not only of states but the
effects of recognition of governments, see the work
by EEK listed below and the book by DELUPIS on
International Law and the Independent State, listed in
Section 1.8. For the function of non-recognition as a
'sanction' in international law see the works by BRIGGS,
listed below. Recognition is most accurately
conceived as a unilateral act, see Section 5.6 (the
work by PFLUGER), but may occasionally, especially
when there is a treaty on the matter, be construed as
a conventional act, see SUY listed in Section 5.6.1.

AUFRICHT, H, 'Principles and practices of
   recognition by international organizations', Am. J.
   Int. Law, vol 43 (1949), pp 679-704

BLIX, H, 'Contemporary aspects of recognition',
   Acad. Droit Int. Recl. Cours, vol 130 (1970),
   pp 587-704

BOT, B R, Non-recognition and Treaty Relations
   (Leiden: Sijthoff/Dobbs Ferry, NY: Oceana, 1968)

BRIGGS, H W, 'Non-recognition in the courts; the
   ships of the Baltic republics', Am. J. Int. Law
   (1943), p 585

BRIGGS, Herbert W, 'Non-recognition of title by
   conquest and limitations on the doctrine', Am. Soc.
   Int. Law Proc. (1940), pp 72-82

BRIGGS, H W, 'Recognition of states: some
   reflections on doctrine and practice', Am. J. Int.
   Law, vol 43 (1949), pp 113-21

BROWN, P M, 'The legal effects of recognition', Am.
   J. Int. Law, vol 44 (1950), pp 617-40

BROWN, P M, 'La reconnaissance des nouveaux états
   et des nouveaux gouvernements', Annu. Inst.
   Droit Int. (1934), pp 302-57

BROWN, P M, 'La reconnaissance des nouveaux états
   et des nouveaux gouvernements', Annu. Inst.
   Droit Int. (1936), vol 2, pp 175-255

See also 'Résolutions votées par l'Institut au cours de sa XLe session', Annu. Inst. Droit Int. (1936), vol 2, pp 289-310, resolution 3 (pp 300-5)

CAVARE, L, 'La reconnaissance de l'état et le Manchukuo', Rev. Gén. Droit Int. Public (1935), p 5

CHARPENTIER, J, La Reconnaissance internationale et l'évolution du droit des gens (Paris: Pedone, 1956)

CHEN, Ti-Chiang, The International Law of Recognition, edited by L C Green (London: Stevens & Sons, 1951)

COHN, E J, Review of Lauterpacht's Recognition in International Law, Law Quarterly Review, vol 64 (1948), pp 404-8

EEK, H, 'Nya stater och nya regimer', in Skrifter åt minnet av C A Reutersköld (Helsingfors, 1945)

EEKELAAR, J M, 'Rhodesia: the abdication of constitutionalism', Modern Law Review, vol 32 (1969), pp 19-34

ERICH, R, 'La naissance et la reconnaissance des états', Acad. Droit Int. Recl. Cours, vol 13 (1926), pp 431-41

FRENZKE, Dietrich, Die Kommunistische Anerkennungslehre: Die Anerkennung von Staaten in der osteuropäischen Völkerrechtstheorie, (Köln: Verlag Wissenschaft und Politik, 1972)

GARNER, J, 'Non-recognition of illegal territorial annexations and claims to sovereignty', Am. J. Int. Law, vol 30 (1936), pp 679-88

GEMMA, Scipione, 'Les gouvernements de fait', Acad. Droit Int. Recl. Cours, vol 4 (1924), pp 293-414

GRAHAM, M W, The Diplomatic Recognition of the Border States (Berkeley, Calif: University of California Press, 1935). Part I, Finland. Part II, Estonia. Part III, Latvia.

GREIG, D W, 'The Carl-Zeiss case and the position of an unrecognized government in English law', Law Quarterly Review, vol 83 (1967), pp 96-145

GUTIERREZ, Alberto Ostria, La doctrina del no-reconocimiento de la conquista en America (Rio de Janeiro, 1938). 158 pp.

HILL, Chesney, 'Recent policies of non-recognition', Int. Conciliation, no 293 (1933), pp 357-477

JOHNSON, D H N, 'The Minquiers and Ecrehos case', Int. & Comp. Law Q., vol 3 (1954), pp 189-216

JOHNSON, D H N, 'Decisions of English courts during 1951-2 involving questions of public or private international law. A. Public international law', Br. Yearb. Int. Law, vol 29 (1952), pp 455-76. Especially case 6 (pp 462-4)

KELSEN, H, 'Recognition in international law', Am. J. Int. Law, vol 35 (1941), pp 605-17

KUNZ, J L, 'Critical remarks on Lauterpacht's Recognition in International Law', Am. J. Int. Law, vol 44 (1950), p 713

KUNZ, J, 'Die Anerkennung der Staaten und Regierungen im Völkerrecht', in Handbuch des Völkerrechts, edited by Stier-Somlo, vol 2, sec 3 (Stuttgart: Verlag von W Kohlhammer, 1928)

LAGARDE, E, La Reconnaissance du gouvernement des Soviets (Paris: Payot, 1924)

LANGER, R, Seizure of Territory: The Stimson Doctrine and Related Principles (Princeton, 1947). 314 pp.

LARNAUDE, F, 'Les gouvernements de fait', Rev. Gen. Droit Int. Public (1921), p 487

LAUTERPACHT, H, Recognition in International Law (London: Cambridge University Press, 1947)

LAUTERPACHT, H, 'Recognition of insurgents as a de facto government', Modern Law Review, vol 3 (1939/40), pp 1-20

LAUTERPACHT, H, 'Règles générales du droit de la paix', Acad. Droit Int. Recl. Cours, vol 62 (1937),

pp 94-422. Especially ch 6 'La reconnaissance des
états' (pp 244-80)
LAUTERPACHT, H, 'The principle of non-recognition
in international law' in Legal Problems in the Far
Eastern Conflict, edited by Quincy Wright with
H Lauterpacht, E M Borchard, & Phoebe Morrison
(New York: Institute of Pacific Relations, 1941),
pp 129-56
MacCORKLE, Stuart Alexander, American Policy of
Recognition towards Mexico (Baltimore, Md: Johns
Hopkins Press, 1933)
MacGIBBON, I C, 'The scope of acquiescence in
international law', Br. Yearb. Int. Law, vol 31
(1954), pp 143-86
McNAIR, A D, 'The Stimson doctrine of non-recognition',
Br. Yearb. Int. Law (1933), p 65
MIDDLEBUSH, Frederick Arnold, 'Non-recognition as
a sanction of international law', American Society
of International Law Proceedings (1933), pp 40-55
MISRA, K P, 'India's policy of recognition of states and
governments', Am. J. Int. Law, vol 55 (1961),
pp 398-424
PADELFORD, N, 'Non-recognition of title by conquest',
American Society of International Law Proceedings
(1940), pp 82-8
PATEL, Satyaurata Ramdas, Recognition in the Law
of Nations (Bombay: N M Tripathi, 1959). 122 pp.
ROSENNE, S, 'Recognition of states by the United
States', Br. Yearb. Int. Law, vol 26 (1949), pp
437-47
SALMON, Jean J A, La Reconnaissance d'état
Quatre cas: Manchoukouo, Katanga, Biafra, Rhodésie
du Sud (Paris: Librairie Armand Colin, 1971). 286 pp.
SCELLE, G, 'La reconnaissance des insurgés et la
guerre espagnole', Die Friedens-Warte, vol 37
(1937), pp 65-70

SCHACHTER, O, 'The development of international law through the legal opinions of the United Nations secretariat', Br. Yearb. Int. Law, vol 25 (1948), pp 91-132. Especially sec 5 'The recognition of new states' (pp 109-15)

SHARP, R H, 'Non-recognition as a legal obligation', Thesis. Geneve, 1934

SPIROPOULOS, J, Die de-facto Regierung im Völkerrecht (Verlag des Instituts für internationales Recht an der Universität Kiel, 1926)

VENTURINI, G, Il riconoscomento nel diritto internazionale (Milano, 1946)

WALDOCK, C H M, 'Disputed sovereignty in the Falkland Islands Dependencies', Br. Yearb. Int. Law, vol 25 (1948), pp 311-53

WALKER, W L, 'Recognition of belligerency and grant of belligerent rights', Grotius Soc. Trans., vol 23 (1937), pp 177-210

WEHBERG, H, 'Die Stimson-Doktrin', in Fundamental Problems of International Law, Festschrift für Jean Spiropoulos (Bonn, 1957), pp 433-43

WILLIAMS, Sir John Fischer, ' "Recognition" ',Grotius Soc. Trans. vol 15 (1929), pp 53-81

WILLIAMS, Sir John Fischer, 'The new doctrine of "recognition" ', Grotius Soc. Trans., vol 18 (1932), pp 109-29

WILLIAMS, Sir John Fischer, 'La doctrine de la reconnaissance en droit international et ses développements récents', Acad. Droit Int. Recl. Cours, vol 44 (1933), pp 199-314

WILLIAMS, Sir John Fischer, 'Some thoughts on the doctrine of recognition in international law', Harvard Law Review, vol 47 (1933/4), pp 776-94

WRIGHT, Q, 'Some thoughts about recognition', Am. J. Int. Law, vol 44 (1950), pp 548-59

WRIGHT Q, 'The Stimson note of January 7, 1932', Am. J Int. Law, vol 26 (1932), pp 342-8

WRIGHT, Q, 'Non-recognition of title by conquest', American Society of International Law Proceedings (1940), p 80
YOKOTA, Kisaburo, 'The recent development of the Stimson doctrine', Pacific Affairs, vol 8 (1935), pp 133-43

7.6   TERRITORY OF STATES

7.6.1   LEGAL NATURE

BASTID, S, 'Les problèmes territoriaux dans la jurisprudence de la Cour internationale de justice', Acad. Droit Int. Recl. Cours, vol 107 (1962), pp 391-5
SCHÖNBORN, W, 'La nature juridique du territoire', Acad. Droit. Int. Recl. Cours, vol 30 (1929), pp 81-189

7.6.2   NEIGHBOURHOOD RELATIONS BETWEEN STATES

See also Section 11 on responsibility
ANDRASSY, J, 'Les relations internationales de voisinage', Acad. Droit Int. Recl. Cours, vol 79 (1952), pp 73-182

7.6.3   BOUNDARIES OF STATES

Boundaries of states is a subject which can hardly be studied without reference to state practice, see the books listed in Section 1.4. On marine boundaries see Sections 7.8.2 and 7.8.5.2.
BEGGS, S W, International Boundaries (New York, 1940)
CUKWURAH, A O, The Settlement of Boundary Disputes in International Law (Manchester:

Manchester University Press/New York, Oceana, 1967). 267 pp.

JONES, Stephen B, Boundary making: Handbook for Statesmen, Treaty Editors and Boundary Commissioners (Washington, DC: Carnegie Endowment for International Peace, 1945). 268 pp.

LAPRADELLE, P de, La Frontière: Etude de droit international (Paris, 1928)

LUARD, Evan, The International Regulation of Frontier Disputes (New York: Praeger/London: Thames & Hudson, 1970). 247 pp.

MANCE, Sir Harry Osborne, Frontiers, Peace Treaties, and International Organization (London: Oxford University Press, 1946). x + 196 pp.

NELSON, L D M, 'The arbitration of boundary disputes in Latin America', Ned. Tijdschr. Int. Recht (1973), pp 267-94

VISSCHER, Charles de, Problèmes de confins en droit international public (Paris: Editions A Pédone, 1969)

7.6.4 PARTICULAR FRONTIERS

GRABSKI, S, The Polish-Soviet Frontier (London, 1943)

IRELAND, Gordon, Boundaries, Possessions and Conflicts in South America (Cambridge, Mass, 1938). 345 pp.

IRELAND, Gordon, Boundaries, Possessions and Conflicts in Central and North America and the Caribbean (Cambridge, Mass, 1941). 432 pp.

KRÜLLE, Siegrid, Die Völkerrechtlichen Aspekte des Oder-Neisse-Problems (Berlin: Duncker & Humblot, 1970). 391 pp.

McEWEN, A C, International Boundaries of East Africa (London: Oxford University Press, 1971)

WOOLSEY, L H, 'The Polish boundary question', Am. J. Int. Law, (1944), p 441

7.6.5 ACQUISITION OF TERRITORY

See also Sections 7.6.7 on Arctic and Antartic areas, 10.5 on acquisition by conquest in war and 5.6.2.5 on acquiescence and estoppel.

BLUM, Y Z, Historic Titles in International Law (Den Haag: Nijhoff, 1965)

GENET, R, 'Notes sur l'acquisition par occupation et le droit des gens traditionnel', Rev. Droit Int. & Légis. Comp., vol 15 (1934), pp 285-342; pp 416-50

HEYDTE, F A F von der, 'Discovery, symbolic annexation and virtual effectiveness in international law', Am. J. Int. Law, vol 29 (1935), pp 448-91

JENNINGS, R Y, Acquisition of Territory in International Law (Manchester: Manchester University Press/Dobbs Ferry, NY: Oceana, 1963)

LANGER, R, Siezure of Territory (Princeton, NJ: Princeton University Press, 1947)

JOHNSON, D H N, 'Consolidation as a root of title in international law', Cambridge Law Journal (1955), pp 215-25

JOHNSON, D H N, 'Acquisitive prescription in international law', Br. Yearb. Int. Law, vol 27 (1950), pp 332-54

KELLER, Arthur S, LISSITZYN, O J, & MANN, F A, Creation of Rights of Sovereignty through Symbolic Acts 1400-1800 (New York, 1938; reissued by AMS Press, New York)

7.6.6 LOSS OF TITLE TO TERRITORY

BECKETT, W E, 'Les questions d'intérêt général au point de vue juridique dans la jurisprudence de la Cour permanente de justice internationale', Acad. Droit. Int. Recl. Cours, vol 50 (1934), pp 189-310. Especially Ch 2, sec 2R, 'La perte de la souveraineté territoriale par abandon' (pp 252-5)

7.6.7 ARCTIC AND ANTARCTIC TERRITORIES

AUBURN, F M, 'The white desert', Int. & Comp. Law Q., vol 19 (1970), pp 229-56

BALCH, T W, 'The Arctic and Antarctic regions and the law of nations', Am. J. Int. Law, vol 4 (1910), pp 265-75

DOLLOT, R, 'Le droit international des espaces polaires', Acad. Droit Int. Recl. Cours, vol 75 (1949), pp 121-91

FITZMAURICE, Sir Gerald, 'The general principles of international law considered from the standpoint of the rule of law', Acad. Droit Int. Recl. Cours, vol 92 (1957), pp 1-227. Especially sec 86 (iii), 'Ice territory' (p 155)

HAYTON, R D, 'The "American" Antarctic', Am. J. Int. Law, vol 50 (1956), pp 583-610

LAKHTINE, W, 'Rights over the Arctic', Am. J. Int. Law, vol 24 (1930), pp 703-17

SHEDAL, G, Acquisition of Sovereignty over Polar Areas (Oslo, 1931)

On 'international areas' - that is, Arctic and Antarctic regions as well as the oceans - see also

KISH, J, The Law of International Spaces (Leiden: Sijthoff, 1973). 236 pp.

7.6.8 DISPUTED TERRITORIES

GOEBEL, J, The Struggle for the Falkland Islands (New Haven, Conn: 1927; reissued 1971 by Kennikat Press, Port Washington, NY)

MARSTON, G, 'International law and the Sabah dispute', Australian Year Book of International Law (1967), pp 103-52

ORITZ, Legal Aspects of the North Borneo Question (London, 1964)

WALDOCK, C H M, 'Disputed sovereignty in the
   Falkland Island Dependencies', Br. Yearb. Int.
   Law, vol 25 (1948), pp 311-53
See also
ORENT, B, & REINSCH, P, 'Sovereignty over islands
   in the Pacific', Am. J. Int. Law, vol 35, pp 443-61

7.6.9 SERVITUDES

REID, H D, International Servitudes in Law and
   Practice (Chicago, Ill, 1932)
VÁLI, F A, Servitudes of International Law, 2nd
   edition (London: Stevens & Sons, 1958)
See also DELUPIS, International Law and the Independent
   State, listed in Section 1.8

7.6.10 RIGHT OF TRANSIT
        OF LANDLOCKED STATES

In the seventeenth century Grotius claimed that
landlocked states have a right of transit over the
territory of other states to reach the sea. Modern
works on this topical and controversial subject are
not numerous but the works listed below give some
treatment of it. On the rights of passage of landlocked
states, see also, DELUPIS, International Law and
the Independent State, listed in Section 1.8.
DELUPIS, I, (née Detter), Landlocked States and the
   Law of the Sea, Scandinavian Studies in Law, (1975)
KRENZ, F E, International Enclaves and Rights of
   Passage: With Special Reference to the Case
   concerning Right of Passage over Indian Territory
   (Genève, 1961)
MERRYMAN, J H, & ACKERMAN, E D, International
   Legal Development and the Transit Trade of Land-
   locked States: The Case of Bolivia (Hamburg, 1969)

PALAZZOLI, C, 'De quelques développements
récents du droit des gens en matière d'accès à la
mer de pays dépourvu de littoral', Rev. Gén.
Droit Int. Public, vol 70 (1966), pp 667-735
SARUP, Amrit, 'Transit trade of land-locked Nepal',
Int. & Comp. Law Q., vol 21 (1971), p 287
THIERRY, Hubert, 'Les états privés de littoral
maritime', Rev. Gén. Droit Int. Public, vol 62
(1958), p 612

7.7 INTERNATIONAL COMMUNICATIONS

See also Sections 7.8.7 (on international waterways),
7.9.1 (on the right to fly), 13.24.2.24.3 (on the
Universal Postal Union), 13.24.2.24.4 (on the
International Telecommunications Union), 13.24.2.24.
14 (on the International Civil Aviation Organization)
and 7.9.5.2 (on telecommunication by satellite).
ALEXANDROWICZ, C H, The Law of Global
 Communications (New York/London: Columbia
 University Press, 1971). xiv + 195 pp.
BOURQUIN, Maurice, 'L'organisation internationale
 des voies de communication', Acad. Droit Int.
 Recl. Cours, vol 5 (1924), pp 159-210
McWHINNEY, E, (ed), The International Law of
 Communications (Dobbs Ferry, NY: Oceana/Leiden:
 Sijthoff, 1971). 170 pp.

7.8 LAW OF THE SEA

The great names with respect to the study of the law
of the sea are, above all, GIDEL and COLOMBOS as
listed below and these writers hold, in spite of their
works being published some time ago, fairly progressive views which were adopted by an ever
increasing number of states during discussion in
preparation for the conference on the law of the sea
held in 1974.

It is also necessary to refer to important case law, for example to the Anglo-Norwegian Fisheries case (see Section 1.4).

7.8.1 GENERAL

For historical background, see
OUDENDIJK, J K, Status and Extent of Adjacent Waters: A Historical Orientation (Leiden: Sijthoff, 1970). 160 pp.
and vol 4 of VERZIJL's International law in Historical Perspective, listed in Section 2.2. For basic documents of, for example, the Geneva conventions and UN resolutions, see
ODA, S, The International Law of the Ocean Development: Basic Documents (Leiden: Sijthoff, 1972-4). 2 vols.

ALEXANDER, Lewis, (ed), The Law of the Sea, International Rules and Organizations for the Sea. Proceedings of the Third Annual Conference of the Law of the Sea Institute, 24 June - 27 June, 1968 (Kingston, RI, 1969)
ALVARADO, G T, El Dominion del Mar (Guayaquil, 1968)
ALVARADO, G T, Derecho Internacional Maritimo (Guayaquil, 1970)
ALVAREZ, A, Los Nuevos Principios del Derecho del Mar (Montevideo, 1969)
AZCARRAGA y BUSTAMENTE, J L, Derecho Internacional Maritimo (Barcelona, 1970)
AZUNI, D, Sistema Universale dei Principi del Diritto Maritimo dell'Europa (1795), tr Johnson, New York, 1803
BAILEY, Sir K, 'Australia and the Law of the Sea', Adelaide Law Review, vol 1 (1960), p 1

BARABOLYA, et al, Manual of Maritime Law (Moscow, 1966; US Navy translation, 1968)

BEESLEY, J A, 'Some unresolved issues on the law of the sea', Natural Resources Lawyer (1971), p 629

BOWETT, D W, The Law of the Sea (Manchester: Manchester University Press/Dobbs Ferry, NY: Oceana, 1967). vii + 117 pp

BOWETT, D W, 'The second United Nations conference on the law of the sea', Int. & Comp. Law Q., vol 9 (1960), p 415

BROWN, E D, The Legal Regime of Hydrospace (London: Stevens & Sons, 1971). xx + 236 pp.

BURKE, W T, 'Some Comments on the 1958 Conventions', Proceedings of the American Society of International law (1959), p 197

BUTLER, William E, The Soviet Union and the Law of the Sea (Baltimore, Md: Johns Hopkins Press, 1971). xiii + 245 pp.

BUTLER, W, 'Some recent developments in Soviet Maritime law', in The Law of the Sea, edited by Alexander (Rhode Island: The Law of the Sea Institute, 1971)

CHAPPELL, D, 'Conference on the law of the sea', Tasmanian University Law Review, vol 1 (1959), p 323

CHARLIER, R E, 'Résultats et enseignements des conférences du droit de la mer', Annu. Fr. Droit Int., vol 6 (1960), p 63

COLOMBOS, C J, The International Law of the Sea, 6th edition (London: Longmans, 1967). 886 pp.

COLOMBOS, C J, 'The unification of maritime law in time of peace', Br. Yearb. Int. Law, vol 21 (1944), p 96

DEAN, A H, 'Achievements at the law of the sea conference', Proceedings of the American Society of International Law, vol 53 (1959), p 186

DEAN, A H, 'Second Geneva conference on the law of the sea: the fight for freedom of the seas', Am. J. Int. Law, vol 54 (1960), p 751
DEAN, A H, 'Second United Nations conference on the law of the sea: a response', Am. J. Int. Law, vol 55, p 675
DUPUY, R J, The Law of the Sea: Current Problems (Leiden: Sijthoff, 1974). 200 pp.
EEK, H, The Hydrological Cycle and the Law of Nations (Studia juridica Stockholmiensia 22) (Stockholm, 1965)
EEK, H, Världshavens Frihet och Fred (Stockholm: Bokforlaget Aldus/Bonniers, 1971). 153 pp.
EICHHORN, K, Die Bodenseefischerei in ihrer Geschichtlichen Entwicklung und ihrer Regelung in Internationalen und Einzelstaatlichen Recht (Würzburg, 1930)
FERRON, O de, Le Droit international de la mer (Paris/Genève, 1960). 2 vols.
FITZMAURICE, G, 'Some results of the Geneva conference on the law of the sea', Int. & Comp. Law Q., vol 8 (1959), p 73
FOCSANEAU, L, 'Le droit international maritime de l'océan Pacifique et de ses mers adjacentes', Annu. Fr. Droit Int., vol 7 (1961), p 173
FRANKLIN, C M, 'The law of the sea: some recent developments', Southern California Law Review, vol 33 (1960), p 357
GARCIA AMADOR Y RODRIGUEZ, F V, Latin America and the Law of the Sea (Rhode Island: The Law of the Sea Institute, 1972)
GARCIA AMADOR, F V, 'The Latin American contribution to the development of the law of the sea', Am. J. Int. Law, vol 68 (1974), pp 33-50
GARCÍA ROBLES, A, 'Second United Nations conference on the law of the sea - a reply', Am. J. Int. Law, vol 55 (1961), p 669

GANNINI, A, 'La seconda conferenza del diritto del mare', Rivista del Diritto della Navigazione, vol 26 (1960), p 3

GIDEL, Gilbert, Le Droit international public de la mer (Paris: Chateauroux, 1932-4). 3 vols. Vol 1 'Introduction - la haute mer', vol 2 'Les eaux intérieures, vol 3 'La mer territoriale et la zone contigue'

GRZYBOWSKI, K, 'The Soviet doctrine of mare clausum and politics in the Black and Baltic Seas', Journal of Central European Affairs, vol 14 (1954/5), p 320

HARTINGH, F, de, Les Conceptions soviétiques du droit de la mer (Paris, 1960)

HJERTONSSON, Karin, (née Oldfeldt), The New Law of the Sea, Influence of Latin American States on Recent Developments of the Law of the Sea (Stockholm: Norstedt/Leiden: Sijthoff, 1973)

HOOG, V G, Die Genfer Seerechtkonferenzen von 1958 und 1960 (Frankfurt/Berlin, 1961). 138 pp.

JESSUP, P C, 'Geneva conference on the law of the sea: a study in international law-making', Am. J. Int. Law, vol 52 (1958), p 730

JESSUP, P C, 'United Nations conference on the law of the sea', Columbia Law Review, vol 59 (1959), p 234

JESSUP, P C, 'The law of the sea around us', Am. J. Int. Law, vol 55 (1961), p 104

JOHNSON, Bo, Suveraniti i havet och Luftrummet. Souveraineté sur la mer at dans les airs. Avec un condensé en français (Stockholm: P A Norstedt & Söners Forlag, 1972). 414 pp.

JOHNSON, D H N, Recent Developments in the Law of the Sea, 1958-64 (London, 1965)

JOHNSON, D H N, 'The preparation of the 1958 Geneva conference on the law of the sea', Int. & Comp. Law Q., vol 8 (1959), p 122

JOHNSON, D H N, 'The Geneva conference on the law of the sea', Yearb. World Aff., vol 13 (1959), p 68

MÜNCH, F, 'Die Internationale Seerechtzkonferenz in Genf 1958', Arch. Völkerrechts, vol 8 (1959), pp 180-208

NIELD, R R, Alternative Forms of International Regime for the Ocean (Towards a better use of the Ocean) (Uppsala: SIPRI, 1969)

LAY, S, Houston, CHURCHILL, R, & NORDQUIST, M, New Directions in the Law of the Sea: Documents (London: British Institute of International and Comparative Law, 1973). 2 vols.

MacCHESNEY, Brunson, US Naval War College. International Law Situation and Documents 1956. Situation, Documents and Commentary on Recent Developments in the International Law of the Sea, vol 51 (Washington, 1957). 629 pp.

McDOUGAL, M S, 'Crisis in the law of the sea: community perspectives versus national egoism', Yale Law Journal, vol 67 (1958), p 539

McFEE, W, The Law of the Sea (London, 1951)

MANLEY, R H,'The Geneva conferences on the law of the sea as a step in the international law-making process', Albany Law Review, vol 25 (1961), p 17

MEYER-LINDENBERG, H, 'Seerechtliche Entwicklungstendenzen auf den Genfer Konferenzen von 1958 und 1960', Z. Ausl. Öff. Recht & Völkerrecht, vol 21 (1961), p 38

MOLODTSOV, S, 'Codifying the law of the sea', Sov. Ezheg. Mezhdunar. Prava (1958), p 237. In Russian with English summary.

ODA, S, 'Japan and the United Nations conference on the law of the sea', Jap. Annu. Int. Law, vol 3 (1959), p 65

PATEY, J, 'La conférence des Nations Unies sur le droit de la mer', Rev. Gén. Droit Int. Public, vol 62 (1958), p 446

QUENEUDEC, J P, Droit maritime international (Paris, 1971). 383 pp.
REIFF, H, The United States and the Treaty Law of the Sea (Minneapolis, Minn, 1959)
ROSEMAN, D M, 'Geneva conference on the law of the sea: convention on fishing and conservation of the living resources of the high seas', Boston B J, vol 3 (1959), p 28
SANDIFORD, R, 'Conférence de Genève sur le droit de la mer', Rev. Int. Fr. Droit Gens, vol 28 (1959) p 18
SANDIFORD, R, 'Deuxième conférence sur le droit de la mer, Genève 15 mars - 26 avril 1960', Rev. Int. Fr. Droit Gens., vol 30 (1961), p 67
SHALOWITZ, A, Shore and Sea Boundaries (Washington DC, 1962-4)
SIMMONDS, R R, 'Law of the sea: the second Geneva conference', Law Journal, vol 110 (1960), p 507
SMITH, H A, The Law and Custom of the Sea, 3rd edition (London: Stevens, 1959)
SØRENSON, M, 'Law of the sea', Int. Conciliation no 520 (1958), p 195
STEVENSON, J R, & OXMAN, B H, 'The preparation for the law of the sea conference ', Am. J. Int. Law, vol 68 (1974), pp 1-32
SWAN, C, & WEBERHORST, J, 'The conference on the law of the sea: a report', Michigan Law Review, vol 56 (1958), p 1132
Law of the Sea (London: Society of Comparative Legislation and International Law, 1958)
The Law of the Sea. National Policy Recommendations. Proceedings of the Fourth Annual Conference of the Law of the Sea Institute June 23 - June 26, 1969 (Kingston, R I: University of Rhode Island, 1970). vi + 533 pp.
TAO CHENG, 'Communist China and the law of the sea', Am. J. Int. Law (1969), p 37

VATTEL, E de, The Abridgement of All the Sea-Laws (London, 1613)
VERZIJL, J H W, 'Conference of the law of the sea', Ned. Tijdschr. Int. Recht, vol 6 (1959)
VISSER 'T HOOFT, H Ph V, Les Nations Unies et la conservation des ressources de la mer (Den Haag, Nijhoff, 1958)
WERNER, A R, Traité de droit maritime international (Genève, 1964)
YEPES, J M, 'Les nouvelles tendances du droit international de la mer et le droit international américain', Rev. Gén. Droit Int. Public, vol 60 (1956), p 10
ZACKLIN, R, The Changing Law of the Sea: Western Hemisphere Perspectives (Leiden: Sijthoff, 1974). 279 pp.

7.8.2 TERRITORIAL WATERS

On territorial waters there is a host of different works. The importance of the question of the width of territorial waters has somewhat decreased since states now concentrate on claims for 'zones', mainly for fishing purposes, and less on full jurisdiction over territorial waters. See also, Section 7.8.4 on special zones. For the width of territorial waters and of zones, see also above on law of the sea in general and, for a geographical-economic interpretation, DELUPIS, International Law and the Independent State, listed in Section 1.8.

ALEXANDER, Lewis, 'Breadths of territorial and other offshore zones', in The Law of the Sea: International Rules and Organizations for the Sea: Proceedings of the Third Annual Conference of the Law of the Sea Institute, 24 June - 27 June 1968, edited by L Alexander (Kingston, RI, 1969)

AUBERT, L M B, 'La mer territoriale de la Norvège', Rev. Gén. Droit Int. Public, vol 1 (1894), p 429

AUBY, J M, 'Les problèmes de la mer territoriale devant la Cour internationale de justice', J, Droit Int., vol 80 (1953), p 24

BATY, T, 'Three-mile limit', Am. J. Int. Law, vol 22 (1928), p 503

BUSTAMENTE y SIRVÉN, A S de, El Mar Territorial (Havana, 1930)

BUTLER, W E, The Law of Soviet Territorial Waters (New York: Praeger, 1967)

BUTLER, W E, 'New Soviet legislation on straight base lines', Int. & Comp. Law Q., vol 20 (1971), p 750

CAICEDO CASTILLA, José Joaquin, 'La conferencia de Ciudad Trujillo sobre mar territorial', Rev. Esp. Derecho Int., vol 9 (1956), p 731

FENN, P T, 'Origins of the theory of territorial waters', Am. J. Int. Law, vol 20 (1926), p 465

FENN, P T, The Origin of the Right of Fisheries in Territorial Waters (Cambridge, Mass, 1926)

GARCÍA ROBLES, A, La Anchura del Mar Territorial (Mexico, 1966)

GARCÍA SAYAN, E, Notas sobre Soberania Maritima de Peru: Defensa de las 200 Milas de Mar Peruano ante las Recientes Transgressiones (Lima, 1955)

GIHL, T, 'Utgångspunkten for territorialhavets beräkning', Statens Offentliga Utredningar (1965), p 1

GIHL, T, 'Gränsen för Sveriges territorialvatten', Statens Offentliga Utredningar (1930), p 6

GROS ESPIELL, Hector, 'La mer territoriale dans l'Atlantique sud-américain', Annu. Fr. Droit Int., vol 16 (1970), pp 743-63

HALE, R W, 'Territorial waters as a test of codification', Am. J. Int. Law, vol 24 (1930), p 65

HEINZEN, B G, 'Three-mile limit: preserving the freedom of the sea', Stanford Law Review, vol 11 (1959), p 597

JESSUP, P C, Law of Territorial Waters and Maritime Jurisdiction (New York, 1927; reissued by Kraus Reprint Corporation, New York)

JOHNSON, D H N, 'Developments since the Geneva conferences of 1958 and 1960: Anglo-Scandinavian agreements concerning the territorial sea and fishing limits', Int. & Comp. Law Q., vol 10 (1961), p 587

KENNEDY, W P M, 'Foreign fishing vessels in Canadian territorial waters', South African Law Times, vol 1 (1932), p 134

KENT, H S K, 'The historical origins of the three-mile limit', Am. J. Int. Law, vol 48 (1954), p 537

KLEIN, C B, 'The territorial waters of archipelagos', Federal Bar Journal, vol 26 (1966), p 316

KOLODKIN, A, 'Territorial waters and international law', Int. Aff. no 8 (August 1969), p 78

LAPRADELLE, A, de, 'Le droit de l'état sur la mer territoriale', Rev. Gén. Droit Int. Public (1898)

McDOUGAL, M S, & BURKE, W T, 'The community interest in a narrow territorial sea: inclusive versus exclusive competence over the oceans', Cornell Law Quarterly, vol 45 (1960), p 171

MEDINA ORTEGA, M, 'Derecho de pesa y mar territorial español', Rev. Esp. Derecho Int. (1963), p 61

MEYER, C V, The Extent of Jurisdiction in Coastal Waters (New York, 1937)

NIKOLAEV, A N, Territorial'noe More (Moscow, 1969)

O'CONNELL, D P, 'Problems of Australian coastal jurisdiction', Br. Yearb. Int. Law, vol 34 (1958), p 199

O'CONNELL, D P, The juridical nature of the territorial sea, Brit. Yearb. Int. Law, (1971), pp 303-384
ODA, S, 'The extent of the territorial sea', Jap. Annu. Int. Law, vol 6 (1962), p 7
REEVES, J S, 'The codification of the law of territorial waters', Am. J. Int. Law, vol 24 (1930), p 225
RÖRIG, F, Zur Rechtsgeschichte der Territorialgewässer: Reede, Strom, und Küstengewässer (Berlin, 1949)
ROUSSEAU, C, 'Décret-loi brésilien du 25.4.69 modifiant l'étendue de la mer territoriale', Rev. Gén. Droit Int. Public (1970), p 410
ROUSSEAU, C, 'Décret uruguayien étendant les limites de la mer territoriale', Rev. Gén. Droit Int. Public (1970), p 567
ROUSSEAU, C, 'L'extension de l'étendue d'eaux territoriales', Rev. Gén. Droit Int. Public (1970), p 1101; (1971), p 487
SCHAPIRO, L B, 'The limits of Russian territorial waters in the Baltic', Br. Yearb. Int. Law, vol 27 (1950), pp 439-48
SELAK, C B, Jr, 'Fishing vessels and the principle of innocent passage', Am. J. Int. Law, vol 48 (1954), p 627
TEITELBOIM, Sergio, 'Los paises del Pacifico y el mar territorial', Estudios Internacionales, vol 3 (1970), p 38
WALKER, W L, 'Territorial waters: the cannon shot rule', Br. Yearb. Int. Law, vol 22 (1945), p 210
YEPES, E, 'El problema del mar territorial jurisdiccional y de la plataforma submarina ante el nuevo derecho internacional', Revista Universita Bogotà (1955), p 45

7.8.2.1 INNOCENT PASSAGE AND FREEDOM OF NAVIGATION

KHOSHKISH, Anoushiravan, The Right of Innocent Passage (Genève, 1954). 168 pp.
RAESTAD, A, 'La chasse à la baleine en mer libre: un question de legislation internationale devant la société des nations', Rev. Droit Int. (1928), p 595
BALDONI, Claudio, 'Les navires de guerre dans les eaux territoriales étrangères', Acad. Droit Int. Recl. Cours, vol 65 (1938), pp 185-303
JONES, J Mervyn, 'The Corfu Channel case: merits', Br. Yearb. Int. Law, vol 26 (1949), pp 447-53
ZWANENBERG, Anna van, 'Interference with ships on the high seas', Int. & Comp. Law Q., vol 10 (1961), pp 785-817

7.8.2.2 HOT PURSUIT

BECK, J S H, 'The doctrine of hot pursuit', Canadian Bar Review, vol 9 (1931)
BOSE, H v, Die Nacheile im Völkerrecht (Baruth: Mark-Berlin, 1935). 48 pp.
MARTENS, H L, Das Recht der Nacheile zur See (Grömitz in Holstein, 1937). 212 pp.
MASSIN, J, La Poursuite en droit maritime (Paris, 1937). 108 pp.
ODDINI, M, Il diritto di inseguimento e la zone contigua (Genova, 1952). 16 pp.
POULANTZAS, Nicholas, The Right of Hot Pursuit in International Law (Leiden: Sijthoff/New York: Humanities Press, 1969). xvi + 451 pp.
WILLIAMS, G L, 'The juridical basis of hot pursuit', Br. Yearb. Int. Law (1939), pp 83-97
See also
HERSHEY, A S, 'Incursions into Mexico and the doctrine of hot pursuit', Am. J. Int. Law, vol 13 (1919), pp 557-69

7.8.3 CONTIGUOUS ZONE

FATTAL, Antoine, Les Conférences des Nations Unies et la convention de Genève du 29 avril 1958 sur la mer territoriale et la zone contiguë (Beirut: Librairie du Liban, 1968). 319 pp.

MASTERSON, William E, Jurisdiction in Marginal Seas: with Special Reference to Smuggling (New York, 1929; reissued by Kennikat Press, Port Washington, NY, 1970)

ODA, S, 'The concept of the contiguous zone', Int. & Comp. Law Q. (1962), pp 131-53

7.8.4 SPECIAL 'ZONES'

Recently an ever increasing number of states have made extensive claims to zones for various purposes, mainly for fishing. See also Section 7.8.2 on territorial waters, and the work by BURKE in Section 7.8.6.2.

ALEXANDER, L M, (ed), The Law of the Sea: Offshore Boundaries and Zones (Columbus, Ohio: Ohio State University Press, 1967). 321 pp.

ALEXANDER, L, 'Offshore claims and fisheries in northwest Europe', Yearb. World Aff. (1960), p 236

ALLEN, E W, 'Control of fisheries beyond three miles', Washington Law Review, vol 14 (1939), p 91

ALLEN, E W, 'Developing fishery protection', Am. J. Int. Law, vol 36 (1942), p 115

ALLEN, E W, 'Legal limits of coastal fishery protection', Washington Law Review, vol 21 (1946), p 1

ALLEN, E W, 'The fishery proclamation of 1945', Am. J. Int. Law, vol 45 (1951), p 177

ALLEN, E W, 'A new concept for fishery treaties', Am. J. Int. Law, vol 46 (1952)

ANDERSON, C P, 'Exploitation of the products of the sea', Am. J. Int. Law, vol 20 (1926), p 752

AZZAM, T, 'Dispute between France and Brazil over lobster fishing in the Atlantic', Int. & Comp. Law Q., vol 13 (1964), p 1453

BAYITCH, S A, Interamerican Law of Fisheries: An Introduction with Documents (New York, 1957)

BAYITCH, S A, 'International fishery problems in the western hemisphere', Miami Law Quarterly, vol 10 (1956), p 499

CAMPBELL, E, 'Regulation of Australian coastal fisheries', Tasman UL Rev., vol 1 (1960), p 405

CAMPBELL, N J, 'International law developments concerning national claims to and in offshore areas', Tulane Law Review, vol 33 (1959), p 339

CHAPMAN, W M, 'United States policy on high seas fisheries', US Department of State Bulletin, vol 20 (1949), p 67; p 80

CHAPMAN, W M, Concerning Fishery Jurisdiction and the Regime of the Deep Sea Bed (Towards a Better Use of the Ocean) (Uppsala: S I P R I, 1969)

CHARTERIS, A H, 'Trawling in prohibited areas', Juridical Review, vol 21 (1909), p 181

DAGGETT, A P, 'The regulation of maritime fisheries by treaty', Am. J. Int. Law, vol 28 (1934), p 693

DAVIS, M, Iceland Extends its Fisheries Limits (Oslo, 1963)

DINH, Nguyen Quoc, 'La revendication des droits preferentiels de pêche en haute mer, devant les conférences des Nations Unies sur le droit de la mer de 1958 et 1960', Annu. Fr. Droit Int., vol 6 (1960), p 77

DOUENCE, J C, Droit de la mer et développement économique sur la côte occidentale d'Afrique', Rev. Gén. Droit Int. Public, vol 71 (1967), pp 110-42

FINLAY, L W, 'Rights of coastal nations to the continental margins', Natural Resources Lawyer (1971), p 668
FLEISCHER, C A, Fiskerijurisdiksjon (Oslo, 1963). 425 pp.
FLEISCHER, C A, 'Fiskerigrensespörsmålet. Utvikklingen etter Haag Dommen av 1951', Nord. Tidsskr. Int. Ret, vol 34 (1964), p 158
FLEISCHER, C A, 'Norway's policy on fisheries', in Developments in the Law of the Sea 1958-1964 (London: British Institute of International and Comparative Law, 1965)
GOLDIE, L F E, 'Occupation of the sedentary fisheries off the Australian coasts', Sydney Law Review, vol 1 (1953), p 84
GOTTLIEB, A E, 'Canadian contribution to the concept of a fishing zone in international law', Can. Yearb. Int. Law, vol 2 (1964), p 55
GREEN, L C, 'Anglo-Norwegian fisheries case, 1951', Modern Law Review, vol 15 (1952), p 373
GUTMANN, F, Die Internationalen Verträge über die Nordseefischerei (Leipzig, 1912)
Iceland, Ministry of Foreign Affairs, The Icelandic Fishing Limits (Reykjavik, 1959)
IRELAND, G, 'The north Pacific fisheries', Am. J. Int. Law, vol 36 (1942), p 400
JESSUP, P C, 'The Pacific coast fisheries', Am. J. Int. Law, vol 33 (1939), p 129
JOHNSON, D H N, 'Icelandic fish limits', Int. & Comp. Law Q., vol 1 (1952), p 71; p 350
JOHNSON, R W, 'Fishery developments in the Pacific', in Developments in the Law of the Sea 1958-1964 (London: British Institute of International and Comparative Law, 1965)
JOHNSON, D M, The International Law of Fisheries (New Haven, Conn: Yale University Press, 1965). 554 pp.

KEHDEN, M I, Die Inanspruchsnahme von
Meereszonen und Meeresbodenzonen durch
Küstenstaten (Hamburg, 1971). 214 pp.
NELSON, L D M, 'The patrimonial sea', Int. & Comp.
Law Q., vol 22 (1973), pp 668-86
NWOGUGU, E I, 'Problems of Nigerian offshore
jurisdiction', Int. & Comp. Law Q., vol 22 (1973),
p 349
OUDENDIJK, J K, Status and Extent of Adjacent Waters:
A Historical Orientation (Leiden: Sijthoff, 1970).
160 pp.
KOERS, A W, International Regulation of Marine
Fisheries: (West Byfleet: Fishing News (Books) Ltd.,
1973). 368 pp.
LADOR-LEDERER, J J, 'L'évolution du droit international des pêcheries', J. Droit Int., vol 85 (1958),
p 634
LEONARD, L L, International Regulation of Fisheries
(Washington, 1944)
LEVY, G, La Condition juridique et économique des
pêcheurs français de Terre Neuve et d'Islande
(Toulon, 1931)
MacDONALD, R St J, 'Some aspects of international
fisheries control in United States-Canadian
relations', Rev. Hell. Droit Int., vol 7 (1954), p 194
MIKHAILOV, V S, 'International law and the regulation
of fisheries and other maritime industries in the
Pacific', Sov. Yezheg. Mezhdunar. Prava (1960),
p 189. In Russian with English summary.
MORIN, J Y, 'La zone de pêche exclusive du Canada',
Can. Yearb. Int. Law, vol 2 (1964), p 77
ODA, S, 'Japan and the international fisheries', Jap.
Annu. Int. Law, vol 4 (1960), p 50
ODA, S, 'The 1958 Geneva convention on the fisheries:
its immaturities', Die Friedens-Warte, vol 55 (1960),
p 317
OHIRA, Z, 'Fishery problems between Soviet Russia
and Japan', Jap. Annu. Int. Law, vol 2 (1958), p 1

OHIRA, Z, & KUWAHARA, T, 'Fishery problems between Japan and the People's Republic of China', Jap. Annu. Int. Law, vol 3 (1959), p 109

PLATON, C G, 'Contiguous zones for fishing purposes', Philippine Law Journal, vol 37 (1962), p 774

RIESENFELD, S A, Protection of Coastal Fisheries under International Law (Washington, 1943)

ROBERTSON, W S, 'International co-operation in fisheries conservation', US Department of State Bulletin, vol 30 (1954), p 297

ROSENOW, B J, 'Fishing rights and North American-Japanese treaty problems', Washington Law Review, vol 38 (1963), p 223

SELAK, C B, 'Proposed international convention for the high seas fisheries of the north Pacific ocean', Am. J. Int. Law, vol 46 (1952), p 323

WOODLIFFE, J. C, 'Inshore fisheries and international law', Law Journal, vol 113 (1963), p 428

WOODLIFFE, J C, 'European fishing limits: some recent developments', Law Journal, vol 114 (1964), p 601

YOUNG, R, 'Saudi Arabian offshore legislation', Am. J. Int. Law, vol 43 (1949), p 531

7.8.5 SUBMERGED MARINE AREAS

7.8.5.1 GENERAL

LAUTERPACHT, H, 'Sovereignty over submarine areas', Br. Yearb. Int. Law, vol 27 (1950), pp 415-19

7.8.5.2 SUBMARINE BOUNDARIES

PADWA, David J, 'Submarine boundaries', Int. & Comp. Law Q., vol 9 (1960), pp 628-53
On a particular dispute:

GIDEL, G, 'Le querelle des "Tidelands" aux Etats-Unis de la proposition Nye (1937) au "Submerged Lands Act" (22 Mai 1953) et au "Outer Continental Shelf Lands Act" (7 Mai 1953)' in Festgabe für Makarov (1958)

7.8.5.3 CONTINENTAL SHELF

ALVARADO GARAIOCA, T, 'Continental shelf and the extension of the territorial sea', Miami Law Quarterly, vol 10 (1956), p 490

ARAMBURU y MENCHACA, A A, 'Character and scope of the rights declared and practised over the continental sea and shelf', Am. J. Int. Law, vol 47 (1953), p 120

AUGUSTE, B, The Continental Shelf: The Practice and Policy of the Latin American States with Special Reference to Chile, Ecuador and Peru (Genève/ Paris, 1960). 408 pp.

AZCARRAGA (y BUSTAMENTE) de J L, La Plataforma Submarina y el Derecho Internacional (Madrid, 1952)

AZCARRAGA y BUSTAMENTE, José Luis de,'La Sentencia del Tribunal Internacional de Justicia sobre los Casos de la Plataforma Continental del Mar del Norte (20 de Febrero de 1969)', Rev. Est. Derecho Int., vol 22 (1969), p 527

BOUCHEZ, Leo J, 'The North Sea continental shelf cases', Journal of Maritime Law and Commerce, vol 1 (1969), p 113

BUTLER, William, 'The Soviet Union and the continental shelf', Am. J. Int. Law, vol 63 (1969), p 103

ELY, Northcutt, 'The United States seabed minerals policy', Natural Resources Lawyer, vol 4 (1971), p 597

FRIEDMANN, W, 'The North Sea continental shelf cases: a critique', Am. J. Int. Law, vol 64 (1970), p 229

GIDEL, G C, 'A propos des bases juridiques des prétensions des états riverains sur le plateau continental: les doctrines du "droit inhérent" ', Z. Ausl. Öff. Recht & Völkerrecht, vol 19 (1959), p 81

GOLDIE, L F E, 'Australia's continental shelf: legislation and proclamations', Int. & Comp. Law Q., vol 3 (1954), p 535

GREEN, L C, 'The continental shelf', Current Legal Problems, vol 4 (1951), p 54

GRISEL, E, 'The lateral boundaries of the continental shelf and the judgment of the International Court of Justice in the North Sea continental shelf case', Am. J. Int. Law (1970), p 562

KUNZ, J L, 'Continental shelf and international law: confusion and abuse', Am. J. Int. Law, vol 50 (1956), p 828

LANG, J, Le Plateau continental de la mer du nord: Arrêt de la Cours internationale de justice 20/2/69 (Paris 1970). 163 pp.

LOPEZ VILLAMIL, H, La Plataforma Continental y los Problemas Juridicos del Mar (Madrid, 1958)

MOUTON, M, The Continental Shelf, (Den Haag, 1952). 367 pp.

O'CONNELL, D P, 'Sedentary fisheries and the Australian continental shelf', Am. J. Int. Law, vol 49 (1955), p 185

ODA, S, 'A reconsideration of the continental shelf doctrine', Tulane Law Review, vol 32 (1957), p 21

PUIG, 'Mar territorial, mar epicontinental y plataforma continental', Jurisprudencia Argentina (1964)

ROUSSEAU, C, 'Chroniques des faits internationaux',
Rev. Gén. Droit Int. Public, vol 75 (1971), pp
759-876. Pages 813-14, 'Colombie et Venezuela:
Difficultes entre les deux états au sujet de la
délimitation du plateau continental dans la golfe du
Venezuela'
SCELLE, G, Plateau continental et le droit international (Paris, 1955)
SCELLE, G, 'Plateau continental et droit international',
Rev. Gén. Droit Int. Public, vol 59 (1955), pp 5-62
SLOUKA, Z J, International Custom and the Continental
Shelf (Den Haag: Nijhoff, 1968)
STONE, O, 'United States legislation relating to the
continental shelf', Int. & Comp. Law Q., vol 17
(1968), p 103
VALLEE, C, Le Plateau continental dans le droit
positif actuel (Paris, 1971). 359 pp.
VALLAT, F A, 'The continental shelf', Br. Yearb.
Int. Law, vol 23 (1946), p 333
YOUNG, R, 'Recent developments with respect to the
continental shelf', Am. J. Int. Law, vol 42 (1948),
p 849
YOUNG, R, 'Sedentary fisheries and the convention on
the continental shelf', Am. J. Int. Law, vol 55 (1961),
p 359

7.8.5.4 SEABED AND OCEAN FLOOR

See also Section 7.8.5.3 on continental shelf
COLLIARD, C A, DUPUY, R J, POLVECHE, I, &
VAISSIERE, R, Le Fond des mers (Paris: Armand
Colin, 1971). 205 pp.
EVENSEN, J, Muligheter og Rettigheter på
Havbunnen (Oslo, 1970)
HURST, C, 'Whose is the bed of the sea?', Br. Yearb.
Int. Law, vol 4 (1923/4), pp 34-43

JENNINGS, R Y, 'The United States draft treaty on the international seabed area: basic principles', Int. & Comp. Law Q., vol 20 (1971), p 433

KÜHNE, W, Das Völkerrecht und die Militärische Nützung des Meeresbodens (Leiden: Sijthoff, 1974). 200 pp.

MANGONE, Gerard, J, The United Nations, International Law and the Bed of the Seas. Oceans Series 303 (Washington: Woodrow Wilson International Center for Scholars, 1972). 44 pp.

MENGOZZI, P, Il regime giuridico internazionale del fondo marino (Milano: Giuffré, 1971). 321 pp.

SZTUCKI, J, (ed), Symposium on the International Regime of the Sea-Bed: Proceedings (Roma: Accademia Nazionale dei Lincei, 1970). 767 pp.

VALLAT, F A, 'Ownership of the sea-bed: United States of America v. State of California', Br. Yearb. Int. Law, vol 24 (1947), p 382

YOUNG, R, 'Further claims to areas beneath the high seas', Am. J. Int. Law, vol 43 (1949), p 790

YOUNG, R, 'The legal status of submarine areas beneath the high seas', Am. J. Int. Law, vol 45 (1951), p 225

7.8.6   THE HIGH SEAS

See also Grotius's Mare liberum listed in Section 2.1.

7.8.6.1   GENERAL

ACCIOLY, H, 'La liberté des mers et le droit de pêche en haute mer', Rev. Gén. Droit Int. Public, vol 61 (1957), p 193

ALFIN Y DELGADO, F, El Mundo Submarino y el Derecho (Madrid, 1959)

BIERZANEK, R, 'La nature juridique de la haute mer', Rev. Gén. Droit Int. Public, vol 65 (1961), p 259

CRICHTON, G H, 'Grotius on the freedom of the seas', Juridical Review, vol 53 (1941), p 226
ELY, N, 'The United States seabed minerals policy', Natural Resources Lawyer, vol 4 (1971), p 597
FEDOZZI, Prospero, 'La condition juridique des navires de commerce', Acad. Droit Int. Recl. Cours, vol 10 (1925), pp 1-222
FULTON, T W, Sovereignty of the Sea (Edinburgh/London, 1911)
GIDEL, G, 'Explosions nucléaires experimentales et liberté de la haute mer', in Festschrift für Jean Spiropoulos (Bonn, 1957)
LAUTERPACHT, H, 'Sovereignty over submarine areas', Br. Yearb. Int. Law, vol 27 (1950), p 376
McDOUGAL, Myres S, & BURKE, William T, The Public Order of the Oceans: Contemporary International Law of the Sea (New Haven, Conn: Yale University Press, 1962)
McDOUGAL, M S, BURKE, W T, & VLASIC, I A, 'Maintenance of public order at sea and the nationality of ships', Am. J. Int. Law, vol 54 (1950), p 25
MacKAY, R A, Preliminary Report on the International Control of Fisheries on the High Seas, with Particular Reference to the Pacific (Honolulu, 1929)
MOLEN, J, 'The principle of abstention and freedom of the seas', Ned. Tijdschr. Int. Recht, Liber amicorum J P A François (1959), p 203
PAPANDREOU, A, La Situation juridique des pêcheries sédentaires en haute mer (Athens, 1958)
POTTER, P B, The Freedom of the Seas in History, Law and Politics (New York, 1924)

7.8.6.2 RESOURCES OF THE
SEA AND THE OCEANS

See also Sections 7.8.4 on 'special zones' and 7.8.5.1

on the seabed and ocean floors.
ANDRASSY, J, International Law and the Resources of the Sea (New York/London: Columbia University Press, 1970)
BURKE, W T, 'Contemporary legal problems in ocean development', in Towards a Better Use of the Ocean (Stockholm: International Peace Research Institute, 1969)
BURKE, W T, Towards a Better Use of the Ocean. A Study of the Legal Problems (London: Gerald Duckworth & Co Ltd/New York: Humanities Press Inc, 1970). 231 pp.
FRIDMAN LUTZKAYA, J, El Desarrollo del Derecho Internacional en la Conservación de los Recursos Vivos del Mar (Mexico City, 1956)
FRIEDMANN, Wolfgang, The Future of the Oceans (New York: George Braziller, 1971/London: Dennis Dobson, 1972). 132 pp.
GARCÍA AMADOR Y RODRÍGUEZ, F V, The Exploitation and Conservation of the Resources of the Sea, 2nd edition (Leiden: Sijthoff, 1963)
GROS, A, 'La convention sur la pêche et la conservation des ressources biologiques de la haute mer', Acad. Droit Int. Recl. Cours, vol 97 (1959), p 1
HENKIN, L, Law for the Sea's Mineral Resources (New York: Institute for the Study of Science in Human Affairs, Columbia University, 1968)
JESSUP, P C, 'L'exploitation des richesses de la mer', Acad. Droit Int. Recl. Cours, vol 29 (1929), p 405
JESSUP, P C, 'International protection of whales', Am. J. Int. Law, vol 24 (1930), p 751
JONES, E B, Law of the Sea: Oceanic Resources (Dallas, Tex: Southern Methodist University Press, 1972). xiv + 162 pp.
KOERS, A W, International Regulation of Marine Fisheries (West Byfleet, Surrey: Fishing News (Books) Ltd, 1973). 368 pp.

KOLODKIN, A L, Mirovo: Okean: Mezhdunarodno-
pravovoy Rezhim; Osnovnye Problemy (The World
Ocean: International Legal Regime: Basic problems)
(Moscow, 1973). 232 pp.
League of Nations, 'Report on the exploitation of the
products of the sea by León Suárez M J to the
committee of experts for the progressive codification
of international law', Am. J. Int. Law, vol 20,
special number (1926), p 231
McDOUGAL, Myres S, & BURKE, William T, The
Public Order of the Oceans: A Contemporary
International Law of the Sea (New Haven, Conn:
Yale University Press, 1962). xxv + 1226 pp.
ODA, S, 'New trends in the regime of the seas: a
consideration of the problems of conservation and
distribution of marine resources', Z. Ausl. Öff.
Recht & Völkerrecht, vol 18 (1957), p 61
ODA, S, International Control of Sea Resources
(Leiden, 1963)
ODA, S, The International Law of the Ocean Develop-
ment: Basic Documents (Leiden: Sijthoff, 1972).
xiv + 519 pp.
VISSER 'T HOOFT, H Ph, Les Nations unies et
la conservation des ressources de la mer (Den
Haag: Nijhoff, 1958). 425 pp.
WENK, Edward, The Politics of the Ocean (Seattle,
Wash: University of Washington Press, 1973).
xviii + 590 pp.

7.8.7 INTERNATIONAL WATERWAYS

The standard of work on waterways in general is by
BAXTER listed in Section 7.8.7.2

7.8.7.1 RIVERS AND DRAINAGE BASINS

AGORO, I O, 'The establishment of the Chad Basin
Commission', Int. & Comp. Law Q., vol 15 (1966),

pp 542-50

ALSTYNE, W W van, 'The justiciability of international river disputes: A study in the case method', Duke Law Journal (1964), pp 307-40

BATSTONE, K K, 'The utilization of the Nile waters', Int. & Comp. Law Q., vol 8 (1959), pp 532-58

BERBER, F J, Rivers in International Law (London, 1959)

BOURNE, C B, 'The right to utilize the waters of international rivers', Can. Yearb. Int. Law, vol 3 (1965), pp 187-264

COLLIARD, C A, 'Evolution et aspects actuels du régime juridique des fleuves internationaux', Acad. Droit Int. Recl. Cours, vol 125 (1968), pp 343-442

EYSINGA, W J M van, 'Les fleuves et canaux internationaux', Bibliotheca Visseriana. vol 2 (1924), pp 123-57

FORTUIN, H, 'The regime of navigable waterways of international concern and the statute of Barcelona', Ned. Tijdschr. Int. Recht (1960), pp 125-43

GARRETSON, A H, HAYTON, R D, & OLMSTEAD, C J, The Law of International Drainage Basins (Dobbs Ferry, NY: Oceana, 1967). 916 pp.

GRIFFIN, W L, 'The use of waters of international drainage basins under customary international law', Am. J. Int. Law, vol 53 (1959), pp 50-80

HIRSCH, A M, 'Utilization of international rivers in the Middle East', Am. J. Int. Law, vol 50 (1956), pp 81-100

JOHNSON, R W, 'Freedom of navigation for international rivers: what does it mean?', Michigan Law Review, vol 62 (1963/5), pp 465-84

KAECKENBECK, G, International Rivers (London: Historical Section, UK Foreign Office, 1920)

KENWORTHY, W, 'Joint development of international rivers', Am. J. Int. Law, vol 54 (1960), pp 592-602

KÜLZ, H R V, 'Further water disputes between India and Pakistan', Int. & Comp. Law Q., vol 18 (1969), pp 713-38

LAYLIN, J G, & BIANCHI, R L, 'The role of adjudication in international river disputes: the Lake Lanoux case', Am. J. Int. Law, vol 53 (1959), pp 30-49

L'HUILLIER, J, 'Les conventions conclues par la France sur l'utilisation de la force motrice des cours d'eau internationaux', Annu. Fr. Droit Int. (1958), pp 692-711

POMPE, C A, 'The Nile Waters question', in Symbolae Verzijl Presentées au Professeur J H W Verzijl à l'occasion de son LXX-ième anniversaire (Den Haag: Nijhoff, 1958), pp 275-94

SAUSER-HALL, Georges, 'L'utilisation industrielle des fleuves internationaux', Acad. Droit Int. Recl. Cours, vol 83 (1953), pp 465-586

SMITH, H A, The Economic Uses of International Rivers (London: University of London, 1931)

TECLAFF, L A, The River Basin in History and Law (Den Haag: Nijhoff, 1967). 228 pp.

WINIARSKI, B, 'Principes généraux du droit fluvial international', Acad. Droit Int. Recl. Cours, vol 45 (1933), pp 79-217

WOLFROM, M, L'utilisation autres que le navigation des eaux, des fleuves, lacs et canaux internationaux (Paris: Pédone, 1964)

7.8.7.2 INTEROCEANIC CANALS

For Suez, see also under nationalization, Section

BADAWI, A H, 'Le statut international du canal de Suez: aperçu historique', in Spiropoulos Festschrift (Bonn, 1957)

BAXTER, R R, The Law of International Waterways with particular Regard to Interoceanic Canals

(Cambridge, Mass: Harvard University Press, 1964). 371 pp.
MENSBRUGGHE, Y van der, Les Garanties de la liberté de navigation dans le canal de Suez (Paris, 1964)
MINER, Dwight Carroll, The Fight for the Panama Route: Story of the Spooner Act and Hay-Herran Treaty (New York: Columbia University Press, 1940; reissued 1966 by Octagon Books, New York)
OBIETA, Joseph A, The International Status of the Suez Canal, 2nd edition (Den Haag: Nijhoff, 1970). 164 pp.
VISSCHER, P de, 'Les aspects juridiques fondamentaux de la question de Suez', Rev. Gén. Droit Int. Public, vol 62 (1958), pp 400-45

7.8.7.3 INTERNATIONAL STRAITS

BRÜHL, E, International Straits (Copenhagen: Nyt Nordisk Forlag Arnold Busck, 1947). 2 vols.
DELUPIS, I, née Detter, Supertankers och internationella sund, Festskrift till Eeek, Schmidt och Ljungman (Stockholm: 1975)
LEIFER, M, & NELSON, L D M, 'Conflict of interest in the Straits of Malacca', Int. Aff. (UK) (1973), pp 190-203
VISSCHER, F de, 'La nouvelle convention des détroits', Rev. Droit Int. & Légis. Comp., vol 17 (1936), pp 669-718

7.8.7.4 BAYS AND GULFS

BOUCHEZ, L J, The Regime of Bays in International Law (Leiden, 1964)
LAURIA, F, Il regime giuridico delle baie e dei golfi (Napoli: Casa Ed. Dott. E. Jovene, 1970). 213 pp.

STROHL, Mitchell P, The International Law of Bays (Den Haag: Nijhoff, 1963). 426 pp.

7.8.7.5 PORTS AND HARBOURS

HAAS, R, 'Régime international des zones franches dans les ports maritimes', Acad. Droit Int. Recl. Cours, vol 21 (1928), pp 375-427
LAUN, Rudolf, 'Le régime international des ports', Acad. Droit Int. Recl. Cours, vol 15 (1926), pp 1-143

7.8.7.6 LAKES

PIPER, Don Courtney, The International Law of the Great Lakes (Durham, NC: Duke University Press, 1967). 165 pp.
SELAK, C B, 'United States-Canadian Great Lakes fisheries convention', Am. J. Int. Law, vol 50 (1956), p 122

7.9 LAW OF THE AIRSPACE

'Air law' is a subject which sometimes goes beyond the boundaries of international law to deal with comparative aspects of civil law. The champions of rights of states in general, as a subject of public international law are Lord McNAIR and Professor D H N JOHNSON whose works on air law and rights in airspace respectively, listed below are the basic textbooks on the subject. 'Space law' is now a topical subject and a vast amount has been published about it. For damage caused by extra-terrestial experiments, see Section 11 on responsibility. On the International Civil Aviation Organization, see Section 13.24.2.24.14

7.9.1 THE RIGHT TO FLY

CHENG, Bin, 'The right to fly', Grotius Soc. Trans.,
  vol 42 (1956), p 121
COOPER, J C, El Derecho de Volar (Buenos Aires:
  ed. La Collection Aeronautica, 1950)

7.9.2 SOVEREIGNTY AND THE
      EXTENT OF NATIONAL AIRSPACE

See also B JOHNSON on Suveränitet, listed in
Section 7.8.1.
CONAC, Gerard, 'L'affaire relative à l'incident
  aérien du 27 juillet 1955 entre Israel et la
  Bulgarie devant la Cour internationale de justice',
  Rev. Gén. Droit Int. Public, vol 64 (1960), p 711
COSTADOAT, Pasini, El espacio aereo (Buenos Aires,
  1955)
DINU, Madeline C, 'State sovereignty in the
  navigable airspace', Journal of Air Law and
  Commerce, vol 17 (1950), pp 43-53
EEK, H, Statens maktsfär i luftrummet (Uppsala,
  1942)
EYMESS, V, Die Lufthoheit und ihre Beschränkungen
  (Rostock, 1940)
FAUCHILLE, P, 'Le domaine aérien et le régime
  juridique des aérostats', Rev. Gén. Droit Int.
  Public, vol 8 (1901), p 414
FAUCHILLE, P, 'Régime juridique des aérostats',
  Annu. Inst. Droit Int., vol 19 (1902), p 86
FAUCHILLE, P, 'Régime des aérostats et de la
  télégraphie sans fils', Annu. Inst. Droit Int., vol 21
  (1906), p 297
FENWICK, Charles G, 'How high is the sky?' Am. J.
  Int. Law, vol 52 (1958)
GEORGIADES, E, 'Du nationalisme aérien à
  l'internationalisme spatial ou le mythe de la

souveraineté aérienne', Revue française de droit
aérien, vol 16 (1962), p 150
HAUPT, G, Der Luftraum (Breslau, 1931)
HAYTON, R D, 'Jurisdiction of the littoral state in the
"air frontiers" ', The Philippine I L Journal, vol 3
(1964), p 369
HEAD, Juan L, 'ADIZ: international law and contiguous
airspace', Alberta Law Review, vol 3 (1964), p 182
JOHNSON, D H N, Rights in Air Space (Manchester:
Manchester University Press/Dobbs Ferry, NY:
Oceana, 1965)
KISLOV, A, & KRILOV, S, 'State sovereignty in air-
space', in U S Congress, Legal Problems of Space
Exploration: A Symposium (Washington, DC: US
Government Printing Office, 1961), p 1037
LA PRADELLE, Paul de, 'Les frontières de l'air',
Acad. Droit Int. Recl. Cours, vol 86 (1954)
LA PRADELLE, Paul de, 'Espace et relations inter-
nationales', Revue générale aérienne, vol 25 (1962),
p 244
LISSITZYN, O, 'The treatment of aerial intruders in
recent practice and international law', Am. J. Int.
Law, vol 47 (1953), pp 559-89
LISSITZYN, O, 'Some legal implications of the U-2 and
RB-47 incidents', Am. J. Int. Law, vol 56 (1962),
pp 135-42
LYCKLAMA à NIJHOLT, J F, Air Sovereignty (Den
Haag, 1910)
MATTE, N M, De la mer territoriale à l'air
'territorial' (Paris, 1965)
MURCHISON, J T, The Contiguous Air Space Zone in
International Law (Ottawa, 1955)
NIJHOLT, Lycklama, Air Sovereignty (Den Haag, 1910)
PENG, M M, Le Statut juridique de l'aéronef militaire
(Den Haag: Nijhoff, 1957). 129 pp.
PENG, M M, 'Le vol à haute altitude et l'article
premier de la Convention de Chicago, 1944', Rev.
Barreau Prov. de Quebec, vol 12 (1952), p 277

SAA, Pavez, Evolución historico juridico de la
doctrina sobre et domino aereo (Santiago, 1948)
RODE-VERSCHOOR, I H Ph de, 'Quelques aspects de
la juridiction sur la haute mer et sur les eaux
territoriales en droit aérien', Rev. Hell. Droit
Int., vol 17 (1961), p 395
SPAIGHT, J M, Aircraft in Peace and the Law
(London, 1919)
WANG, Ming, 'La delimitación de la soberania vertical',
Thesis.Sección de Derecho Aeronautico del Espacio,
del Instituto Francisco de Vitoria, Madrid, 1965
WRIGHT, R, 'Legal aspects of the U-2 incident',
Am. J. Int. Law, vol 54 (1960), pp 836-54
ZARGES, A N, 'Die Grenze des Staatsgebiets un
Luftraum unter Berücksichtigung von Fragen des
Weltraums', Thesis.Marburg 1959

7.9.3   AIR LAW AND TRANSPORT

See above all the work by CHENG
CHENG, Bin, The Law of International Air Transport
(London: Stevens & Sons, 1964)
COOPER, J C, Air Law, a Field of International Thinking
Transport and Communications Rev., vol 4 (1951),
p 3
DOHM, John, (ed), Rules of the Air (Bloomington, Ill:
McKnight & McKnight Publishing Co, 1954). 182 pp.
HOMBOURG, R, 'Etendues et limites du droit aérien,
Revue générale aérienne, vol 19 (1956), pp 140-144
JENNINGS, R V, 'International civil aviation and the
law', Br. Yearb. Int. Law (1945), p 192
KROELI, Joseph, Traité de droit international public
aérien (Paris, 1934)
LACOMBE, J - SAPORTA, Les Lois de l'air (Paris,
1953)
LE GOFF, Marcel, Manuel de droit aérien (Paris,
1956)

LEMOINE, M, Traité de droit aérien (Paris, 1947)
LITVINE, Max, Droit aérien: Notions de droit belge
  et de droit international (Bruxelles: Etablissements
  Emile Bruylant, 1970). 363 pp
LODRUP, P, Luftrett, vol 1 (Oslo, 1965)
MAPELLI, Lopez Enrique, El contrato de transporte
  aéreo internacional, ed Teenos, Madrid, 1968
MATEESCO, Mircea, Institutiuni de Drept Aerian
  (Bucharest, 1947)
MATEESCO, Mircea, Le Droit maritime et le droit
  aérien de l'URSS à l'heure de la coexistence
  pacifique (Paris: Pédone, 1967)
McNAIR, A D, (Baron McNair), The Law of the Air,
  3rd edition by M. R E Kerr & A H M Evans (London:
  Stevens & Sons, 1964)
RIESE, O, Luftrecht (Stuttgart, 1949). 556 pp.
RIESE, O, & LACOUR, J T, Précis de droit aérien
  (Paris, 1951)
SAND, Peter, 'Die Entwicklung des Luftfahrtrechts in
  der Sowjetunion', Ost. Europa Recht (1964), p 176
SHAWCROSS, C N, & BEAUMONT, K M, Air Law,
  3rd edition by P B Keenan, A Lester & P Martin
  (London: Butterworths, 1966). 3 vols
SUNDBERG, J W F, Aircharter (Stockholm, 1961).
  587 pp.
WAGNER, W, International Air Transportation as
  affected by State Sovereignty (Bruxelles, 1970).
  248 pp.
WASSENBERG, H A, Aspects of Air Law and Civil Air
  Policy in the Seventies (Den Haag, 1970). 165 pp.

7.9.4 SPACE LAW

Numerous works of varying quality and originality have
been published in recent years. The works by
COOPER and FAWCETT, as well as the book by MATTE,
are the standard works. The recent work by LACHS is
of a particularly high standard.

ABRANCHES, Dunshee de, Espacio exterior y responsabilidade internacional (Rio de Janiero, 1964)

ADAMS, T R, 'The outer space treaty: an interpretation in light of the no-sovereignty provision', Harvard International Law Journal, vol 9 (1968), p 150

ARMSTRONG, Cole A, Report submitted to the 10th IAF Conference on Space Law held in Belgrade (Yugoslavia) in September 1967

AUGER, R, European Space Research Organization (Paris: Compagnie générale française, 1963)

BAUZA, Araujo, Hacia un derecho astronautico, (Montevideo, 1957)

BERKNER, Lloyd V, 'Space research: a permanent peacetime activity', Peacetime Uses of Outer Space, edited by Simon Ramo (New York: McGraw-Hill, 1961), p 6

BOURELY, M G, 'The European organization for cooperation on the space question', VIth Conference on Space Law, publication of the International Astronomical Federation, 1963

BÖHME, W, 'Lufthoheit und Weltraumflug', Zeitschrift für Luftrecht und Weltraumrechtsfragen, vol 5 (1956), p 186

British Institute of International and Comparative Law, Current Problems in Space Law: A Symposium (London, 1966)

CHAUMONT, Charles, Problèmes de droit international de l'espace extra-atmosphérique (Paris: Institut des hautes études internationales, 1959)

CHAUMONT, C, Le Droit de l'espace (Paris: Presses Universitaires de France, éd. Que sais-je?, 1960)

CHENG, Bin, 'The extra-terrestrial application of international law', Current Legal Problems, vol 18 (1965), p 143

CHENG, Bin, 'United Nations Resolutions on outer space:"instant" international customary law?' Indian J. Int. Law, vol 5 (1965), p 41

CHENG, Bin, 'Le traité de 1967 sur l'espace', J. Droit Int., vol 95 (1968), p 644

CHENG, Bin, 'Analogies and fictions in air and space law', Current Legal Problems, vol 21 (1968), p 147

CHEPROV, Ivan, 'Global or American space communications system', Int. Aff. (USSR), vol 12 (1964), p 69

CHRISTOL, C Q, 'The international law of outer space', in International Law Studies 1962, Naval War College, Newport, Rhode Island (Washington, DC: US Government Printing Office, 1966), pp 394-5

COCCA, Aldo Armando, Teoria del Derecho Interplanetario (Buenos Aires: ed. Bibliografica Argentina, 1957)

COHEN, Dean Maxwell, (ed), Law and Politics in Space (Proceedings of the First Conference on the Law of Outer Space organized by the Institute of Air and Space Law, McGill University, Montreal 1964) (Montreal: McGill University Press, 1964)

COLINO, Richard E, 'INTELSAT: doing business in outer space', Columbia Journal of Transnational Law, vol 6 (1967)

COLLIARD, C A, KISS, A C, & MALAVIALLE, A M, (ed), Le Droit de l'espace: Bulletin d'analyses et d'information (Paris: éd. Technique et économique, 1971). 153 pp.

COOPER, J C, Explorations in Aerospace Law (Montreal: McGill University Press, 1968)

COOPER, J C, 'State sovereignty in space: developments 1910 to 1914', in Beiträge zum Internationalen Luftrecht, Festschrift für Alex Meyer (Düsseldorf, 1954)

COOPER, J C, 'Legal problems of upper space', Am. Soc. Int. Law Proc. (1956), pp 85-115

COOPER, J C, 'The problem of a definition of "air space" ', in Proceedings of the First Colloquium on the Law of Outer Space, edited by A G Haley & W Heinrich (New York: Springer-Verlag, 1959), p 38

COOPER, J C, 'Legal Problems of Upper Space', in US Congress, Legal Problems of Space Exploration: Symposium (Washington, DC: US Government Printing Office, 1961), p 71

COOPER, J C, 'High altitude flight and national sovereignty', in US Congress Legal Problems of Space Exploration: Symposium (Washington, DC: US Government Printing Office, 1961), p 3

COOPER, J C, 'International control of outer space', Zeitschrift für Luftrecht und Weltraumrechtsfragen, vol 9 (1960), p 291; vol 10 (1961), p 103

COOPER, J C, 'Aerospace law: subject matter and terminology', Journal of Air Law and Commerce, vol 29 (1963), p 89

COOPER, J C, 'The manned orbiting laboratory: a major legal and political decision', American Bar Association Journal, vol 51 (1965), p 1137

COOPER, J C, 'Some crucial questions about the space treaty', Air Force and Space Digest (March 1967), p 107

CRANE, Robert D, 'Soviet attitudes toward international space law', Am. J. Int. Law, vol 56 (1962)

CRANE, Robert D, 'The beginnings of Marxist space jurisprudence', Am. J. Int. Law, vol 57 (1963)

CSABAFI, I A, The Concept of State Jurisdiction in International Space Law. A Study in the Progressive Development of Space Law in the United Nations (Den Haag: Nijhoff, 1971). xv + 197 pp.

DARWIN, H G, 'The outer space treaty', Br. Yearb. Int. Law, vol 42 (1967), pp 278-89

DEMBLING, Paul, & ARONS, Daniel M, 'Space law and the United Nations', Journal of Air Law and Commerce, vol 32 (1966), pp 329-30

DEMBLING, P, & ARONS, D M, 'The evolution of the outer space treaty', Journal of Air Law and Commerce, vol 33 (1967), p 430

DIEDREKS & VERSCHOOR, 'New developments in space law: the first convention on space law', IDA, vol 26 (1968), p 128

FASAN, F, Weltraumrecht (Mainz: Kransakoff, 1965)

FAWCETT, J E S, International Law and the Uses of Outer Space (Manchester: Manchester University Press/Dobbs Ferry, NY: Oceana, 1968)

FRUTKIN, A W, International Cooperation in Space (Englewood Cliffs, NJ 1965)

GÀL, G, Space Law (Leiden: Sijthoff/Dobbs Ferry, NY: Oceana, 1969). 320 pp.

GÀL, G, 'Air space and outer space', in US Congress, Legal Problems of Space Exploration: A Symposium (Washington, DC: US Government Printing Office, 1961), p 1148

GALLOWAY, Eileen (ed), Legal Problems of Space Exploration. A Symposium 87th Cong. 1st Session Senate (Washington, DC: US Government Printing Office, 1961)

GALLOWAY, Eileen, 'The United Nations ad hoc committee on the peaceful uses of Outer Space: accomplishments and implications for legal problems', in Second Colloquium on the Law of Outer Space London, 1959, Proceedings (1960)

GOEDHUIS, Daniel, 'Some trends in the political and legal thinking on the conquest of space', Ned. Tijdschr. Int. Recht, vol 9 (1962), p 121

GOEDHUIS, D, 'Reflections on the evolution of space law', Ned. Tijdschr. Int. Recht, vol 13 (1966), p 109

GORE, Albert, 'Contemporary practice of the United States relating to international law, outer space and military uses', Am. J. Int. Law, vol 57 (1963)

HALEY, A W G, Space Law and Government (New York: Meredith Publishing Company, 1963)

HALEY, A G, & HEINRICH, W, (eds), Proceedings of the First Colloquium on the Law of Outer Space (New York: Springer-Verlag, 1959)

HALEY, Andrew G, & SCHWARTZ, Mortimer D, (eds), Proceedings of the Eights Colloquium on the Law of Outer Space (South Hackensack, NJ: Fred B Rothman & Co, 1966)

HALL, R Cargill, 'Rescue and return of astronauts on earth and in outer space', Am. J. Int. Law, vol 63 (1969)

HANNOVER, Prince Heinrich von, 'Luftrecht und Weltraum', Thesis. Göttingen, 1953

HEIERMAN, J H, 'International Civil Aviation Organization and outer space', ICAO Bulletin, vol 21, no 3 (1966), p 3

HINGORANI, C R, 'La souveraineté sur l'espace extra atmospherique', Revue générale aérienne, vol 20 (1957), p 248

HOGAN, J C, 'Legal terminology for the upper regions of the atmosphere and for the space beyond the atmosphere', Am. J. Int. Law, vol 51 (1957), p 362

HOMBURG, R, 'Droit astronautique et droit aérien', Revue générale aérienne, vol 21 (1958), p 15

JENKS, C W, 'International law and activities in space', Int. & Comp. Law Q., vol 5 (1956), p 103

JENKS, C W, 'Le droit international des espaces célestes', Annu. Inst. Droit Int. (1963), pp 382-407

JENKS, C W, Space Law (London: Stevens & Sons, 1965)

JESSUP, Philip, & TAUBENFELD, Howard G, Controls for Outer Space and the Antarctic Analogy (New York, 1959)

KOPAL, V, 'Treaty on principles governing the activities of states in the exploration and use of outer space, including the moon and other celestial bodies', Yearb. Air & Space Law (1966), p 477

KROELL, J, 'Eléments créateurs d'un droit astronautique', Revue générale aérienne, vol 16 (1953), p 222
KUCHEROV, S, 'Legal problems of outer space', in Proceedings of the Second Colloquium on the Law of Outer Space, edited by A G Haley & W Heinrich (New York: Springer-Verlag, 1960)
KUHFELD, A M, 'The space age legal dilemma', in US Congress, Legal Problems of Space Exploration: A Symposium (Washington, DC: US Government Printing Office, 1961), p 773
LACHS, Manfred, 'The international law of outer space', Acad. Droit Int. Recl. Cours, vol 113 (1964), p 7
LACHS, Manfred, The Law of Outer Space: an Experiment in Contemporary Lawmaking (Leiden: Sijthoff, 1972)
LA PRADELLE, P de, 'La charte de l'espace et des corps célestes', Revue générale aérienne, vol 30 (1967), p 131
LAY, S Houston, & TAUBENFELD, Howard J, The Law Relating to Activities of Man in Space (Chicago, Ill: University of Chicago Press, 1970)
LI, Kuo-Lee, 'For a more rational legal regime of aerospace continuum - a proposal', Unpublished thesis submitted to the Institute of Air and Space Law, McGill University, Montreal, April 1968
LIPSON, Leon, & KATZENBACH, N de B, 'The law of outer space', in US Congress, Legal Problems of Space Exploration: A Symposium (Washington, DC: US Government Printing Office, 1961), p 882
LISSITZYN, Oliver, 'The American position on outer space and Antarctica', Am. J. Int. Law, vol 53 (1959), p 131
LÜST, R, 'Die gegenwärtigen Probleme der Weltraumforschung', Mitteilungen der Alexander von Humboldt-Stiftung, No 6 (1953), p 15

MACHADO, Hugo de Chunha, 'Treaty for the exploration and use of outer space', in Proceedings of the Tenth Colloquium on the Law of Outer Space, edited by Mortimer D Schwartz (South Hackensack, NJ: Fred B Rothman & Co, 1968), p 219

MANKIEWICZ, René H, 'L'ordre juridique dans l'espace extra-atmosphérique', Annu. Fr. Droit Int., vol 5 (1959), p 153

MANKIEWICZ, René H, 'The regulation of activities in extra-aeronautical space, and some related problems', McGill Law Journal, vol 8 (1961/2), p 211

MARKOV, Marko G, 'Liberté de l'espace extra-atmosphérique, Revue générale de l'air,' vol 14 (1951), p 327, p 330

MARKOV, M G, 'Liberté de l'espace et stations interplanétaires', Revue générale de l'air, vol 24 (1961), p 327

MARKOV, M G, 'Utilisation pacifique de l'espace extra-atmosphérique', Revue générale de l'air, vol 25 (1962), p 235

MARKOV, M G, 'Le traité de droit cosmique', Revue générale de l'air et de l'espace, vol 31 (1968), p 41; p 42

MATTE, Nicholas Mateesco, Aerospace Law (London: Sweet & Maxwell, 1969). 501 pp.

MATTEESCO, M, 'Le traité du 27 janvier 1967 et la réglementation des activités spatiales', Revue générale de l'air et de l'espace, vol 31 (1968), p 27

McDOUGAL, M S, 'The emerging customary law of space', in Proceedings of the conference on the Law of Space and of Communication System NASA SP-44 Washington, DC, (1964)

McDOUGAL, Myers S, LASSWELL, H D, & VLASIC, Ivan, Law and Public Order in Space (New Haven, Conn: Yale University Press, 1963)

McDOUGAL, Myres, & LIPSON, Leon, 'Perspectives for a law of outer space', Am. J. Int. Law, vol 52 (1958), p 412

McMAHON, J F, 'Legal aspects of outer space', Br. Yearb. Int. Law, vol 38 (1962), p 339

McMAHON, J F, 'Legal aspects of outer space: recent developments', Br. Yearb. Int. Law, vol 41 (1965/6), p 417

McWHINNEY, E & BRADLEY, M, New Frontiers in Space Law (Leiden: Sijthoff/Dobbs Ferry, NY: Oceana, 1969). 132 pp.

MENTER, Martin, 'Astronautical law', US Congress, Legal Problems of Space Exploration, Symposium (Washington, DC: US Government Printing Office, 1961)

MEYER, Alex, Rechtsprobleme des Weltraumgebiets, Luft- und Weltraumrechtliche Gegenwartsfragen (Düsseldorf, 1958)

MEYER, A, 'L'importance d'une limite entre l'espace aérien et extra-atmosphérique', Zeitschrift für Luftrecht und Weltraumrechtsfragen, vol 11 (1962), p 106

NOZARI, F, The Law of Outer Space (Stockholm: Norstedt, 1973)

ODISHAW, Hugh, The Challenge of Outer Space (Chicago, Ill: University of Chicago Press, 1962)

OSNITSKAYA, G A, 'International law problems of the conquest of space', in US Congress, Legal Problems of Space Exploration: A Symposium (Washington, DC: US Government Printing Office, 1961), p 1089

PAPACOSTAS, Alkis-Basile N, 'L'influence de l'activité spatiale sur la notion de la souveraineté', Rev. Fr. Droit Aér. (1968), p 265

PEPIN, E, 'The legal status of the airspace in the light of progress in aviation and astronautics', McGill Law Journal, vol 3 (1956)

PEPIN, Eugène, 'Space penetration', Am. Soc. Int. Law Proc. (1958), p 229

PERGENT, J, 'Le domaine spatial', Revue generale de l'air et de l'espace, vol 30 (1967), p 366

PIGNOCHET, A, La Commission internationale de navigation aérienne (Paris, 1936)

POULANTZAS, Nicholas M, 'Development or retrogression of international law in view of outer space activities?' IDA (1965), p 156

PROBST, R, Le Droit de l'espace: Cours d'introduction au droit aérien (Zürich, 1969)

QUADRI, R, Droit international cosmique, Acad. Droit Int. Recl. Cours, vol 98 (1959), p 510

RAMO, Simon, Peacetime Uses of Outer Space (New York: McGraw-Hill, 1961)

RATCLIFFE, J A, The use of outer space for scientific and technological purposes. Current Problems in Space Law, Symposium, British Institute of International and Comparative Law, International Law Series. No 6 London, 1966

RAUCHHAUPT, F W von, 'Über Weltraumrecht', Zeitschrift für Luftrecht und Weltraumrechtsfragen, vol 11 (1962), p 230

REHM, G W, 'Einige Völkerrechtliche Betrachtungen zu sowietischen Souveranitatsanspruchen im Liftraum', Zeitschrift für Luftrecht und Weltraumrechtsfragen, vol 8 (1959), p 175

RICHARDSON, J E, 'Private property rights in the air space at common law', Canadian Bar Review, vol 31 (1953), p 117

SCHACHTER, Oscar, 'A preview of space law problems: early unilateral positions', in US Congress, Legal Problems of Space Exploration: A Symposium/ Washington, DC: US Government Printing Office, 1961), p347

SCHWARTZ, L E, International Organizations and Space Cooperation (Durham, N C: Duke University Press, 1962)

SMIRNOFF, Michael S V, 'Les efforts de la FIA dans l'élaboration des normes du droit de l'espace', Rev. Fr. Droit Aér., vol 14 (1960), p 278

TAGER, Thomas E, 'The legality of the military use of outer space', LL.M. thesis submitted to the Institute of Air and Space Law, McGill University, Montreal, 1967

TAUBENFELD, Howard J, (ed), The Space and Society (Dobbs Ferry, NY: Oceana, 1964)

TEMPESTA, Adalberto, 'La communità internazionale e l'uso dello spazio', IDA, vol 4 (1962), p 322

TERROU, Fernand, 'La liberté de l'information à l'ère spatiale', in Les Télécommunications par satellites (Paris: Editions Cujas, 1968), p 175

TERROU, F, 'The need for international agreements', in Communication in the Space Age (Amsterdam: UNESCO, 1968)

VALLADAO, Haroldo, 'The law of interplanetary space', in Proceedings of the Second Colloquium on the Law of Outer Space, edited by A G Haley & W Heinrich (New York: Springer-Verlag, 1960)

VALLADAO, H, 'Droit interplanétaire et droit "inter Gentes" Planétaire', in Internationalrechtliche und Staatrechtliche Abhandlungen (Düsseldorf: Gebr. Hermes, 1960)

VASQUEZ, Modesto Seura, Introducción al Derecho Internacional Cosmico (Escuela Nacional de Ciencias Politicas y Sociales, Universidad Nacional de Mexico, 1961)

VASQUEZ, M S, 'El principio de utilizaciones pacificas del espacio extra-atmosferico', IDA, vol 8 (1963), p 351

VASQUEZ, M S, Cosmic International Law (Detroit, Mich: Wayne State University Press, 1965). 293 pp.

VERPLAETSE, Julian G, 'Relationships between air law and the law of outer space', IDA, vol 12 (1964), p 364

VERPLAETSE, J G, 'Autour de l'article IV du traité de droit cosmique du 27 janvier 1967', Revue générale de l'air, vol 31 (1968), p 45

VLASIC, Ivan A, 'The growth of space law 1957-1965: achievements und issues', Yearb. Air & Space Law (1965), p 167

VLASIC, I A, 'The space treaty: a preliminary evaluation', California Law Review, vol 55 (1967), p 507

WASSENBERG, H A, Post-War International Civil Aviation Policy and the Law of the Air, 2nd edition (Den Haag, 1962)

WRIGHT, Christopher, 'The United Nations and outer space', in The Challenge of Outer Space, edited by Hugh Odishaw (Chicago, Ill: University of Chicago Press, 1962)

ZHUKOV, G P, 'Practical problems of space law', International Affairs (USSR), vol 5 (May 1963), pp 27-8

ZHUKOV, G P, 'Kosmischeskoye pravo izdatelstvo', Mezhdunaranye otnoshenija (1966)

ZHUKOV, G P, 'Qu'est-ce que l'espace cosmique?' Revue générale de l'air et de l'espace, vol 31 (1968), p 56

ZHUKOV, G P, Weltraumrecht (Berlin: Verlag Arno Spitz, 1968)

ZYLICZ, M, 'Sur quelques problèmes du droit astronautique', Rev. Gén. Droit Int. Public, vol 62 (1958), p 655

7.9.5 SATELLITES

7.9.5.1 GENERAL

BERESFORD, Spencer M, 'Surveillance aircraft and satellites: a problem of international law', Journal of Air Law and Commerce, vol 27 (1960), pp 107-9

COOPER, J C, 'Raketen und Satelliten: Das Recht und unsere national Politik', Zeitschrift für Luftrecht, vol 7 (1958), p 394

SOBAGHAN, Joseph R, 'Reconnaissance satellites: legal characterization and possible utilization for peace-keeping', McGill Law Journal, vol 13 (1967), p 463

7.9.5.2 TELECOMMUNICATIONS BY SATELLITES

See also Section 13.24.2.24.4 on the International Telecommunications Union.

CATALA-FRANJOU, Nicole, 'Résponsabilite civile et pénale pour émissions retransmises par les satellites de télécommunications', in Les Télécommunications par satellites (Paris: Editions Cujas, 1968), p 187

CHAYES, A, FAWCETT, J, et al, Satellite Broadcasting (London: Oxford University Press, 1973). xviii + 159 pp.

COCCA, A A, 'Preliminary report of special working group on telecommunications by satellites'. Submitted at the XIth Colloquium of Space Law, New York, October 1968

COCCA, A A, 'Legal problems arising from the establishment of one or several systems of telecommunication by satellites'. Report submitted to the Xth Symposium on the Law of Outer Space, IAF, Belgrade, September 1967

DOYLE, S, 'Legal problems arising from the establishment of one or several systems of telecommunications by satellite: the record up to the present time'. Study prepared for presentation at the Xth Symposium on the Law of Outer Space, IAF. Belgrade, Spetember 1967

DOYLE, Stephen, 'International satellite communication', McGill Law Journal, vol 11 (1965), p 142

ESTEP, Raymond, 'Some international aspects of communications satellite systems', Northwestern

University Law Review, vol 58 (1963), p 237
ESTEP, Samuel D, & KIERSE, Amelia L, 'Space communications and the law: adequate international control after 1963?' Michigan Law Review, vol 60 (1962), p 887
FELDMAN, George J, 'International arrangements for satellite communications', in Law & Politics in Space, edited by Dean Maxwell Cohen (Montreal: McGill University Press, 1964), p 23
GARDNER, Richard N, 'Space meteorology and communications: a challenge to science and diplomacy', US Department of State Bulletin, vol 48, no 1246 (13 May 1963), p 740
GOTLIEB, A E, & DALPEN, C H, 'Dual-satellite broadcasting: a case study in the development of the law of space communications', Can. Yearb. Int. Law, vol 7 (1969), pp 33-60
GUEPIN, Claude, 'Les télécommunications par satellites aux Etats-Unis: La Communication Satellite Corporation (COMSAT)', in Les Telecommunications par satellites (Paris: Editions Cujas, 1968), p 33
JONES, Erin B, Earth Satellite Télécommunications Systems and International Law (Austin, Tex: University of Texas Press, 1970). xii + 167 pp.
KATZENBACH, Nicholas de B, 'Communications satellites', in World Peace Through Law (The Athens World Conference Lectures) (St Paul, Minn: West Publishing Company, 1964), p 520
PEPIN, E, 'Comment recevoir l'organisation internationale mondiale future des télécommunications par satellites', in Les Télécommunications par satellites (Paris: Editions Cujas, 1968), p 295
THOMAS, D D, 'Les satellites de communications: une nouvelle ère de coopération internationale', ICAO Bulletin, vol 24, no 2 (February 1969), pp 3-4

ZHUKOV, G P, 'Worldwide telecommunication system
by satellite: legal aspects', in Proceedings of the
Ninth Colloquium on the Law of Outer Space,
edited by Mortimer D Schwartz (South Hackensack,
NJ: Fred B Rothman, 1967), p 91

7.9.6 PLANETS

On recent treaties on celestial bodies see LACHS,
listed in Section 7.9.4.
BROOKS, Eugene, 'National control of natural
planetary bodies: preliminary consideration',
Journal of Air Law and Commerce, vol 32 (1966),
p 321
COOPER, J C, 'Who will own the moon? The need for
an answer', Journal of Air Law and Commerce,
vol 32 (1966), p 165
CZABAFI, Imre, 'The law of celestial bodies',
Indian J. Int. Law, vol 6 (1966), p 223
FERRER, Manuel Augusto, Problemas de derecho
espacial en torno a los objetos actualmente puestos
en la luna (Universidad Nacional Cordoba, 1968)
MARKOV, M G, 'La lune et le droit international',
Rev. Gén. Droit Int. Public, vol 68 (1964), p 431
MARKOV, M G, 'Moon landing and international law',
IDA, vol 9 (1964), p 23

7.10 IMMUNITY FROM JURISDICTION

Problems of immunity cannot be studied in all their
complexity within the framework of public international
law: it is a subject also to which conflict among law
writers has given ample attention. I have therefore
included only a selection of the vast literature on this
subject. For early literature see the 1926 bibliography
listed above under Section 1.2.
See also Section 13.12 on immunities and
privileges of international organizations.

7.10.1   IMMUNITY OF STATES

7.10.1.1   IMMUNITY IN GENERAL

Actes du colloque conjoint des 30 & 31/1/1969. L'Immunité de juridiction et d'exécution des états: à propos du projet de convention du Conseil de l'Europe (Bruxelles, 1971)

ANDERSON, C F, 'Immunity of a state from suit in the Supreme Court by a foreign government without the state's consent', Am. J. Int. Law, vol 28 (1934), p 527

ANZILOTTI, D, 'L'essenzione degli stati stranieri dalla giurisdizione', Riv. Diritto Int., vol 5 (1910), p 477

BELMAN, M J, 'New departures in the law of sovereign immunity', Am. Soc. Int. Law Proc. (1969), pp 182-4

BISHOP, W W, 'General course of public international law', Acad. Droit Int. Recl. Cours, vol 115 (1965), pp 147-470. Especially pp 325-8

BISHOP, W W, 'New United States policy limiting sovereign immunity', Am. J. Int. Law, vol 47 (1953), p 93

BOGUSLAVSKIJ, M M, Staatliche Immunität, (translated from the 1962 Russian edition) (Berlin, 1965)

BRINTON, J Y, 'Suits against foreign states', Am. J. Int. Law, vol 25 (1931), p 50

CARTER, P B, Sovereign immunity: substantiation of claims', Int. & Comp Law Q., vol 4 (1955)

CAVARE, L, 'L'immunité de juridiction des états étrangers: rapport fait à l'Académie internationale de droit comparé, session des Londres 1950', Rev. Gén. Droit Int. Public (1954), p 177

COHN, E J, 'Gerichtsbarkeit über fremde Staaten', in Wörterbuch des Völkerrechts, vol 1 (Berlin: Verlag Walter de Gruyter, 1960), p 661

DUNBAR, N C H, 'Controversial aspects of sovereign immunity in the case of some states', Acad Droit Int. Recl. Cours, vol 132 (1971), pp 197-362
DYNOVSKY, C v, (ed), Unzulässigkeit einer Zwangsvollstreckung gegen ausländische Staaten (Berlin, 1910)
ESSEN, Jan Louis Frederick van, Immunities in International Law (Leiden: Sijthoff, 1955)
FAIRMAN, 'Some disputed applications of the principle of state immunity', Am. J. Int. Law, vol 22 (1928), pp 568-9
FITZMAURICE, Sir Gerald G, 'State immunity from proceedings in Foreign Courts', Br Yearb. Int. Law, vol 14 (1933), p 101
GIHL, T, Staters immunitet vid främmände domstolar, SVJT, 1944
GMÜR, E A, 'Zur Frage der gerichtlichen Immunität fremder Staaten', SJIR, vol 7 (1950), p 9
GREEN, B C, 'Standing to sue of foreign governments in courts of the United States', Syracuse Law Review, vol 16 (1965), p 797
HEYMANN, E, 'Zur Frage der Gerichtsbarkeit über fremde Staaten', AcP, vol 121 (1923), p 149
JENKS, C W, International Immunities (London: Stevens, 1961). xxxvii + 178 pp
LALIVE, J F, 'L'immunité de juridiction des états et des organisations internationales', Acad. Droit Int. Recl. Cours, vol 84 (1953), p 205
LAUTERPACHT, H, 'Jurisdictional immunities of foreign states', Br. Yearb. Int. Law, vol 28 (1951), p 220
LOEWENFELD, E, (Discussion on state immunity), International Law Association Report of the Forty-fifth Conference held at Lucerne August 31st to September 6th 1952 (London: ILA, 1953)

MÜNCH, F, 'Immunität fremder Staaten in der deutschen Rechtssprechung bis zu den Beschlüssen des Bundesverfassungsgerichts vom 30. Oktober 1962 und 30. April 1963', Z. Ausl. Öff. Recht. & Völkerrecht, vol 24 (1964), p 265

MICHAELS, David B, International Privileges and Immunities: A Case for a Universal Statute (Den Haag: Nijhoff, 1971)

PRAAG, L, van, 'La question de l'immunité de juridiction des états étrangers et celle de la possibilité de l'exécution des jugements qui les condamnent', Rev. Droit Int. & Légis. Comp, ser 3, vol 15 (1934), pp 652-82; vol 16 (1935), pp 100-37

PUGH, R C, & McLAUGHLIN, J, 'Jurisdictional immunities of foreign states', New York University Law Review, vol 41 (1966), p 25

RIAD, Fouad A M, 'L'entreprise publique et semi-publique en droit international privé', Acad. Droit Int. Recl. Cours, vol 108 (1963), pp 561-668; especially ch 2, sec 2, 'Rattachement de l'immunité de l'entreprise à celle de l'état'

SINCLAIR, I M, 'The European convention on state immunity', Int. & Comp. Law Q., vol 22 (1973), p 254

STRÖMBERG, H, Främmande statschefers civilprocessuella immunitet jämförd med staters och diplomaters immunitet, Nord. Tidsskr. Int. Ref., 1958, p 12

SUY, E, 'Immunity of states before Belgian courts and tribunals', Z. Ausl. Öff. Recht & Völkerrecht (1967), pp 660-92

UNDÉN, Ö, Rättegång mot främmande stat, in Juridiska fakultetens Uppsala Minnesskrift (Uppsala 1929)

VINCKE, C, 'Certain aspects de l'évolution récente du problème de l'immunité de juridiction des états', Can Yearb. Int. Law, vol 7 (1969), p 224-54

WATKINS, R D, The State as Party Litigant (Baltimore, Md: Johns Hopkins Press, 1927)

WEIS, P, 'Compétence ou incompétence des tribunaux à l'égard des états étrangers', Acad. Droit Int. Recl. Cours, vol 1 (1923), p 525

7.10.1.2 IMMUNITY FOR STATE TRADING ACTIVITIES

The standard work is that by SUCHARITKUL. See also Section 14.4 on state trading.

BRANDON, M, 'Sovereign immunity of government owned corporations and ships', Cornell Law Quarterly (1954), p 425

FENSTERWALD, B, Jr, 'Sovereign immunity and Soviet state trading', Harvard Law Review, vol 63 (1950), p 614

GARNER, J W, 'Immunity of state owned ships employed in commerce', Br. Yearb. Int. Law, vol 6 (1925), p 128

SCHMITTHOFF, C M, 'The claim of sovereign immunity in the law of international trade', Int. & Comp. Law Q., vol 7 (1958), p 452

SEIDL-HOHENVELDERN, I, 'Commercial arbitration and state immunity', in International Trade Arbitration, edited by Domke (New York, 1958), pp 87-92

SETSER, V G, 'The immunities of the state and government economic activities', Law and Contemporary Problems, vol 24 (1959), p 291

THOMMEN, T K, The Legal Status of Government Merchant Ships in International Law (The Hague: Nijhoff, 1962)

SUCHARITKUL, Sompong, State Immunities and Trading Activities in International Law (London: Stevens, 1959)

WEDDERBURN, K W, 'Sovereign immunity of foreign public corporations', Int. & Comp. Law Q., vol 6 (1957), p 290

7.10.1.3 IMMUNITY OF EXILE GOVERNMENTS

BRANDWEINER, H, 'Zur Lehre von den Exilregierungen' Österr. Z. Öff. Recht, vol 3 (1950/1), pp 497-519

FLORY, M, Le Statut international des gouvernements réfugiés et le cas de la France Libre 1939-1945 (Paris: Pédone, 1952)

JUMEAU, A, 'Le refuge du gouvernement national à l'étranger', Doctorate thesis Aix-en-Provence, 1941

KIMMINICH, O, 'Völkerrechtsfragen der exilpolitischen Betätigung', Arch. Völkerrechts, vol 10 (1962/3), pp 132-65

MATTERN, Karl Heinz, Die Exilregierung (Tübingen: Mohr, 1953). vii + 77 pp.

OPPENHEIMER, F W, 'Governments and authorities in exile', Am. J. Int. Law (1942), p 568

7.10.2 IMMUNITY OF DIPLOMATS

For some late trands see a brief account in DELUPIS, Independence, listed in Section 1.8.

For more on diplomats, see Section 7.11.1.

American Institute of International Law, Project No 16 entitled 'Diplomatic Protection' (1925)

BAGINYAN, K, & LAZAREV, M, Review of D B Levin, Diplomatic Immunity (Moscow, 1949), in Soviet State and Law, no 2 (February, 1951), pp 91-2, reprinted in Current Digest of the Soviet Press 3 (26 May, 1951), pp 3-5

BARNES, William, 'Diplomatic immunity from local jurisdiction', US Department of State Bulletin, vol 43 (1 August, 1960), pp 173-82

BINET, Henri T P, 'Recent developments affecting diplomatic privileges and immunities', J. Comp. Legis. & Int. Law, vol 13 (1931), pp 84-90

BRANDON, Michael, 'Report on diplomatic immunity by an interdepartmental committee on state immunities', Int. & Comp. Law Q., vol 1 (1952), pp 358-61

BROOKFIELD, S H, 'Immunity of the subordinate personnel of a diplomatic mission', Br. Yearb. Int. Law, vol 19 (1938), pp 151-60

BROWN, Peter Campbell, 'The defense of diplomatic immunity', Insurance Law Journal, no 334 (November, 1950), pp 812-17

CARDOZO, M H, 'Judicial deference to State Department suggestions: recognition of prerogative or abdication to usurper?' Cornell Law Quarterly, vol 48 (1963)

CARDOZO, Michael H, 'Diplomatic immunities, protocol and the public', Journal of International Affairs, vol 17, no 1 (1963), pp 61-9

COHEN, M, 'Espionage and immunity: some recent problems', Br. Yearb. Int. Law, vol 25 (1948), p 404

DEAK, F, Immunity, diplomatic', in Encyclopedia of the Social Sciences (New York: The Macmillan Company, 1932), vol 7, pp 595-7

DEAK, Francis, 'Classification, immunities and privileges of diplomatic agents', Southern California Law Review, vol 1 (1928), pp 209-52; pp 332-54

DEENER, David R, 'Some problems of the law of diplomatic immunity', Am. J. Int. Law, vol 50 (1956), pp 115-20

DEHAUSSY, J, 'The inviolability of diplomatic residences', J Droit. Int., vol 83 (1956), p 596

DINSTEIN, Yoram, Diplomatic immunity from jurisdiction: ratione materiae', Int. & Comp. Law Q., vol 15 (1966), pp 76-89

'Diplomatic intercourse and immunities', Am. J. Int. Law, vol 53 (1959), pp 253-91

'Diplomatic privileges and immunities', External Affairs, vol 11 (November, 1959), pp 374-8

FELLER, A H, 'A seventeenth century problem in the application of Prohibition laws to foreign diplomats', Am. J. Int. Law, vol 28 (1934), pp 349-51

GIULIANO, M, 'Les relations et immunités diplomatiques', Acad. Droit Int. Recl. Cours, vol 100 (1960), pp 81-202

GUTTERIDGE, Joyce A C, 'Immunities of the subordinate diplomatic staff', Br. Yearb. Int. Law, vol 24 (1967), pp 148-59

GORDON, J C, 'Diplomatic immunity', Foreign Service Journal, vol 29 (January, 1952), pp 23, 46-7

HERSHEY, Amos Shartle, Diplomatic Agents and Immunities (Washington: Government Printing Office, 1919)

HILL, Martin, Immunities and Privileges of International Officials (Washington: Carnegie Endowment, 1947). xiv + 281 pp.

HILL, Chesney, 'Sanctions constraining diplomatic representatives to abide by the local law', Am. J. Int. Law, vol 25 (1931), pp 252-69

HOLLAND, D C, 'Diplomatic immunity in English law', Current Legal Problems, vol 4 (1951), pp 81-106

HURST, Cecil, 'Les immunités diplomatiques', Acad. Droit Int. Recl. Cours, vol 12 (1926), pp 115-245

HURST, Sir Cecil J B, 'Diplomatic immunities: modern developments', Br. Yearb. Int. Law, vol 10 (1929), pp 1-13

HUSSEY, Luther, N, 'The negligent diplomat', Journal of the Bar Association of the District of Columbia, vol 13 (April, 1946), pp 148-53

JANOUSEK, Jeseph O, 'Some aspects of the law of diplomatic immunity', Journal of the Bar Association of the District of Columbia, vol 8 (May, 1941), pp 183-96

JONES, J Mervyn, 'Immunities of servants of diplomatic agents and the statute of Anne 7 c 12', J. Comp. Legis. & Int. Law, vol 22 (1940), pp 19-31

KEITH, A Berriedale, 'The exterritoriality of ambassadors', J. Comp. Legis & Int. Law, vol 12 (1930), pp 126-8

KERLEY, Ernest L, 'Some aspects of the Vienna conference on diplomatic intercourse and immunities', Am. J. Int. Law, vol 56 (1962), pp 88-129

KING, John Kerry, The Privileges and Immunities of the Personnel of International Organizations (Odense: Strandberg, 1949). xiv + 282 pp.

LYONS, A B, 'The conclusiveness of the Foreign Office certificate', Br. Yearb. Int. Law, vol 23 (1946), pp 240-81

LYONS, A B, 'Conclusiveness of the "suggestion" and certificate of the American State Department', Br. Yearb. Int. Law, vol 24 (1947), pp 116-210

LYONS, A B, 'Conclusiveness of the statements of the executive: Continental and Latin American practice', Br. Yearb. Int. Law, vol 25 (1948), pp 180-210

LYONS, A B, 'Claims of diplomatic immunity: some special aspects', Br. Yearb. Int. Law, vol 26 (1949), pp 433-7

LYONS, A B, 'Immunities other than jurisdictional of the property of diplomatic envoys', Br. Yearb. Int. Law, vol 30 (1953), pp 116-51

LYONS, A B, 'Personal immunities of diplomatic agents', Br. Yearb. Int. Law, vol 31 (1954), pp 299-340

LYONS, A B, 'The Foreign Office certificate: some recent tendencies', Br. Yearb. Int. Law, vol 33 (1957), pp 302-10

LYONS, A B, 'Diplomatic immunities: some minor points', Br. Yearb. Int. Law, vol 34 (1958), pp 368-74

MONROE, D C, 'Privileges and immunities', Journal of Criminal Law and Criminology, vol 37 (1947), pp 480-3

MURRAY, John J, 'The Görtz-Gyllenborg arrest: a problem in diplomatic immunity', Journal of Modern History, vol 28 (1956), pp 325-37

OGDON, Montell, 'The growth of purpose in the law of diplomatic immunity', Am. J. Int. Law, vol 31 (1937), pp 449-65

OGDON, Montell, Juridical Bases of Diplomatic Immunity (Washington, DC: John Byrne & Co, 1936)

PANHUYS, H F van, 'In the borderland between the act of state doctrine and questions of jurisdictional immunity', Int. & Comp Law Q, vol 13 (1964), p 1193

PREUSS, L, 'Foreign diplomats and the Prohibition laws', Michigan Law Review, vol 30 (1932), pp 333-48

PREUSS, Lawrence, 'Capacity for legation and the theoretical basis of diplomatic immunities', New York University Law Quarterly Review, vol 10 (1932), pp 170-87

RAESTAD, A, 'La protection diplomatique des nationaux à l'étranger', Rev. Droit Int., vol 7 (1933), pp 493-544

REEVES, J S, 'Diplomatic privileges and immunities', Am. J. Int. Law, vol 26 (1932), supp vol part 1 pp 19-187

REIFF, Henry, Diplomatic and Consular Privileges, Immunities, and Practice (Cairo: Ettemad Press, 1954)

SCHWELB, E, 'Restrictions on diplomatic priviletes', Modern Law Review, vol 7 (1944), pp 223-7

SCHWELB, Egon, 'The Diplomatic Privileges (Extension) Act, 1944', Modern Law Review, vol 8 (1945), pp 50-63

SCHWARZENBERGER, G, 'Diplomatic immunity', Modern Law Review, vol 5 (1941), pp 64-6
SIMMONDS, K R, 'The "rationale" of diplomatic immunity', Int. & Comp. Law Q., vol 12 (1962), pp 1204-10
SLATIN, L, 'De la juridiction sur des agents diplomatiques', J. Droit Int., vol 2, p 329
SMITH, Ernest H, 'Tax immunities of diplomats under Canadian federal law', Canadian Tax Journal, vol 8 (1960), pp 318-24
STIRLING, Patrick, 'The immunities of diplomatic agents', Law Journal, vol 108 (18 April 1958), pp 243-4; (13 June 1958), pp 375-6
STONE, O M, 'Families personal and diplomatic', Modern Law Review, vol 22 (1959), pp 193-4
STOWELL, ELLERY C, 'Diplomatic privileges and immunities', Am. J. Int. Law, vol 20 (1926), pp 735-8
TAYLOR, J T, 'Diplomatic immunity', Criminal Law Review (April 1955), pp 230-4
THORNELY, P W, 'Extraterritoriality', Br. Yearb. Int. Law, vol 7 (1926), pp 121-34
TUNKIN, G, 'Vienna convention on diplomatic relations', International Affairs (USSR), no 6 (June 1961), pp 51-6
UNITED NATIONS. 'Conference on diplomatic intercourse and immunities', Am. J. Int. Law, vol 55 (1961), pp 1044-77
WILSON, Clifton, E, Diplomatic Privileges and Immunities (Tucson, Ariz: University of Arizona Press, 1967)
YOUNG, E, 'The development of the law of diplomatic relations', Br. Yearb. Int. Law, vol 40 (1964), pp 141-82
YOUNG, Richard, 'Diplomatic immunities', American Bar Association Journal, vol 39 (1953), pp 839-40

ZEILEISSEN, C, Die abgabenrechtlichen Privilegien in den diplomatischen und konsularischen Beziehungen (Wien: Wilhelm Braumüller, 1971). 153 pp

7.10.3. IMMUNITY OF CONSULS

For more on consuls, see Section 7.11.2 especially the standard books by LEE.

BECKETT, Sir W Eric, 'Consular immunities', Br. Yearb. Int. Law, vol 21 (1944), p 34

DINSTEIN, Yoram, Consular Immunity from Judicial Process with Particular Reference to Israel (Jerusalem: Institute for Legislative Research and Comparative Law, 1966). 89 pp

7.10.4 IMMUNITY OF FOREIGN FORCES

Association of the Bar of the City of New York Report on Status of Forces Agreements (New York, April 1958)

BALDWIN, Gordon B, 'Foreign jurisdiction and the American soldier', Wisconsin Law Review (January 1958)

BARTON, G P, 'Foreign armed forces: qualified jurisdictional immunity', Br. Yearb. Int. Law (1954), p 341

BATHURST, M E, 'Jurisdiction over friendly foreign armed forces, the American law', Br. Yearb. Int. Law, vol 23, p 338

BAXTER, R R, 'Criminal jurisdiction in the NATO status of forces agreement', Int. & Comp. Law Q. (1958), p 72

BENTWICH, N, 'The United States of America, Visiting Forces Act, 1942', Modern Law Review, vol 6 (1942), p 68

BLOM-COOPER, L J, 'Legal status of visiting forces in Britain', The Solicitor (November 1957), p 296

BODSON, Nicole, 'Statut juridique des forces internationales de l'OTAN en France', Mémoire à l'Institut des hautes études internationales (Paris, 1958)

BRICKER, John W, 'Safeguarding the rights of American servicemen abroad', The JAG Journal (October 1953)

BRINTON, J Y, 'The Egyptian mixed courts and foreign armed forces', Am. J. Int. Law, vol 40 (1946), p 737

CHALUFOUR, Aline, 'Le Statut juridique des forces alliées pendant la guerre 1914-1918', Thesis. Paris, 1927

COUTANT, Pierre, 'Le statut des forces des états parties au traité de l'Atlantique nord', Revue administrative (1953)

DRAPER, G I A D, Civilians and the Nato Status of Forces Agreement (Leiden: Sijthoff, 1966)

ELLERT, 'The US as a receiving state', Dickinson Law Review, vol 63, p 75

FAIRMAN, C, & KING, A, 'Taxation of friendly foreign forces', Am. J. Int. Law (1944), p 258

FLORY, Maurice, 'Les bases militaires à l'étranger', Annu. Fr. Droit Int. (1955), p 3

GOODHART, Arthur L, 'The legal aspects of the American forces in Great Britain', American Bar Association Journal (November 1942)

HALL, 'Criminal jurisdiction over civilians accompanying American armed forces overseas', Harvard Law Review (1958), p 712

HERMOSO, A, 'Jurisdiction over friendly foreign armed forces', Lawyers Journal, vol 23 (1958), p 1

KALSHOVEN, F, 'Criminal jurisdiction over military persons in the territory of a friendly foreign power', Ned. Tijdschr. Int. Recht (April 1958), p 165

KING, A, 'Jurisdiction over friendly armed forces', Am. J. Int Law (1942), p 539

KING, A, Further developments concerning jurisdiction over friendly armed forces', Am. J. Int. Law (1946), p 257

KURATOWSKI, 'International law and the naval military and air force courts of foreign governments in the UK', Grotius Soc. Trans, vol 28 (1942), p 1

LAZARETT, S, Le Statut des forces de l'Organisation du traité de l'Atlantique nord et son application en France (Paris: Pédone, 1964). xii+ 548 pp.

LAZARETT, Serge, Status of Military Forces under Current International Law (Leiden: Sijthoff, 1971). xv + 458 pp.

LEVIE, Howard S, 'The NATO SOFA: Legal safeguards for American serviceman,' American Bar Association Journal (April 1958)

LEVIE, 'Some legal problems arising under the NATO status of forces agreement and the administrative agreement with Japan', Federal Bar Journal, vol 17 (1957), p 620

MICHELWAITE, Claude B, 'The NATO status of forces agreement', The Judge Advocate Journal (October 1954), p 15

MURPHY, 'Basic issues in the NATO status of forces agreement', US Department of State Bulletin, vol 33 (August 1955), p 178

MERON, Theodor, 'Some reflections on the status of forces agreements in the light of customary international law', Int. & Comp. Law Q., vol 6 (1957), p 689

NORTHWESTERN Law Review, (1955), p 349. Report on the NATO status of forces agreement and international law

ORFIELD, Lester B, 'Jurisdiction of foreign courts over crimes committed abroad by American military personnel', South Carolina Law Quarterly (Spring 1956), p 346

PANHUYS, H F van, 'Some recent developments of international law in respect of the conflicts of jurisdiction resulting from the presence of foreign armed forces in the territory of a state', Ned. Tijdschr. Int. Recht (July 1955)

PINTO, R, 'Notes sur les personnels civils employés par les forces', l'Actualité juridique, vol 2 (1954), p 365

PLANTEY, A, 'La réparation des dommages causes dans la métropole par les membres des Forces alliées de 1944 à 1946', Dalloz, (1950)

RE, Edward D, 'The NATO status of forces agreement and international law', Northwestern University Law Review (July 1955), p 349

ROUSE, & BALDWIN, 'Exercise of criminal jurisdiction under the NATO status of forces agreement', Am. J. Int. Law, vol 51 (1957), p 29

SCHUCK, E G, 'Concurrent jurisdiction under the NATO SOFA', Columbia Law Review (1957), p 355

SCHWARTZ, Murray L, 'International law and the NATO SOFA', Columbia Law Review (December 1953), p 1091

SCHWELB, Egon, 'The status of the US forces in English law', Am. J. Int. Law (1944), pp 50-73

SCHWELB, E, 'The jurisdiction over members of the allied forces in Great Britain', Czechoslovak Year Book of International Law (1942), p 147

SCHWENK, Edmund H, 'Comparative study of the law of criminal procedure in NATO countries under the NATO SOFA', North Carolina Law Review, vol 57, p 358

SNEE, J M, 'NATO agreements on status: "Travaux préparatoires" ', Naval War College International Law Studies (1961)

SNEE, Joseph M, & PYE, Kenneth A, Status of
  Forces Agreements and Criminal Jurisdiction
  (Dobbs Ferry, NY: Oceana, 1957)
STAMBUK, George, American Military Forces
  Abroad (Columbus, Ohio: Ohio State University
  Press, 1963)
STANGER, Roland J, 'Criminal jurisdiction over
  visiting armed forces', Naval War College International Law Studies 1957-1958'
VILLACRES, J, 'Les bases stratégiques et le droit
  international américain', Thesis. Paris, 1950
VIGNES, D, 'L'affaire Girard et le statut des forces
  américaines stationnees en territoire étranger',
  Annu Fr. Droit Int. (1957), p 304
VOELCKEL, M, 'L'application aux forces navales de
  la convention de Londres du 19 juin 1951', Annu.
  Fr. Droit Int. (1962), p 744
WHITTON, John B, 'L'exercice de la compétence pénale
  à l'égard des forces américaines à l'étranger',
  Rev. Gén. Droit Int. Public, vol 63 (1959), pp 5-20

7.10.5 OTHER IMMUNITY

BARTOŠ, M, 'Le statut des missions speciales de la
  diplomatie ad hoc', Acad. Droit Int. Recl. Cours,
  vol 108 (1963), pp 431-560
VOLLENHOVEN, C van, 'Diplomatic prerogatives of
  non-diplomats', Am. J. Int. Law, vol 19 (1925),
  pp 469-74
WATTS, A D, 'Jurisdictional immunities of special
  missions: the French property commission on
  Egypt', Int. & Comp. Law Q., vol 12 (1963), pp 1383-99

7.11 LAW OF DIPLOMATS AND CONSULS

The law of diplomats is probably the oldest part of
international law and, consequently, the literature is

enormous on this subject. However, international law is a dynamic subject and I have sought to include certain works which reflect the changing conditions of the modern diplomat. Reference must be made to the work of the International Law Commission and the recent Vienna Convention, see Section 1.1 For immunity of diplomats see Section 7.10.2. In the section below I have also included works on 'ad hoc' diplomats; for their immunity see Section 7.10.5.

7.11.1 DIPLOMATS

7.11.1.1 HISTORY

ADAIR, E R, The Extraterritoriality of Ambassadors in the Sixteenth and Seventeenth Centuries (London, 1929)
COWAN, Margaret, 'Origins of diplomatic immunity in England', The Solicitor, 4 (April 1965), pp 104-17
NAHLIK, S E, Narodziny Nowozytnej Dyplomacji (Naissance de la Diplomatie Moderne) (Wroclaw, 1971). 286 pp.
NUMELIN, Ragnar, The Beginnings of Diplomacy (New York: Philosophical Library, 1950)

7.11.1.2 FUNCTIONS OF DIPLOMATS AND PROTECTION OF NATIONALS

See also Section 7.12.13 on the treatment of aliens and Section 7.12.16 on protection by forces. The works by SATOW and SEN listed below are the standard books on the subject.

BARBIER, Robert L, 'Intervention diplomatique d'un état pour la protection des droits de son national résident à l'étranger (Bergerac: Imprimerie Générale du Sud-Ouest, 1935). 236 pp.
BORCHARD, E M, 'Protection diplomatique des nationaux à l'étranger', Annu Inst. Droit Int. (1931), pp 230-455

BORCHARD, E M, The Diplomatic Protection of Citizens Abroad, or the Law of International Claims (New York: The Banks Law Publishing Co, 1922) xxxvii + 988 pp.

BRIGGS, H W, La Protection diplomatique des individus en droit international: la nationalité des réclamations (Genève: Institut de droit international, 1963). 124 pp.

CORBETT, P E, Law in Diplomacy (Gloucester, Mass: Peter Smith, 1959)

DALLOZ, (ed), Répertoire Agent Diplomatique (Paris)

DOEHRING, K, Die Pflicht des Staates zur Gewährung diplomatischen Schutzes, Deutsches Recht und Rechtsvergleichung (Köln/Berlin, 1959)

DUNN, Frederick Sherwood, The Protection of Nationals (Baltimore, Md: The Johns Hopkins Press, 1932; reissued by Kraus Reprint Corporation, New York). xi + 228 pp.

DURANTE, F, 'Doppi a o plurima cittadinanza nella protezione diplomatico, Riv. Diritto, Int. (1956) p 173

FELLER, A H, & HUDSON, M O, A Collection of the Diplomatic and Consular Laws and Regulations of Various Countries (New York, 1933). 2 vols

FISCHEL, Wesley R, The End of Extraterritoriality in China (Berkeley, Calif: University of California Press, 1952)

FODERE, Pradier, Cours de droit diplomatique (1899). 2 vols

GROSSEN, J M, 'Nationalité et protection diplomatique', in. Festgabe Gutzwiller (1959)

HARDY, M, Modern Diplomatic Law (Manchester: Manchester University Press/Dobbs Ferry, NY: Oceana, 1968)

HOCHEPIED, J P, La Protection diplomatique des sociétés et des actionnaires (Paris 1965)

JOSEPH, C, Nationality and Diplomatic Protection (Leiden: Sijthoff/New York: Humanities Press Inc, 1969). 271 pp.
KRASKE, Erich, Handbuch des Auswärtigen Dienstes (Tübingen: JCB Mohr (Paul Siebeck), 1957)
LEIGH, G I F, 'Nationality and diplomatic protection', Int. & Comp. Law Q., vol 20 (1971), p 453
MOUSSA, F, Manuel de pratique diplomatique: L'Ambassade (Bruxelles: Etablissements Emile Bruylant, 1972). xii + 411 pp.
NASCIMENTO E SILVA, G E, do, Diplomacy in International Law (Leiden: Sijthoff, 1973). xv + 217 pp
OBERTHUR, K, 'Der Anspruch des deutschen Staatsangehörigen auf diplomatischen und konsularischen Schutz gegenüber anderen Staaten', Dissertation. Köln, 1965
PLISCHKE, Elmer, Conduct of American Diplomacy, 3rd edition (New York: Van Nostrand Reinhold, 1967)
PARRY, C, Some considerations upon the protection of individuals in international law, Acad. Droit Int. R. Cours, 1956, II, p. 705
RAESTAD, A, 'Diplomatisk beskyttelse av landsmenn i utlandet', Nord. Tidsskr. Int. Ret, vol 4 (1933), pp 3-29; 157-78
REDLICH, Marcellus Donald, International Law as a Substitute for Diplomacy, 2nd edition (Chicago, Ill; Independent Publishing Co, 1929). 208 pp.
SATOW, Sir Ernest, A Guide to Diplomatic Practice, 4th edition by Sir Neville Bland (London: Longmans, Green & Co, 1957)
SEN, B, A Diplomat's Handbook of International Law and Practice (Den Haag: Nijhoff/New York: International Publications Service, 1965)
STUART, GRAHAM H, American Diplomatic and Consular Practice, 2nd edition (New York: Appleton-Century-Crofts, Inc, 1952)

STUART, Graham, 'Le droit et la pratique diplomatiques et consulaires', Acad. Droit Int. Recl. Cours, vol 48 (1934), pp 459-70

TCHERNOFF, N, Protection des nationals residant à l'étranger (Paris 1899)

THAYER, Charles W, Diplomat (New York: Harper & Brothers, 1959)

TORRES BERNARDEZ, S, 'La conférence des Nations Unies sur les relations consulaires', Annu. Fr. Droit Int. (1963), p 78

TOSTI, G, 'Dei limiti giuridici della così detta protezione del cittadino all'estero', Riv. Diritto Int. (1915), p 374

WATERS, Maurice, The Ad Hoc Diplomat: A Study in Municipal and International Law, (Den Haag: Nijhoff, 1963)

VERDROSS, Alfred, 'The second congress of Vienna', United Nations Review, vol 8 (May 1961), pp 12-14; p 51

VISSCHER, P de, 'La protection diplomatique des personnes morales', Acad. Droit Recl. Cours, vol 102 (1961) pp 395-511

YOUNG, Eileen, 'The development of the law of diplomatic relations', Br. Yearb. Int. Law, vol 40 (1964), pp 141-82

7.11.1.3   EXTRA-TERRITORIAL ASYLUM

Extraterritorial asylum can, according to most writers, only be granted in very exceptional circumstances on the premises, for example, of a foreign embassy or legation. On this problem in general see:

FRANCIONI, F, Asilo diplomatico (Milano: Giuffré, 1973). 249 pp.

MORGENSTERN, F, 'Diplomatic asylum', Law Quarterly Review, vol 67 (1951), p 362

MORGENSTERN, F, ' "Extra territorial" asylum',
Br. Yearb. Int. Law, vol 25 (1948), pp 236-61
RONNING, C Neale, Diplomatic Asylum: Legal Norms
and Political Reality in Latin American Relations
(Den Haag: Nijhoff, 1965). v + 242 pp.
UERIA, J, Derecho de asilo diplomatico (Montevideo,
1961)

7.11.1.4   IMMUNITY OF DIPLOMATS

See Section 7.10.2.

7.11.2   CONSULS

7.11.2.1   FUNCTIONS IN GENERAL

LEE, Luke T, Consular Law and Practice (London:
Stevens, 1961). xxii + 431 pp.
LEE, L T, Vienna Convention on Consular Relations
(Leiden: Sijthoff, 1966). 315 pp.
MARESCA, A, Le relazione consolari (Milano: Giuffré,
1966). 897 pp.
NASCIMENTO E SILVA, G E do, 'The Vienna
conference on consular relations', Int. & Comp.
Law Q., vol 13 (1964), p 1214
PIGGOTT, Francis, Extraterritoriality Law relating
to Consular Jurisdiction and Residence in
Oriental Countries (London: William Clowes & Sons
Ltd, 1907)
ZOUREK, J, 'Some theoretical problems of consular
law', J Droit Int., vol 90 (1963), pp 4-67
ZOUREK, J, Le statut et les fonctions des consuls',
Acad. Droit Int. Recl. Cours, vol 106 (1962), pp
365-497

7.11.2.2   IMMUNITY OF CONSULS

See Section 7.10.3

7.12 HUMAN RIGHTS

Human rights may be one of the most expanding subjects of international law although, at the same time, it is often under attack for the obvious lack of guarantees and sanctions. Among the vast literature on the subject I draw attention to the works by LAUTERPACHT and DROST and, as far as Europe is concerned, to the books and articles by ROBERTSON. To many, the rights of aliens surpass those of nationals (see Section 7.12.13 on the treatment of aliens) although there is a trend, as suggested in my own book on Independence (listed under 1.8) to equate at least some basic human rights of a citizen with those of an alien. See also Section 12.2.5 on war crimes and Section 10.6 and 10.11 on humanitarian law in war and in civil war.

7.12.1 HISTORY

Annalen der Rechte des Menschen, des Bürgers und der Völker (Königsberg, 1794). 89 pp.
BAYET, A, Histoire de la déclaration des droits de l'homme. Du 89 politique au 89 économique (Paris, 1939). 172 pp.
PLANITZ, H, 'Das Naturrecht und die Menschenrechts' Juristische Blätter, 70, no 51 (13 March 1948), pp 111-14
RITTER, G, 'Ursprung und Wesen der Menschenrechte' Historische Zeitschrift, 169, no 2 (August 1949), pp 233-63
SALANDER, G A, Vom Werden der Menschenrechte. Ein Beitrag zur modernen Verfassungsgeschichte unter Zugrundlegung der virginischen Erklärung der Rechte vom 12.Juni 1776 (Leipzig, 1926). 98 pp.
VERZIJL, J H W, Human Rights in Historical Perspective (Haarlem, 1958). 115 pp
VOIGT, A, Geschichte der Grundrechte (Stuttgart, 1948). 227 pp.

7.12.2 HUMAN RIGHTS IN GENERAL

See also Section 6.4.3 on the individual as a subject of international law. The standard works are those by Professor ROBERTSON.

ASBECK, F M van, De mens in het volkenrecht. Groningen-Djakarta 1949. Gedenkboek uitgegeven ter gelegenheid van het vijf en twintig jarig bestaan van het rechtswetenschappelijk hoger onderwijs in Indonesië

BASTID, P, 'Les garanties internationales des droits de l'homme d'après la tradition de la France', Académie diplomatique internationale séances et travaux, vol 8, no 1 (1934), pp 13-16

BARTOLOMEI, D M, La protezione dei diritti umani nell'ordinamento internazionale (Roma, 1958). 116 pp

BENES, E, 'The rights of man and international law', Czechoslovak Yearbook of International Law (March, 1942), pp 1-6

BENTWICH, N, The International Protection of Individual Rights (Nottingham, 1935). 24 pp.

BENTWICH, N, 'Human rights: The problem of national and international protection', British Survey, vol 8, no 10 (July 1947), pp 1-15

BOBBIO, N, 'Presente e avvenire dei diritti dell' uomo', Comunità internazionale, vol 23 (1968), p 5

BONGER, H, Lehre der Menschenrechten: Thomas Jefferson (Arnhem: Van Loghum Slaterus, 1951). 73 pp.

BONNEVIE, C, Menneskerett, individets og folkets: En rettspolitisk studie (Oslo, 1953). 56 pp.

BRACHT, Hans Werner, 'Die Idee der Menschenrechte im Staats- und Völkerrechtsverständnis des Marxismus-Leninismus', Die Menschenrechte, pp 322-54

BRIGGS, H W, 'The "rights of aliens" and international protection of human rights', in Aspects of Liberty, edited by Milton R Konvitz & Clinton Rossiter (New York: Johnson Reprint Corporation, 1958)

BRUNET, R, 'La garantie internationale des droits de l'homme depuis la Charte de San Francisco', Rev. Egypt. Droit Int., vol 6 (1950), pp 103-64

CADIEUX, C, 'Les droits de l'homme en regard du droit international', Revue du Burreau, vol 22 (1962), p 18

CAMARGO, P P, La Protección Juridica de los Derechos Humanos y de la Democratia en America (Mexico: Excelsior, 1960)

CARRO, V D, Derechos y deberes del hombre. Discurso de recepción de y contestación de José Maria Trias de Bes (Madrid, 1954). 165 pp.

CASSIN, René, (ed), Amicorum Discipulorumque Liber: Problèmes de protection internationale des droits de l'homme (Paris: Pédone, 1969-71). 4 vols

CIASULLO, A L, El hombre y la communidad internacional (Montevideo, 1954). 154 pp.

COSENTINI, F, 'Les droits internationaux de l'homme', Rev. Droit Int. Sci. Dipl. & Polit., vol 13 (1935), pp 167-89

COURSTER, B H, 'L'évolution du droit international humanitaire', Acad. Droit Int. Recl. Cours, vol 99 (1960), pp 357-465

CUADRA, H, La Protección Internacional de los Derechos Humanos (Mexico: Instituto de Investigaciones Juridicas, 1970). 308 pp.

DEL RUSSO, A L, 'Dimensions and relevance of human rights under the rule of law', World Peace Through Law Conference, (1965)

DEL RUSSO, A L, 'International law of human rights: a pragmatic approach', William & Mary Law Review, vol 9 (1968), p 749

DEL RUSSO, A L, International Protection of Human
  Rights (Washington, DC: Lerner Law Book Co
  Inc, 1971). 361 pp.
DIETZE, C, Über die Formulierung der Menschenrechte
  (Berlin, 1956). 178 pp.
DROST, Pieter N, Human Rights as Legal Rights
  (Leiden: Sijthoff, 1951). 272 pp.
DUMAS, J, 'La sauvegarde internationale des droits de
  l'homme', Acad. Droit Int. Recl. Cours, vol 59
  (1937), p 1
EIDE, Asbjörn, & SCHOU, August, (eds), International Protection of Human Rights: Proceedings
  of the Seventh Nobel Symposium, Oslo, September
  25-27, 1967 (New York/Chichester: Interscience/
  Stockholm: Almqvist & Wiksell, 1968). 300 pp.
ERMACORA, F, 'Die Menschenrechte und der
  Formalismus', Juristische Blätter, vol 84 (1962)
ERMACORA, F, Handbuch der Grundfreiheiten und
  der Menschenrechte (Wien, 1963)
EUSTATHIADES, C Th, Les Sujets du droit international et la responsabilité internationale:
  Nouvelles tendances (Leiden, 1955), 236 pp.
EZEJIOFOR, G, Protection of Human Rights under
  the Law (London: Butterworths, 1964). 292 pp.
FRANGULIS, A F, 'La défense des droits de l'homme et
  des libertés individuelles devant le forum des
  nations civilisées', Académie diplomatique
  internationale séances et travaux, vol 8, no 1
  (1934), pp 17-23
FRAZIER, R H, 'Essentials of law necessary to
  guarantee individual rights in world organization',
  Conference (Third International) of the Legal
  Profession, 1950, d 17
FRIEDRICH, 'Rights, liberties, freedom: a reappraisal', American Political Science Review,
  vol 57 (1963), p 841

GADOLIN, Carl Axel Johan von, 'Gerechtigkeit, Menschenrechte und Asylrecht unter besonderer Berücksichtigung der nordischen Länder', in Die Menschenrechte, pp 46-61

GALLINA, G, La chiesa cattolica con le organizzazione internazionale per i diritti umani (Roma, 1968)

GANJI, M, International Protection of Human Rights (Genève/Paris, 1962). 318 pp.

GARCIA BAUER, C, Los derechos humanos preocupación universal (Guatemala, 1960)

GELLHORN, Walter, Ombudsmen and Others: Citizen's Protectors in Nine Countries (Cambridge, Mass: Harvard University Press, 1966)

GLASER, 'Les droits de l'homme à la lumière du droit international positif', in Mélanges Rolin (1964), p 104

GOLDBERG, 'The need for a world court of human rights', Howard Law Journal, vol 11 (1965), p 621

GOLDSCHMIDT, R, 'La protección juridica de la vida privada', 12, no 36 (September-December 1959), pp 13-29

GOLSONG, H, 'A critique: law and human rights', World Justice (1961), p 348

GOSLINGA, W J, De rechten van den mensch en burger Een overzicht der Nederlandsche geschriften en verklaringen ('s-Gravenhage, 1936). 186 pp.

GUETZEVITCH, B M, 'La défense des droits de l'homme et la Charte des Nations Unies', Bataille de la paix

GUGGENHEIM, P, 'Die völkerrechtliche Schutz der Menschenrechte', Die Friedens-Warte, vol 49 (1949), pp 177-90

GUGGENHEIM, P, 'La Tutela internazionale dei diritto dell'uomo', Comunità internazionale (1949), p 3

GURADZE, Heinz, Der Stand der Menschenrechte im Völkerrecht (Göttingen: Otto Schwartz, 1956). 236 pp.

GUTZWILLER, M. 'Menschenrechte und Kodifikation des Völkerrechts. Glossen zur 42. Konferenz der International Law Association, Prag, 31.August bis 6.September 1947', Die Friedens-Warte, vol 47 (1947), pp 298-305

HAMBURGER, E, 'The rights of man and international relations', Acad. Droit Int. Recl. Cours, vol 97 (1959), p 293

Handbuch der Theorie und Praxis der Grundrechte (Berlin 1954-)

HENKIN, L, 'The constitution, treaties and international human rights', University of Pennsylvania Law Review, vol 116 (1968), p 1012

HOLCOMBE, A N, Human Rights in the Modern World (New York/London, 1948). 162 pp.

HUBER, M, 'Le droit des gens et l'humanité', Revue internationale de la croix-rouge, 34 no 404 (August 1952), pp 646-69

HULA, E, 'International law and the protection of human rights', in Law and Politics in the World Community (1953), pp 161-88

JANSSEN-PEVTSCHIN, J V, & VAN WELKENHUYZEN, A, 'La convention de sauvegarde des droits de l'homme et des libertés fondamentales et le fonctionnement des juridictions belges', Chronique de la politique extérieure 15, no 3 (June 1962), pp 199-246

JANOWSKY, N, 'Auswirkungen der europäischen Konvention zum Schutze der Menschenrechte und Grundfreiheiten auf das österreichische Recht', Juristische Blätter (21 March 1959), pp 145-8

JENKS, C W, Social Justice in the Law of Nations (London: Oxford University Press, 1970)

KUTNER, L, World Habeas Corpus (Dobbs Ferry, NY: Oceana, 1962). 296 pp

KUTNER, L, 'World habeas corpus: human rights and world community', De Paul Law Review, vol 17 (1967), p 1

LACHANCE, Le Droit et les droits de l'homme (Paris: Presses universitaires de France, 1959)

LADOR-LEDERER, J J, International Group Protection: Aims and Methods in Human Rights (Leiden: Sijthoff, 1968)

LALIVE, P A, 'The protection of human rights within the framework of existing regional organizations', in Human Rights in National and International Law edited by A H Robertson (Manchester: Manchester University Press/Dobbs Ferry, NY: Oceana, 1968), p 330

LAUTERPACHT, H, 'The law of nations, the law of nature and the rights of man', Grotius Soc. Trans., vol 29 (1944), pp 1-33

LAUTERPACHT, H, 'The international protection of human rights', Acad. Droit Int. Recl. Cours, vol 70 (1947), pp 1-108

LAUTERPACHT, H, International Law and Human Rights (London: Stevens, 1950). xvi + 475 pp.

LE FUR, L, 'La protection internationale des droits de l'homme', Affaires étrangères, vol 1 (April 1931), pp 85-90

LIMBURG, J, 'Internationale rechtsbescherming van de belangen van particulieren', Mededelingen van de Nederlandse Vereniging voor internationaal Recht, no 19 (June 1934), pp 11-32

LUARD, E, The International Protection of Human Rights (New York: Praeger/London: Thames & Hudson, 1967)

MANDELSTAM, A, 'Das Problem der Menschen- und Bürgerrechte im "Institut de droit international" ', Die Friedens-Warte (1928), p 350

MANDELSTAM, A, 'La déclaration des droits internationaux de l'homme, adoptée par l'Institut de droit international', Rev. Droit Int.(1930), p 59

MANDELSTAM, A, 'La protection internationale des droits de l'homme', Acad. Droit Int. Recl. Cours, vol 38 (1931), p 125

MANDELSTAM, A N, La Protection internationale des droits de l'homme (Paris, 1932). 108 pp
MARCIC, R, 'Die Menschenrechte... Eine Antwort', Juristische Blätter, vol 84 (1962), p 303
McDOUGAL, M S, LASSWELL, H D, & CHEN, Lung-chu, 'Human rights and world public order', am. J. Int. Law, vol 63 (1969), p 237
MENDIZABAL, A, 'Les droits de l'homme. Du droit naturel au droit international', Doctrines politiques modernes (1947), pp 65-84
MIRKINE-GUETZÉVITCH, B, 'La protection internationale des droits de l'homme', Revue politique et parlementaire, vol 48 (1946), p 3
MODINOS, P, 'Un instrument efficace pour la sauvegarde des libertés humaines', Le Monde diplomatique (1960), p 3
MOSKOWITZ, Moses, The Politics and Dynamics of Human Rights (Dobbs Ferry, NY: Oceana, 1968)
MOSLER, H, 'Protection of human rights by international legal procedures', Georgetown Law Journal, vol 52 (1964), p 800
NEDJATI, Z M, Human Rights and Fundamental Freedoms (Nicosia: Zavallis Press, 1972). xxii + 228 pp.
PADIRAC, R, 'Les droits de l'homme devant les instances internationales,' Revue politique et parlementaire (1956), p 50
PARDOS PEREZ, J L, 'Les Droits de l'homme en droit interne et en droit international (Bruxelles, 1968)
PARRY, C, 'Some considerations upon the protection of individuals in international law', Acad. Droit. Int. Recl. Cours, vol 90 (1956), pp 653-726
ROBERTSON, A H, 'The international protection of human rights', Workpaper Geneva World Conference on World Peace Through Law D 18. 488 (1967)

ROBERTSON, A H, (ed), Human Rights in National and International Law (Manchester: Manchester University Press/Dobbs Ferry, NY: Oceana, 1968). xvi + 396 pp.
ROBERTSON, A H, Human Rights in the World (Manchester: Manchester University Press, 1972). viii + 280 pp.
RODRIGUEZ, L V, Protección de Derechos Humanos (Quito: Editorial Casa de la Cultura Ecuatoriana, 1972). 28 pp.
ROMMEN, H, 'Vers l'internationalisation des droits de l'homme', Justice dans le monde, vol 1, no 2 (December 1959), pp 147-77
RUSIS, 'The international protection of human rights', US Library of Congress Quarterly Journal (1968), p 244
SALGADO, P, Direitos e deveres do homem (Rio de Janeiro, 1953). 259 pp.
SANDIFER, D V, & SCHEMAN, L D, The Foundation of Freedom: the Interrelationship Between Democracy and Human Rights (New York: Praeger, 1966)
SCHÄTZEL, W, 'Humanität und Völkerrecht', G I R (1957), pp 393-400
SCHWARZENBERGER, G, 'The rights of man', in Festgabe für Carlo Schmid zum 65. Geburtstag (Tübingen, 1962), pp 193-8
SCHWELB, E, Human Rights and the International Community (1964)
SCHWELB, E, 'Civil and political rights: the international measures of implementation', Am. J. Int. Law, vol 62 (1968), p 827
SLOAN, F Blaine, 'Human rights, the United Nations and international law', Acta scandinavica juris gentium, vol 20 (1950), pp 23-42
SMYRNIADIS, G, 'Les droits de l'homme et leur protection internationale', Rev. Hell. Droit Int. (1952), p 63

SOCINI, R, La protezione internazionale dei
  diritti dell'uomo (Firenze, 1950)
SPERDUTI, G, L'individuo nel diritto internazionale
  (Milano, 1950)
SPERDUTI, G, 'Protezione dei diritti umani', in
  Enciclopedia del Diritto, vol 12 (Milano, 1969)
SVARLIEN, O, 'International law and the individual',
  Journal of Public Law, vol 4 no 1 (Spring 1955),
  pp 138-49
SYMPOSIUM on the international law of human rights
  (Washington 1965). 367 pp.
TENEKIDES, C G, 'La protection internationale des
  intérêts privés', Rev. Droit Int. (1932), pp 89-111
VALLAT, Sir Francis, (ed), An Introduction to the
  Study of Human Rights (London: Europa Publications,
  1972). xvi + 127 pp.
VISSCHER, Ch de, 'Les droits fondamentaux de l'homme,
  base d'une restauration du droit international.
  Rapport. Session de Lausanne de l'Institut de droit
  international, août 1947', Annu. Inst. Droit Int.
  (1947), pp 1-13
WALDOCK, Sir Humphrey, 'Human rights in
  contemporary international law', Int. & Comp. Law
  Q., vol 11 (1965), supp. p 13
WEBER, W, 'National courts and human rights - the
  Fujii case', Am. J. Int. Law, vol 45 (1959), p 621
WESSNER, H P M, 'Die Menschenrechte', Das
  Menschenrecht (German Federal Republic), 15, no
  5 (October 1960), pp 1-7
WRIGHT, Q, 'National courts and human rights: the
  Fujii case', Am. J. Int. Law, vol 45 (1951), pp
  62-82
WRIGHT, Q, 'Freedom and human rights under inter-
  national law', in Aspects of Liberty, edited by
  Milton R Konvitz & Clinton Rossiter (New York:
  Johnson Reprint Corporation, 1958), pp 181-211

YANGUAS MESSIA, J Ma, 'La garantia internacional de los derechos de la persona humana', ARACMP 8, 2 (1956), pp 97-111

YELTEKIN, N, La Nature juridique des droits de l'homme (Lausanne, 1950). 247 pp.

7.12.3 SPECIAL HUMAN RIGHTS AND PARTICULAR VIOLATIONS OF SUCH RIGHTS

See also Sections 7.12.18 (on refugees), 7.12.13 (on aliens), 2.4 (on jus cogens), 11 (on responsibility), 7.12.5 (on human rights in particular countries), and Section 12.1 on international criminal law.

ARONEANU, E, 'Discrimination: a threat to peace', World Veteran, 9, no 96 (May 1960), pp 14-16

BAUER, Elmar F, Die völkerrechtswidrige Entführung (Berlin: Duncker & Humblot, 1968). 208 pp.

BOURQUIN, J, La Liberté de la presse (Lausanne, 1950).

BÜLCK, Hartwig, Die Zwangsarbeit im Friedensvölkerrecht: Untersuchung über die Möglichkeit und Grenzen allgemeiner Menschenrechte (Göttingen: van den Hoeck & Ruprecht, 1953). 227 pp.

CASSESE, A, 'Il controlo internazionale sul rispetto della libertà sindecale vel quadro delle attuali tendenze in materia di protezione internazionale dei diritto dell'uomo', Comun. & Stud. vol 12 (1966), p 291

DUGARD, C J R, 'The legal effect of United Nations resolutions on apartheid', South African Law Journal, vol 83 (1966), pp 44-59

GREEN, L C, 'Human rights and the colour problem', Current Legal Problems, vol 3 (1950), pp 236-62

HARRIS, D, 'The right to a fair trial in criminal proceedings as a human right', Int. & Comp Law Q., vol 16 (1967), p 352

JENKS, C W, The International Protection of Freedom of Association for Trade Union Purposes (Leiden, 1956). 115 pp.
JENKS, C W, The International Protection of Trade Union Freedom (London: Stevens, 1957). xi + 592 pp.
JENKS, C W, Human Rights and International Labour Standards (London: Stevens, 1960)
KUTNER, Luis (ed), The Human Right to Individual Freedom: A Symposium on World Habeas Corpus (Coral Gables, Fl: University of Miami Press, 1970). 249 pp.
KRAUS, H, 'Staats- und völkerrechtliche Betrachtungen zur Rechtsstellung des Fremden. Ein Beitrag zum Gleichheitsproblem', Forschungen und Berichte aus dem öffentlichen Recht (1955), pp 89-99
LANARES, P, La Liberté religieuse dans les conventions internationales et dans le droit public général (Paris 1964), 286 pp.
LANARES, P, La Liberté dans les conventions internationales et dans le droit public général (1964). 286 pp.
LEMKIN, R, 'Le crime de génocide', Rev. Droit Int. Sci. Dipl. & Polit., vol 24 (1946), pp 213-23
LEVI, Sandri, 'La libertà sindacale e la contrattazione collettiva nella reglamentazione internationale', Rivista di diritto del lavoro (1955), p 215
MAIER-REIMER, H, 'Die Gleichberechtigung der Frau', Deutsche Rechts-Zeitschrift, 5, no 13, (5 July 1950), pp 289-94
MARGIOTTA BROGLIO, G, La protezione internazionale della libertà religiosa nella Convenzione europea dei diritti dell'uomo (Milano, 1967)
MOLEN, G H J van der, 'Discrimination and human rights', Free University Quarterly, vol 7, part 4 (March 1961)

PANHUYS, H F van, Het verdrag van Rome, de reclame en de commerciële televisie (1962). 23 pp. Uitgave Onafhankelijke televisie exploitatie maatschappij (OTEM)

PINO DIAZ, Rosa, & SEIDA GOMEZ, Vila, 'Derechos politicos de la mujer en el derecho comparado americano', Revista de derecho y legislacion, 38 nos 458-60 (July-September 1949), pp 99-112

PROSPERETTI, G, 'La libertà sindacale e l'org. int. del lav.', Rassegna del Lavoro (1959), p 857

SCHINDLER, D, Gleichberechtigung von Individuen als Problem des Völkerrechts (Zürich, 1957)

SCHWELB, E, 'Marriage and human rights', Am. J. Comp. Law, vol 12 (1963), pp 337-83

TEUBEN, H N, Recht op arbeid in historie en in verklaring van mensenrechten. Theorie van het gepositiveerde rechtsbeginsel. Right to work in history and in declaration of rights (Assen, 1955). 162 pp.

TRUBEL, H, & HAINKA, F, Das Versammlungsrecht. Ausführlicher Kommentar zum Versammlungsgesetz. Alle mit dem Versammlungsrecht zusammenhängenden Gesetze (Hamburg, 1953). 176 pp.

UNGER, A, 'The human right to travel: a measure of the progress of co-existence', Law in the Service of Peace (December 1955), pp 5-13

VELU, J, 'Le régime de l'arrestation et de la détention préventive à la lumière de l'évolution du droit international', Revue de droit pénal et de criminologie (1965/6), p 724

WENGLER, W, 'Le droit de la libre disposition des peuples comme principe du droit international', Rev. Hell. Droit Int., vol 10 (1957), pp 26-39

7.12.4 RIGHTS OF MINORITIES

AZCARATE, P de, League of Nations and National Minorities: An experiment, translated from the

Spanish by Eileen E Brooke, (Washington 1945). 216 pp
BAGLEY, T H, General Principles and Problems in the International Protection of Minorities: A Political Study (Gèneve, 1950). 222 pp.
CLAUDE, I L, Jr, 'The nature and status of the sub-commission on prevention of discrimination and protection', Int. Organ., vol 5 (1951), pp 300-12
CLAUDE, I L, Jr, National Minorities: An International Problem (Cambridge, 1955; reissued by Greenwood Press, Westport, Conn). 248 pp.
FEINBERG, N, La question des minorités à la conférence de la paix (Paris, 1929)
FISCHER, A, Hearings on the Genocide Convention, Sub-Committee of the Senate For. Rels. Committee 81st Congress, 2nd sess. (1950)
FOUQUES-DUPARC, J, La Protection des minorités de race, de langue ou de réligion (Paris, 1922)
GOTLIEB, A E, (ed), Human Rights, Federation and Minorities (1970)
JUNCKERSTORFF, H K, World Minorities (Calcutta, 1961). 244 pp.
KOROWICZ, M St, Górnoślaska Ochrona Mniejśzosci 1922-37 (The Upper Silesian Protection of Minorities) (Katowice, 1938)
KUNZ, J L, 'The present status of international law for the protection of minorities', Am. J. Int. Law (1954), p 282
LANGENHOVE, Fernand van, 'Le problème de la protection des populations aborigènes aux Nations Unies', Acad. Droit Int. Recl. Cours, vol 89 (1956), pp 321-435
LANNING, 'The rights of minorities', in Mélanges offerts à P Modinos (Paris, 1968), p 183
MANDELSTAM, 'La protection des minorités', Acad. Droit Int. Recl. Cours, vol (1923), p 368
MESSINEO, A, Il problema delle minoranze nazionali (Roma, 1946). 265 pp.

MODÉEN, T, The International Protection of National Minorities in Europe (Turku: Åbo Akademi, 1961). 182 pp.

NOVA, R de, 'Protezione internazionale delle minoranze e diritti dell'uomo', Diritto Internazionale, vol 20, no 1 (1966), pp 3-16

OSTROROG, L, 'Les droits de l'homme et des minorités de droit musulman', Académie diplomatique internationale séances et travaux, vol 1 (January-March 1930), pp 16-21

PORDEA, G A, 'La protection internationale des minorités et la déclaration des droits de l'homme', Rev. Droit Int. Sci. Dipl. & Polit., vol 27 (1949), pp 276-84

ROBINSON, J, Das Minoritätenproblem und seine litteratur (Berlin, 1928)

ROBINSON, KARBACH, LASSERSON, & VICHNIAK, Were the Minorities Treaties a Failure? (New York, 1943)

ROSTING, H, 'Protection of minorities by the League of Nations', Am. J. Int. Law, vol 17 (1923), pp 641-60

ROSTING, H, Protection des minorités par la Société des Nations (Genève, 1925)

ROSTING, Helmer, 'De moderne minoritetstraktater', Nord. Tidsskr. Int. Ret, vol 9 (1938), pp 52-82

ROSTING, H, 'Die modernen Minderheitsverträge', Acta scandinavica juris gentium, vol 9 (1938), pp 14-48

SABELLI, dei, Nazioni e minoranze etniche (Milano, 1928)

SCHECHTMAN, J B, 'Decline of the international protection of minority rights', Western Political Quarterly, 4 no 1 (March, 1951), pp 1-11

SCHMID, E, Wie können nationale Minderheiten geschützt werden (Berlin, 1921)

SERENI, P A, 'Il diritto internazionale delle minoranze', Riv. Diritto Int., vol 65 (1929)

STONE, Julius, International Guarantees of Minority Rights (London: Oxford University Press, 1932). 188 pp.

TCHIRKOVITCH, S, La protection de l'individu et des minorités nationales d'après les traités diplomatiques du début du XVIIIème siècle à nos jours. Cours. (Paris, 1948), 142 pp.

THOMPSON, Virginia, & ADLOFF, Richard, Minority Problems in Southeast Asia (Stanford, Calif, 1955; reissued 1970 by Russell & Russell, New York). 295 pp.

TUREGG, K E v, Minderheitenrecht. Untersuchungen zum Recht der völkischen Minderheiten (Köln, 1950). 208 pp.

VERZIJL, J H E, 'Internationale vaststelling van de rechten van den mensch, in verband met het minderhedenprobleem', De Volkenbond, vol 9, nos 9/10 (June-July 1934), pp 253-7

VIEFHAUS, E, Die Minderheitenfrage und die Entstehung der Minderheitenschutzverträge auf der Pariser Friedenskonferenz 1919. Eine Studie zur Geschichte des Nationalitätenproblems im 19. und 20. Jahrhundert (Würzburg, 1960). 244 pp.

7.12.5 HUMAN RIGHTS IN PARTICULAR COUNTRIES

There has been much written on the implementation of human rights in various countries. The works listed below are a small selection of the vast material. For human rights in Latin America see also Section 7.12.11, and, for various aspects of the European Convention, see Section 7.12.10.3.

AMACHREE, T, 'Fundamental freedoms in Nigeria', Howard Law Journal, vol 11 (1965), p 463

BAFFREY, M, Le droit de réunion en Angleterre et en France (Paris, 1937). 213 pp.

BERNARDINI, A, 'L'Italia e le convezione universale in materia di diritti dell'uomo', Riv. Diritto Int. (1967), p 107

CABRANES, J A, 'Human rights and non-intervention in the inter-American system', Michigan Law Review, vol 65 (1967), p 1147

CABRANES, J A, 'Protection of human rights by the Organization of American States', Am. J. Int. Law, vol 62 (1968), p 889

CASSESE, A, 'L'efficacia delle norme italiane di adattamento alla convenzione europe dei diritti dell'uomo', Rivista di diritto internazionale privato e processuale (1969), p 918

DAY, B, Le Canada et les droits de l'homme. Le concept des droits de l'homme dans la politique étrangère et la constitution du Canada (Paris, 1953). 154 pp.

DERWENT, G H Johnstone, 'Les garanties internationales des droits de l'homme d'après la tradition de la Grande-Bretagne', Académie diplomatique internationale séances et travaux, vol 8, no 1 (1934), pp 9-13

FABOZZI, C, 'La conv. europ. dei diritti dell'uomo nell'ordinamento italiano', TEMI (1963), p 798

FENWICK, Ch G, 'Pan-American action for protection of human rights', American Academy of Political and Social Science Annals, 243 (January 1946),

GOSLINCA, W J, De rechten van den mensch en burger. Een overzicht der Nederlandsche geschriften en verklaringen ('s Gravenhage, 1936). 186 pp.

GLEDHILL, A, Fundamental Rights in India (London, 1955). 134 pp.

HUDSON, M O, 'Charter provisions of human rights in American law', Am. J. Int. Law, vol 44 (1950), p 2

LAUTENSCHLÄGER, K, Die Bedeutung der Grundrechte im Sowjetsystem am Beispiel der UdSSR (1962). 279 pp.
MADHAVTIRTHA, S, Human Rights. Based on Indian Social Philosophy and Dharma. Compared with Human Rights adopted by UNO and by the Constitution of India (Bombay, 1953). 199 pp.
NAKAMURA, K, 'Korean repatriation question and positive international law', Jap. Annu. Int. Law, no 4 (1960), pp 68-78
PRINS, W F, 'De vrijheid van verplaatsing van de Nederlander', Personeel Statuut, 11, no 1 (January 1960), pp 1-15
Protection (La) internationale des droits de l'homme dans le cadre européen. Travaux du colloque organisé par la Faculté de droit et des sciences politiques et économiques de Strasbourg en liaison avec la Direction des droits de l'homme du Conseil de l'Europe, 14-15 novembre 1960, (Paris, 1961). 429 pp.
RAMASWAMY, M, Fundamental Rights: A Constitutional and Juridical Study with particular Reference to India in the Light of the Experience of the United States of America and the United Kingdom (New Delhi, 1946). 252 pp.
RAPPARD, W E, 'Human rights in mandated territories', Annals of the American Academy of Political and Social Science, 243 (January 1946), pp 118-23
SANDIFER, D V, 'Human rights in the inter-American system', Howard Law Journal, vol 11 (1965), p 430
SCHWARZENBERGER, G, 'The protection of human rights in British state practice', Current Legal Problems, vol 1 (1948), pp 152-69
SCHWELB, E, 'The Austrian state treaty and human rights', Int. & Comp. Law Q. (1956), p 265

TRISKA, J F, 'The individual and his rights in the European community: an experiment in international law', Tulane Law Review, vol 31 (1957), pp 283-302

VASAK, K, 'Les droits de l'homme et l'Afrique', Revue Juridique et Politique (1967), p 273

VASAK, K, 'Intégration régionales et droits de l'homme: situation en Afrique et en Amérique', in Synthèses (Bruxelles, 1969), p 93

VISSCHER, Ch. de, 'Human rights in Roman law countries', Annals of the American Academy of Political and Social Science, 243, (January 1946), pp 53-9

WOLD, 'Den europäiske menneskeretts Konvensjon og Norge', Legal Essays in Honour of Fred Castberg (1963), p 353

7.12.6 UNIVERSAL AND REGIONAL APPROACH TO HUMAN RIGHTS

See also Section 7.12.5.

GUYOMAR, G, 'Nations Unies et organisations régionales dans la protection des droits de l'homme', Revue générale de droit international public, vol 68, no 3 (July-September 1964), pp 687-707

LALIVE, P A, 'La protection des droits de l'homme dans le cadre des organisations régionales existantes', in Les Droits de l'homme en droit interne et droit international (Bruxelles, 1968)

MODINOS, P, 'Coexistence de la Convention européenne des droits de l'homme et du Pacte des droits civils et politiques des Nations Unies', Revue des droits de l'homme (1968), p 41

MOURA, La Protection juridictionelle des droits de l'homme et les organisations régionales (Paris, 1958)

PINTO, R, 'Régionalisme et universalisme dans la
    protection des droits de l'homme', in International
    Protection of Human Rights, Proceedings of the
    Seventh Nobel Symposium, Oslo, September 25-27
    1967 (New York/Chichester: Interscience/Stockholm:
    Almqvist & Wiksell, 1968), p 177
QUINTANO-RIPOLLES, A, 'La protección de los derechos
    humanos en lo universal y lo regional', Rev. Esp.
    Derecho Int. (1965), p 437
VALTICOS, N, 'Universalité des droits de l'homme et
    diversité des conditions nationales', in Problèmes de
    la protection internationale des droits de l'homme:
    en honneur R Cassin (Paris, 1969), p 383
VASAK, K, 'Vers la création de commissions
    régionales des droits de l'homme', in Problèmes
    de la protection internationale des droits de
    l'homme: en honneur du R Cassin, vol 1 (Paris,
    1969), p 467

7.12.7   CONVENTIONS ON HUMAN
         RIGHTS IN GENERAL

On the United Nations Covenants see below in
Section 7.12.8.3 and for the European Convention see
Section 7.12.10.3
BACALU, J, 'Het verdragsrecht betreffende de
    rechten van de mens', Rechtskundig Weekblad
    (Antwerpen), 21, no 26 (16 March 1958), pp 1321-42
CAPOTORTI, F, Patti internazionali sui diritti
    dell'uomo (Studio introduttivo) (Padova, 1967)
GARCIA, E A, 'Anteproyecto de tratado internacional
    sobre protección de los derechos humanos',
    Revista del Colegio de Abogados de Buenos Aires, 3
    (1950)
GARDNER, R, 'The three human rights treaties: good
    law and good policy', International Lawyer, vol 1
    (1967), p 633

KERTESZ, S D, 'Human rights in the peace treaties',
  Rights (International human), 1949 (II), pp 627-46
MARTIN, A, 'Human rights in the Paris peace treaties',
  Br. Yearb. Int. Law (1947), pp 392-8
MARTIN, A, 'Human rights in the Paris peace
  treaties: problems of interpretation and enforcement'
  (report; for the discussions see p 45 etc) Reports
  of the 43d Conference of the International
  Law Association, 1950 (1948), pp 139-54
MOURGEON, 'Les pactes internationals relatifs aux
  droits de l'homme', Annu. Fr. Droit Int. (1967),
  p 326
SCHWELB, E, 'International conventions on human
  rights', Int. & Comp. Law Q., vol 9 (1960), pp
  654-75
SEIDL-HOHENVELDERN, I, 'Die internationale
  Flüchtlingskonvention von 1951 in der Praxis.
  Internationalrechtliche und staatsrechtliche
  Abhandlungen', Festschrift für Walter Schätzel zu
  seinem 70. Geburtstag (1960), pp 441-51
SIMON, M, 'La convention des droits de l'homme et
  le droit pénal international', Revue international
  de droit pénal 21, no 2, (1950), pp 163-78

7.12.8   HUMAN RIGHTS AND
         THE UNITED NATIONS

7.12.8.1   GENERAL

BRUNET, René, Garantie internationale des droits de
  l'homme d'après la charte de San-Francisco
  (Genève: Ch Grasset, 1947). 383 pp.
CAPOTORTI, F, 'Le Nazioni Unite per il progresso
  dei diritti dell'uomo: risultati e prospetti',
  Comunità internazionale (1967), p 18
CAREY, J, 'UN double standard on human rights', Am.
  J. Int. Law, vol 60 (1966), p 792

CAREY, J, UN Protection of Civil and Political Rights (Syracuse, NY: Syracuse University Press, 1970). xii + 205 pp.
CHAKRAVARTI, R, Human Rights and the United Nations (Calcutta, 1958). 218 pp.
CLARK, Roger Stenson, A United Nations Commissioner for Human Rights (Den Haag: Nijhoff, 1972). 186 pp.
ERMACORA, F, Der Minderheitenschutz in der Arbeit der Vereinten Nationen (Wien/Stuttgart, 1964). 118 pp
EWELL, M, Manacles for Mankind: An Analysis of UNO's Championship of Human Rights, 2nd edition (Chulmleigh, Devon: Britons Publishing Co, 1964). 104 pp.
GARCIA BAUER, C, 'Los derechos en las Naciones Unidas', Revista de la Asocición guatemalteca de derecho international, no 1 (January 1954), pp 17-35
GLASER, S, 'La protection des droits de l'homme et la charte des Nations Unies', Revue de droit pénale et de criminologie 30, no 4 (January 1950), pp 357-92
GREEN, J F, The United Nations and Human Rights (Dubuque, Iowa: William C Brown Co, 1956). 194 pp.
KUTNER, L, 'A proposal for a United Nations writ of habeas corpus and an international court of human rights', Tulane Law Review, vol 28 (1954), pp 417-41
McDOUGAL, M S, & BEBR, G, 'Human rights in the United Nations', Am. J. Int. Law, vol 58 (1964), pp 603-41
LAUTERPACHT, H, 'Human rights, the charter of the United Nations, and the International bill of the rights of man', (Report and discussion. Appendix: the rapporteur's draft, May 1948) Reports of the 43d Conference of the International Law Association, 1950 (1948), pp 29-138

LAUTERPACHT, H, 'The charter of the United Nations and human rights and fundamental freedoms', Österr. Z. Öff. Recht, vol 3 (1950), pp 19-29

MIRKINE-GUETZÉVICH, B, 'L'ONU et la doctrine moderne des droits de l'homme', Rev. Gén. Droit Int. Public, vol 55 (1951)

MOSKOWITZ, M, Human Rights and World Order: The Struggle for Human Rights in the United Nations (Dobbs Ferry, NY: Oceana, 1958).

NEAL, M, 'The United Nations and human rights', Int. Conciliation, no 489 (March 1953), pp 111-74

POBLETE TRONCOSO, M, 'Los derechos humanos y las Naciones Unidas', R D (Concepción, Chile), vol 21, no 85 (July-September 1953)

SLOAN, F B, 'Menneskerettighederne, De Forenede Nationer og folkeretten', Nord. Tidsskr. Int. Ret, vol 20 (1950), pp 69-83

7.12.8.2 THE UNIVERSAL DECLARATION ON HUMAN RIGHTS

ANTONOPOULOS, H, 'L'influence de la déclaration universelle des droits de l'homme sur les constitutions contemporaines', Politique, Revue internationale des doctrines et des institutions, 13 (January-March 1961), pp 1-33

ASBECK, F M van, The Universal Declaration of Human Rights and its Predecessors (1679-1948) (Leiden: E J Brill, 1949). 99 pp.

CASSIN, René, 'La declaration universelle et la mise en oeuvre des droits de l'homme', Acad. Droit Int. Recl. Cours, vol 79 (1951), pp 237-367

CASSIN, R, 'Twenty years after the Universal Declaration', International Commission of Jurists Journal, vol 8 (1968), p 1

FRIESENHAHN, 'La dichiarazione universale dei diritti dell'uomo', Jus (1951), p 55

HUMMELL, R, Die Menschenrechte und die
  Erklärung der allgemeinen Menschenrechte der UN
  vom 10, Dezember 1948 im Recht des Saarlandes
  (Saarbrucken, 1955). 219 pp.
JIMENEZ DE ARECHAGA, E, 'The background to
  article 17 of the Universal Declaration', International Commission of Jurists Journal, vol 8
  (1968), p 34
LAUTERPACHT, H, An International Bill of the Rights
  of Man (New York: Columbia University Press, 1945)
  x + 230 pp.
LAUTERPACHT, H, 'The Universal Declaration of
  Human Rights', Br. Yearb. Int. Law (1948), p 354
MIRKINE GUETZEVITCH, B, 'Quelques problèmes de
  la mise en oeuvre de la Déclaration universelle des
  droits de l'homme', Acad. Droit Int. Recl. Cours,
  vol   (1953), p 255
POLAK, C H F, 'Behoren sociale grondrechten als
  vervat in de internationale verklaring van de
  rechten van de mens (art 22 e v) ook voor ons recht
  aanvaard, in de grondwet verankers en wettelijk
  nader omschreyen to worden? Praeadvies',
  Handelingen der Juristenvereniging, 83, I, no 1
  (1953), pp 184-256
ROBINSON, N, The Universal Declaration of Human
  Rights: Its Origin, Significance, Application and
  Interpretation (New York, 1956). 173 pp.
SCHWELB, E, 'The nature of obligations of states
  parties to the International covenant on civil and
  political rights', in Problèmes de la protection des
  droits de l'homme: en l'honneur de R Cassin
  (Paris, 1969), vol 1, p 301
SCOTT, J B, 'La déclaration internationale des
  droits de l'homme, adoptée par l'Institut de droit
  international à la session de New-Yorck, le 12
  octobre 1929, 437e anniversaire de la découverte
  du nouveau monde', Rev. Droit Int. & Légis. Comp.
  (1930), p 79

SEIDL-HOHENVELDERN, I, 'Die Allgemeine
Deklaration der Menschenrechte als Rechtsquelle',
Juristische Blätter, 74, no 23 (6 December 1952),
pp 558-9
SOHN, L B, 'The Universal Declaration of Human
Rights', International Commission of Jurists
Journal, vol 8 (1968), p 7
SPERDUTI, G, 'La dichiarazione universale dei
diritti dell'uomo, Comunità internazionale (1950),
p 216
UNESCO, Autour de la nouvelle declaration
universelle des droits de l'homme (Paris, 1949),
236 pp. With contributions by Mahatma Gandhi,
Harold J Laski, Quincy Wright etc.
UNESCO, La Declaración universal de derechos del
hombre. Trabajos del seminario efectuado en la
Habana par la Unesco y la Academia interamericana
de derecho comparado e internacional, Agosto 4-16
de 1952 (Havana, 1953). 347 pp.
VERDOODT, A, Naissance et signification de la
déclaration universelle des droits de l'homme
(Louvain/Paris, 1964). 356 pp.

7.12.8 3   THE UNITED NATIONS COVENANTS

See also above in Section 7.12.7 for conventions in
general, and below Section 7.12.17 on statelessness.

BRÜGEL, 'Die Menschenrechtskonventionen der
Vereinten Nationen', Europa-Archiv (1967), p 329
FERGUSON, C C,'The United Nations human rights
covenants: problems of ratification and
implementation', Am. Soc. Int. Law Proc. (1968),
p 83
NEWMAN, 'Natural justice, due process and the new
international covenants on human rights', Public
Law (1967), p 274
see also

CHAFEE, Z, 'Federal and state powers under the
United Nations covenant on human rights',
Wisconsin Law Review (1951)
MacCHESNEY, B, 'Should the United States ratify the
covenants? A question of merits, not of constitutional
law', Am. J. Int. Law, vol 62 (1968), p 912
NATHANSON, L, 'Constitutional problems involved in
adhesion by the US to a convention for the protection
of human rights and fundamental freedoms',
Cornell Law Quarterly, vol 56 (1965), p 235

7.12.8.4   THE UNITED NATIONS CONVENTION
AGAINST RACIAL DISCRIMINATION

LERNER, N, The UN Convention on the Elimination of
all Forms of Racial Discrimination: A Commentary
(Leiden: Sijthoff, 1970). 132 pp.
SCHWELB, E, 'The international convention on the
elimination of all forms of racial discrimination',
Int. & Comp. Law Q., vol 15 (1966), p 996

7.12.9   THE RED CROSS CONVENTIONS

See also Sections 10.6 and 10.11 on humanitarian law in
war and civil war, and Section 13.5 on the Red Cross.

7.12.10   HUMAN RIGHTS AND EUROPE

The various sections below are all interwoven, but I
have divided the material into several interrelated
subsections.

7.12.10.1   EUROPEAN HUMAN RIGHTS
IN GENERAL

ALCIATOR, Maurizio, FOIS, Paolo, et al, Essais
sur les droits de l'homme en Europe. (1ère-
série) (Torino/Paris, 1959)

GOLSONG, H, 'La défense des droits de l'homme en Europe', in Sciences humaines et intégration européenne (1960), p 85
LEIFER, M, 'Human rights in the European Comminity', Australian Outlook, vol 15 (1961), p 169
MORRISON, Clovis C, The Developing European Law of Human Rights (Leiden: Sijthoff, 1967). 247 pp.
ROBERTSON, A H, Human Rights in Europe (Manchester: Manchester University Press, 1963). ix + 280 pp.
RUSSO, del, 'L'istituto dell'habeas corpus: contributo della common law ai diritti umani d'Europa', 2nd Human Rights Conference, Villa Monastero Varenna, Italy, 1969
SIDJANSKI, D, 'La protection internationale et européenne des droits de l'homme. Fondement et consequences', Rev. Egypt.Droit Int., vol 12, no 1 (1956)
SIMON, M, 'Le Conseil de l'Europe et la protection des droits de l'homme', Rev. Droit Int. Sci. Dipl. & Polit., vol 28 (1950), pp 30-8
TIEDEMANN, K, 'Eine europäische Erklärung der Rechte des Strafgefangenen', Juristen Zeitung no 8 (19 April 1962), pp 245-8

7.12.10 2 HUMAN RIGHTS AND THE EUROPEAN COMMUNITY

PESCATORE, Pierre, 'Les droits de l'homme et l'intégration européenne', Cah. Droit. Eur. (1968), pp 629-57
PESCATORE, Pierre, 'Fundamental rights and freedoms in the system of the European Communities', Am. J. Comp. Law (1970), pp 343-51
RUPP, Hans Heinrich, 'Die Grundrechte und das Europäische Gemeinschaftsrecht', Neue juristische Wochenschrift (1970), pp 353-9

TRISKA, J F, 'The individual and his rights in the
European Community: an experiment in international
law', Tulane Law Review, vol 31 (1957), pp 283-302
ZIEGER, Gottfried, Das Grundrechtsproblem in den
Europäischen Gemeinschaften (Tübingen: Mohr,
1970). Recht und Staat, numbers 384-385

7.12.10.3 THE EUROPEAN CONVENTION
ON HUMAN RIGHTS

See also Section 7.12.10.1 on human rights in Europe
and note the work by ROBERTSON listed under 7.12.10.1.
For the European Court and Commission see further
Sections 7.12.10.5 and 7.12.10.6.
BEDDARD, 'Status of the European convention of
  human rights in domestic law', Int. & Comp. Law
  Q., vol 16 (1967), p 206
BÜRGENTHAL, Th, 'The domestic status of the
  European convention on human rights: a second
  look', International Commission of Jurists Journal,
  vol 7 (1966), p 55
CHIAVARIO, A, La convenzione europea dei diritti
  dell'uomo nel sistema delle fonti normaltive in
  materia penale (Milano, 1969)
COMTE, A, 'The application of the European convention
  on human rights in municipal law', International
  Commission of Jurists Journal, vol 4 (1962), p 94
DIEZ DE VELASCO, 'Mecanismos de garantia y
  medios procesales de proteccion creados por la
  Convencion Europea de los Derechos del hombre',
  in Libro Homenaje a D Nicolas Perez Serrano
  (1959), vol 2, p 585
ECHTERHÖLTER, R, "Die Europäische
  Menschenrechtkonvention in der juristischen
  Praxis', Juristenzeitung (1956), p 144
EHRYN, G, La Convention européenne des droits de
  l'homme (Paris, 1953)

EISSEN, M A, La Convention européenne dite de sauvegarde des droits de l'homme (Strasbourg, 1951). 32 pp.

EISSEN, 'L'autonomie de l'article 14 de la Convention européenne des droits de l'homme dans la jurisprudence de la Communauté', in Mélanges offerts à P Modinos (Paris, 1968), p 122

EUSTATHIADES, C Th, 'La convention de sauvegarde des droits de l'homme et la statut du Conseil de l'Europe', Die Friedens-Warte (1954), p 332; (1955), p 47

FAWCETT, J E S, The Application of the European Convention on Human Rights (Oxford: Clarendon Press, 1969). xii +368 pp.

GOLSONG, H, Das Rechtsschutzsystem der europäischen Menschenrechtkonvention', (Karlsruhe, 1958)

GOLSONG, H, 'The European convention on human rights before the domestic courts', Br. Yearb. Int. Law, vol 38 (1962), p 445

GOLSONG, H, 'The control machinery of the European convention on human rights', Int. & Comp. Law Q., vol 11 (1965), supp.

GOLSONG, H, 'Zur Beurteilung des Art, 6 der Menschenrechtskonvention durch den Verfassungsgerichtshof', Juristische Blätter 83, nos 20-1 (28 October 1962), pp 530-1

GREEN, L C, 'The European convention on human rights', World Affairs (USA), (1951), p 435

GREENBERG, J, & SHALIT, Anthony R, 'New horizons for human rights: the European convention, court, and commission of human rights', Columbia Law Review, 63, no 8 (December 1963), pp 1384-1412

GUGGENHEIM, P, 'Quelques remarques au sujet de l'article 14 de la Convention européenne des droits de l'homme', in Scritti per René Cassin (Paris, 1969)

GURADZE, H, Die Europäische Menschenrechts-
konvention, Kommentar (Berlin/Frankfurt a M:
Franz Vahlen GmbH Verlag, 1968)
HERZOG, R, 'Das Grundrecht auf Freiheit in der
Europäischen Menschenrechtskonvention', Archiv
des öffentlichen Rechts, 86, nos 2-3 (September
1961), pp 194-244
HOPKINS, 'European convention on human rights',
Cambridge Law Journal (1966), p 4
KEWENIG, W, 'Die europäische Menschenrechts-
konvention und die Kontrolle des nationalen
Gesetzgebers in Großbritannien', Neue juristische
Wochenschrift (1968), p 2179
KLUG, U, 'Das Verhältnis zwischen der
Europäischen Menschenrechtskonvention und dem
Grundgesetz', in Gedächtnisschrift Peters
(Berlin/Heidelberg/New York, 1967), p 434
KYRIACOPOULOS, E, 'Zur Einwirkung der europäischen
Menschenrechtkonvention', in Festschrift
Spiropoulos (Bonn, 1957), p 285
LACRUZ BERDEJO, J L, Convención Europea de
los Derechos del Hombre (Madrid, 1959)
LØCHEN, Einar, Europas menneskerettighets-
konvensjon (Bergen: Grieg, 1952). 56 pp.
(Chr Michelsens Institutt)
McNULTY, European Convention on Human Rights:
Relationship Between the Individual and the State
(Council of Europe Docs. A 73 607) (1963)
MERLE, M, 'La convention européenne des droits de
l'homme', Rev. Droit Public & Sci. Polit (1951),
p 705
MODINOS, P, La Charte de la liberté de l'Europe
(Brochure no 11 de la Société égyptienne du droit
international) (1951)
NIETO SALE, 'La Convención européa de los
derechos del Hombre', Instituciones europeas,
Zaragoza (1960), p 41

NONNENMACHER, G G, 'La convention de sauvegarde des droits de l'homme', Notre Europe (1953)

PADIRAC, R, 'La convention européenne des droits de l'homme et les réticences de la France', Chronique Sociale de France (1957), p 231

PARTSCH, K J, 'I diritti fondamentali dell'uomo nella Comunità Europea', Comunità internazionale (1956), p 422

PARTSCH, K J, 'Die Europäische Menschenrechtskonvention vor den nationalen Parlamenten', Comunità internazionale (1956-7), p 93

PARTSCH, K J, Die Rechte und Freiheiten der Europäischen Menschenrechtskonvention (Berlin, 1966)

PARTSCH, K J, 'Die Entstehung der europäischen Menschenrechtkonvention', Z. Ausl. Öff. Recht & Völkerrecht (1954), p 631

PELLOUX, R, 'Précedents et caractères généraux de la Convention européenne', in La Protection internationale des droits de l'homme (Paris, 1961), p 63

PFEIFER, G, 'Die rechtliche Bedeutung der europäischen Konvention der Menschenrechte und Grundfreiheiten für Österreich', Juristische Blätter (1958), p 599

PILLING, J, 'The European convention on human rights', Toronto University Faculty Law Review, vol 21 (1963), p 93

ROBERTSON, A H, 'The European convention on human rights: recent developments', Br. Yearb. Int. Law (1951), pp 359-65

ROBERTSON, A H, 'The political background and historical development of the European convention', Int. & Comp. Law Q., vol 11 (1965), supp.

ROLIN, H A, 'La rôle du requérant dans la procédure prévue par la Convention européenne des droits de l'homme', Rev. Hell. Droit Int. (1956), p 3

ROLIN, H A, 'Un texte de droit positif ignoré des juristes belges: la Convention européenne des droits de l'homme', Journal des Tribunaux, vol 73 (1958), p 515

RUSSO, A L del, 'The European bill of rights', Santa Clara Lawyer, vol 4 (1963), p 8

SCHWELB, E, 'The protection of the right of property of nationals under the first protocol to the European convention on human rights', Am. J. Comp. Law, vol 13 (1964), p 518

SIDJANSKI, & CASTANOS, S, 'La Convention Européenne des droits de l'homme', J Droit Int. (1955), p 580

SPERDUTI, G, 'La Convenzione europea dei diritti dell'uomo e il suo sistema di garanzie', Riv. Diritto Int., vol 46 (1963), p 161

SÜSTERHENN, 'L'application de la Convention sur le plan du droit interne', in La Protection internationale des droits de l'homme dans le cadre européen (Paris, 1961), p 303

TAMMES, A J P, 'Hed Europese verdrag tot bescherming van de rechten van de mens en het nationale recht', Medelingen van de Nederlands Vereniging voor internationaal recht, no 43 (November 1960)

THIRLWAY, H W A, 'New jurisdiction: the European convention on human rights', Solicitors Journal, vol 110 (1966), p 299

VASAK, K, 'The European convention of human rights: beyond the frontiers of Europe', Int. & Comp. Law Q., vol 12 (1963), p 1206

VASAK, K, La Convention européenne des droits de l'homme (Paris, 1964)

VELU, J, 'Le problème de l'application aux juridictions administratives des règles de la convention Européenne des droits de l'homme', Rev. Droit Int. & Droit Comp. (1961), p 129

VERDROSS, A, 'La place de la convention européenne des droits de l'homme dans la hiérarchie des normes juridiques', Comun. & Stud., vol 13 (1967), p 3

VIS, L, 'La réparation des violations de la Convention européenne des droits de l'homme', in La Protection internationale des droits de l'homme dans le cadre européen (1961), p 281

VITTA, E, 'Analogie e influenze di diritto publico interno nella Convenzione europea per la salvaguardia dei diritti dell'uomo e delle liberta fondamentali', Rivista trimestriale di diritto pubblico (1958), p 759

WALDOCK, C H M, 'The European convention for the protection of human rights and fundamental freedoms', Br. Yearb. Int. Law (1958), p 36

WALTER, H, 'Der gegenwärtige Wirkungsbereich der Rechtsschutzeinrichtungen der europäischen Menschenrechtskonvention. Unterwerfungserklärungen Belgiens, Grossbritanniens und Schwedens', Z. Ausl. Öff. Recht & Völkerrecht, vol 26 (1966), pp 352-70 with English summary

WEIL, Gordon L, The European Convention on Human Rights: Background, Development, Prospects (Leiden: Sijthoff, 1963)

WEISS, M, Die europäische Konvention zum Schutze der Menschenrechte und Grundfreiheiten (Frankfurt/Berlin, 1954)

7.12.10.4 HUMAN RIGHTS AND THE COMMITTEE OF MINISTERS OF THE COUNCIL OF EUROPE

CASSESE, A, 'L'esercizio di funzioni giuridizionale da parte de Comitato dei ministri del Consiglio d'Europa', Riv. Diritto Int. (1962), p 398

PARDOS PEREZ, J L, Derechos del Hombre en el Consejo de Europa, (Murcia, 1960)

MODINOS, P, 'Les pouvoirs de décision conférés au comité des Ministres du Couseil de l'Europe par l'article 32 de la Convention européenne des droits de l'homme', in Mélanges Henri Rolin (Paris 1964), p 196

WIEBRINGHAUS, H, Die Rom-Konvention für Menschenrechte in der Praxis der Strassburger Menschenrechtskommission: Ein praktischer Kommentar mit allen grundlegenden Texten zur Tätigkeit der Kommission auf dem Gebeit der Individualbeschwerden (Saarbrücken, 1959). 172 pp.

7.12.10.5 EUROPEAN COMMISSION ON HUMAN RIGHTS

An outstanding work on this subject is the book by MONCONDUIT listed below.

BUERGENTHAL, 'Confrontation de la jurisprudence des tribunaux nationaux avec la jurisprudence des organes de la Commission en ce qui concerne les droits judiciaires', in Les Droits de l'homme en droit interne et droit international (Bruxelles, 1968), p 294

DUPUY, R J, 'La Commission européenne des droits de l'homme', Annu. Fr. Droit Int. (1957), p 449

EISSEN, M A, 'Jurisprudence de la Commission européenne des droits de l'homme', Annu. Fr. Droit Int. (1963), p 722

LAUTERPACHT, E, 'Council of Europe: legal questions, European Commission of Human Rights Complaints made by the Greek government in connection with events in Cyprus. Position of national minorities in Europe,' Int. & Comp. Law Q., vol 8 (1958), p 366

LODIGIANI, A, La Commissione nella Convenzione europea dei diritti dell'uomo (Milano, 1970)

MONCONDUIT, F, La Commission européenne des droits de l'homme (Leiden, 1956). 559 pp.

MYERS, D P, 'The European convention on human
  rights', Am. J. Int. Law (1956), p 949
ROLIN, H, 'Le rôle du requérant dans la procedure
  prévue par la Commission européenne des droits
  de l'homme', Rev. Hell. Droit Int., vol 9 (1956),
  pp 3-14
SCHIENDLER, W, 'Die europäische Kommission und
  der europäische Gerichtshof für Menschenrechte',
  Schweizerische Juristen-Zeitung (1960), p 133.
STRYCKMANS, F, 'Het billijk proces volgens de
  Europese commissie der rechten van de mens',
  Rechtskundig weekblad, 30, no 4 (25 September 1966),
  col 177-210, 30, no 5 (2 October 1966), col 233-52
WEIL, G L, 'Decisions on inadmissible applications
  by the European Commission of Human Rights',
  Am. J. Int. Law, vol 64 (1960), p 874
WIEBRINGHAUS, H, 'Jurisprudence et procédure du
  Comité des Ministres du Conseil de l'Europe en
  vertu du premier paragraphe de l'article 32 de la
  Convention européenne des droits de l'homme', in
  Mélanges P Modinos (Paris 1968), p 454
WIEBRINGHAUS, H, 'La règle de l'épuisement
  préalable des voies de recours internes dans la
  jurisprudence de la Commission européenne des
  droits de l'homme', Annu. Fr. Droit Int. (1959),
  p 685
WIEBRINGHAUS, H, 'La protection des droits de
  l'homme dans le cadre du Conseil de l'Europe', Riv.
  Diritto Eur., vol 1 (1961), p 53

7.12.10.6   EUROPEAN COURT
            FOR HUMAN RIGHTS

ALCALA-ZAMORA Y CASTILLO, N, 'Reglamento de
  la Corte Europea de derechos humanos', Bolétin del
  Instituto de derecho comparado de Mexico, 14, 40
  (January-April 1961), pp 89-99

BALLADORE PALLIERI, G, 'Il regolamento della Corte dei diritti dell'uomo', Diritto internazionale, vol 14 (1960), pp 126-35

CASSIN, R, 'La Cour européenne des droits de l'homme', Annu. Eur., vol 7, pp 75-92

EISSEN, M A, 'La Cour européenne des droits de l'homme de la convention du règlement', Annu. Fr. Droit Int., vol 5 (1959)

EISSEN, 'Le premier arrêt de la Cour européenne des droits de l'homme: affaire Lawless, exceptions préliminaires et questions de procédure', Annu. Fr. Droit Int., vol 6 (1960), p 444

GOLSONG, H, 'Der europäische Gerichtshof für Menschenrecht', Juristenzeitung (April 1960), pp 193-8

GOLSONG, H, 'Implementation of international protection of human rights', Acad. Droit Int. Recl. Cours, vol 110 (1963), p 74

GOLSONG, H, 'Quelques réflexions à propos du pouvoir de la Cour européenne des droits de l'homme d'accorder une satisfaction équitable', in Scritti per René Cassin (Paris, 1969), vol 1, p 89

HORVATH, B, 'The European court of human rights', Osterr. Z. Off. Recht, vol 5 (1952), pp 166-91

HUBER, H, 'Der Hauptentscheid des europäischen Gerichtshofes für Menschenrechte in der Sache Lawless', Z. Ausl. Öff. Recht & Völkerrecht, vol 21 (1961), pp 649-66

LALIVE, J F, & VASAK, K, 'Chronique de la jurisprudence de la Commission et de la Cour européenne des droits de l'homme', J. Droit Int., vol 89 (1962), pp 238-89. Also in English

LAUTERPACHT, H, 'The proposed European court of human rights', (followed by discussion), Grotius Soc. Trans., vol 35 (1950), pp 25-47

MATTHIES, H, 'Das erste Urteil des europäischen Gerichtshofs für Menschenrechts; Verfahrensfragen in der Sache Lawless', Z. Ausl. Off. Recht & Völkerrecht, vol 21 (1961), pp 249-58

MOSLER, H, 'Organisation und Verfahren des europäischen Gerichtshofs für Menschenrechte', Z. Ausl. Öff. Recht & Völkerrecht, vol 20 (1960), pp 415-49

MOSLER, H, 'La procédure de la Cour international de justice et de la Cour européenne des droits de l'homme', in Scritti per René Cassin (Paris, 1969), p 1966

PADIRAC, R, 'Les droits de l'homme devant les instances internationales', Revue politique et parlementaire, vol 58, no 567 (April 1956), pp 50-4

PARDOS PEREZ, J L, Derechos del hombre en el Consejo de Europa (Murcia, 1960). 222 pp.

PETRÉN, G, 'La saisie de la Cour européenne par la Commission européenne des droits de l'homme', in Mélanges P Modinos (Paris: Pédone, 1968), p 233

ROBERTSON, A H, 'The European Court of Human Rights', Int. & Comp. Law Q. (1959), pp 396-403

ROLIN, H, 'Has the European Court of Human Rights a future?' Howard Law Journal, vol 11 (1965), p 442

RÖLING, B V A, 'Het individuele klachtrecht in de Europese conventie voor de mensenrechten', Nederlands juristenblad, nos 14-15 (7-14 April 1956), p 293-302, 309-15

SØRENSEN, M, 'La recevabilité de l'instance devant la Cour européenne des droits de l'homme', in Scritti per René Cassin (Paris, 1969), vol 1, p 333

SUY, E, 'De zaak "De Becker" voor het Europese hof der mensenrechten', Rechtskundig tijdschrift voor België, 52, no 2 (1962), pp 131-52

SUY, E, 'De zaak "Lawless" voor het europees gerechtshof voor de mensenrechten', Ned. Tijdschr. Int. Recht, vol 9 (1962), pp 273-93

TARDU, M, 'Le droit de recours des particuliers devant un organe international. Récents développements dans le cadre de la Convention européenne de sauvegarde des droits de l'homme et des libertés fondamentales', Revue de droit international pour le Moyen Orient, 5, no 1 (June 1956), pp 20-41

VERDROSS, A, 'Einige Hauptbestimmungen der Geschäftsordnung des europäischen Gerichtshofes für Menschenrechte', Österr. Z. Öff. Recht, vol 10 (1960), pp 475-9

WEISS, C, 'Die europäische Konvention zum Schutze der Menschenrechte und Grundfreiheiten (mit Wortlaute)'. Dokumente herausgegeben von der Forschungsstelle für Völkerrecht und ausländisches öffentliches Recht der Universität, Hamburg, no 15 (1954)

WESSNER, H P M, 'Der europäische Gerichtshof für Menschenrechte', Das Menschenrecht (Austria), vol 14 (1960), pp 1-4

WIEBRINGHAUS, H, 'Ein internationaler Gerichtshof zum Schutz der Menschenrechte', Die Friedens-Warte, vol 55 (1959), pp 1-25

WIESLER, L, 'Die Rechtsschutzeinrichtungen nach der europäischen Menschenrechtskonvention', Thesis. Tübingen, 1961. 186 pp.

WIESLER, L, 'Der Beginn der Tätigkeit des europäischen Gerichtshofes für Menschenrechte', Europa-Archiv 16, 24 (25 December 1961), pp 735-42

WIESLER, L, Die Rechtsschutzeinrichtungen nach der europäischen Menschenrechtskonvention (n p 1961). 186 pp.

7.12.11 INTER-AMERICAN COMMISSION ON HUMAN RIGHTS

See also Section 7.12.5.

SCHEMAN, L R, 'The Inter-American Commission on

Human Rights', Am. J. Int. Law, vol 59 (1965),
p 335
SCHREIBER, Anna P, The Inter-American Commission
on Human Rights (Leiden: Sijthoff, 1970). 192 pp.
THOMAS & THOMAS, 'Inter-American Commission
on Human Rights', Southwestern Law Journal, vol
20 (1965), p 28
ZANGHI, C, 'La Convenzione inter-americana dei diritti
del'uomo', Comunità internazionale (1970), p 266

7.12.12 HUMAN RIGHTS AND THE
INTERNATIONAL LABOUR ORGANIZATION

See also the works by JENKS listed in Section 7.12.3
on special rights and particular violations.
BLAMONT, 'Human rights and the ILO', Howard Law
Review (1965), p 413
GORMLEY, 'Emergency protection of human rights by
the International Labor Organization', Albany Law
Review, vol 30 (1966), p 13
JUVIGNY, P, 'L'Organisation international du travail
et les droits de l'homme', Scritti in honore di René
Cassin (Paris, 1969), vol 1, p 121
VALTICOS, N, 'L'OIT et sa contribution au principe de
la primauté du droit et à la protection des droits
de l'homme', International Commission of Jurists
Review, vol 9, no 2, p 3
VALTICOS, N, Les droits de l'homme et l'organisation
international du travail', in Mélanges Séfériades
(Athens, 1961), vol 1, p 116
WEAVER, G L P, International Labor Organization
and Human Rights (1966)

7.12.13 TREATMENT OF ALIENS

See also Sections 7.11.12 and 7.12.16 on protection of
nationals, and comments under 7.12.

BAR, C L von, 'L'expulsion des étrangers', Journal du droit international privé (1886), p 5

BASDEVANT, J, 'Etrangers', in Répertoire de droit international, vol 8 (1930), p 1

BISCOTTINI, G, 'La rilevanza degli atti stranieri di certificazione', Foro Padano, vol 3 (1951), p 113

BISCOTTINI, G, 'L'ammissione ed il soggiorno dello straniero', in Scritti in memoria di V E Orlando (Padova, 1955), p 149

BOECK, Charles-Jean-Barthélemy, 'L'expulsion et les difficultés internationales qu'en soulève la pratique', Acad. Droit Int. Recl. Cours, vol 18 (1927), pp 443-650

BOUVE, A, Exclusion and Expulsion of Aliens (New York, 1915)

CUTLER, J Ward, 'The treatment of foreigners', Am. J. Int. Law (1933), p 225

DAWSON, F G & HEAD, J L, International Law Tribunals, and the Rights of Aliens (Syracuse, NY: Syracuse University Press, 1971). xvi + 334 pp.

DELESSERT, Charles, L'établissement et le séjour des étrangers au point de vue juridique et politique (Lausanne: Imprimerie la Concorde, 1924). 608 pp.

DELETRE, Yves, 'Le statut civil de l'étranger en France', in Le Statut de l'étranger et le Marché commun (Paris 1959), pp 73-156

DOEHRING, Karl, Die allgemeinen Regeln des völkerrechtlichen Fremdenrechts und das deutsche Verfassungsrecht (Köln: Heymanns, 1963). xi + 205 pp.

EEK, H, Om främlingskap (Stockholm: Norstedt, 1955). 208 pp.

ELENA, L, 'Dei diritti della persona straniera secondo la legge italiana', Arch. Quil, vol 57 & 59

FATOU, Raymond, 'Note sur le problème des étrangers en France, et spécialement sur l'inefficacité, les inconvéments et les dangers des mesures d'expulsion non suivies d'exécution effective', Nouvelle Revue de Droit International Privé, vol 1 (1934), pp 143-8

FEBLOWICZ, S, & LAMOUR, Philippe, Le Statut juridique des étrangers en France (Paris: Librairie Science et Littérature, 1938). 508 pp.

FRANZ, F, 'Das Völkerrecht als Quelle des innerdeutschen Aufenthalts- und Niederlassungrechts der Fremden', Deutsches Verwaltungsblatt (1965), pp 457-67

FRASER, C F, Control of Aliens in the British Commonwealth of Nations (London: The Hogarth Press, 1940). 304 pp.

FRISCH, W, Das Fremdenrecht (Berlin, 1910)

GIBSON, William Marion, Aliens and the Law (Chapel Hill, NC: University of North Carolina Press, 1940). xvii + 200 pp.

GUIDI, 'Espulsione respulsione e internamento di stranieri', in Enciclopedia giuridica, vol 3 (1911), p 336

HAMBRO, E, Norwegian Law of Aliens (Oslo, 1950)

HAMBRO, E, Norsk fremmedrett (Oslo: Gyldendal, 1950). 238 pp.

HAMBRO, E, 'Brief summary of Nordic treaty law concerning the position of aliens', Jus gentium (Denmark), vol 1 (1949), pp 340-58

HEALY, T H, 'La condition juridique de l'étranger spécialement aux Etats-Unis', Acad. Droit Int. Recl. Cours, vol 27 (1929), pp 401-96

ISAY, H, Das deutsche Fremdenrecht (Berlin, 1923)

JEMOLO, A C, 'L'espulsione delle straniero', Foro italiano (1952), p 108

KOBARG, W, Ausweisung und Abweisung von Ausländern (Berlin, 1930)

LADAME, Paul, A, Le Rôle des migrations dans le monde libre (Geneve/Paris, 1958). xvi + 525 pp.

LUSENA, C, Diritto di espulsione degli stranieri (Firenze, 1891)

MARTINI, Alexis, L'Expulsion des étrangers (Paris: Sirey, 1909). xxv + 370 pp.
MONZANI, M, Il diritto di espellere gli stranieri (Modena, 1899)
ROTH, Andreas Hans, The Minimum Standard of International Law Applied to Aliens (Lciden: Sijthoff, 1949). 194 pp.
SCHÄTZEL, D, 'Les limites à la souveraineté de l'état en matière d'immigration et de naturalisation', Integration, vol 4 (1957), pp 52-65
STEINBACH, Peter A, Untersuchungen zum Internationalen Fremdenrecht (Bonn/Köln: Röhrscheid, 1931). 134 pp.
STOERK, F, 'Staatsuntertanen und Fremde', in Holtzendorff Handbuch, vol 2, p 637
VERDROSS, A von, 'Les règles internationales concernant le traitement des étrangers', Acad. Droit Int. Recl. Cours, vol 37 (1931), pp 323-412

7.12.14 NATIONALITY

It is often important to establish the nationality of a person in order to ascertain whether he may enjoy the rights of an alien (and according to many writers these rights surpass the human rights enjoyed by a citizen) and also the protection of the diplomats of his home state. I have included the question of nationality in this section although it has, naturally, also other and different implications.
BAR-YAACOV, Nissim, Dual Nationality (London: Stevens, 1961). xxvii + 297 pp.
LAPENNA, Ernesto, La Cittadinanza nel diritto internazionale generale (Milano: Dott A Giuffré, 1966). 226 pp.
MAKAROV, Aleksandr Nikolaevich, Allegemeine Lehren des Staatsangehörigkeitsrechts (Stuttgart: Kohlhammer, 1947). 397 pp.

MAKAROV, A N, 'Règles générales du droit de la nationalité', Acad. Droit Int. Recl. Cours, vol 74 (1947), pp 269-378

MASSFELLER, Franz, Deutsches Staatsangehörigkeitsrecht von 1870 bis zur Gegenwart, 2nd edition (Frankfurt am Main/Berlin: Metzner, 1955). 455 pp.

MEIER, B, Der Staatsangehörige und seine Rechte, insbesondere seine Vermögensrechte, im System des Völkerrechts. Studie über die dogmatische Berechtigung und Auswirkung wirtschaftsrechtlicher Vorstellungen in den Gedankengängen des Völkerrechts (Jena, 1927)

PANHUYS, H F van, The Role of Nationality in International Law (Leiden: Sijthoff, 1955). 256 pp.

PARRY, C, Nationality and Citizenship Laws of the Commonwealth and of the Republic of Ireland (London: Stevens, 1957-60). 2 vols

PARRY, Clive, 'The duty to recognise foreign nationality laws', Z. Ausl. Öff. Recht & Völkerrecht, vol 19 (1958), pp 337-68

PFEIFFER, C, Das Problem der effektiven Staatsangehörigkeit (Leipzig, 1933)

QUADRI, R, La sudditanza nel diritto internazionale (Padova, 1936)

SCERNI, G, Sulla espulsione del territorio dello stato', in Scritti di onore di Tomasso Perassi (Milano, 1957). 161 pp.

SCHÄTZEL, W, 'Die Staatsangehörigkeit der politischen Flüchtlinge', Arch. Völkerrechts, vol 5 (1955), pp 63-79

SCHATZEL, Walter, 'De-facto-Staatsangehörigkeit und De-facto-Staatenlosigkeit', in Völkerrecht und rechtliches Weltbild, (1960), pp 217-27

WEIS, P, Nationality and Statelessness in International Law (London: Stevens, 1956). xxviii + 338 pp.

WEIS, P, Staatsangehörigkeit und Staatenlosigkeit im gegenwärtigen Völkerrecht (Berlin: De Gruyter, 1962). iv + 28 pp.

ZVENKO, R Rode, 'Dual nationality and the doctrine of dominant nationality', Am. J. Int. Law, vol 53 (1959), pp 142-3
See also
HECKER, Gottfried, Der völkerrechtliche Wohnsitzbegriff; Untersuchungen in Anknüpfung an den griechisch-türkischen Streit über den Bevolkerungsaustausch (Wurzburg/Bavaria, 1930). xviii + 87 pp.

7.12.15 PASSPORTS

BISCOTTINI, G, 'Il passaporto e la sua natura giuridica', in Scritti in onore di Perassi (Milano, 1957), vol 1, p 199
DIPLOCK, W J K, 'Passports and protection in international law', Grotius Soc. Trans., vol 32 (1947)
GARGAS, S, Das internationale Passproblem (Den Haag, 1927)
GORMLEY, W Paul, The Procedural Status of the Individual before International and Supranational Tribunals (Den Haag: Nijhoff, 1966). 206 pp.
MAULL, H, Die rechtliche natur des Reisepass (München, 1930)
REALE, E, 'Le problème des passeports', Acad. Droit Int. Recl. Cours, vol 10 (1934), p 89
TURACK, Daniel C, The Passport in International Law (Lexington, Mass: Lexington Books/London: D C Heath, 1972)
VALLOTON, G, Le Passeport (Lausanne, 1933)
WEHBERG, H, Das Passwesen (Gladbach, 1923)

7.12.16 PROTECTION OF NATIONALS

See under 'diplomatic protection' (Section 7.11.1.2) and also, for protection by forces

OFFNUTT, Milton, The Protection of Citizens abroad by the Armed Forces of the United States (Baltimore, Md: Johns Hopkins Press, 1928). 170 pp.

7.12.17 STATELESSNESS

FRANÇOIS, J P A, 'Le problème des apatrides', Acad. Droit Int. Recl. Cours, vol 53 (1935), pp 288-376
KUHN, A K, 'International measures for the relief of stateless persons', Am. J. Int. Law, vol 30 (1936), pp 495-9
LESSING, Hans, La obligación internacional de admisión de apatridas (Buenos Aires: Impr. de la Universidad, 1944). 73 pp.
RAESTAD, A, 'Statsløse personer og deres rettsstilling', Nord. Tidsskr. Int. Ret, vol 5 (1934), pp 177-90
RAESTAD, Arnold, 'Les apatrides ("statsløse") et leur condition légale', Acta scandinavica juris gentium, vol 6 (1935), pp 57-72
RAESTAD, Arnold, Statut juridique des apatrides et des réfugiés (Bruxelles, 1936)
ROBINSON, N, Convention relating to the Status of Stateless Persons. Its History and Interpretation: A Commentary (New York: Institute of Jewish Affairs, 1955). iv + 161 pp.
SCELLE, Georges, 'Le problème de l'apatridie devant la Commission du droit international de l'ONU', Die Friedens-Warte, vol 52 (1953-5), pp 142-53
SCHEFTEL, J, 'L'apatridie des réfugiés russes', J. Droit Int., vol 61 (1934), pp 36-69
TRACHTENBERG, B, 'La situation des apatrides', Revue de droit international privé, vol 28 (1933), pp 588-619
TRACHTENBERG, B, 'L'expulsion des apatrides', Rev. Droit Int. & Légis. Comp., vol 63 (1936), pp 552-63

WEIS, P, 'Convention relating to the status of stateless persons', Int. & Comp. Law Q., vol 10 (1961), pp 255-64

WEIS, P, 'The United Nations convention on the reduction of statelessness, 1961', Int. & Comp. Law Q., vol 11 (1962), pp 1073-96

7.12.18 REFUGEES

See also Section 7.12.13 on treatment of aliens. A comprehensive treatment of the subject is the recent work by GRAHL-MADSEN, listed below.

AUDINET, Eugène, 'Les Heimatloses et leur condition juridique', J. Droit Int. (1925), pp 882-96

BALOGH, Elemer, 'World peace and the refugee problem', Acad. Droit Int. Recl. Cours, vol 75 (1949), pp 363-507

BENTWICH, Norman, The Refugees from Germany April 1933 to December 1935 (London: George Allen & Unwin, 1936). 228 pp.

CAPPELLI, Fiorella, 'La convenzione del 28 luglio 1951 relativa allo statuto del rifugiati', Roma Università degli studi di Roma, Facultà di Giurisprudenza (academic year 1959/60). 257 pp (typescript)

CASSESE, Antonio, 'Sul soggiorno del rifugiato politico in Italia', Riv. Diritto Int., vol 42 (1959), pp 653-61

FIELDS, Harold, The Refugee in the United States (New York: Oxford University Press, 1938). xii + 229 pp.

FLORY, Maurice, Le Statut international des gouvernements réfugiés et le cas de la France libre 1939-1945 (Paris: Pédone, 1952). xi + 311 pp.

FRANZ, F, 'Der Asylfall Geza Györfi und die Flüchtlingsregelung im Ausländerpolizeirecht', Juristische Rundschau (1964), pp 81-7

FRINGS, Paul, Das internationale Flüchtlingsproblem 1919-1950 (Frankfurt am Main: Frankfurter Hefte, 1951). 295 pp + tables

GOY, Raymond, 'La jurisprudence française sur la qualité de réfugié', Annu. Fr. Droit Int. (1961), pp 943-57

GRAHL-MADSEN, A, The Status of Refugees in International Law (Leiden: Sijthoff, 1966-72). 2 vols

GRAHL-MADSEN, A, 'Commentary on the refugee convention 1951', (Genève, 1963). Typescript.

GUILLEMINET, Raymond, La Notion de réfugié statutaire (Lyon: Université, 1958). xiv + 329 pp.

HAMBRO, E, The Problem of Chinese Refugees in Hong Kong (Leiden: Sijthoff, 1955). x + 214 pp.

HAMRELL, Sven, (ed), Refugee Problems in Africa (Uppsala, The Scandinavian Institute of African Studies, 1967). 123 pp.

HANSSON, Michael, Flyktningsproblemet og Folkeforbundet (Oslo: Cammermeyer, 1938). 32 pp.

HEUVEN-GOEDHART, G J van, 'The work of the United Nations High Commissioner for Refugees', Interpreter Releases, vol 30 (1953), pp 314-25

HEUVEN-GOEDHART, G J van, 'The problem of Refugees', Acad. Droit Int. Recl. Cours, vol 82 (1953), pp 261-371

HOLBORN, L W, 'The legal status of political refugees, 1920-1938', Am. J. Int. Law, vol 32 (1938), pp 680-703

HOLBORN, L W, 'The United Nations and the refugee problem', Yearb. World Aff., vol 6 (1952), pp 124-48

HOLBORN, Louise Wilhelmine, The International Refugee Organization (London: Oxford University Press, 1956). xiv + 805 pp.

HSU, Fu-yung, La protection des réfugiés par la Société des Nations, (Lyon: Bosc Frères (Riou), 1935) 157 pp.

JAHN, Eberhard, 'The work of the Asian-African Legal Consultative Committee on the legal status of refugees', Z. Ausl. Öff. Recht & Volkerrecht, vol 27 (1967), pp 122-38

JENNINGS, R Y, 'Some international law aspects of the refugee questions', Br. Yearb. Int. Law, vol 20 (1939), pp 98-114

JOKSIMOVIC, Ilija, Le Statut juridique des réfugiés politiques et des apatrides selon le nouveau droit international (Paris, 1951). 282 pp.

KIMMINICH, O, Der internationale Rechtsstatus des Flüchtlings (Köln: Heymann, 1962). 492 pp.

KRENZ, F E, 'The refugee as subject of international law', Int. & Comp. Law Q., vol 15 (1966), p 90

LACHAZE, Marcel, Les étrangers dans le droit public français (Paris: Dalloz, 1928). Also published under the title: Du status juridique de l'étranger au regard du droit public français

LAFITTE, F, The Internment of Aliens (Harmondsworth: Penguin, 1940). 256 pp.

LANGROD, G, 'La charte du réfugié politique', Revue politique et parlementaire, vol 57 (1955), pp 276-85

LEIBHOLZ, G, 'Die völkerrechtliche Stellung der "Refugees" im Kriege', Arch. Völkerrechts, vol 2 (1949), pp 129-59

LINDT, August R, 'Le Haut-Commissariat des Nations Unies pour les réfugiés et son oeuvre', Revue internationale de la Croix rouge, vol 41 (1959), pp 435-53

MAKAROV, A N, 'Das internationale Flüchtlingsrecht und die Rechtsstellung heimatloser Ausländer nach dem Bundesgesetz vom 25. April 1951', Z. Ausl. Öff. Recht & Völkerrecht, vol 14 (1952), pp 431-62

MELANDER, Göran, Flyktingar och asyl (Stockholm: Norstedt, 1972). 275 pp.

MÜLLER, Edward J, Grundzüge der Stellung des Flüchtlings im geltenden Völkerrecht (Fribourg, Paulusdruckerei, 1952). xii + 63 pp.

NATHAN-CHAPOTOT, Roger, Les Nations Unies et les réfugiés (Paris: Pédone, 1949). Also published under the title: La qualification internationale des réfugiés et personnes déplacées dans le cadre des Nations Unies

POULIN, G, 'Le problème des réfugiés', Schweiz. Jahrb. Int. Recht, vol 3 (1946), pp 95-196

PROUDFOOT, Malcolm Jarvis, European Refugees 1939-52 (London: Faber & Faber, 1957). 542 pp.

READ, J M, 'The United Nations and refugees: changing concepts', Int. Conciliation, no 537 (1962), p 60

REUT-NICOLUSSI, E, 'Displaced persons in international law', Acad. Droit Int. Recl. Cours, vol 2 (1948), p 65

ROGGE, Heinrich, 'Das Flüchtlingsproblem als international Rechtsfrage', Int. Recht & Dipl. (1958), pp 28-41; 236-41

SALOMON, R, Les Réfugiés (Paris, 1963)

SARRAUTE, R, & TAGER, P, 'Le nouveau statut international des réfugiés; Convention de Genève du 28 juillet 1951', Revue critique de droit international privé, vol 42 (1953), pp 245-87

SCHÄTZEL, Walter, & VEITER, Theodor, (eds), Handbuch des internationalen Flüchtlingsrechts (Wien/Stuttgart: Braumüller, 1960). viii + 372 pp.

SCHECTMAN, J B, The Refugees in the World: Displacement and Integration (New York: Barnes, 1962)

SCHNYDER, Felix, 'Les aspects juridiques actuels du problème des réfugiés', Acad. Droit Int. Recl. Cours, vol 115 (1965), pp 335-450

SCHÜLER, Alfred, 'Zum Begriff des Fluchtlings in 160 BEG', Rechtssprechung zur Wiedergutmachung (1965), pp 147-50

SCHWARZ, Leo W, Refugees in Germany Today (New York: Twayne, 1957). 172 pp.
SEIDL-HOHENVELDERN, Ignaz, 'Die internationale Flüchtlingskonvention von 1951 in der Praxis', in Internationalrechtliche und staatsrechtliche Abhandlugen (1960), pp 441-52
SIMPSON, John Hope, The Refugee Problem (London: Oxford University Press, 1939). xv + 637 pp.
SMALL, J M, 'Quelques aspects du problème des jeunes réfugiés', Revue internationale de l'enfant (1959), pp 85-100
STEDINGK, Yvonne von, Die Organisation des Flüchtlingswesens in Österreich seit dem Zweiten Weltkrieg (Wien: Braumüller, 1970). vii + 160 pp.
THOMASHEFSKY, Joseph M, The Development of International Protection of Refugees (New York: University, 1949). 111 pp.
TREMEAUD, H, 'Les réfugiés sous mandat du Haut Commissaire des Nations Unies', Rev. Gen. Droit Int. Public, vol 63 (1959), pp 478-506
VEITER, Theodor, & KLEIN, Friedrich, (eds), Die Menschenrechte: Entwicklung, Stand, Zukunft: mit besonderer Berücksichtigung des Flüchtlingsrechts in den wichtigsten Flüchtlingsaufnahmestaaten (Wien: Braumüller, 1966). vii + 406 pp.
VERNANT, Jacques, The Refugee in the Post-War World (London: George Allen & Unwin, 1953). xvi + 827 pp.
Vertreibung, Zuflucht, Heimat, Expulsion, Refuge, Domicile (Wien: Braumüller, 1962). 231 pp.
WEIS, P, 'Legal aspects of the convention of 28 July 1951 relating to the status of refugees', Br. Yearb. Int. Law, vol 30 (1953), pp 478-89
WEIS, P, 'Die Genfer Flüchtlingskonvention vom 28. Juli 1951', Jahrb. Int. & Ausl. Öff. Recht, vol 4 (1954), pp 53-62
WEIS, P, 'The international protection of refugees', Am. J. Int. Law, vol 48 (1954), pp 193-221

WEIS, P, 'Le statut international des réfugiés et apatrides', J. Droit Int. (1956), p 3

WEIS, P, 'The Hague agreement relating to refugee seamen', Int. & Comp. Law Q., vol 7 (1958), pp 334-48

WEIS, P, 'The concept of the refugee in international law', J. Droit Int., vol 87 (1960), pp 928-1001. Also published separately as UN Doc. HCR/INF/49, Geneve 1961

WEIS, P, 'Human rights and refugees', Lecture given at Yale University Law School 7 November 1967. UN Doc MHCR/14/68

WEIS, P, 'The 1967 protocol relating to the status of refugees and some questions of the law of treaties', Br. Yearb. Int. Law (1967), pp 39-70

WERNER, H, 'Quelques aspects juridiques du problème des réfugiés', Zeitschrift für Schweizerisches Recht, vol 63 (1944), pp 361-93

Zellerbach Commission, European Refugee Problems 1959 (New York, 1959). 96 pp.

ZINK, Karl Friedrich, Das Asylrecht in der Bundesrepublik Deutschland nach dem Abkommen vom 28.Juli 1951 über die Rechtsstellung der Flüchtlinge unter besonderer Berücksichtigung der Rechtssprechung der Verwaltungsgerichte (Nürnberg, 1962). xxi + 259 pp.

ZYPTHEN-ADELER, H, 'Legal and political protection of refugees', Jus Gentium (Denmark), vol 2 (1951), pp 141-64

7.12.19 ASYLUM

For extraterritorial asylum, or diplomatic asylum, see above, Section 7.11.1.3. For modern aspects of asylum see GRAHL-MADSEN's work listed in Section 7.12.1.18, and, also the anthology, Asylrecht als Menschenrechte and the Heilbronn Colloquium listed

below.
ANTALOVSKY, Eugen, 'Das Asylrecht der politischen Flüchtlinge', Integration, vol 4 (1957), pp 9-17
Asylrecht als Menschenrechte: Flüchtlingsfragen im Weltjahr der menschenrechte (ed. T. Veiter). (Vienna: Braumüller 1969) 165 pp.
BAHRAMY, A, Le Droit d'asile (Paris: Rousseau, 1938). 162 pp.
BALDONI, C, 'Studi sull'asilo in diritto internazionale L'asilo sul proprio territorio e sulle navi in alto mare', Archivio di diritto pubblico (1938), p 20
BERGENDAL, Ragnar, 'Krigsförbrytare och asylrätt', Svensk Juristtidning, vol 30 (1957), pp 80-8
BOLESTA-KOZIEBRODZKI, Léopold, Le Droit d'asile (Leiden: Sijthoff, 1962). 374 pp.
CASTRÉN, Erik, 'Asylrätten', Nord. Tidsskr. Int. Ret, vol 16 (1945), pp 7-19
Conférence internationale pour le droit, Paris 1936. Préface de Léon Jouhaux (Paris: Bureau international pour le respect du droit d'asile et l'aide aux réfugiés, 1937). xvi + 168 pp.
DIMITRIJEVIC, Vojin, Utočište na teritoriji strane države-teritorijalni azil (Beograd: Pravni fakultet, 1969). 176 pp.
DOEHRING, K, 'Asylrecht und Statsschutz', Z. Ausl. Öff. Recht & Völkerrecht, vol 26 (1966), pp 33-58
FRANZ, F, Das Asylrecht der politisch verfolgten Fremden nach internationalem und deutschem Recht (Berlin: Ernst Reuter, 1961). 153 pp.
FRANZ, F, 'Asylrecht und Asylverordnung', Deutsche Verwaltungsblatt (1963), pp 125-33
GARCIA-MORA, Manuel R, International Law and Asylum as a Human Right (Washington,DC: Public Affairs Press, 1956). vi + 171 pp.

GRAHL-MADSEN, A, 'The European tradition of
   Asylum and the development of refugee law',
   JPR (1966), pp 278-89
GRAHL-MADSEN, A, 'Asylretten i Norden', Tidsskrift
   for Rettsvitenskap, vol 80 (1967), pp 302-25
GREEN, L C, The Right of Asylum in International
   Law (Singapore: University of Malaya, 1961). 19 pp.
GRÜTZNER, Heinrich, 'Auslieferungsverbot und
   Asylrecht', in Die Grundrechte, vol 2, pp 583-604
HÄFLIGER, Hans, Das Asylrecht nach Völkerrecht und
   nach dem schweizerischen öffentlichen Recht
   (Davos, 1943). vii + 103 pp.
HAMBRO, Edvard, 'Asylrett og utleveringsplikt',
   Tidsskrift for Rettsvitenskap (1960), pp 29-58
HAMBRO, E, 'Auslieferungspflicht und Asylrecht',
   ZGS, vol 73 (1961), pp 657-68
Heilsbronn-Colloquium 1963: Abgelehnte Asylbitten
   (Augsburg: Hofmann-Druck, 1963) Schriftenreihe
   der Deutschen Nansen-Gesellschaft, Heft 3. 122 pp.
HENRICHS, Wilhelm, 'Zum Asylrecht der de-facto-
   Staatenlosen', Integration, vol 4 (1957), pp 29-39
KAMANDA, A M, 'Territorial asylum and the protection
   of political refugees in public international law
   (Genève: Carnegie Endowment, 1971). iv + 242 pp.
   (Mimeographed). (Colloquium on the Law of
   Territorial Asylum, Bellagio, April 13-15 1971)
KIMMINICH, Otto, 'Gibt es immanente Grenzen des
   Asylrechts?' 3rd International Colloquium on
   Asylum 1965 Bochum
KIMMINICH, Otto, 'Zur Theorie der immanenten
   Schranken des Asylrechts', Juristen Zeitung (1965),
   pp 739-45
KIMMINICH, O, Asylrecht (Berlin: Luchterhand,
   1968). 180 pp
KIMMINICH, Otto, 'Asyl in Stutzpunkten der UN-Truppe'
   ZfP (1961), pp 235-40
LAHARMY, Le Droit d'asile (Paris, 1938)

LERCHE, Peter, 'Das Asylrecht ist unverwirkbar', in Festschrift für Adolf Arndt (1972), pp 199-214
METTGENBERG, 'Das politische Asyl und seine Grenzen', Z. Völkerrecht (1932), p 731
MEYER, Heinrich, 'Neues zum Asylrecht', Monatsschrift für Deutsches Recht (1953), pp 534-6
MORENO QUINTANA, L, Derecho de asilo (Buenos Aires, 1952)
MORGENSTERN, Felice, 'The right of asylum', Br. Yearb. Int. Law, vol 26 (1949), pp 327-57
PERASSI, T, 'L'asile en droit international public', Report to the Institut de droit international, 1950
PISANI, G, Delitto politico, estradizione, diritto d'asilo (Washington, 1956)
RAESTAD, A, 'Asylretten', Nord. Tidsskr. Int. Ret, vol 8 (1937), pp 147-59
REALE, Egidio, 'Le droit d'asile', Acad. Droit Int. Recl. Cours, vol 63 (1938), pp 469-601
RECHT, The Right of Asylum (New York, 1935)
SCELLE, G, 'Chronique sur le droit d'asile', Rev. Gén. Droit Int. Public (1913)
SCHAEFFER, Rolf, 'Das Asylrecht in der Bundesrepublik Deutschland', Vereinte Nationen, vol 11 (1963), pp 44-50
SIBLEY, J, 'Le droit d'asile en Angleterre depuis la loi des étrangers', J. Droit Int. (1907), p 29
SINHA, S Prakash, Asylum and International Law (Den Haag: Nijhoff, 1971). xii + 366 pp.
TOBAY, Borgoni, L'asile interne devant le droit international (Paris, 1911)
TURPIN, Jean, Nouveaux Aspects juridiques de l'asile politique: Le Litige hungaro-yougoslave devant la Société des Nations (Paris: Maisonneuve, 1937). 251 pp.
UDINA, M, 'La Dichiarazione delle Nazioni Unite sull' "Asilo Territoriale" ', Communità Internazionale, vol 23, no 2 (1968)

UDINA, Manlio, 'L'asilo politico territoriale nel diritto internazionale e secondo la Costituzione Italiana', Diritto Internazionale, vol 21 (1967), pp 258-72

VEITER, Theodor, (ed), Asylrecht als Menschenrecht: Flüchtlingsfragen im der Menschenrechte (Wien: Braumüller, 1969). viii + 165 pp.

WEIS, P, 'The United Nations declaration on territorial asylum', Can. Yearb. Int. Law (1969), pp 92-149

WEIS, P, 'Recent development in the law of territorial asylum', Revue des Droits de l'Homme, vol 1 (1968), pp 378-96

WEIS, P, 'Territorial asylum', Indian J. Int. Law, vol 6 (1966), pp 173-94

WEIS, P, 'Legal aspects of the problem of asylum', vol 51 (1964), pp 283-93

WEIS, P, 'The right of asylum in the context of the protection of human rights in regional and municipal law', International Review of the Red Cross (1966)

7.12.20 EXTRADITION

See also the work by BAUER under 7.12.3.

CARDOZO, M H, 'When extradition fails is abduction the solution?' Am. J. Int. Law, vol 55 (1961), p 127

CLARKE, E, A Treatise upon the Law of Extradition, and the practice

GREEN, L C, 'Recent practices in the law of extradition', Current Legal Problems, vol 6 (1953), pp 274-96

HAMBRO, E, 'Extradition and asylum: a note', Jahrbuch für internationales Recht, vol 11 (1962), pp 106-13

HAMBRO, E, 'Noen bemerkninger om den nordiske utleveringslov', Stud. Jur. no 5 (1961), pp 9-14

HAMBRO, E, 'New trends in the law of extradition and asylum', The Western Political Quarterly, vol 5 (1952), pp 1-19

Harvard Law School, Research in International Law, 'Extradition, jurisdiction with respect to crime, law of treaties', Am. J. Int. Law, vol 26 (1935), supp

HONIG, F, 'Extradition by multilateral convention', Int. & Comp Law Q., vol 5 (1956), p 549

LAMMASCH, Heinrich, Auslieferungspflicht und Asylrecht (Leipzig: Duncker & Humblot, 1887). xvi + 912 pp.

LAMMASCH, H, Das Recht der Auslieferung wegen politischer Verbrechen (Wien: Manz, 1884). iii + 109 pp.

MERCIER, André, 'L'extradition', Acad. Droit Int. Recl. Cours, vol 33 (1930), pp 167-240

MOORE, J B, A Treatise on Extradition and Interstate Rendition (Boston: Boston Book Co, 1891). 2 vols.

PANHUYS, H F van, 'Le traité d'extradition en tant que source de droits pour les individus', in Le Droit pénal international, pp 57-74

REEVES, J S, 'Extradition treaties and the death penalty', Am. J. Int. Law, vol 18 (1924), p 298

ROLIN, Alberic, Baron, 'Quelques questions rélatives à l'extradition', Acad. Droit Int. Recl. Cours, vol 1 (1923), pp 177-227

SHEARER, I A, Extradition in International Law (Manchester: Manchester University Press/Dobbs Ferry, NY: Oceana, 1971). xxiii + 283 pp.

7.13 LAW OF TREATIES

On the vast subject of the law of treaties there are numerous treatises, both of the subject as a whole and of particular issues. The works by Lord McNAIR are, to the English speaking reader, of basic importance.

There is recent work by Professor Reuter to which I
may draw attention as, in spite of its deceivingly modest
title, it constitutes one of the most outstanding contributions to international law. It is not possible to
study the subject in any depth without reference to the
work of the International Law Commission, see Section
1.1.

7.13.1 LAW OF TREATIES: HISTORY

See also the work by Oliver listed in Section 7.13.2.

BETTANINI, A M, Introduzione allo studio della
 storia dei trattati (Padova: Cedam, 1944)
GEMMA, S, Storia dei trattati e degli atti diplomatici
 europei dal congresso di Vienna (1815) ai giorni
 nostri, revised edition (Firenze, Barbera, 1949).
 viii + 507 pp.
NAVA, S, Lezioni di storia dei trattati e politica
 internazionale (Firenze: Soc. an. editrice
 universitaria, 1944). 274 pp.
OLIVER, C T, 'Historical development of international
 law: contemporary problems of treaty law', Acad.
 Droit Int. Recl. Cours (1955), vol 2, pp 417-50
RAPISARDI-MIRABELLI, A, Storia dei trattati e delle
 relazioni internazionali (Milano: Istituto per gli
 studi di politica internazionale, 1940). 381 pp.
RAY, J, 'La communauté internationale d'après les
 traités du XVIe siècle à nos jours', Annales
 sociologiques, ser C, 3, pp 14-49
ROUSSEAU, C, La Théorie générale des traités internationaux (Cours de droit international rédigé
 d'après les notes et avec l'autorisation de C
 Rousseau) (Paris: Les Cours de droit, 1959). 345 pp.
VEDOVATO, G, La competenza a stipulare i trattati
 nella storia delle relazioni internazionali (Firenze:
 Le Monnier, 1939). 166 pp.

ZEMANEK, K, 'Die Entwicklung des völkerrechtlichen Vertragrechtes', Österr. Z. Öff. Recht, vol 6 (1954), pp 378-98

7.13.2 LAW OF TREATIES IN GENERAL

AGO, R, 'Droit des traités à la lumière de la Convention de Vienne, Introduction', Acad. Droit Int. Recl. Cours, vol 139 (1971), pp 297-332
BITTNER, Ludwig, Die Lehre von den völkerrechtlichen Vertragsurkunden (Berlin/Leipzig, 1924)
DETTER, Ingrid, Essays on the Law of Treaties (London: Sweet & Maxwell/Stockholm: Norstedts, 1967)
FRANGULIS, A F, Théorie et pratique des traités internationaux (Paris: Académie diplomatique internationale, 1934). iv + 208 + ciii pp. Académie diplomatique internationale séances et travaux, vol 8, nos 2, 3 & 4
HARASZTI, G, Some Fundamental Problems of the Law of Treaties (Budapest: Akadémiai Kiadó, 1973). 439 pp.
HOIJER, O, Les Traités internationaux (Paris: Editions internationales, 1928). 2 vols.
JESSUP, P C, 'Modernization of the law of international contractual agreements', Am. J. Int. Law, vol 41 (1947), p 378
KELSEN, H, 'Contribution à la théorie du traité international', Revue internationale de la théorie du droit, vol 10 (1936), pp 253-92
McNAIR, A D, The Law of Treaties (Oxford: Clarendon Press, 1961)
MARESCA, A, Il diritto dei trattati. La convenzione codificatrice di Vienna 23 maggio 1969 (Milano: Giuffré, 1971). 895 pp.
METALL, R A, 'Quelques observations sur la théorie du traité international', Archives de philosophie du droit et de sociologie jur., vol 10 (1940), pp 186-94

OLIVER, C T, 'Historical development of international law: Contemporary problems of treaty law', Acad. Droit Int. Recl. Cours, vol 2 (1955), p 417
READ, J E, 'International agreements', The Canadian Bar Review, vol 26 (1948), pp 520-32
REUTER, Paul, Introduction au droit des traités (Paris: Librairie Armand Colin, 1972). 236 pp.
ROSENNE, Shabtai, The Law of Treaties. A Guide to the Legislative History of the Vienna Convention (Leiden: Sijthoff/Dobbs Ferry, NY: Oceana, 1970). 443 pp.
SURSALOV, V M, Osnovnye voprosy teorii mezhdunarodnogo dogovora/Theoretical Basic Question on Treaties (Moscow, 1959)
SIBERT, M, Les Traités internationaux (Cours de droit international public rédigé d'après les notes et avec l'autorisation de M Sibert) (Paris: Les Cours de droit, 1953). 184 pp.
THOMAS, Ann van Wynen, & THOMAS, A J, Jr, International Treaties (Den Haag, 1950)
TRISKA, J F, & SLUSSER, R M, The Theory, Law and Policy of Soviet Treaties (Stanford, Calif: Stanford University Press, 1962). 608 pp.
VITTA, E, Studi sui trattati (Torino: Giappichelli, 1958). 100 pp.
YEPÈS, J M, 'Le droit des traités', Rev. Droit Int. Sci. Dipl. & Polit., vol 32 (1954), pp 135-92

7.13.3 DEFINITION OF TREATIES

BRANDON, M, 'Analysis of the terms "treaty" and "international agreement" for purposes of registration under article 102 of the United Nations charter', Am. J. Int. Law, vol 47 (1953), pp 49-69
BUSTAMENTE Y SIRVEN, A S De, 'Définition des traités', in Mélanges Streit, vol 1 (1939), pp 113-20
FENWICK, C G, 'When is a treaty not a treaty?' Am. J. Int. Law, vol 46 (1952), p 296

JONES, J M, 'International agreements other than "inter-state treaties" - modern developments', Br. Yearb. Int. Law (1944), p 111

MYERS, D P, 'The names and scope of treaties', Am. J. Int. Law, vol 51 (1957), pp 574-605

RAPISARDI-MIRABELLI, A, 'La classification des traités internationaux', Rev. Droit Int. & Légis. Comp., ser 3, vol 4 (1923), p 653

7.13.4 CLASSIFICATION OF TREATIES

See also Section 7.13.5.3 on law-making treaties.

DECLEVA, M, Rapporti e coordinamento fra i trattati internazionali (Pubblicazioni dell'Instituto di dir. internazionale e leg. comp. della Università di Triesta, 1949, no 18). Also in Annali triestini (1949), pp 151-99

DEHAUSSY, J, Le problème de la classification des traités et le projet de la convention établi par la commission du droit international des Nations Unies, (Mélanges Guggenheim, Genève 1968), p 308

RAPISARDI-MIRABELLI, Andrea, 'La classification des traités internationaux', Rev. Droit Int. & Legis Comp., ser 3, vol 4 (1923), p 653

7.13.5 NATURE AND FUNCTION OF TREATIES

7.13.5.1 GENERAL

ALLEN, F E, The Treaty as an Instrument of Legislation (New York, 1952)

CHAILLEY, P, La Nature juridique des traités internationaux (Paris, 1932)

FAWCETT, J E S, 'The legal character of international agreements', Br. Yearb. Int. Law (1953), pp 381-400

GIHL, T, International Legislation (Uppsala, 1937)

HOULARD, M, La Nature juridique des traités internationaux et son application au théories de la nullité, de la caducité et de la révision des traités (Bordeaux: Delmas, 1936). 159 pp.

KRAUS, H, 'Système et fonctions des traités internationaux', Acad. Droit Int. Recl. Cours, vol 4 (1934), p 311

MARCOVITCH, L, 'L'ONU et le vote des lois internationales', Rev. Gén. Droit Int. Public, vol 57 (1951), pp 55-72

McNAIR, A D, 'The functions and different legal character of treaties', Br. Yearb. Int. Law, vol 11 (1930), p 100

NISOT, J, 'Des clauses juridiquement superflues dans les traités internationaux', Rev. Droit Int. & Legis. Comp.(1938)

WRIGHT, Q, 'The legal nature of treaties', Am. J. Int. Law, vol 10 (1916), p 706

7.13.5.2 CHARACTER OF MULTILATERAL TREATIES

JENKS, C W, 'Les instruments internationaux à caractere collectif', Acad. Droit Int. Recl. Cours, vol 3 (1939), pp 448-553

LACHS, M, 'Les conventions multilatérales et les organisations internationales contemporaines', Annu. Fr. Droit Int. (1956), pp 334-42

LACHS, M, 'Le développement et les fonctions des traités multilatéraux', Acad. Droit Int. Recl. Cours, vol 2 (1957), pp 229-341

LACHS, M, 'Evolutionen des Kollektivvertrages. Wandlungen und Änderungen Kollektivnormen', Jahrb. Int. Recht, vol 8 (1959), pp 23-34

LERICHE, A, 'Quelques réflexions sur l'adoption et la conclusion des accords multilatéraux deposes auprès du secrétaire général de l'Organisation des Nations Unies', Revue de droit international pour le Moyen-Orient, vol 3 (1954), pp 254-65

LERICHE, A, 'L'évolution récente de la société internationale et les traités multilatéraux', Rev. Droit Int. Sci. Dipl. & Polit., vol 29 (1951), pp 16-37

SYDOW, G de, 'De la conclusion et la rédaction des traités collectifs', Acta scandinavica juris gentium, vol 21 (1951), pp 83-101

WALSH, Thomas J, The Multilateral Treaty (Washington, 1929)

7.13.5.3 LAW-MAKING TREATIES

On earlier discussion of the classification of treaties according to their material contents into 'traités-lois' and 'traités-contrats', see also the works on classification above in Section 7.13.4 and general textbooks by French writers like ROUSSEAU and SCELLE under Section 1.8.

REGLADE, M, 'De la nature juridique des traités internationaux et du sens de la distinction des traités-lois et des traités-contrats', Rev. Droit Public & Sci. Polit., vol 31 (1924), pp 505-40

7.13.5.4 RIGHT OF PARTICIPATION IN COLLECTIVE TREATIES

LUKASHUK, I I, 'Parties to treaties - the right of participation', Acad. Droit Int. Recl. Cours, vol 135 (1972), pp 231-328

SCHACHTER, O, NAWAZ, M, & FRIED, J, Towards Wider Acceptance of UN Treaties. A UNITAR Study (New York: Arno Press, 1971). 190 pp.

7.13.5.5 REGIONAL TREATIES

FREYTAGH-LORINGHOVEN, A von, 'Les ententes régionales', Acad. Droit Int. Recl. Cours, vol (1936), p 585

KREZDORN, F J, 'Les Nations Unies et les accords régionaux'. Thesis. Speyer am Rhein, 1954

PORDEA, G A, 'Pactes régionaux et sécurité collective. Article écrit pour honorer la mémoire de V Vespasien Pella', Rev. Droit Int. Sci. Dipl. & Polit., vol 31 (1953), p 412

7.13.5.6 AGREEMENTS IN SIMPLIFIED FORM

BENOIST, J, 'La force obligatoire pour les tribunaux des accords diplomatiques en forme simplifiée', Juris classeur périodique, la semaine juridique XXVI, 13 (27 March 1952)

BORCHARD, E, 'Shall the executive agreement replace the treaty?' Am. J. Int. Law, vol 38 (1944), pp 637-43

BYRD, Elbert M, Jr, Treaties and Executive Agreements in the United States (Den Haag, 1960)

CHAYET, C, 'Les accords en forme simplifiée', Annu. Fr. Droit Int. (1957), pp 3-13

DEVAUX, J, 'La conclusion des traités internationaux en forme s'écartant des règles constitutionnelles et dite "conclusion en forme simplifiée" ', Rev. Int. Fr. Droit Gens., vol 1 (1936), pp 299-309

MARCUS-HELMONS, S, 'Les accords en forme simplifiée et le droit constitutionnel', Annales de droit sociale politique, vol 21 (1961), pp 293-313

ROUSSOS, G, 'Les accords en forme simplifiée en droit international', Rev. Hell. Droit Int., vol 5 (1952), pp 248-55

UDINA, M, 'Gli accordi internazionali in forma
semplificata e la costituzione italiana', in Studi in
onore di Guido Zanobini (Milano 1962), vol 4, pp
467-88
VEICOPOULOS, N, 'Accords internationaux conclus en
forme simplifiée et gentlemen's agreements', Rev.
Droit Int. Sci.Dipl. & Polit., vol 27 (1949), p 162
WEINSTEIN, J L, 'Exchanges of notes', Br. Yearb.
Int. Law (1952), pp 205-26

7.13.5.7   AGREEMENTS WITH
           OTHER THAN STATES

See also Sections 13.4 on treaties of organizations,
14.9 on concessions and economic development agreements, and 14.8 on state contracts.
WENGLER, W, 'Agreements of states with other
parties than states in international relations', Rev.
Hell. Droit Int., vol 8 (1955), pp 113-30 and in
Schriftenreihe (1957), pp 149-64

7.13.5.8   AGREEMENTS WITH PRIVATE-LAW
           SUBJECTS AND STATE CONTRACTS

Note that many lawyers claim that agreements between
states and private-law subjects are never governed by
international law. See Section 14.8 on state contracts,
and Section 14.9 on concessions and economic
development agreements, and Section 4.10 on state loans.

7.13.5.9   CONCORDATS

CATALANO, G, Problematica giuridica dei
concordati (Milano, 1963). 222 pp.
EHLER, S Z, 'The recent concordats', Acad. Droit
Int. Recl. Cours, vol 3 (1961), p 1

KLEYNTJENS, J, 'Les concordats avec les pays
allemands. (Efforts du Saint-Siège en faveur de la
paix)', Rev. Droit Int. Sci. Dipl. & Polit, vol 27
(1949), p 47, 349; vol 28 (1950), p 416
LA BRIERE, Y de, 'Le droit concordataire dans la
nouvelle Europe', Acad. Droit Int. Recl. Cours,
vol 1, (1938), p 367
LUCIEN-BRUN, J, 'La politique concordataire de Pie
XII', Annu. Fr. Droit Int. (1955), p 218
LUCIEN-BRUN, J, 'Le problème concordataire en
Allemagne et en Autriche', Annu. Fr. Droit Int
(1958), p 242
RUZE, Robert, 'A propos des trois derniers concordats
du Saint-Siège avec la Lettonie, la Bavière et la
Pologne', Rev. Droit Int. & Légis. Comp., ser 3,
vol 7 (1926), p 5
SALOMON, J, 'La politique concordataire des états
depuis la fin de la deuxième guerre mondiale', Rev.
Gén. Droit Int. Public, vol 59 (1955), p 570
SUY, E, Le Concordat du Reich de 1933 et le droit des
gens. Quelques réflexions sur la question concord-
ataire en Allemagne (Tamise (Belgium): De
Maeyer-De Bock, 1958). v + 90 pp.

7.13.6 THE TIME OF CREATION OF LEGAL BONDS

BERNHARDT, Rudolf, 'Völkerrechtliche Bindungen in
den Vorstadien des Vertragsschlusses', Z. Ausl.
Öff. Recht & Völkerrecht, vol 18 (1957), p 652

7.13.7. THE BINDING CHARACTER OF TREATIES
AND THE RULE PACTA SUNT SERVANDA

See Section 2.3 on the nature of international law and
Section 17.13.11.2 on breaches, and Section 11 on
responsibility.

ADAMKIEWICZ, W, 'Pacta sunt servanda'. Conference (Third international) of the legal profession, 1950
BERNHARDT, R, 'Völkerrechtliche Bindungen in den Vorstadien des Vertragsschlusses', Z. Ausl. Öff. Recht & Völkerrecht, vol 18 (1958), pp 652-90
C. (A M), 'Le fondement du respect des traités et les motifs de la crise des traités', Rev. Droit Int. Sci. Dipl. & Polit., vol 20 (1942), pp 177-86
KEITH, A B, 'The sanctity of treaties', Czechoslovak Yearbook of International Law (1942), pp 104-28
KUNZ, J L, 'The meaning and the range of the norm pacta sunt servanda', Am. J. Int. Law, vol 39 (1945), pp 180-97
LE FUR, L, 'La force obligatoire des traités', Archives de philosophie du droit et de sociologie jur., vol 10 (1940), pp 85-109
MAHADEVAN, T M P, 'Kautilya on the sanctity of pacts', Indian Yearbook of International Affairs (1956), pp 342-9
NISOT, J, 'La force obligatoire des traités signés, non encore ratifiés', J. Droit Int., vol 57 (1930), p 873
PADOUX, G, 'The binding force of treaties', The Chinese Social and Political Science Review, vol 7 (1922), pp 94-116
PAPACOSTAS, B G, 'Le principe "pacta sunt servanda" et l'organisation des Nations Unies', Rev. Hell. Droit Int., vol 6 (1953), pp 231-8
RICE, W G, & MAYDA, J, 'Some thoughts on the binding force of international treaties', Wisconsin Law Review, 1956, no 2, pp 186-95
SHURSHALOV, V M, 'Juridical content of the principle pacta sunt servanda and its realization in international relations', Sov. Ezheg. Mezhdunar. Prava (1958), pp 150-68. In Russian with an English summary

SHURSHALOV, V M, 'Der juristische Inhalt des
Prinzips pacta sunt servanda und seine Verwirklichung in den internationalen Beziehungen', in
Gegenwartsprobleme des Völkerrechts (Berlin, 1962),
pp 132-51

SIBERT, M, 'Le principe "pacta servanda" à partir du
Moyen Age jusqu'aux débuts des temps modernes',
The Indian Yearbook of International Affairs (1956),
pp 38-45

SIDJANSKI, D, & CASTANOS, S, 'De la clause "pacta
sunt servanda" ', Rev. Droit Int. Sci. Dipl. & Polit.,
vol 31 (1953), pp 299-306

STINSON, J W, 'La sanction du droit des gens et la
force obligatoire des traités', Rev. Droit Int. &
Légis. Comp., ser 3, vol 5 (1924), p 425

TAUBE, M de, 'L'inviolabilité des traités', Acad.
Droit Int. Recl. Cours, vol 2 (1930), p 291

VERDROSS, A von, 'Der Grundsatz "pacta sunt servanda"
und die Grenze der "guten Sitten" im Völkerrecht',
Z. Öff. Recht, vol 16 (1936), pp 79-86

WEHBERG, H, 'Pacta sunt servanda', Am. J. Int. Law,
vol 53 (1959), p 775

WHITTON, J B, 'La regle "pacta sunt servanda" ',
Acad. Droit Int. Recl. Cours, vol 3 (1934), p 147

WILD, P S, Jr, 'Treaty sanctions', Am. J. Int. Law,
vol 26 (1932), p 488

7.13.8 CONCLUSION OF TREATIES

7.13.8.1 CONCLUSION OF TREATIES AND
TREATY-MAKING POWER IN GENERAL

Cf. Section 6.1 on personality in general and Section
13.7 on personality of organisations. See also Section
13.14 on treaty-making power of organisations,
13.24.2.6 (UN), 13.24.2.24.12 (UNESCO), and
13.24.3.12.14 (European Countries).

ARNOLD, R, Treaty-making Procedure (Oxford/ London, 1933)

BAILAS, Demetrios, Das Problem der Vertragesschliessung und der vertragsbegrundende Akt (Göttingen, 1962). (Göttinger rechtswissenschaftliche Studien, vol 43)

BABINSKI, L, 'Méthodes de conclusion des traités internationaux', (Rapport au congrès international de droit comparé à la Haye en août 1932), Thémis polonaise, ser 3, vol 7

BALLADORE PALLIERI, G, 'La formation des traités dans la pratique internationale contemporaine', Acad. Droit Int. Recl. Cours, vol 1 (1949), pp 465-545

BASDEVANT, J, 'La conclusion et la rédaction des traités et des instruments diplomatiques autres que les traités', Acad. Droit Int. Recl. Cours, vol 5 (1926), pp 539-642

BASDEVANT, J, & MIRKINE-GUETZEVITCH, B, 'Méthodes de conclusion des traités internationaux', Rev. Droit Int. Sci Dipl. & Polit., vol 11 (1933), pp 210-17

BERNHARDT, R, 'Der Abschluss völkerrechtlicher Verträge im Bundesstaat', Beiträge zum ausländischen öffentlichen Recht und Völkerrecht, no 32 (1957)

BLIX, H, Treaty-making Power (London: Stevens & Sons/New York: Praeger, 1960). 414 pp.

BRANDON, M, 'Final clauses in multilateral conventions', Int. & Comp. Law Q., vol 4 (1951), pp 469-74

CRANDALL, S B, Treaties: Their Making and Enforcement, 2nd edition (Washington 1916)

FAIRMAN, C, 'Competence to bind the state to an international engagement', Am. J. Int. Law, vol 30 (1936), pp 439

HUBER, J, Le Droit de conclure des traités internationaux (Lausanne: Payot, 1951). 171 pp. Thesis. Université de Lausanne, Faculté de droit

JENKS, C W, 'The need for an international legislative drafting bureau', Am. J. Int. Law, vol 39 (1945), p 163

LINDSTEDT, A L, Sammanfattning av de allmänna principerna för traktaträttens olika system (Stockholm, 1950). 27 pp

LUKASHUK, I I, Strouktora i forma mezdhunarodnykh dogovorov (1960). 131 pp. (Moscow)

PALLIERI, C B, 'La formation des traités dans la pratique internationale contemporaine', Acad. Droit Int. Recl. Cours, vol 1 (1949), p 465

PARRY, C, 'Some recent developments in the making of multipartite treaties', Grotius Soc. Trans., vol 36 (1951), pp 149-89

REIFF, H, 'A form book for standard treaty clauses', Am. J. Int. Law, vol 40 (1946), p 640

SABA, H, 'Certains aspects de l'évolution dans la technique des traités et conventions internationales', Rev. Gén. Droit Int. Public, vol 54 (1950), p 417

SPERDUTI, G, Rilevanza internazionale delle dispozioni costituzionale sulla stipulazione dei trattati e suoi limiti. Scritti di diritto internazionale in onore di Tomaso Perassi, vol 2 (1957), pp 301-33

STUYT, A M, 'Inwerkingtreding van verdragen', Themis (1953), 4, pp 387-404

TELDERS, B M, 'Méthodes de conclusion des traités internationaux. Rapport général', Mémoires de l'Académie internationale de droit comparée, vol 2 no 3 (1935), pp 676-81

WILDHABER, L, 'Rechtsvergleichende Bemerkungen zur sogenannten vertragsschliessenden Gewalt', Z S W (86, I Halbband, heft 1), pp 33-62

VISSCHER, Paul de, 'De la conclusion des traités internationaux. Etude de droit constitutionnel comparé et de droit international (Bruxelles: Bruylant, 1943). 294 pp.

ZOTIADES, G B, 'Staatsautonomie und die Grenzen der Vertragsfreiheit im Völkerrecht', Österr. Z. Öff. Recht, vol 17 (1967), pp 90-112

7.13.8.2 COLONIAL CLAUSES

LIANG, Yuen-Li, 'Colonial clauses and federal clauses in United Nations multilateral instruments', Am. J. Int. Law, vol 45 (1951), p 108

7.13.8.3 FEDERAL STATES AND TREATIES

DECOUFLE, A, 'Le clause fédérale dans les traités internationaux', Revue de droit contemporain (December 1958), pp 81-92

GHOSH, R C, Treaties and Federal Constitutions: Their Mutual Impact (Calcutta: World Press, 1961). 343 pp.

HORAK, J N J B, Les Limitations constitutionnelles au pouvoir de traiter dans les régimes fédéraux (Paris, 1957). 119 pp.

HENDRY, J M, Treaties and Federal Constitutions (Washington, 1955)

HOFFMANN, S, 'Système fédéral et accords internationaux. Etats-Unis', Rev. Droit Public & Sci. Polit, vol 59 (1953), pp 21-156

LIANG, Yuen-Li, 'Colonial clauses and federal clauses in United Nations multilateral instruments', Am. J. Int. Law, vol 45 (1951), pp 108-28

LOOPER, R B, ' "Federal state" clauses in multilateral instruments', Br. Yearb. Int. Law (1955/6), pp 162-203

NETTL, J P, 'The treaty enforcement power in federal constitutions', The Canadian Bar Review, vol 28 (1950), pp 1051-70

O'CONNELL, D P, 'Some problems of the interaction of international law and constitutional law in federal states', Grotius Soc. Trans., vol 43 (1957), pp 159-72

TAYLER, W L, Federal States and Labor Treaties. Relations of Federal States to the International Labor Organization. (A study of the origin and application of art 19, par 9, of its constitution) (New York, 1935). 171 pp.

TURLINGTON, E, 'The legal effect of treaties in municipal law; the special position of federal states', Am. Soc. Int. Law Proc. (1951), pp 76-82

7.13.8.4 CONCLUSION OF TREATIES AND THE PRACTICE OF PARTICULAR COUNTRIES

7.13.8.4.1 GREAT BRITAIN

Some of these works have a bearing also on the effect of treaties: see Section 7.13.13.2

DU PLOOY, R A, 'Treaties and inter-governmental agreements between Commonwealth and foreign states and between Commonwealth states inter se, with special reference to the Union of South Africa', Thesis. Köln, 1958. 196 pp.

FAWCETT, J E S, 'Treaty relations of British overseas territories', Br. Yearb. Int. Law (1949), pp 86-107

LEWIS, Malcolm M, 'The treaty-making power of the Dominions', Br. Yearb. Int. Law (1925), p 31

MAENECKE, R, Die rechtliche Stellung der britischen Dominien bein Abschluss internationaler Verträge (Leipzig: Scholl, 1938). xv + 199 pp.

STEWART, R B, 'Treaty-making procedure in the British dominions', Am. J. Int. Law, vol 32 (1938), pp 467-87

STEWART, R B, Treaty Relations of the British Commonwealth of Nations (New York: Macmillan, 1939). 503 pp.

WADE, E C S, & PHILLIPS, G G, Constitutional Law, 8th edition by A W Bradley (London: Longmans, 1970)

7.13.8.4.2 FRANCE

CORAIL, J L, de, 'Le rôle des Chambres en matière de politique extérieure', Rev. Droit Public & Sci. Polit., vol 72 (1956), pp 770-853

HOLLOWAY, K, 'Recent constitutional developments in France: With special reference to the treaty-making power', Ned. Tijdschr. Int. Recht, vol 11 (1964), pp 132-83

PINTO, R, 'La règlementation constitutionnelle de la conclusion des traités internationaux devant la jurisprudence administrative et judiciaire', l'Actualité juridique, Z, 10 (20 October 1954), pp 125-8; 12 (20 December 1954), p 166

ROUSSEAU, Ch, 'La ratification des traités en France depuis 1946', in L'Evolution du droit public: Etudes offertes à Achille Hestre (1956), p 473-92

ROUSSEAU, Ch, 'Le régime actuel de la conclusion et de la publication des traités diplomatique', Travaux du comité français et de droit international privé, 1955, pp 149-75

ROUSSEAU, Ch, 'Le régime actuel de conclusion des traités en France'. La technique et les principes du droit public (Etudes en l'honneur de Georges Scelle) (1950), pp 565-84

ROUSSEAU, Ch, 'Le régime actuel de publication des traités en France', Recueil Dalloz de doctrine, de jurisprudence et de législation, (3 December 1953), pp 169-74

7.13.8.4.3 GERMANY

ABENDROTH, W, 'Die Völkerrechtliche Bindung Gesamtdeutschlands durch Verträge seiner

Staatsfragmente', Gegenwartsprobleme des
internat. Rechtes u. der Rechtsphil (1953), pp 145-
64
BEGRIFF und Wesen des sozialen Rechtsstaates. Die
auswärtige Gewalt der Bundesrepublik, Berichte
von E. Forsthoff, W Grewe, etc. Tagung der
deutschen Staatsrechtslehrer zu Bonn am 15 und 16
Oktober 1953 (Berlin: de Gruyter & Co, 1954). 267
pp. Veröffentlichungen der Vereinigung der
deutschen Staatsrechtslehrer, 12.
BERNHARDT, R, Der Abschluss völkerrechtlicher
Verträge im Bundesstaat. Eine Untersuchung zum
deutschen und ausländischen Bundesstaatsrecht
(Köln/Berlin: Heymann, 1957). 208 pp.
GROSS, G S, 'Völkerrecht und Aussenpolitik nach
dem Bonner Grundgesetz'. Thesis. Mainz, 1954.
107 pp.
HAAS, D, Abschluss und Ratifikation internationaler
Verträge (Allemagne occidentale). Archiv des
öffentlichen Rechts (1953), pp 381-9
KRAUS, H, 'Die Zuständigkeit der Länder der
Bundesrepublik Deutschland zum Abschluss von
Kulturabkommen mit auswärtigen Staaten nach dem
Bonner Grundgesetz', Arch. Völkerrechts, vol 3
(1952), pp 414-27
MEISSNER, H O, Vollmacht und Ratifikation bei
völkerrechtlichen Verträgen nach deutschem Recht
(Göttingen, 1934). 99 pp.
MENZEL, E, 'Die auswärtige Gewalt der Bundes-
republik in der Deutung des Bundesverfassungsgerichts
Arch. Öff. Rechts, vol 79 (1954), pp 326-49
MUENCH, F, 'Droit international et droit interne
d'après la Constitution de Bonn', Rev. Int. Fr.
Droit Géns., vol 19 (1950), pp 5-20
WEBER, W, 'Die Vereinbarkeit des Verteidigungs-
beitrags mit dem Grundgesetz', Arch. Öff. Rechts,
vol 78 (1952), pp 129-48

7.13.8.4.4 BELGIUM

DURIEUX, J, 'La Constitution belge dans l'Europe de demain', Journal des tribunaux (15 March 1953), pp 166-7

MASQUELIN, J, 'La nécessaire révision de l'article 68 de la constitution (belge)', Journal des tribunaux (28 June 1959), pp 433-5

VISSCHER, P de, 'Droit international public - Traité internationaux - Accords en forme simplifiée. - Assentiment parlementaire. - Lois budgétaires', Journal des tribunaux (20 May 1956), pp 339-41

VLIEBERGH, H, 'De l'effet de l'assentiment des chambres aux traités conclus par le roi', Rev. Droit Int. & Droit Comp., vol 28 (1951), pp 7-22

XIIIme Journée Interuniversitaire d'études juridiques. Gand, 30 mai 1953. La revision de la Constitution', Annales de droit et de sciences politiques, vol 13, no 53 (1953), pp 229-330

7.13.8.4.5 ITALY

MONACO, R, 'Die internationalen Verträge und die neue italienische Verfassung', Österr. Z. Öff. Recht, vol 6 (1954), pp 285-302

7.13.8.4.6 NETHERLANDS

DUYNSTEE, F J F M, Grondwetsherziening 1953. De nieuwe bepalingen omtrent de buitenlandse betrekkingen in de grondwet (Deventer: Kluwer, 1954)

ERADES, L, 'Promulgation and publication of international agreements and their internally binding force in the Netherlands', Ned. Tijdschr. Int. Recht, Liber amicorium J P A François (July 1959), pp 93-9

PANHUYS, H F van, 'Pays Bas. La révision récente des dispositions constitutionnelles relatives aux relations internationales', Rev. Droit Public & Sci. Polit., vol 71 (1955), pp 330-56

ZANDEN, J W van der, 'Verdrag gaat voor wet, ook in nationale rechtsbetrekkingen', (Zwolle 1952) Thesis Leiden. Summaries in English and French. xii + 244 pp.

ZIMMERMAN, E, 'Die Neuregelung der auswärtigen Gewalt in der Verfassung der Niederlande', Z. Ausl. Öff. Recht & Völkerrecht, vol 15 (1953), pp 164-218

7.13.8.4.7 SWITZERLAND

BERENSTEIN, A, 'La ratification des conventions internationales du travail et la législation interne (notamment suisse)', Die Friedens-Warte, vol 53 (1956), pp 136-65

FEHLMANN, P R, 'Der Beitritt der Schweiz zu einer Weltorganisation für kollektive Sicherheit als verfassungsrechtliches Problem', Thesis. Zürich 1951. 103 pp.

GUGGENHEIM, P, Staatsverträge (Genève, 1942)

LOOPER, R B, 'The treaty power in Switzerland', Am. J. Comp. Law, vol 7 (1958), pp 178-94

RICE, W G, 'The position of international treaties in Swiss law', Am. J. Int. Law, vol 46 (1952), pp 641-66

TRINKLER, B, 'Der Abschluss von Staatsverträgen in der Schweiz', Thesis. Muri-Bern 1954. v + 87 pp.

ZUMSTEIN, H, Die staatsrechtliche Beschwerde wegen Verletzung von Staatsverträgen (Zürich: Polygraphischer Verlag, 1952). 163 pp.

7.13.8.4.8 SWEDEN

BLOCH, Joachim-Dieter, Der Abschluss von Staatsverträgen nach schwedischem Recht (Berlin/Leipzig, 1934)
BLOCH, Joachim-Dieter, 'Der Abschluss von Staatsverträgen nach schwedischem Recht', Z. Ausl. Öff. Recht & Völkerrecht, vol 6 (1934), pp 25-52
EEK, H, 'Makten över Utrikes ärendena', Smärre Utredningar Stockholm (1951-4), pp 100-16

7.13.8.4.9 DENMARK

ANDERSON, S V, 'Article twenty of Denmark's new constitution', Am. J. Int. Law, 50 (1956), pp 654-9

7.13.8.4.10 USSR

'Act on the procedure of ratification and denunciation of the international treaties of the USSR', Slavonic Review, vol 27, no 40 (1939), pp 464-5
'Gesetz vom 20.8.1938 betr. Ratifizierung und Kündigung von zwischenstaatlichen Vertragen der USSR', Zeitschrift für osteurop. Recht, new ser, vol 5, no 6 (1938), pp 392-4

7.13.8.4.11 LUXEMBOURG

PESCATORE, P, Conclusion et effet des traités internationaux selon le droit constitutionel, les usages et la jurisprudence du Grand-Duché de Luxembourg (Luxembourg: Office des imprimés de l'état, 1964). 110 pp.

7.13.8.4.12 GREECE

KYRIACOPOULOS, E, 'Le droit international et la constitution hellénique de 1952', Gegenwartsprobleme d. internationalen Rechtes und d. Rechtsphilosophie (1953), pp 201-12

7.13.8.4.13 ISRAEL

LAPIDOTH ESCHELBACHER, Ruth, La Conclusion des traités internationaux en Israël (Paris: Pédone, 1962). 111 pp.

7.13.8.4.14 UNITED STATES

BYRD, E M, Treaties and Executive Agreements in the United States (Den Haag: Nijhoff, 1960). x + 276 pp
CATUDAL, H M, 'How a trade agreement is made (in the United States of America)', The Department of State Bulletin, vol 38, no 964 (1958), pp 286-90
DEAN, A H, 'The Bricker amendment and authority over foreign affairs', Foreign Affairs, vol 32 (1953), p 1-19
DELAUME, G R, 'De l'application et de l'interprétation des traités par les tribunaux internes dans les relations franco-américaines', J. Droit Int., vol 80 (1953), pp 584-635. With English translation.
DULLES, J F, 'The making of treaties and executive agreements', The Department of State Bulletin, vol 28, no 721 (1953), pp 591-5
DULLES, J F, 'US constitution and UN charter: an appraisal', The Department of State Bulletin, vol 29, no 741 (1953), pp 307-10
ELY, R B, III, 'The treaty-making power: The constitutionality of international courts', American Bar Association Journal, vol 36 (1950), pp 738-41; 800-03

FINCH, G A, 'The need to restrain the treaty-making power of the United States within constitutional limits', Am. J. Int. Law, vol 48 (1954), pp 57-82

HERTER, Ch A, 'Relation of the House of Representatives to the making and implementation of treaties', (Followed by discussion). Am. Soc. Int. Law Proc. (1951), pp 55-65

HOFFMANN, S, 'Système féderal et accords internationaux. Etats-Unis', Rev. Droit Public & Sci. Polit., vol 59 (1953), pp 121-56; 374-414; 649-79

LEVITT, A, The President and the International Affairs of the United States (Los Angeles, Calif: Parker & Co, 1954). xi + 87 pp.

MacBRIDE, R L, Treaties versus the Constitution (Caldwell, Idaho: Caxton, 1955). 89 pp.

MacCHESNEY, B, HATCH, V, et al, 'The treaty power and the constitution: the case against amendment', American Bar Association Journal, vol 40 (1954), pp 203-10, 248-60

McCLURE, W, International Executive Agreements: Democratic Procedure under the Constitution of the United States (New York: Columbia University Press, 1941). xxii + 449 pp.

PARK, C S, 'The treaty-making power in the United States', K J I L, vol 8, no 2 (September 1963), pp 377-88

PREUSS, L, On amending the treaty-making power: a comparative study of the problem of self-executing treaties. Michigan Law Review, vol 51 (1953), pp 1117-42

SAVARIT, R, 'Les traités internationaux dans la constitution des Etats-Unis et la proposition d'amendment du senateur Bricker', Rev. Int. Droit Comp., vol 7 (1955), pp 132-43

SCHÖNHERR, K H, 'Die Entrechtung des amerikanischen Senats im treaty-making-verfahren', Staat und Recht, vol 6 (1957), pp 471-85

SURRENCY, E C, 'The treaty law of the United States', Int. & Comp. Law Q., vol 14 (1965), pp 602-12

WHITTON, J B, & FOWLER, J E, 'Bricker amendment - fallacies and dangers', Am. J Int. Law, vol 48 (1954), pp 23-56

WHITTON, J B, 'L'amendement Bricker', Rev. Droit Public & Sci. Polit., vol 70 (1954), pp 714-21

WOOLSEY, L H, 'The new policy regarding United Nations treaties', Am. J. Int. Law, vol 47 (1953), pp 449-51

WORLEY, F, Treaty Law and the Constitution. A Study of the Bricker Amendment (New York/Washington: American Enterprise Association, 1953). 50 pp.

WRIGHT, Q, 'Congress and the treaty-making power', Am. Soc. Int. Law Proc.,(1952), pp 43-69

7.13.8.4.15 AUSTRALIA

DOEKER, G, The Treaty-making Power in the Commonwealth of Australia (Den Haag: Nijhoff, 1966). 279 pp.

7.13.8.4.16 CANADA

FRANCK, T, 'The Bricker amendment in Canada .. a rose-coloured optical illusion', Nebraska Law Review, vol 34 (1954), pp 59-66

GRENON, J Y, 'De la conclusion des traités et de leur mise en oeuvre au Canada', Canadian Bar Review, vol 40, no 2 (May 1962), pp 151-64

SZABLOWSKI, G J, 'Creation and implementation of treaties in Canada', Canadian Bar Review, vol 34 (1956), pp 28-59

7.13.8.4.17   BRAZIL

ACCIOLY, H, 'Suspensão da ratificação dc tratadu internacional', Boletim da Sociedade brasil de dir. internacional, vol 4, no 7 (January-June 1948), pp 164-6
ACCIOLY, H, 'A conclusão de atos internacionais no Brasil', Boletim da Sociedade brasil de dir. internacional, vol 9 (1953), pp 58-63
ACCIOLY, H, 'Ainda o problema da ratificação dos tratados, em face da constituição brasiliera', Boletim da Sociedade brasil de dir. internacional, vol 7 (1951), pp 5-19
CARNEIRO, L, 'Acordos por troca de notas e aprovação pelo congresso nacional', Boletim da Sociedade brasil de dir. internacional, vol 7 (1951), pp 129-42
RANGEL, V M, 'La procédure de conclusion des accords internationaux au Brésil', R F D, vol 55 (1960), pp 153-71

7.13.8.4.18   INDIA AND PAKISTAN

BINDER, L, 'The new constitution of Pakistan and the treaty-making powers', Pakistan Horizon, vol 8 (1955), pp 351-61
LOOPER, R B, 'The treaty power in India', Br. Yearb. Int. Law (1955/6), pp 300-07

7.13.8.4.19   JAPAN

COLEGROVE, K W, 'The treaty-making power in Japan', Am. J. Int. Law (1931), pp 270-97
TAKANO, YUICHI, 'Conclusion and validity of treaties in Japan: Constitutional requirements', Jap. Annu. Int. Law, vol 8 (1964), p 9

7.13.8.4.20 VIETNAM

HA VINH PHUONG, 'La négociation et la signature
des accords commerciaux par le Viet-Nam',
Revue juridique et politique de l'Union française,
vol 7 (1953), pp 492-9

7.13.8.5 RATIFICATION

On the equivalent procedure in international
organizations, 'approval', see the article by DETTER
listed in Section 13.14

ACCIOLY, H, 'Suspensão da ratificação de tratado
  internacional', Boletim da Sociedade brasil de dir.
  internacional, vol 4, no 8 (July-December 1948),
  pp 164-6
ACCIOLY, H, 'A ratificação e promulgação dos
  tratados, em face da constituição brasileira',
  Boletim da Sociedade brasil de dir. internacional,
  vol 4, no 7 (January-June 1948), pp 5-11
ACCIOLY, H, 'Ainda o problema da ratificação dos
  tratados, em face da constituição federal
  brasileira', Boletim da Sociedade brasil de dir.
  internacional, vol 7, nos 13-14 (1951), pp 5-19
ALTEA, Conde de, 'La ratificación de los convenios
  internacionales de trabajo', Conferencia dada ...
  para la Asociación española para la Sociedad de
  las naciones el dia 3 le febrero de 1925. Madrid
  1925. 38 pp.
BERENSTEIN, A, 'La ratification des conventions
  internationales du travail et la législation interne
  (Notamment suisse)', D W, vol 53, no 2 (1956),
  pp 136-65
BLIX, H, 'The requirement of ratification', Br. Yearb.
  Int. Law (1953), p 352
BÖLGER, B, 'De ratificatie van de (ontwerp-)
  verdragen der internationale arbeidsconferenties',

Economisch Statistische Berichte (13 October 1926), p 898

BOGAERT, E van, 'De volkenrechtelijke grondslagen der bekrachtiging van verdragen', Tijdschrift voor bestuurswetenschappen en publiek recht, vol 11 (1956), pp 219-25

CABALEIRO MARTINEZ, E, 'La ratificación de los tratados internacionales en el derecho español', Estudios juridico-sociales. Homenaje al Profesor Luis Legaz y Lacambra (1960), pp 1189-1200

CALOGEROPOULOS-STRATIS, S, 'La ratification des traités d'après les constitutions récentes', Rev. Hell. Droit Int., vol 2 (1949), p 33

CAMARA, J S, The Ratification of International Treaties (Toronto: The Ontario Publishing Company, 1949). xii + 173 pp.

DEHOUSSE, F, La ratification des traités. Essai sur les rapports des traités et du droit interne (Paris: Recueil Sirey, 1935). 222 pp.

FITZMAURICE, G G, 'Do treaties need ratification?' Br. Yearb. Int. Law (1934), p 113

FREYMOND, P, 'La ratification des traités et le problème des rapports entre le droit international et le droit interne', Thesis. Lausanne 1947. 175 pp.

GEORGOPOULOS, C, La Ratification des traités et la collaboration du Parlement. Etude de droit constitutionnel grec et comparé (Paris: Librairie générale de droit et de jurisprudence, 1939). 132 pp

HERZOG, B, Der Begriff der Ratifikation und die Bedeutung seiner Technik für das Völkerrecht (Kiel, 1929). 126 pp.

JEZE, G, 'La ratification par le parlement des accords avec l'Angleterre et les Etats-Unis pour le règlement des dettes interalliées n'est pas nécessaire', Rev. Droit Public & Sci.Polit. (1927), p 92

JONES, J M, Full Powers and Ratification (London: Cambridge University Press, 1946)
JONES, J M, 'The retroactive effect of the ratification of treaties', Am. J. Int. Law, vol 29 (1935), p 51
LIANG, Yuen-Li, 'The use of the term " acceptance" in United Nations multilateral instruments', Am. J. Int. Law, vol 44 (1951), pp 342-9
MARCY, C, 'A note on treaty ratification', American Political Science Review, vol 47, no 4 (December 1953), pp 1130-3
NERI, S, 'Sulla ratifica dei trattati in diritto internazionale','Sulla ratificazione dei trattati in diritto int vol 29 (1962), pp 63-106
NERI, S, 'Sull' "applicazione provvisoria" dei trattati internazionali non ancora ratificati', Rivista di studi politici internazionali, vol 24 (1962), pp 588-91
NICOLOPOULOS, G, L'Acte de ratification et sa place dans la procédure diplomatique de la conclusion des traités (Lyon, 1942). 166 pp.
POLENTS, O E, Ratifikatsiia mezdhunarodnykh dogovorov (Moscow/Leningrad: Izdatelstvo Akademii naouk SSSR, 1950). 63 pp.
ROUSSEAU, Ch, 'La ratification des traités en France depuis 1946', in l'Evolution du droit public. Etudes offertes à Achille Mestre (1956), pp 473-92
SCHEUFFLER, H, 'Die Ratifikationen im Weltpostverein', Z. Völkerrecht, vol 24 (1940), pp 50-69
SCHEUFFLER, 'Die Ratifikationen im Weltpostverein', vol 67 (1942), pp 260-90
SIMEONOFF, I, 'La ratification des traités internationaux', Rev. Droit Int. Sci. Dipl. & Polit., vol 26 (1948), pp 257-62
TRISKA, Jan F, & SLUSSER, Robert M, 'Ratification of treaties in Soviet theory, practice and policy', Br. Yearb. Int. Law (1958), p 312

WEGMANN, Friedrich, Die Ratifikation von
Staatsverträgen. Insbesondere das Verhältniss der
Ratifikation zur parlamentarischen Zustimmung
beim Verträgsabschluss (Berlin, 1892)
WILCOX, F O, 'The ratification of League conventions:
an examination of the problem of giving effect to
agreements between states', Geneva Special Studies,
vol 6, no 2 (1935), pp 3-35
WILCOX, F, The Ratification of International Con-
ventions. A Study of the Relationship of the
Ratification Process to the Development of
International Legislation (London: Allen & Unwin,
1935). 349 pp.
ZANNINI, W, 'L'adesione ai trattati internazionali',
Studi nelle scienze giuridiche e sociali, vol 28
(1946)

7.13.8.6   REGISTRATION OF TREATIES

AREVALO Y CARRENO, C, 'El registro de los
tratados en las Naciones Unidas', Revista Peruana de
Derecho Internacional, vol 14 (1954), pp 3-13
BOUDET, F, 'L'enregistrement des accords internationaux', Rev. Gén. Droit Int. Public, vol 64
(1960), p 596
BRANDON, M, 'Analysis of the terms "treaty" and
"international agreement" for purposes of
registration under article 102 of the United Nations
charter', Am. J. Int. Law, vol 47 (1953), p 49
BRANDON, M, 'The validity of non-registered
treaties', Br. Yearb. Int. Law (1952), p 186
BROCKERS, A, & BOSKEY, S, 'Theory and practice
of treaty registration with particular reference to
agreements of the International Bank', Ned.
Tijdschr. Int. Recht, vol 4 (1957), pp 159-92;
277-300

CANYES, M S, Registration of treaties in the Pan American Union. Bulletin of the Pan American Union, vol 79 (1945), pp 638-45; vol 80 (1946), pp 571-5

DEHOUSSE, Maurice, L'Enregistrement des traités. Essai de droit international public (Paris: Recueil Sirey/Liège: Wykmans, 1929). 77 pp.

EUSTATHIADES, C Th, (Registration of treaties with the League of Nations)(in Greek), in Etudes de droit international 1929-59, vol 2 (Athens, 1959), pp 3-33

GECK, W K, 'Die Registrierung und Veröffentlichung völkerrechtlicher Verträge', Z. Ausl. Öff. Recht., & Völkerrecht vol 22 (1962), pp 113-211

HUDSON, M O, 'Registration of treaties by the Pan American Union', Am. J. Int. Law, vol 38 (1944), pp 98-9

HUDSON, M O, 'Legal effect of unregistered treaties in practice, under article 18 of the covenant', Am. J. Int. Law, vol 28 (1934), p 546

HUDSON, M O, 'Registration of United States treaties at Geneva', Am. J. Int. Law, vol 28 (1934), p 342

HUDSON, M O, 'The registration and publication of treaties', Am. J. Int. Law, vol 19 (1925), p 273

HUDSON, M O, 'The registration of treaties', Am. J. Int. Law, vol 24 (1930), p 752

HUDSON, M O, 'The registration of treaties of the United States', Am. J. Int. Law, vol 22 (1926), p 852

KIERNIK, S, 'Registration and publication of treaties and international agreements', The Diplomatic Yearbook (1951), pp 40-4

LAMBIRIS, J, 'L'enregistrement des traités d'après l'article 18 du pacte de la Société des Nations', Rev. Droit Int. & Légis. Comp., ser 3, vol 7 (1926), p 697

MODÉEN, Tore, The Deposit and Registration of Treaties in International Organizations.

Possible Application of the Rules of the Vienna Convention on the Law of Treaties (Åbo, Finland: Åbo Akademi, 1971). 20 pp.
REITZER, L, 'L'enregistrement des traités internationaux', Rev. Gén. Droit Int. Public', vol 44 (1937), p 67

7.13.8.7 DEPOSITARIES OF TREATIES

BROCKERS, A, & BOSKEY, S, 'Theory and practice of treaty registration with particular reference to agreements of the International Bank', Ned. Tijdschr. Int. Recht, vol 4 (1957), pp 159-92; 277-300
DEHAUSSY, J, 'Le dépositaire de traités', Rev. Gén. Droit Int. Public, vol 56 (1952), p 489
DIEZ DE VELASCO, M, 'Naturaleza juridica y functiones del depositario de tratados', Riv. Diritto Int., vol 41 (1958), pp 390-413
EAGLETON, C, 'The handling of treaties by the Secretariat of the United Nations. Report of the Committee to study legal problems of the United Nations. Presented by its chairman Clyde Eagleton and commented by I S Kerno', Am. Soc. Int. Law Proc. (1951), pp 139-51
KISS, A-Ch, 'Les fonctions du Secrétaire général du Conseil de l'Europe comme dépositaire des conventions européennes', Annu. Fr. Droit Int., vol 2 (1956), pp 680-8
OULIANOVA, N N, 'Depozitarii mnogostoronnevo dogovora', Sov. Yezheg. Mezhdunar. Prava (1965), pp 335-46
OTTAWA-RENE, F, Das Verbot der Geheimverträge. Artikel 18 der Volkerbundsatzung (Dresden, 1933). 54 pp.
ROSENNE, S, 'The depositary of international treaties', Am. J. Int. Law, vol 61 (1967), p 923

VELASCO, Manuel Diez de, 'Naturaleza juridica y funciones del depositario de tratados', Riv. Diritto Int., vol 41 (1958), p 390

7.13.9 EFFECT OF TREATIES

7.13.9.1 RESERVATIONS TO TREATIES

INFORME sobre el efecto jurídico de las reservas a los tratados multilaterales. Informe preparado por el comite jurídico interamericano, a solicitud del consejo de la organización de los estados americanos, para ser considerado en la 3a. reunión del consejo interamericano de jurisconsultos en México (Washington, DC: Union panamericana, 1955). 38 pp.

REPORT on the juridical effect of reservations to multilateral treaties. Report prepared by the inter-American juridical committee at the request of the Council of the Organization of American States, to be considered at the 3rd meeting of the inter-American council of jurists to be held in Mexico city (Washington, DC: Pan American Union, 1955). 36 pp.

ACCIOLY, H, 'Efeito juridico das reservas a tratados multilaterais', Boletim da Sociedade brasil de dir. internacional, vol 11, nos 21-2 (1955), pp 157-73

ANDERSON, D R, 'Reservations to multilateral conventions: a re-examination', Int. & Comp. Law Q., vol 13 (1964), p 450

BALDONI, C, 'Zur Theorie und praxis der Vorbehalte in den Staatsverträgen', Revue international de la théorie du droit, nos 3-4 (1929/30), pp 178-92

BALLADORE PALLIERI, G, 'Apuntes sobre el problema de las reservas en las convenciones colectivas', Escuela de funcion. internac., Madrid, Vol 50 (1957), pp 73-98

BELAUNDE MOREYRA, A, 'Las reservas a las convenciones multilaterales', Revista peruana de derecho internacional, vol 14 (1954), pp 14-57
BISHOP, W W, Jr, 'Reservations to treaties', Acad. Droit Int. Recl. Cours, vol 2 (1961), p 245
COX, W W, 'Reservations to multipartite conventions', Am. Soc. Int. Law Proc. (1952), pp 26-35
CRAYEN, A D von, 'Die Vorbehalte im Völkerrecht. (Untersuchung über gewisse, mit "Vorbehalt" bezeichnete Bedingungen des Staatsvertragsrechts)', Thesis. Zürich 1938. 100 pp.
ENZWEILER, J A, 'Der Vorbehalt in den Konvention innerhalb der Vereinten Nationen', Annales universitatis saraviensis, vol 6, no 1 (1958)
FENWICK, C G, 'Reservations to multilateral conventions: the report of the International Law Commission', Am. J. Int. Law, vol 46 (1952), 330, pp 119-23
FENWICK, C G, 'Reservations to multilateral treaties. (Report submitted by the Department of international law of the Pan American Union)', Anuario juridico interamericano (1950-51), pp 27-36
FITZMAURICE, G, 'Reservations to multilateral conventions', Int. & Comp. Law Q., vol 11 (1953), pp 1-26
GOMEZ ROBLEDO, A, 'Las reservas en los tratados multilaterales', Revista de la Escuela nacional de jurispr., vol 7 (1957), pp 11-34
GOPALAKRISHNAN, R, 'Reservations to multipartite treaties', vol 4 (1955), pp 168-209
GOUBINE, V F, (The USSR and reservations to multilateral treaties), Sov. Ezheg. Mezhdunar. Prava (1959), pp 126-43
HENKIN, L, 'The treaty makers and the law makers: the Niagara reservation', Columbia Law Review, vol 56 (1956), pp 1151-82

HERRERA PELLERANO, H, 'Las reservas en los tratados multilaterales', Boletin de información diplom. (November-December 1958), pp 38-46

HUDSON, M O, 'Reservations to multipartite international instruments', Am. J. Int. Law, vol 32 (1938), p 330

HOLLOWAY, K, Les Réserves dans les traités internationaux (Paris: Librairie générale de droit et de jurisprudence, 1958). 378 pp.

JOBST, III, V, 'Reservations to multipartite treaties', Am. J. Int. Law, vol 31 (1937), p 318

JULLY, L, 'Les réserves aux conventions multilaterales" Die Friedens-Warte, vol 51 (1952), pp 254-75

KAPPELER, D, Les Réserves dans les traités internationaux (Basel: Verlag für Recht und Gesellschaft, 1958). xvi + 101 pp.

KERNO, I, 'Réserves à la convention pour la prévention du crime de génocide', Rev. Droit Int., vol 29 (1951), p 214

KHADJENOURI, M, 'Réserves dans les traités internationaux', Thesis. Université de Genève, 1953. 256 pp.

LAUTERPACHT, H, 'Some possible solutions of the problem of reservations to treaties', Grotius Soc. Trans., vol 38 (1953), p 97

LIAN, Yuen-Li, 'The practice of the United Nations with respect to reservations to multipartite instruments', Am. J. Int. Law, vol 44 (1950), p 117

MALKIN, H W, 'Reservations to multilateral conventions', Br. Yearb. Int. Law (1926), p 141

MONACO, R, 'Le riserve agli accordi internazionali e la competenza parlamentare', Riv. Diritto Int., vol 37 (1954), pp 72-81

OGAWA, Y, (Codification of the rules on reservations by the International Law Commission). (In Japanese with an English summary) J I L D, vol 66 (1967), pp 62-98

PARK, T S, 'The legal effect of reservation and understanding in American law', Korean J. Int. Law, vol 7 (September 1962), pp 333-50
PILLOUD, C, 'Die Vorbehalte zu den Genfer Abkommen von 1949', Revue international de la Croix-rouge, German supp. (1958)
PODESTA COSTA, L A, 'Les réserves dans les traités internationaux', Rev. Droit Int., vol 21 (1938), p 1
RUDA, J M, 'Las reservas a las convenciones multilaterales', Rev. Derecho Int. & Cienc. Dipl., vol 12 (1963), pp 7-85
SANDERS, W, 'Reservations to multilateral treaties in the act of ratification or adherence', Am. J. Int. Law, vol 33 (1939), p 488
SCHEIDTMANN, U, Der Vorbehalt beim Abschluss Völkerrechtlicher Verträge (Berlin/Grunewald: Verlag fur Staatswissenschaften und Geschichte, 1934). viii + 80 pp.
STEFFAN, B A, 'Der Völkerrechtliche Vorbehalt. Gelnhausen'. Thesis. Frankfurt am Main, 1937. 57 pp.
SCHERMERS, H G, 'The suitability of reservations to multilateral treaties', Ned. Tijdschr. Int. Recht, vol 6 (1959), p 350
SHATZKY, B, 'La portée des réserves dans le droit international', Rev. Droit Int. & Légis. Comp., vol 14 (1933), p 216
VITTA, E, Le riserve nei trattati (Torino: Giappichelli, 1957). 145 pp.
YUEN-LI LIANG, & HSUAN-TSUI LIU, 'The third session of the International Law Commission; review of its work by the General Assembly. (Reservations to multilateral conventions)', Am. J. Int. Law, vol 46 (1952), pp 483-503; 667-81

7.13.9.2 INTERPRETATION OF TREATIES

7.13.9.2.1 GENERAL

FACHIRI, A P, 'Interpretation of treaties', Am. J. Int. Law, vol 23 (1929), pp 745-52

FAIRMAN, C, 'The interpretation of treaties', Grotius Soc. Trans., vol 20 (1935), pp 123-39

FITZMAURICE, G G, 'The law and procedure of the International Court of Justice: Treaty interpretation and certain other treaty points', Br. Yearb. Int. Law (1951), pp 1-28; (1957), pp 323-9

FITZMAURICE, G, 'De l'interprétation des traités', Annu. Inst. Droit Int., vol 46 (1956), p 317

BERLIA, G, 'Contribution à l'interprétation des traités', Acad. Droit Int. Recl. Cours, vol 114 (1965), pp 283-333

BRACHT, H W, 'Die Auslegung internationaler Verträge in der sowjetischen Völkerrechtslehre', Osteuroparecht, vol 7 (1961), pp 66-81

BROWN, P M, 'The interpretation of treaties', Am. J. Int. Law, vol 23 (1929), pp 819-24

CHENG, C H, 'Essai critique sur l'interprétation des traités dans la doctrine et la jurisprudence de la Cour permanente de justice internationale', Thesis. Paris, 1941. 107 pp.

DEGAN, V D, L'Interprétation des accords en droit international (Den Haag, 1963).

EHRLICH, L, Interpretacja traktatow, (Warsaw, 1957) Droit Int. Recl. Cours, vol 4 (1928), pp 1-145

IDEM, Interpretacja tratkatow,(Warsaw, 1957)

JOKL, M, De l'interprétation des traités normatifs d'après la doctrine et la jurisprudence internationales (Paris: Pédone, 1936). viii + 194 pp.

LAUTERPACHT, H, 'De l'interprétation des traités. Rapport et projet de résolutions présentés lors de la session de Bath de l'Institut de droit international', Annu. Inst. Droit Int., (1950), vol 1, p 366

LAUTERPACHT, H, 'De l'interprétation des traités. Observations complémentaires et projet de résolutions lors des travaux préparatoires de la session de Sienne 1952', Annu. Inst. Droit Int. (1952), vol 1, p 197 Nouveau projet... d'Aix', vol 45 (1954), p 225
NERI, S, Sull'interpretazione dei trattato nel diritto internazionale (Milano: Giuffré, 1958). xxv + 309 pp.
VISSCHER, Ch de, Problèmes d'interprétation judiciaire en droit international public (Paris, 1963).
WRIGHT, Q, 'The International Court of Justice and the interpretation of multilateral treaties', Am. J. Int. Law, vol 41 (1947), pp 445-52

7.13.9.2.2 INTERPRETATION OF MULTILINGUAL TEXTS

DICKSCHAT, D A, 'Problèmes d'interprétation des traités européens résultant de leur plurilinguisme', Rev. Belg. Droit Int., vol 3 (1968), pp 40-60
DÖLLE, H, 'Zur Problematik mehrsprachiger Gesetzes- und Vertragstexte', Rabels Z. Ausl. & Int. Privatrecht, vol 26 (1961), pp 4-39
HARDY, J, 'Interpretation of plurilingual treaties by international courts and tribunals', Br. Yearb. Int. Law, vol 37 (1961), pp 72-155
HUDSON, M O, 'Languages used in treaties', Am. J. Int. Law, vol 26 (1932), pp 368-72
MAKAROV, A N, 'Zur Auslegung mehrsprachiger Staatsverträge', in Recueil d'études de droit international en hommage à Paul Guggenheim (Genève, 1968). pp 403-25
METALL, R A, 'Fremdsprachige Staatsverträge', Z. Öff. Recht (1930), pp 357-89

7.13.9.2.3 INTERPRETATION OF
CONSTITUTIONS OF ORGANIZATIONS

See also Section 8.11.10 on the advisory jurisdiction of the ICJ and Section 13.24.2.3 on interpretation of the Charter of the UN.

ENGEL, S,'"Living"international constitution and the world court. (The subsequent practice of international organs under their constituent instrument)', Int. & Comp. Law Q., vol 16 (1967), pp 865-910

GORDON, E, 'The World Court and the interpretation of constitutive observations on the development of an international constitutional law', Am. J. Int. Law, vol 59 (1965), pp 794-833

HEXNER, E P, 'Interpretation of public international organizations of their basic instruments', Am. J. Int. Law, vol 53 (1959), pp 341-70

HEXNER, E P, 'Teleological interpretation of basic instruments of public international organization', in Law, State and International Legal Order: Essays in Honour of H Kelsen, edited by Salo Engel & R A Metall (Knoxville, Tenn: University of Tennessee Press, 1964), pp 119-38

RAJU, G S, & CHANDRASEKHARA RAO, P, 'The specialised agencies and their interpretative mechanism', Indian J. Int. Law, vol 1 (1961), pp 613-28

VISSCHER, Ch de, 'L'interprétation judiciaire des traités d'organisation internationale', Diritto internazionale, vol 41 (1958), pp 177-87

7.13.9.2.4 OTHER SPECIAL QUESTIONS

JENKS, C W, 'The interpretation of international labour conventions by the International Labour Office', Br. Yearb. Int. Law, vol 20 (1939), pp 132-41

KUHN, A K, 'Interpretation of the "high contracting parties" in the air traffic convention', Am. J. Int. Law, vol 35 (1941), p 132

LACHS, M, 'La restitution de l'or monétaire. Un problème de l'interprétation des traités', J. Droit Int. vol 88 (1961), pp 4-37. In English and French

MacDOUGAL, M S, 'The international law commission's draft articles upon interpretation: textuality redivivus', Am. J. Int Law, vol 61 (1967), p 992

METZGER, S D, 'Treaty-interpretation and the United States-Italy air transport arbitration', Am. J. Int. Law, vol 61 (1967), p 1007

O'CONNELL, D P, 'State succession and problems of treaty interpretation', Am. J. Int. Law, vol 58 (1964), pp 41-6

VISSCHER, Ch de, 'L'interprétation de l'accord aérien France-Etats-Unis du 27. mars 1946', Rev. Belg. Droit Int. (1966), pp 1-7

7.13.9.2.5 METHODS OF INTERPRETATION

See also Section 13.24.2.3.1 on the interpretation of the Charter.

FAVRE, A, 'Interprétation objectiviste des traités internationaux', Schweiz. Jahrb. Int. Recht, vol 17 (1960), pp 75-98

HARASZTI, G, 'Historical interpretation of international treaties', Questions of International Law (Budapest, 1966), pp 66-88

HEXNER, E P, 'Teleological interpretation of basic instruments of public international organizations', in Law, State and International Legal Order. Essays in Honour of Hans Kelsen, edited by Salo Engel & R A Metall (Knoxville, Tenn: University of Tennessee Press, 1964), pp 119-38

LAUTERPACHT, H, 'Restrictive interpretation and the principle of effectiveness in the interpretation of treaties', Br. Yearb. Int. Law, vol 36 (1949), pp 48-85

MORRISON, C C, 'Restrictive interpretation of sovereignty-limiting treaties; the practice of the European human rights system', Int. & Comp. Law Q., vol 19 (1970)

NAGY, K, (Authentic interpretation of international treaties), Acta Universitatitis Szegediensis, vol 10 (1963), p 4. In Hungarian with French and Russian summaries

POLITIS, N, 'Méthodes d'interprétation du droit conventionnel', in Mélanges Gény, (Paris, 1934), vol 3, pp 374-82

STONE, J, 'Fictitional elements in treaty interpretation - a study in the international judicial process', S L R, vol 1, no 3 (1953/5), pp 344-68

SULTAN, H, 'The special function of the principle of restrictive interpretation', in Mélanges offerts à Juraj Andrassy, edited by V Ibert (Den Haag: Nijhoff, 1968), pp 294-306

VISSCHER, Ch de, 'Remarques sur l'interprétation dite textuelle des traités internationaux', Ned. Tijdschr. Int. Recht, vol 6 (1959), supp. 'Varia juris gentium ... Liber amicorum ... F P A François'

VOÏCU, I, De l'interprétation authentique des traités internationaux (Paris, 1968)

7.13.9.2.6 ROLE OF THE PREAMBLE

YOU, P, Le Préambule des traités internationaux (Fribourg, 1941)

YOU, P, 'L'interprétation des traités et le rôle du préambule des traités dans cette interprétation', Rev. Droit Int. Sci. Dipl. & Polit., vol 20 (1942), pp 25-45

7.13.9.2.7 ROLE OF TRAVAUX PREPARATOIRES

LAUTERPACHT, H, 'Les travaux préparatoires et l'interprétation des traités', Acad. Droit Int. Recl. Cours, vol 2 (1934), pp 709-817
LAUTERPACHT, H, 'Some observations on the preparatory work in the interpretation of treaties', Harvard Law Review, vol 48 (1935), pp 549-91
ROSENNE, S, 'Travaux préparatoires', Int. & Comp. Law Q., vol 12 (1963), pp 1378-83
SHARMA, S P, 'The I L C draft and treaty interpretation with special reference to preparatory works', Indian J. Int. Law, vol 8 (1968), pp 367-98
SPENCER, J H, L'Interprétation des traités par les travaux préparatoires (Paris, 1934). 209 pp.

7.13.9.2.8 INTERPRETATION BY COURTS IN GENERAL

BERNHARDT, Rudolf, Die Auslegung völkerrechtlicher Verträge insbesondere in der neueren Rechtsprechung internationaler Gerichte (Köln/Berlin, 1963)
GROSS, L, 'Treaty interpretation: the proper role of an international tribunal', Am. Soc. Int. Law Proc. (1969), pp 108-22
SCHECHTER, A H, Interpretation of Ambiguous Documents by International Administrative Tribunals (London, 1964)
SCHWARZENBERGER, G, 'Peace treaties before international courts and tribunals', Indian J. Int. Law, vol 8 (1968), p 1-8

7.13.9.2.9 INTERPRETATION BY PCIJ

For more on the PCIJ, see Section 8.10.
CHENG, C H, 'Essai critique sur l'interprétation des

traités dans la doctrine et la jurisprudence de la Cour permanente de justice internationale', Thesis. Paris 1941

WILSON, R R, 'Interpretation of treaties. Contributions of the Permanent Court of International Justice to the development of international law', Am. Soc. Int. Law Proc. (1930), pp 39-45

HUDSON, M O, 'International engagements and their interpretation by the Permanent Court of International Justice', in Legal Essays in Tribute to Orrin Kip McMurray (Berkeley, Calif: 1935), pp 187-220

HYDE, C C, 'The interpretation of treaties by the Permanent Court of International Justice', Am. J. Int. Law, vol 24 (1930), pp 1-19

7.13.9.2.10 INTERPRETATION BY ICJ

For more on the ICJ, see Section 8.11

GORDON, E, 'The World Court and the interpretation of constitutive treaties', Am. J. Int. Law, vol 59 (1965), pp 794-833

HAMBRO, E, 'Quelques remarques sur la jurisprudence de la Cour internationale de justice en matière d'interprétation des traités, notamment de la Charte des Nations Unies', Annales de la Faculté d'Istanbul (1952), pp 299-316

HAMBRO, E, 'The interpretation of multilateral treaties by the International Court of Justice', Trans Grotius Soc., vol 39 (1953), pp 235-55

HOGG, J F, 'The International Court: rules of treaty interpretation', Minnesota Law Review, vol 43 (1959) pp 369-441; vol 44 (1959), pp 5-73

LIACOURAS, P J, 'The International Court of Justice and development of useful "rules of interpretation" in the process of treaty interpretation', Am. Soc. Int. Law Proc., vol 59 (1965), pp 161-9

WRIGHT, Q, 'The International Court of Justice and the interpretation of multilateral treaties', Am. J. Int. Law, vol 41 (1947), pp 115-52

7.13.9.2.11 INTERPRETATION BY NATIONAL COURTS

Cf. certain entries under 7.13.13.2 on treaties in the municipal sphere.
See also Section 13.24.3.12.6.5.3 on the prejudicial system of the European Communities
BASDEVANT, J, 'Le rôle du juge dans l'interprétation des traités diplomatiques. Exposé dans la séances du 29 avril 1949 de l'Association Henri Capitant suivi de discussion', Travaux de l'Ass. H. Capitant (1950), vol 5, pp 107-27 and Revue de droit international privé, vol 38 (1949), pp 413-33
BATIFFOL, H, 'Interprétation des traités diplomatiques par les tribunaux judiciaires', Travaux du Comité français de droit international privé 19/20 (1958/9), pp 99-121
BAYER, W F, 'Auslegung und Ergänzung internationaler vereinheitlicher Normen durch staatliche Gerichte', Zeitschrift für ausländisches und internationales Privatrecht, vol 20 (1955), pp 603-42
BENOIST, J, 'L'interprétation des traités d'après la jurisprudence française', Rev. Hell.Droit Int., vol 6 (1953), pp 103-16
DELAUME, G R, 'De l'application et de l'interprétation des traités par les tribunaux internes dans les relations franco-américaines/Application and interpretation of treaties by the internal courts in Franco-American relations', J. Droit Int., vol 80 (1953), pp 584-635
DAVID, G, 'De l'interprétation des traités diplomatiques par l'authorité judiciaire', Thesis. Nancy 1909

HYDE, C C, 'The interpretation of treaties by the Supreme Court of the United States', Am. J. Int. Law, vol 23 (1929), pp 824-8

McNAIR, A D, 'L'application et l'interprétation des traités d'après la jurisprudence britannique', Acad. Droit Int. Recl. Cours, vol 1 (1933), pp 251-307

NAUROIS, L de, Les Traités internationaux devant les juridictions nationales (Paris, 1934)

PERGLER, C, Judicial Interpretation of International Law in the United States (New York, 1928)

STASSINOPOULOS, M, 'Remarques sur la jurisprudence française relative a l'interprétation des traités internationaux', Rev. Gén. Droit Int. Public, vol 73 (1969), pp 5-29

SINCLAIR, I M, 'The principles of treaty interpretation and their application by the English courts', Int. & Comp. Law Q., vol 12 (1963), pp 508-51

TENNANT, J S, 'The judicial process of treaty interpretation in the United States Supreme Court', Michigan Law Review, vol 30 (1932), pp 1016-39

WAELBROECK, M, Traités internationaux et juridictions internes (Bruxelles, 1969), pp 204-17

YI-TING-CHANG, The Interpretation of Treaties by Judicial Tribunals (London/New York, 1933)

7.13.9.2.12 INTERPRETATION BY COURTS OF ARBITRATION

BLÜHDORN, R, 'Le fonctionnement et la jurisprudence des tribunaux arbitraux mixtes', Acad. Droit Int. Recl. Cours, vol 41 (1932), pp 141-243

MENDELSSOHN-BARTHOLDY, A, 'Le rôle des tribunaux arbitraux mixtes dans l'interprétation des traités internationaux', Acad. Dipl. Int. séances et travaux (1933), pp 27-39

7.13.9.2.13   INTERPRETATION BY
             ADMINISTRATIVE TRIBUNALS

BASTID, Suzanne, 'Les tribunaux administratifs et leur jurisprudence', Acad. Droit Int. Recl. Cours, vol 2, (1957), especially pp 474-6
SCHECHTER, A, Interpretation of Ambiguous Documents by International Administrative Tribunals (London, 1964)

7.13.9.2.14   INTERPRETATION BY THE COURT
             OF THE EUROPEAN COMMUNITIES

For more on the Court, see Section 13.24.3.12.6.5;
McMAHON, J, 'The Court of the European Communities judicial interpretation and international organization', Br. Yearb. Int. Law (1961), p 320
MONACO, R, 'Les principes d'interprétation suivis par la Cour de justice des Communautés européennes', in Mélanges Rolin (Paris, 1964), pp 217-27
DEGAN, V, 'Procédés d'interprétation tirés de la jurisprudence de la Cour de justice des Communautés européennes', Rev. Trimest. Droit Eur. (1966), pp 189-227

7.13.10   MODIFICATION OF TREATIES

7.13.10.1   GENERAL

GIRAUD, E, 'Modification et termination des traités collectifs. Rapports presentés à la sess. de Bruxelles de l'Institut de droit internat. Onzième Commission, mars, 1960',

7.13.10.2   REVISION OF TREATIES

For revision of constitutions of organisations see 13.17 (in general), 13.24.2.3.2 (UN).

AUER, P de, 'Revision of treaties', Grotius Soc. Trans., vol 18 (1932), p 155

BLIX, H, 'The rule of unanimity in the revision of treaties: A study of the treaties governing Tangier', Int. & Comp. Law Q., vol 5 (1956), p 447, 581

EIBE, J von, 'Einige Fälle von Vertragsrevision im XIX. Jahrhundert', Z. Ausl. Öff. Recht & Völkerrecht, vol 5 (1935), pp 269-92

ENGEL, S, 'Les clauses de révision dans les traités supranationaux multilatéraux de l'après-guerre', Rev. Droit Int. & Légis. Comp., ser 3 (1939), pp 529-58

ESCHER, R H von, 'Die Revision der internationalen Vereinbarungen'. Dissertation. Zürich 1947. 171 pp.

GOES VAN NATERS, M van der, 'La revision des traités supranationaux', Ned. Tidschr. Int. Recht (1959), 'Liber amicorum, J P A François', pp 120-31

HAUCHMANN-TCHERNIAK, T, 'La SdN est-elle en mesure d'arriver à la revision des traités?' Rev. Droit Int., vol 17 (1939), p 1

HOYT, E C, The Unanimity Rule in the Revision of Treaties (Den Haag, 1959)

JENKS, C W, 'The revision of international labour conventions', Br. Yearb. Int. Law, vol 14 (1933), pp 43-64

JONES, H H, 'Amending the Chicago convention and its technical standards - can consent of all member states be eliminated?' Journal of Air Law and Commerce, vol 16 (1949), pp 185-213

JONES, F L, 'Treaty revision and art. XIX of the covenant of the League of Nations', Grotius Soc. Trans., vol 19 (1933), p 13

LECA, J, Les Techniques de révision des conventions internationales (Paris, 1961)

LIANG, Yuen-Li, 'The question of revision of a multilingual treaty text', Am. J. Int. Law, vol 47 (1953), p 26

MODEROW, W, 'The revision of treaties and the interests of peace', in Studies in Polish and Comparative Law (London, 1945), pp 70-97

MRAZEK, I, (Revision clauses in international agreements) (In Polish), Państwo i prawo, vol 13 (1958), pp 605-20

NICOLOFF, A M, 'La révision des traités et la charte des Nations Unies', Rev. Droit Int. Sci. Dipl. & Polit, vol 24 (1946), pp 55-66; 224-35; vol 25 (1947), pp 101-10

ROHNFELDER, G, 'Die Revision internationaler Verträge nach Billigkeit dargestellt an der Genfer Generalakte (1928) 1949 un der Europäischen Konvention zur friedlichen Streiterledigung (1957)', Dissertation. München 1962

SCELLE, G, Théorie juridique de la révision des traités (Paris, 1936)

SCELLE, G, 'La révision dans les conventions générales. Rapport préliminaire lors des travaux préparatoires de la session de Bruxelles, 1948', Annu. Inst. Droit Int. (1947), p 1; (1948), p 175

SCELLE, G, 'La Société des Nations et la révision des traités. Etude juridique par Albert Wigniolle', Rev. Gén. Droit Int. Public, vol 41 (1934), p 90

SCELLE, G, & WEHBERG, H, 'La révision des traités du point de vue juridique, I et II: Rapports présentés au XXIXme congrès universal de la paix Vienne, sept. 1932', Movement pacifiste, nos 5-6 (1932), p 53. Société des Nations, vol 14 (1932), p 514

SCHWELB, E, 'The amending procedure of constitutions of international organizations', Br. Yearb. Int. Law, vol 31 (1954), pp 48-95

SORENSEN, M, 'The modification of collective treaties without the consent of all the contracting parties', Nord. Tidsskr. Int. Ret., vol 9 (1938), pp 150-73

STEED, W, 'The revision of the peace treaties', Grotius Soc. Trans., vol 19 (1933), p 115

TOBIN, H J, 'The role of the great powers in treaty revision', Am. J. Int. Law, vol 28 (1934), p 487

VONCKEN, J, 'La revision des grandes conventions humanitaires', Rev. Droit Int., vol 21 (1938), pp 357-72

YAKEMTCHOUK, R, 'La révision des traités multilatéraux en droit international', Rev. Gén.Droit Int. Public, vol 60 (1956), pp 337-500

YAKEMTCHOUK, R, 'La technique de révision des traités multilatéraux', Annales de droit et de sciences politiques, vol 16 (1956), pp 173-201

7.13.10.3 TERMINATION OF TREATIES

See also Section 7.13.11.4 on unequal treaties.

AUFRICHT, H, 'Supersession of treaties in international law', Cornell Law Quarterly, vol 37, no 4 (1952), pp 655-700

CAPOTORTI, F , 'L'extinction et la suspension des traités', Acad. Droit Int. Recl. Cours, vol 134 (1971), pp 417-588

GARNER, J W, & JOBST III, V, 'The unilateral denunciation of treaties by one party because of alleged non-performance by another party or parties', Am. J. Int. Law, vol 29 (1935), p 569

GIRAUD, E, 'Modification et termination des traités collectifs. Rapports présentés à la session de Bruxelles de l'Institut de droit international. Onzième Commission, mars 1960'.

GIRAUD, E, 'La notion de temps dans les relations et le droit international', in Scritti di diritto internazionale in onore di T Perassi (1957), vol 1 pp 461-86

HOFBAUER, K, 'L'inexécution cause d'extinction du traité international', Rev. Droit Int., vol 20 (1937), pp 92-103

LISSITZYN, O J, 'Duration of executive agreements. Editorial comment', Am. J. Int. Law, vol 54 (1960), p 869

McNAIR, A D, 'La terminaison et la dissolution des traités', Acad. Droit Int. Recl. Cours, vol 2 (1923), p 459

MOLEN, G H J van der, 'Het völkenrechtelijk aspect van de eenzijdige opzegging der Nederlands-Indonesische Unie', Antirevolutionaire staatkunde vol 26, nos 2-3 (1956), pp 33-42

MONACO, R, 'Die Aufhebung der zwischenstaatlichen Rechtsregeln', Z. Öff. Recht, vol 19 (1939), pp 78-113

MONACO, R, 'L'abrogazione delle norme giuridiche internazionali', in Scritti giur. in onore di S Romano (1940), vol 3, pp 233-263

ROUSSEAU, Ch, 'La dénonciation des traités de Locarno devant le droit international', Paix par le droit, vol 46 (1936), pp 118-98

SCHWELB, E, 'Termination or suspension of the operation of a treaty as a consequence of its breach', Indian J. Int. Law, vol 7 (1967), pp 309-34

SINHA, Bhek Pati, Unilateral Denunciation of Treaty because of Prior Violations of Obligations by other Party (Den Haag: Nijhoff, 1966). xx + 232 pp.

TOBIN, H J, The Termination of Multipartite Treaties (New York: Columbia University Press/London: King & Sons, 1933). 321 pp.

TOBIN, H J, 'Is Belgium still neutralized? A study in the termination of treaties', Am. J. Int. Law (1932), pp 511-32

WILSON, G G, 'Duration of treaties', Am. J. Int. Law, vol 36 (1942), p 447

WOOLSEY, L H, 'The unilateral termination of treaties', Am. J. Int. Law, vol 20 (1926), p 346

WRIGHT, Q, 'The termination and suspension of treaties', Am. J. Int. Law, vol 61 (1967), p 1000

7.13.10.4 FUNDAMENTAL CHANGES AND CLAUSULA REBUS SIC STANTIBUS

BERGER, P, 'Zur Klausel "rebus sic stantibus" ', Österr. Z. Öff. Recht, vol 4 (1951), pp 27-51

BOGAERT, E van, 'Le sens de la clause "rebus sic stantibus" dans le droit des gens actuel', Rev. Gén. Droit Int. Public, vol 70 (1966), pp 49-74

BRACHT, H W, 'Die clausula rebus sic stantibus in der sowjetischen Völkerrechtslehre', Int. Recht & Dipl., nos 3-4 (1961), pp 190-203

BRIERLY, J L, 'Some considerations on the obsolescence of treaties', Grotius Soc. Trans., vol 11 (1926), pp 11-20

BRIGGS, H W, 'The Attorney General invokes rebus sic stantibus', Am. J. Int. Law, vol 36 (1942), p 89

BRIGGS, H W, 'Rebus sic stantibus before the Security Council: The Anglo-Egyptian question', Am. J. Int. Law, vol 43 (1949), p 762

BURCKHARDT, W, 'La clausula rebus sic stantibus en droit international', Rev. Droit Int. & Légis. Comp., ser 3, vol 14 (1933), p 5

FAIRMAN, C, 'Implied resolutive conditions in treaties', Am. J. Int. Law, vol 29 (1935), p 219

FEINBERG, N, 'The legal validity of the undertaking concerning minorities and the clausula rebus sic stantibus', Hebrew University, Faculty of Law. Studies in Law. Scripta hierosolymitana, vol 5, pp 95-131

GENET, R, 'Le problème de la clause rebus sic stantibus. Caducité ou révision', Rev. Gén. Droit Int. Public, vol 37 (1930), p 287

GARNER, J W, 'The doctrine of rebus sic stantibus and the termination of treaties', Am. J. Int. Law, vol 21 (1927), p 509

GHOBASHY, O Z, 'Treaties and changed conditions', Egyptian Economic and Political Review (April 1958), pp 13-17

GRANFELT, H, 'Striden kring rebus sic stantibus. självbestämmelserätten och minoritetsrätten: ett förspel till världskriget 1939', Nord. Tidsskr. Int. Ret, vol 16 (1945), pp 20-60

LIPARTITI, C, 'La clausola "rebus sic stantibus" e le circostanze propizie al suo funzionamento e fondamento', Rev. Droit Int. Sci. Dipl. & Polit., vol 18 (1940), pp 219-33

LISSITZYN, O J, 'Treaties and changed circumstances', Am. J. Int. Law, vol 61 (1967), p 895

POCH DE CAVIEDES, A, 'De la clause "rebus sic stantibus" à la clause de révision dans les conventions internationales', Acad. Droit Int. Recl. Cours, vol 118 (1966), pp 109-204

POTTER, P B, 'Article XIX of the covenant of the League of Nations: a study in the problem of international government', Geneva Special Studies, vol 12, no 2 (1941), pp 9-98

RAJA, C K N, 'Clausula sic stantibus', Sarada Vilasa Law College Journal, no 6 & 7

ROS, E J, 'La clausula "rebus sic stantibus", Cómo la consideran los clásicos del derecho internacional', Revista de la Facultad de der. y ciencia soc. (Buenos Aires), vol 9, no 38 (1954), pp 558-64

SALVIOLI, Gabriele, 'Sulla clausola "rebus sic stantibus" nei trattati internazionale. A proposito del libro di E Kaufmann, Das Wesen des Völkerrechts und de Clausola rebus sic stantibus, Tübingen 1911', Riv. Diritto Int., vol 8 (1914), p 264

SIMEONOFF, I, 'La clause "rebus sic stantibus" en droit international', Rev. Droit Int., vol 27 (1949), p 35

TENEKIDES, C G, 'Le principe rebus sic stantibus, ses limites rationnelles et sa récente évolution', Rev. Gen. Droit Int. Public, vol 41 (1934), p 273

VERPLAETSE, J G, 'Apuntes sobre la doctrina "rebus sic stantibus" en el derecho international a la luz de algunos casos actuales', Rev. Esp. Derecho Int., vol 4 (1951), pp 113-33

VERZIJL, J H, 'Le principe "rebus sic stantibus" en droit international public', in Internationalrechtliche und staatsrechtliche Abhandlungen. Festschrift für Walter Schatzel zu seinem 70. Geburtstag, pp 515-29

WILLIAMS, J F, 'The permanence of treaties. The doctrine of rebus sic stantibus, and article 19 of the covenant of the League', Am. J. Int. Law, vol 22 (1928), p 89

WILSON, G G, 'Treaties and changing conditions', Am. J. Int. Law, vol 29 (1935), p 307

WILSON, G G, 'Treaties and status quo', Am. J. Int. Law, vol 27 (1933), p 104

WRIGHT, Q, 'Article 19 of the League covenant and the doctrine "rebus sic stantibus" ', Am. Soc. Int. Law Proc. (1936), pp 55-86

7.13.11 VALIDITY OF TREATIES

7.13.11.1 VALIDITY IN GENERAL

See also the theory enunciated in DELUPIS, International Law and the Independent State (see Section 1.8) on the validity of treaties restricting territorial sovereignty

ATASSY, A, Les vices de consentement dans les traités internationaux à l'exclusion des traités de paix (Genève: Imprimérie du commerce, 1929). 101 pp.

BRANDNER, K, 'Pacta contra bonos mores im Völkerrecht', Jahrbuch d. Konsularakademie zu Wien (1937), pp 33-43

BRIGGS, H W, 'The validity of the Greenland agreement', Am. J. Int. Law, vol 35 (1941), pp 506-13

BRIGGS, H W, 'Procedures for establishing the invalidity or termination of treaties under the International Law Commission's 1966 draft articles on the law of treaties', Am. J. Int. Law, vol 61 (1967), p 976

DENNEMARK, Sigurd, 'Quelle est la loi selon laquelle on tranche la question de la validité d'un accord sur la compétence internationale', Ned. Tijdschr. Int. Recht, vol 9, Special Issue (1962), p 118

ELIAS, T O, 'Problems concerning the validity of treaties', Acad. Droit Int. Recl. Cours, vol 134 (1971), pp 333-416

GECK, Wilhelm Karl, Die völkerrechtlichen Wirkungen verfassungswidriger Verträge. Zugleich ein Beitrag zum Vertragsschluss im Verfassungsrecht der Staatenwelt (Köln/Berlin, 1963)

GOELLNER, A, Pré-caducité, caducité, et désuétude en matière de droit international public. (Essai juridique) (Paris, 1939). 246 pp.

GUGGENHEIM, P, 'La validité et la nullité des actes juridiques internationaux', Acad. Droit Int. Recl. Cours, vol 2 (1949), pp 191-268

GUGGENHEIM, P, 'La validité et la nullité des actes juridiques internationaux', Acad. Droit Int. Recl. Cours, vol 1 (1949), pp 191-268

SHATZKY, B, 'La validité des traités', Rev. Droit Int., vol 11 (1933), pp 545-92

SURSALOV, V M, Osnovanija dejstvitel nosti mezdunarodnych dogovorov (Moscow, 1957)

TALALAEV, A N, (Annulment of international agreements in the history and practice of the Soviet state) (In Russian with English summary) Sov. Ezheg. Mezhdunar. Prava (1959), pp 144-57

VERDROSS, A von, 'Anfechtbare und nichtige Staatsverträge', Z. Öff. Recht, vol 15 (1935), pp 289-99
VERDROSS, A von, 'Forbidden treaties in international law: comments on Professor Garner's report on "the law of treaties" ', Am. J. Int. Law, vol 32 (1937), pp 571-7
VERDROSS, A von, 'Trattati "contra bones mores" ', Riv. Diritto Int., vol 29 (1937), pp 3-11
VERZIJL, J H W, 'La validité et la nullité des actes juridiques internationaux', Rev. Droit Int., vol 15 (1935), pp 284-339
VITTA, E, La Validité des traités internationaux (Leiden: Brill, 1940). xii + 247 pp.

7.13.11.2   BREACH OF TREATIES

Cf. Section 7.13.7 on the binding character of treaties.
GHOBASHY, O Z, 'Violation of treaties', Egyptian Economic and Political Review (September 1959), pp 15-19
MYERS, Denys P, 'Violation of treaties: Bad faith, nonexecution and disregard', Am. J. Int. Law, vol 11 (1917), p 794
WRIGHT, Quincy, 'The denunciation of treaty violators', Am. J. Int. Law, vol 32 (1938), pp 526-35

7.13.11.3   TREATIES AND COERCION

CAVAGLIERI, Arrigo, 'La violenza come motivo di nullità dei trattati', Riv. Diritto Int., vol 27 (1935), p 4
BUZA, L, 'Der Zwang im Völkerrecht', Z. Völkerrecht, vol 21 (1937), pp 420-40
TOMSIČ, I, La Reconstruction du droit international en matière des traités. Essai sur le problème des

vices du consentement dans le conclusion des
  traités internationaux (Paris: Pédone, 1931). 118 pp.
VISSCHER, F de, 'Des traités imposés par la
  violence', Rev. Droit Int. & Légis. Comp., ser 3,
  vol 12 (1931), p 513
WEIDNER, R, 'Der erzwungene Vertrag im
  Völkerrecht'. Thesis. Berlin, 1939. 89 pp.
WENNER, G, Willensmängel im Völkerrecht (Zürich:
  Polygraphischer Verlag, 1940). 422 pp.

7.13.11.4 UNEQUAL TREATIES

(By an unequal treaty some authors mean an imposed
one. Others claim that the contents of a treaty may
alone make it an unequal one. For a more complete
list of bibliographic references on this topic see
Delupis Section 1.8, p. 30).
BUELL, R L, 'The termination of unequal treaties',
  Am. Soc. Int. Law Proc. (1937), pp 90-100
DETTER, I, 'The problem of unequal treaties', Int. &
  Comp. Law Q., vol 15 (1966), pp 1069-89
FRENZKE, D, 'Der Begriff des ungleichen Vertrages
  im sowjetisch-chinesischen Disput', OT vol 11 (June
  1965), pp 69-103
HOLMBÄCK, Å, 'Principles of international morality
  (unequal treaties) - Les principes de morale inter-
  nationale (traités inégaux). Rapport, suivi de
  discussions', Compte rendu de la XXXVIIe
  conférence de l'Union interparlementaire (1949),
  pp 272-309
NOZARI, F, Unequal treaties in International Law,
  Stockholm 1971
THONNES, August, 'Das Ende der ungleichen
  Verträge in China', Arch. Völkerrechts, vol 4 (1953/
  4), p 158
TSENG YU-HAO, The Termination of Unequal Treaties
  in International Law. Studies in Comparative

Jurisprudence and Conventional Law of Nations (Shanghai, China: Commercial Press, 1933). ii + 550 pp.
WOOLSEY, L H, 'China's termination of unequal treaties', Am. J. Int. Law, vol 21 (1927), p 289

7.13.12 EFFECT OF WAR ON TREATIES

'Accordi bilaterali fra l'Italia ed altri stati rimessi in vigore in base all'art. 44 del trattato di pace', Riv. Diritto Int., vol 36 (1953), pp 273-83
'Notification handed by US ambassador J M Allison to the Japanese minister for foreign affairs on April 22, 1953 regarding prewar agreements with Japan', Department of State Bulletin, vol 28, no 725 (1953), pp 721-2
'Revival of pre-war treaties and agreements between the UK of Great Britain and Northern Ireland and the Governments of Bulgaria, Finland, Hungary, Italy and Roumania (with text of the note of UK Ambassador at Rome to the Italian Minister for foreign affairs, March 13, 1948)', Int. Law Q., vol 2 (1948), pp 535-8
AMBERG, R, & HARHAMMER, Allen, Zur Wiederanwendung von Konventionen durch die Deutsche Demokratische Republik (Mit der Bekanntmachung von 39 wiederanwendbaren Abkommen vom Minister f. Auswärtige Angelegenheiten, Dr Bolz, 16 April 1959)', Deutsche Aussenpolitik (July 1959), pp 764-9; 812-14
BRANDON, M, & LERICHE, A, 'Suspension of rights and obligations under multilateral conventions between opposing belligerents on account of war', Am. J. Int. Law, vol 46 (1952), pp 532-7
CASTEL, J G, 'Effect of war on bilateral treaties: comparative study', Michigan Law Review, vol 51 (1953), pp 566-73

CURTI GIALDINO, A, Gli effetti della guerra sui trattati (Milano: Giuffré, 1959). xi + 271 pp.
CURTI GIALDINO, A, 'Circa gli effetti della seconda guerra mondiale sulla convenzione italo-francese del 3 juin 1930. (Note sous l'arrêt en cassation du 3 mai 1957, Soc. Fornaci Stazzano c Rancillo)', Riv. Diritto Int. (1959), pp 121-33
CURTI GIALDINO, A, 'Rimessa in vigore del diritto convenzionale prebellico in base all'art. 44 del trattato di pace e norme interne sulla stipulazione degli accord internazionali', Riv. Diritto Int., vol 43 (1960), pp 124-34
DENNIS W C, 'The effect of war on treaties', Am. J. Int. Law, vol 23 (1929), p 602
ERADES, L, 'De invloed van oorlog op de geldigheid van verdragen', Thesis. Leiden 1938. xiii + 402 pp.
ERADES, L, 'De invloed, die de Nederlandse rechtspraak met betrekking tot verdragen aan de oorlog toekende', Ned. Tidschr. Int. Recht, vol 3 (1956), pp 105-28. With English summary
GRIMM, F, Die Vorkriegsvertrage nach dem Friedensvertrag und das Verfahren vor den gemischten Schiedsgerichtshofen nach dem Stande vom 1. März 1921, nebst einem Anhang, etc (Essen, 1921)
HURST, C J B, 'The effect of war on treaties', Br. Yearb. Int. Law (1921/2), p 37
KAUFMANN, E, 'Die völkerrechtlichen Vorkriegsverträge', Z. Ausl. Öff. Recht & Völkerrecht, vol 19 (1958), pp 225-33
KEELEY, J R, 'The effect of end of war on pre-war treaties between the belligerents', Grotius Soc. Trans., vol 12 (1927), p 7
KEGEL, G, Die Abwicklung von Vorkriegsverträgen der deutschen Wirtschaft mit dem Ausland. Zugleich ein Beitrag zum Problem der Geschäftsgrundlage (Tübingen: Mohr, 1948). 18 pp. Beiheft Deutsche Rechts-Zeitschrift, 3.

KLEIN, F, 'Kriegsausbruch und Staatsverträge', Jahrb. Int. & Ausl. Öff. Recht (1954), pp 26-57
KUGELMEIER, A M, 'Die Einwirkung des Krieges auf Staatsverträge unter Berücksichtigung der Bestimmungen des Friedensvertrages von Versailles', Thesis. Bonn 1929. 73 pp.
LA PRADELLE, A, 'The effect of war on private law treaties', Int. Law Q., vol 2 (1948), p 555
LA PRADELLE, P de, 'Une solution jurisprudentielle de "droit des gens" du problème de l'effet de la guerre sur les traités', in Technique et principes du droit public. Etudes en l'honneur de G Scelle (1950), pp 463-87
LAYTON, R, 'The effect of measures short of war on treaties', University of Chicago Law Review, vol 30 (1962), pp 96-119
LEANZA, U, 'Intorno agli effetti della guerra sui trattati', Riv. Diritto Int., vol 40 (1957), pp 226-44
LESSER, S T, 'Treaty provisions dealing with the status of pre-war bilateral treaties (in the courts of the United States)', Michigan Law Review, vol 51 (1953), pp 573-82
McINTYRE, S H, Legal Effect of World War II on treaties of the United States (Den Haag: Nijhoff, 1958). x + 392 pp.
McNAIR, A D, 'Les effets de la guerre sur les traités', Acad. Droit Int. Recl. Cours, vol 1 (1937), pp 523-85
McNAIR, A D, War and Treaties (Oxford Pamphlets on World Affairs, no 37) (1942)
MONACO, R, 'Les conventions entre belligérants', Acad. Droit Int. Recl. Cours, vol 2 (1949), p 273
RANK, R, Einwirkung des Krieges auf die nichtpolitischen Staatsverträge (Uppsala: Almqvist & Wiksell, 1949). 234 pp. (Publications de l'Institut suédois de droit international, 8)
PLISCHKE, E, 'Reactivation of prewar German treaties', Am. J. Int. Law, vol 48 (1954), pp 245-64

SCELLE, G, 'De l'influence de l'état de guerre sur le droit conventionnel (à propos d'un récent arrêt de cassation)', J. Droit Int., vol 77 (1950), p 26
SCHINDLER, D, 'Relations de la Suisse avec les puissances alliées et les puissances de l'Axe, avant et après les capitulations. (Au point de vue du droit international public)', Schweiz. Jahrb. Int. Recht, vol 3 (1946), pp 199-218
WOLFF, E, Vorkriegsverträge in Friedensverträgen (Berlin: De Gruyter & Co/Tübingen: Mohr, 1949). xii + 196 pp.

7.13.13 TRANSFORMATION OF TREATIES INTO INTERNAL LAW

See also Section 3.3.2 on the relationship between international law and municipal law and cross-references under 3.3.1. See also certain entries under 7.13.8.4 and Section 13.24.3.12.6.5.3 on the prejudicial system of the European Communities, and Section 13.24.3.12.18 on the law of the European Communities and the law of member states.
DEHAUSSY, J, 'Les conditions d'application des normes conventionnelles sur le for interne français', J. Droit Int. (1960), p 702

7.13.13.1 TRANSFORMATION IN GENERAL

ERADES, L, 'Promulgation and publication of international agreements and their internally binding force in the Netherlands', Ned. Tijdschr. Int. Recht, Liber amicorum J P A François, (July 1959), pp 93-9
GUGGENHEIM, P, 'Die Nicht-veröffentlichungspflichtigen Verträge nach Völkerrecht und schweizerischem Bundesstaatsrecht', Staat and Wirtschaft, Festgab H Nawiasky (24 August 1950), pp 91-107

LANGNER, A von Georg, & WENGLER, W, 'Die Rechtsnatur der Bekanntmachung über das Inkrafttreten völkerrechtlicher Verträge für den Staatsbürger', Neue Juristische Wochenschrift, vol 15, no 6 (8 February 1962), pp 233-88

LEVEL, P, 'La publication en tant que condition d'application des traités par les tribunaux nationaux', Rev. Crit. Droit Int. Priv. (1961), pp 83-104

NARAYANA RAO, K, 'Parliamentary approval of treaties in India', Indian Yearb. Int. Aff. (1960/1), pp 22-39

NISOT, J, 'Le traité signé doit-il, par l'effet d'une obligation internationale, être soumis au parlement en vue de sa ratification?' J. Droit Int. (1930), p 878

REIFF, H, 'The proclaiming of treaties in the United States. (Outline of the views of Dr Hunter Miller)', Am. J. Int. Law, vol 44 (1950), pp 572-6

ROUSSEAU, Ch, 'Le régime actuel de publication des traités en France', Recueil Dalloz de doctrine, de jurisprudence et de legislation (3 December 1953), pp 169-74

SOTO, J de, La Promulgation des traités (Paris: Pédone, 1945). 108 pp.

7.13.13.2 EFFECT OF TREATIES IN THE MUNICIPAL SPHERE AND THE QUESTION OF HIERARCHY OF NORMS

Note cross-references under 7.13.13.

ANDERSON, C P, 'Treaties as domestic law', Am. J. Int. Law, vol 29 (1935), p 472

AUBERT, J F, 'L'autorité, en droit interne, des traités internationaux', Zeitschrift für Schweizerisches Recht, vol 81 (1962), pp 265-87

BIAL, L C, 'Some recent French decisions on the relationship between treaties and municipal law', Am. J. Int. Law, vol 49 (1955), pp 347-55

BIOUX, J, La position de la jurisprudence français vis-à-vis des traités internationaux. Etude de droit public interne (Lille, 1933). 323 pp.

BENOIST, J, 'L'interprétation des traités d'après la jurisprudence française', Rev. Hell. Droit Int., vol 6 (1953), pp 103-16.

FABOZZI, C, L'attuazione dei trattati internazionali (Milano, 1961)

GINSBURG, George, 'The validity of treaties in the municipal law of the socialist states', Am. J. Int. Law, vol 59 (1965), p 523

GREVTSOVA, T P, (International treaties in the system of sources of Soviet national law) (In Russian with an English summary), Sov. Ezheg. Mezhdunar. Prava (1963), pp 171-9

HAYOIT DE TERMICOURT, R, 'Conflict tussen het verdrag en de interne wet', Rechtskundig weekblad, vol 27, no 2 (15 September 1963), col 73-91

HAYOIT DE TERMICOURT, R, 'Le conflit "Traité-loi interne"', Journal des tribunaux, vol 78, no 4414, pp 481-6

HEURON, A de, 'L'autorité des traités internationaux en droit public suisse', Thesis. Neuchâtel 1937. 96 pp.

HÖGTUN, G, 'Incorporation of international treaties in a state's legal system, with special reference to the Council of Europe', Nord. Tidsskr. Int. Ret, vol 28 (1958), pp 62-9

HÖGTUN, G, 'Inkorporasjon av mellem-statlige avtaler i en stats rettssystem med saerlig henblikk pä Europaradet', Nord. Tidsskr. Int. Ret, vol 28 (1958), pp 149-55

HYDE, C C, 'The interpretation of treaties by the Supreme Court of the United States', Am. J. Int. Law (1929), p 824

IRANI, P, The Incorporation of Treaties in Indian
   Law (Bombay: Asia Publishing House, 1961), pp 103-
   14
KAISER, J, 'Die Erfüllung der völkerrechtlichen
   Verträge des Bundes durch die Länder', Z. Ausl. Off.
   Recht & Volkerrecht (1958), pp 526-58
KAUFMANN, E, 'Traité international et loi interne',
   Riv. Diritto Int., vol 41 (1958), pp 369-89
KAUFMAN, E, 'Traité international et loi interne', in
   Mélanges en l'honneur de Gilbert Gidel (Paris, 1961),
   pp 383-400
KOPELMANAS, Lazare, 'Du conflit entre le traité inter-
   national et la loi interne. Quelques remarques au
   sujet des rapports du droit interne et du droit inter-
   national', Rev. Droit Int. & Légis. Comp., ser 3,
   vol 18, (1937), p 88; 310
LAPIDOTH, R, 'De la valeur interne des traités internationaux dans le droit isrélien (precédé par l'état
   des choses sous mandat britannique)', Rev. Gen
   Droit Int. Public, vol 63 (1959), pp 65-93; 221-47
MacBRIDE, R L, Treaties versus the Constitution
   (1955). 89 pp.
MARTINEZ BAEZ, A, 'La constitución y los tratados
   internacionales. Estudios sobre el tratado
   Mexicano-Norteamericano sobre aguas internacionales
   (3 février 1944)', Revista de la Escuela nacional de
   jurisprudencia, vol 8, no 30 (April-June 1946), pp
   167-81; 183-91
MASQUELIN, J, 'L'action réciproque des traités et
   des lois', Annales de droit et de sciences politiques,
   vol 13 (1953), pp 133-56
McNAIR, A D, 'Treaties and sovereignty', Symbolae
   Verzijl (Den Haag: Nijhoff, 1958), pp 222-37
McNAIR, A D, 'L'application et l'interprétation des
   traités d'après la jurisprudence britannique', Acad.
   Droit Int. Recl. Cours, vol 1 (1933), pp 251-307

MENZEL, E, 'Die Geltung internationaler Verträge im innerstaatlichen Recht', Sonderheft der Zeitschrift für ausländisches und internationales Privatrecht (no 21), pp 401-13

MESTRE, A, 'Les traités et le droit interne', Acad. Droit Int. Recl. Cours, vol 4 (1931), pp 233-306

MILLETTE, Anne Marie Jacomy, L'Introduction et l'application des traités internationaux au Canada (Paris, 1970)

MIRONOV, N V, (Correlation between international treaties and national law) (In Russian with an English summary). Sov. Ezheg. Mezhdunar. Prava (1963), pp 150-70

MOLTMANN, G, 'Technik und Sicherung des Vollzugs völkerrechtlicher Verträge in Deutschland und England', Thesis. Hamburg 1936

MONACO, R, 'Die internationalen Verträge und die neue italienische Verfassung', Österr. Z. Öff. Recht, vol 6 (1954), pp 285-302

MOUSKHELY, M, 'Le traité et la loi dans le système constitutionnel français de 1946', Z. Ausl. Öff. Recht & Völkerrecht, vol 13 (1950), pp 98-117

MURACCIOLE, L, 'Revue de jurisprudence française en matière internationale (1951). Les traités internationaux', Rev. Droit Public & Sci. Polit., vol 69 (1953), 515-28

PAPACOSTAS, A N, 'L'autorité des conventions internationales en Grèce', Rev. Hell. Droit Int., vol 15 (1962), pp 361-7

PAPALAMBROU, A, 'Le problème de la "transformation" et la question de la validité des actes étatiques "contraires" au droit international. (Avec un aperçu de la doctrine et de la jurisprudence grecques)', Rev. Hell. Droit Int., vol 3 (1950), pp 234-69

PASTOR RIDRUEJO, J A, 'La estipulación y la eficacia interna de los tratados en el derecho español', Rev. Esp. Derecho Int.. vol 17 (1964), pp 39-59

PESCATORE, P, 'L'autorité, en droit interne, des traités internationaux selon la jurisprudence luxembourgeoise', Pasicrise luxembourgeoise, 1962, pp 97-115

PESCATORE, P, Conclusion et effet des traités internationaux selon le droit constitutionnel, les usages et la jurisprudence du Grand-Duché de Luxembourg (Luxembourg, 1964)

PREUSS, L, 'The execution of treaty obligations through internal law. System of the United States and of some other countries', Am. Soc. Int. Law Proc. (1951), pp 82-100

REIFF, H, 'The proclaiming of treaties in the United States. (Outline of the views of Dr H. Miller)', Am. J. Int. Law, vol 44 (1950), pp 572-6

RICE, W G, 'The position of international treaties in Swiss law', Am. J. Int. Law, (1952), pp 641-66

RIGAUX, F, 'Les conflits de la loi nationale avec les traités internationaux', Rapport au VIIe Congrès international de droit comparé, Bruxelles (1966), p 269

RIPHAGEN, W, 'Iets over de betekenis der structuur van verdragen en besluiten van internationale instellingen voor de internationale en de interne rechtsorde', in Opstellen aangeboden aan Prof. mr dr van den Bergh ter gelegenheid van zijn aftreden als hoogleraar in het nederlandse staatsrecht aan de Universiteit van Amsterdam (1960), pp 192-210

ROZMARYN, S, 'Les traités internationaux dans le droit constitutionnel de la République populaire de Pologne', in Mélanges offerts à Henri Rolin (Paris, 1964), pp 311-27

SALVIOLI, G, 'Qualche riflessione sulla legge e il trattato', Z. Ausl. Öff. Recht. & Völkerrecht, vol 19 (1958), pp 385-8

SANTA PINTER, J J, 'Legislación nacional argentina versus tratados internacionales', Rev. Esp. Derecho Int., vol 11, pp 587-97

SAVARIT, R, 'Les traités internationaux dans la constitution des Etats-Unis et la proposition d'amendement du senateur Bricker', Rev. Int. Droit Comp., vol 7 (1955), pp 132-43

SCHWARZENBERGER, G, 'International law in early English practice', Br. Yearb. Int. Law (1948), pp 52-90

SEPULVEDA, C, 'La autoridad de los tratados internacionales en el derecho interno', Boletin del Instituto de derecho comparado de México, vol 15, no 45 (September-December 1962), pp 511-19

SEPULVEDA, C, 'La situación de los tratados en el orden legal Mexicano'. Comunicaciones Mexicanas al VI congreso internacional de derecho comparado (1962), pp 203-17

SHATZKY, B, 'Le problème de la priorité des traités à l'égard des lois', J Droit Int. (1933), pp 45-52

SIDENBLADH, Karl, 'Traktat och lag i praktiken', Svensk juristtidning, vol 50 (1965), p 600

STICHELE, M van der, 'Zal de UNO de wetten van de USA maken? Het "Bricker draft amendment" als oplossing van enkele moeilijkheden door de Amerikaanse grondwet gesteld', Ars aequi, vol 4 (1955), pp 232-7

TAYLOR, Paul B, 'The execution of treaties in the United States', Thesis. Columbia University 1951

TARAZI, Salah el Dine, 'La superiorité du traité sur la loi dans la nouvelle constitution syriénne', Revue de droit international pour le Moyen-Orient, vol 3 (1954), pp 177-84

VERBAET, Ch, 'Du conflit entre le traité et la loi. De leurs forces respectives devant le pouvoir judiciaire. (Droit belge et droit comparé)', J T O M, vol 9, no 98 (15 August 1958), pp 113-15

VIGNES, D, 'L'autorité des traités internationaux en droit interne', Travaux et recherches de l'institut de droit comparé de l'université de Paris, pp 475-85

VISSCHER, P de, 'Les positions actuelles de la doctrine et de la jurisprudence belges à l'égard du conflit entre le traité et la loi', in Mélanges Guggenheim (Genève, 1968), pp 605-12

WINKLER, G, 'Der Verfassungsrang von Staatsverträgen. Eine Untersuchung des geltende österreichischen Verfassungsrechtes', Österr. Z. Öff. Recht, vol 10 (1960), pp 514-39

7.13.13.3 SELF-EXECUTING TREATIES

ERADES, L, 'Poging tot ontwarring van de "self-executing" knoop', Nederlandse jurisprudentie, no 37 (2 November 1963), pp 845-53

ERADES, L, 'Le problème des dispositions directionment applicables (self-executing) des traités internationaux et son application aux traités instituant une communauté européenne', Rev. Hell. Droit Int., vol 17 (1964), pp 221-39

EVANS, A E, 'Self-executive treaties in the United States of America', Br. Yearb. Int. Law (1953), pp 178-205

GORDON, W C, 'International law - self-executing treaties - the genocide convention', Modern Law Review, vol 48, no 6 (April 1950), pp 852-60

PREUSS, L, 'On amending the treaty making power: a comparative study of the self-executing treaties', Modern Law Review, vol 51, no 8 (June 1953), pp 1117-42

VASAK, K, 'Was bedeutet die Aussage: ein Staatsverträg sei "self-executing"?' Juristische Blätter 83, no 24 (23 December 1961), pp 621-2

WIJMEN, P C E van, 'Self-executingness van volkenrechtelijke overeenkomsten', Ars aequi, vol 12 (1962), pp 1-8

7.13.13.4 COMPATIBILITY OF TREATIES WITH CONSTITUTIONS

ABDORRAN-BOUROUMAND, La Licéité constitutionelle de la conclusion des traités instituant une communauté supranationale (Geneve/Tehran, 1956)

CAPITANT, R, 'La constitutionnalité des traités européens', Année politique et économique, vol 30, pp 274-9

GOOSSENS, Ch, 'La Communauté européenne du charbon et de l'acier et le régime constitutionnel de la Belgique', Rev. Droit Public & Sci Polit., vol 71 (1955), pp 98-115

HAURI, Kurt, Die Verfassungsmässigkeit der Staatsverträge (Bern, 1962)

KLEFFENS, A van, 'Europese integratie en grondwet', Nederl. juristenblad, no 8 (1952), pp 165-72

KOPELMANAS, L, 'Du conflit entre le traité international et la loi interne. Quelques remarques au sujet des rapports du droit interne et du droit international', Rev. Droit Int. & Légis. Comp., ser 3, vol 18 (1937), pp 88; 310

MONACO, R, Osservazioni sulla costituzionalità degli accordi internazionali (Milano, 1958). 16 pp. Comitato nazionale per la celebrazione del primo decennale della promulgazione della costituzione (27 Dicembre 1947-17 Dicembre 1957). Estratto dal Vol II Studi sulla costituzione.

MOSCONI, F, 'Norme straniere e controllo di costituzionalità e di legittimità internazionale', Diritto internazionale, vol 14 (1960), pp 426-39

SCELLE, G, 'De la prétendue inconstitutionnalité interne des traités. (A propos du Traité sur la "Communauté européenne de défense")', Rev. Droit Public & Sci. Polit., vol 68 (1952), pp 1012-28

WRIGHT, Q, 'The constitutionality of treaties', Am. J. Int. Law, vol 13 (1919), p 242

7.13.13.5 COMPATIBILITY WITH
OTHER TREATIES

AUFRICHT, H, 'Supersession of treaties in international law', Cornell Law Quarterly, vol 37 (1952), pp 655-700
JENKS, C, 'The conflict of law-making treaties', Br. Yearb. Int. Law (1953), pp 401-53
LAUTERPACHT, H, 'The Covenant as the "higher law"', Br. Yearb. Int. Law (1936), p 54
MAROTTA RANGEL, V, Do conflito entre a Carta das Naçoes Unidas e os demais acordos internacionais (São Paulo, 1954). 139 pp.
VERDROSS, A von, 'Forbidden treaties in international law', Am. J. Int. Law, vol 31 (1937), p 571
VERDROSS, A von, 'Jus dispositivum and jus cogens in international law', Am. J. Int. Law, vol 60, (1966), pp 55-63
WRIGHT, Q, 'Conflicts between international law and treaties', Am. J. Int. Law, vol 11 (1917), p 566

7.13.14 TREATIES AND THIRD PARTIES

See also Sections 13.15 on international relations of international organizations, 13.24.2.20 on the UN and non-members, and 13.24.3.12.15 on the European Communities and third states

7.13.14.1 GENERAL

ARÉCHAGA, E J de, 'Treaty stipulations of third states', Am. J. Int. Law, vol 50 (1956), p 338
BALLREICH, H, 'Völkerrechtliche Verträge zu Lasten Dritter', Völker- und Staatsrechtliche Abhandlungen (1954), pp 1-26
DOLD, G, Stipulations for a Third Party (London, 1948)

ENRIQUES, G, 'Sugli effetti giuridici dei trattati internazionali per i terzi', Riv. Diritto Int., vol 25 (1933), pp 24-37

GELLERMANN, K P, Völkerrechtliche Verträge zu Lasten Dritter (München, 1963). 145 pp.

GIARDINA, A, Comunità europee e stati terzi (Napoli, 1964). 243 pp.

GROTTANELLI DE SANTI, G, 'Il principio "pacta tertiis nec nocent nec iuvant" e le'attuali tendenze internazionali'. Studi senesi in memoria di Ottotin Vannoni (1957), pp 765-801

JIMENEZ DE ARECHAGA, E, 'Treaty stipulations in favor of third states', Am. J. Int. Law, vol 50 (1956), pp 338-57

JIMENEZ DE ARECHAGA, E, 'La estipulacion en favor de terceros estados en el derecho internacional', in Estudios jurídicos en memoria de J Irurera Goyena (Madrid, 1955), pp 301-414

KELSEN, H, 'Traités internationaux à la charge d'états tiers', in Mélanges Mahaim, vol 2 (1935), pp 164-72

KOJANEC, G, Trattati e terzi stati. Limiti soggettivi di validita delle zonne positive dell'ordinamento internazionale (Padova, 1961). 251 pp.

KRUGER, H, 'Geschäftsführung ohne Aufträge für die Völkergemeinschaft', Völker- und Staatsrechtliche Abhandlungen (1954), pp 169-204

McNAIR, A D, 'A note on pacta tertiis', Ned. Tijdschr. Int. Recht Liber amicorum J P A François (July 1959), pp 188-193

McNAIR, A D, 'Treaties producing effects "erga omnes" ', Scritti di diritto internazionale in onore di Tomaso Perassi (Milano, 1957), vol 2, pp 21-35

PAHR, W P, 'Der Verträge zu Lasten Dritter im Völkerrecht', Österr. Z. Öff. Recht, vol 6 (1955), pp 600-10

PASTOR RIDRUEJO, J A, 'Los efectos de los acuerdos internacionales respecto a los terceros', Rev. Esp. Derecho Int., vol 13, pp 387-411

POMPE, C A, 'Toepassing van multilaterale verdragen op derde staten', Themis, no 4 (1951), pp 322-44

RIZ A PORTA, G G, Der Vertrag zu Günsten Dritter im Völkerrecht (Zürich, 1942). 77 pp.

ROUCOUNAS, E, 'Le traité et les états tiers', Rev. Hell. Droit Int. (1964), pp 299-365

ROXBURGH, R F, International Conventions and Third States. A Monograph (London 1917)

SCRIMALI, A, Efficacia dei trattati rispetto ai terzi stati (Palermo: Domino, 1938). 149 pp.

SCRIMALI, A, 'Dell'efficacia dei trattati sfavoreoli ai terzi stati', Rev. Droit Int. Sci. Dipl. & Polit., vol 16 (1938), pp 243-57; vol 17 (1939), pp 23-30

SCRIMALI, A, 'Natur und Grundlage der Rechtsverbindlichkeit des Völkerrechts mit besonderer Berucksichtigung der Wirksamkeit der internationalen Verträge und übereinkommen fur jene Staaten, die nicht an ihrer Gestaltung teilgenommen haben', Z. Öff. Recht, vol 21 (1941), pp 190-216

WINKLER, C H, Verträge zu Gunsten und zu Lasten Dritter im Völkerrecht (Leipzig: Hoske, 1932). xiv + 124 pp.

WUNSCHIK, J, Die Wirkung der völkerrechtlichen Verträge für dritte staaten (Bern, 1930). 75 pp.

VERDROSS, A, von, 'Le Nazioni e i terzi stati', La comunità internazionale, vol 2 (1947)

7.13.14.2 MOST-FAVOURED-NATION CLAUSES

Most-favoured-nation clauses are one form of treaties of benefit to third parties. One recent and valuable article is the Hague course by VIGNES listed below.

BONHOEFFER, Klaus, Die Meistbegünstigung im modernen Völkerrecht (Berlin, 1930)

CATUDAL, H M, 'The most-favoured-nation clause and the courts', Am. J. Int. Law, vol 35 (1941), p 41

CLUTE, R, & WILSON, R, 'The Commonwealth and favored-nation usage', Am. J. Int. Law (1958), pp 455-68

DOMKE, M, & Hazard, J N, 'State trading and the most-favoured-nation clause', Am. J. Int. Law, vol 52 (1958), p 55

HAZARD, J N, 'Commercial discrimination and international law', Am. J. Int. Law, vol 52 (1958), p 495

JAHNKE, L G, 'The European Economic Community and the most-favoured-nation-clause', Can. Yearb. Int. Law, vol 1 (1963), p 252

KUNG, E, 'Zur Problematik der Meistbegünstigung', Weltwirtschaftliche Archiv, vol 67 (1951), pp 21-58. With summaries in English and French.

LACHARRIERE, G de, 'Aspects récents de la clause de la nation la plus favorisée', Annu. Fr. Droit Int. (1961), p 10

LOHER, A, Die Meistbegünstigungsklausel (1949). 125 pp

NOLDE, B, 'La clause de la nation la plus favorisée et les tarifs préférentiels', Acad. Droit Int. Recl. Cours, vol 1 (1932), p 1

NOLDE, B, 'Les effets de la clause de la nation la plus favorisée en matière de commerce et de navigation. Rapport lors de la 15me commission des travaux préparatoires de la session de Paris, 1934', Annu. Inst. Droit Int. (1934), p 414; (1936), vol 2, p 39; 289

NOLDE, B, 'Problèmes modernes du régime de la nation la plus favorisée', Rev. Droit Int. & Légis Comp., ser 3, vol 14 (1933), p 185

OPPENHEIM, H F, La clause de la nation la plus favorisée dans la pratique internationale de la

Suisse(Zürich: Editions polygraphiques, 1948).
214 pp.
PAPAS, C N, 'Clause of the "most favored nation"
with Egypt', Rev. Hell. Droit Int., vol 14 (1961),
p 226
PESCATORE, P, La clause de la nation la plus
favorisée dans les conventions multilatérales,
rapport présenté à l'Institut de droit international,
1968
ROESNER, P, 'Die Meistbegünstigungsklausel in den
bilateralen Handelsverträgen der Bundesrepublik
Deutschland', Dissertation. Heidelberg 1964. 140 pp
ROSSILLION, C, 'La clause de la nation la plus
favorisée dans la jurisprudence de la Cour international de justice', J. Droit Int., vol 82 (1955),
p 76. Also in English
SCHIAVONE, Guiseppe, 'Uguaglianza di trattamento e
clausola della nazione più favorita nell'accordo
generale sulle tariffe doganali e sul commercio
(GATT)', Riv. Diritto Int., vol 46 (1963), p 366
SCHWARZENBERGER, G, 'The most-favoured-nation
standard in British state practice', Br. Yearb. Int.
Law (1945), p 96
SERENI, Angelo Piero, 'Il trattaménto della nazione
più favorita', Riv. Diritto Int., vol 24 (1932), p 53;
201; 405
SNIJDER, R C, The Most Favoured Nation Clause. An
Analysis with Particular Reference to Recent
Treaty-practice and Tariffs (New York, 1948).
264 pp.
SUNDBOM, I, Mest-gynnad-nations-klausulen i
nutidens handelsavtal. Forelasningar över utrikes
handelns rättsliga problem, 1946, 2
VELASCO, R, La clausula de la nación mas
favorecida (Lima, 1962). 163 pp.
VIGNES, D, 'La clause de la nation la plus favorisée et
sa pratique contemporaine - problèmes posés par

la Communauté économique européenne', Acad.
Droit Int. Recl. Cours, vol 130 (1970), pp 207-350
VISSER, L E, 'La clause de "la nation la plus
favorisée" dans les traités de commerce', Rev.
Droit Int. & Légis. Comp, ser 2, vol 4 (1902), p
66; 159; 270
WRIGHT, Quincy, 'The most-favoured-nation clause',
Am. J. Int. Law, vol 21 (1927), p 760

8 Settlement of Disputes and International Tribunals

8.1 SETTLEMENT OF DISPUTES IN GENERAL

Settlement of disputes must obviously be studied in close conjunction with already existing case law providing both substantive and procedural rules for the solving of conflicts (see above Section 1.4). For connected problems see Section 9 on international peacekeeping and Section 13.24.2.22.23 on peacekeeping by the United Nations and its forces.

MORELLI, G, Nuovi studi sul processo internazionale (Milano: Giuffré, 1972). 173 pp.
Report of a Study Group of the David Davies
  Institute of International Studies, International Disputes: the Legal Aspects (London, 1972). (Europa Publ.)
Disputes (London, 1972). (Europa Publ.)
REUTER, P, Cours de droit international public, les modes de solution des conflits internationaux (Paris: Cours de droit, 1958)

8.2 CONCILIATION

COT, J P, International Conciliation (London: Europa, 1972/Paris: Pédone, 1968, in French)

ETREMOTT, 'Organisation de la Conciliation Comme moyen de prévenir la guerre', Acad. Droit Int. Recl. Cours, vol 59 (1937), pp 103-222

HAMZEH, F S, International Conciliation (Amsterdam: Djambatan, 1965). 175 pp.

REVEL, G, 'Rôle et caractère des commissions de conciliation', Rev. Gén. Droit Int. Public (1931), p 564

VULCAN, C, La Conciliation dans le droit international actuel (Paris, 1932)

WEHBERG, H, 'Die Vergleichkommissionen im modernen Völkerrecht', in Festgabe fur Makarov (Stuttgart, 1958), p 551

8.3 NEGOTIATION

KAASIK, N, 'La clause des negociations diplomatiques dans le droit international positif et dans la jurisprudence de la Cour internationale de justice', Rev. Droit Int. & Légis. Comp (1933), p 62

8.4 GOOD OFFICES

PECHOTA, V, The Quiet Approach. A Study of the Good Offices Exercised by the United Nations Secretary-General in the Cause of Peace (New York: UNITAR, 1972). vi + 92 pp.

8.5 MEDIATION

SCHÜCKING, W, Das völkerrechtliche Institut der Vermittlung (Kristiania, 1923)

POLITIS, N, 'L'avenir de la médition', Rev. Gén. Droit Int. Public (1910), p 130

8.6 COMMISSIONS OF INQUIRY

HYDE, C C, 'The place of commissions of inquiry and concilation treaties in the peaceful settlement of international disputes', Br. Yearb. Int. Law (1929), p 96

POLITIS, N, 'Les commissions internationales d'enquête', Rev. Gén. Droit Int. Public (1912), p 149

8.7 INTERNATIONAL ADJUDICATION IN GENERAL

ANAND, R P, Studies in International Adjudication (Delhi: Vicas Publications, 1969). 298 pp.

ANDRASSY, J, Medunarodno pravosude. Ustrojstvo i postupak (Zagreb, 1948). 230 pp.

BARCLAY, Sir Thomas, The New Method of Adjusting International Disputes and the Future (London: Constable, 1917)

BASTID, Susanne, La fonction juridictionnelle dans les relations internationales (Paris: Les Cours de droit, 1957). 435 pp.

BERLIA, G, 'Jurisprudence des tribunaux internationaux en ce qui concerne leur competence', Acad. Droit Int. Recl. Cours, vol 88 (1955), p 109

CASTBERG, Frede, 'L'Excès de pouvoir dans la justice internationale', Acad. Droit Int. Recl. Cours, vol 35 (1931), p 357

DELBEZ, L, Les Principes généraux du contentieux international (Paris, 1962). 340 pp.

DARBY, W E, International Tribunals. A Collection of the various Schemes Which Have Been Propounded and of Instances in the Nineteenth Century, 4th edition (London: J M Dent & Co, 1904)

FALK, A, ARON, T M, TIMBERG, S, & STANGER, R J, Essays on International Jurisdiction (Columbus, 1961). 94 pp.
FASCHING, H W, 'Die Aufgaben der internationalen und übernationalen Gerichtsbarkeit', Österr. Z. Öff. Recht, vol 10 (1960), pp 169-224
FINKELSTEIN, Maurice, 'Judicial self-limitation', Harvard Law Review, vol 37 (1923/4), p 338
GRIEVES, Forest L, Supranational and International Adjudication (Urbana, Ill: University of Illinois Press, 1970). xv + 266 pp.
GUCKEL, P, Die Streitbeilegungsvorschriften in den Satzungen der internationalen Organisationen mit Ausnahme der Vereinten Nationen und der europäischen Gemeinschaften (Bonn, 1962). 217 pp.
HAMBRO, E, Folkerettspleie (Oslo, 1956). 272 pp.
HAMMARSKJÖLD, Å, Juridiction internationale (Leiden: Sijthoff, 1938). 896 pp.
HARDY, Jean, 'The interpretation of plurilingual treaties by international courts and tribunals', Br. Yearb. Int. Law, vol 37 (1961), p 72
HELDRICH, Andreas, Internationale Zuständigkeit und Any ndbares Rechts (Tübingen: J C B Mohr (Paul Siebeck), 1969). xx + 279 pp.
HUBER, Max, 'Classification des conflits justiciables', (Commentary) Annu. Inst. Droit Int., vol 29 (1922), p 241
HUDSON, M O, International Tribunals. Past and Future (Washington, 1944). 287 pp.
IACCARINO, U, Della c. d. competenza sulla competenza dei tribunali internazionali (Napoli: Morano, 1962). 136 pp.
JENKS, C Wilfred, 'Compétence obligatoire des instances judiciaires et arbitrales internationales', Annu. Inst. Droit Int., (1959), vol 2, p 57

JENKS, C W, The Prospects of International Adjudication (London: Stevens/Dobbs Ferry, NY: Oceana, 1964)

KATZ, M, The Relevance of International Adjudication (Cambridge, Mass: Harvard University Press, 1968). 655 pp.

KELSEN, Hans, 'Compulsory adjudication of international disputes', Am. J. Int. Law, vol 37 (1934), p 397

KRISPI, I, To diethnes dikastiron tou organismou Inomenon Ethnon (Athens, 1959). 480 pp.

LARSON, A, When Nations Disagree. A Handbook on Peace through Law (Baton Rouge, La: Louisiana State University Press, 1961). 251 pp.

McNAIR, A D, The Development of International Justice, Two Lectures Delivered at the Law Center of New York University in December 1953 (New York, 1954)

MORELLI, G, 'La théorie générale du procès international', Acad. Droit Int. Recl. Cours, vol 61 (1937), p 257

MORRIS, C, 'Peace through law: the role and limits of adjudication', University of Pennsylvania Law Review, vol 109 (1960/1), p 212

POLITIS, N, La Justice internationale (Paris: Hachette, 1924)

See also the work by CHENG listed in Section 5.5.2.

8.8 ARBITRATION AND ITS PROCEDURE

The standard work is that by SIMPSON & FOX.

ACREMENT, Albert, La Procédure dans les arbitrages internationaux (Paris: Imprimerie Sueur-Charruey, 1905)

American Arbitration Association, A Dictionary of Arbitration and its Terms, Labour, Commercial, International: A Concise Encyclopedia of Peaceful Dispute Settlement (Dobbs Ferry, NY: Oceana, 1970)

AUDRY, Léon, La Revision de la sentence arbitrale (Paris: E Duchemin, 1914)
BALASKO, A, Causes de nullité de la sentence arbitrale en droit international public (Paris: Editions A Pédone, 1938)
BAYER, F, 'Das Wesen der internationalen Schiedsgerichtsbarkeit - Vermittlung und Schiedsgerichtsbarkeit in den Haager Konventionen, der Völkerbundsatzung und der Satzung der Vereinten Nationen', Dissertation. München 1953
BISHOP, C M, International Arbitral Procedure (Washington: J Byrne & Co, 1931)
BOREL, Eugene, 'Les voies de recours contre les sentences arbitrales', Acad. Droit Int. Recl. Cours, vol 52 (1935), p 1
CARLSTON, K S, The Process of International Arbitration (New York: Columbia University Press, 1946)
CAVARE, L, 'La notion de juridiction international', Annu. Fr. Droit Int. (1956), pp 496-501
CHAPAL, P, L'Arbitrabilité des differends internationaux (Paris, 1967)
CORY, Helen, Compulsory Arbitration on International Disputes (New York: Columbia University Press, 1932; reissued 1972 by Kraus Reprint Co, New York)
GOLDSCHMIDT, R, 'Projet de règlement pour les tribunaux arbitraux internationaux', Rev. Droit Int. & Legis. Comp., ser 1, vol 6 (1874), p 421
GUERMANOFF, Dimitri, L'Excès de Pouvoir de l'arbitre (Paris: Université de Paris, 1929)
GUYOMAR, G, 'Le règlement de la Cour permanente d'arbitration relatif aux conflits internationaux entre deux parties dont une seulement est état', Annu. Fr. Droit Int. (1962), pp 377-90
JOHNSON, D H N, 'The constitution of an arbitral tribunal', Br. Yearb. Int. Law, vol 30 (1953), pp 152-77

RALSTON, Jackson H, International Arbitral Law and Procedure (Boston/London: Ginn, 1910). xiv + 352 pp.

REVON, Michel, L'Arbitrage international, son passé, son présent, son avenir (Paris: A Rousseau, 1892)

ROUARD DE CARD, Edgard, Droit international l'arbitrage international dans le passé, le présent, et l'avenir (Paris: A Durand et Pedone-Lauriel, 1877)

RUEGGER, P, 'Schiedsklauseln in neuen Kollektiv-Verträgen zur Kodification des internationalen rechts', in I s A Festschrift für Walter Schatzel zu seinem 70. Geburtstag, (1960), pp 407-17

MERIGNHAC, A, Traité théorique et pratique de l'arbitrage international (Paris: Larose, 1895)

SALVIOLI, G, 'Sul potere dell'arbitro a pronunciarsi sulla sua competenza', Diritto Internazionale, vol 13 (1959), p 119

SHAMMA, S, 'Arbitration, conciliation and other means of resolving international disputes', in World Peace through Law Center Conference Report (1963), p 112

SIMPSON, J L, & FOX, H, International Arbitration: Law and Practice (London: Stevens, 1959). 330 pp.

SOHN, L B, 'The function of international arbitration today', Acad. Droit Recl. Cours, vol 108 (1963), pp 1-113

SUMMERS, L M, 'International arbitration', World Peace through Law Center Conference Report (1965), p 299

VERDROSS, A, 'L'excès de pouvoir de juge arbitral dans le droit international public', Rev. Droit Int. & Légis. Comp., ser 3, vol 9 (1928), p 225

VIGNANO, A T de, 'Algunas observaciones sobre el poder del arbitro (o del juez internacional) para pronunciarse sobre la propria competencia', Rev. Esp. Derecho Int., vol 15 (1962), pp 439-44

WILSON, Robert R, International Agreements for Obligatory Arbitration (Doctorate Thesis - Harvard University) Limited publication 1957
WILSON, Robert R, 'Reservation clauses in agreements for obligatory arbitration', Am. J. Int. Law, vol 23 (1929), p 68

8.9 INTERNATIONAL TRIBUNALS IN GENERAL: LAW AND PROCEDURE

GROSSEN, J M, Les Presomptions en droit international public (Neuchâtel: Delachaux et Niestlé, 1954)
RALSTON, J H, The Law and Procedure of International Tribunals, revised edition (Stanford, Calif: Stanford University Press, 1926)
RALSTON, J H, The Law and Procedure of International Tribunals. Supplement to the 1926 Revised Edition (Stanford, Calif: Stanford University Press, 1936)
SALVIOLI, G, 'Problèmes de procédure dans la jurisprudence internationale', Acad. Droit Int. Recl. Cours (Leyde, 1958), p 64
SCHLOCHAUER, H J, 'Die Entwicklung der internationalen Schiedsgerichtbarkeit', Arch. Völkerrechts, vol 10 (1962/3), p 1
SCHWARZENBERGER, G, International Law as Applied by International Courts and Tribunals (London: Stevens, 1957-68). 2 vols.
SERENI, A P, Principi generali di diritto e processo internazionale (Milano, 1955). 98 pp.
SOHN, Louis B, 'International tribunals: past, present and future', American Bar Association Journal, vol 46, p 23
SOUBEYROL, J, 'Jurisprudence et juridictions internationales', Annu. Fr. Droit Int. (1951), p 232
STOLL, J A, L'Application et l'interprétation du droit interne par les juridictions internationales (Université libre de Bruxelles, 1962). 225 pp.

URBANEK, H, 'Die Überprufüng und Aufhebung nationaler Urteile durch internationale Gerichte', Thesis. Bonn 1957. 176 pp.

VISSCHER, C de, Problèmes d'interprétation judiciaire en droit international public (Paris: A Pédone, 1963)

WHITE, Gillian, The Use of Experts by International Tribunals (Syracuse, NY: Syracuse University Press, 1965). 259 pp.

WITENBERG, J C, & DESRIOUX, J, 'L'Organisation judiciaire: la procédure et la sentence internationales (Paris: A Pédone, 1937)

8.9.1 SPECIAL PROCEDURAL ASPECTS AND MECHANISMS OF LITIGATION

BOS, M, De procesvoorwaarden in het volkenrecht/ Les conditions du procès en droit international public (Dordrecht, 1951). 280 pp.

BOS, Maarten, Les Conditions du procès en droit international public (Leiden, 1957) (19 Bibliotheca Visseriana)

SMITH, C, The Relation between Proceedings and Premises (Oslo: Universitets Forlager, 1962). 138 pp.

8.9.2 NON-LIQUET

LAUTERPACHT, H, 'Some observations on the prohibition of non-liquet and the completeness of the law', in Symbolae Verzijl Présentées au Professeur J H W Verzijl à l'occasion de son LXX-ième anniversaire (Den Haag: Nijhoff, 1958), pp 169-221

STONE, J, 'Non-liquet and the function of law in the international community', Br. Yearb. Int. Law (1959), p 129

8.9.3 PLEA OF DOMESTIC JURISDICTION

See also Section 3 on the relationship between international law and internal law, Section 8.11.9 on domestic jurisdiction and the ICJ, and Section 9.24.2.10 on the UN and domestic jurisdiction.

BRIERLY, J L, 'Matters of domestic jurisdiction', Br. Yearb. Int. Law, vol 6 (1925), p 8

GUERRERO, J Gustave, 'La qualification unilatérale de la compétence nationale', in Grundprobleme des Internationalen Rechts, ed. Constantopoulos (1957), p 207

WALDOCK, C H M, 'The plea of domestic jurisdiction before international legal tribunals', Br. Yearb. Int. Law, vol 31 (1954), p 96

VAUCHER, M, Le Problème de la justiciabilité et de la non-justiciabilité en droit international des differends dits 'politiques' ou 'non-juridiques' et les notions de compétence exclusive et de compétence nationale (article 15, 8 du Pacte de la SdN et article 2 7 de la Charte de l'O N U (Montreux, 1951). 256 pp.

8.9.4 EXHAUSTION OF LOCAL REMEDIES

CHAPPEZ, Jean, La Règle de l'épuisement des voies de recours internes (Paris: Editions A Pédone, 1972). xii + 263 pp.

FAWCETT, J E S, 'The exhaustion of local remedies: substance or procedure', Br. Yearb. Int. Law, vol 31 (1954), p 452

HAESLER, T, The Exhaustion of Local Remedies in the Case Law of International Courts and Tribunals (Leiden, 1968). 169 pp.

LAW, Castor H P, The Local Remedies Rule in International Law, (Travaux de juridiction internationale) (Genève: Librairie E Droz/Paris: Librairie Minard, 1961)

MERON, Theodor, 'The incidence of the rule of exhaustion of local remedies', Br. Yearb. Int. Law, vol 35 (1959), p 83

8.9.5 INTERIM MEASURES

COCATRE-ZILGIEN, A, 'Les mesures conservatoires en droit international', Rev. Egypt. Droit Int., vol 11 (1955), p 73
DUMBAULD, E, Interim Measures of Protection in International Controversies (Den Haag: Nijhoff, 1932)
GUGGENHEIM, Paul, 'Les measures conservatoires dans la procédure arbitrale et judiciaire', Acad. Droit Int. Recl. Cours, vol 40 (1932), p 649

8,9.6 JUDGMENTS EX AEQUO ET BONO

AYCINENA SALAZAR, L, El procedimiento "ex aequo et bono" y la controversia Angloguatemalteca sobre Belice. Guatemala, 1949. Tesis Brasil
BERLIA, G, Essai sur la portée de la clause de jugement en équité en droit des gens (Paris, 1937)
CALOYANNI, M, 'The organisation of international justice, justiciable and political disputes, and the prospects thereof', Grotius Soc. Trans., vol 23 (1937), pp 71-84
FRIEDMANN, W, The Contribution of English Equity to the Idea of an International Equity Tribunal (London, 1935)
The Functions of an International Equity Tribunal (London, 1944)
GARCIA BAUER, C, 'El procedimiento ex-aequo et bono (I). La controversia sobre Belice y el procedimiento ex-aequo et bono (II)', Revista de la Asociación guatemalteca de derecho internacional, January 1959 (no 3), pp 7-30

HABICHT, M, 'Le pouvoir du juge international de statuer "ex aequo et bono" ', Acad. Droit Int. Recl. Cours, vol 49 (1934), pp 277-371

HABICHT, M, The Power of the International Judge to Give a Decision 'ex aequo et bono', (London, 1935)

HOHENWART, G, 'Der materiellrechtliche Begriff der Billigkeit im Völkerrecht', Jahrbuch der Konsularakademie zu Wien (1937), pp 43-50

MUNRO, H, 'The international equity tribunal', The New Commonwealth, vol 6 (1937/8), pp 207-8; 229-30; vol 7 (1938/9), pp 13-14

SCHEUNER, U, 'Decisions ex aequo et bono by international courts and arbitral tribunals', in International Arbitration: Liber amicorum for Martin Domke, edited by P Sanders (Den Haag: Nijhoff, 1967), pp 275-88

SIMONS, W, & SCHÜCKING, W, 'Critique de l'ouvrage de Karl Strupp: Das Recht des internationalen Richters, nach Billigkeit zu entscheiden (Frankfurter Abhandlungen zum modernen Völkerrecht, 10) Leipzig 1930', Juristische Wochenschrift, (1932), vol 1, pp 25-7

SOHN, L B, 'Arbitration of international disputes ex aequo et bono', in International Arbitration: Liber amicorum for Martin Domke, edited by P Sanders (Den Haag: Nijhoff, 1967), pp 330-7

STRUPP, K, Das Recht des internationalen Richters, nach Billigkeit zu entscheiden (Frankfurter Abhandlungen zum modernen Völkerrecht, 20) (Leipzig, 1930)

STRUPP, K, 'Le droit du juge international de statuer selon l'équité', Acad. Droit Int. Recl. Cours, vol 33 (1930), pp 351-481

YOTIS, Ch, 'De l'influence de la notion de "Justice et d'Equité" sur l'application des traités de paix par les tribunaux arbitraux mixtes', J. Droit Int., vol 50 (1923), pp 249-55

8.9.7 FORUM PROROGATUM

Cf. Section 8.11.5 on forum prorogation of the ICJ, especially the article by WALDORF.
WINIARSKI, B, 'Quelques réflexions sur le soisdisant forum prorogatum en droit international', in Grundprobleme des Internationalen Rechts, ed Constantopoulos (1957), p 445

8.9.8 EXCESS OF POWER BY COURTS

LAPRADELLE, Albert de, 'L'excès de pouvoir de l'arbitre', Rev. Droit Int., vol 2 (1928), p 5
LAUTERPACHT, Sir Hersch, 'The legal remedy in case of excess jurisdiction', Br. Yearb. Int. Law, vol 9 (1928), p 117

8.9.9 EXECUTION OF JUDGMENTS

See also Sections 9.5 on international control and 9.6 on sanctions in general.
DUMAS, J, Les Sanctions de l'arbitrage international (Paris, 1905)
GUYOMAR, G, Le Défaut des parties à un différend devant les juridictions internationales. Etude de droit international public positif (Paris, 1960). 242 pp.
HAMBRO, Edward Isak, L'Exécution des sentences internationales (Paris: Sirey, 1936)
NANTWI, E K, The Enforcement of International Judicial Decisions and Arbitral Awards in Public International Law (Leiden, 1966)
REISMAN, W Michael, Nullity and Revision. The Review and Enforcement of International Judgments and Awards (New Haven, Conn: Yale University Press, 1971). xvi + 900 pp.

8.9.10 COURTS AND INDIVIDUALS: RIGHTS OF PETITION

See also Section 6 on subjects of international law, and Sections 7.12.10.5 and 7.12.10.6 on the European Commission and Court of Human Rights.

BAR, L von, 'Die Errichtung eines ständigen internationalen Gerichtshofes für Klagen von Privatpersonen gegen fremde Staaten', Z. Völkerrecht, vol 7 (1913), p 429

BAUMGARTEN, F, 'Le protection des intérêts des particuliers devant les juridictions internationales', Rev. Droit Int. & Légis. Comp., ser 3, vol 13 (1932), pp 742-99

CHRISTOL, Carl Q, 'Remedies for individuals under world law', Northwestern University Law Review, vol 56 (1961), pp 65-86

DURANTE, F, Ricorsi individuali ad organi internazionali, Controbuto alla teoria della personalità internazionale dell'individuo (Milano: Giuffré, 1958)

FEINBERG, N, 'La pétition en droit international', Acad. Droit Int. Recl. Cours., vol 2 (1932), pp 525-644

FLEURY, L, Un Nouveau Progrès de la justice internationale: l'accès des particuliers aux tribunaux internationaux (Paris, 1932)

GORMLEY, W P, 'An analysis of the future procedural status of the individual before international tribunals', University of Detroit Law Journal, vol 39 (1961), pp 38-88

HALLIER, H J, Völkerrechtliche Schiedsinstanzen für Einzelpersonen und ihr Verhältnis zur innerstaatlichen Gerichtsbarkeit, Eine Untersuchung der Praxis seit 1945 (Köln/Berlin/Bonn/München: Carl Heymanns Verlag, 1962)

MEURER, Ch, 'Klagen von Privatpersonen gegen auswärtige Staaten', Z. Völkerrecht, vol 8 (1914), p 1

PILOTTI, M, 'Le secours des particuliers devant les juridictions internationales', in Grundprobleme des Internationalen Rechts, Festschrift Jean Spiropoulos (Bonn, 1957). p 351

POULANTZAS, N M, 'The individual before international jurisdictions', Rev. Hell. Droit Int., vol 15 (1962)

JIMÉNEZ DE ARECHAGA, 'L'arbitrage entre les états et les sociétés privées étrangères', in Mélanges Gidel (Paris, 1961), p 367

REUTER, P, 'Quelques remarques sur la situation juridique des particuliers en droit international public', in La Technique et les principes du droit (Etudes en l'honneur de George Scelle) (Paris: Librairie générale de droit et de jurisprudence, 1950), pp 535-52

SCHULE, D, Le Droit d'accès des particuliers aux juridictions internationales (Paris: Domat Mortchrestien, 1934)

SEFERIADES, S, 'Le problème de l'accès des particuliers à des juridictions internationales', Acad. Droit Int. Recl. Cours, vol 1 (1935), pp 1-120

VEDEL, G, 'Le Problème de l'arbitrage entre gouvernements ou personnes de droit public et personnes de droit privé: Rapport vor dem 1. Congrès International de l'Arbitrage 1961', Revue de l'Arbitrage (1961), p 116

8.10 PERMANENT COURT OF INTERNATIONAL JUSTICE (PCIJ)

8.10.1 GENERAL

ANDREAE, J P Fockema, An Important Chapter in the History of Legal Interpretation: The Jurisdiction

of the First Permanent Court of International
Justice (1922-1940) (Leiden: Sijthoff, 1948). 109 pp.
BRUNS, Viktor, 'La Cour permanente de justice internationale, son organisation et sa compétence',
Acad. Droit Int. Recl. Cours, vol 62 (1937), p 551
BUSTAMANTE, Antonio S de, The World Court
(trans by Read) (New York: Macmillan, 1925)
ENRIQUE, Giuliano, 'L'Acceptation sans réciprocité
de la juridiction de la Cour permanente de justice
internationale', Rev. Droit Int. & Légis. Comp.,
ser 3, vol 13 (1932), p 834
FACHIRI, Alexander P, The Permanent Court of
International Justice, 2nd edition (London: Oxford
University Press, 1932)
FEINBERG, Nathan, La Juridiction de la Cour
permanente de justice dans le système de la
protection internationale des minorités (Paris: A
Rousseau, 1931)
FEINBERG, N, 'La juridiction et la jurisprudence de
la Cour permanente de justice internationale en
matière de mandats et de minorités', Acad. Droit
Int. Recl. Cours., vol 59 (1937), p 591
FELLER, A H, 'Conclusions of the parties in the procedure of the Permanent Court of International
Justice', Am. J. Int. Law, vol 25 (1931), p 490
FISCHER, G, Les Rapports entre l'Organisation
internationale du travail et la Cour permanente de
justice (Paris: Pédone, 1946)
HUDSON, Manley O, The Permanent Court of International Justice, 2nd edition (New York: Macmillan,
1943)
LAUTERPACHT, H, The Development of International
Law by the Permanent Court of International
Justice (London: Longman, Green & Co, 1934)
MAGYARY, Géza, La Juridiction de la Cour
permanente de justice internationale (Paris: Les
Editions internationales, 1931)

SCERNI, Mario, 'La procédure de la Cour permanente de justice internationale', Acad. Droit Int. Recl. Cours, vol 65 (1938), p 565

RUDSTEIN, Simon, 'La Cour permanente de justice internationale comme instance de recours', Acad. Droit Int. Recl. Cours., vol 43 (1933), p 1

SALVIOLI, Gabriele, 'La Corte permanente di giustizia internazionale', Rev. Diritto Int., vol 15 (1923), p 11

SALVIOLI, Gabriele, 'La jurisprudence de la Cour permanente de justice internationale', Acad. Droit Int. Recl. Cours., vol 12 (1926), p 1

SALVIOLI, Gabriele, 'Les rapports entre le jugement sur la compétence et celui sur le fond dans la jurisprudence internationale', Rev. Gen. Droit Int. Public, vol 36 (1929), p 108

SCHLOCHAUER, H J, 'Ständiger Internationaler Gerichtshof', in Wörterbuch des Völkerrechts, ed K Strupp & H J Schlochauer (Berlin: de Gruyter, vol 3, 1960-2), p 341

8.10.2 ADVISORY JURISDICTION OF THE PCIJ

Cf. Section 8.11.10 on the advisory jurisdiction of the ICJ.

GOODRICH, Leland M, 'The nature of the advisory opinions of the Permanent Court of International Justice', Am. J. Int. Law (1938), pp 738-58

McNAIR, Arnold, 'The Council's request for an advisory opinion from the Permanent Court of International Justice', Br. Yearb. Int. Law, vol 7 (1926), p 1

PHILIPSE, A, Les Fonctions consultatives de la Cour permanente de justice internationale (Lausanne: Librairie Payot & cie, 1928)

8.10.3 OPTIONAL CLAUSE OF THE PCIJ

Cf Section 8.11.6 on the optional clause of the ICJ

ENRIQUES, G, 'L'acceptation sans réciprocité de la juridiction obligatoire de la Cour permanente de justice internationale', Rev. Droit Int. & Légis Comp., ser 3, vol 13 (1932), p 834

PERASSI, T, 'I caratteri formali della clausola facoltativa sulla giurisdizione obligatoria della Corte permanente de giustizia internationazionale', Riv. Diritto Int., vol 24 (1932), p 127

WILLIAMS, Sir John Fischer, 'The optional clause', Br. Yearb. Int. Law, vol 11 (1930), p 63

8.11 INTERNATIONAL COURT OF JUSTICE (ICJ)

On numerous aspects relevant to the law and procedure applied by the ICJ see Section 8.9 on tribunals in general and their procedure. On the important question of domestic jurisdiction, see the work by Waldock listed in Section 8.9.3. For cases dealt with by the World Court see in Section 8.9.3 above under case law, Sections 1.4.3.2 and 1.4.3.3. In the section below I have also included some articles from the abundant works commenting on specific cases to illustrate the general competence of the Court.

8.11.1 GENERAL

ANAND, R P, Compulsory Jurisdiction of the International Court of Justice (Bombay: Asia Publishing House, 1961)

ANDRASSY, J, 'Betrachtungen über die Zuständigkeit des Internationalen Gerichtshofes', Z. Ausl. Öff. Recht & Völkerrecht, vol 19, nos 1-3 (Festgabe A N Makarov) (August 1958)

BASTID, S, 'La jurisprudence de la Cour internationale de justice', Acad. Droit Int. Recl. Cours, vol 78 (1951), pp 575-86

BRIGGS, H W, 'Interhandel: The Court's judgment of March 21, 1959, on the preliminary objections of the United States', Am. J. Int. Law, vol 53 (1959), p 547

BRIGGS, H W, 'La compétence incidente de la Cour internationale de justice en tant que compétence obligatoire', Rev. Gen. Droit Int. Public, vol 64 (1960), p 217

CAFLISCH, Lucius C, 'The recent judgment of the International Court of Justice: the case concerning the aerial incident of July 17, 1955', Am. J. Int. Law, vol 54 (1960), p 855

CHENG, B, 'Revision of judgments of the I L O administrative tribunal by the ICJ', The Solicitor, vol 24, nos 4-5 (April-May 1957), pp 102-4; 132-5

DEBBASCH, C, 'La compétence "ratione temporis" de la C I J dans le système de la clause facultative de juridiction obligatoire', Rev. Gén. Droit Int. Public, vol 64 (1960), pp 230-59

DUBISSON, M, Cour internationale de justice (Paris: R Richon et R Durand-Auzias, 1964)

EHRLICH, L, Karta Narodów Zjednoczonych wraz ze statutem Miedzynarodowego Trybunału sprawiedliwosci. Uwagi wstepne, teksty, komentarze (Krakow, 1946). 119 pp.

EISEMANN, P, COUSSIRAT-COUSTERE, V, & HUR, P, Petit Manuel de la jurisprudence de la Cour internationale de justice, 2nd edition (Paris: Pédone, 1971)

ELIAN, George, The International Court of Justice (Leiden: Sijthoff). 150 pp.

ENGEL, Salo, 'The compulsory jurisdiction of the International Court of Justice', Georgetown Law Journal, vol 40 (1951/2), p 41

ESSEN, J L F van, 'De bevoegdheid van het Internationale hof van justitie', Nederlands Juristenblad, no 32 (28 September 1957), pp 693-700

EVRIGENIS, D J, La C I J et le droit interne. Problèmes des éléments latents de la règle de droit international (Thessaloniki, 1958). 40 pp.

FARMANFARMA, Ali Naghi, The Declared Jurisdiction of the International Court of Justice (Montreux: Imprimérie Ganguin & Laubscher, 1952)

FARMANFARMA, A N, The Declaration of the Members Accepting the Compulsory Jurisdiction of the International Court of Justice (The Interpretation of Article 36, Paragraph 2, of the Statute of the I C J) (Montreux, 1952). 192 pp.

FARTACHE, M, 'De la compétence de la C I J dans l'affaire de l'Anglo-Iranian Oil Co', Rev. Gén. Droit Int. Public, vol 57 (1953), pp 584-612

FITZMAURICE, Sir Gerald, 'The law and procedure of the International Court of Justice, international organizations and tribunals', Br. Yearb. Int. Law, vol 29 (1952), pp 1-62

FITZMAURICE, Sir Gerald, 'The law and procedure of the International Court of Justice, 1951-54 Treaty Interpretation and other treaty points', Br. Yearb. Int. Law, vol 33 (1957), p 203

FITZMAURICE, Sir Gerald, 'The law and procedure of the International Court of Justice 1951-54. Questions of jurisdiction, competence and procedure', Br. Yearb. Int. Law, vol 34 (1958), p 1

FLEMING, D F, The United States and the World Court (New York, 1945)

FOSTER, W F, 'Fact finding and the World Court', Can. Yearb. Int. Law (1969), p 150

GROSS, Leo, 'Some observations on the International Court of Justice', Am. J. Int. Law, vol 56 (1962), p 33

GROSS, Leo, 'The jurisprudence of the World Court: thirty-eighth year (1959)', Am. J. Int. Law, vol 57 (1963), p 571

GROSS, Leo, 'The International Court of Justice: consideration of requirements for enhancing its role in the international legal order', vol 65 (1971), p 253

GROSS, Leo, 'The time element in the contentious proceedings in the International Court of Justice', Am. J. Int. Law, vol 63 (1967), pp 74-85

GUYOMAR, G, Commentaire du règlement de la Cour internationale de justice (Paris: Pédone, 1973). 535 pp.

GUGGENHEIM, P, 'L'élaboration d'une clause modèle de compétence obligatoire de la C I J. Rapport', RAPPORTS présentés à la session de Sienne (1952) de l'Institute de droit international, Genève (October, 1951)

HACKWORTH, G H, 'The International Court of Justice and the codification of international law', American Bar Review, vol 32 (1946)

HAMBRO, E, The Jurisdiction of the I C J (Paris, 1951). 94 pp.

HAMBRO, E, 'Some observations on the compulsory jurisdiction of the International Court of Justice', Br. Yearb. Int. Law, vol 25 (1948), p 133

HAMBRO, E, 'Jurisdiction of the International Court of Justice', Acad. Droit Int. Recl. Cours, vol 76 (1950), p 125

HENKIN, L, 'The Connally reservation revisited and, hopefully, contained', Am. J. Int. Law, vol 65 (1971), pp 374-7

HOGG, James, 'The International Court: rules of treaty interpretation', Minnesota Law Revue, vol 43 (1958/9), p 369

HOGG, James, 'The International Court: rules of treaty interpretation II', Minnesota Law Review, vol 44 (1959/60), p 5

HUDSON, M O, 'Compulsory jurisdiction of the International Court of Justice', Am. Soc. Int. Law Proc. (1946), p 12

HUDSON, M O, 'The World Court: America's declaration accepting jurisdiction', American Bar Association Journal, vol 23 (1946), p 832
JIMENEZ DE ARECHAGA, Eduardo, 'The International Court of Justice and the judicial settlement of international disputes', in International Law in a Changing World, (1963), pp 54-63
JENKS, C W, 'Compétence obligatoire des instances judiciaires et arbitrales internationales', Annu. Inst. Droit Int., vol 2 (1959), pp 55-177
JESSUP, Philip, 'The International Court of Justice of the United Nations', Foreign Policy Reports, vol 21 (August 1945), p 154
JESSUP, Philip, 'The International Court of Justice and legal matters', Illinois Law Review, vol 42 (1948), p 273
JONES, Mervyn, 'Corfu Channel Case - jurisdiction', Grotius Soc. Trans., vol 35 (1949), p 91
JULLY, L, 'Le premier arrêt de la Cour internationale de justice', Die Friedens-Warte, vol 48 (1948), p 144
KRYLOV, S B, Mezhdounarodnyi soud Organizatsii obiedinennykh natsii. (Voprossy mejdounarodnoyo prava i protessa v evo praktike za desiat let 1947-1957)(Moscow, 1958). 167 pp.
LAUTERPACHT, H, The Development of International Law by the International Court (London: Stevens, 1958). 408 pp.
LAWSON, R C, 'The problem of the compulsory jurisdiction of the World Court', Am. J. Int. Law, vol 46 (1952), pp 219-38
LIACOURAS, P J, The International Court of Justice: Materials on the Record of the I C J in Contentious Proceedings (Durham, NC, 1962). 2 vols.
LISSITZYN, O J, The International Court of Justice: Its Role in the Maintenance of International Peace and Security (New York, 1951; reissued 1972 by Octagon Books, New York). 118 pp.

MARTI DE VESES PUIG, M del C, 'La condición jurídica de los funcionarios internacionales y el tribunal internacional de justicia', Rev. Esp. Derecho Int., vol 10 (1957), pp 373-420

MENSCHAAR, C L, 'De verplichte rechtsmacht van het Internationale Gerechtshof', Wordende wereld, vol 9, no 9 (September 1957), pp 4-6

MICHAL, V, Posudky mezinárodního soudu s funkcí rozsudku (Praha, 1959). 224 pp.

MIGLIAZZA, A, 'La giurisprudenza della Corte internazionale di Giustizia', Comun. & Stud., vol 7 p 582

PERRIN, G, 'L'Affaire de l'Interhandel-Phase des exceptions préliminaires', Ann. Suisse Droit Int., vol 16 (1959), p 73

POLYANSKII, N N, Mezdhunarodnyi soud (Moscow, 1951) 235 pp.

PASTOR RIDRUEJO, J A, La jurisprudencia del Tribunal internacional de La Haya (Sistematización y comentarios) (Madrid, 1962). 504 pp.

ROSENNE, SHABTAI, 'Res judicata: some recent decisions of the International Court of Justice', Br. Yearb. Int. Law, vol 28 (1951), p 365

ROSENNE, SHABTAI, The International Court of Justice. An Essay in Political and Legal Theory (Leiden: Sijthoff, 1957)

ROSENNE, SHABTAI, The Time Factor in the Jurisdiction of the International Court of Justice (Leiden: Sijthoff, 1960)

ROSENNE, SHABTAI, The World Court (Leiden: Sijthoff/Dobbs Ferry, NY: Oceana, 1962)

ROSENNE, SHABTAI, The Law and Practice of the International Court (Leiden: Sijthoff/New York: Humanities Press, 1965). 2 vols.

SCHLOCHAUER, H J, 'Internationaler Gerichtshof', in Wörterbuch des Völkerrechts, vol 2 (Berlin: Verlag de Gruyter, 1961), p 96

SCHWARZENBERGER, Georg, 'Trends in the practice of the World Court', Current Legal Problems (1951)

SCHWELB, E, 'The process of amending the statute of the International Court of Justice', Am. J. Int. Law, vol 64 (1970), p 880

SCHACHOR-LANDAU, C, 'The judgment of the International Court of Justice in the aerial incident case between Israel and Bulgaria', Arch. Völkerrechts, vol 8 (1960), p 277

SHIHATA, I F I, The Power of the International Court of Justice to Determine its own Jurisdiction, Compétence de la Compétence (Den Haag: Nijhoff, 1965)

SOHN, L B, 'The jurisdiction of the International Court of Justice', American Bar Association Journal, vol 35 (1949)

STARACE, V, La Competenza della Corte Internazionale de Giustizia in Materia Contenziosa (Napoli: Casa Ed Dott. Jovene, 1970). 189 pp.

STARKE, J G, The New Rules of the International Court of Justice (Canberra: Australian State University, 1973)

SUY, E, 'Die Zukunft der international Gerichtsbarkeit', Arch. Völkerrechts, vol 8 (1960), pp 421-5

SYATAUW, J J G, Decisions of the I C J A Digest (Leiden, 1962). 237 pp.

VERZIJL, J H W, 'Cour internationale de justice - affaire relative a certains emprunts norwegiens', Ned. Tijdschr. Int. Recht, vol 4 (1957), p 373

VERZIJL, J H W, 'The International Court of Justice in 1959', Ned. Tijdschr. Int. Recht, vol 6 (1959), p 362; vol 7 (1960), p 1

VISSCHER, C de, Aspects récents du droit procédural de la Cour internationale de Justice (Paris: Pédone, 1966)

WEHBERG, H & GOLDSCHMIDT, H W, Der internationale Gerichtshof: Entstehungsgeschichte, Analyse, Dokumentation (Berlin: Verlag Arno Spitz, 1973). 115 pp.
WEFELMEIER, H J, 'Der internationale und der europäische Gerichtshof, Vergleich und Abgrenzung', Dissertation. Köln 1968.

8.11.2 JUSTICIABLE AND NON-JUSTICIABLE DISPUTES

BRUNS, 'Politische und Rechtsstreitigkeiten', Z. Ausl. Öff. Recht & Völkerrecht, vol 3 (1933), p 445
CHAPAL, P, L'Arbitrabilité des différends internationaux (Paris: Pédone, 1967). 294 pp.
SOHN, Louis B, 'Exclusion of political disputes from judicial settlement', Am. J. Int. Law (1944), p 694
WILLIAMS, J F, 'Justiciable and other disputes', Rev. Droit Int. & Légis. Comp., ser 3, vol 9 (1928), p 263
VERZIJL, J H W, 'La classification des différends internationaux', Rev. Droit Int. & Légis. Comp., ser 3, vol 6 (1925), p 732

8.11.3 ELECTION OF JUDGES

BAXTER, R R, 'The procedures employed in connection with the United States nominations for the International Court in 1960', Am. J. Int. Law, vol 55 (1961), p 445
GUERRERO, M J G, 'La composition de la Cour internationale de justice et ses garanties statutaires', Annu. Inst. Droit Int., vol 2 (1952), pp 439-52
HOGAN, W N, 'The Ammoun case and the election of judges to the International Court of Justice', Am. J. Int. Law, vol 59 (1965), pp 908-12

SIMPSON, J L, 'The 1960 elections to the International
Court of Justice', Br. Yearb. Int. Law, vol 37
(1961), pp 527-35
SUH, I R, 'Voting behaviour of national judges in international courts', Am. J. Int. Law, vol 63 (1969),
pp 224-36

8.11.4 INDIVIDUAL AND
DISSENTING OPINIONS

ANAND, R P, 'The role of individual and dissenting opinions in international adjudication', Int. & Comp. Law Q., vol 15 (1965), pp 788-808

8.11.5 FORUM PROROGATUM

For forum prorogatum in general, see Section 8.9.7.
Among the works there, note especially the article by
WALDOCK
ROSENNE, S, 'The forum prorogatum in the international Court of Justice', Rev. Hell. Droit Int., vol 6
(1953), p 1
STILLMUNKES, P, 'Le "forum prorogatum" devant la
Cour permanente de justice internationale et la
Cour internationale de justice', Rev. Gén. Droit Int.
Public, vol 68 (1964), p 665
WALDOCK, C H M, 'Forum prorogatum or
acceptance of a unilateral summons to appear before
the International Court', Int. Law, Q., vol 2 (1948),
p 337
WINIARSKI, B, 'Quelques reflexions sur le soi-disant
forum prorogatum en droit international', in
Festschrift Spiropoulos (Bonn, 1957), p 445

8.11.6 THE OPTIONAL CLAUSE OF THE ICJ

For the PCIJ optional clause, see Section 8.10.3

CECCHETTO, R, 'La posizione dell'Italia rispetto all'art. 37 dello statuto della Corte internazionale di giustizia', Riv. Diritto Int., vol 39 (1956), p 339

FACHIRI, A P, 'Repudiation of the optional clause', Br. Yearb. Int. Law (1939), pp 52-8

HIGGINS, A P, The British Acceptance of Compulsory Arbitration under the Optional Clause and its Implications (London, 1930)

JESSUP, P C, 'Acceptance by the United States of America of the optional clause of the International Court of Justice', Am. J. Int. Law, vol 39 (1945), p 745

LAUTERPACHT, H, 'The British reservations to the optional clause', Economica (UK), vol 10 (1930), pp 137-72

MacDONALD, R St J, 'The new Canadian declaration of acceptance of the compulsory jurisdiction of the International Court of Justice', Can. Yearb. Int. Law (1970), p 3

VERZIJL, J H W, 'The system of the optional clause', International Relations (UK), (October 1959), pp 585-610

VULCAN, C, 'La clause facultative', Nord. Tidsskr. Int. Ret., vol 18 (1947/8)

WALDOCK, C H M, 'Decline of the optional clause', Br. Yearb. Int. Law, vol 32 (1956), p 244

WILCOX, Francis, 'The United States accepts compulsory jurisdiction', Am. J. Int. Law, vol 40 (1946), p 699

see also the articles by PERASSI and WILLIAMS listed in Section 8.10.3.

8.11.7 RESERVATIONS TO OPTIONAL CLAUSE

BRIGGS, Herbert, 'Reservations to the acceptance of compulsory jurisdiction of the International Court

of Justice', Acad. Droit. Int. Recl. Cours, vol 93
(1958), p 229
IANKOV, A, 'Rezervite v deklaratsiite za priemane
zadaljitelnata iourisdiktsiia na mejdounarodniia sad
i tiakhnoto vliianie varkhou kompetentnostta na
sada', (Godichnik na Sofiiskiia ouniversitet)
Iouriditcheski fakoultet, 52 (1961), pp 453-598.
Summaries in Russian and French
JENNINGS, R Y, 'Recent cases on automatic reservations to the optional clause', Int. & Comp. Law Q.,
vol 7 (1958), p 349
LAUTERPACHT, H, 'The British reservations to the
optional clause', Economica (UK), vol 10 (1930),
pp 137-72
MAUS, B, Les Réserves dans les déclarations
d'acceptation de la juridiction obligatoire de la C I J
(Genève/Paris: E Droz, 1959). 214 pp.
YANKOV, A, 'Les réserves dans les déclarations
d'acceptation de la juridiction obligatoire de la
Cour internationale de justice', Yearbook of the
University of Sofia (1961)

8.11.8 PRELIMINARY OBJECTIONS

ABI-SAAB, G, Les Exceptions préliminaires dans la
procédure de la Cour internationale (Paris: Pédone,
1967)
DOLLEMAN, J, Preliminaire excepties voor het
Internationaal gerechtshof (Leiden, 1949). 200 pp.
GRISEL, E, Les Exceptions d'incompétence et
d'irrecevabilité dans la procédure de la Cour internationale de justice (Bern: Lang, 1968)

8.11.9 PLEA OF DOMESTIC JURISDICTION

See also Section 8.9.3, especially the article by
WALDOCK and cross-references mentioned in that
section.

PREUSS, L, 'The International Court of Justice, the Senate and matters of domestic jurisdiction', Am. J. Int. Law, vol 40 (1946), p 726

ROLIN, Henri, 'The International Court of Justice and domestic jurisdiction', Int. Organ., vol 8 (1954), p 36

8.11.10 ADVISORY JURISDICTION OF THE ICJ

Cf. Section 8.10.2 on the advisory jurisdiction of the PCIJ.

BASAK, Adam, Decisions of the UN Organs in the Judgments and Opinions of the ICJ (Wrocfaw, 1969)

CHENG, B, 'The scope and limits of the advisory jurisdiction of the International Court of Justice', The Solicitor, vol 24 (1957), pp 187-91; 219-22; 244-8

GREIG, D W, 'The advisory jurisdiction of the International Court and the settlement of disputes between states', Int. & Comp. Law Q., vol 15 (1966), p 325

HAMBRO, E, 'The authority of the advisory opinions of the ICJ', Int. & Comp. Law Q., vol 3 (1954), pp 2-22

HUDSON, M O, 'The effect of advisory opinions of the World Court', Am. J. Int. Law, vol 42 (1948), pp 630-2

HUMBER, P O, 'The authority of advisory opinions of the ICJ and the acceptance of the second opinion by the General Assembly', Die Friedens-Warte, vol 51 (1952), pp 143-50

KEITH, K J, The Extent of the Advisory Jurisdiction of the International Court of Justice (Leiden: Sijthoff, 1971). 271 pp.

PRATAP, D, The Advisory Jurisdiction of the International Court (London: Oxford University Press, 1972). xvi + 292 pp.

POMERANCE, M, The Advisory Function of the Inter-

national Court in the League and UN Eras (Baltimore, Md: Johns Hopkins Press, 1973). xv + 440 pp.
ROSENNE, Sh, 'On the non-use of the advisory competence of the International Court of Justice', Br. Yearb. Int. Law, vol 39 (1963), pp 1-53
ROSENNE, Sh, 'The advisory competence of the International Court of Justice', Rev. Droit. Int. & Légis. Comp., ser 3, vol 30 (1952), pp 10-39
SLOAN, F B, 'Advisory jurisdiction of the International Court of Justice', California Law Review, vol 38 (1950), pp 830-59
WARTBURG, W v, 'Der Internationale Gerichtshof in seiner Rolle als Gutachtenerteiler', Thesis. Basel 1963

see also:
GROSS, L, 'The International Court of Justice and the United Nations', Acad. Droit Int. Recl. Cours, vol 120 (1967), pp 312-440
HAMBRO, E, 'The relations between the ICJ and international organizations', Western Political Quarterly (1950), pp 326-34
JENKS, C W, 'The status of international organizations in relation to the ICJ', Grotius Soc. Trans., vol 32 (1947), pp 1-41
KERNO, I S, L'Organisation des Nations Unies et la CIJ (Paris, 1952). 68 pp.
SEIDL-HOHENVELDERN, I, 'Der Zugang internationaler Organisationen zum Internationalen Gerichtshof', Die Friedens-Warte, vol 54 (1957), pp 16-28
ZOLLIKOFER, P L, Les Relations prévues entre les institutions spécialisées des Nations Unies et la Cour internationale de justice (Leiden, 1955)

8.11.11 EXECUTION OF JUDGMENTS

See also Sections 8.9.9. on execution of judgments

in general, 9.5 on international control and 9.6 on sanctions.

ROSENNE, Shabtai, 'L'exécution et la mise en vigueur des décisions de la Cour internationale de justice', Rev. Gén. Droit Int. Public, vol 57 (1953), pp 532-83

VULCAN, Constantin, 'L'exécution des décisions de la Cour internationale de justice d'après la Charte des Nations Unies', Rev. Gén. Droit Int. Public, vol 51 (1947), pp 187-205

8.12 ADMINISTRATIVE TRIBUNALS

8.12.1 ADMINISTRATIVE TRIBUNALS IN GENERAL

BASTID, S, Les Tribunaux administratifs internationaux et leur jurisprudence (Leiden, 1958). 175 pp.

BEDJAOUI, M, 'Jurisprudence comparée des tribunaux administratifs internationaux en matière d'excès de pouvoir', Annu. Fr. Droit Int. (1956), pp 482-96

CHENG, B, 'Nature and scope of the jurisdiction of international administrative tribunals', The Solicitor, vol 24, no 6 (June 1957), pp 160-4

CHIESA, F, 'Les juridictions administratives internationales. (Rapport présenté au IXe congrès international des sciences administratives, Istambul, 6-14 IX 1953)', Revue international des sciences administratives, vol 20 (1954), pp 67-88

COMBA, A, 'Cenni introduttivi allo studio delle giurisdizioni amministrative delle organizzazioni internazionali', Diritto Internazionale, vol 21 (1967) pp 313-47

COMBA, A, Le giurisdizioni amministrative delle organizzazioni internazionali (Torino, 1967)

HEYMAN, J F, 'Les juridictions administratives

internationales', Thesis. Dijon 1958. 2 vols. vol 1 'L'organisation et la procédure', vol 2 'Le recours et ses suites'

HUET, P, 'Tribunaux administratifs des organisations internationales', J. Droit Int., vol 77 (1950), pp 336-76

Juridictions administratives internationales. Introduction, discussions et résolution (Round table, Istamboul, 7 septembre 1953) Publications de l'Institut international des sciences administratives, 1954 (congrès d'Istamboul), pp 19-31

KING, J K, International Administrative Jurisdiction (Bruxelles, 1952)

POELJE, G A van, 'Internationale administratieve rechtspraak', (Tribunaux administratifs et cour européenne. Rapports présentes au congrès de l'Institut international des sciences administratives, septembre 1953. Textes français) Bestuurswetenschappen, vol 8, no 1 (January, 1954), pp 1-22

RUZIE, D, 'Bulletin de jurisprudence administrative internationale, (Tribunal administratif de l'ONU; Tribunal administratif de l'OIT; Commission de recours de l'OECE; Cour de Justice des Communautés Européennes) (1958-1960)', J. Droit Int., vol 89 (1962), pp 476-527. In French and English

SCHECHTER, A, Interpretation of Ambiguous Documents by International Administrative Tribunals (London: Stevens, 1964). 183 pp.

SEYERSTED, F, 'Settlement of internal disputes of intergovernmental organizations by internal and external courts', Z. Ausl. Öff. Recht & Völkerrecht, vol 24 (1964), pp 1-121

8.12.2 ADMINISTRATIVE TRIBUNALS OF THE UNITED NATIONS

DEHAUSSY, J, 'La procédure de réformation des

jugements du Tribunal administratif des Nations Unies', Annu. Fr. Droit Int. (1956), pp 460-81
FRIEDMANN, W. & FATOUROS, A A, 'The United Nations administrative tribunal', Int. Organ., vol 11 (1957), pp 13-29
HONING, F, 'Awards of the UN Administrative Tribunal. The advisory opinion of the ICJ', Law Journal, 104, no 4621 (20 August 1954), pp 534-5
Judgements of the United Nations Administrative Tribunal. Numbers 1/70 - 1950/1957 (New York, 1958)
LANGROD, G, 'La fonction publique internationale à la lumière des tendances, et des réalistions à l'ONU au cours des années 1957 et 1958', Annales universitatis saraviensis, vol 7 (1959), pp 141-90
LANGROD, G, 'La jurisprudence du Tribunal administratif des Nations Unies (1950-1953)', Rev. Droit Int., vol 37 (1954), pp 243-98
LANGROD, G, 'La réforme 1955 du tribunal administratif des Nations Unies', Z. Ausl. Öff. Recht. & Völkerrecht, vol 17 (1956), pp 249-310
LANGROD, G, 'Le tribunal administratif des Nations Unies', Rev. Droit Public & Sci. Polit., vol 57 (1951), pp 71-104

8.12.3 ADMINISTRATIVE TRIBUNAL OF THE ILO

Cf. Section 13.24.2.24.5.

ARONSTEIN, G, 'Les tribunaux administratifs et le statut des fonctionnaires internationaux', Journal des Tribunaux, vol 70 (1955), pp 561-3
CHENG, B, 'Revision of judgments of the ILO by the ICJ', The Solicitor, vol 24 (1957), pp 102-4, 132-5
DREYFUS, S, 'Tribunal administratif de l'OIT (jugements nos. 25-30)', Annu. Fr. Droit Int. (1957), pp 246-53

GAMILLSCHEG, F, 'Die Rechtsprechung des Verwaltungsgerichts der Internationalen Arbeitsorganisation 1947-1957. (Wortlaut, Satzung u. Verfahrensordnung, S 176-182)', Arch. Völkerrechts, vol 7 (1958), pp 120-8

LANGROD, G, 'Les réalisations jurisprudentielles du "Tribunal administratif international" de Genève', Rev. Droit Int. & Droit Comp., vol 32 (1955), pp 7-29

MARTI DE VESES PUIG, M del C, 'La condición jurídica de los funcionarios internacionales y el Tribunal internacional de justicia', Rev. Esp. Derecho Int., vol 10 (1957), pp 373-420

MERCIER, J, 'L'indépendance des fonctionnaires internationaux dans la jurisprudence du Tribunal de l'OIT (notamment sur les jugements 13, 15, 17, 18 19, 21, 22, 23 et 24)', Le Droit au service de la paix (June 1956), pp 23-39

MERCIER, J, 'Tribunal administratif de l'OIT (Jurisprudence)', Annu.Fr. Droit Int. (1955), pp 296-312

ORCASITAS LLORENTE, L, 'Dictamen del Tribunal internacional de 23 de octubre de 1956 sobre validez de la decisiones adoptadas por el Tribunal administrativo de la OIT en el recurso planteado por varios empleados de la UNESCO', Rev. Esp. Derecho Int., vol 10 (1957), pp 153-9

VERZIJL, J H W, 'The ICJ - Judgments of the Administrative Tribunal of the ILO upon complaints made against the UNESCO', Ned. Tijdschr. Int. Recht, vol 6 (1957), pp 236-53

VIGNES, C H, 'Jurisprudence internationale. Tribunal administratif de l'OIT jugement no 53 du 6 octobre 1961, Affair Wakley', Rev. Gén. Droit Int. Public, vol 66 (1962), pp 638-48

WATTS, A D, 'Recent decisions of the ILO Administrative Tribunal. (Note on judgments nos 17, 18, 19 and

21 concerning staff members of UNESCO)', Int. & Comp.Law Q., vol 5 (1956), pp 483-90

WOLF, F, 'Le tribunal administratif de l'OIT', Rev. Gén. Droit Int. Public, vol 58 (1954), pp 279-314

WOLF, F, 'Note sur la quatrième session du Tribunal administratif de l'OIT (Analyse des jugements nos 12, 13 et 15)', Rev. Gén. Droit Int. Public, vol 59 (1955), pp 137-48

8.13 SPECIAL TRIBUNALS AND PROJECTED TRIBUNALS

See also Section 7.12.10.6 on the European Court for Human Rights.

BESLY, E F W, 'The International Tribunal in Saarland', Annu. Eur. (1960), pp 106-24

FELLER, A H, The Mexican Claims Commissions, 1923-24 (New York, 1935)

MAXWELL FYFE, D, 'Towards an international penal court' (Etude écrite en mai 1949. Avec traduction française). Revue internationale de droit pénal, vol 21 (1950), pp 17-25

MORELLI, G, 'Il tribunale delle Nazioni Unite in Libia', Riv. Diritto Int., vol 26 (1953), pp 105-8

SEIDL-HOHENVELDERN, Ignaz, The Austrian-German Arbitral Tribunal (Syracuse, NY: Syracuse University Press, 1972). xv + 261 pp.

VIGNES, D, 'Un tribunal administratif international juge de litiges de droit privé du travail', Rev. Droit Int. & Droit Comp., vol 37 (1960), pp 233-8

9 Peace, International Security and Sanctions

In this part of the bibliography I have listed works which deal with peacekeeping in the international community. Some of these works bear on questions of extra-juridical character but I have sought to limit the selection to what is relevant to a scholar of public international law. See also Section 8 on peaceful settlement of disputes, Section 13.24.2.22 on UN peacekeeping and Section 13.24.2.23 on UN Forces. See also McDOUGAL listed under 1.8 and McDOUGAL-FELICIANO listed under 9.7.

9.1 HISTORY OF PEACE

BEALES, A C F, The History of Peace (London: G Bell & Sons, 1931). 355 pp.
FORSTER, Kent, The Failures of Peace: The Search for a Negotiated Peace during the First World War (Washington: American Council on Public Affairs, 1947). 157 pp.
GROB, Fritz, The Relativity of War and Peace: A Study in Law, History and Politics (New Haven, Conn: Yale University Press, 1949). 402 pp.

9.2 INTERNATIONAL SECURITY

ARON, Raymond, Paix et guerre entre les nations 3rd edition (Paris: Calmann-Lévy, 1962). English translation, Peace and War: A Theory of International Relations, tr by R Howard & A Baker Fox (London: Weidenfeld & Nicolson, 1966)

BAXTER, Richard R, 'Constitutional forms and some legal problems of international military command', Br. Yearb. Int. Law (1952), p 325

BEALES, A C F, The History of Peace (London: G Bell & Sons, 1931)

BEATON, L, The Struggle for Peace (London: George Allen & Unwin, 1966)

BERNAL, J D, World without War (London: Routledge & Kegan Paul, 1958)

BLOOMFIELD, Lincoln P, et al, International Military Forces (Boston, Mass: Little, Brown & Co, 1964)

BOSE, Robert, Sociologie de la Paix (Paris: Spes, 1965)

BOULDING, Kenneth, Conflict and Defense: A General Theory (New York: Harper & Brothers, 1962)

BOURQUIN, Maurice, (ed), Collective Security. A record of the 7th and 8th International Studies Conferences, Paris 1934, and London 1935. International Institute of Intellectual Co-operation, Paris 1936

BOURQUIN, Maurice, 'Le problème de la sécurité internationale', Acad. Droit Int. Recl. Cours, vol 49 (1934), pp 473-542

BUTLER, Harold, Peace or Power (London: Faber & Faber, 1947)

CALDWELL, W E, Hellenic Conceptions of Peace (New York: Columbia University Press, 1919)

Carnegie Endowment for International Peace, Perspectives on Peace 1910-1960 (London: Stevens & Sons, 1960)

CARR, Edward Hallett, Conditions of Peace (London: Macmillan, 1944)

CALVOCORESSI, Peter, World Order and New States: Problems of Keeping the Peace (London: Chatto & Windus, 1962)

CHAUMONT, Ch, 'Facteurs nouveaux de la sécurité collective', Cahiers des Nations Unies, no 16

DAVIES, David, An International Police Force (London: Ernest Benn, 1952)

DRAPER, G I A D, 'Regional arrangements and enforcement action', Rev. Egypt. Droit Int., vol 20 (1964) p 1

FALK, Richard A, & MENDLOVITZ, Saul H, (eds), The Strategy of World Order (New York: World Law Fund, 1966). Vol 1 'Toward a theory of war prevention', vol 2 'International law', vol 3 'The United Nations', vol 4 'Disarmament and economic development'

FALK, Richard A, Legal Order in a Violent World (Princeton, NJ: Princeton University Press, 1968). 610 pp.

GALLOIS, Pierre M, Paradoxes de la paix (Paris: Presses du temps présent, 1967)

HABICHT, Max, Post-War Treaties for the Pacific Settlement of International Disputes (Cambridge, Mass, 1931). 1109 pp.

HEKHUIS, Dale J, McGLINTOCK, Charles G, & BURNS, Arthur L, (eds), International Stability: Military, Economic, and Political Dimensions (New York: Wiley, 1964)

HEMLEBEN, Sylvester John, Plans for World Peace through Six Centuries. (Chicago, Ill: University of Chicago Press, 1945)

HIGGINS, Rosalyn, Conflict of Interests: International Law in a Divided World (London: The Bodley Head, 1965)

HINSLEY, F H, Power and the Pursuit of Peace (London: Cambridge University Press, 1963)

Institute for Social Research, Oslo, Research for Peace: Essays by Professor Quincy Wright, and others (Amsterdam: North-Holland Publishing Co., 1954)

International Peace Research Association, Proceedings of Inaugural Conference, July 2-5, 1965 (Assen: Van Gorcum & Co, NV, 1966)

International Sociological Association, The Nature of Conflict: Studies on the Sociological Aspects of International Tension (Paris: UNESCO, 1957)

KELSEN, H, Law and Peace in International Relations (Cambridge, Mass, 1942). 181 pp.

KELSEN, Hans, Peace through Law (Chapel Hill, NC: University of North Carolina Press, 1944)

KELSEN, Hans, Collective Security under International Law, US Naval War College International Law Studies, vol 49 (1954)

KELSEN, Hans, 'La technique du droit international et l'organisation de la paix', Rev. Droit Int. & Légis. Comp., vol 15 (1934), pp 5-24

KEYNES, J M, The Economic Consequences of the Peace (London: Macmillan, 1920)

KIRK, Grayson, (ed), Some Problems of International Policing (New York: Council on Foreign Relations, 1944)

KISKER, G W, (ed), World Tension: The Psychopathology of International Relations (New York: Prentice-Hall, 1951)

KULSKI, W W, 'The Soviet system of collective security compared with the western system', Am. J. Int. Law, vol 44 (1950), pp 453-76

LANGE, Christian L, 'Histoire de la doctrine pacifique sur le développement du droit international', Acad. Droit Int. Recl. Cours, vol 13 (1926), pp 175-422

LIPSKY, George A, (ed), Law and Politics in the World Community (Berkeley, Calif: University of California Press, 1953)

LUARD, Evan, Peace and Opinion (London: Oxford University Press, 1962)

LYONS, F S L, Internationalism in Europe, 1815-1914 (Leiden: Sijthoff, 1963)
McNAIR, A D, 'Collective security', Br. Yearb. Int. Law, vol 17 (1936), pp 152-64
MAY, M A, A Social Psychology of War and Peace (New Haven, Conn: Yale University Press, 1948)
NATHAN, Otto, & NORDEN, Heinz (ed), Einstein on Peace (New York: Simon & Schuster, 1960)
NAWAZ, M K, et al, The Legal Principles governing Friendly Relations and Co-operation among States (Leiden: Sijthoff, 1966)
PANNWITZ, Rudolf, Der Friede (Nürnberg: Verlag Hans Carl, 1950)
PITERSKII, Nikolai, International Security Forces (Moscow: Novosti Press Agency Publishing House, 1966)
PRICE, Peter, Power and the Law: A Study in Peaceful Change (Genève: Librairie E Droz, 1954). 155 pp.
RAAFAT, Waheed, Le Problème de la sécurité internationale (Paris, 1930). 684 pp.
RAPPARD, William E, The Quest for Peace (Cambridge, Mass: Harvard University Press, 1940)
REDSLOB, Robert, Le Problème de la paix (Basel: Verlag für Recht und Gesellschaft, S A, 1954)
REVES, E, The Anatomy of Peace (London: George Allen & Unwin, 1946)
RICHARDSON, Lewis F, Arms and Insecurity (Chicago, Ill: Quadrangle Books, 1960)
RICHARDSON, Lewis F, Statistics of Deadly Quarrels (Chicago, Ill: Quadrangle Books, 1960)
SCHACHTER, O, 'The uses of law in international peace-keeping', Virginia Law Review, vol 50 (1964)
SCHELLING, T C, Arms and Influence (New Haven, Conn: Yale University Press, 1966)
SCHLOCHAUER, Hans-Jürgen, Die Idee des Ewigen Friedens (Bonn: Ludwig Röhrscheid, 1953)

SCHWARZENBERGER, Georg, Power Politics. A Study of World Society, 3rd edition (London: Stevens & Sons, 1964)
SETON-WATSON, Hugh, Neither War nor Peace (London: Methuen, 1960)
STARKE, J G, An Introduction to the Science of Peace (Leiden: Sijthoff, 1968). 214 pp.
STAWELL, F Melian, The Growth of International Thought (London: Home University Library, Thornton Butterworth Ltd, 1929)
SIBERT, M, 'La sécurité internationale et les moyens proposés pour l'assurer de 1919 a 1925', Rev. Gén. Droit Int. Public, vol 32 (1925), pp 194-237
STONE, Julius, Legal Controls of International Conflict (London, 1954). 851 pp
TAUBENFELD, Howard J, 'International armed forces and the rules of war', Am. J. Int. Law, vol 45 (1951), pp 671-9
THOMAS, W Bryn, An International Police Force, (London: Allenson & Co, 1936)
VEBLEN, T, An Inquiry into the Nature of Peace and the Terms of its Perpetuation (New York: Augustus M Kelly, 1964)
WAELDER, Robert, Psychological Aspects of War and Peace (Genève: Geneva Research Centre, 1939)
WEHBERG, Hans, Theory and Practice of International Policing (London: Constable and Co, 1935)
'La police internationale', Acad. Droit Int. Recl. Cours, vol 48 (1934), pp 1-132
WILLIAMS, W L, Intergovernmental Military Forces and World Public Order (Leiden: Sijthoff/Dobbs Ferry, NY: Oceana, 1971)
WYNNER, Edith, & LLOYD, Georgia, Searchlight on Peace Plans, revised edition 1949 (New York: E P Dutton)

9.3 DISARMAMENT

BOGDANOV, O V, 'Outlawry of war and disarmament', Acad. Droit Int. Recl. Cours, vol 133 (1971), pp 15-42

BULL, Hedley, The Control of the Arms Race, 2nd edition (New York: Frederick A Praeger, 1965)

BURTON, J W, Peace Theory: Preconditions of Disarmament (New York: Alfred A Knopf, 1962)

FISHER, Adrian S, 'Outlawry of war and disarmament', Acad. Droit Int. Recl. Cours, vol 133 (1971), pp 389-412

FURET, M F, Le Désarmement nucléaire (Paris: Pedone, 1973)

GARCIA ROBLES, A, 'Mesures de désarmement dans des zones particulières: le traité visant l'interdiction des armes nucléaires en Amérique latine', Acad. Droit Int. Recl. Cours, vol 133 (1971), pp 43-134

GOTLIEB, Alan, Disarmament and International Law (Toronto: The Canadian Institute of International Affairs, 1965)

HAZARD, John N, 'Post-disarmament international law', Am. J. Int. Law, vol 61 (1967), p 83

KOROVIN, E A, 'The USSR and disarmament', International Conciliation, no 292 (1933), pp 291-354

MARTIN, Andrew, Legal Aspects of Disarmament (London: British Institute of International and Comparative Law, 1963)

NEIDLE, 'Peace-keeping and disarmament', Am. J. Int Law, vol 57 (1963), pp 46-72

WEHBERG, H, 'Völkerbund und einsetige Abrüstung', Nord Tidsskr. Int. Ret, vol 2 (1931), pp 21-39

9.4 PEACEFUL COEXISTENCE

Peaceful coexistence is a term which has been used for some time by international lawyers from the socialist states. In recent years it has also been adopted by many Western lawyers for the analysis of peaceful cooperation by states.

BRETTON, P, & CHAUDET, J P, La Coexistence pacifique (Paris: Librairie Armand Colin, 1971). 327 pp.

DURDENEVSKY, V N, & LAZAREV, M I, Pyat' printsipov mirnogo sosushchestvovaniya (The Five Principles of Peaceful Coexistence) (Moscow, 1957). German edition, Berlin (DDR), 1959. 114 pp.

FIFIELD, Russell H, 'The five principles of peaceful coexistence', Am. J. Int. Law, vol 52 (1958), pp 504-10

RAMUNDO, Bernard A, Peaceful Coexistence: International Law in the Building of Communism (Baltimore, Md: Johns Hopkins Press, 1967). 262 pp.

LYON-CAEN, Gérard, 'Le droit international et la coexistence pacifique des états relevant des systèmes opposés', J. Droit Int., vol 79 (1952), pp 48-83

McWHINNEY, Edward, Peaceful Coexistence and Soviet-Western International Law (Leiden: Sijthoff; New York: Humanities Press, 1964), 135 pp.

TUNKIN, Grigory I, 'Coexistence and international law', Acad. Droit Int. Recl. Cours, vol 95 (1958), pp 1-81

9.5 INTERNATIONAL CONTROL

In this section I have listed works on the control of execution of international obligations. For execution of judgments see above in Section 8.9.9

ASBECK, F M, van, 'Quelques aspects du contrôle international non-judiciaire de l'application par les gouvernements de conventions internationales', Ned. Tijdschr. Int. Recht, Liber amicorum JPA François (July 1959), pp 27-41

BERTHOUD, P, Le Contrôle international de l'exécution des conventions collectives (Genève: Imprimerie de Saint-Gervais, 1946). 359 pp.

CASSESE, A, Il Controllo internazionale. Contributo alla teoria delle funzione di organizzazione dell' ordinamento internazionale (Milano: Giuffré, 1971). xi + 314 pp.
KAASIK, N, Le Contrôle en droit international (Paris, 1933). 399 pp.
KOPELMANAS, L, 'Le contrôle international', Acad. Droit Int. Recl. Cours, vol 77 (1950)
KRÜGER, H, 'Sicherung völkerrechtlicher Verpflichtungen', in Worterbuch des Völkerrechts, edited by K Strupp & H J Schlochauer (Berlin: de Gruyter, 1960-2), vol 3, p 269
LLOYD, W B, Jr 'Enforcement of world law', World Affairs (USA), vol 109, no 4 (December 1946), pp 273-9
RIDEAU, J, Juridictions internationales et contrôle du respect des traités constitutifs des organisations internationales (Paris, 1969)
SCHWEBEL, Stephen M, (ed), The Effectiveness of International Decisions. Papers of a Conference of the American Society of International Law and the Proceedings of the Conference (Dobbs Ferry, N Y: Oceana/Leiden: Sijthoff, 1971). 538 pp.
SYMONIDES, J, Kontrola miedzynorodowa (Toruń, 1964)
VOSSKAMP, H W, Mittel und Methoden der Sicherung der Vertragserfüllung in internationalen Zusammenschlüssen und Vereinigungen (Bonn, 1966)
WHITE, Th R, Methods of enforcing international law. Conference (second international) of the legal profession at the Hague. (International bar association) 1948
ZANGHI, C, La funzione di controllo negli enti internazionali (Milano, 1966)

9.6 SANCTIONS IN GENERAL

The problem of sanctions has a close bearing on the nature of international law as a whole (see Section 2.3). For various types of sanctions, see Section 9.7 on legitimate use of force, Section 9.8 on intervention, Section 9.12 on reprisals, Section 9.13 on blockade in peace and Section 9.2 on international security, as well as Section 13.24.2.21 on UN sanctions, Section 13.23 on sanctions of organisations in general, Section 13.24.2.22 on UN peacekeeping and Section 13.24.2.23 on UN forces.

HSU MO, 'The sanctions of international law', Grotius Soc. Trans., vol 35 (1949), pp 3-14

KUNZ, J L, 'Sanctions in international law', Am. J. Int. Law, vol 54 (1960), pp 324-7

ROYAL Institute of International Affairs, International Sanctions: A report by a Group of Members of the Royal Institute of International Affairs (New York/London/Toronto, 1938). 247 pp.

9.7 USE OF FORCE

The international community may be a primitive one as far as the density of the legal system is concerned. It has, however, now progressed to the stage where force is prohibited unless it is deployed as authorized sanctions. The standard book, although it is now twelve years old, is the one by BROWNLIE listed below. The study of use of force is not feasible without close analysis of state practice as reflected in case law, see above Section 1.4 for basic cases like the Corfu Channel case. See also Sections 9.9 on aggression and 10.1 on war

BARDELEBEN, Herbert von, Die zwangsweise Durchsetzung im Völkerrecht (Leipzig, 1930). 90 pp.

BOWETT, D W, 'The use of force in the protection of nationals', Grotius Soc. Trans., vol 43 (1957), pp 111-26

BRIERLY, J L, 'International law and resort to armed force', Cambridge Law Journal, vol 4 (1932), pp 308-19

BROWNLIE, I, International Law and the Use of force by States (Oxford: Clarendon Press, 1963)

BROWNLIE, I, 'Recent appraisals of legal regulation of the use of force', Int. & Comp. Law Q., vol 8 (1959), pp 707-21

BUZA, Ladislaus, 'Der Zwang im Völkerrecht', Z. Völkerrecht, vol 21 (1937), pp 420-40

FREEMAN, Harrop A, Coercion of States in International Organization (Philadelphia: The Pacifist Research Bureau, 1944)

FREI, P H, Die völkerrechtliche Wertung des Ultimatums (Köln, 1938)

GORDON, E, 'Evolution de la notion d'agression en droit international public', in Mélanges offerts à Ernest Mahaim (Paris, 1935), vol 2 pp 134-45

HIGGINS, Rosalyn, 'The legal limits to the use of force by sovereign states: United Nations practice', Br. Yearb. Int. Law, vol 37 (1961), pp 269-319

HINDMARSH, A E, Force in Peace. Force Short of War in International Relations (Cambridge, Mass, 1933). 249 pp.

McDOUGAL, Myres S, & FELICIANO, Florentino P, Law and Minimum World Public Order: The Legal Regulation of International Coercion (New Haven, Conn: Yale University Press, 1961). xxvii + 872 pp.

McDOUGAL, M S, 'Legal regulation of resort to international coercion: aggression and self-defence in policy perspective', Yale Law Journal, vol 68 (1958/9), pp 1057-1165

McDOUGAL, M S, 'The initiation of coercion: a multi-temporal analysis', Am. J. Int. Law, vol 52 (1958), pp 241-59

PETRASCU, Nicolas N, Les Mesures de contrainte internationale qui ne sont pas la guerre, entre états membres de la Société des Nations (Paris, 1927). 210 pp.

SKUBISZEWSKI, K, 'Use of force by states: collective security: law of war and neutrality', in Manual of Public International Law, edited by Max Sørensen (London: Macmillan/New York: St Martin's Press, 1968), pp 739-854

VISSCHER, C de, 'L'interdiction du recours à la force dans l'organisation internationale', in Rechtsfragen der internationalen Organisation. Festschrift für Hans Wehberg zu seinem 70 Geburtstag, edited by W Schätzel & H J Schlochauer (Frankfurt am Main, 1956), pp 395-403

WALDOCK, Sir Humphrey, 'The regulation of the use of force by individual states in international law', Acad. Droit Int. Recl. Cours, vol 81 (1952), pp 451-517

WEHBERG, H, 'L'interdiction du recours à la force; le principe et les problèmes qui se posent', Acad. Droit Int. Recl. Cours, vol 78 (1951), pp 7-115

WIDMER, Hans, Der Zwang im Völkerrecht. Eine Abhandlung und Kritische Darstellung des Sanktionsproblems im internationalen Leben (Leipzig, 1936). 150 pp.

WILHELM, René-Jean, 'La réalisation du droit par la force ou la menace des armes (considérations sur l'arrêt de la Cour internationale de justice en l'affaire du détroit de Corfou)', Annu. Suisse Droit Int., vol 15 (1958), pp 93-130

9.8 INTERVENTION

Intervention is sometimes used to denote any mingling into another state's affairs, thus even mere discussion of internal matters would, to some, constitute intervention. To most lawyers, intervention is used as a term to denote something more forceful

and the act is therefore better studied in a section
parallel to that of use of force. See also Section 9. 24. 2.
10 on the UN and domestic jurisdiction, Section 8. 9. 3
on the plea of domestic jurisdiction and Section 8. 11. 9
on domestic jurisdiction and the ICJ. See also Section
10. 13 on particular disputes and Section 9. 9 on
aggression.

ALVAREZ, Alejandro, The Monroe Doctrine (New
 York, 1924). 573 pp.
ARONEANU, Eugene, 'La guerre internationale
 d'intervention pour cause d'humanité', Revue inter-
 nationale de droit pénal, vol 19 (1948), pp 173-244
ARONEANU, Eugène, 'L'intervention d'humanité et la
 declaration universelle des droits de l'homme', Rev.
 Droit Int. Sci. Dipl. & Polit., vol 33 (1955), pp 126-
 33
ATIENZA, G, El Principio Internacional de no Inter-
 vención y los Doctrinas Americanas (1949)
BALLADORE PALLIERI, Giorgio, 'L'intervento come
 istituto giuridico internazionale', in Annali dell'
 Istituto di scienze giuridiche dell'Università di
 Messina, vol 4 (1929-30)
BALLADORE-PALLIERI, Giorgio, 'Quelques aspects
 juridiques de la non-intervention en Espagne', Rev.
 Droit Int. & Légis. Comp., ser 3, vol 18 (1937),
 pp 285-309
BATY, Thomas, 'Note sur la doctrine de Monroe', Rev.
 Droit Int. & Légis. Comp., vol 9 (1928), pp 157-72
BERNARD, Montague, On the Principle of Non-
 Intervention. A lecture delivered in the hall of All
 Souls College (Oxford/London, 1860). 36 pp.
CALVO, Carlos, et al, 'La doctrine de Monroe', On
 the Drago doctrine. Rev. Droit Int. & Légis.
 Comp., ser 2, vol 5 (1903), pp 597-623
CAVAGLIERI, Arrigo, L'intervento nella sua
 definizione giuridica. Saggio di diritto internazionale
 (Bologna, 1931). 164 pp.

CAVAGLIERI, Arrigo, Nuovi studi sull'intervento: Biblioteca di diritto pubblico e corporativo, vol 1 (Roma 1928). 81 pp.

DUPUY, René-Jean, 'Agression indirecte et intervention sollicitée à propos de l'affaire libanaise',

ERBER, P 'Die Intervention im modernen Völkerrecht', Thesis. Erlangen 1931.

ESMEIN, 'La théorie de l'intervention internationale', in Mélanges de droit international public, vol 2

FABELA, Isidro, Intervention (Paris, 1961). 236 pp.

FEDOZZI, Prospero, Saggio sull'intervento (Modena, 1898)

FENWICK, C G, 'Intervention by way of propaganda', Am. J. Int. Law, vol 35 (1941), p 626

FENWICK, C G, 'The Monroe doctrine and the declaration of Lima', Am. J. Int. Law, vol 33 (1939) pp 257-68

FENWICK, C G, 'Intervention: individual and collective', Am. J. Int. Law, vol 39 (1945), pp 645-63

FENWICK, C G, 'Has the specter of intervention been laid in Latin America?' Am. J. Int. Law (1956), pp 636-9

FENWICK, C G, 'Intervention and the inter-American rule of law', Am. J. Int. Law, vol 53 (1959), pp 873-6

FLOCKHER, Adolph von, De l'intervention en droit international (Paris, 1896). 70 pp.

FLOCKHER, Adolph von, 'Les conséquences de l'intervention', Rev. Gén. Droit Int. Public, vol 3 (1896), pp 329-33

GARCIA-ARIAS, L, 'La intervención internacional por causa de humanidad', in Fundamental Problems of International Law, Festschrift für Jean Spiropoulos, pp 163-71

GEFFCKEN, Friedrich Heinrich, Das Recht der Intervention (Hamburg, 1887). 50 pp.

GILMOUR, D R, 'The meaning of "intervene" within article 2 (7) of the United Nations Charter; an historical perspective ', Int. & Comp. Law Q., vol 16 (1967), pp 330-51

GHIRARDINI, G, 'A proposito di intervento', Riv. Diritto Int. (1913), pp 89-105

GUERRERO, Jose Gustavo, 'La question de l'intervention a la VIe Conférence Panaméricane', Rev. Gén. Droit Int. Public, vol 36 (1929), pp 40-51

HAGEDAN, H, 'Wandlungen des Interventionsrechtes in der Geschichte', Thesis. Freiburg i/B 1933

HAUTEFEUILLE, Laurent Basile, Le Principe de non-intervention et ses applications (Paris, 1863). 67 pp.

HELLER, Karl, 'Die Frage der Zulässigkeit der völkerrechtlichen Intervention', Dissertation. Erlangen, Leipzig 1915. 34 pp.

HERSHEY, Amos Shartle, 'The Calvo and Drago Doctrines', Am. J. Int. Law, vol 1 (1907), pp 26-45

HETTLAGE, Karl M, 'Die Intervention im System der modernen Völkerrechtslehre', Niemeyers Z. Int. Recht, vol 37 (1927), pp 11-88

HODGES, H G A M, The Doctrine of Intervention (Princeton, NJ: The Banner Press, 1915). 288 pp.

HYDE, Charles Cheney, 'Intervention in theory and in practice', Illinois Law Review, vol 6 (1911), pp 1-16

HYDE, C C, 'Legal aspects of the Japanese pronouncement in relation to China. A discussion of the Japanese claim to rights analogous to those accruing under the Monroe doctrine', Am. J. Int. Law, vol 28 (1934), pp 431-43

KEBEDGY, Michel S, De l'intervention, théorie générale et étude spéciale de la question de l'Orient (Paris, 1890). 224 pp.

KOMARNICKI, T, 'L'intervention en droit international moderne', Rev. Gén. Droit Int. Public, vol 60 (1956), pp 521-68

KRAUS, Herbert, Die Monroedoktrin in ihren Beziehungen zur amerikanischen Diplomatie und zum Völkerrecht (Berlin, 1913). 480 pp.
LADOR-LEDERER, J J, 'Intervention - Historical stocktaking', Nord. Tidsskr. Int. Ret, vol 29 (1959), pp 127-41
LAUTERPACHT, Elihu, 'Intervention by invitation', Int. & Comp. Law Q., vol 7 (1958), pp 102-8
LAUTERPACHT, H, 'L'intervention pour cause d'humanité', in Vitoria et Suarez, contributions de théologiens au droit international moderne (Paris, 1939). 228 pp.
LIMBURG, Stirum, J P van Tets, 'Over de völkenrechtelijke interventie', Thesis. Leiden 1895. 93 pp.
LINGELBACH, William Ezra, 'The doctrine and practice of intervention in Europe', American Academy of Political Science Annals, vol 16 (1900), pp 1-32
MOSLER, Hermann, Die Intervention im Völkerrecht (Berlin, 1937). 89 pp.
MOULIN, H A, La Doctrine de Drago (Paris, 1908). 368 pp.
PENNISI, 'Appunti per una teoria giuridica dell'intervento', Jus Gentium (Denmark), vol 3 (1940), p 1
PERKINS, Dexter, The Monroe Doctrine, 1826-1867 (Baltimore/London, 1933). 580 pp.
PERKINS, Dexter, 'The Monroe Doctrine, 1867-1907 (Baltimore/London, 1937). 480 pp.
PIRADOV, A S, & STARUSHENKO, G B, 'Non-intervention and contemporary international law', Sov. Ezheg. Mezhdunar. Prava (1958), p 230. With summary in English
POTTER, P B, 'L'intervention en droit international moderne', Acad. Droit Int. Recl. Cours, vol 32 (1930), pp 606-90
ROUSSEAU, Ch, 'La non-intervention en Espagne', Rev. Droit Int. & Légis Comp., vol 19 (1938), pp 217-80; 473-549; 700-75; vol 20 (1939), pp 114-49

SCERNI, G, 'Sull'intervento', in Scritti giuridici per Santi-Romano (Padova, 1939)
SCHNEIDER, J, Die Intervention im Völkerrecht (Erlangen, 1928)
SCHWARZ, U, Confrontation and Intervention in the Modern World (Dobbs Ferry, NY: Oceana, 1970)
SHAH, Nasim Hasan, 'Discovery by intervention: the right of a state to seize evidence located within the territory of the respondent state', Am. J. Int. Law, vol 53 (1959), pp 595-612
STOWELL, Ellery C, Intervention in International Law (Washington, 1921). 558 pp.
STRUPP, K, 'L'intervention en matière financière', Acad. Droit Int. Recl. Cours, vol iii (1925), pp 5-124
TEUBAUM, H, Die völkerrechtliche Intervention (Greifswald, 1918)
THOMAS, Ann van Wynen, & THOMAS, A J, Non-Intervention. The Law and its Import in the Americas (Dallas, 1956). 476 pp.
TROLLIET, Pierre, Essai sur l'intervention en droit international public (Lausanne, 1940). 104 pp.
VALVERDE, Antonio, L, La intervención, estudio de derecho internacional público (Habana, 1902). 195 pp.
WACHTER, Alfred von, Die völkerrechtliche Intervention als Mittel der Selbsthilfe (München, 1911). 67 pp.
WALKER, A, 'Die Intervention im Sinne des Völkerrechtes und ihre prinzipielle Zulässigkeit', Thesis. Freiburg i/B, 1929
WILCOX, Francis O, 'The Monroe doctrine and World War II', American Political Science Review, vol 36 (1942), pp 434-53
WRIGHT, Q, 'Subversive intervention', Am. J. Int. Law, vol 54 (1960), pp 521-35
WRIGHT, Q, 'Intervention and Cuba, in 1961', Am. Soc. Int. Law Proc., vol 55 (1961), pp 2-19
ZANNINI, Walter, 'Dell'intervento', Studi nelle scienze giuridiche e sociali, vol 31 (1950), pp 1-44

9.9 AGGRESSION AND ITS DEFINITION

Aggression is one form of illegitimate use of force (see Section 9.7 on use of force in general). Note the recent UN Resolution on definition of the use of force GA/RES/3314 of 14th December 1974. See also Section 10.13 on particular disputes.

ALFARO, Ricardo J, 'La Cuestión de la Definición de la Agresion', Rev. Derecho Int., vol 59 (1951), pp 361-80

ALFARO, Ricardo J, 'La question de la définition de l'agression', Rev. Droit Int. Sci. Dipl. & Polit., vol 29 (1951), pp 367-87

AMADO, Gilberto, 'La question de la définition de l'agression', Rev. Droit Int. Sci. Dipl. & Polit., vol 30 (1952), pp 147-55

ARONEANU, E, La Définition de l'agression (Paris, 1958). 405 pp.

ARONEANU, E, 'Les formes de l'agression', Rev. Droit Int. Sci. Dipl. & Polit., vol 36 (1958), pp 401-11

BAAK, J Carel, 'Das Völkerrecht und das Problem des Angriffs', Z. Öff. Recht, vol 6 (1925), pp 367-80

BAAK, J Carel, 'Völkerrechtliche Betrachtungen über Angriff und Verteidigung', Die Friedens-Warte, vol 26 (1926), pp 377-9

BAGINYAN, K A, 'The forty-year struggle of the Soviet Union for outlawing aggression', Sov. Ezheg. Mezhdunar Prava (1958), p 169. With English summary

BAGINYAN, K A, 'The question of the definition of agression', Sovietskoe gosudarstvo i pravo, no 1 (1955), pp 59-67

BALICKI, Jan, Pojęcie agresji w prawie miedzynarodowym (Warsaw, 1952)

BASTID, Paul, 'Définition de l'agresseur', in Dictionnaire diplomatique (Paris: Académie diplomatique internationale), vol 3, p 1

BILFINGER, Carl, 'Die russische Definition des Angreifers', Z. Ausl. Öff. Recht. & Völkerrecht, vol 7 (1937), pp 483-96

BLIX, Hans, Sovereignty. Aggression and Neutrality. Three Lectures (Uppsala: The Dag Hammerskjöld Foundation, 1970). 62 pp.

BOURGEOIS, Léon V, 'Définition de l'agression', Europe nouvelle, no 344 (20 September 1924). pp 1229-31

BRAATØY, B, 'The quest for treaty definitions of aggression', Acta scandinavica juris gentium, vol 5 (1934), pp 29-40

BRIERE, R P Y, 'Définition de l'agresseur', in Dictionnaire diplomatique (Paris: Académie diplomatique internationale), vol 3, pp 2-4

BRIERE, R P Y, 'Un nouveau progrès sur la route du droit: la définition de l'agresseur', Esprit international, vol 7 (1933), pp 616-25

BROMS, B, The Definition of Aggression in the United Nations (Abo: Turun Yliopisto, 1968). 162 pp.

CHAUMONT, Charles, 'Explication juridique d'une définition de l'agression', Annu. Fr. Droit Int. (1956), pp 521-9

DIAMANDESCO, Jean, Le Problème de l'agression dans le droit international public actuel (Paris, 1936). 252 pp.

DONNEDIEU DE VABRES, 'Un traité multilatéral pour la définition de "l'aggresseur"', L'année politique française et étrangère (1933), pp 400-4

EAGLETON, C C, 'The attempt to define aggression', Int. Conciliation, no 264 (1930), pp 579-650

GRANFELT, H, 'Om begreppet anfall och anfallskrig; historisk belysning', Acta scandinavica juris gentium, vol 17 (1946), pp 9-35

GUGGENHEIM, Paul, 'Das Problem der völkerrechtlichen Feststellung des Angreifers', Völkerbund, no 13 (April 1932)
HERTZ, W, 'Le problème de l'agression en droit international', Rev. Int. Théorie, vol 9 (1935), pp 203-8
HERTZ, W, 'Das Problem des völkerrechtlichen Angriffs', Z. Öff. Recht, vol 15 (1935), pp 300-29
HERTZ, WILHELM G, Das Problem des völkerrechtlichen Angriffs (Leiden, 1936). 183 pp.
JESSUP, P, 'The crime of aggression and the future of international law', Political Science Quarterly, vol 62 (1947), pp 1-10
KELSEN, H, 'E possibile e desiderabile definire l'aggressione?' in Scritti di diritto internazionale in onore di Tomaso Perassi (Milano, 1957), vol 2, p 1
KOMARNICKI, Wacław, 'La définition de l'agresseur dans le droit international moderne', Acad. Droit Int. Recl. Cours, vol 75 (1949), pp 5-110
KOPELMANAS, Lazare, 'The problem of aggression and the prevention of war', Am. J. Int. Law, vol 31 (1937), pp 244-57
LEDERER, Z J, 'La définition de l'agresseur', Rev. Droit Int. Sci. Dipl. & Polit, vol 13 (1935), pp 119-25
LE FUR, Louis-Erasme, 'Les Conventions de Londres (1933) et la définition de l'agresseur', Rev. Droit Int. Sci. Dipl. & Polit., vol 11 (1933), pp 179-91
LU-CHUN-KAI, 'La Notion juridique de l'agression en droit international public', Thesis. Caen/Paris 1938
MAKTOS, John, 'Définition de l'agression', Rev. Droit Int. Sci. Dipl. & Polit., vol 30 (1952), pp 5-9
MANDELSTAM, A N, 'Réflexions sur la constatation de l'agression (Athens, 1939)
MORAWIECKI, Wojciech, Walka o definicje agresji w prawie miedzynarodowym, (Warsaw, 1956). 422 pp.

PAL, R, 'What is aggressive war?' Indian Law Review, vol 4 (1950), pp 99-142

PAL, R, 'The definition of aggression', Indian Yearb. Int. Aff. (1954), p 341

PIOTROWSKI, G, 'Où en sommes-nous sur le problème de l'agression?' Rev. Droit Int. Sci. Dipl. & Polit., vol 35 (1957), pp 169-83; 289-303

PORDEA, G A, 'L'agression, ses critères déterminatifs et sa définition', Rev. Droit Int. Sci. Dipl. & Polit., vol 30 (1952), pp 367-83

RADOJKOVIC, M, La Définition de l'agresseur (Belgrade, 1934)

REICHHELM, Konrad, Der Angriff. Eine völkerrechtliche Untersuchung über den Begriff. Internationale Abhandlungen, 27 (Berlin/Grünewald, 1927 & 1934)

RÖLING, B V A, 'The question of defining agression', in Symbolae Verzijl (Den Haag: Nijhoff, 1958), p314

SCHIRMER, Gregor, 'Zum Kampf um das völkerrechtliche Verbot der Aggression', Staat und Recht (DDR), vol 7 (1958), pp 870-92

SCHÖCKING, W, 'Die definition des Angriffs', Völkerbund, no 12 (April 1932)

SERRA, Enrico, L'aggressione internazionale (Milano, 1946). 204 pp.

SIDJANSKI, D, & CASTAÑOS, Stelios, 'L' "aggresseur" et l' "aggression" au point de vue idéologique et réel', Rev. Droit Int. Sci. Dipl. & Polit., vol 30 (1952), pp 44-55

SOHN, L B, 'The definition of aggression', Virginia Law Review, vol 45 (1959), pp 697-701

STEINLEIN, Wilhelm, Der Begriff des nicht herausgeforderten Angriffs in Bündnisverträgen seit 1870 und insbesondere im Locarno-Vertrag, Dissertation Frankfurt. Frankfurter Abhandlungen zum Kriegsverhütungsrecht, Heft 5 (Leipzig, 1927). 134 pp.

STONE, J, Aggression and World Order: A Critique of United Nations Theories of Aggression (London, 1958). 226 pp.
THIRRING, Hans, 'Was ist Aggression?' Österr. Z. Öff. Recht, vol 5 (1952/3), pp 226-42
THERY, René, La Notion d'agression en droit international (Paris, 1937). 256 pp.
THOMAS, Ann van Wynen, & THOMAS, A J, Jr, The Concept of Aggression in International Law (Dallas, Tex: Southern Methodist University Press, 1972). xi + 114 pp.
VIGNOL, René, 'Définition de l'agresseur dans la guerre', Thesis. Montpellier, Paris 1933. 174 pp
WRIGHT, Q, 'The concept of aggression in international law', Am. J. Int. Law, vol 29 (1935), pp 373-95
WRIGHT, Q, 'The prevention of aggression', Am. J. Int. Law, vol 50 (1956), pp 514-32
ŽOUREK, Jaroslav, 'La définition de l'agression et le droit international. Développements récents de la question', Acad. Droit Int. Recl. Cours, vol 91 (1957), pp 755-860

9.10 SELF-DEFENCE

See also Section 9.11 on self-help and necessity.
AL CHALABI, Hassan Abdel Hadi, La Légitime Défense en droit international (Cairo, 1952)
ARNOLD-FORSTER, W, 'Order and self-defence in the world community', Problems of Peace, vol 5 (1930), pp 230-55
BAGINYAN, K A, 'Armed aggression under the pretext of self-defence', Sov. Gos. i Pravo (1959), pp 121-7
BOWETT, D W, Self-Defence in International Law (Manchester: Manchester University Press, 1958). 287 pp.

BOWETT, Derek W, 'Collective self-defence under the charter of the United Nations', Br. Yearb. Int. Law, vol 32 (1955/6), pp 130-61
BUZZATI, G C, L'offesa e la difesa nella guerra secondo i moderni ritrovati. Studio di diritto internazionale (Roma, 1888)
CALOGEROPOULOS, S S, 'La légitime défense', Rev. Hell. Droit Int., vol 6 (1953), pp 217-30
CASTBERG, Frede, 'Le droit international et la défense', Acta scandinavica juris gentium, vol 1 (1930), pp 1-18; 81-7
CURTIS, George Ticknor, The Case of the Virginius Considered with Reference to the Law of Self-defense', (New York, 1874). 40 pp.
DELIUANIS, J, La Légitime Défense en droit international public moderne (Paris, 1971)
DINH, Nguyen Quoc, 'La légitime défense d'après la Charte des Nations Unies', Rev. Gén. Droit Int. Public, vol 52 (1948), pp 223-54
EISENBERG, A, 'La legitima defensa en el derecho internacional', Revista de la Facultad de Derecho y Ciencias sociales (Montevideo), vol 10 (1959), pp 925-48
GIRAUD, Emile, 'La théorie de la légitime défense', Acad. Droit Int. Recl. Cours, vol 49 (1934), pp 687-438
GREEN, L C, 'Armed conflict, war and self-defence', Arch. Völkerrechts, vol 6 (1956/7), pp 387-438
KELSEN, H, 'Collective security and collective self-defence under the Charter of the United Nations', Am. J. Int. Law, vol 42 (1948), pp 783-96
KUNZ, J L, 'Individual and collective self-defense in article 51 of the Charter of the United Nations', Am. J. Int. Law, vol 41 (1947), pp 872-9
LAMBERTI ZANARDI, P, La legitima difese nel diritto internazionale (Milano: Giuffré, 1972). 251 pp.

LAUN, Rudolf, 'Angriff und Verteidigung', Z. Völkerrecht, vol 10 (1917/18), pp 504-46

NINČIĆ, D, 'Legitimate defence in the new international law', Jugoslovenski revija za medunarodno pravo, vol 2 (1955), p 180

SCELLE, G, 'L'agression et la légitime défense dans les rapports internationaux', L'esprit international, vol 10 (1936), pp 372-93

SCHWARZENBERGER, G, 'The principle of self-defence in international judicial practice', in Estudios de derecho internacional. Homenaje al Profesor Camilo Barcia Trelles, (1958), pp 213-19

VISSCHER, Charles de, La Belgique et les juristes allemands (Lausanne/Paris, 1916). 134 pp.

VISSCHER, Charles de, Belgium's Case. A Juridical Enquiry (London, 1916). 164 pp.

ZANARDI, P L, La legittima difesa nel Diritto Internazionale (Milano: Giuffré, 1972). xi + 313 pp.

9.11 SELF-HELP AND NECESSITY

Cf. Section 9.10 on self-defence.

BORSI, Umberto, 'Ragione di guerra e stato di necessità nel diritto interzationale', Riv. Diritto Int., vol 10 (1916), pp 157-94

CAVAGLIERE, A, 'Lo stato di necessità nel diritto internazionale', Rivista italiana per le scienze giuridiche, vol 60 (1917/18), p 171

FAATZ, Adolf, 'Notwehr und Notstand im Völkerrecht', Doctorate dissertation. Greifswald, 1919

HAZAN, Edouard Tawfik, L'Etat de necessité en droit pénal interétatique et international (Paris, 1949). 159 pp.

HERTEL, A, 'Notstand und Notwehr im Völkerrecht', Doctorate dissertation. Greifswald, 1918

HERTZ, W, 'Die Theorie der Notwehr im Volkerrecht', Warte, vol 35 (1935), pp 137-42

HINDMARSH, Albert E, 'Self-help in time of peace',
  Am. J. Int. Law, vol 26 (1932), pp 315-26
KOHLER, Josef, Not kennt kein Gebot. Die Theorie
  des Notrechtes und die Ereignisse unserer Zeit
  (Berlin/Leipzig, 1915). 39 pp.
RAPISARDI-MIRABELLI, Il tema di stato di necessità
  nel diritto internazionale (Paris, 1919), and
  Rivista italiana per la scienze giuridiche, vol 62
  (1919), p 170
RODICK, Burleigh Cushing, The Doctrine of Necessity
  in International Law (New York, 1928), 206 pp.
SCHÖN, Paul, 'Zur Lehre von den völkerrechtlichen
  nichtkriegemschen Mitteln der Selbsthilfe',
  Z. Völkerrecht, vol 20 (1936), pp 14-64
SCHÖNBORN, Walther, Die Besetzung von Vera Cruz
  (Zur Lehre von den völkerrechtlichen Selbsthilfeakten)
  mit einem Anhang: Urkunden zur Politik des Präsidenten Wilson gegenüber Mexico (Stuttgart, 1914).
  60 pp.
SPERDUTI, Giuseppe, 'Introduzione allo studio delle
  funzioni della necessità nel diritto internazionale',
  Riv. Diritto Int., vol 35 (1943), pp 19-103
STEGER, F S E, 'Notwehr und Notstand im
  Völkerrecht', Dissertation. Freiburg, 1927
STILZ, Richard, Notstand im Völkerrecht (Coburg,
  1930)
VISSCHER, Ch de, 'Les lois de la guerre et la théorie
  de la nécessité', Rev. Gén. Droit Int. Public, vol
  24 (1917), pp 74-108
WEIDEN, Paul, 'Necessity in international law',
  Grotius Soc. Trans., vol 24 (1938), pp 105-32

9.12 REPRISALS

See also the book by VISSCHER listed in Section 11.1
BAENZIGER, Jakob, 'Die Repressalien im
  Völkerrecht'. Dissertation. Freiburg, 1925. 60 pp.

COLBERT, Evelyn Speyer, Retaliation in International Law (New York, 1948). 228 pp.

DUCROCQ, Louis, 'Représailles en temps de paix; blocus pacifique, suivi d'une étude sur les affaires de Chine (1900-1901)', Thesis. Paris, 1901. 237 pp.

KALSHOVEN, F, The Law of Belligerent Reprisals (Leiden: Sijthoff, 1971). 387 pp.

KELLER, Ludwig, Die Nichtkriegsche Militärische Gewaltmassnahme, ihre Abgrenzung von Krieg und ihre Zulässigkeit als Repressalie und Notwehrakt. Völkerrechtliche Monographien, Heft 11 (Berlin, 1934). 137 pp.

LA BRIERE, R P Yves de, 'Evolution de la doctrine et de la pratique en matière de représailles', Acad. Droit Int. Recl. Cours, vol 22 (1928), pp 241-93

MACCOBY, Simon, 'Reprisals as a measure of redress short of war', Cambridge Law Journal, vol 2 (1924), pp 60-73

POLITIS, Nicolas, 'Les représailles entre états membres de la SDN', Rev. Gén. Droit Int. Public, vol 31 (1924), pp 5-16

RITTER, W, Die Repressalienhandlung (Giesser, 1930)

SCHUMANN, Erich, Die Repressalien. Rostocker Abhandlungen, Heft 3 (Rostock, 1927)

SEFERIADES, Stelio, 'La question des représailles armées en temps de paix, en l'état actuel du droit des gens', Rev. Droit Int. & Légis Comp., ser 3, vol 17 (1936), pp 138-64

VENEZIA, Jean-Claude, 'La notion de représailles en droit international public', Rev. Gén. Droit Int. Public, vol 44 (1960), pp 465-98

WESTLAKE, J, 'Reprisals and war', Law Quarterly Review, vol 25 (1909), pp 127-37

9.13 BLOCKADE

On the guarantee of Cuba see p.396 and the articl MacCHESNEY listed below and also WHITEMAN, Digest, listed in Section 1.4.2, vol 4, pp 523-24. On blockade in war see general works under 10.1.

AGO, R, 'Il blocco marittimo', Le vie del mondo (1940), p 97

BARES, Charles, Le Blocus pacifique (Toulouse, 1898). 160 pp.

BRUNS, J, 'Die brittische Seesperre un die Neutralen', Z Ausl. Öff. Recht & Völkerrecht, vol 9 (1943), p 505

FALCKE, Horst P, Le Blocus pacifique (Leipzig, 1919). 316 pp.

FALCKE, Horst P, 'Die Friedensblockade', Zeit für int. Privat- und öff. Recht, vol 19 (1909), p 67

FALCKE, Horst P, 'Die Friedensblockade', Niemeyers Z. Int. Recht, vol 28 (1919/20), pp 33-182

FAUCHILLE, Paul, Du blocus maritime. Etude de droit international et de droit comparé (Paris, 1882). 406 pp.

HOGAN, Albert Edmond, Pacific Blockade (Oxford, 1908). 183 pp.

MALKIN, H W, 'Blockade in modern conditions', Br. Yearb. Int. Law (1922/3), p 87

MacCHESNEY, B, Some comments on the 'guarantee' of Cuba, 57 Am. J. Int. Law, (1963) p 592

McDOUGAL, M S, 'The Soviet-Cuban quarantine and self-defense', Am. J. Int. Law, vol 57 (1963), p 597

MONACO, R, La guerra al commercio marittimo nemico (Milano, 1942). p 24

PARRY, Clive, 'British practice in some nineteenth century Pacific blockades', Z. Ausl. Öff. Recht & Völkerrecht, vol 8 (1938), pp 672-88

SCERNI, G, 'L'influenza del blocco sul commercio marittimo neutrale', Comun. & Stud., vol 1, p 31

SÖDERQUIST, Nils, Le Blocus maritime (Stockholm, 1908). 307 pp.

STAUDACHER, Hermann, Die Friedenblockade, ein Beitrag zur Theorie und Praxis des nichtkriegerischen Selbsthilfe (Leipzig, 1909)

TACHI, S, (Pacific blockade in international law and the measure of prevention of ingress and egress of Chinese vessels) (Japanese text). J I L D, vol 37 (January 1938)
TEYSSAIRE, J, Le Blocus pacifique (Paris, 1910)
WESTLAKE, J, 'Le blocus pacifique', Rev. Droit Int. & Légis, Comp., ser 2, vol 11 (1909), pp 203-16
On the Cuban Quarantine see:
CHAYES, A, Law and the Quarantine of Cuba, For Aff. (US) (1965), no 3, pp 550-557
CHRISTOL, C Q, & DAVIS, C R, Maritime Quarantine: The Naval Interdiction of Offensive Weapons and Associated Material to Cuba, 1962, Am. J. Int. Law, vol 57 (1963), pp 525-546
D'ESTEFANO, M A, La Curantena y el Derecho Internacional, Politica Internacional No 4 (Habana, 1963)
FENWICK, C G, The Quarantine Against Cuba: Legal or Illegal? Am. J. Int. Law, vol 57 (1963), pp 588-592
KOLODKIN, A L, Morskaja blokada i sovremennoe mezhdunaronoe pravo, Sovetskoe gosudarvtvo i pravo (Moscow, 1963) no 4, pp 92-104
MALLISON, W T, Jr, Limited Naval Blockade or Quarantine Interdiction, National and Collective Defense Claims Valid under International Law, Am. J. Int. Law, vol 57 (1963), pp 592-597
McDOUGAL, M, The Soviet Cuban Quarantine and Self Defense, Am. J. Int. Law, vol 57 (1962), pp 597-604
MEEKER, L, Defensive Quarantine and the Law, Am. J. Int. Law, vol 57 (1963), pp 515-525
PACHTER, H M, Collision Course - The Cuban Missile Crisis and Coex NY, (London 1963) (includes documents)
WRIGHT, Q, The Cuban Quarantine, Am. J. Int. Law, vol 57 (1963), p 546

10 War and Armed Conflicts

10.1 GENERAL

Many works on the laws of war have become obsolete as modern international law has changed to outlaw all forms of aggressive war (see Section 10.2 on legitimacy of war and Section 12.2.5 on war crimes). In the Section below I have included some older works as well as fresh material to illustrate the recent progress of international law in this respect. On the use of force in general see Section 9.7 and compare Section 9.9 on aggression and Section 9.2 on international security.

BALLADORE-PALLIERI, G, La guerra (Padova: CEDAM, 1935)

BALLADORE-PALLIERI, G, Diritto Bellico, 2nd edition (Padova: CEDAM, 1954)

BAILEY, S D, Prohibitions and Restraints in War (London: Oxford University Press, 1972). 194 pp.

BALLIS, William, The Legal Position of War: Changes in its Practice and Theory from Plato to Vattel (Den Haag: Nijhoff, 1937). 188 pp.

BATY, T, & MORGAN, S H, War - Its Conduct and Legal Results (London: John Murray, 1915). 555 pp.

BATY, T, 'The suppression of war', Quarterly Review (1929), pp 177-99

BAXTER, R R, 'The definition of war', Revue égyptienne de droit international, vol 16 (1960), pp 1-14

BEAUFORT, D, La Guerre comme instrument de secours ou de punition (Den Haag: Nijhoff, 1933). 185 pp.
BORCHARD, E M, ' "War" and "peace",' Am. J. Int. Law, vol 27 (1933), pp 114-17
BOUTHOUL, G, Les Guerres: Eléments de polémologie (Paris: Payot, 1951)
BRETTON, P, Le Droit de la guerre (Paris: Librairie Armand Colin, 1970). 95 pp.
BROUCKERE, Louis de, 'La prévention de la guerre', Acad. Droit Int. Recl. Cours, vol 50 (1934), pp 1-83
BUCHAN, Alastair, War in Modern Society. An Introduction (London: C A Watts & Co, 1966)
CADOUX, C J, The Early Christian Attitude to War (London, 1919)
CALEGORYPOULOS-STRATIS, S, 'La souveraineté des états et les limitations au droit de guerre', Rev. Hell. Droit Int., vol 2 (1949), pp 153-67
CANTRIL, H, (ed), Tensions that Cause Wars (Urbana, Ill: University of Illinois Press, 1951)
CASTRÉN, Erik, The Present Law of War and Neutrality (Helsinki, 1954). 630 pp. (Annales Academiae Scientarum Fennicae, Ser B)
CHOWDHURY, Roy, Military Alliances and Neutrality in War and Peace (London: Longmans, 1967)
CLARK, G N, War and Society in the Seventeenth Century (London: Cambridge University Press, 1958)
DELBEZ, Louis, 'La notion juridique de guerre', Rev. Gen. Droit Int. Public, vol 57 (1953), pp 177-209
DESCHAMPS, E E F, 'Le droit international nouveau. L'influence de la condamnation de la guerre sur l'évolution juridique internationale', Acad. Droit Int. Recl. Cours, vol 31 (1930), pp 393-559
DEVEZE, A, Le Droit des gens et de la guerre (Paris: Les Editions internationales/Bruxelles: Emile Bruylant, 1937)

EAGLETON, C, 'The attempt to define war', Int.
  Conciliation, no 291 (1933), pp 235-87
EAGLETON, C, 'Form and function of the declaration
  of war', Am. J. Int. Law, vol 32, (1938), pp 19-35
EAGLETON, C, 'Judicial determination of the end of
  the war', Columbia Law Review, vol 47 (1947), pp
  255-68
EAGLETON, C, 'When did the war begin?' Columbia
  Law Review, vol 47 (1947), pp 742-8
ENRIQUES, Giuliano, 'Considerazioni sulla teoria
  della guerra nel diritto internazionale', Riv. Diritto
  Int., vol 20 (1928), pp 27-49; 149-73
FRIEDMANN, L, The Law of War - A Documentary
  History (New York: Random House, 1972). 2 vols.
  1737 pp.
GHIL, T, Folkrätt under krig och neutralitet, 2nd ed
  (Stockholm: KFs Bokförlag 1943)
GOHLER, Hans, Freies Kriegsführungsrecht und
  Kriegsschuld. Abhandlungen des Instituts für Politik,
  ausländisches öffentliches Recht und Völkerrecht an
  der Universität Leipzig, Heft 17 (Leipzig, 1931).
  114 pp.
GREENSPAN, Morris, The Modern Law of Land
  Warfare (Berkeley/Los Angeles, 1959). 724 pp.
GROB, F, The Relativity of War and Peace (New
  Haven, Conn: Yale University Press, 1949). 902 pp.
HIGGINS, A Pearce, War and the Private Citizen
  (London: P S King & Son, 1912). 200 pp.
HILLEKE, Heinrich, Der Kriegsbegriff und seine
  Stellung in der Weltordnung: eine völkerrechtliche
  Untersuchung, Göttinger Diss (Leipzig, 1932). 81 pp.
HOLLAND, T E, The Laws and Customs of War on Land
  as defined by the Hague Convention of 1899 (London:
  Harrison & Sons, 1904). 70 pp.
KAHN, Herman, On Escalation (New York: Frederick
  A Praeger, 1965)

JÄGERSKIÖLD, Stig, Handbok: Folkrätt under neutralitet och krig (Stockholm: Allmänna förlaget 1971)
KALSHOVEN, F, The Law of Warfare (Leiden: Sijthoff, 1973). 232 pp.
KAPPUS, Georg, Der völkerrechtliche Kriegsbegriff in seiner Abgrenzung gegenüber den militärischen Repressalien (Breslau, 1936). 82 pp.
KERR, Philip, 'The outlawry of war', Journal of the Royal Institute of International Affairs, vol 7 (1928), pp 361-88
KEYDEL, Hans, Das Recht zum Kriege im Völkerrecht. Frankfurter Abhandlungen zum modernen Völkerrecht, Heft 24 (Leipzig, 1931). 80 pp.
KHADDURI, Majid, The Law of War and Peace in Islam (London, 1940)
KHADDURI, Majid, War and Peace in the Law of Islam (Baltimore, 1955). 321 pp.
KOTZSCH, Lothar, The Concept of War in Contemporary History and International Law (Genève: Librairie Droz, 1956). 310 pp.
KRUSE-JENSEN, C, Krigens rett (Oslo: Gyldendal, 1952). 223 pp.
KUEI, Tsung Yao, 'Der Krieg als völkerrechtliches Institut, insbesondere der Kriegsbegriff', Thesis. Bern, 1945
KUNZ, J, Kriegsrecht und Neutralitätsrecht (Wien: Julius Springer, 1935). 335 pp.
McDOUGAL, M S, & FELICIANO, Florentino P, 'International coercion and world public order: The general principles of the law of war', Yale Law Journal, vol 67 (1957/8), pp 771-845
MARTIN, C E, 'The legal position of war and neutrality during the last twenty-five years', Am. Soc. Int. Law Proc. (1932), pp 137-79
MAURICE, Sir John Frederick, Hostilities without Declaration of War: from 1700 to 1870 (London: HMSO, 1883)

McNAIR, A D, & WATTS, A D, The Legal Effects of War, 4th edition (London: Cambridge University Press, 1966)
McNAIR, A D, 'The legal meaning of war and the relation of war to reprisals', Grotius Soc. Trans., vol 11 (1926), pp 29-51
MEYROWITZ, H, 'Le statut des saboteurs dans le droit de la guerre', Revue de droit pénal militaire et de droit de la guerre, vol 5 (1966), pp 121-76
MEYROWITZ, H, Le Principe de l'égalité des belligerants devant le droit de la guerre (Paris: Pédone, 1970)
MILLS, W, & REAL, J, The Abolition of War (New York: Macmillan, 1963)
GREENSPAN, Morris, The Modern Law of Land Warfare (Berkeley/Los Angeles, 1959). 724 pp.
OLIVI, Augusto, La dottrina della guerra e i suoi limiti giuridici nel diritto internazionale (Modena, 1929)
OTLET, Paul, Les Problèmes internationaux et la guerre (Genève/Paris, 1916). 501 pp.
PHILLIPSON, C, Termination of War and Treaties of Peace (London: T F Unwin, 1916)
RAPISARDI-MIRABELLI, Andrea, Il significato della guerra nella scienza del diritto internazionale (Roma, 1910)
REITH, Charles, Police Principles and the Problems of War (London: Oxford University Press, 1940). 152 pp.
RIDDER, Helmut, 'La guerra y el derecho de guerra en el derecho internacional y en la doctrina internacionalista', Revista de estudios politicos (March-April 1957), pp 31-50
ROLLAND, L, 'Les pratiques de la guerre aérienne', Rev. Gén. Droit Int. Pub., vol 23 (1916), p 497
ROY, Nirmal Kumar, International Law: Peace, War and Neutrality (Calcutta: Eastern Law House, 1965). 424 pp.

RUMPF, Helmut, 'Is a definition of war necessary?' Boston University Law Review, vol 18 (1938), pp 687-714

RUMPF, Helmut, 'Der Unterschied zwischen Krieg und Frieden', Arch. Völkerrechts, vol 2 (1949), pp 40-50

RUMPF, Helmut, 'Zur Frage der Relativität des Kriegsbegriffs', Arch. Völkerrechts, vol 6 (1956), pp 51-5

SALVIOLI, Gabriele, 'Considerazioni sulla guerra', Riv. Diritto Int., vol 37 (1954), pp 161-7

SALVIOLI, Giuseppe, Le Concept de la guerre juste chez les écrivains antérieurs à Grotius (trans. from the Italian), 2nd edition (Paris, 1918)

SCELLE, G, 'De l'influence de l'état de guerre sur le droit conventionnel', J. Droit Int., vol 77 (1950), pp 26-87

SCHÄTZEL, W, 'Aggressionskrieg und Haager Kriegsrecht', Nord. Tidsskr. Int. Ret., vol 24 (1954), pp 17-31

SCHÄTZEL, W, 'Die Theorie des Krieges bei Francisco de Victoria und der moderne Angriffskrieg', Nord. Tidsskr. Int. Ret., vol 25 (1955), pp 79-98

SCHINDLER, D, & TOMAN, J, (eds), The Law of Armed Conflicts: A Collection of Conventions, Resolutions and Other Documents (Leiden: Sijthoff, 1973). 795 pp.

SCHWARZENBERGER, G, 'From the laws of war to the law of armed conflict', Journal of Public Law, vol 17 (1968), pp 61-77

SHOTWELL, J T, War as an Instrument of National Policy (New York, 1928/London, 1929). 300 pp.

SMITH, The Law and Customs of the Sea, (1948) See 7.8.1

SPAIGHT, J M, Air Power and War Rights, 3rd edition (London: Longmans Green, 1947)

SOFRONIE, Georges, Le Problème des limitations du droit de belligérance (Bucharest, 1934)

STRACHEY, A, The Unconscious Motives of War (London: George Allen & Unwin, 1957)
STRISOWER, Leo, Der Krieg und die Völkerrechtsördnung (Wien, 1919). 146 pp.
SWANTON, J R, Are Wars Inevitable? (Washington, DC: Smithsonian Institution, 1943)
TAMBARO, G, 'Das Recht, Krieg zu fuhren', Niemeyers Z. Int. Recht, vol 24 (1914), pp 41-77
TAUBENFELD, Howard J, 'International armed forces and the rules of war', Am. J. Int. Law, vol 45 (1951), pp 671-9
TUCKER, Robert W, The Law of War and Neutrality at Sea (Washington, DC: US Naval War College, 1957) International Law Studies, vol 45. 448 pp.
TUCKER, Robert W, 'The interpretation of war under present international law', Int. Law Q., vol 4 (1951), pp 11-38
VANDERPOL, A, La Doctrine scolastique du droit de guerre (Paris, 1919). 534 pp.
VERZIJL, J H W, 'De aanwijzing van den aanvaller bij internationale conflicten', Weekblad voor het recht, nos 12644, 12645 (1933)
VOM KRIEG, & VOM FRIEDEN, Festschrift der Universität Zürich zum siebzigsten Geburstag von Max Huber (Zürich: Schulthess & Co, 1944). 323 pp.
WALTZ, K N, Man, The State and War: a Theoretical Analysis (New York: Columbia University Press, 1959)
WEHBERG, H, Krieg und Eroberung im Wandel des Völkerrechts (Frankfurt a M/Berlin, 1953). 136 pp.
WEHBERG, H, 'L'interdiction du recours à la force: Le principe et les problèmes qui se posent', Acad. Droit Int. Recl. Cours, vol 78 (1951)
WEHBERG, H, 'Das Kriegsproblem in der neueren Entwicklung des Völkerrechts', Die Friedens-Warte, vol 38 (1938), pp 129-49
Why War? Exchange of letters between Albert

Einstein and Sigmund Freud. (Paris: International Institute of Intellectual Co-operation, 1933)

WRIGHT, Quincy, A Study of War (Chicago, Ill: University of Chicago Press, 1942) Second edition, A Study of War: With a Commentary on War since 1942 (Chicago, Ill: University of Chicago Press, 1965)

WRIGHT, Quincy, The Role of International Law in the Elimination of War (Manchester: Manchester University Press, 1961)

WRIGHT, Quincy, 'The new law of war and neutrality', Ned. Tijd. Int. Ret., vol 6 Liber amicorum J P A François (July 1959), pp 412-24

WRIGHT, Quincy, 'Changes in the conception of war', Am. J. Int. Law, vol 18 (1924), pp 755-67

WRIGHT, Quincy, 'When does war exist?' Am. J. Int. Law, vol 26 (1932), pp 362-8

10.2 LEGITIMACY OF WAR

See also Section 10.3 on pacts against war

BALLADORE-PALLIERI, G, 'Il problema della guerra lecita nel diritto internazionale commune e nell'ordinamento giuridico della Società delle Nazioni' Riv. Diritto Int., vol 22 (1930), pp 342-62; 509-25 vol 23 (1931), pp 32-53; 149-70; 352 seq; 464 seq.

BLUM, Rolf, Das System der verbotenen und erlaubten Kriege in Völkerbundssatzung, Locarno-Vertrage und Kellogg-Pakt. Frankfurter Abhandlungen zum modernen Völkerrecht, Heft 31 (Leipzig, 1932). 44 pp

BRIERE, R P Y de la, Le Droit de juste guerre: tradition théologique: adaptations contemporaines (Paris, 1938). 207 pp.

CALOGEROPOULOS-STRATIS, S, Jus ad Bellum. Le droit de recourir à la guerre (Athens, 1950). 134 pp.

CALOGEROPOULOS-STRATIS, S, 'Le droit de recourir à la guerre d'après la doctrine et la pratique', Revue de droit international pour le Moyen Orient, vol 3 (1954), pp 266-303

ELBE, Joachim von, 'The evolution of the concept of just war in international law', Am. J. Int. Law, vol 33 (1939), pp 665-88

FEINBERG, Nathan, The Legality of a 'State of War' after the cessation of hostilities under the Charter of the United Nations and the Covenant of the League of Nations (Jerusalem, 1961). 86 pp.

GABUS, Eric, La Criminalité de la guerre (Genève, 1953)

GARCIA-ARIAS, Luis, La guerra preventiva y su licitud (Oviedo, 1956). 25 pp.

GARCIA-ARIAS, Luis, La guerra liberadora y su licitud (Saragossa, 1957). 134 pp.

KUNZ, J, 'Bellum iustum and bellum legale', Am. J. Int. Law, (1951), p 528

KYM, Chong Soo, 'The effects of the illegality of war', Korean Journal of International Law, vol 4 (1959), pp 87-104

LAUTERPACHT, H, 'Rules of warfare in an unlawful war', in Law and Politics in the World Community. Essays on Hans Kelsen's Pure Theory and Related Problems in International Law (Berkeley/Los Angeles, 1953), pp 89-113

MIRKINE-GUETZÉVICH, B, 'La renonciation à la guerre et le droit interne', L'esprit international, vol 4 (1930), pp 546-62

MORRISON, Charles Clayton, The Outlawry of War: A Constructive Policy for World Peace (Chicago, 1927/London, 1928). 300 pp.

NUSSBAUM, A, 'Just war - A legal concept?' Michigan Law Review, vol 42 (1943), pp 453-79

NYS, Ernest, Le Droit de la guerre et les précurseurs de Grotius (Bruxelles, 1882)

REGOUT, Robert, La Doctrine de la guerre juste de saint Augustin à nos jours d'après les théologiens et les canonistes catholiques (Paris: Pédone, 1935). 342 pp.

RUNDSTEIN, Szymon, 'Les paradoxes juridiques de la justification de la guerre', Rev. Droit Int. & Légis. Comp., ser 3, vol 19 (1938), pp 776-90

RUTGERS, V H, Strafbaarstelling van de aanvalsoorlog (Amsterdam, 1928)

SCELLE, G, 'Quelques refléxions sur l'abolition de la compétence de guerre', Rev. Gén. Droit Int. Public, vol 58 (1954), pp 5-22

SCELLE, G, 'Jus in bello jus ad bellum', Ned. Tijdschr. Int. Recht, vol 6, Liber Amicorum J P A François (July 1959), pp 292-304

SCHWARZENBERGER, G, 'Legal effects of illegal war', in Völkerrecht und Rechtliches Weltbild. Festschrift für Alfred Verdross (Wien: 1960), pp 243-52

STURZO, Luigi, The International Community and the Right of War, translated by Barbara Barclay Carter (London, 1929). 294 pp. French edition 1931; first Italian edition revised, Bologna 1954

TUCKER, R W, The Just War. A Study in Contemporary American Doctrine (Baltimore, Md: Johns Hopkins Press, 1960). 207 pp.

WEHBERG, Hans, Die Achtung des Krieges (Berlin, 1930). 195 pp.

WEHBERG, Hans, The Outlawry of War (New York, 1931). 149 pp.

WEHBERG, Hans, 'Le problème de la mise de la guerre hors la loi', Acad. Droit Int. Recl. Cours, vol 24 (1928), pp 146-306

WEHBERG, Hans, 'Gibt es nach Ratifikation des Kelloggpakts noch ein Kriegsrecht?' Friedens-Warte, vol 29 (1929), pp 115-16

WRIGHT, Q, 'The outlawry of war', Am. J. Int. Law, vol 19 (1925), pp 76-103

WRIGHT, Q, 'The outlawry of war and the law of war', Am. J. Int. Law, vol 47 (1953), pp 365-76

10.3 PACTS AGAINST WAR

ALVAREZ, A, 'Deux pactes régionaux pour supprimer la guerre: les Conventions de Londres et le projet du Ministre des Affaires Etrangères de l'Argentine', Bulletin interparlementaire, vol 13 (1933), pp 121-8
BILFINGER, C, 'Die Kriegserklärung der Westmächte und der Kelloggpakt', Z. Ausl. Öff. Recht. & Völkerrecht, vol 10 (1940), pp 1-23
BILFINGER, C, Das wahre Gesicht des Kelloggpaktes: angelsächsischer Imperialismus im Gewande des Rechts (Essen, 1942)
BORCHARD, Edwin, M, 'The Kellogg treaties sanction war', Z. Ausl. Öff. Recht & Völkerrecht, vol 1 (1929), pp 126-31
BORCHARD, Edwin, M, 'The multilateral treaty for the renunciation of war', Am. J. Int. Law, vol 23 (1929), pp 116-20
BOYE, T, 'Shall a state which goes to war in violation of the Kellogg-Briand pact have a belligerent's right in respect of neutrals?' Am. J. Int. Law, vol 24 (1930), pp 766-70
BRIERLY, James Leslie, 'Some implications of the Pact of Paris', Br. Yearb. Int. Law, vol 10 (1929), pp 208-10
BROWN, Philip Marshall, 'The interpretation of the general pact for the renunciation of war', Am. J. Int. Law, vol 23 (1929), pp 374-9
BROWN, Philip Marshall, 'Japanese interpretation of the Kellogg pact', Am. J. Int. Law, vol 27 (1933), pp 100-2
CALOGEROPOULOS-STRATIS, S, Le Pacte général de renonciation à la guerre: étude juridique (Paris, 1931). 246 pp.

COHN, Georg, 'Kellogg-Verträg und Völkerrecht', Z. Völkerrecht, vol 15 (1929), pp 169-82

COLOMBOS, C John, 'The Paris pact, otherwise called the Kellogg pact', Grotius Soc. Trans., vol 14 (1928), pp 87-101

ERICH, Rafael Waldemar, 'Les traités de non-agression entre membres et non-membres de la Société des Nations', Rev. Droit Int. & Légis Comp., vol 7 (1926), pp 613-21

GARNER, James Wilford, 'The Geneva protocol for the Pacific settlement of international disputes', Am. J. Int. Law, vol 19 (1925), pp 123-32

GEROULD, James Thayer, Selected Articles on the Pact of Paris (New York, 1929). 287 pp.

GONSIOROWSKI, Miroslas, 'The legal meaning of the pact for the renunciation of war', American Political Science Review, vol 30 (1936), pp 653-80

HARRIMAN, E A, 'The legal effect of the Kellogg-Briand treaty', Boston University Law Review, vol 9 (1929), pp 239-52

HASSMANN, Heinz, Der Kellogg-Pakt und seine Vorbehalte (Würzburg, 1930). 95 pp.

HUDSON, Manley Ottmer, 'The Geneva protocol', Foreign Affairs, vol 3 (1924), pp 226-35

HUDSON, M O, 'The Budapest resolutions of 1934 on the Briand-Kellogg pact of Paris', Am. J. Int. Law, vol 29 (1935), pp 92-4

HUDSON, M O, By Pacific Means. The Implementation of Article Two of the Pact of Paris (New Haven/London, 1935). 200 pp.

HYDE, C C, 'Secretary Hull on the Kellogg-Briand pact', Am. J. Int. Law, vol 35 (1941), pp 117-18

JOHNSON, David H N, 'The draft code of offences against the peace and security of mankind', Int. & Comp. Law Q., vol 4 (1955), pp 445-68

JESSUP, Philip Caryl, 'The Argentine anti-war pact', Am. J. Int. Law, vol 28 (1934), pp 538-41

KEEN, F N, 'The preamble to the pact of Paris',
Grotius Soc. Trans., vol 21 (1935), pp 177-90
KOROVIN, Evgenii A, 'Pakt Kelloga i prisoedinenie
k nemu SSSR', Sovetskoe pravo, no 6 (1928), pp
26-48
KUNZ, Josef Laurenz, 'Der Kellogg-Pakt', Mitteilungen
der Deutschen Gesellschaft für Völkerrecht, vol 9
(Berlin, 1929), pp 75-101
LA PRADELLE, Albert de, 'Le projet de traité sud-
américain pour prévenir la guerre', Rev. Droit Int.,
vol 10 (1932), pp 425-32
LAUTERPACHT, H, 'The pact of Paris and the Budapest
articles of interpretation', Grotius Soc. Trans.,
vol 20 (1935), pp 178-206
LYSEN, A, (Ed), Le Pacte Kellogg. Documents
concernants le traité multilatéral contre la guerre
signé à Paris le 27 Aout 1928 (Leiden, 1928). 95 pp.
MANDELSLOH, A, L'Interprétation du Pacte Briand-
Kellogg par les gouvernements et les parlements des
états signataires (Paris, 1934). 162 pp, and in Rev.
Gén. Droit Int. Public, vol 40 (1933), pp 537-605;
vol 41 (1934), pp 179-269
MANDELSLOH, A V, L'Interprétation du Pacte Briand-
par les organes de la Société des Nations', Rev.
Gén. Droit Int. Public, vol 42 (1935), pp 241-92
MAKOWSKI, Julien, 'Le Pacte Kellogg', Bull. de
l'Inst. Interméd., vol 21 (1929), pp 10-20
MILLER, David Hunter, The Geneva Protocol (London
1925), 279 pp.
MILLER, David Hunter, The Peace Pact of Paris (New
York/London, 1928). 294 pp.
MILLER, David Hunter, 'Le Pacte de Paris ou traité
Briand-Kellogg', Anneé politique française et
étrangère, vol 4 (1929), pp 1-33
SCHÜCKING, Walther, Das Genfer Protokoll
(Frankfurt a M, 1924). 22 pp.

MYERS, Denys P, Origin and Conclusion of the Paris
   Pact, 12 World Peace Foundation Pamphlets, no 2
   (Boston, 1920). 227 pp.
RAESTAD, Arnold, 'Guerre et moyens pacifiques:
   quelques observations au sujet de projet d'incorporer
   le contenu du Pacte Kellogg dans le Pacte de la
   Société des Nations', Rev. Droit Int. Sci. Dipl.
   & Polit., vol 7 (1931), pp 555-66. Also in Festskrift
   tillägnad Eriks Marks von Würtemberg. 11 May
   1931, (Stockholm), p 494
RAMBERT, Georges, Le Droit de la guerre et le Pacte
   Briand-Kellogg (Lausanne, 1931). 47 pp.
RUTENBERG, Gregory, 'The Baltic states and the
   Soviet Union', Am. J. Int. Law, vol 29 (1935), pp
   598-615
RUTGERS, V H, 'La mise en harmonie du Pacte de la
   Société des Nations avec le Pacte de Paris', Acad.
   Droit Int. Recl. Cours, vol 38 (1931), pp 1-123
SAAVEDRA LAMAS, Carlos, 'Le projet de traité sud-
   américain pour prévenir la guerre', Rev. Droit
   Int., vol 10 (1932), pp 433-60
SOTTILE, Antoine, Règlement pacifique des différends
   internationaux dans le protocole adopté par la Ve
   assemblée de la Société des Nations le 2 octobre
   1924 (Paris, 1924)
SOTTILE, Antoine, 'Le système de l'arbitrage, de la
   sécurité et de la réduction des armements dans le
   protocole adopté le 2 octobre 1924', Rev. Droit Int.
   Sci. Dipl. & Polit., vol 2 (1924), pp 227-53
SPIROPOULOS, J, 'Draft code of offences against the
   peace and security of mankind', Rev. Hell. Droit
   Int., vol 3 (1950), pp 141-98
STIMSON, Henry L, 'The pact of Paris: three years of
   development', Foreign Affairs, vol 11, supp. no
   1 (1932/3)
VANDY, Francois, 'Le pacte Kellogg', Rev. Gén. Droit
   Int. Public, vol 37 (1930), pp 5-18

VERDROSS, Alfred von, 'Die Ausnahmen von
  Kriegsverbote des Kellogg-Pakts', Die Friedens-
  Warte, vol 30 (1930), pp 65-6
WASMUND, Günther, Die Nichtangriffspakte. Zugleich
  ein Beitrag zu dem Problem des Angriffsbegriffes
  (Leipzig, 1935). 126 pp.
WEBER, Paul, Die Verteidigungspflicht der
  Gliedstaaten des Völkerbundes nach den Normen des
  Völkerbundsvertrages (Zürich, 1932). 224 pp.
WEHBERG, Hans, Das Genfer Protokoll betreffend die
  friedliche Erledigung internationaler Streitigkeiten
  (Berlin, 1927). 189 pp.
WEHBERG, Hans, 'Le protocole de Genève', Acad.
  Droit Int. Recl. Cours, vol 7 (1925), pp 1-150
WEHBERG, Hans, 'Quelques remarques sur le
  protocole de Genève', Rev. Droit Int. & Légis. Comp.,
  ser 3, vol 5 (1924), pp 548-63
WEHBERG, Hans, 'Die Hauptlücke des Kelloggpakts',
  Die Friedens-Warte, vol 29 (1929), pp 225-31
WHEELER-BENNETT, J W, Information on the
  Renunciation of War (1927-8) (London, 1928). 191 pp.
WILLIAMS, Sir John Fischer, 'The Geneva protocol of
  1924', Journal of the British Institute of International
  Affairs, vol 3 (1924), pp 282-304
WILLIAMS, Sir John Fischer, 'The Covenant of the
  League of Nations and war', Cambridge Law
  Journal, vol 5 (1933), pp 1-21
WILLIAMS, Sir John Fischer, 'Recent interpretations of
  the Briand-Kellogg pact', International Affairs (UK),
  vol 14 (1935), pp 346-68
WRIGHT, Q, 'The meaning of the pact of Paris', Am.
  J. Int. Law, vol 27 (1933), pp 39-61

10.4   OCCUPATION

CAVARE, Louis, 'Quelques notions générales sur
  l'occupation pacifique. Etude particulière de

l'occupation de Haute-Silesie', Rev. Gén. Droit Int. Public, vol 31 (1924), pp 339-71

CYBICHOWSKI, Z, 'Das völkerrechtliche Okkupationsrecht', Z. Völkerrecht, (1934), p 29

DEBBASH, Odile, L'occupation militaire (Paris: Pichon, 1962)

FEILCHENFELD, E, The International Economic Law of Belligerent Occupation (Washington, DC, 1942; reissued 1971 by Johnson Reprint Corp., New York)

GLAHN, G v, The Occupation of Enemy Territory, A Commentary on the Law and Practice of Belligerent Occupation (Minneapolis, Min: University of Minnesota Press, 1957). 350 pp.

FINCH, George Augustus, 'The legality of the occupation of the Ruhr Valley', Am. J. Int. Law, vol 17 (1923), pp 724-33

GRABER, D A, The Development of the Law of Belligerent Occupation 1863-1914 - A Historical Survey (New York: Columbia University Press, 1949)

JENNINGS, R Y, 'Government in commission', Br. Yearb. Int. Law, vol 23 (1946), pp 112-41

KAFKA, G E, ·'Österreich, die Besatzung und die Grundlagen der Völkerrechtsgemeinschaft', Österr. Z. Öff. Recht, vol 6 (1954), pp 348-77

KELSEN, H, 'The legal status of Germany according to the declaration of Berlin', Am. J. Int. Law, vol 39 (1945), pp 518-26

KLINGHOFFER, H, Les Aspects juridiques de l'occupation de l'Autriche par l'Allemagne (Rio de Janeiro, 1943)

McNAIR, Arnold Duncan, 'The legality of the occupation of the Ruhr', Br. Yearb. Int. Law, vol 5 (1924), pp 17-37

ROBIN, Raymond, Des occupations militaires en dehors des occupations de guerre (etude d'histoire diplomatique et de droit international)(Paris, 1913). 824 pp.

ROSS, Alf, 'Denmark's legal status during the occupation', Jus Gentium (Denmark), vol 1 (1949), pp 3-21

SCHWARZENBERGER, G, 'The law of belligerent occupation', Nord. Tidsskr Int. Ret (1960), pp 10-24

SCHUSTER, Ernest, J, 'The question as to the legality of the Ruhr occupation', Am. J. Int. Law, vol 18 (1924), pp 407-18

SAUSER-HALL, G, 'L'occupation de guerre et les droits privés', Annu. Suisse Droit Int. (1944), p 58

SAUSER-HALL, G, 'L'occupation de l'Allemagne par les Puissances Alliées', Annu. Suisse Droit Int. (1946), p 9

UHLER, O M, Der völkerrechtliche Schutz der Bevölkerung eines besetzten Gebiets gegen Massnahmen der Okkupationsmacht (Zürich: Polygraphischer Verlag, 1950)

WEHBERG, H, 'Hat Japan durch die Besetzung der Mandschurei das Völkerrecht verletzt', Die Friedens-Warte, vol 32 (1932), pp 1-13

10.5 CONQUEST BY ANNEXATION

Cf. Section 7.6.5 on acquisition of territory.

BINDSCHEDLER, Rudolf L, 'Annexion', in Wörterbuch des Völkerrechts, edited by K Strupp & H J S Schlochauer, vol 1 (Berlin: de Gruyter, 1960), pp 68-71

HYDE, C C, 'Conquest today', Am. J. Int. Law, vol 30 (1936), pp 471-6

McMAHON, Matthew M, Conquest and Modern International Law: The Legal Limitations on the Acquisition of Territory by Conquest (Washington, 1940). 233 pp.

MARTINI, R de, The Right of Nations to Expand by Conquest (Washington, 1955)

SCHÄTZEL, Walter, 'Die Annexion im Völkerrecht',
   Arch. Völkerrechts, vol 2 (1950), pp 1-28
WESTLAKE, John, 'The nature and extent of the title
   by conquest', Law Quarterly Review, vol 17 (1901),
   pp 392-401
WRIGHT, Herbert Francis, 'The legality of the
   annexation of Austria by Germany', Am. J. Int. Law,
   vol 38 (1944), pp 621-35

10.6 HUMANITARIAN LAW IN WAR

See also Section 10.11 on humanitarian law in
civil war.
DRAPER, G I A D, 'The Geneva conventions of 1949',
   Acad. Droit Int. Recl. Cours, vol 114 (1965), pp
   59-165
GUTTERIDGE, J A C, 'Geneva conventions of 1949',
   Br. Yearb. Int. Law, vol 26 (1949), pp 294-326
PICTET, J, 'The XXth international conference of the
   Red Cross: results in the legal field', Journal of
   the International Commission of Jurists, vol 7 (1966),
   pp 3-19
PICTET, J, Le droit humanitaire et la protection des
   victimes de la guerre (Leiden: Sijthoff, 1973). 152 pp.
LA PRADELLE, P de, 'Réflexions sur la XXIe
   conférence internationale de la Croix-Rouge (Istanbul
   6-13 septembre 1969)', Rev. Gén. Droit Int. Public,
   vol 74 (1970), pp 261-88
SCHLÖGEL, A, 'Völkerrechtliche Probleme auf der
   XX. Internationalen Rotkreuzkonferenz 1965 in Wien',
   Jahrb. Int. Recht, vol 13 (1967), pp 245-62
TOMAN, J, Index to the Geneva Conventions for the
   Protection of War Victims of 12 August 1949
   (Leiden: Sijthoff, 1973). 194 pp.
VERRI, P, 'Considérations sur l'application dans les
   conflits modernes des articles 3 et 4 des Conventions

de Genève de 1949', Revue de droit pénal militaire
et de droit de la guerre, vol 11 (1972), pp 93-103
WILHELM, A, 'Le caractère des droits accordés à
l'individu dans les conventions de Genève',
Revue internationale de la Croix Rouge (1950),
p 561

10.7 PERMISSIBILITY OF
CERTAIN WEAPONS

BAILEY, Sydney D, Prohibitions and Restraints in War
(London: Oxford University Press, 1972). xiii + 194
pp.
A Swedish Working Group: Torgil Wulff, Bo Janzon,
Lars Olof Olofson, Torsten Petré, and Bo Lydbeck,
Conventional Weapons, Their Deployment and
Effect from a Humanitarian Aspect: Recommendations
for the Modernization of International Law,
(Stockholm, 1973)

10.8 BIOLOGICAL WARFARE

BOTHE, M, Das völkerrechtliche Verbot des
Einsatzes chemischer und bakteriologischer Waffen
(Köln: Carl Heymanns Verlag, 1973). xiv + 397 pp.
THOMAS, A V W, & THOMAS, A J, Jr, Legal Limits
on the Use of Chemical and Biological Weapons.
International Law 1899-1970 (Dallas, Tex: Southern
Methodist University Press, 1970). x + 332 pp.

10.9 NUCLEAR WEAPONS

See also Section 11 on responsibility.
ALEKSEYEV, A, 'Non-proliferation talks', Int. Aff.
(USSR), vol 5 (1968), p 21

BLACKETT, Patrick Maynard Stuart, Atomic Weapons and East-West Relations (London: Cambridge University Press, 1956). 107 pp.

DELCOIGNE, G, & RUBINSTEIN, G, Non-prolifération des armes nucléaires et systèmes de contrôle (Bruxelles: Editions de l'Institut de Sociologie, 1970). 214 pp.

FISCHER, Georges, The Non-Proliferation of Nuclear Weapons translated from French by D Willey (London: Europa, 1971). 270 pp.

McDOUGAL, M S, & SCHLEI, M S, 'The hydrogen bomb tests in perspective: lawful measures for security', Yale Law Journal, vol 64 (1955), pp 648-710

McVITTY, Marion H, 'Disarmament negotiations - 1956-1962', in Legal and Political Problems of World Order, compiled and edited by Saul H Mendlovitz (New York, 1962), pp 659-60

MARGOLIS, E, 'The hydrogen bomb experiments and international law', Yale Law Journal, vol 64 (1955), p 621

SINGH, M Nagendra, Nuclear Weapons and International Law (London, 1959). 267 pp.

SINGH, M Nagendra, 'The right of self-defence in relation to the use of nuclear weapons', Indian Yearb. Int. Aff. (1956), pp 3-37

see also:

STEIN, E, 'Impact of new weapons technology on international law: selected aspects', Acad. Droit Int. Recl. Cours, vol 133 (1972), pp 233-388

SCHWARZENBERGER, G, The Legality of Nuclear Weapons (London, 1958). 61 pp.

WILLRICH, Mason, Non-Proliferation Treaty: Framework for Nuclear Arms Control (Charlottesville, Va: The Michie Company, 1969)

10.10 CIVIL WAR AND UNCONVENTIONAL WARFARE BY GUERILLAS

See also numerous works listed in Section 10.13

CASTRÉN, E, Civil War (Helsinki, 1966)

FALK, R, (ed), The International Law of Civil War (Baltimore, Md: Johns Hopkins Press, 1971). 425 pp.

FERAUD-GIRAUD, L J D, 'De la reconnaissance de la qualité de belligérants dans les guerres civiles', Rev. Gén. Droit Int. Public, vol 13 (1896), pp 277-91

JANOS, A C, 'Unconventional warfare', Framework and analysis', World Politics, vol 15 (1962/3), pp 636-46

KALSHOVEN, F, 'The position of guerrilla fighters under the law of war', Revue de droit pénal militaire et de droit de la guerre, vol 11 (1972), pp 55-91

KANE, W E, Civil Strife in Latin America. A Legal History of US Involvement (Baltimore, Md: The Johns Hopkins Press, 1972). ix + 240 pp.

KHAN, R, 'Guerrilla warfare and international law', International Studies, vol 9 (1967), pp 103-27

KING, C R, 'Revolutionary war, guerrilla warfare, and international law', Case Western Reserve Journal of International Law, vol 4 (1972), pp 91-123

KLEUT, P, 'Guerre de partisans et droit international', Jugoslovenska revija za medunarodno pravo, (1956), no 1, pp 94-104

LUARD, Evan, The International Regulation of Civil Wars (London, 1972)

OGLESBY, R R, Internal War and the Search for Normative Order (Den Haag: Nijhoff, 1971)

McCUEN, J J, The Art of Counter-revolutionary War. The Strategy of Counter-insurgency (London: Faber & Faber, 1966)

MEYROWITZ, H, 'Guérilla et le droit de la guerre. Problèmes principaux', Rev. Belg. Droit Int., vol 7 (1971), pp 56-72

MODELSKI, G, The International Relations of Internal War. Research Monograph no 11 (Princeton, NJ: Center of International Studies, 1961)

NURICK, L, & BARRETT, R W, 'Legality of guerrilla forces under the laws of war', Am. J. Int. Law, vol 40 (1946), 563-83

PARET, P, & SHY, J W, Guerrillas in the 1960s (New York, 1962)

PINTO, R, 'Les règles du droit international concernant la guerre civile', Acad. Droit Int. Recl. Cours, vol 114 (1965), pp 451-553

ROUGIER, Antoine, Les Guerres civiles et le droit des gens (Paris, 1903). 569 pp.

SINGH, B, & KO-WANG MEI, Theory and Practice of Modern Guerrilla Warfare (London: Asia Publishing House, 1971)

SIOTIS, J, Le Droit de la guerre et les conflits armés d'un caractère non-international (Paris, 1958)

TAULBEE, J L, 'Retaliation and irregular warfare in contemporary international law', The International Lawyer, vol 7 (1973), pp 195-204

TRAININ, I P, 'Questions of guerrilla warfare in the law of war', Am. J. Int. Law, vol 40 (1946), pp 534-62

WEHBERG, H, 'La guerre civile et le droit international' Acad. Droit Int. Recl. Cours, vol 63 (1938), pp 7-123

10.11 HUMANITARIAN LAW IN CIVIL WAR

See also Section 10.6 on humanitarian law in war

AMELIN, A B, (International law protection for participants in civil and national-liberation wars), Sov. Ezheg. Mezhdunar. Prava (1958), pp 397-407. In Russian with English summary

BOISSIER, L, 'Les troubles intérieurs et l'action du Comité international de la Croix-Rouge', Bulletin interparlementaire, vol 39 (1959), pp 164-71

BRANDWEINER, H, 'Das Partisanenproblem und die Genfer Konventionen vom 12.August 1949', Juristische Blätter, vol 71 (1950), pp 261-4

BRAUN, U, Die Anwendung der Genfer Zivilkonvention in Kriegen nicht-internationalen Charakters (Winterthur, 1962)

DRAGIC, D, & JAKOVLJEVIC, B, (Le droit international de la guerre et la protection des blessés et malades dans la guerre de libération nationale), Jugoslovenska revija zu medunarodno pravo, vol 8 (1961), pp 238-45. In Serbo-Croatian with French summary

FARER, T, 'Humanitarian law and armed conflicts: toward the definition of "international armed conflict",' Columbia Law Review, vol 71 (1971), pp 37-72

FARER, T J, 'The humanitarian laws of war in civil strife: towards a definition of "international armed conflict" ', Rev. Belg. Droit Int., vol 7 (1971), pp 20-55

FORD, W J, 'Resistance movements and international law', International Review of the Red Cross, vol 7 (1967), pp 515-31; vol 8 (1968), pp 7-15

GIRAUD, E, 'Le respect des droits de l'homme dans la guerre internationale et dans la guerre civile', Revue de droit public et de la science politique (1958), pp 613-75

HOOKER, W S, Jr, & SAVASTEN, D H, 'The Geneva convention of 1949: application in the Vietnamese conflict', Virginia Journal of International Law, vol 5 (1965), pp 243-65

JAKOVLEVIC, B, & PATRNOGIC, J, 'The urgent need to apply the rules of humanitarian law to so-called internal armed conflicts', International Review of the Red Cross (1961), pp 250-7

MERTENS, P, 'Modalités de l'intervention du Comité international de la Croix-Rouge dans le conflit du Nigéria', Annu. Fr. Droit Int. (1969), pp 183-209

PINTO, R, 'Hanoï et la convention de Genève', Le Monde 27, 28-29 December 1969, (26, nos 7762, 7763), pp 2; 5

SEIDL-HOHENVELDERN, I, & PATRNOGIC, J, 'La protection des populations civiles dans les conflits armés de caractère non-international', Annales de droit international médical, no 17 (June 1968), pp 12-24

SIORDET, F, 'Commentaire de l'article 3 de la IIIe convention de Genève', Revue internationale de la Croix-Rouge, vol 40 (1958), pp 635-53

SIORDET, F, 'Les Conventions de Genève et la guerre civile', Revue internationale de la Croix-Rouge, vol 32 (1950), pp 104-22; 187-212

VEUTHEY, M, 'Règles et principes de droit international humanitaire applicables dans la guérilla', Rev Belg. Droit Int., vol 7 (1971), pp 505-39

ZORGBIBE, C, 'Pour une réaffirmation du droit humanitaire des conflits armés internes', J. Droit Int., vol 97 (1970), pp 658-83

10.12 NEUTRALITY

In this Section I have listed a few works on neutrality and its various complex aspects. See also Section 9.2 on international security and compare Section 10.1 on war.

BINDSCHEDLER, H, 'Die Neutralität im modernen Völkerrecht', Z. Ausl. Öff. Recht & Völkerrecht, vol 17 (1956/7), p 1

BOYE, T, 'Quelques aspects du développement des règles de la neutralité', Acad. Int. Recl. Cours vol 2 (1938), p 157

GALINA, A, (Neutrality in contemporary international law), Sov. Ezheg. Mezhdunar. Prava (1958), p 225. In Russian with English summary

GUGGENHEIM, P, 'La securité collective et le problème de la neutralité', Annu. Suisse Droit Int. (1945), p 9

GUGGENHEIM, P, 'Der Neutralitätsbegriff im allgemeinen Völkerrecht und in der internationalen Organisationen', in Festschrift für Verdross, (1971), p 119

GRIEVE, 'The present position of neutral states', Grotius Soc. Trans., vol 33 (1948), p 99

HAMMASKJÖLD, Å, 'La neutralité en général', Bibliotheca Visseriana, vol 3 (1924)

JESSUP, P, Neutrality: Its History, Economics and Law (New York, 1935-6; reissued 1972 by Shoe String Press, Hamden, Conn). 4 vols

KOMARNICKI, T, 'The place of neutrality in the modern system of international law', Acad. Droit Int. Recl. Cours, vol 1, (1952), p 395

LALIVE, Jean-Flavien, 'International organization and Neutrality', Br. Yearb. Int. Law, vol 24 (1947), pp 72-89

LA RUCHE, Francis, La Neutralité de la Suède, (Paris 1953)

MIELE, M, 'Neutralità', Novissima digesta italiana, vol 11, p 234

MIELE, Alberto, L'Estraneità ai Conflitti Armati secondo il Diritto Internazionale. Vol 1, Origini ed Evoluzione del Diritto di Neutralità; vol 2, La Disciplina Positiva delle Attività Statuali (Padova: Cedam, 1970). xii + 241 pp. (vol 1); xi + 585 pp. (vol 2)

NICHOLS, A, Neutralität und amerikanische Waffenausfuhr, insbesondere in Bezug auf den Pakt von Paris (Berlin, 1932). 145 pp.

NOVA, R de, 'La neutralità nel sistema della Società della Nazioni del Patto Kellogg', Annali di scienze politiche, vol 6 (1934), pp 237-54; vol 7 (1935), pp 109-45

ÖRVIK, T, The Decline of Neutrality 1914-1941 (Oslo, 1953)

POLITIS, N, 'La Neutralité et la paix (Paris, 1935). 229 pp. Translated into English as Neutrality and Peace (Washington, 1935). 99 pp.

SCHINDLER, 'Aspects contemporaines de la neutralité', Acad. Droit Int. Recl. Cours, vol 2, (1967), p 225

STEINER, G, 'Die Internierung von Armeeangehörigen Kriegführender Mächte in neutralen Staaten', (Bern, 1947)

TAUBENFELD, H J, 'International actions and neutrality', Am. J. Int. Law (1953), p 377

UNDÉN, O, Alliansfrihet i terrorbalansens varld, NTIL, (1957), p 205

UNDÉN, O, Neutralitet och folkrätt (Stockholm 1939)

VERDROSS, A, 'Neutrality within the framework of the United Nations organization', in Symbolae Verzijl (Den Haag: Nijhoff, 1958), pp 410-18

WALDKIRCH, G, 'Militärische Rechte und Plichten des neutralen Staates im Luftkrieg', Jahrb. Int. Recht (1954), p 151

WRIGHT, Q, 'Present status of neutrality', Am. J. Int. Law (1940), p 391

WYSS, Georg, Die Rechtsstellung des entwichenen Kriegsgefangenen im neutralen Staat (Bern: Haupt, 1945). 104 pp.

10.13 PARTICULAR DISPUTES

See also Sections 7.5.4 on formation of particular states, 10.6 on humanitarian law in war and 10.10 on civil war.

CLEEF-GREENBERG, E V, 'Law and the conduct of the Algerian revolution', Harvard International Law Journal, vol 11 (1970), pp 37-72

GARNER, J W, 'Questions of international law in the Spanish civil war', Am. J. Int. Law, vol 31 (1937), pp 66-73

HULL, R H & NOVOGROD, J C, Law and Vietnam (Dobbs Ferry, NY: Oceana, 1968)

JESSUP, P, 'The Spanish rebellion and international law', Foreign Affairs, vol 15 (1937), pp 260-79

KHAN, 'The United Nations and Kashmir', Thesis. Utrecht 1955

KORBEL, J, 'The Kashmir dispute and the UN', Int. Organ. (May 1949), pp 278-87

LA PRADELLE, P de, 'Les événements de'Espagne', Rev. Droit Int., vol 18 (1936), pp 153-71

LAUTERPACHT, H, ' "Resort to war" and the interpretation of the Covenant during the Manchurian dispute', Am. J. Int. Law, vol 28 (1934), pp 43-60

LE FUR, Louis-Erasme, Etude sur la guerre hispano-américaine de 1898 envisagée au point de vue de droit international public (Paris, 1899). 316 pp.

LIANG, Yuen-Li, 'Rechtsprobleme des Mandschureikonflikts', Z. Völkerrecht, vol 17 (1933), pp 1-12

MANDELSLOH, A v, 'Der chinesisch-japanische Konflikt vor dem Völkerbund und der Brusseler Konferenz', Z. Ausl. Öff. Recht & Völkerrecht, vol 8 (1938), pp 84-99

MANDELSTAM, André N, La Société des Nations et les puissances devant le problème arménien (Paris 1926). 355 pp.

MANDELSTAM, A N, Le Conflit italo-éthiopien devant la Société des Nations (Paris, 1937). 577 pp.

MAKAROV, A N, 'Der sowjetrussischfinnische Konflikt', Z. Ausl. Öff. Recht & Völkerrecht, vol 10 (1940/1), pp 294-331

McNAIR, A, 'The law relating to the civil war in Spain', Law Quarterly Review, vol 53 (1937), pp 471-99

MEYROWITZ, H, 'Le droit de la guerre dans le conflit vietnamien', Annu. Fr. Droit Int. (1967), pp 153-201

MOORE, John Norton, Law and the Indo-China War (Princeton, NJ: Princeton University Press, 1972). 794 pp.

PADELFORD, Norman Judson, 'The international non-intervention agreement and the Spanish civil war', Am. J. Int. Law, vol 31 (1937), pp 578-603

PADELFORD, Norman Judson, 'International law and the Spanish civil war', Am. J. Int. Law, vol 31 (1937), pp 226-43

PADELFORD, Norman Judson, International Law and Diplomacy in the Spanish Civil Strife (New York, 1939). 710 pp.

POTTER, P B, 'The principal legal and political problems involved in the Kashmir case', Am. J. Int. Law (1950), pp 361-3

NOSTITZ-WALLWITZ, Oswalt von, 'Die diplomatische Vorgeschichte des Abessinienkonfliktes', Z. Ausl. Öff. Recht & Völkerrecht, vol 5 (1935), pp 760-802

NOSTITZ-WALLWITZ, Oswalt von, 'Die Entwicklung des Abessinienkonfliktes bis zum Beginn der Sanktionen', Z. Ausl. Öff. Recht & Völkerrecht, vol 6 (1936), pp 496-537

RABBATH, Edmond, 'L'intervention militaire des USA au Liban (juillet-octobre, 1958)', Revue de droit international pour le Moyen Orient, vol 8 (1959-60), pp 1-20

RAO, H S Gururaj, Legal Aspects of the Kashmir Problem (Bombay: Asia Publishing House, 1967). 379 pp.

ROLIN, Henri, 'Der italienisch-abessinische Konflikt', Die Friedens-Warte, vol 36 (1936), pp 236-45

ROUSSEAU, Charles, Le Conflit italo-éthiopien devant le droit international (Paris, 1938). 275 pp. Composed of Articles from Rev. Gén. Droit Int. Public, vol 43 (1936), pp 546-88; vol 44 (1937), pp 4-42; 169-98; 291-329; 681-728; vol 45 (1938), pp 53-123

SARAILIEFF, Georges V, 'Le Conflit gréco-bulgare d'octobre 1925 et son règlement par la Société des Nations.' Thesis. Grenoble. (Amsterdam, 1928). 165 pp.

ALBRECHT, D, Der chinesisch-japanische Konflikt und das Völkerrecht (Leipzig, 1933). 164 pp.

BASDEVANT, Jules, 'L'action coercitive anglo-germano-italienne contre le Venezuéla (1902-1903)', Rev. Gén. Droit Int. Public, vol 11 (1904), pp 362-458

BENTON, Elbert Jay, International Law and Diplomacy of the Spanish-American War (Baltimore, 1908). 300 pp.

BOHAN, Richard T, 'The Dominican case: unilateral intervention', Am. J. Int. Law, vol 60 (1966), p 809

FALK, Richard A, (ed), The Vietnam War and International Law (Princeton, NJ: Princeton University Press, 1967-72). 3 vols

GARNER, J W, International Law and the World War 2 vols (1920). 524,504 pp.

GARNER, J W, 'Settlement of the Graeco-Bulgarian dispute', Am. J. Int. Law, vol 20 (1926), pp 337-9

GOTTSCHALK, Egon, 'Die völkerrechtliche Hauptprobleme des Mandschureikonfliktes', Z. Völkerrecht, vol 17 (1933), pp 188-259; 289-341

GREEN, Leslie Claude, 'The nature of the "war" in Korea', Int. Law Q., vol 4 (1951), pp 462-8

HUDSON, M O, The Verdict of the League. China and Japan in Manchuria. The Official Documents with Notes and an Introduction (Boston, 1933). 102 pp.

HUDSON, M O, The Verdict of the League. Colombia and Peru at Leticia. The Official Documents with Notes and an Introduction (Boston, 1933). 88 pp.

MOORE, John Norton, Law and the Indo-China War (Princeton, NJ: Princeton University Press/London: Oxford University Press, 1973). xxxiii + 794 pp.

SCELLE, G, 'La guerre civile espagnole et le droit des gens', Rev. Gén. Droit Int. Public, vol 45 (1938), pp 265-301; 649-57; vol 46 (1939), pp 197-228

SERENI, Angelo Piero, 'La fine del conflitto italo-etiopico e il diritto internazionale', Riv. Diritto Int., vol 28 (1936), pp 404-33

SHINOBU, Jumpei, International Law in the Shanghai Conflict (Tokyo, 1933). 267 pp.

SPIROPOULOS, Jean, 'Sur l'éxistence de l'état de guerre entre la Grèce et l'Albanie', Rev. Hell. Droit Int., vol 7 (1948), pp 370-5

VISSCHER, Ch de, 'L'interprétation du Pacte au lendemain du différend italo-grec', Rev. Int. & Légis. Comp., vol 5 (1924), pp 213-30; 377-96

VISSCHER, Ch de, 'Le conflit anglo-égyptien et la Société des Nations', Rev. Droit Int. & Légis Comp., vol 5 (1924), pp 564-89

WEBER, H, Der Vietnam-Konflikt - Bellum Legale? (Hamburg: Alfred Metzner Verlag, 1970). 336 pp.

WILLOUGHBY, Westel Woodbridge, The Sino-Japanese Controversy and the League of Nations (Baltimore, 1935). 733 pp.

WOOLSEY, Lester Hood, 'The Chaco Dispute', Am. J. Int. Law, vol 28 (1934), pp 724-9

WOOLSEY, Lester Hood, 'The Japanese in Kulangsu', Am. J. Int. Law, vol 33 (1939), pp 526-30

WRIGHT, Q, 'The test of aggression in the Italo-Ethiopian war', Am. J. Int. Law, vol 30 (1936), pp 45-56

WRIGHT, Q, 'Opinion of Commission of Jurists on Janina-Corfu affair', Am. J. Int. Law, vol 18 (1924), pp 536-44

WRIGHT, Q, 'United States intervention in the Lebanon', Am. J. Int. Law, vol 53 (1959), pp 112-25

WRIGHT, Q, 'The Goa incident', Am. J. Int. Law, vol 56 (1962), pp 617-32

YEPES, Jesús María, Le Conflit entre la Colombie et le Pérou (affaire de Léticia) devant le droit international (Paris, 1933). 112 pp.

YEPES, Jesús María, 'L'affair de Léticia entre la Colombie et le Pérou. Etude historique et juridique', Rev. Droit Int., vol 11 (1933), pp 133-71

11 *Responsibility*

11.1 GENERAL

See also Section 6.1 on personality.
Responsibility is related to the problem of personality in so far as only a 'subject' of international law can be held responsible for breaches of international law. Thus, the individual must enjoy at least sone degree of personality as we know that, at least after the Second World War, state practice shows that individuals may be held internationally responsible for at least certain crimes. On responsibility in general, see the works listed below and, also, the chapters on responsibility in the Hague courses by Jules BASDEVANT, QUADRI, REUTER and SØRENSEN, listed under general works in Section 1.8

ACCIOLY, H, 'Principes généraux de la responsibilité internationale d'après la doctrine et la jurisprudence', Acad. Droit Int. Recl. Cours, vol 96 (1959), pp 353-70

ANZILOTTI, D, Teoria generale della responsibilità dello stato nel diritto internazionale (Firenze, 1902)

CARLEBACH, A, Le Problème de la faute et sa place dans la norme du droit international (Paris: Pichon et Durand-Auzias, 1962)

COHN, G, 'La théorie de la responsibilité internationale' Acad. Droit Int. Recl. Cours, vol 68 (1949), pp 207-325

EAGLETON, Clyde, The Responsibility of States in
    International Law (New York: The New York
    University Press, 1928). xxiv + 291 pp.
EAGLETON, Clyde, 'International organization and the
    law of responsibility', Acad. Droit Int. Recl. Cours,
    vol 76 (1950), pp 319-425
EUSTATHIADES, C Th, 'Les sujets de droit inter-
    national et la responsabilité internationale. Nouvelles
    tendances', Acad. Droit Int. Recl. Cours, vol 84
    (1953), pp 397-633
GARCIA-AMADOR, 'State responsibility in the light
    of the new trends of international law', Am. J. Int.
    Law, vol 49 (1955), p 339
GARCIA-AMADOR, F V, 'La responsabilité interna-
    tionale de l'état. La responsabilité des organisations
    internationales', Rev. Droit Int. Sci. Dipl. & Polit.,
    vol 34 (1956), pp 146-52
GARCIA-AMADOR, F V, 'State responsibility, some
    new problems', Acad. Droit Int. Recl. Cours, vol 94
    (1958), pp 369-491
JIMÉNEZ DE ARÉCHAGA, Eduardo, 'International
    responsibility', in Manual of Public International
    Law, edited by Max Sørensen (London: Macmillan/
    New York: St Martin's Press, 1968), pp 531-603
KELSEN, Hans, 'Unrecht und Unrechtsfolge im
    Völkerrecht', Z. Off. Recht, vol 12 (1932), pp 481-
    608
LEVINE, D B, La Responsabilité des états dans le
    droit internationale contemporain (Paris, 1967)
LILLICH, R B, 'Toward the formulation of an
    acceptable body of law concerning state responsibility',
    Syracuse Law Review, vol 16 (1965), p 721
MAGARASEVIC, A, 'International responsibility of
    states in the United Nations International Law
    Commission: a comment', Jugoslovenska Revija za
    Medunarodno Pravo, (1958), no 1, pp 42-50. In
    English and French

MURPHY, C F, Jr, State responsibility for injuries to aliens', New York University Law Review, vol 41 (1966), p 125

PREUSS, Lawrence, 'International responsibility for hostile propaganda against foreign states', Am. J. Int. Law, vol 28 (1934), pp 649-68

SALVIOLI, G, 'La responsabilité des états et la fixation des dommages et interêts par les tribunaux internationaux', Acad. Droit Int. Recl. Cours, vol 28 (1929), pp 235-86

THORNEYCROFT, E, Personal Responsibility and the Law of Nations (Den Haag: Nijhoff, 1961). 87 pp.

VISSCHER, Ch de, 'La responsibilité des états', Bibliotheca Visseriana, vol 2, pp 87-119

11.2 ABUSE OF RIGHTS

FAWCETT, J E S, 'Détournement de pouvoir by international organisations', Br. Yearb. Int. Law, vol 33 (1957), pp 311-16

KISS, A C, L'Abus de droit en droit international (Paris: Librairie générale de droit et de jurisprudence, Pichon-Auzias, 1953)

POLITIS, N, 'Le problème des limitations de la souveraineté et la théorie de l'abus des droits dans les rapports internationaux', Acad. Droit Int. Recl. Cours, vol 6 (1925), pp 1-121

SCHLOCHAUER, H J, 'Die Theorie des abus de droit im Völkerrecht', Z. Völkerrecht (1933), p 373

SERENI, A P, L'abuso di diritto nei rapporti internazionali (Milano, 1930)

TRIFU, S, La notion de l'abus du droit dans le droit international (Paris, 1940)

see also

Chapter 7 of GUGGENHEIM'S Hague course on La validité et la nullité des actes, listed under general works in Section 1.8 and VALENTINE's Jurisdiction

of the Court of the Communities to annul executive
action, listed in Section 13. 24. 13. 12. 6. 5.

11.3 RESPONSIBILITY FOR NUCLEAR ACTIVITY

See Section 10. 9 on nuclear weapons.
ARANGIO-RIUZ, G, 'Some international legal
  problems of the civil uses of nuclear energy', Acad.
  Droit Int. Recl. Cours, vol 107 (1962), p 503
FURET, M F, 'La non-prolifération des armés
  nucléaires', Rev. Gén. Droit Int. Public, vol 4
  (1967), pp 1015-16
FURET, Marie-Françoise, Expérimentation des armés
  nucléaires et droit international public (Paris:
  Pédone, 1955)
GIGOJ, S, 'International regulation of civil liability
  for nuclear risk', Int. & Comp. Law Q., vol 14
  (1965), pp 809-44
HARDY, M J L, 'International protection against
  nuclear risks', Int. & Comp. Law Q., vol 10 (1961),
  pp 739-59
HARDY, M J L, 'Nuclear liability: the general
  principles of law and further proposals', Br. Yearb.
  Int. Law, vol 36 (1960), pp 223-49
PELZER, Norbert, Rechtsprobleme der Beseitigung
  Radioaktiver Abfälle in das Meer (Göttingen: Institut
  für Völkerrecht, 1970). xl + 216 pp.
McDOUGAL, M S, & SCHLEI, N A, 'The hydrogen
  bomb tests in perspective: lawful measures for
  security', Yale Law Journal, vol 64 (1954/5), p 648
D'AMATO, A, 'Legal aspects of the French nuclear
  tests, Am. J. Int. Law, vol 61 (1967), p 66

11.4 RESPONSIBILITY FOR POLLUTION

DANZIG, A L, Marine Pollution - A Framework for
  International Control. Oceans Studies Programme

(Washington: Woodrow Wilson International Center for Scholars, 1972). 65 pp.
RABIN, Edward H, & SCHWARTZ, Mortimer D, (eds), The Pollution Crisis. Official Documents (Dobbs Ferry, NY: Oceana, 1971). 510 pp.

11.5 RESPONSIBILITY FOR OTHER SPECIFIC ACTS

AKEHURST, M, 'State responsibility for the wrongful acts of rebels an aspect of the Southern Rhodesia problem', Br. Yearb. Int. Law, vol 43 (1968/9), pp 49-70

BAXTER, R R, 'Reflections on codification in light of the international law of state responsibility for injuries to aliens', Syracuse Law Review, vol 16 (1965), p 745

BOHME, Eckart, Tankerumfälle auf dem Hohen Meer (Hamburg: Forschungsstelle für Völkerrecht der Universität Hamburg, 1969). 92 pp.

DEPIEREUX, Stefan, Die völkerrechtliche Haftung des Staates bei Ausbreitungen gegen diplomatische Missionen (Bonn, Universitat, 1957)

DYKE, Vernon van, 'The responsibility of state for international propaganda', Am. J. Int. Law, vol 34 (1940), pp 58-73

EAGLETON, Clyde, 'The responsibility of the state for the protection of foreign officials', Am. J. Int. Law, vol 19 (1925), pp 293-314

FITZGERALD, Gerald F, 'The participation of international organizations in the proposed international agreement on liability for damage caused by objects launched into outer space', Can. Yearb. Int. Law, (1965), p 271

FREEMAN, A V, 'Responsibility of states for unlawful acts of their armed forces', Acad. Droit Int. Recl. Cours, vol 88 (1955) pp 267-415

FREEMAN, Alwyn, The International Responsibility of States for Denial of Justice (London: Longmans Green & Co, 1938). xix + 758 pp.

HALLBRONNER, K, 'Liability for damage caused by spacecraft', Z. Ausl. Off. Recht & Völkerrecht, vol 30 (1970), pp 125-41

HALEY, Andrew W G, 'Space vehicle torts', University of Detroit Law Journal, vol 36 (1959), p 294

HOCH, F, 'Die völkerrechtliche Verpflichtung der Staaten durch Regierungsakte', Thesis. Zurich, 1947

HORSFORD, C E S, 'National and personal responsibility for space activities', Int. & Comp. Law Q., vol 20 (1970), p 547

JAHRREISS, H, Die Rechtspflicht der Bundesrepublik Deutschland zur Entschädigung für Reparations- und Demilitarisierungseingriffe der Kriegsgegner des Reiches in Privatvermögen, Rechtsgutachten (Köln, 1950)

JESCHEK, Hans-Heinrich, Die Verantwortlichkeit der Staatsorgane nach Völkerstrafrecht. Eine Studie zu den Nürnberger Prozessen (Bonn, 1952). 420 pp.

PAZARCI, H, Responsabilité internationale des états en matière contractuelle (Ankara: University of Ankara, 1973). xiv + 144 pp.

LA PRADELLE, P de, & LARNAUDE, F, 'Examen de la responsabilité pénale de l'empereur Guillaume II d'Allemagne', Rev. Droit Int. & Légis Comp., vol 46 (1919), pp 131-59

LUME, R D, 'Individual responsibility for aggressive war: the crime against peace', Queensland Law Journal, vol 3 (1959), pp 333-55

QUENEUDEC, J P, La Responsabilité internationale de l'état par les fautes personnelles de ses agents (Paris: Pichon et Durand Auzias, 1966). 275 pp.

RAESTAD, A, 'Statens ansvar for skade som forvoldes på utlendingers person og eiendom', Tidsskrift for Rettsvitenskap (1930), pp 163-76

ROY, S N Guha, 'Is the law of responsibility of states for injuries to aliens a part of universal international law?' Am. J. Int. Law, vol 55 (1961), pp 863-91

ROY, S N G, 'The responsibility of the state for injuries to aliens', Österr. Z. Öff. Recht, vol 12 (1962), pp 128-87

SOHN, L B & BAXTER, R R, 'Responsibility of states for injuries to the economic interests of aliens', Am. J. Int. Law, vol 55 (1961), p 545

WRIGHT, Philip Quincy, 'The legal liability of the Kaiser', American Political Science Review, vol 13 (1919), pp 120-8

ZELLWEGER, Die völkerrechtliche Verantwortlichkeit der Staaten für die Presse unter besonderer Berücksichtigung der schweizerischen Praxis (Zürich: Polygraphischer Verlag, 1949). 144 pp.

11.6 REPARATION

Reparation cannot be studied without reference to case law, for example the famous Reparation for Injuries Case, see cases in Section 1.4.

Duty to make reparation may occur as a result of a 'criminal act', see Section 12.1, or following any other breach of international law such as a violation of a treaty, see Sections 7.13.7 and 7.13.11.2, or other specific activity or passivity, see Sections above in this chapter. On injury to aliens see also Sections 7.11.1.2 and 7.12.13.

BISSONETTE, P A, La Satisfaction comme mode de réparation en droit international (Annemasse, 1952)

BURNETT, Philip Mason, Reparation at the Paris Peace Conference from the Standpoint of the American Delegation (New York, 1949). 2 vols.

CAMUZET, Luce, L'Indemnité de guerre en droit international (Paris, 1928). 218 pp.

EVGENEV, V V, Mezhdunarodno-pravovoe regulirovanie reparatsiy posle vtoroi mirovoi voiny (International Legal Regulation of Reparations after the Second World War) (Moscow, 1950)

REITZER, Ladislas, La Réparation comme consequence de l'acte illicite en droit international (Paris, 1938). 239 pp.

PERSONNAZ, J, La Réparation du Préjudice en Droit International Public (Paris, 1938)

YNTEMA, H E, 'The treaties with Germany and compensation for war damage', Columbia Law Review, vol 24 (1924), pp 134-43

WHITEMAN, M M, Damages in International Law (Washington, DC: US Government Printing Office, 1937-43). 3 vols.

see also Chapter V of Fitzmaurice's Hague Course on Economic, Financial and Commercial Clauses of the Peace Treaties, listed under general works in Section 1.8.

12 International Criminal Law

On the fairly 'new' subject of international criminal law see the following works. One standard book is that by MUELLER and WISE listed below. An international 'crime' is not any breach of international law but restricted (although not yet clearly defined) to concern illegitimate use of force (see Section 9.7), piracy, hijacking, terrorism and crimes of war (see Section 10) including aggression (Sedtion 9.9) and crimes against humanity (Sections 10.6, 10.11 and 7.12).

12.1 GENERAL

BASSIOUNI, M C, & NANDA, V P, A Treatise on International Criminal Law, (Springfield, Ill: Charles C Thomas, 1973). 2 vols.
DROST, P, The Crime of State (Leyden, 1959)
GALBE, J L, Crimenes y justicia de guerro (Havana, 1950)
GIHL, Torsten, 'Angående begreppet "folkrättsbrott"', Nord. Tidsskr. Int. Ret., vol 23 (1952), pp 240-56
GLASER, S, Introduction à l'étude du droit international pénal (Bruxelles/Paris, 1954). 208 pp.
GLASER, S, Droit international pénal conventionnel (Bruxelles: Emile Bruylant, 1970)

KEENAN, Joseph B, & BROWN, Brendan F, Crimes against International Law (Washington, 1950). 226 pp

KELSEN, H, Unrecht und Unrechtsfolge im Völkerrecht (1932)

KELSEN, H, Le Droit Pénal International. Recueil d'études en hommage à Jacob Maarten van Bennelen (Leiden: Brill, 1965)

LEGROS, 'L'avenir du droit pénal international', in Mélanges Rolin (1964), p 183

MUELLER, G O W, & WISE, E M, International Criminal Law (London: Sweet & Maxwell/South Hackensack, NJ: Fred B Rothman, 1965). 660 pp.

PAL, R, Crimes in International Relations (Calcutta, 1955). 439 pp.

PARRY, C, 'Some considerations upon the content of a draft code of offences against the peace and security of mankind', Int. Law Q., vol 3 (1950), pp 208-27

PELLA, Vespasian V, La Criminalité collective des états et le droit pénal de l'avenir, (Bucharest/Paris, 1925). 360 pp. 2nd ed. 1931 (in Spanish)

PELLA, V V, 'Towards an international criminal court', Am. J. Int. Law, vol 44 (1950), pp 37-68

PELLA, V V, 'Fonctions pacificatrices du droit pénal supranational et fin du système traditionnel des traités de paix', Rev. Gén. Droit Int. Public, vol 51 (1947), pp 1-27

PELLA, V V, 'La justice pénale internationale', Rev. Droit Int. Sci.Dipl. & Polit., vol 42 (1945), pp 85-139

PELLA, V V, 'La codification du droit pénal international', Rev. Gén.Droit Int. Public, vol 56 (1952), pp 337-459

PHILLIMORE, Sir Walter (Lord Phillimore), 'An international criminal court and the resolution of the committee of jurists', Br. Yearb. Int. Law, vol 3 (1922), pp 79-86

QUINTANO-RIPOLLES, A, Tratado de derecho penal internacional et internacional penal, vol 1 (Madrid, 1955), 676 pp.

REUT-NICOLUSSI, E, 'Zum Problem der Friedenssicherung durch Strafgerichtsbarkeit' in Gegenwartsprobleme des internationalen Rechts und der Rechtsphilosophie. Festschrift für Rudolf Laun, edited by D S Constantinopoulos and H Wehberg (Hamburg, 1953), pp 367-78

SALDAÑA, Quintiliano, 'La justice pénale internationale', Acad. Droit Int. Recl. Cours, vol 10 (1925), pp 223-429

SEIDL-HOHENFELDERN, I, 'Völkerrechtswidrige Akte fremder Staaten vor innerstaatlichen Gerichten', in Recht im Wandel, Beiträge zu Strömungen und Fragen im heutigen Recht (Köln, 1964), p 591

SCHÜLE, A, 'Völkerrechtliches Delikt', in Wörterbuch des Völkerrechts, vol 1 (Berlin: Verlag Walter de Gruyter, 1960), p 326

STONE, J & WOETZEL, R K, (eds), Towards a Feasible International Criminal Court (Genève, 1970)

STRUPP, Karl, Das völkerrechtliche Delikt (Berlin, 1920). 223 pp.

VERDROSS, Alfred von, Die völkerrechtswidrige Kriegshandlung und der Strafenspruch der Staaten (Berlin, 1920). 116 pp.

12.2 SPECIFIC CRIMES

12.2.1 AIR PIRACY AND HIJACKING

There is an overwhelming amount of writing on air piracy and hijacking as one might expect on a subject of such topical importance. The section below covers certain aspects of hijacking, as well as the problem of jurisdiction of crimes committed on board aircraft.

McWHINNEY'S and AGRAWALA'S monographs are of particular interest.

AGRAWALA, S K, Aircraft Hijacking and International Law (Bombay: N M Tripathi/Dobbs Ferry, NY: Oceana, 1973). 243 pp.

CHENG, B, 'Crimes on board aircraft', Current Legal Problems, vol 12 (1959), pp 177-207

FITZGERALD, G F, 'The development of international rules concerning offenses and certain other acts committed on board aircraft', Can. Yearb. Int. Law (1963), pp 230-57

FITZGERALD, G F, 'Development of international legal rules for the repression of the unlawful seizure of aircraft', Can. Yearb. Int. Law (1969), pp 269-97

FITZGERALD, G F, 'Offenses and certain other acts committed on board aircraft, the Tokyo convention of 1963', Can. Yearb. Int. Law (1964), pp 191-204

FOLCHI, M O, Los delictos aeronauticos (Buenos Aires: Astrea, 1970)

FOLCHI, M O, Delicto a bordo de aeronaves (Buenos Aires: Abeledo-Perrat, 1964). 139 pp.

JOHNSON, D H N, 'Hijacking, why governments must act', Aeronautical Journal, vol 14 (1970), p 143

LA PRADELLE, P de, 'Le détours d'aéronefs et le droit international', Revue Générale de l'air et l'espace (1969), pp 249-69

McWHINNEY, E, Aerial Piracy and International Law (Dobbs Ferry, NY/ Leiden: Sijthoff, 1971). 213 pp.

SCHWARZENBERGER, G, 'Hijackers, guerilleros and mercenaries', Current Legal Problems, vol 24 (1971), pp 257-82

SHUBBER, S, Jurisdiction over Crimes on Board Aircrafts (Den Haag: Nijhoff, 1973). 369 pp.

SIMBERG, J W F, 'La piratérie aérienne', Revue international du droit pénal, vol 41 (1970), pp 165-78

VILLAMIN, M L, Piracy and Air Law (Montreal:
Institute of Air and Space Law, McGill University,
1962)
VISSCHER, C de, 'Le droit pénal international en
matière de navigation aérienne', Rev. Droit Int. &
Légis. Comp., ser 3, vol 17 (1936), pp 118-37

12.2.2 MARITIME PIRACY

Piracy at sea has taken on increased importance
since a ship, the Santa Maria, was seized in 1961.
This incident caused an influx in the writings of
scholars on a subject fairly neglected in recent years.
On the historical background, see the classics listed
in Section 2.1
SESTIER, J M, La Piraterie dans l'antiquité (Paris:
    A Marescq, 1880). 320 pp.
On the measures of the League of Nations see:
MÜLLER, A, Die Piraterie im Völkerrecht unter
    besonderer Berücksichtigung des Entwurfes der
    Völkerbund-Kommission un der Regierungsäusse-
    rungen (Grünberg: Ritter, 1929). 80 pp.
On modern rules:
ARIAS, L G, La pirateria como delito del derecho de
    gentes (Saragosa: Fac. de derecho, 1961). 47 pp.
GOYARD, C, 'L'affaire du Santa Maria', Rev. Gén.
    Droit Int. Public, vol 66 (1962), pp 123-42
GREEN, L C, 'The Santa Maria: rebels or pirates',
    Br. Yearb. Int. Law, vol 37 (1961), pp 496-505
JEANNEL, J, La Piraterie (Paris: A Rousseau, 1963)
JOHNSON, D H N, 'Piracy in modern international
    law', Grotius Soc. Trans., vol 43 (1957), pp 63-85
WORTLEY, B A, 'Pirata non mutat dominium', Br.
    Yearb. Int. Law, vol 24 (1947), pp 258-72

12.2.3 RADIO PIRACY

The works listed below do not, apart from ROUSSEAU's article on a specific incident, limit themselves to questions relating to radio piracy. On the regulation of the radio spectrum in general, see Section 13.24.2.24.4 on the International Telecommunications Union.

EVENSEN, J, Aspects of International Law Relating to Modern Radio Communications (Leiden: Sijthoff, 1965) 111 pp.

LEIVE, David M, International Telecommunications and International Law: The Regulation of the Radio Spectrum (Leiden: Sijthoff, 1970). 386 pp.

ROUSSEAU, C, 'Légalité au regard du droit international de l'opération de police entreprise le 17 décembre 1964 par les autorités néerlandaises contre la station émettrice de télévision Radio TV Noordsee édificié sur une ile artificielle en haute mer à 6 milles de la côte hollandaise', Rév. Gen. Int. Public, vol 69 (1965), pp 365-84

SØRENSEN, M, 'Private broadcasting from the high seas', in Legal Essays, Attribute to Frede Castberg (Copenhagen/Stockholm/Gothemburg, 1963). pp 319-331

WOODLIFFE, J C, 'Some legal aspects of private broadcasting in the North Sea', Ned Tijdschr. Int. Recht, vol 12 (1965), pp 365-84

12.2.4 TERRORISM

On terrorism as an entirely new form of crime against the international society see:

BRACH, 'The Inter-American convention on the kidnapping of diplomats', Columbia Journal of Transnational Law, vol 10 (1971), pp 392-412

FRANCK, T M, & LOCKWOOD, B B J, Preliminary thoughts towards an international convention on

terrorism', Am. J. Int. Law, vol 68 (1974), pp 69-90
ROZAKIS, C L, 'Terrorism and the internationally protected persons in the light of the ILC's draft articles', Int. & Comp Law Q., vol 23 (1974), pp 32-72

12.2.5 OTHER SPECIAL CRIMES

In this section I have listed works on specific crimes apart from those listed above. I have here included also war crimes, but I may also refer to Section 12.2.6 on war crimes trials, Section 11 on responsibility and Section 10 on war.

BOURQUIN, Maurice, 'Crimes et délits contre la sûreté des états étrangers', Acad. Droit Int. Recl. Cours, vol 16 (1927), pp 117-246

DICKINSON, 'The defamation of foreign governments', Am. J. Int. Law, vol 22 (1928), p 840

DROST, Pieter N, The Crime of State - Genocide. UN Legislation on International Criminal Law (Leiden: Sijthoff, 1959)

DROST, Pieter N, The Crime of State - Humanicide. International Governmental Crime against Individual Human Rights (Leiden: Sijthoff, 1959)

GREEN, L, 'Political offences, war crimes and extradition', Int. & Comp Law Q., vol 11 (1962), p 329

KELSEN, H, 'Punishment of war criminals', California Law Review, vol 31 (1943), p 530

LACHS, Manfred, War Crimes (London: Stevens, 1945). viii + 108 pp.

LAUTERPACHT, H, 'Revolutionary propaganda by governments', Grotius Soc. Trans., vol 13 (1927), pp 143-64

LAUTERPACHT, H, 'Revolutionary activities by private persons against foreign states', Am. J. Int. Law, vol 22 (1928), pp 105-30

MENGELLE, F de Marosy, ' "Crimes against Peace" and international law', Revista española, vol 3 (1950), pp 459-72
RÖLING, B V A, Strafbarheid van de agressieve oorlog (Groningen, 1950)
SCHAFER, M, 'Crimes against peace', Thesis. Genève, 1952.
VOLCHKOV, A F, 'Aggression as an international crime', Sovietskoe gosudarstvo i pravo, no 6 (1951), pp 72-4
YOKOTA, K, 'War as an international crime', in Fundamental Problems of International Law: Festschrift für Jean Spiropoulos (Bonn, 1957), p 453
PELLA, V V, La Guerre - Crime et les criminels de guerre (Paris/Genève, 1946). 208 pp.
PELLA, Vespasian V, 'La repression des crimes contre la personnalité de l'état', Acad. Droit Int. Recl. Cours, vol 33 (1930), pp 671-837
POMPE, C A, Aggressive War. An International Crime (Den Haag, 1953). 382 pp.
WRIGHT, Q, 'Subversive intervention', Am. J. Int. Law, vol 54 (1960), pp 521-35
UNDEN, Östen, Om krigets kriminalisering (Stockholm, 1929)

12.2.6 WAR CRIMES TRIALS

The standard work is that by WOETZEL. For documentary material see Judgment (Nuremberg), Dull (Tokyo), Poliakov (Eichmann) listed below
On the war trials:
APPLEMAN, John F, Military Tribunals and International Crimes (Indianapolis: Bobbs-Merrill, 1954). 421 pp.
BAADE, H, 'The Eichmann trial: some legal aspects', Duke Law Journal, vol 3 (1961), p 400
BASU, K K, 'Tokyo trials', Indian Law Review, vol 3 (1949), pp 25-30

BENTON, W E, & GRIMM, G, (eds), Nuremberg: German Views of the War Trials (Dallas, Tex: Southern Methodist University Press, 1955). 230 pp.

BIRKETT, Sir William Norman, 'International legal theories evolved at Nuremberg', Int. Aff. (UK), vol 23 (1947), pp 317-25

DONNEDIEU DE VABRES, 'Le jugement de Nuremberg et le principe de la légalité des délits et des peines', Revue de droit pénal et de criminologie, vol 27 (1946/7), pp 813-33

DONNEDIEU DE VABRES, 'Le procès de Nuremberg devant les principes modernes du droit pénal international', Acad. Droit Int. Recl. Cours, vol 70 (1947), pp 481-580

DULL, P S, & UNEMURA, M T, The Tokyo Trials: a Functional Index to the Proceedings of the International Military Tribunal for the Far East (Ann Arbor: University of Michigan Press, 1962). 94 pp.

GLASER, Stefan, 'La charte du tribunal de Nuremberg et les nouveaux principes du droit international', Schweizerische Zeitschrift für Strafrecht, vol 62 (1948), p 13

GLASER, Stefan, 'Les lois de Nuremberg et le droit international', Schweizerische Zeitschrift für Strafrecht, vol 67 (1953), pp 321-59

GLUECK, Sheldon, War Criminals: their Prosecution and Punishment (New York, 1944). 250 pp.

GLUECK, Sheldon, 'The Nurnberg trial and aggressive war', Harvard Law Review, vol 59 (1945/6), pp 396-456

GLUECK, Sheldon, The Nuremberg Trial and Aggressive War (New York, 1946). 121 pp.

GRAVEN, Jean, 'De la justice internationale à la paix: les enseignements de Nuremberg', Rev. Droit Int. Sci. Dipl. & Polit., vol 24 (1946), pp 183-210; vol 25 (1947), pp 3-17

GREEN, 'Legal issues of the Eichmann trial', Tulane Law Review, vol 37 (1963), p 641
GREEN, L C, 'Aspects juridiques du procès Eichmann', Annu. Fr. Droit Int., vol 9 (1963), pp 150-90
GREWE, Wilhelm, & KUSTER, Otto, Nürnberg als Rechtsfrage: eine Diskussion, (Stuttgart, 1947). 111 pp.
GROSS, L, 'The punishment of war criminals: the Nuremberg trial', Ned. Tijdschr. Int. Recht, vol 3 (1956), pp 10-24
HEINZE, Kurt, & SCHILLING, Karl, (eds), Die Rechtsprechung der Nürnberger Militärtribunal. Sammlung der Rechtsthesen, der Urteile und gesonderten Urteilsbegrundungen der dreizehn Nürnberger Prozesse (Bonn, 1952). 356 pp.
HORWITZ, Solis, 'The Tokyo trial', Int. Conciliation, no 465 (1950), pp 473-584
JACKSON, Robert Houghwout, 'Nürnberg in retrospect', Canadian Bar Review, vol 27 (1949), pp 761-81
JACKSON, Robert Houghwout, The Nürnberg Case as Presented by Robert H Jackson, Chief of Counsel for the United States, Together with Other Documents, (New York, 1947). 270 pp.
JANECZEK, E, Nuremberg Judgment in the Light of International Law (Genève, 1949). 142 pp.
Judgment of the International Military Tribunal for the Trial of German Major War Criminals. Nuremberg 30th September and 1st October 1946 (London: HM Stationery Office) Cmd. 6964
KAUL, F K, Der Fall Eichmann (Berlin, 1963). 365 pp.
KELSEN, H, 'Will the judgment of the Nuremberg trials constitute a precedent in international law?' Int. Law Q. (1947), p 165
KILMUIR, Viscount (Sir David Maxwell Fyfe). Nuremberg in Retrospect (Holdsworth Club, University of Birmingham), 1956, 18 pp.

KNIERIEM, August von, Nürnberg: rechtliche und menschliche Probleme (Sttutgart, 1953). 574 pp.

KNIERIEM, August von, The Nuremberg Trials, translated from the German by Elizabeth D Schmitt (Chicago, 1959). 561 pp.

KRANZBÜHLER, Otto, 'Nürnberg als Rechtsproblem', in Um Recht und Gerechtigkeit, Festgabe für Erich Kaufmann (Stuttgart/Köln, 1950), pp 219-37

LASOK, 'The Eichmann trial', Int. & Comp. Law Q., vol 11 (1962), p 355

LAWRENCE, Sir Geoffrey (Lord Oaksey), 'The Nuremberg trial', Int. Aff. (UK), vol 23 (1947), pp 151-9

LEVENTHAL, Harold, HARRIS, Sam, WOOLSEY, John M, & FARR, Warren F, 'The Nuremberg verdict', Harvard Law Review (1946/7), pp 857-907

LINZE, The Trial of Adolf Eichmann (Los Angeles: Holloway House, 1961)

MARIDAKIS, Georges, 'Un précédent du procès de Nuremberg tiré de l'histoire de la Grèce ancienne', Rev. Hell. Droit Int., vol 5 (1952), pp 1-16

MASSAREK, Eduard, Nürnberg. Zum Prozeß gegen die Hauptkriegsverbrecher (Wien, 1947). 178 pp.

MAUGHAM, Viscount, UNO and War Crimes (London, 1951). 144 pp.

MINEAR, Richard H, Victor's Justice: The Tokyo War Crimes Trial (Princeton, NJ: Princeton University Press, 1972). xv + 229 pp.

PAPADATOS, P A, Le Procès Eichmann (Genève: Droz, 1964)

PAPADATOS, P A, The Eichmann Trial (London: Stevens, 1964)

PAL, R, International Military Tribunal for the Far East, Dissentient Judgment of Justice Pal (Calcutta/London, 1953). 701 pp.

POLIAKOV, L, Le Procès de Jerusalem (Paris, 1963)

POLYANSKY, Nokolai Nikolayevich, Mezhdunarodnoye pravosudie i prestupniki voiny (International Justice and War Criminals) (Moscow/Leningrad: Izdatel'stvo Akademii nauk SSR, 1945)

POLYANSKY, N N, Mezhdunarodny Voyenny Tribunal (The International Military Tribunal) (Moscow: Yuridicheskoye izdatel'stvo Ministerstva yustitsii SSR, 1946)

RAGINSKY, M Y, & ROZENBLIT, S Y, Mezhdunarodny protsess glavnykh yaponskikh voyennykh prestupnikov (The International Trial of Chief Japanese War Criminals) (Moscow/Leningrad: Izdatel'stvo Akademii nauk SSR, 1950)

RAPPAPORT, M J, Mezhdunarodno-pravovyye voprosy suda nad glavnymi yaponskimi prestupnikami voiny (Trial of Major Japanese War Criminals, Questions of International Law Concerning) in Uchenyye zapiski Leningradskogo gosudarstvennogo universiteta (Scientific Notes of Leningrad State University)

RÖLING, B V A, 'The Tokyo trial and the development of international law', Indian Law Review, vol 7 (1953), pp 4-14

RÖLING, B V A, 'On aggression, on international criminal law, on international criminal jurisdiction', Ned. Tijdschr. Int. Recht, vol 2 (1955), pp 167-96; 279-89

RUSSELL, E F L R, The Record: The Trial of Adolf Eichmann

SCHICK, F B, 'The Nuremberg trial and the international law of the future', Am. J. Int. Law, vol 41 (1947), pp 770-94

SCHICK, F B, 'The Nuremberg trial and the development of an international criminal law', Juridical Review, vol 59 (1947), pp 193-207

SCHICK, F B, 'War criminals and the law of the United Nations', University of Toronto Law Journal, vol 7 (1947/8), pp 27-67

SCHICK, F B, 'Crimes against peace', Journal of Criminal Law, vol 38 (1947/8), pp 445-65
SCHWARZENBERGER, Georg, International Law and Totalitarian Lawlessness (London, 1943). 168 pp.
SCHWARZENBERGER, Georg, 'Jus Pacis ac Belli?' Am. J. Int. Law, vol 37 (1943), pp 460-79
SCHWARZENBERGER, Georg, 'The judgment of Nuremberg', Tulane Law Review, vol 21 (1946/7), pp 329-61
SCHWARZENBERGER, Georg, 'The problem of an international criminal law', Current Legal Problems, vol 3 (1950), pp 263-96
SOTTILE, A, 'Les criminels de guerre et le nouveau droit pénal international, seul moyen efficace pour assurer la paix du monde', Rev. Droit Int. Sci. Dipl. & Polit., vol 23 (1945), pp 225-48
SPIROPOULOS, J, 'Formulation of the Nuremberg Principles', Rev. Hell Droit Int., vol 4 (1951), pp 129-62
STIMSON, H, 'The Nuremberg trial: landmark in law', Foreign Affairs, vol 25 (1946/7), pp 179-89
TAYLOR, Telford, Les Procès de Nuremberg. Crimes de guerre et droit international (Paris, 1949)
TAYLOR, Telford, 'The Nuremberg war crimes trials', Int. Conciliation, no 450 (1949), p 241
TAYLOR, Telford, The Nuremberg Trials (New York, 1949)
TREVES, A, 'Jurisdictional aspects of the Eichmann Case', Minnesota Law Review, vol 47 (1963), p 557
WEHBERG, H, 'Die völkerrechtliche Verantwortlichkeit von Individuen wegen Friedensbruchs im Zeitalter des Völkerbundes', in D S Constantinopoulos and H Wehberg, (eds) Gegenwartsprobleme des internationalen Rechtes und der Rechtsphilosophie, Festschrift für Rudolf Laun, edited by D S Constantinopoulos & H Wehberg (Hamburg, 1953), pp 379-94

WOETZEL, Robert K, The Nuremberg Trials in International Law (London/New York, 1960). 287 pp. With a postlude on the Eichmann case (London: Stevens, 1962). 317 pp.

WRIGHT, Quincy, 'The law of the Nuremberg trial', Am. J. Int. Law, vol 41 (1947), pp 38-72

WRIGHT, Quincy, 'Legal positivism and the Nuremberg judgment', Am. J. Int. Law, vol 35 (1948), p 42

WRIGHT, Sir Robert Alderson, (Lord Wright), History of the United Nations War Crimes Commission and the Development of the Laws of War, UNWCC (London: HMSO, 1948). 592 pp.

ZOUREK, J, 'The Nuremberg principles as a decisive stage in the development of international law', Review of Contemporary Law (December, 1961), pp 105-26

13 International Organisations

In this part of the bibliography I have listed works on the evolution of international organizations. I have initially included a section on international conferences which may be conceived as the origin of such organizations although they are also important in their own right in the contemporary international society.

13.1 INTERNATIONAL CONFERENCES

HUDSON, M O, 'Procedure of international conferences and procedure for the conclusion and drafting of treaties', Am. J. Int. Law, vol 20 (1926), p 747. Cf. special supp. p 204

PASTUHOV, V D, A Guide to the Practice of International Conferences (Washington, 1945)

POTTER, P B, 'Développement de l'organisation internationale (1815-1914)', Acad. Droit Int. Recl. Cours, vol 2 (1938), p 71

SCELLE, G, 'L'évolution des conférences internationales/The evolution of international conferences', Bulletin international des sciences sociales, vol 5 (1953), pp 257-303; International Social Science Bulletin, vol 5 (1953), pp 241-57

13.2 HISTORY OF INTERNATIONAL ORGANIZATIONS

MANGONE, G J, A Short History of International Organization (New York: McGraw-Hill, 1954). ix + 326 pp.
WEHBERG, H, 'Entwicklungsstufen der internationalen Organisation', Die Friedens-Warte, vol 52 (1954), pp 193-218

13.3 INTERNATIONAL INSTITUTES

13.3.1 INSTITUT INTERNATIONAL DE COOPERATION INTELLECTUELLE/ INTERNATIONAL INSTITUTE OF INTELLECTUAL COOPERATION

Institut international de coopération intellectuelle, L'Institut international de coopération intellectuelle 1925-1946 (Paris, 1946). 599 pp.
OTLET, Paul, Centre Intellectuel Mondial au service de la Société des Nations (Bruxelles: Union des Associations Internationales, 1919). 28 pp. (Publication no 88)
Union des associations internationales, Sur l'organisation du travail intellectuel à créer au sein de la Société des Nations. Rapport et voeu présentés par l'Union des Associations Internationales (Bruxelles, 1920). 20 pp. (Publication no 95)

13.3.2 INSTITUT INTERNATIONAL d'AGRICULTURE/INTERNATIONAL INSTITUTE OF AGRICULTURE

DOR, Louis, 'L'Institut international d'agriculture', La Vie Internationale, fasc 4 (1912), pp 429-454 (Office

Central des Associations Internationales, Bruxelles, Publication no 37)

FUSINATO, G, 'La personalità giuridica dell'Instituto internazionale d'agricoltora', Riv. Diritto Int. (1914), p 149

Institut international d'agriculture, L'Activité de l'Institut international d'agriculture, conditions et caractéristiques actuelles de l'agriculture dans le monde. Exposé général de G de Michelis (Roma, 1928). 371 pp.

Institut international d'agriculture, L'Activité de l'Institut international d'agriculture pendant la guerre (1940-1945) (Roma, 1945). 110 pp.

Institut international d'agriculture, L'Institut international d'agriculture: organisation, activité, resultats (Roma: Caso, 1927). 47 pp.

Institut international d'agriculture, Quelques aspects de l'activité de l'Institut international d'agriculture (1905-1940) (Roma, 1941). 136 pp.

International Institute of Agriculture, The International Institute of Agriculture: organization, activity and results (Roma, Caso, 1927). 51 pp.

13.3.3 OFFICE INTERNATIONAL D'HYGIENE PUBLIQUE/INTERNATIONAL OFFICE FOR PUBLIC HEALTH

ABT, G, Vingt-cinq ans d'activité de l'Office international d'hygiène publique, 1900-1933 (Paris: OIHP, 1933). 140 pp.

13.4 UNIONS

See also Sections 13.24.2.24.3 on the Universal Postal Union and 13.24.2.24.4 on the International Telecommunications Union.

DESCHAMPS, E, Les Offices internationaux et leur avenir (Bruxelles: Hayez, 1894). 106 pp.

KAUFMANN, Wilhelm, 'Les unions internationales de nature économique', Acad. Droit Int. Recl. Cours, vol 77 (1924), pp 181-289

LA FONTAINE, Henri, Organisation internationale et collective du travail intellectuel (Bruxelles: Lombaerts, 1894). (Bibliothèque internationale de l'Alliance scientifique universelle, vol 1, fasc. 4, pp 260-340)

MOYNIER, G, Les Bureaux internationaux des unions universelles (Paris: A Cherbuliez, 1892). 174 pp.

MYERS, Denys P, Non-sovereign Representation in Public International Organs. Congrès mondial des Associations internationales. Deuxième session: Gand-Bruxelles, 15-18 juin 1913. Organisé par l'Union des associations internationales (Bruxelles: Union des associations internationales, 1913). 69 pp. (Publication no 60, sec. 4)

RAPISARDI-MIRABELLI, A, 'Théorie générale des unions internationales', Acad. Droit Int. Recl. Cours, vol 7 (1925), pp 341-93

REIFF, Henry, 'The United States and international administrative unions: Some historical aspects', Int. Conciliation, no 332 (1937), pp 625-57

ROSSELLO, P, Les Précurseurs du Bureau international d'éducation. Un aspect inédit de l'histoire de l'éducation et des institutions internationales (Genève: Bureau international d'éducation, 1943). 303 pp.

ROSSELLO, P, Forerunners of the International Bureau of Education (London: Evans Brothers, 1944)

SCHNECKEBIER, Laurence Frederick, International Organizations in which the United States Participates (Washington, DC: The Brookings Institution, 1935). x + 363 pp. (Institute for Government Research of the Brookings Institution, Studies in Administration, no 30)

TOLL, Baron Benno von, Die internationalen Bureaux der allgemeinen Verwaltungsvereine (Tübingen: H Laupp, 1910). vii + 115 pp.

ZACHARIADE, Z, 'Le Statut financier des services publics internationaux (Paris: Domat-Montchrestien, 1938). 181 pp. (Thesis. Université de Paris)

13.5 NON-GOVERNMENTAL ORGANIZATIONS

On the function of the Red Cross see further Sections 10.6 on humanitarian law in war and 10.11 on humanitarian law in civil war.

BISSELL, T S G, 'International Committee of the Red Cross and the protection of human rights', Human Rights Journal, vol 1 (1968), pp 255-74

KENNEDY, E M, 'International humanitarian assistance: proposals for action', The Virginia Journal of International Law, vol 12 (1972), pp 299-308

KNITEL, H G, 'Rôle de la Croix-Rouge dans la protection internationale des droits de l'homme', Österr. Z. Öff. Recht, vol 19 (1969), pp 1-36

SPEECKAERT, G P, 'On the structure and functioning of international non-governmental organizations', Associations internationales/International Associations, vol 18, no 3 (March 1966), pp 140-50

STOSIC, B D, Les Organisations non-gouvernementales et les Nations Unies (Genève/Paris, 1964)

UMOZURIKE, U O, 'The 1949 Geneva conventions and Africa', Indian J. Int. Law, vol 11 (1971), pp 205-18

WENGLER, W, 'Bemerkungen zu den Verträgen nichtstaatlicher Verbände und ihre Organe mit Staaten und Staatsorganen', in Scritti in onore di Th. Perassi, vol 2 (1957), pp 421-46

13.6 INTERNATIONAL ORGANIZATIONS IN GENERAL

The theory and practice of international organisations have attracted more attention in France and Italy and on the continent in general than in Anglo-Saxon countries. For conceptual analysis see above all, the works by Paul REUTER.

AGO, Roberto, 'Considerazioni su alcuni sviluppi dell' organizzazione internazionale', La Comunità internazionale, (October, 1952), pp 527-67

AGO, R, Die internationalen Organisationen und ihre Funktionen im inneren Tätigbereich der Staaten, in Festschrift für Hans Wehberg (Frankfurt, 1956)

AGO, R, 'International organisations and their functions in the fields of internal activities of states', Nord. Tidsskr. Int. Ret, vol 27 (1957), pp 1-18

AGO, R, GIULIANO, M, MONACO, R, et al., Contributi allo studio della organizzazione internazionale (Padova: Cedam, 1957). iii + 290 pp.

ALEXANDROWICZ, C H, World Economic Agencies: Law and Practice (London, 1962)

ARANGIO RUIZ, G, 'Rapporti contrattuali fra Stati ed organizzazione internazionale (per una teoria dualista delle unioni di stati)', Archivio giuridico 'Filippo Serafini', vol 139 (1950), pp 7-158

ARES, R, L'Eglise catholique et l'organisation de la société internationale contemporaine, 1939-1949; les faits, les principes, le programme (Montréal: Les Facultés de philosophie et de théologie de la Compagnie de Jésus, 1949). 169 pp. (Jesuits, Montreal, Faculty of Philosophy, Studia collegii maximi, vol 7)

BALCELLS, M, Organizaciones internacionales (Barcelona, 1962)

BARENTS, Internationaal Recht, internationale organisaties en internationale betrekkingen,

Volkenrechtlije opstellen ter ere van Baron van Asbeck en J H W Verzijl (Zwolle, 1957)

BASTID, S, Le Droit des organisations internationales (Paris: Cours polycopie D E S, 1951-2)

BASTID, S, Cours d'institutions internationales (Paris, 1955)

BASTID, S, 'De quelques problèmes juridiques posés par le développement des organisations internationales', Festschrift für Jean Spiropoulos (Bonn, 1957)

BASTID, S, 'Place de la notion d'institution dans une théorie générale des organisations internationales', L'évolution du droit public, Etudes en l'honneur d'Achille Mestre (Paris, 1956)

BIBIER, M, La Communauté internationale et ses institutions. Les juridictions internationales, l'organisation internationale du travail, l'organisation des Nations Unies, les ententes régionales (Paris: Recueil Sirey, 1949). 248 pp.

BILFINGER, C, 'Vom politischen und nicht politischen Recht in organisatorischen Kollektivverträgen', Z. Ausl. Öff. Recht. & Völkerrecht, vol 13 (1950), pp 615-53

BODMER, H, 'Die stellung der Staaten in den internationalen Organisationen unter besonderer Berücksichtigung der Kleinstaaten', Dissertation. Winterthur, 1955.

BORATYNSKI, S, 'Przedmiot i metodologia stosunków międzynarodowych. Z teorii organizacji międzynarodowych', Sprawy międzynarodowe, vol 21 (1968), pp 117-21

BOWETT, D W, The Law of International Institutions, 2nd edition (London: Stevens & Sons, 1970). xviii + 384 pp.

CARMOY, Guy de, Les Organisations économiques internationales (Cours donné à l'Université de Paris, Institut d'Etudes politiques, 1949-1950) (Paris: Les Cours de droit). 2 vol, 338 pp. duplic.

CHAUMONT, Ch, Les Organisations internationales (Cours donné à l'Université de Paris, Institut d'Etudes politiques, 1948-1949) (Paris: Les Cours de droit) 2 vols, 185 pp. duplic.

COLLIARD, C A, Institutions internationales, 3rd edition (Paris, 1966)

CORSINI, V, Codice delle organizzazioni internationali (Milano: Giuffré, 1958). 1287 pp.

CUEVAS CANCINO, F, Tratado sobre la organización internacional (Mexico, 1962)

DELUPIS, Ingrid (nee Detter) Ekonomisk integrationsrätt (Stockholm: Almqvist & Wiksell, 1974)

DUPUY, R-J, 'L'organisation internationale et l'expression de la volunté générale', Rev. Gén Droit Int. Public, vol 61 (1957), pp 527-79

FAVILLI, V, Sulla teoria degli organi in diritto internazionale (Trieste, 1949)

FAWCETT, J E S, 'The place of law in international organizations', Br. Yearb. Int. Law (1960)

FAWCETT, J E S, & HIGGINS, Rosalyn, (eds), Law in Movement: Essays in Honour of John McMahon (London, 1974)

FLORIO, F, La natura giuridica delle organizzazioni internazionali (Milano, 1949)

FLORIO, F, Le organizzazioni internazionali (Milano: Giuffré, 1949). 156 pp.

GARCIA ARIAS, L, Poder universal u organización internacional. Derecho de gentes y organiz. internacional, vol 1 (1956), pp 65-99

GOETHEM, F v, Nieuwe vormen van internationale gemeenschapsorganisatie (Antwerpen, 1955)

HOFFMANN, Stanley, Organisations internationales et pouvoirs politiques des états (Paris: A Colin, 1954). 427 pp. (Fondation nationale des sciences politiques, cahier 52)

JAENICKE, Günther, 'Die Sicherung des übernationalen Charakters der Organe internationaler Organisationen', Z Ausl. Öff. Recht & Völkerrecht, vol 14 (1951)

JENKS, C W, 'Some constitutional problems of international organizations', Br. Yearb. Int. Law, vol 22 (1945), pp 11-72

JENKS, Clarence Wilfred, 'Co-ordination: a new problem of international organization. A preliminary survey of the law and practice of inter-organizational relationships', Acad. Droit Int. Recl. Cours, vol 77 (1950), pp 157-302

JENKS, C W, 'The contribution of the international organisation to the development of procedures of peaceful change', New Commonwealth Quarterly, vol 4 (1939), pp 361-79

JENKS, C W, 'Co-ordination in international organization: an introductory survey', Br. Yearb. Int. Law (1951), pp 29-89

JENKS, C W, The Proper Law of International Organizations (London: Stevens/Dobbs Ferry, NY: Oceana, 1962)

JESSUP, Philip C, LANDE, Adolph, & LISSITZYN, Oliver J, International Regulation of Economic and Social Questions (New York: Carnegie Endowment for International Peace, 1955). 173 pp.

KUNZ, J L, 'General international law and the law of international organisations', Am. J. Int. Law, vol 47, pp 456-62

LACHS, M, 'Le rôle des organisations internationales dans la formation du droit international', Mélanges offerts à Henri Rolin (Paris, 1964), pp 156-70

LADOR-LEDERER, J J, 'L'importance des organisations consultatives internationales en matière juridique', Die Friedens-Warte, vol 55 (1959), pp 115-37

MONACO, Riccardo, Lezioni di organizzazione internazionale, 2nd edition (Torino, 1965). 2 vols:

vol 1 'Diritto delle istituzioni internazionali', vol
2 'Diritto degli enti economici internazionali'
MORAWIECKI, W, Organizacje międzynarodowe
(Warszawa, 1965)
MORENO QUINTANA, L M, & SHAW, C M Bollini,
'Los órganos internacionales', Revista de la
Facultad de der. y ciencias soc., vol 4, no 15
(1949), pp 787-821; Revista del Instit. de der.
internacional, vol 2, nos 7-8 (1949), pp 155-89
MIGLIAZZA, A, Il fenomeno dell'organizzazione e la
comunità internazionale (Milano, 1958)
MOSLER, H, 'La organización internacional y la
distribución de competencias', Escuela de Funcion-
arios Internacionales, Cursos y conferencias, año
academico, 1955-1956 (Madrid, 1957)
PINTO, R, 'Cours d'institutions internationales',
(Paris: Les Cours de droit, 1964-5)
POBLETE TRONCOSO, M, La comunidad inter-
nacional contemporanea. Relaciones y organismos
internacionales (Santiago de Chili, 1958)
RAEYMAEKER, O de, 'Neue Perspektiven in der
Entwicklung der internationalen Organisationen/
Nouveaux aspects de l'organisation intern', Inter-
nationales Jahrbuch der Politik (1955), pp 3-33
REUTER, P, Institutions internationales (Paris:
Presses universitaires de France, 1955). 426 pp.
Translated into English as: International Institutions
(London: Allen & Unwin, 1958). 316 pp.
REUTER, P, Les Organisations internationales. Cours
professé à la Faculté de droit de Paris (Paris, 1955).
501 pp.
REUTER, P, 'Organisations internationales et
évolution du droit', in Evolution du droit public,
Etudes offertes à Achille Mestre (1956)
ROHN, P, 'A legal theory of international organizations',
Turk. Yearb. Int. Relat., vol 5 (1964), pp 19-54

RUSSETT, Alan de, Strengthening the Framework of Peace: A Study of Current Proposals for Amending, Developing, or Replacing Present International Institutions for the Maintenance of Peace (London: Royal Institute of International Affairs, 1950). xiii + 225 pp.

ROYER, Jean, Les Organisations économiques internationales (Cours donné à l'Université de Paris, Institut d'Etudes politiques, 1947-1948) (Paris: Les Cours de droit, 1948). 238 pp.

SCHERMERS, H G, International Institutional Law (Leiden: Sijthoff, 1972-4). 3 vols. Vol 1 'Structure', vol 2 'Functioning and legal order', vol 3 'Teaching and cases'

SEIDL-HOHENVELDERN, I, Das Recht der internationalen Organisationen einschliesslich der supranationalen Gemeinschaften (Köln, 1967)

SERENI, A P, Le organizzazioni internazionali (Milano, 1959)

SØRENSEN, M, Grundtraek af international organisation (Copenhagen: Munksgaard, 1952). 184 pp.

SØRENSEN, M, 'Nyere udvihlingslinier i international organisation', Statsvetenskaplig tidskrift för politik, statistik ekonomi, vol 2 (1951), pp 113-29

SUMMERS, Robert Edward, The United States and International Organizations (New York: The H W Wilson Co, 1952). 194 pp.

TAMMES, A J P, Hoofdstukken van internationale organisatie. Part 1 (Den Haag: Nijhoff, 1951) xi + 283 pp.

TOKAREVA, P A, 'Stanovlenie sistemy mezdhunarodnykh organizatsiy sotsialistitcheskikh gosudarstv', Sovetskoe gosudarstvo i pravo, no 37 (October 1967) pp 64-72

WEGNER, A, 'Aktuelle Gedanken zum Problem der internationalen Organisation', (Review of Festschrift für Hans Wehberg), Int. Recht & Dipl., vol 3 (1957), pp 239-63

13.7 PERSONALITY OF INTERNATIONAL ORGANIZATIONS

See also Section 6.1 on personality in general, the work by CARROZ listed in Section 13.14 and the work by WRIGHT listed in Section 13.24.2.6.

BALLADORE PALLIERI, G, 'La personalità delle organizzazioni internazionali', Diritto Internazionale, vol 14 (1960), pp 230-55

BOUDET, F, Contribution à l'étude de la personnalité des organisations internationales (Paris, 1955)

CARROZ, J, & PROBST, Y, Personnalité juridique internationale et capacité de conclure des traités de l'ONU et des institutions specialisés (Paris, 1953)

CONFORTI, B, 'La personalità internazionale delle unioni di stati', Studi senesi, vol 77 (1965), pp 23-52; Diritto Internazionale, vol 18 (1964), pp 324-43

JENKS, C W, 'The legal personality of international organizations', Br. Yearb. Int. Law, vol 22 (1945), pp 267-75

PRZEWOZNIK, B, 'Personnalité juridique internationale des organisations internationales. Revue critique des organisations internationales. Revue critique des tendences principales de la doctrine contemporaine', Annales universitatis Marie Curie-Sklodowskaa, vol 11 (1964), pp 125-57

SEIDL-HOHENVELDERN, I, 'The legal personality of international and supranational organizations', Rev. Egypt. Droit Int., vol 21 (1965), pp 35-72

SEYERSTED, F, International personality of intergovernmental organizations. Its scope and its validity vis-à-vis non members. Do the capacities really depend upon the constitutions? (Delhi, 1964). 110 pp. Also in Indian J. Int. Law, vol 4 (1964), pp 1-74; 233-65

SEYERSTED, F, Objective international personality of intergovernmental organisations. Do their capacities really depend upon the conventions establishing them? (Copenhagen, 1963). 112 pp.

ZEMANEK, K, 'Internationale Organisationen als Handlungseinheiten in der Völkerrechtsgemeinschaft', Österr. Z. Öff. Recht, vol 7 (1956), pp 335-72

13.8 CIVIL SERVANTS OF INTERNATIONAL ORGANIZATIONS

BASDEVANT, S, 'Les fonctionnaires internationaux', Dissertation. Paris, 1931

BASTID, S, 'El derecho de las organizaciones internacionales europeas', Revista de la Facultad de Derecho y Ciencias Sociales, Montevideo (1955)

BASTID, S, Le statut juridique des fonctionnaires de l'ONU, the United Nations, Ten Years of Legal Progress, (n.p., n.d.)

CAHIER, Ph, 'Le droit interne des organisations internationales', Rev. Gén. Droit Int. Public, vol 67 (1963), pp 563-602

CHAUMONT, Ch, 'Perspectives d'une théorie du service public à l'usage du droit international contemporain', in Etudes en l'honneur de G Scelle (1950)

LANGROD, George, The International Civil Service, its Origins, its Nature, its Evolution (Leiden, 1963). 358 pp.

LANGROD, George, 'Problèmes fondamentaux de la fonction publique internationale, Revue internationale des sciences administratives (1953)

SCHLOCHAUER, H J, Der Rechtsschutz gegenüber der Tätigkeit internationaler und übernationaler Behörden (Frankfurt am Main: Klostermann, 1952). 39 pp.

13.9 RULES OF PROCEDURE

On rules of procedure and procedure in general of
organizations few monographs have been written. See
the work listed below and, also, the book by DETTER
listed in Section 13.16
KAPPELMANN, 'Die Geschäftsordnungen internationaler
 Organisationen unter besonderer Berücksichtigung
 der Allgemeinen Versammlung der Vereinigten
 Nationen', Dissertation. Mainz, 1956

13.10 VOTING IN ORGANIZATIONS

See, above all, the work by RICHES listed below, the
work by HOYT listed in Section 7.13.10.2 and that by
LJUBISAVIJEVIC listed in Section 13.24.3.12.8. See
also, Section 13.24.2.9 on voting in the UN.
DIEFENBACHER, Einstimmigkeitsprinzip und
 Mehrheitsbeschlüsse in internationalen Organisationen
 (Basel, 1953)
GARCHON, C, Le droit de veto. Etude positive du mode
 de vote dans les organismes internationaux (Alger,
 1949)
HILL, D J, 'Unanimous consent in international
 organizations', Am. J. Int. Law (1928)
KOO, Wellington, Jr, Voting Procedure in International
 Political Organisations (New York: Columbia
 University Press, 1947; reissued by AMS Press,
 New York)
RICHES, Cromwell Adams, Majority Rule in Inter-
 national Organization. A Study of the Trend from
 Unanimity to Majority Decision (Baltimore: The
 Johns Hopkins Press, 1940). viii + 322 pp.
SCHWARTZ-LIEBERMANN, Wahlendorff, v,
 Mehrheitsentscheidung und Stimmenwägung
 (Tübingen, 1953)
UBERTAZZI, G M, Il principio di unanimità negli organi
 collegiali internazionali (Milano, 1953)

13.11 BUDGET QUESTIONS
       OF ORGANIZATIONS

COLLIARD, C A, 'La procédure budgétaire des organisations internationales', Revue de science et de législation financières (1958), pp 237-60; 437-60

13.12 HEADQUARTER AGREEMENTS,
       IMMUNITIES AND PRIVILEGES

Cf. Section 7.10 on immunity in general and Section 13.24.2.18 on immunity of the UN

ALUWALIA, K, The Legal Status, Privileges and Immunities of the Specialized Agencies of the United Nations and Certain other International Organizations (Den Haag, 1964)

CAHIER, P, Etude des accords de siège conclus entre les états où elles resident (Milano, 1959)

GOY, R, 'Le droit d'accès au siège des organisations internationales', Rev. Gén. Droit Int. Public, vol 66 (1962), pp 357-70

JENKS, Clarence Wilfred, The Headquarters of International Institutions. A Study of their location and Status (London, 1945). 102 pp. (Royal Institute of International Affairs. Postwar problems, no 8)

KUNZ, J L, 'Privileges and immunities of international organizations', Am. J. Int. Law (1947)

MACHOWSKI, J, (Right of free access to the headquarters of an international organisation) Pánstwo i Prawo, vol 18 (1963), pp 477-83. In Polish with English and Russian summaries

13.13 SUSIDIARY ORGANS
       OF ORGANIZATIONS

REUTER, P, 'Les organes subsidaires des organisations internationales', in Hommage au Président Basdevant (Paris, 1960)

13.14 TREATY-MAKING POWER OF ORGANIZATIONS

See Section 6.1 on personality, and Section 13.7 on personality of organizations. See also the works by PARRY and KASME listed in Section 13.24.2.6, Section 13.24.2.24.12 on UNESCO and Section 13.24.3.12.14 on the treaty-making power of the European Communities. Cf. Section 7.13.8.1 on treaty-making power, and Section 13.24.2.24.2 on external relations of the specialized agencies.

CHIU, Hungdah, The Capacity of International Organizations to Conclude Treaties, and Special Legal Aspects of the Treaties so Concluded (Den Haag: Nijhoff, 1966). 225 pp.

DETTER, I, 'The organs of international organizations exercising their treaty-making power', Br. Yearb. Int. Law, vol 38 (1962), p 421

LACHS, M, 'Les conventions multilatérales et les organisations internationales contemporaines', Annu. Fr. Droit Int. (1956), pp 334-42

LUKASHUK, I, 'An International Organization as a Party to International Treaties', Soviet Yearbook of International Law (1960)

LÖRCHER, G, Der Abschluss Völkerrechtlicher Verträge nach dem Recht der drei europäischen Gemeinschaften (EGKS, EWG und EAG). Ein Beitrag zur Rechtsstellung organisierter Staaten Verbindungen (1965). 235 pp.

MEGRET, J, 'Le pouvoir de la Communaute économique européenne de conclure des accords internationaux', Rev. Marche Commun, no 75 (December, 1964). pp 529-36

RAUX, J, 'La procédure de conclusion des accords externes de la Communauté européenne de l'énergie atomique', Rev. Gén. Droit Int. Public, vol 69 (1965), pp 1019-50

PILIDIS, 'La capacité de conclure des traités des organisations internationales', Dissertation. Paris, 1952.
POULANTZAS, N M, 'Une disposition malencontreuse de l'accord d'association de la Grèce à la communauté économique européenne', Rev. Hell. Droit Int., vol 16 (1963)
SCHNEIDER, J W, Treaty-making Power of International Organizations (Genève/Paris, 1959)
SMETS, P F, & MERTENS, P, 'Le "treaty-making power" de l'UNESCO', Rev. Gén.Droit Int. Public, vol 70 (1966), pp 916-60
SOCINI, R, 'Sui trattati delle organizzazioni internazionali', Rivista di studi politici internazionali, vol 18 (1961), pp 422-57
SOCINI, R, Gli accordi internazionali delle organizzazioni intergovernative (Padova, 1962)
VALKI, L, 'The juristic personality and treaty-making power of international organizations', Questions of International Law (1968), pp 285-308
WENGLER, W, 'Agreements of states with other parties than states in international relations', Schriftenreihe (1957), pp 149-64
ZEMANEK, K, Das Vertragsrecht der Internationaler Organizationen (Wien, 1957)

13.15 INTERNATIONAL RELATIONS OF ORGANIZATIONS

See also Sections 13.24.2.20 on the UN and 13.24.3.12.5 on the European Communities.
DECLEVA, M, 'Relazioni e collagamenti tra le unioni internazionali', Comun. & Stud. (1950), pp 160-73
DUPUY, R J, 'Le droit des relations entre les organisations internationales', Acad. Droit Int. Recl. Cours, vol 100 (1960), pp 457-589
HOLLENWEGER, P, Die Assoziation von Staaten mit internationalen Organisationen (Zürich, 1967)

JENKS, C W, 'Coordination: a new problem of international organization', Acad. Droit Int. Recl. Cours, vol 77 (1950), pp 151-303

JÉNKS, C W, 'Coordination in international organization: an introductory survey', Br. Yearb. Int. Law, vol 28 (1951), pp 29-89

MONACO, R, 'Coordinamento tra enti internazionali', Riv. Diritto Int., vol 40 (1957), pp 181-201

RIPHAGEN, W, 'Enige juridische aspecten van de betrekkingen tussen internationale instellingen', International Spectator, vol 9, no 21 (1955), pp 685-733

SEIDL-HOHENVELDERN, I, 'Rechtsbeziehungen zwischen Internationale Organisationen und den einzelnen Staaten', Arch. Völkerrechts, vol 4 (1953), pp 30-58

WENGLER, W, 'Agreements of states with other parties than states in international relations', Rev. Hell. Droit Int., vol 8 (1955), pp 113-30

13.16 LAW-MAKING BY ORGANIZATIONS

In this section I have listed works dealing with the competence of organizations to bind their member states and to issue staff rules, rules of procedure and to make financial regulations. The matter has attracted renewed attention since the legislative processes of the European Communities have been in focus. Some of the works listed below, like my own book on law-making, seek to cover organizations, even the communities by inserting them in categories according to their complexity. Others like MALINTOPPI, only deal with 'recommendations' which may, or may not, contribute to law-making. Two recent works merit some attention: that by ALEXANDROWICS and that by YEMIN. However, both are restricted to dealing with the specialized agencies and the UN, whereas the apex of law-making by

organization is the European Communities. The work by
YEMIN is well documented and is a scholarly work of
high standard.
See also Section 13.24.7.3 on resolutions of the General
Assembly, Section 5.6.3 on acts by international organizations as sources of international law. See also other
powers exercised by organizations, such as the treatymaking function in general Section 13.14, of the UN,
13.24.2.6 and of the European Communities, 13.24.3.
12.14.

ALEXANDROWICS, C H, The Law Making Function of
the Specialized Agencies of the United Nations
(Sydney: Angus and Robertson, 1973). 181 pp.

BODDA, G, I regolamenti degli enti autarchici
(Torino, 1932)

CAPOTORTI, F, 'Sulla competenza a stipulare degli
organi di unioni', Comun. & Stud., vol 7 (1955)

DETTER, Ingrid, Law Making by International Organizations (Stockholm, 1965)

GLAESNER, H J, 'Übertragung Rechtsetzender Gewalt
auf internationale Organisationen in der völkerrechtlichen Praxis', Die Öffentliche Verwaltung (1959)

JASPAR, E J E M H, La Compétence législative et
réglementaire des organes collectifs en droit de gens
(Liège, 1936)

MALINTOPPI, A, La raccomandazioni internazionali
(Milano, 1958)

MARTINEZ-USEROS, J, 'Naturaleza jurídica de los
preceptos reguladores de la actividad administrativa
internacional', Revista General de Legislación y
Jurisprudencia (1946)

MERLE, M, 'Le pouvoir réglementaire des institutions
internationales', Annu. Fr. Droit Int. (1958), pp 341-
60

MONACO, R, 'L'autonomia normative degli enti internazionali', in Scritti di dir. internaz. in onore di
Tomaso Perassi, vol 2 (1957), pp 135-68

NAGEL, H, 'Einige rechtsvergleichende Bemerkungen zu den Empfehlungen der Vereinten Nationen, des Europarates und des Nordischen Rates', Int. Recht & Dipl., vol 3 (1958), pp 223-35

SABA, H, 'L'activité quasi-législative des institutions spécialisées des Nations Unies', Acad. Droit Int. Recl. Cours, vol 111 (1964), pp 603-90

SCERNI, M, Saggio sulla natura giuridica delle norme emanate dagli organi creati con atti internazionali (Genova, 1930)

SCHEUNER, U, 'Die Rechtsetzungsbefugnis internationaler Gemeinschaften', in Völkerrecht und rechtliches Weltbild. Festschrift für Alfred Verdross (1961), pp 229-42

SCHLÄFEREIT, H, Rechtsetzung durch internationale Organisationen. Ein Beitrag zur Lehre von der Souveränität (Kiel, 1952)

SKUBISZEWSKI, K, Uchwały prawtwórcze organizacji międzynarodowych. Przegląd zagadnien i analiza wstępna (Poznan, 1965). 240 pp. (Law making resolutions of international organizations. Survey of problems and preliminary analysis). Summary in English

SKUBISZEWSKI, K, 'Enactment of law by international organizations', Br. Yearb. Int. Law, vol 41 (1965/6), pp 198-274

SKUBISZEWSKI, K, 'Forms of participation of international organizations in the law making powers', Int. Organ., vol 18 (1964), pp 790-805

TAMMES, A J P, 'Besluitvorming bij internationale organisatie', Rechtsgeleerd Magazijn Themis, nos 4-5 (1945/6), pp 485-511

VIRALLY, M, 'La valeur juridique des recommandations des organisations internationales', Annu. Fr. Droit Int. (1956), pp 66-97

YEMIN, Edward, Legislative Powers in the UN and the Specialized Agencies (Leiden, 1969)

See also

SEIDL-HOHENVELDERN, I, 'Rechtsbeziehungen zwischen Internationalen Organisationen und den einzelnen Staaten', Arch. Völkerrecht, vol 4 (1953), pp 30-58

13.17 REVISION OF CONSTITUTIONS

The revision of the constitution of an international organization could be thought to constitute a law-making function, see the works by DETTER and YEMIN listed in Section 13.16 and Sections 13.24.3.12 (on the European Communities) and 13.24.3.18 (on the OAS) On revision of the Charter see Section 13.24.2.3.2 and for revision of treaties in general see Section 7.13.10.2.

GOES v NATERS, M v d, 'La révision des traités supranationaux', Ned. Tijdschr. Int. Recht, vol 6 (1959), pp 120-31

HÖBERG-PETERSEN, B, 'Revisions-og aendrings bestemmelser i internationale organisations statututter', Nord. Tidsskr. Int. Ret, vol 36 (1966), pp 39-47

PHILLIPS, L H, 'Constitutional revision in the specialized agencies', Am. J. Int. Law, vol 62 (1968), pp 654-78

SCHWELB, E, 'The amending procedure of constitutions of international organizations', Br. Yearb. Int. Law, vol 31 (1954), pp 49-95

ZACKLIN, R, The Amendment of the Constitutive Instruments of the United Nations and Specialized Agencies (Leiden: Sijthoff, 1968). 216 pp.

13.18 EXERCISE OF POWER OF ORGANIZATIONS

See also Section 11 on responsibility.

FAWCETT, J E S, '"Détournement de pouvoir" by

international organizations', Br. Yearb. Int. Law, vol 33 (1957), pp 311-16

KRUSE, H, 'Implied powers and implied limitations', Arch. Völkerrechts, vol 4 (1953), pp 169-82

MEIER, G, 'Das Recht der internationaler Organisationen zur Schaffung und Bevollmachtigung eigener Organen', Arch. Völkerrechts, vol 12 (1964/5), pp 14-33

ROUTER-HAMERAY, Bernard, Les Compétences implicites des organisations internationales (Paris: L G D J, 1962). Bibliothèque de droit international, vol 25

13.19 EXCESS OF POWER OF ORGANIZATIONS

See also Section 11 on responsibility.

LAUTERPACHT, E, 'The legal effect of illegal acts of international organisations', Cambridge Essays in International Law. Essays in Honour of Lord MacNair (1965), pp 88-121

SEIDL-HOHENVELDERN, I, 'Die völkerrechtliche Haftung für Handlungen internationalen Organisationen im Verhältnis zu Nichtmitgliedstaaten', Österr. Z. Öff. Recht (1961)

13.20 RELATIONSHIP BETWEEN ORGANIZATIONS AND MUNICIPAL LAW

See also Section 3 on the relation between international law and internal law, Section 7.13.13 on the relation of treaties to internal law, and Section 13.24.3.12.18 on effect of acts of the European Communities in internal law.

AGO, Robert, 'International organizations and their functions in the field of internal activities of states', Nord. Tidsskr. Int. Ret, vol 27 (1957), pp 1-18

MOSLER, 'Internationale Organisationen und Staatsverfassung', in Festschrift für Hans Wehberg (Frankfurt, 1956)
SCHLUTER, Bernhard, Die Innerstaatliche Rechsstellung der internationalen Organisationen unter besonderer Berücksichtigung der Rechtslage in der Bundesrepublik Deutschland (Köln: Carl Heymanns Verlag, 1972). xiii + 200 pp.

13.21 MEMBERSHIP OF ORGANIZATIONS

See also Section 13.24.2.19 on membership of the UN, 7.5.3 on state succession, 7.5.5 on new states.
AKZIN, B, New States and International Organizations (Paris, 1955)
DECLEVA, M, 'La qualità di membro delle organizzazioni internazionali', Diritto Internazionale, vol 18 (1964), pp 187-250
DÖLL, B, Völkerrechtliche Kontinuitätsprobleme bei internationalen Organisationen (Berlin, 1967)
FEINBERG, N, 'Unilateral withdrawal from an international organization', Br. Yearb. Int. Law, vol 39 (1963), pp 189-219
HAHN, H J, 'Continuity in the law of international organization', Österr. Z. Öff. Recht, vol 13 (1964), pp 167-239
MOSLER, H, 'Die Aufnahme in internationale Organisationen', Z. Ausl. Öff. Recht & Völkerrecht, vol 19, p 275
SINGH, N, Termination of Membership of International Organisations (London: Stevens, 1958). 209 pp.
SOHN, L B, 'Expulsion or forced withdrawal from an international organization', Harvard Law Review, vol 77 (1964), pp 1381-425

13.22 NEW STATES AND ORGANIZATIONS

AKZIN, B, New States and International Organizations. A Report Prepared on behalf of the International Political Science Association (Paris: Unesco, 1955). 200 pp.

13.23 SANCTIONS OF ORGANIZATIONS

See also Section 9.6 on sanctions in general and 13.24.2.21 on sanctions of the UN
OLDENHAGE, G, Die Reaktionsmassnahmen internationaler Organisationen gegen Pflichtverletzungen ihrer Mitgliedstaaten (Rechtskarakter, Rechtsformen, Rechtsproblemen) (Göttingen, 1963)

13.24 PARTICULAR ORGANIZATIONS

13.24.1 LEAGUE OF NATIONS

ANDRASSY, J, 'La souveraineté de la Société des Nations', Acad. Droit Int. Recl. Cours, vol 61 (1937), pp 641-762
BOURGEOIS, Léon, Le Pacte de 1919 et la Société des Nations (Paris: Bibliothèque-Charpentier, 1919)
BOURGEOIS, Leon, L'oeuvre de la Societe des Nations (1920-23) (Paris: Payot, 1923). 456 pp.
BURTON, M E, 'The Assembly of the League of Nations', Thesis. Columbia University, 1941
CORBETT, P, 'What is the League of Nations', Br. Yearb. Int. Law, vol 5 (1924), pp 119-48
DAVIS, Harriet Eager, Pioneers in World Order. An American Appraisal of the League of Nations (New York: Columbia University Press, 1945). x + 272 pp.
ELES, G T, Le Principe de l'unanimité dans la Société des Nations et les exceptions de ce principe (Genève, 1935)

FEINBERG, 'L'exclusion de la Société des Nations et le principe de l'unanimité', Rev. Droit Int. Sci. Dipl. & Polit. (1955)

FOURES, R, Des développements apportés par la S D N à la notion de représentation étatique (Paris, 1939)

HILL, Martin, The Economic and Financial Organization of the League of Nations, a Survey of Twenty-five Years' Experience (Washington: Carnegie Endowment for International Peace, 1946). xv + 168 pp. (Studies in the administration of international law and organizations, no 6)

HOWARD-ELLIS, Charles, The Origin, Structure and Working of the League of Nations (London: Allen & Unwin, 1928). 528 pp.

KNUDSON, John Immanuel, A History of the League of Nations (Atlanta, Ga: T E Smith & Co, 1938). vi + 445 pp.

LEMOINE, G X, La Nature juridique de la Société des Nations (Paris, 1939)

MARBURG, Theodore, Development of the League of Nations Idea; Documents and Correspondence of Theodore Marburg (New York: Macmillan, 1932). 2 vols.

MARTIN, W, 'La nature juridique de la SDN des Nations', Rev. Droit Int., vol 3 (1929), pp 403-31

MATHIEU, M, 'L'évolution de l'idée de la Société des Nations', Thesis. Nancy, 1923. 268 pp

MORLEY, Felix, The Society of Nations: Its Organization and Constitutional Development (Washington: The Brookings Institution, 1932). 678 pp.

MYERS, Denys P, Handbook of the League of Nations: A Comprehensive Account of its Structure, Operation and Activities (Boston: World Peace Foundation, 1935). 411 pp.

NISOT, J, 'La structure juridique de la Société des Nations', J. Droit Int. (1928), pp 329-38

OPPENHEIM, L, 'Le caractère essentiel de la
  Société des Nations', Rev. Gén. Droit Int. Public,
  vol 26 (1919), pp 234-44
OTLET, Paul, Constitution mondiale de la Société des
  Nations. Le nouveau droit des gens (Genève, Edition
  Atar/Paris, Editions G Gres, 1917). 253 pp.
RAY, Jo, Commentaire du Pacte de la Société des
  Nations, (Paris: Sirey, 1930-35). 1 vol + 4 supp.
SCHIFFER, Walter, Répertoire des questions de droit
  international général exposées devant la Société des
  Nations, 1920-1940 (Genève: Geneva Research
  Centre, 1943)
SCHÜCKING, W, & WEHBERG, H, Die Satzung des
  Völkerbundes, 3rd edition (Berlin: Vahlen, 1931).
  794 pp.
SCHWARZENBERGER, Georg, The League of Nations
  and World Order: A Treatise on the Principle of
  Universality in the Theory and Practice of the
  League of Nations (London: Constable, 1936). xvii +
  191 pp.
WALTERS, Francis P, A History of the League of
  Nations (London: Oxford University Press, 1952).
  xxiv + 833 pp. 2 vols.
WILLIAMS, J F, 'The status of the League of Nations
  in international law', Int. Law Association, vol 34
  (1926), pp 675-95
YEPES, J M, & PEREIRA DA SILVA, F C,
  Commentaire théorique et pratique du pacte de la
  Société des Nations et des Statuts de l'Union
  panaméricaine (Paris, 1934-9). 3 vols.

13.24.2 UNITED NATIONS

13.24.2.1 HISTORY

BENTWICH, N, From Geneva to San Francisco: An
  Account of the International Organisation of the

New Order (London: Gollanez, 1946). 111pp.

BOURQUIN, Maurice, Vers une nouvelle Société des Nations (Neuchâtel, La Baconnière, 1945). 281 pp.

DAMALAS, B V, La Réorganisation de l'économie mondiale. Les tentatives infructueuses de la SDN et les efforts actuels de l'ONU (Paris: Presses universitaires de France, 1947). 525 pp.

GOLAY, P W, La Charte des Nations Unies et ses antécédents (New York, 1947). 215 pp. Thesis. Université de Bâle, Haute Faculté de Droit, 1945

RUSSELL, Ruth B, & MUTHER, Jeannette E, A History of the United Nations (Washington, 1958). 1140 pp.

13.24.2.2 UNITED NATIONS IN GENERAL

The standard work is the monograph by KELSEN
See also cases on UN law by SOHN listed under 1.4.2.

ARECHAGA, Jimenez de, Derecho constitucional de las Naciones Unidas (Madrid, 1958). 642 pp.

BARRAINE, R, La Réglementation des rapports internationaux et l'Organisation des Nations Unies, (Paris: Librairie générale de droit et de jurisprudence, 1946). 319 pp.

BINDSCHEDLER, R L, 'La délimitation des compétences des Nations Unies', Acad. Droit Int. Recl. Cours, vol 108 (1963), pp 312-422

BOBROV, R L, (The legal character of the United Nations), Sov. Ezheg. Mezhdunar. Prava (1959), pp 229-42. In Russian with an English summary

CHAUMONT, Ch, L'Organisation des Nations Unies, 2nd edition (Paris, 1959)

CHAUMONT, Ch, 'L'esprit conquérant des Nations Unies et l'extension de leur compétence', in Nations Unies, Chantiers de l'avenir, vol 2, pp 78-95

CHAUMONT, Ch, 'L'équilibre des organes politiques des Nations Unies et la crise de l'Organisation', Annu. Fr. Droit Int. (1965), pp 428-46

COHEN, Benjamin V, The United Nations: Constitutional Developments, Growth and Possibilities (Cambridge, Mass: Harvard University Press, 1961)

EVATT, Herbert Vere, The United Nations (London/Melbourne, 1948). 148 pp.

FAKHER, Hossein, The Relationships among the Principal Organs of the United Nations (Genève: Imprimerie Centrale, 1950). ix + 200 pp. (Université de Genève: Institut Universitaire des Hautes Etudes Internationales)

GOODRICH, L M, The United Nations (London: Stevens, 1960). x + 419 pp.

GROSS, Ernest A, The United Nations: Structure for Peace (New York: Harper & Brothers, 1962)

GUTTERIDGE, J A C, The United Nations in a Changing World (London: Manchester University Press/Dobbs Ferry, NY: Oceana, 1969). vii + 111 pp.

HALDERMAN, John W, The United Nations and the Rule of Law: Charter Development through the Handling of International Disputes and Situations (Dobbs Ferry, NY: Oceana, 1966). 248 pp.

HIGGINS, R, The Development of International Law through the Political Organs of the United Nations (London: Oxford University Press, 1963)

JIMENEZ DE ARECHAGA, E, Derecho constitucional de las Naciones Unidas (Madrid, 1958). 653 pp.

KELSEN, Hans, The Law of the United Nations (New York: Praeger, 1964). 994 pp.

KOPELMANAS, Lazare, L'organisation des Nations Unies, vol 1 'L'organisation constitutionnelle des Nations Unies', fasc. 1 'Les sources constitutionnelles de l'ONU' (Paris: Sirey, 1947). 327 pp.

NICHOLAS, H G, The United Nations as a Political Institution, 4th edition (London: Oxford University Press, 1971)

PFEIFENBERGER, W, Die Vereinten Nationen (Salzburg: Universitätsverlag Anton Pustet, 1971). 662 pp.
ROBINSON, J, 'Metamorphosis of the United Nations', Acad. Droit Int. Recl. Cours, vol 94 (1958), pp 493-592
ROSS, Alf, The United Nations: Peace and Progress (Totowa, NJ: The Bedminster Press, 1966)
SAYRE, P, 'United Nations law', Canadian Bar Review, vol 25 (1947), pp 809-22
SCHACHTER, O, 'The relation of law, politics and action in the United Nations', Acad. Droit Int. Recl. Cours, vol 109 (1963)
SCHACHTER, O, 'The quasi-judicial role of the Security Council and the General Assembly', Am. J. Int. Law, vol 58 (1964)
SCHEUNER, Ulrich, 'Eine Internationale Sicherungsmacht im Dienate der Vereinten Nationen', Z. Ausl. Öff. Recht & Völkerrecht, vol 19 (1959), pp 389-415
UDINA, M, L'Organizzazione delle Nazione Unite. Introduzione e Testi Annotati, 2nd edition (Padova: Cedam, 1973). xiii + 247 pp.
VALLAT, F, 'The General Assembly and the Security Council of the United Nations', Br. Yearb. Int. Law (1952), pp 63-105
VANDENBOSCH, Amry, & HOGAN, W N, The United Nations: Background, Organization, Functions, Activities (New York: McGraw-Hill, 1952; reissued by Greenwood Press, Westport Conn)
VERDROSS, Alfred von, 'Idées directrices de l'ONU', Acad. Droit Int. Recl. Cours, vol 83
VERGEZ, Henriquez Homero, Las Naciones Unidas (Ciudad Trujillo: Editora Arte y Cine, 1952). 321 pp.
VIRALLY, M, L'Organisation Mondiale (Paris: Armand Colin, 1972). 587 pp.
VISSCHER, P de, 'Observations sur le fondement et la mise en oeuvre du principe de la responsabilité de

l'ONU', Rev. Droit Int. & Droit Comp., vol 40 (1963), pp 165-76

WEISSBERG, Guenter, The International Status of the United Nations (London: Stevens, 1961). xii + 228 pp.

WRIGHT, Quincy, International Law and the United Nations (London: Asia Publishing House, 1960). 134 pp

WRIGHT, Q, 'The juridical personality of the United Nations', Am. J. Int. Law, vol 43 (1949), pp 509-16

13.24.2.3 CHARTER OF THE UN

The standard work is that by GOODRICH, HAMBRO and SIMONS. For conflicts between the Charter and other international agreements see MAROTTA RANGEL, listed under 7.13.13.5.

BENTWICH, Norman & MARTIN, Andrew, A Commentary on the Charter of the United Nations (London: Routledge & Kegan Paul, 1950)

BRIERLY, J L, 'The Covenant and the Charter', Br. Yearb. Int. Law (1946)

BRIERLY, J L, The Covenant and the Charter (London: Cambridge University Press, 1947)

EAGLETON, C, 'International law and the charter of the UN', Am. J. Int. Law, vol 39 (1945), p 751

GOODRICH, Leland M, HAMBRO, Edvard, & SIMONS, Anne Patricia, Charter of the United Nations, Commentary and Documents, 3rd edition (New York: Columbia University Press, 1969). 732 pp.

GROSS, L, 'The Charter of the United Nations and the Lodge Reservations', Am. J. Int. Law, (1947), p 534

GUTTERIDGE, J, The UN in a Changing World, International Law Association 1969

SCHWARZENBERGER, G, 'Report (of the) Committee on the review of the Charter of the United Nations', International Law Association, Edinburgh Conference,

1954 (London: International Law Association, 1954), p 98

ROSS, Alf, Constitution of the United Nations: Analysis of Structure and Function (Copenhagen: Ejnar Munksgaard, 1950). 236 pp.

RUSSELL, Ruth B, & MUTHER, Jeannette E, A History of the United Nations Charter (Washington, 1958). 1140 pp.

NEMOURS, A, La Charte des Nations Unies; étude comparative de la Charte avec: les propositions de Dumbarton Oaks, le Covenant de la Société des Nations, les conventions de La Haye, les propositions et doctrines inter-américaines (Port-au-Prince: Deschamps, 1945). 188 pp.

MENESES PALLARES, A, Carta y estructura de las Naciones Unidas; esquema del estatuto mundial (Quito: Casa de la Cultura Ecuatoriana, 1952). 368 pp.

13.24.2.3.1 INTERPRETATION OF THE CHARTER

See also Section 8.11 on the ICJ and Section 7.13.9.2 on interpretation of treaties.

BARNETT, S W, Interpretation of the UN Charter by the International Court of Justice (np 1958)

KOCOT, K, Sposoby interpretacji Karty Narodów Zjednoczonych. (Methods of interpreting the United Nations charter) (Warszawa, 1957). Summaries in Russian and French

MUSHKAT, M, 'De quelques problèmes relatifs à l'interprétation de la charte et aux transformations de structure des Nations Unies', Rev. Hell. Droit Int. vol 17 (1964), pp 240-80

'POLLUX', 'The interpretation of the Charter', Br. Yearb Int. Law, vol 23 (1946), pp 54-82

SCHACHTER, O, 'Interpretation of the Charter in the Political organs of the United Nations', in Law, State, and International Legal Order. Essays in

Honor of Hans Kelsen edited by S Engel & R A
Metall (Knoxville, Tenn: University of Tennessee
Press, 1964), pp 269-83

13.24.2.3.2 REVISION OF THE CHARTER

For revision of constitutions of organisations in general
see Section 13.17, and for revision of treaties see
Section 7.13.10.2.
AZCARRAGA, J L, de, La Carta de las Naciones Unidas
  y su possible reforma (Madrid, 1955)
CASTRÉN, E, 'Revision av Förenta Nationernas Stadga',
  Nord Tidsskr. Int. Ret (1955)
ENGEL, S, 'Procedures for the de facto revision of
  the Charter', Am. Soc. Int. Law Proc. (1965), pp
  108-16
GIRAUD, E, 'La révision de la Charte des Nations
  Unies', Acad. Droit Int. Recl. Cours, vol 90 (1956),
  pp 307-467
KONISHI, M, La Révision de la Charte des Nations
  Unies (Paris, 1967)
KOPAL, V, & MRAZEK, I, Otázka revise charty OSN
  (Praha, 1957)
MOROZOV, G I, 'O Novykh Planakh Revizii Ustava OON'
  (On new plans concerning the revision of the UN
  Charter) Sovetskoe Gosudarstvo i Pravo, vol 5 (1959),
  pp 116-24
Revision of the United Nations Charter: A Symposium.
  (Bombay: Oxford University Press, 1956). iii + 145
  pp.

13.24.2.4. LEGAL PERSONALITY OF THE UN

See Section 6.1 on personality in general and
Section 13.7 on personality of organizations.
WRIGHT, Q, 'The jural personality of the United
  Nations', Am. J. Int. Law (1949)

13.24.2.5 IMPLIED POWERS OF THE UN

Implied powers of organizations cannot be studied without reference to case law, for example, to the Reparation for Injuries Case, see for case law, Section 1.4.

KHAN, Rahmatullah, Implied Powers of the United Nations (Delhi: Vikas Publications, 1970). xii + 236 pp.

13.24.2.6 TREATY-MAKING POWER OF THE UN

The basic work is the monograph by KASME. Cf. Section 13.14 on treaty-making power of organisations in general.

CARROZ, J, & PROBST, Y, Personnalité juridique internationale et capacité de conclure des traités de l'ONU et des institutions spécialisées (Paris: Foulon, 1953). 91 pp.

KASME, Badr, La Capacité de l'Organisation des Nations Unies de conclure des traités (Paris: Pichon & Durand-Auzias, 1960). 214 pp. (Bibliothèque de droit international, vol 12)

LIANG, Y, 'The use of the term "acceptance" in United Nations treaty practice', Am. J. Int. Law, vol 44 (1950), pp 342-9

PARRY, C, 'The treaty-making power of the United Nations', Br. Yearb. Int. Law, (1949), p 108

PASZKOWSKI, M, (Origins of the treaty-making power of the United Nations), Państwo i Prawo, vol 17 (1962), pp 796-803. In Polish with English, French and Russian summaries

ROSENNE, S, 'United Nations treaty practice', Acad. Droit Int. Recl. Cours, vol 2 (1954), pp 275-444

13.24.2.7 THE GENERAL ASSEMBLY

13. 24. 2. 7. 1   COMPETENCE AND GENERAL

See also UN peacekeeping, Section 13. 24. 2. 22.

ALKER, Hayward R, & RUSSETT, Bruce M, World Politics in the General Assembly (New Haven, Conn: Yale University Press, 1965). 326 pp.

BAILEY, Sydney D, The General Assembly of the United Nations: A Study of Procedure and Practice, revised edition (New York: Praeger, 1964)

BOUSHEHRI, M, 'L'Assemblée générale de l'Organisation des Nations Unies et le règlement pacifique des conflits internationaux', Dissertation. Paris, 1952

BRUGIERE, P, Les Pouvoirs de l'Assemblée générale des Nations Unies en matière politique et de sécurité (Paris, 1955). 431 pp.

CHU TZE-FEN, 'La compétence de l'Assemblée générale des Nations Unies', Thesis. Paris, 1952. 101 pp.

KOLASA, J, Rules of Procedure of the United Nations General Assembly. A Legal Analysis (Wrocław, 1967)

LADAME, Paul-Alexis, 'L'Assemblée Générale des Nations Unies', Thesis. Université de Genève. Institut Universitaire des Hautes Etudes Internationales

LANG, Y, 'The General Assembly and the progressive development of international law', Am. J. Int. Law', vol 42 (1948), p 66

LIANG, Y, 'Methods and procedures of the General Assembly dealing with the legal and drafting questions', Am. J. Int. Law, vol 47 (1953), pp 70-83

RAZI, M, 'La compétence de l'Assemblée Générale de l'Organisation des Nations Unies, Essai d'une distinction entre les pouvoirs de recommandation et les pouvoirs de décision de l'Assemblée', Dissertation. Genève, IHEI, 1951

VALLAT, F A, The Competence of the United Nations General Assembly, Acad. Droit Int. Recl. Cours, vol 97 (1959), pp 203-92

13.24.2.7.2 UNITING FOR PEACE RESOLUTION

ANDRASSY, J, 'Uniting for peace', Am. J. Int. Law (1956)
JOHNSON, 'The uniting for peace resolution', Annual Review of the UN Affairs (1951), pp 239-53
WOOLSEY, L H, 'The uniting for peace resolution', Am. J. Int. Law (1951), pp 129-37

13.24.2.7.3 EFFECT OF RESOLUTIONS OF THE GENERAL ASSEMBLY

There has been some discussion on whether the resolutions or, technically, 'recommendations' of the General Assembly are 'binding' or whether they produce some other legal effects for the addressees. On this controversial subject see DETTER and YEMIN listed in Section 13.16 and also:
ASAMOAH, O, 'The legal effects of resolutions of the General Assembly', Columbia Journal of Transnational Law, vol 3 (1965), pp 210-30
ASAMOAH, O Y, The Legal Significance of the Declarations of the General Assembly of the United Nations (Den Haag: Nijhoff, 1966) xvii + 274 pp.
CASTAÑEDA, Jorge, Legal Effects of United Nations Resolutions (New York: Columbia University Press, 1969). 243 pp.
CASTAÑEDA, Jorge, 'Valeur juridique des résolutions des Nations Unies', Acad. Droit Int. Recl. Cours, vol 129 (1970), pp 205-332
FALK, R A, 'On the quasi legislative competence of the G A', Am. J. Int. Law, vol 60 (1966), pp 782-91

IVRAKIS, S, 'The regulation making power of the United Nations', Rev. Hell. Droit Int., vol 9 (1956), pp 80-92
JOHNSON, D H N, 'The effect of resolutions of UN General Assembly', Br. Yearb. Int. Law (1955/6)
LANDE, G R, 'The changing effectiveness of General Assembly resolutions', Am. Soc. Int. Law Proc., vol 58 (1964), pp 162-73
MALINTOPPI, A, 'Il valore delle raccomandazioni adottate da conferenze delle Nazioni Uniti', Riv. Diritto Int., vol 44 (1961), pp 604-23
MARCOVITCH, L, 'L'ONU et la vote des lois internationales', Rev. Gén. Droit Int. Public, vol 57 (1953), pp 55-72
PANEBIANCO, M, 'Raccomandazioni delle Nazioni Unite e libertà degli stati membri', Annuario di diritto internazionale (1966), pp 268-90
PIOTROWSKI, G, Les résolutions de l'Assemblée Générale des Nations Unies et la portée du droit conventionnel. I', Rev. Droit Int. Sci. Dipl. & Polit., vol 33 (1955), pp 111-25
SLOAN, F B, 'The binding force of a recommendation of the General Assembly of the UN', Br. Yearb. Int. Law (1948)
QUAL, Lino Di, Les Effets des resolutions des Nations Unies (Paris; Librairie générale de droit et de jurisprudence, 1967). x + 283 pp (Bibliothèque de Droit International, vol 37.)
VERDROSS, A, 'Kann die Generalversammlung der Vereinten Nationen das Völkerrecht weiterbilden?' Z. Ausl. Öff. Recht & Völkerrecht, vol 26 (1966), p 690

13.24.2.8 SECURITY COUNCIL

See further, peacekeeping by the UN in Section 13.24.2.22 and settlement of disputes in Section 8.

ARECHAGA, Jimenez de, 'Le traitement des différends internationaux par le Conseil de Sécurité', Acad. Droit Int. Recl. Cours, vol 85 (1954)
BAILEY, Sydney D, Voting in the Security Council (Bloomington, Ind: Indiana University Press, 1969). 275 pp.
BOYD, Andrew, Fifteen Men on a Powder Keg. A History of the UN Security Council (London: Methuen, 1971). 383 pp.
FLORY, M, 'L'ONU et les opérations de maintien de la paix', Annu. Fr. Droit Int. (1965), pp 446-67
GENTILE, F C, 'Competenza del Consiglio di Sicurezza et del Assemblea generale in materia di mantenimento o ristabilimento delle pace', Comun. & Stud., vol 5 (1953), pp 285-354
KAHNG, Tae Jin, Law, Politics, and the Security Council. An Inquiry into the Handling of Legal Questions Involved in International Disputes and situations, 2nd edition (Den Haag: Nijhoff, 1969). 268 pp.
KERLEY, E L, 'The powers of investigation of the Security Council', Am. J. Int. Law (1961), p 892
SCHACHTER, O, 'The quasi judicial role of the Security Council and the General Assembly', Am. J. Int. Law (1964), pp 960-5

13.24.2.9 VOTING IN THE UN

See also sections on voting in organizations in general (13.10) and voting in the European Communities (13.24.3.12.8). Discussions on voting in the world organization have usually centred round the right of veto in the Security Council and the so-called double veto.
DAY, G, Le Droit de veto dans l'Organisation des Nations Unies (Paris: Pédone, 1952). 238 pp.

GROSS, E A, 'The question of Laos and the double veto in the Security Council', Am. J. Int. Law (1960), pp 118-31

GROSS, L, 'Voting in the Security Council: abstention from voting and absence from meetings', Yale Law Journal, vol 60 (1951), p 209

McDOUGAL, M S, & GARDNER, R N, 'The veto and the Charter: an interpretation for survival', Yale Law Journal, vol 60 (1951), pp 258-92. Also in Studies in World Public Order by M S McDougal et al. (New Haven, Conn: Yale University Press, 1960), p 718

RUDZINSKI, A, 'The so-called double veto', Am. J. Int. Law (1951)

VALLAT, F A, 'Voting in the General Assembly of the United Nations', Br. Yearb. Int. Law, vol 31 (1954), p 273

WISE, R L, 'Veto cannot bar UN General Assembly from establishing a peace keeping force', American Bar Association Journal, vol 51 (1965), pp 1169-72

13.24.2.10   UN AND DOMESTIC JURISDICTION

The UN is not entitled to deal with 'internal matters' or matters within the domestic jurisdiction of a state unless there is a threat to international peace and security. On what matters are sheltered behind the wall of domestic jurisdiction see below and, also, Sections 8.9.3 (on domestic jurisdiction and international tribunals), 8.11.9 (on domestic jurisdiction and the ICJ), 9.8 (on intervention) and 13.24.2.22 (on UN peacekeeping).

RAJAN, M S, United Nations and Domestic Jurisdiction, 2nd edition (London: Asia Publishing House, 1961). 539 pp.

13.24.2.11 ECOSOC

DELBEZ, L, 'Les pouvoirs du ECOSOC des Nations Unies', in Etudes Scelle, vol 1

FINER, Herman, The United Nations Economic and Social Council (Boston: World Peace Foundation, 1946). 121 pp.

SHARP, Walter, The United Nations Economic and Social Council (New York: Columbia University Press, 1969). 322 pp.

13.24.2.12 SECRETARIAT

BAILEY, Sydney D, The Secretariat of the United Nations (New York: Carnegie Endowment for International Peace, 1964). 128 pp.

BIRNBAUM, Karl E, 'Hammarskjöld and die Funktionen der Vereinigten Nationen wahrend der Kongo-Krise', Europa Archiv, vol 17 (1962), pp 533-48

EEK, H, 'The Secretariat as a principal organ of the United Nations', Nord. Tidsskr. Int. Ret (1953)

GORDENKER, Leon, The UN Secretary-General and the Maintenance of Peace (New York: Columbia University Press, 1967). 380 pp.

KOUZBARI, 'Les pouvoirs politiques du Secrétaire Général des Nations Unies', Dissertation. Paris, 1959

LANGROD, G, 'Le Secrétariat de l'Organisation des Nations Unies', AVR (1956)

ROVINE, Arthur W, The First Fifty Years, the Secretary General in World Politics 1920-1970 (Leiden: Sijthoff, 1970)

SCHACHTER, O, 'The development of international law through the legal opinions of the UN Secretariat', Br. Yearb. Int. Law (1948), pp 91-132

FOCSANEANU, L, 'Le droit interne de l'ONU', Annu. Fr. Droit Int. (1957), pp 315-49
VIRALLY, M, 'Le rôle politique du Secrétaire général des Nations Unies', Annu. Fr. Droit Int. (1958), pp 360-99

13.24.2.13 TRUSTEESHIP COUNCIL, MANDATES AND TRUSTEESHIP AGREEMENTS

Although the problem of mandates could have been treated above under the League of Nations where, chronologically, they belong, I have thought it more convenient for a reader to find material on such mandates in this section, which primarily deals with trusteeship matters of the UN, to which most mandate questions are, of course, intimately linked.

BADIALI, G, 'La struttura dell'accordo di amministrazione fiduciaria e il problema degli "Stati direttamente interessanti"', Comun. & Stud., vol 9 (1957), pp 73-115

CAPOTORTI, F, 'Natura e carretteri degli accordi di amministrazione fiduciaria', Riv. Diritto Int., vol 38 (1955), pp 185-228; 457-513

CHOWDHURI, R N, International Mandates and Trusteeship Systems, A Comparative Study (Den Haag, 1955). 328 pp.

DUNCAN HALL, H, Mandates Dependencies and Trusteeships (London: Stevens, 1948)

GROSS, L, 'United Nations trusteeship and League of Nations mandate systems', India Quarterly, vol 4, (1948), pp 224-40

LEROY, P, 'La nature juridique des accords de tutelle', Rev. Gen. Droit Int. Public, vol 69 (1965), pp 977-1018

MARSTON, G, 'Termination of trusteeship', Int. & Comp. Law Q., vol 18 (1969), p 1

PARRY, C, 'The legal nature of trusteeship agreements', Br. Yearb. Int. Law, vol 27 (1950), pp 164-85

SAYRE, F B, 'Legal problems arising from the United Nations trusteeship system', Am. J. Int. Law, (1948)

THULLEN, George, Problems of the Trusteeship System: A Study of Political Behaviour in the United Nations (Gèneve, 1964). 217 pp.

TOUSSAINT, C E, The Trusteeship System of the UN (London, 1956)

VEDOVATO, G, 'Les accords de tutelle', Acad. Droit Int. Recl. Cours, vol 76 (1950), pp 609-700

See also

DUGARD, J, 'The revocation of the mandate for South West Africa', Am. J. Int. Law, vol 62 (1968), pp 78-97

HIGGINS, Rosalyn, 'The advisory opinion on Namibia: which UN resolutions are binding under article 25 of the Charter?' Int. & Comp. Law Q., vol 21 (1972), p 270

SLONIM, S, South West Africa and the United Nations: An International Mandate in Dispute (Baltimore, Md: Johns Hopkins Press, 1973). xiv + 409 pp.

13.24.2.14 SUBSIDIARY ORGANS OF THE UN

13.24.2.14.1 TAB AND TECHNICAL ASSISTANCE

There is one standard work on technical assistance:

FEUER, G, Les Aspects juridiques de l'assistance technique dans le cadre des Nations Unies et des institutions specialisées (Paris, 1957)

13. 24. 2. 14. 2 DEVELOPMENT AID

ALTHEIM, F, Entwicklungshilfe im Altertum. Die
  großen Reiche und ihre Nachbarn (Reinbek, 1962)
BAADE, H, Handbuch der Entwicklungshilfe
  (Baden-Baden/Bonn, 1960)
MEYER-CORDING, U, 'Regionalpolitik und
  Entwicklungshilfe durch die europäische Investitions-
  bank', Vortrag am 22.11.1965 vor dem Industrie-
  Club Düsseldorf

13. 24. 2. 14. 3 THE ECONOMIC
                 COMMISSIONS OF THE UN

GREGG, Robert W, 'The UN Regional Commissions and
  integration in the underdeveloped regions', Int.
  Organ., vol 20 (1966), pp 208-32
MAGEE, James S, 'ECA and the paradox of African
  cooperation', Int. Conciliation, no 580 (November
  1970). 64 pp.
MYRDAL, Gunnar, 'Twenty years of the United Nations
  Economic Commission for Europe', Int. Organ.,
  vol 22 (1968), pp 617-28
SIOTIS, Jean, 'The Secretariat of the United Nations
  Economic Commission for Europe and European
  economic integration, the first ten years', Int.
  Organ., vol 19 (1965), pp 177-202
SIOTIS, Jean, 'ECE in the emerging European system',
  Int. Conciliation, no 561 (January 1967). 72 pp.
WIGHTMAN, D, Economic Co-operation in Europe - A
  Study of the United Nations Economic Commission for
  Europe (London, 1956)
WIGHTMAN, D, Toward Economic Co-operation in Asia
  The United Nations Economic Commission for Asia
  and the Far East (New Haven, Conn: Yale University
  Press, 1963). 400 pp.

13.24.2.14.4   INTERNATIONAL
               LAW COMMISSION

See also Section 1.1.
BRIGGS, Herbert W, The International Law
  Commission (Ithaca, NY: Cornell University Press,
  1965). 380 pp.

13.24.2.14.5   UNCTAD

EL-NAGGAR, S, 'The United Nations Conference on
  Trade and Development', Acad. Droit Int. Recl.
  Cours, vol 128 (1969), pp 241-346
HAGRAS, Kamal M, United Nations Conference on Trade
  and Development: A Case Study in UN Diplomacy
  (New York: Praeger, 1965). 171 pp.

13.24.2.15   INTERNAL LAW OF THE UN

Some have written on the 'internal' law of the UN and below I mention one monograph and an article on this subject. It may be pointed out that not all writers agree that it is helpful to distinguish 'internal' law. Staff rules and rules of procedure are most adequately studied in connection with financial regulations but the latter, at least some of them, are not 'internal' as they are addressed to the member states. I have suggested in my Law Making, listed in Section 13.16, that acts of organizations are more appropriately classified as primary (those necessary in any organization, e.g., on staff, procedure and finance) and operative acts (those which differ from each organization according to their objective and purpose).
DURANTE, F, L'ordinamento interno delle Nazione
  Unite (Milano, 1964)
FOCSANEANU, L, 'Le droit interne de l'Organisation
  des Nations Unies', Annu. Fr. Droit Int. (1957)

13.24.2.16 FINANCES OF THE UN

See Section 13.11 on budgetary questions in general
BISHOP, P V, 'Canada's policy on the financing of UN peace keeping operations', International Journal (Canada), vol 20 (1965), pp 463-83
GROSS, E A, 'Expenses of the UN for peace keeping operations: The advisory opinion of the ICJ', Int. Organ. (1963), pp 1-36
MOROZOV, 'Behind the UN financial crisis', Int. Aff. (USSR), (June 1964), pp 23-9
SALMON, A, 'Aspects juridiques des difficultés financières de l'ONU', Cours Institut des Hautes Etudes Internationales, 1963-4
SINGER, J David, Financing International Organization: The United Nations Budget Process (Den Haag: Nijhoff, 1961)
SOMMER, The Finances of the United Nations (Zürich, 1951)
STOESSINGER, J B, Financing of UN Peace and Security Operations (Washington, DC: The Brookings Institution, 1962)
STOESSINGER, John, Financing the United Nations System (Washington, DC: The Brookings Institution, 1964)

13.24.2.17 HEADQUARTER AGREEMENTS OF THE UN

See headquarter agreements of organizations in general in Section 13.12.
BRANDON, M, 'The legal status of the premises of the UN', Br. Yearb. Int. Law, vol 28 (1950), pp 90-113

13.24.2.18 PRIVILEGES AND IMMUNITIES OF THE UN

See also privileges of organizations in general in Section 13.12 and Section 7.10 on immunity.

BOGDANOV, O V, Pravovye voprosy prebyvanitya OON v SSH A (Privilegii i immounity OON)', (Moscow, 1962). (Legal questions of the presence of the UN in the USA - privileges and immunities of the UN)

LIANG, Y, 'The legal status of the United Nations in the United States', Int. Law Q., vol 2 (1948), pp 577-602

13.24.2.19 MEMBERSHIP OF TIIE UN

See also membership of organizations in general in Section 13.21

BRIGGS, H W, 'Membership in the proposed general international organization', Am. J. Int. Law, vol 39 (1945), p 101

GORDON, F, Advisory Opinion - Admission to Membership in the United Nations', Michigan Law Review (1949)

HUMBER, P O, 'Admission to the United Nations', Br. Yearb. Int. Law (1947)

KATZAROV, C, 'Die Stellung der Nichtmitglieder der Vereinten Nationen', Arch. Völkerrechts (1951) pp 1-22

SHOU-SHENG-HSUEH, 'L'ONU et les états non-membres', Thesis. Gèneve, 1953

SÖDER, J, Die Vereinten Nationen und die Nichtmitglieder (Bonn, 1956)

SPERDUTI, G, 'Il principo della buona fede et l'ammissione di nuovi membri nelle Nazione Unite', La Communite Internazionale (1952), p 42

TOBIASSEN, Lief Kr, The Reluctant Door. The Right of Access to the United Nations (Washington, DC: Public Affairs Press, 1969). vi + 413 pp.

13.24.2.20 UN AND NON-MEMBERS

See also treaties and third states in Section 7.13.14 and the European Communities and third states in Section 13.24.3.12.15.
HSUEH, S S, L'Organisation des Nations Unies et les états non membres (Ambilly, 1953)
KATZAROV, C, 'Die Stellung der Nichtmitglieder der Vereinigten Nationen', Arch. Völkerrechts (1955/6), p 5
SÖDER, J, Die Vereinigten Nationen und die Nichtmitglieder, Zum Problem der Weltstaatenordnung (Bonn, 1956)

13.24.2.21 UN SANCTIONS

See also sanctions in general in Section 9.6.
CAVARE, L, 'Les sanctions dans le cadre de l'ONU', Acad. Droit Int. Recl. Cours (1952), pp 191-291
COHEN, B V, 'Principles governing the imposition of sanctions under the United Nations charter', Am. Soc. Int. Law Proc. (1951), pp 153-9

13.24.2.22 UN PEACEKEEPING

See also Sections 13.24.2.10 (on the UN and domestic jurisdiction), 13.24.2.8 (on the Security Council), 13.24.2.7.2 (on the Uniting for peace resolution), 9.8 (on intervention) and 9.13 (on blockade). Works on military and political aspects are excluded.
ALESSI, 'L'evoluzione della prassi delle NU relative al mantenimento della pace', Riv. Diritto Int. (1964), pp 519-65

BHUTTO, Z A, Peace-keeping by the United Nations (Karachi, 1967)
BROOK, D, Preface to Peace: The UN and the Arab Israel Armistice System', (Washington, 1964)
CAVARE, L, 'Les sanctions dans le cadre de l'Organisation des Nations Unies', Acad. Droit Int. Recl. Cours, vol 1 (1952), pp 191-291
CLAUDE, Inis, 'The United Nations and the Use of Force', Int. Conciliation (March 1961)
DEHAUSSY, J, 'La crise du Moyen-Orient et l'ONU', J. Droit Int., no 4, (1968), pp 853-88
FABRI, 'Le misure provisorie nel sisteme di sicurezza delle Nazioni Unite', Riv. Diritto Int. (1964), p 186
FLORY, M, 'L'organisation des Nations Unies et les opérations de maintien de paix', Annu. Fr. Droit Int. (1965), pp 446-68
GOODRICH, & SIMONS, A P, The United Nations and the Maintenance of International Peace and Security (Washington, 1957)
GREEN, 'United action for peace', Int. Law Q. (April 1951), pp 216-19
GROSS, E A, The United Nations: Structure for Peace (New York, 1962)
HIGGINS, Rosalyn, United Nations Peacekeeping 1946-1967. Documents and Commentary (London: Oxford University Press, 1969-70). 2 vols. Vol 1 'The Middle East', vol 2 'Asia'
ISENBURG, M, 'L'uso della forza da parte della Nazioni Unite', Thesis. University of Milan, 1961
KARAOSMANOGLU, A L, Les Actions militaires coercitives et non coercitives des Nations Unies (Genève: Droz, 1970)
KHAN, 'Peace keeping powers of the UN General Assembly', Int. Aff. (UK) (1965), pp 317-32
LANGENHOVE, Fernand van, La Crise du système de sécurité collective des Nations Unies (Den Haag, 1958)

MANIN, Philippe, L'Organisation des Nations Unies et le maintien de la paix. Le respect du consentement de l'état (Paris: Librairie Générale de Droit et de Jurisprudence, 1971). iv + 343 pp.

SELIGMAN, Eustace, 'The legality of US quarantine action under the United Nations Charter', American Bar Association Journal, vol 49 (1963), p 142

SOHN, L B, 'Authorization of the United Nations to maintain and establish peace and security', Am. J. Int. Law (1958)

SPATAFORA, 'Gli interventi collettivi delle NU e il parere della CIJ', Riv. Diritto Int. (1964), p 23

TANDON, Y, 'Consensus and authority behind United Nations peacekeeping operations', Int. Organ, vol 21 (1967), pp 254-83

ZICCARDI, P, 'L'intervento collettivo delle Nazioni Unite e nuovi poteri del Assemblea generale', Comunità internazionale (1957), p 223

13.24.2.23 UN FORCES

In this section I have gathered some of the most important works on the UN forces and UN factfinding commissions. I have also included reference works on the Korean affair although to many it was not UN forces who acted in that instance but collective forces under US command as the Security Council could not validly have taken a decision to intervene in the absence of one permanent member, the USSR. On this legality, see DETTER, Law Making, listed in Section 13.16. Among the numerous works on the UN forces those by BOWETT and SEYERSTED listed below are basic. See also Rosalyn HIGGINS's book listed in Section 13.24.2.22.

ARMSTRONG, 'The UN experience in Gaza', Foreign Affairs (1957), p 600

ATTIA, Gamal el Din, 'Les forces armées des NU en Corée et au Moyen-Orient', Thesis. Genève, 1963

BASTID, S, 'L'action militaire franco-britannique en Egypte et le droit des Nations Unies', in Mélanges Gidel, p 49

BENTON, Wilbourn E, 'United Nations action in the Suez crisis', in Tulane Studies in Political Science, vol 4 'International law and the Middle East crisis', (New Orleans: Tulane University Press, 1957)

BOWETT, D W, with the assistance and collaboration of G P BARTON, etc. United Nations Forces: A Legal Study of United Nations Practice (London: Stevens, 1964)

BUIL, O, 'De Forente Nasjoners Observatorgruppe i Lebanon i 1958', Norsk Militaert Tidsskrift, vol 129 (1959), pp 543-70

BURNS, & HEATHCOTE, Peace keeping by UN Forces: from Suez to the Congo (London, 1963)

CHAUMONT, Ch, 'La situation juridique des états membres à l'égard de la Force d'urgence des Nations Unies', Annu. Fr. Droit Int. (1958), pp 399-439

DALE, T, 'Sikkerhetsstyrker for FN', Norsk Militaert Tidsskrift, vol 134 (1964), pp 540-51

DRAPER, G, 'The legal limitation upon the employment of weapons by the UN forces in the Congo', Int. & Comp. Law Q. (1963), pp 387-413

ESPERSON, O, FN - styrker i retlig belysning (Copenhagen, 1965)

FLORY, M, 'La Mission d'information des Nations Unies au Yémen', Annu Fr. Droit Int. (1963), pp 612-26

FLORY, M, 'Force internationale des Nations Unies et pacification intérieure de Chypre', Annu. Fr. Droit Int. (1964), pp 458-78

FLORY, M, 'Le retrait de la Force d'urgence des Nations Unies', Annu. Fr. Droit Int. (1968) pp 377-88

FRANKESTEIN, L'ONU devant le conflit coréen (Paris: Pédone, 1952)
FRYE, W R, A UN Peace Force (New York, 1957)
GOODRICH, L M, 'Korea, collective measures', Int. Conciliation (October 1953)
GOODRICH, & ROSNER, G, 'The United Nations Emergency Force', Int. Organ.(1957), pp 413-30
HALDERMAN, J W, 'Legal basis for UN armed forces', Am. J. Int. Law (1962), pp 971-96
HOFFMANN, S, 'The UN in the Congo labyrinth', Int. Organ. (1962), pp 331-61
HOLMES, 'The United Nations in the Congo', International Journal (Canada), vol 16, no 1
JOHNSON, 'The Korean question and the UN', Nord. Tidsskr. Int. Ret, vol 26 (1956)
KRIVITCHKOVA, E S, Vooroujennye sily OON (Mezdhunarodnopravovye voprossy) (Moscow, 1965). (Armed forces of the UN. Questions on international law)
LACHARRIERE, Guy de, 'La polémique sur les opérations de maintien de la paix des Nations Unies', Politique Etrangère (1966), pp 319-35
LAUTERPACHT, Elihu, (ed), The UN Emergency Force: Basic Documents (London: British Institute of International and Comparative Law, 1960)
LECLERCQ, C, L'ONU et l'affaire du Congo (Paris: Payot, 1964)
LOURIE, 'The UN military observer group in India and Pakistan', Int. Organ. (February 1955), pp 19-32
MILLER, Schachter, ' Legal aspects of United Nations in Congo', Am. J. Int. Law (1961), pp 1-29
O'BRIEN, C C, Mission au Katanga (Paris, 1964)
POIRIER, P, 'La Force internationale d'urgence', Thesis. Paris, 1962
POTTER, P B, 'Legal aspects of the situation in Korea', Am. J. Int. Law (1950), p 709

RIAD, A, 'The UN action in the Congo and its legal basis', Revue égyptienne de droit international, vol 17 (1961)
RIKHYE, General, 'UN operations in Congo', Foreign Affairs (July 1962), pp 552-61
ROSNER, Gabriella, The United Nations Emergency Force (New York: Columbia University Press, 1963)
RUSSEL, R B, UN Experience with Military Forces: Political and Legal Aspects (Washington Institute for Defence Analysis, paper 27)
SCHACHTER, O, 'Preventing the internationalization of international conflict, a legal analysis of the UN Congo experience', Am. Soc. Int. Law Proc. (1963)
SEYERSTED, F, 'United Nations forces: some legal problems', Br. Yearb. Int. Law, (1961), pp 351-476
SEYERSTED, F, United Nations Forces in the Law of Peace and War (Leiden, 1966)
SOHN, L B, 'The authority of the United Nations to establish and maintain a permanent UN force', Am. J. Int. Law (1958), p 229
VIRALLY, M, 'Les Nations Unies et l'affaire du Congo', Annu. Fr. Droit Int. (1960), pp 557-97
WRIGHT, Q, 'Legal aspects of the Congo situation', experience', Am. Soc. Int. Law Proc. (1951), p 165
WRIGHT, 'Legal aspects of the Congo situation', Quarterly Journal of the Indian School of International Studies (July 1962), pp 1-23

13.24.2.24   THE SPECIALIZED AGENCIES

13.24.2.24.1   GENERAL

ADAM, H T, Les Organismes internationaux spécialisés. Contribution à la theorie générale des établissements publics internationaux (Paris, 1965-67). 3 vols.
BECKEL, Graham, Workshops for the World: the Specialized Agencies of the United Nations (New York: Abelard-Schuman, 1954). 213 pp.

BLAU, G, 'Les institutions specialisées', Rev. Gén. Droit Int. Public, vol 51 (1947), pp 155-71
LABEYRIE-MENAHEM, C, Des Institutions specialisées. Problèmes juridiques et diplomatiques de l'administration internationale (Paris: Pédone, 1953). 168 pp.
MALINTOPPI, A, 'Gli istituti specializzati e la loro posizione respetto all'ONU', Riv. Diritto Int., vol 45 (1962), pp 217-36
PAUW, F de, 'De gespecialiseerde organisaties van de Verenigde Naties', Rechtskundig Weekblad, 25 (1962, no 39) cols 2001-10
SCHERMERS, H G, De Gespecialiseerde Organisaties, hun bouw en inrichting (Leiden, 1957). 221 pp.

13.24.2.24.2 EXTERNAL RELATIONS

See also, treaty-making power of organizations in general in Section 13.14
FRIED, J H E, 'Relations between the UN and the ILO' American Political Science Review, vol 41 (1947), pp 963-77
LAWRENCE, W Ph D, 'Operational relationships among the United Nations specialized agencies', Rev. Droit Int. Sci. Dipl. & Polit., vol 43 (1965), pp 151-62
SHARP, W S, 'Agreements between the United Nations and the specialized agencies', Int. Organ., vol 1 (1947), pp 460-74; vol 2 (1948), pp 247-67

13.24.2.24.3 UNIVERSAL POSTAL UNION (UPU)

BLAYAC, Raoul, 'Origine, évolution et organisation de l'Union postale universelle', Thesis. Université de Montpellier, 1932
CODDING, G A, Jr, The Universal Postal Union: Coordinator of the International Mails (New York: New York University Press, 1964)

MENON, M A K, 'Universal Postal Union', Int. Conciliation, no 552 (March 1965). 64 pp.

MIR ESKANDARI, A N, 'L'institution internationale specialisée des PTT (UPU)', Thesis. Université de Paris, Faculté de Droit, 1951

SCHEUFFLER, H, 'Die Ratifikationen im Weltpostverein', L'Union postale, vol 67, no 11 (November 1942), pp 260-90; Z. Völkerrecht, vol 24 (1940), pp 50-69. With translations into French, English and Spanish

SCHRÖDER, Carl, Der Weltpostverein. Geschichte seiner Gründung und Entwicklung in 25 Jahren (Bern: Wyss, 1900). 341 pp.

SLY, John F, 'The genesis of the Universal Postal Union. A study in the beginnings of international organization', Int. Conciliation, no 223 (1927), pp 395-443

13.24.2.24.4 INTERNATIONAL TELE-
COMMUNICATIONS UNION (ITU)

See also telecommunications by satellite in Section 7.9.5.2.

CODDING, George A, The International Telecommunication Union: An Experiment in International Cooperation (Leiden: Brill, 1952). 505 pp.

EVENSEN, Jens, 'Aspects of international law relating to modern radio communications', Acad. Droit Int. Recl. Cours, vol 115 (1965), pp 477-583

GLAZER, J, Henry, 'The law making treaties of the International Telecommunications Union through time and in space', Michigan Law Review, vol 60 (1962), p 290

LOIVE, David M, International Telecommunications and International Law: the Regulation of the Radiospectrum (Leiden: Sijthoff/Dobbs Ferry, NY: Oceana, 1970). 386 pp.

JASENTULIYANA, 'Regulatory functions of ITU in the field of space telecommunications', Journal of Air Law and Commerce, vol 34 (1968), p 62

STERKY, Håkan, 'Past, present and future telecommunication standardization', Journal UIT (December, 1954), no 12, pp 202e-212e

WILDBOLZ, H, Die Rechtsnatur der Weltnachrichtenverein (Bern, 1946). 118 pp.

13.24.2.24.5 INTERNATIONAL LABOUR ORGANIZATION (ILO)

On the ILO Administrative Tribunal see Section 8.12.3.

13.24.2.24.5.1 GENERAL

ALCOCK, Antony, History of the International Labour Organisation (London: Macmillan Press, 1971). 384 pp.

ARGENTIER, Claude, Les Résultats acquis par l'Organisation permanente du travail de 1919 à 1929 (Paris: Sirey, 1930) xvii + 592 pp.

BARNES, George Nicoll, History of the International Labour Office (London: Williams & Norgate, 1926). xvi+106 pp.

DAHL, Karl Nandrup, 'Kontrollen med gjennomføringen av ILO standarder', TfR, vol 78 (1965), pp 480-95

FISCHER, Georges, Les Rapports entre l'Organisation internationale du travail et la cour permanente de justice internationale. Contribution à l'étude du problème de la séparation des pouvoirs dans le domaine international (Paris: Pédone, 1946). 388 pp.

FOLLOWS, John W, Antecedents of the International Labour Organisation (Oxford: Clarendon Press, 1951). x + 234 pp.

GUERREAU, Maurice, Une Nouvelle Institution du droit des gens: l'Organisation permanente du travail (Paris: Rousseau, 1923). 681 pp.

HAMBURGER, L, 'Die Theorie von den Subjekten und Mitgliedern der Völkerrechtsordnung und die internationale Arbeitsorganisation', Niemeyers Z. Int. Recht, vol 36 (1926), pp 117-96

HIITONEN, Ensio, La compétence de l'Organisation internationale du travail, vol 1 'Compétence de fond', (Paris: A Rousseau, 1929). xlvii + 356 pp.

JENKS, C W, 'The revision of the constitution of the International Labour Organisation', Br. Yearb. Int. Law (1946), pp 303-17

JENKS, C W, 'The application of international labour conventions by means of collective agreements', Z. Ausl. Öff. Recht & Völkerrecht, vol 19 (1958), pp 197-224

JENKS, C W, Social Justice in the Law of Nations: The ILO Impact after Fifty Years (London: Oxford University Press, 1970). 104 pp.

JOUHAUX, Léon, L'Organisation internationale du travail (Paris, 1921) 109 pp.

JOHNSON, G A, The International Labour Organisation (London: Europa Publications, 1970). 363 pp.

LANDY, E A, The Effectiveness of International Supervision, Thirty Years of ILO Experience (London: Stevens, 1966). 268 pp.

MAHAIM, Ernest, 'L'Organisation permanente du Travail', Acad. Droit Int. Recl. Cours, vol 4 (1924), pp 69-221

PHELAN, Edward Joseph, Yes and Albert Thomas (London: Cresset Press, 1936/New York: Columbia University Press, 1949). xvi + 270 pp.

SCELLE, Georges, L'Organisation internationale du travail et le BIT (Paris: M Rivière, 1930). xvi + 333 pp.

SHOTWELL, James T, The Origins of the International Labour Organization under the United Nations system', Press, 1934). 2 vols. 497 + 592 pp.

SULKOWSKI, J, 'The competence of the International labour organization under the United Nations system', Am. J. Int. Law, vol 45 (1951), pp 286-313
SULKOWSKI, J, 'The problem of universal membership in the International Labor Organization', Österr. Z. Öff. Recht, vol 5 (1952), pp 70-100
UDINA, M, 'Formazione del diritto internazionale del lavoro', Primo congresso internaz. di dir. del lavoro, Trieste, 1951, pp 19-39. Rivista di diritto del lavoro, (1951), pp 117-39
WOLF, F, 'L'organisation international du travail, sa composition et les transformations étatiques', Comun. & Stud., vol 9 (1957), pp 46-71

13.24.2.24.5.2 ILO CONVENTIONS AND PARTICULAR STATES

BAILEY, K H, 'Australia and the international labour conventions', International Labour Review, vol 54 (1946), pp 285-308
BLAGOEV, B, 'La Yougoslavie et l'Organisation Internationale du travail', Jugoslovensko revija za medunarodno pravo, (1956), no 1, pp 53-61
BLAGOEV, B, 'Les conventions internationales du travail et leur application en droit interne', Jugoslovenska Revija za Medunarodno pravo, vol 8, no 3 (1961), pp 387-419. In Croatian with a summary in French.
BERENSTEIN, A, 'La ratification des conventions internationales du travail et la législation interne', Die Friedens-Warte, vol 53 (1956), pp 136-65
CALHOUN, L J, The International Labour Organization and United States Domestic Law (New York/Washington: American Enterprise Association, 1953). 49 pp.
DESPRES, J P, Le Canada et l'Organisation internationale du travail (Montréal: Fides, 1947). 273 pp.

JENKS, C W, 'The interpretation of international labour conventions by the International Labour Office', Br. Yearb. Int. Law, vol 20 (1939), pp 132-41

JOBST, III, V, 'The United States and international labor conventions', Am. J. Int. Law, vol 32 (1938), p 135

LANDY, E A, The Effectiveness of International Supervision. Thirty Years of ILO Experience (London: Stevens, 1966)

MALIK, A M, 'Pakistan and ILO', Pakistan Horizon, vol 7 (1954), pp 47-56

SECRETAN, J, 'Swiss constitutional problems and the International Labour Organisation', International Labour Review, vol 56 (1947), pp 1-20

STEWART, R B, 'Canada and international labor conventions', Am. J. Int. Law, vol 32 (1938), p 36

TIMMERMAN, J Aeg, 'The Netherlands and the International Labour Organization', Grotius annuaire international (1940-6), pp 227-40

The United States and the International Labor Organization. Annals of the American Academy of Political and Social Science, vol 310 (March 1957), pp 182-95

VALTICOS, N, 'Conventions internationales du travail et droit interne', Revue critique de droit international privé, vol 44 (1955), pp 251-88

VALTICOS, N, 'The influence of international labour conventions on Greek legislation', International Labour Review, vol 71 (1955), pp 593-615

13.24.2.24.5.3 ILO HEADQUARTERS

See also Section 13.12 on headquarters of organizations in general.

KING, J J, 'La convention sur les privilegès et immunités des institutions spécialisées des Nations Unies dans sa relation avec l'accord entre le Conseil fédéral et l'OIT pour régler le statut juridique de cette organisme en Suisse', Schweiz. Jahrb. Int. Recht, vol 8 (1951), pp 193-4

13.24.2.24.6 BRETTON WOODS NEGOTIATIONS FOR THE WORLD BANK AND THE INTERNATIONAL MONETARY FUND

BACHMANN, Hans, Die Konventionen von Bretton Woods (St Gallen: Fehr, 1945). 140 pp.
BUENOS AIRES. Academia de Ciencias Económicas, Fondo Monetario Internacional y Banco Internacional de Reconstrucción y Fomento (Acuerdos de Bretton Woods) (Editorial Losada, 1945). 187 pp.
GUTT, C, 'Les accords de Bretton Woods et les institutions qui en sont issues', Acad. Droit Int. Recl. Cours, vol 1 (1948), pp 67-165
HEXNER, E P, 'Interpretation of public international organizations of their basic instruments', Am. J. Int. Law, vol 53 (1959), pp 341-70
SACCHETTI, Ugo, Bretton Woods e i piani monetari internazionali (Roma: Edizioni Italiane, 1947). 327 pp. (Societa Italiana per l'Organizzazione Internazionale, Studi 1)
STOKVIS, H J, Bretton Woods en het internationaal monetair bestel (Leiden: H E Stenfert Kroese, 1948). 448 pp.

13.24.2.24.7 INTERNATIONAL BANK FOR RECONSTRUCTION AND DEVELOPMENT (IBRD)

BASCH, Antonin, 'International Bank for Reconstruction and Development 1944-1949', Int. Conciliation, no 455 (November 1949), pp 791-827
BROCHES, A, 'International legal aspects of the World Bank', Acad. Droit Int. Recl. Cours, vol 98 (1959), pp 301-409

LÖWEGREN, Gunnar H, Världsbanken; International
Bank for Reconstruction and Development
(Stockholm: Exportföreningens Forlag, 1953). 53 pp.

13.24.2.24.8 INTERNATIONAL
FINANCE CORPORATION (IFC)

BAKER, James C, The International Finance Corporation
Origin, Operations and Evaluation (New York:
Praeger, 1968). 294 pp.

13.24.2.24.9 INTERNATIONAL
DEVELOPMENT ASSOCIATION (IDA)

WEAVER, James H, The International Development
Association, A New Approach to foreign aid (New
York: Praeger, 1965). 268 pp.

13.24.2.24.10 INTERNATIONAL
MONETARY FUND (IMF)

AKERMALM, Gunnar, Internationella Valutafonden
(Stockholm: Exportföreningens Förlag, 1955). 84 pp.
AUFRICHT, Hans, The International Monetary Fund:
Legal Bases, Structure, Functions (New York, 1964).
126 pp.
CARREAU, D, Le Fonds Monétaire International (Paris:
Librairie Armand Colin, 1970). 270 pp.
CLIFFORD, Happa Belle, 'The organization and
management of the International Monetary Fund; a
case study', Thesis. Washington, 1954. 232 pp.
FAWCETT, J E S, 'The International Monetary Fund
and international law', Br. Yearb. Int. Law, vol 40
(1964), pp 32-76
FLEMING, J Marcus, The International Monetary Fund,
Its Form and Functions, FUND (Washington, 1964).
57 pp.

GOLD, J, 'The interpretation by the International Monetary Fund of its articles of agreement', Int. & Comp. Law Q., vol 3 (1954), pp 256-76

GOLD, J, 'The law and practice of the International Monetary Fund with respect to "stand-by" arrangements', Int. & Comp. Law Q., vol 12 (1963), pp 1-30

GOLD, J, The International Monetary Fund and International Law, FUND (Washington, 1965). 26 pp.

GOLD, J, Fund and Non Member States, some Legal Effects (Washington, 1966)

GOLD, J, Voting and Decisions in the International Monetary Fund (Washington, DC: International Monetary Fund, 1973). xii + 368 pp.

HEXNER, E P, 'Die Rechtsnatur der interpretativen Entscheidungen des Internationalen Währungsfonds', Z. Ausl. Öff. Recht & Völkerrecht, vol 20 (1959), pp 73-82

HORIE, Shigeo, The International Monetary Fund (New York: St Martin's Press, 1964). 209 pp.

MIKESELL, Raymond F, 'The International Monetary Fund 1944-1949 - a review', Int. Conciliation, no 455 (November 1949), pp 828-74

KRASNER, Stephen D, The International Monetary Fund and the Third World, Int. Organ., vol 22 (1968), pp 670-88

See also

CARREAU, Dominique, Souveraineté et Coopération Monétaire Internationale (Paris: Editions Cujas, 1970). ix + 530 pp.

13.24.2.24.11 FOOD AND AGRICULTURE ORGANIZATION (FAO)

CERCLER, R, 'L'organisation internationale de l'agriculture', Revue politique et parlementaire, vol 49 (1947), pp 235-45

GOMEZ ORBANEJA, A, 'La Organización de las Naciones Unidas para la Agricultura y la Alimentación', Escuela de funcionarios internationales, vol 2 (1955-6), pp 403-50

HAASTERT, H F W M van, Het internationaal landbouw instituut (IIA) en de organisatie voor voedsel en landbouw (FAO) (Den Haag, 1947)

HAMBIDGE, Gove, The Story of FAO (Toronto/New York/London, 1955)

MARSEILLAN, L, 'L'organisation des Nations Unies pour l'Alimentation et l'Agriculture (OAA)', Thesis. Université de Paris, Faculte de Droit, 1951. 279 pp.

WEIDENMANN, H U, Entstehung und Aufgabe der Ernährungs- und Landwirtschaftsorganisation der Vereinigten Nationen (FAO) (Aarau, 1951). 159 pp.

YATES, P L, So Bold an Aim: Ten Years of International Co-operation toward Freedom from Want (Roma: FAO, 1955). 174 pp.

On the Headquarter Agreement:

BERNARDINI, A, 'Accordo e contratto di sede tra Italia e FAO', Riv. Diritto Int., vol 46 (1963), pp 26-40

13.24.2.24.12 UNITED NATIONS EDUCATIONAL SCIENTIFIC AND CULTURAL ORGANIZATION (UNESCO)

BENDER, F, UNESCO na zes jaren (Amsterdam: Contact, 1952). 47 pp.

BESTERMAN, Theodore, UNESCO, Peace in the Minds of Men (London: Methuen, 1951). 132 pp.

ENTEZAMI, M F, 'L'organisation de l'UNESCO et ses rapports avec l'ONU', Thesis. Université de Paris, Faculté de Droit, 1952. 202 pp.

HUXLEY, Julian, UNESCO: Its Purpose and its Philosophy (Washington, 1947)

KLINEBERG, Otto, 'UNESCO and the cultural basis for peace', Proceedings of the Academy of Political Science, vol 25 (1953), pp 55-65
LAVES, W H C, & THOMSON, G A, UNESCO, Purpose Progress (Bloomington, Ind: Indiana University Press, 1957)
SHUSTER, George N, UNESCO: Assessment and Promise (New York, 1963)
SMETS, P F, & MERTENS, P, 'Le "treaty-making power" de l'UNESCO', Rev. Gén. Droit Int. Public, vol 70 (1966), pp 916-60
SATHYAMURTHY, Tennalur V I, 'Twenty years of UNESCO', Int. Organ., vol 21 (1967), pp 614-33
TRIPP, B M H, 'UNESCO in perspective', Int. Conciliation, no 497 (March 1954), pp 323-83
On the Headquarter Agreement:
FISCHER, G, 'UNESCO. Accord relatif au siège', Annu. Fr. Droit Int. (1955), pp 393-406

13.24.2.24.13 WORLD HEALTH ORGANIZATION (WHO)

On forerunners of the WHO:
BUCHANAN, Sir G S, International Cooperation in Public Health; its Achievements and Prospects (London: The Lancet, 1934). 60 pp.
On the WHO:
BERKOV, Robert, The World Health Organization, a Study in Decentralized International Administration (Genève/Paris, 1957). 173 pp.
CODDING, George Arthur Jr, 'Contribution of the "WHO" and "ICAO" to the development of international law', Proc. Am. Soc. Int. Law (1965), pp 147-53
FASIHPOUR, H, 'L'Organisation Mondiale de la Santé', Thesis. Université de Paris, Faculté de Droit, 1951. 193 pp.

PAZ SOLDAN, C E, La OMS y la soberania sanitaria de las Americas (Lima: Instituto de medicina social, 1949). 262 pp.
RAOUX, M, 'L'Organisation Mondiale de la Santé et les aspects juridiques de sa fonction épidémiologique', Thesis. Bordeaux, 1955. 58 pp.
ROM, A von, Der bei Ausbleiben staatlicher Ablehnung verbindliche Mehrheitsbeschluss der Weltgesundheitsorganisation (Berlin, 1968)
VONCKEN, J, & LA PRADELLE, P de, 'L'Organisation Mondiale de la Santé', Revue des Deux Mondes (1954), pp 331-41

13.24.2.24.14 INTERNATIONAL CIVIL AVIATION ORGANIZATION (ICAO)

See also Section 7.9.3 on air law and note the work by CODDING listed in Section 13.24.2.24.13.
BUERGENTHAL, Thomas, Law-Making in the International Civil Aviation Organization (Ithaca, NY: Syracuse University Press, 1969). 247 pp.
ERLER, J, Rechtsfragen der ICAO; die internationale Zivilluftfahrtorganisation und ihre Mitgliedstaaten (Köln, 1966)
ERLER, J, Die Internationale Zivilluftfahrtorganisation und ihre Mitgliedstaaten (Köln/Berlin/Munchen: Heymann, 1967)
MANIN, A, L'Organisation de l'aviation civile internationale, autorité mondiale de l'air (Paris, 1970)
SCHENKMAN, J, International Civil Aviation Organization (Gèneve: Droz, 1955). 410 pp.
SAPORTA, M, 'L'élaboration du droit international aérien. (Une proposition d'amendement à l'Acte de Chicago)', Revue général de l'air, vol 15 (1952), pp 413-21
On the Headquarter Agreement:

DAI, P, 'The headquarters agreement between Canada and the ICAO', Can. Yearb. Int. Law, vol 2 (1964), pp 205-14

13.24.2.24.15 INTER-GOVERNMENTAL MARITIME CONSULTATIVE ORGANIZATION (IMCO)

PADWA, D J, 'The curriculum of IMCO', Int. Organ., vol 14 (1960)
JOHNSON, D H N, 'IMCO, first four years', Int. & Comp. Law Q., vol 12 (1963), pp 31-55

13.24.2.24.16 INTERNATIONAL REFUGEE ORGANIZATION (IRO)

HOLBORN, Louise W, The International Refugee Organisation. A Specialised Agency of the United Nations. Its History and Work (London: Oxford University Press, 1956). 805 pp.
RISTELHUEBER, René, 'The International Refugee Organization', Int. Conciliation, no 470 (1951), pp 805
RISTELHUEBER, René, Au secours des réfugiés. L'oeuvre de l'Organisation Internationale pour les Refugiés (OIR) (Paris: Plan, 1951). viii + 319 pp.

13.24.2.24.17 OTHER BODIES ASSOCIATED WITH THE UN

13.24.2.24.17.1 INTERNATIONAL ATOMIC ENERGY AGENCY (IAEA)

FISCHER, G, 'L'accord entre l'ONU et l'agence internationale de l'énergie atomique', Annu. Fr. Droit Int. (1957), pp 375-83

SZASZ, Paul C, The Law and Practices of the International Atomic Energy Agency (IAEA Legal Series no 7) (Wien, 1970). 1176 pp.
On the Headquarter Agreement:
RODGERS, R S, 'The headquarters agreement of the International Atomic Energy Agency of 1 March 1958 at Vienna', Br. Yearb. Int. Law, vol 34 (1958), pp 391-5

13.24.2.24.17.2 GENERAL AGREEMENT FOR TARIFFS AND TRADE (GATT)

BROWN, William Adam Jr, The United States and the Restoration of World Trade. An Analysis and Appraisal of the ITO Charter and the General Agreement on Tariffs and Trade (Washington: Brookings Institution, 1950), xiv + 572 pp.
DAM, Kenneth W, The GATT Law and International Economic Organization (Chicago, Ill: University of Chicago Press, 1970). 480 pp.
FLORY, T, Le GATT, droit international et commerce mondial (Paris: Librairie générale de droit et jurisprudence, 1968)
General Agreement on Tariffs and Trade: An analysis and appraisal for the General Agreement on Tariffs and Trade, prepared by the Fletcher School of Law and Diplomacy for the United States Council of the International Chamber of Commerce. Feb. 1955, 104 pp.
GORTER, W, 'GATT after six years: an appraisal', Int. Organ., vol 8 (1954), pp 1-18
JACKSON, John H, World Trade and the Law of GATT (Indianapolis, Ind: Bobs-Merrill, 1969). 948 pp.
KUNG, Emil, Das allgemeine Abkommen über Zölle und Handel, GATT (Zürich: Polygraphischer Verlag, 1952). 173 pp. (St Gallen, Handelshochschule. Schweizerisches Institut für Aussenwirtschafts- und

Marktforschung. Veröffentlichungen 13).
Supplement published in 1955.
VERNON, Raymond, 'Organizing for world trade', Int. Conciliation, no 505 (November 1955), pp 163-222
WILCOX, Clair, A Charter of World Trade (New York: The Macmillan Co, 1949). xvii + 333 pp.

13.24.3 REGIONAL ORGANIZATIONS

13.24.3.1 GENERAL

BERBER, G, 'Regional organizations: a United Nations problem', Am. J. Int. Law, vol 49 (1955), pp 166-84
BOUTROS-GHALI, B, Contribution à l'étude des ententes régionales (Paris: Pédone, 1949). xv + 247 pp.
CHAUDRI, M A, 'The principle of regional pacts', Pakistan Horizon, vol 8, no 3 (September, 1955), pp 428-36
HEINTZ, Frank Joseph, Regionalism in International Political Organization (Washington: Catholic University of America Press, 1953). 60 pp.
KREZDORN, F J, 'Les Nations Unies et les accords régionaux', Thesis. Speyer am Rhein, 1954. 176 pp.
ORUE Y ARREGUI, José Ramon de, Las dos fases del regionalismo internacional (Valence, 1949). 135 pp.
ORUE Y ARREGUI, José Ramon de, 'Le régionalisme dans l'organisation internationale', Acad. Droit Int. Recl. Cours, vol 53 (1935), pp 7-94
PADELFORD, Norman J, 'Regional organizations and the United Nations', Int. Organ., vol 7 (1954), pp 203-16
SABA, H, 'Les accords régionaux dans la Charte de l'ONU', Acad. Droit Int. Recl. Cours, vol 80 (1952), pp 635-718

VELLAS, Pierre, Le Régionalisme international et l'Organisation des Nations Unies (Paris: Pédone, 1948). 166 pp.

13.24.3.2 EUROPEAN ORGANIZATIONS IN GENERAL

BINDSCHEDLER, R, Rechtsfragen der europäischen Einigung; ein Beitrag zu der Lehre von den Staatenverbindungen (Basel: Verlag für Recht und Gesellschaft, 1954). 424 pp.

CARTOU, Louis, Organisations européennes, 3rd edition (Paris, 1970). 478 pp.

GANSHOF VAN DER MEERSCH, W J, Organisations européennes (Paris, 1966). 580 pp.

LEONARD, Raymond, Vers une organisation politique et juridique de l'Europe. Du projet d'union fédérale européenne aux pactes de sécurité (Paris: Rousseau, 1935). xii + 311 pp.

ROBERTSON, A H, European Institutions, 3rd edition (London: Stevens, 1973). 427 pp.

STEIN, Eric, & HAY, Peter, Law and Institutions in the Atlantic Area: Readings, Cases and Problems (Indianapolis, Ind: Bobbs-Merill Company, 1967). 1151 pp.

13.24.3.3 ORGANIZATION FOR EUROPEAN ECONOMIC COOPERATION (OEEC) & THE ORGANIZATION FOR ECONOMIC COOPERATION AND DEVELOPMENT (OECD)

The OECD has become a universal organization but is listed here because of its regional origin as administrator of the Marshall Aid.

ADAM, H T, L'Organisation européenne de coopération économique (Paris: Librairie générale de droit et de jurisprudence, 1949). 292 pp.

ALEXANDER, Sidney S, The Marshall Plan (Washington: National Planning Association, 1948). 68 pp.

AUBREY, Henry G, Atlantic Economic Co-operation: The Case of the OECD, (New York: Praeger, 1967). 214 pp.

ELKIN, A, 'The Organization for European Economic Cooperation: its structure and powers', Annu. Eur., vol 4 (1956), pp 96-149

FREYMOND, P, 'Les "décisions" de l'organisation européenne de coopération économique (OECE). Contribution à l'étude des procédures à l'effet de conclure des traités', Annuaire Suisse de droit international, vol 11 (1954), pp 65-90

GROSS, Herbert, Der Marshall Plan: Deutschlands Chance (Essen, 1948). 185 pp.

HAHN, H J, 'Die Organisation für Wirtschaftliche Zusammenarbeit und Entwicklung. Das Wirtschaftsrecht des Verbondes und seine Systematie', Arch. Völkerrecht, vol 13 (1966/7), pp 153-293

PEYNER, Henri, Le Plan Marshall peut-il sauver l'Europe? (Paris: Collection de l'Economie, 1948). 234 pp.

PRICE, Harry Bayard, The Marshall Plan and its Meaning (Ithaca, NY: Governmental Affairs Institute, Cornell University Press, 1955). 424 pp.

TEISSEDRE, Jean, Plan Marshall: Naissance et débuts (Paris, 1948). 158 pp. (Actualités scientifiques et industrielles, 1063)

13.24.3.4 COUNCIL FOR MUTUAL ECONOMIC AID (COMECON)

FIUMEL, H de, 'Le statut juridique du Conseil d'assistance économique mutuelle', Annuaire polonais des affaires internationales (1961), pp 74-86

13.24.3.6 EUROPEAN FREE TRADE
ASSOCIATION (EFTA)

See also the relationship between the EEC and GATT
in Section 13.24.3.12.16
DETTER, Ingrid, 'Aspects institutionnels de
l'Association Européenne de Libre Echange', Annu.
Fr. Droit Int. (1960)
LAMBRINIDIS, John S, The Structure, Function and Law
of a Free Trade Area: The European Free Trade
Association (London: Stevens, 1965). 303 pp.
LANGE, Gunnar, 'The European Free Trade Association
Some reflections on its origin, functions and future',
Annu. Europ., vol 11 (1963), pp 3-21
SZOKOLOCZY-SYLLABA, Adrienne, 'Ten years of
EFTA', Journal of World Trade Law, vol 5 (1971),
pp 351-5

13.24.3.7 BENELUX

KARELLE, Jacques, & KEMMETER, Frits de, Le
Benelux Commenté (Bruxelles, 1961)
SCHERMERS, H G, Benelux Economische Unie
(Editie Schuurman & Jordens no 152)

13.24.3.8 COUNCIL OF EUROPE

See also Section 7.12.10 on human rights in Europe.
FOIS, P, 'Gli emendamenti allo Statuto del Consiglio
d'Europa', Riv. Diritto Int., vol 41 (1958), pp 414-29
GELLNER, C R, The Council of Europe: A Brief
Survey of its Origin and Development (Washington:
Library of Congress, Legislative Reference Service,
1951). 24 pp.
GOLSONG, H, & KISS, A Ch, 'Les accords entre le
Conseil de l'Europe et d'autres organisations inter-
gouvernementales', Annu. Fr. Droit Int., vol 4
(1958), pp 477-92

GRZYBOWSKI, A, The Socialist Commonwealth of
  Nations, Organizations and Institutions (New Haven,
  Conn: Yale University Press, 1964)
KASER, Michael, COMECON. Integration Problems of
  the Planned Economies, 2nd edition (London: Oxford
  University Press, 1967). 279 pp.
KORBONSKI, Andrzej, 'Comecon', Int. Conciliation,
  no 549 (September 1964)
KORBONSKI, Andrzej, Theory and Practice of Regional
  Integration: The Case of Comecon, Int. Organ., vol
  24 (1970), pp 942-77
RIBI, Rolf C, Das Comecon, Eine Untersuchung über
  die Problematik der wirtschaftlichen Integration
  sozialistischer Länder (Zürich/St. Gallen, 1970).
  462 pp.
USTOR, E, 'Decision-making in the Council for Mutual
  Economic Assistance', Acad. Droit Int. Recl.
  Cours, vol 134 (1971), pp 163-296

13.24.3.5 NORDIC COUNCIL

ANDERSON, S V, The Nordic Council. A Study of
  Scandinavian Regionalism (Seattle, Wash: University
  of Washington Press, 1967)
LANGROD, G, 'Le Conseil nordique: réalisations
  administratives d'une coopération régionale', Revue
  administrative, no 47 (1955)
NAGEL, H, 'Der Nordische Rat, seine Organe, seine
  Funktionen und seine juristische Natur', Jahrb. Int.
  Recht, vol 6 (1956), pp 199-214
NAGEL, H, 'The Nordic council, its organs, functions
  and juridical nature', Assoc. Auditeurs & Anc.
  Auditeurs Acad. Droit Int. La Haye Annu.(1956),
  pp 51-67
SØRENSEN, M, 'Le Conseil nordique', Rev. Gén. Droit
  Int. Public (1955), pp 63-84

KISS, A Ch, 'Conseil de l'Europe. I. Le Conseil de l'Eutope buts et organisation. II. Les relations extérieures du Conseil de l'Europe. III Contribution du Conseil de l'Europe au developpement du droit européen pendant la periode allant de septembre 1954 à septembre 1955', Annu. Fr. Droit Int., vol 1 (1955), pp 425-54

LAUTERPACHT, E, 'Council of Europe: Legal questions. 1 European commission of human rights. Complaints made by the Greek Government in connection with events in Cyprus; 2 Position of national minorities in Europe', Int. & Comp. Law Q., vol 7 (1958), pp 366-9

MACH, N von, 'Le Conseil de l'Europe et la Charte des Nations Unies', Thesis. Université de Genève/Bonn 1955. 204 pp.

RENCKI, G, L'Assemblée consultative du Conseil de l'Europe. Essai de définition de sa nature juridique (Paris, 1956). 125 pp.

RENTIER, Jeannine, L'activité du Conseil de l'Europe dans le domaine social (Liège: Faculté de Droit de l'Université de Liège, 1955). 210 pp.

ROBERTSON, A H, The Council of Europe, Its Structure, Functions and Achievements, 2nd edition, (London, 1961)

ROHN, P H, Relation between the Council of Europe and international non-governmental organisations. A Thesis. (Doc. pour servir à l'étude des relations non-gouvernementales, no 6) (Bruxelles, 1957)

SØRENSEN, Max, 'The Council of Europe, a new experiment in international organisation', Yearb. of World Aff. (1952), pp 75-97

13.24.3.9 WEST EUROPEAN UNION (WEU)

BORCIER, Paul, The Political Role of the Assembly of WEU (1963). 50 pp.

CAREY, J P C, 'Western European union and the Atlantic community', Foreign Policy Reports, vol 26, no 7 (1950), pp 66-79

CASTAGNE, André, L'Organisation de l'Europe occidentale. Institutions et problèmes (1948-1954) (Paris, 1954), 124 pp.

HERAUD, G, 'La supranationalité dans l'Organisation de l'Union de l'Europe occidentale (Accords de Paris du 23 oct 1954)', Rev. Droit Public & Sci. Polit., vol 71 (1955), pp 304-22

IMBERT, Armand, L'Union de l'Europe occidentale (Paris, 1968). 238 pp.

LAVERGNE, B, 'Analyse et portée des accords de Londres et de Paris', Année politique et économique, vol 27 (1954), pp 437-78

13.24.3.10 NORTH ATLANTIC TREATY ORGANIZATION (NATO)

See also the work by VOSS listed in Section 13.24.3.11.

BASTID, Suzanne, & CLBV, 'Organisation du traité de l'Atlantique du Nord (OTAN): I, II', Annu. Fr. Droit Int (1955), pp 464-90

BECKETT, Sir Eric W, The North Atlantic Treaty, the Brussels Treaty and the Charter of the United Nations. (London: Stevens and Sons, 1950). viii + 75 pp.

BEER, Francis A, Integration and Disintegration in NATO (Athens, Ohio: Ohio University Press, 1969). 330 pp.

BOYD, Andrew, & METSON, William, Atlantic Pact, Commonwealth and United Nations (New York: Hutchinson and Co, 1949). 100 pp. (United Nations Association)

CLBV, 'La personalité juridique de l'OTAN', Annu. Fr. Droit Int. (1955)

COCATRE-ZILGIEN, A, 'Situation de l'Otan depuis les accords de Paris, du 23 oct. 1954', Rev. Gén. Droit Int. Public, vol 60 (1956), pp 80-6

COTTRELL, Alvin, & DOUGHERTY, James E. The Politics of the Atlantic Alliance (New York/London, 1964)

FINCH, G A, 'The North Atlantic pact in international law', Am. Soc. Int. Law Proc. (1949), pp 90-101

HOSKINS, H L, The Atlantic Pact (Washington, DC: Public Affairs Press, 1949). 104 pp.

ISMAY, Lord, OTAN, les cinq premières années 1949-1954 (Paris: Secretariat de l'Otan, 1954). xi + 297 pp.

JCS, 'Problèmes juridiques de l'Otan', Politique étrangère, vol 20 (1955), pp 689-706

KAPLAN, L S, 'NATO and its commentators: the past five years', Int. Organ. (November 1954), pp 447-67

KELSEN, H, 'The North Atlantic defense treaty and the Charter of the United Nations', Nord. Tidsskr. Int. Ret, vol 19 (1949), pp 41-8 (English text); pp 91-9 (Danish text)

KRUGER-SPRENGEL, E, The Role of Nato in the Use of the Sea and the Seabed (Washington, DC: Woodrow Wilson International Center for Scholars, 1972). 45 pp.

PATTERSON, G, & FURNISS, E S, Jr, Nato: A Critical Appraisal. A Report Prepared by -- on the Basis of an International Conference Held at Princeton University from June 19-June 29, 1957 (Princeton NJ: Princeton University Press, 1957. v + 107 pp.

SALVIN, M, 'The NATO', Int. Conciliation, no 451 (1949), pp 373-456

SALVADORI, M, 'Les origines de l'Otan', Revue d'histoire politique et constitutionnelle, vol 4 (1954), pp 34-52

STANLEY, Timothy W, NATO in Transition: The
Future of the Atlantic Alliance (New York/Washington/London: Council of Foreign Relations, 1965).
417 pp.
WARNE, J D, NATO and its Prospects (New York:
Praeger, 1954). 110 pp.

13.24.3.11   WARSAW PACT

GELBERG, L, Układ Warszawski. Studium
prawnomiędzynarodowe (Warszawa, 1957). 203 pp.
KORBONSKI, Andrzej, 'The Warsaw Pact', Int. Conciliation, no 573 (1969)
MEISSNER, Boris, Der Warschauer Pakt (Köln:
Dokumentensammlung, 1966)
VOSS, H, Nordatlantikpakt. Warschauer Vertrag und
die Charta der Vereinten Nationen (Berlin:
Deutscher Zentralverlag, 1958). 55 pp. (Schriftenreihe Völkerrecht)
YAKEMTCHOUK, R, 'Sowjetunion und regionale
Sicherheitsabkommen. Zur Vorgeschichte von Art.
51-54 der Charta der Vereinten Nationen', O-R,
vol 2, no 1 (May 1956), pp 118-93

13.24.3.12   EUROPEAN COMMUNITIES

13.24.3.12.1   GENERAL

CAMPBELL, Alan, Common Market Law (London:
Longmans, 1969). 2 vols with loose-leaf supplements.
CAPOTORTI, F, 'Sulla interpretazione uniforme dei
trattati europei', Riv. Diritto Int., vol 43 (1960),
pp 3-25
CARTOU, Louis, Organisations européennes, 2nd
edition (Paris: Dalloz, 1967)
GANSHOF, van der Meersch, WJ, (ed), Les nouvelles
droit des Communautés européennes (Bruxelles,
1969). 1194 pp.

GOES VAN NATERS, M van der, 'Les fondements du droit parlementaire européen', Ned. Tijdschr. Int. Recht, vol 3 (1956), pp 324-41

HAHN, H J, 'Constitutional limitations in the law of European organisations', Acad. Droit Int. Recl. Cours, vol 108 (1963), pp 193-305

KAPTEYN, P J G, & VERLOREN VAN THEMAAT, P, Inleiding tot het recht van de Europese Gemeenschappen (Deventer, 1970). 408 pp.

PINTO, Roger, Cours d'organisations européennes (Paris: Les Cours de Droit 1960-1961)

PINTO, Roger, Les organisations européennes, 3rd edition (Paris: Payot, 1965)

POLLEDRI, M, & MALLARDO, V, Prospettive di una legislazione comunitaria europea (Bergamo: Mayer, 1958). 210 pp.

PUISSOCHET, J P, L'Elargissement des Communautés européennes (Paris: Editions techniques et économiques, 1974)

REUTER, Paul, Organisations européennes (Paris: Presses Universitaires de France, 1965). Collection 'Themis'

ROBERTSON, A H, 'Legal problems of European integration', Acad. Droit Int. Recl. Cours, vol 1 (1957), pp 105-211

ROBERTSON, A H, European Institutions: Cooperation, Integration, Unification, 3rd edition (London: Stevens, 1973)

13. 24. 3. 12. 2 THE NATURE OF THE EUROPEAN COMMUNITIES

The Communities have been said to be 'different' from other organizations in so far as they are, some claim, 'supranational'. Many writers have criticized this formula as misleading and polemic. However, since the expression is recurring I have listed some articles describing what writers mean by that 'label'. In this section there are also some works on the general nature of the Communities, for example the valuable monograph by PESCATORE, discussing the structure of the Communities which are unquestionably different from other organizations.

DELVAUX, L, 'La notion de supranationalité dans le Traité du 18 avril 1951 instituant la CECA', Actes Officiels, vol 2

EFRON, R, & NANES, A S, 'The Common Market and Euratom treaties: supranationality and the integration of Europe', Int. & Comp. Law Q., vol 6 (1957), pp 670-84

EYSINGA, van, Supranational, Festschrift für Hans Wehberg (Frankfurt, 1956)

JAENICKE, 'Die Europäische Wirtschaftgemeinschaft als übernationale Organisation, Festgabe für Makarov', Z. Ausl. Öff. Recht & Völkerrecht (1958)

JAENICKE, 'Die Sicherung des übernationalen Charakters der Organe internationaler Organisationen', Z. Ausl. Öff. Recht & Völkerrecht (1951/2)

JAENICKE, 'Bundesstaat oder Staatenbund, Zur Rechtsform einer Europäischen Staatengemeinschaft', in Festschrift für Bilfinger (1954)

KUNZ, J, 'Supranational organs', Am. J. Int. Law (1952)

MONACO, R, 'Le Comunità sopranazionali nell'ordinamento internazionale', in Scritti Giuridici in memoria di V E Orlando, vol 2, pp 67-92

LASSALLE, C, 'Contribution à une théorie de la fonction publique supranationale', Rev. Droit Public & Sci. Polit., vol 73 (1957), pp 474-512

LASSALLE, Claude, 'Aspects communautaires de certains actes du droit international', Rev. Gén. Droit Int. Public (1969), pp 987-1017

PESCATORE, P, Droit international et droit communautaire. Essai de réflexion comparative (Nancy: Centre Européen Universitaire, 1969). Pub-

lications du Centre Européen Universitaire de
l'Universite de Nancy - Collection des Conférences
Européennes, no 5
PESCATORE, P, 'L'apport du droit communautaire au
droit international public', Cah. Droit Eur., (1970),
pp 501-25

13.24.3.12.3 THE EUROPEAN COAL AND
STEEL COMMUNITY (ECSC)

The standard work is, in spite of being 21 years old,
the monograph by REUTER.
DIEBOLD, William, Jr, The Schuman Plan, A Study in
Economic Cooperation 1950-1959. 750 pp.
FISCHER, P H, 'Det Europaeiske kul- og stalfaclleskab,
Folkeretlige studier over internationalt sumarbeide',
Dissertation. Copenhagen, 1957
GREEN, L C, 'Legal aspects of the Schuman plan',
Current Legal Problems, (1952), pp 274-94
JAENICKE, 'Die Europäische Gemeinschaft für
Kohle und Stahl, Montan-Union, Struktur und
Funktionen ihrer Organe', Z. Ausl. Öff. Recht &
Völkerrecht (1951/2)
KREYSSIG, G, Révision du Traité instituant la CECA
(Luxembourg: Service des publications de la Communauté européenne, 1958). 57 pp.
LAGRANGE, M, 'L'ordre juridique de la CECA vu à
travers de la jurisprudence de sa Cour de Justice',
Rev. Droit Public & Sci. Polit. (1958)
MASON, Henry L, The European Coal and Steel
Community (Den Haag, 1955)
MATTHIES, H, 'Das Recht der EGKS und die nationalen
Gerichte der Mitgliedstaaten', Juristenzeitung, vol 9
(1954), pp 305-9
MATHIJSEN, Pierre, Le droit de la Communauté
Européenne du Charbon et de l'Acier : Une étude des
sources (Den Haag: Nijhoff, 1957)

MOSLER, H, 'Der Vertrag über die EGKS. Entstehung und Qualifizierung', Z. Ausl. Öff. Recht & Völkerrecht, vol 14 (1951), pp 1-45

NEREE tot BABBERICH, M F F A de, 'L'Assemblée commune de la CECA', Annu. Eur. (1958), pp 65-74

PRIEUR, R, Les Relations internes et externes de la CECA (Paris: Montchrestien, 1958). 311 pp.

RAALTE, E van, 'The treaty constituting the ECSC', Int. & Comp. Law Q., vol 1 (1952), pp 73-85

REUTER, P, La CECA (Paris: Pichon, 1953). 320 pp.

REUTER, P, La Comunidad Europea del Carbón y del Acero como tipo de organización internacional, Escuela de Funcionarios, Cursos y Conferencias, año academico 1955-1956, vol 2 (Madrid, 1957)

P R, Quelques aspects institutionnels du Plan Schuman', Rev. Droit Public & Sci. Polit., vol 57 (1951), pp 105-24

RICHEMONT, de, La Communauté européenne du charbon et de l'acier (Paris, 1954)

RIPHAGEN, W, De juridische struktuur van de Europese Gemeenschap voor Kolen en Staal (Leiden, 1955)

SCHEINGOLD, S A, The Rule of Law in European Integration: The Path of the Scihuman Plan, (New Haven, Conn: Yale University Press, 1965). 331 pp.

SOTO, M J de, 'Les relations internationales de la CECA', Acad. Droit Int. Recl. Cours, vol 2 (1956), pp 29-116

STRANGE, Susan, 'The Schuman plan', Yearb. World. Aff. (1951), pp 109-30

UDINA, M, La personalità internazionale della Comunità europea del carbone e dell'acciaio.

VISSCHER, Paul de, Le Droit public de la Communauté Européenne du Charbon et de l'Acier (Liège: Les Presses Universitaires de Liège, 1956)

13.24.3.12.4 EUROPEAN ECONOMIC
COMMUNITY (EEC)

AXLINE, W A, European Community Law and
  Organizational Development (Dobbs Ferry, NY:
  Oceana, 1968). 215 pp.
CAMPBELL, Alan, Common Market Law (London:
  Longmans/Dobbs Ferry, NY: Oceana, 1969). 2 vols
  and supplements
CATALANO, Nicola, Manuel de droit des Communautés
  Européennes, 2nd edition (Paris: Dalloz et Sirey,
  1965). Collection Eurolibri, vol 9
DIJK, P van, GANSHOF VAN DER MEERSCH, W J,
  PESCATORE, P, RODIERE, R, TREVES, G, &
  ZWEIGERT, K, Diritto delle Comunità europee e
  diritto degli stati membri (Milano: Ferro Edizimi,
  1969). 338 pp.
GANSHOF VAN DER MEERSCH, W J, (ed), Droit des
  Communautés européennes (Bruxelles: Larcier,
  1969). Les Nouvelles
GIDE, Loyrette J, & NOUEL, P H, Dictionnaire du
  Marché Commun (mise à jour) (Paris: Dictionnaires
  Joly, 1968)
GROEBEN, Hans von der, & BOECKH, Hans von,
  Kommentar zum EWG-Vertrag (Baden/Bonn/
  Frankfurt: Lutzeyer, 1958). 2 vols.
HERAUD, G, 'Observations sur la nature juridique de
  la Communauté économique européenne', Rev. Gén.
  Droit Int. Public (1958), pp 26-56
KAPTEYN, P J G, & VERLOREN van THEMAAT, P,
  Inleiding tot het recht van de Europese
  Gemeenschappen. Handboek voor de Europese
  Gemeenschappen (Deventer: Kluwer/Alphen a.d.
  Rijn/Brussels: Samson, 1970)
LIPSTEIN, K, The Law of the European Economic
  Community (London: Butterworth, 1974). 368 pp.

MATHIJSEN, P S R F, A Guide to European Community Law (London: Sweet & Maxwell/New York: Matthew Bender, 1972). 204 pp.
MEGRET, J, LOUIS, J V, VIGNES, D, & WAELBROECK, M, Le Droit de la Communauté économique européenne (Bruxelles: Presses Universitaires de Bruxelles, 1970). 4 vols. Vol 1 'Préambule - principes - libre circulation des marchandises'; vol 2 'Agriculture'; vol 3 'Libre circulation des travailleurs - établissements et services - capitaux - transports'; vol 4 'Concurrence'
PÅLSSON, L, EEC Rätt (Lund: Studentlitteratur 1970)
PARRY, A, & HARDY, S, EEC Law (London: Sweet & Maxwell/New York: Matthew Bender, 1973). 511 pp.
QUADRI, Rolando, MONACO, Riccardo & TRABUCCHI, Alberto, Trattato institutivo della Communita Economica Europea - Commentario (Milano: Giuffré, 1965). 4 vols. Vol 1 'Art 1-84'; vol 2 ' Art 85-136'; vol 3 'Art 137-248'; vol 4 'Appendice - Indice'
SCHRANS, Guy, Inleiding tot het europees economisch recht (Ghent/Louvain: E Story-Scientia, 1969)
WOHLFAHRT, Ernst, EVERLING, Ulrich, GLAESNER, Hans Joachim, & SPRUNG, Rudolf, Die Europäische Wirtschaftsgemeinschaft. Kommentar zum Vertrag. (Berlin/Frankfurt: Vahlen, 1960)
WORTLEY, B A, (ed), An Introduction to the Law of the European Economic Community (Manchester: Manchester University Press, 1972). 134 pp.
WORTLEY, B A, 'La Communauté économique européenne: aspects institutionnels', Annu. Fr. Droit Int. (1957)

13.24.3.12.5 EUROPEAN ATOMIC ENERGY COMMUNITY (EURATOM)

ERRERA, J E Symon, VAN DER MEULEN, J, & VERNAEVE, L, Euratom: Analyse et commentaires du Traité (Bruxelles: Librairie Encyclopédique, 1958). 436 pp.

HAHN, H J, 'Euratom: the conception of an international personality', Harvard Law Review, vol 71 (1958), pp 1001-56

MATHIJSEN, P, 'Problems Connected with the Creation of Euratom', Reprint from a Symposium on European Regional Communities (Durham, 1961)

POLACH, J G, Euratom, its Background, Issues and Economic Implications (New York, 1964)

XXX, 'De quelques aspects des institutions de l'Euratom', Annu Fr. Droit Int. (1958)

13.24.3.12.6 ORGANS OF THE COMMUNITIES

There has been a merger between the executives of the three Communities which also have other organs in common.

13.24.3.12.6.1 COUNCIL

BUERSTEDDE, Sigismund, Der Ministerrat im konstitutionelles System der Europäischen Gemeinschaften (Bruges: De Tempel, 1964). Cahiers de Bruges, NS 9

HOUBEN, P H J M, Les Conseils de Ministres des Communautés Européennes (Leiden: Sijthoff, 1964). Aspects européens, Série C: Politique No 17

13.24.3.12.6.2 COMMISSION

COOMBES, David, Politics and Bureaucracy in the European Community. A Portrait of the Commission of the EEC (London: George Allen & Unwin, 1970)

On the Merger of the Commissions of the EEC and of EURATOM and the High Authority of the ECSC:

GLAESNER, Hans-Joachim, Perspectives d'avenir des organes executifs (Conseil et Commission des Communautés européennes) (Liège: Faculté de Droit/Denn Haag: Nijhoff, 1967). La fusion des Communautés européennes au lendemain des accords de Luxembourg, pp 51-59

HOUBEN, P H J M, 'The Merger of the Executives of the European Communities', Common Market Law Rev., vol 3 (1965), pp 37-74

LOUIS, J V, 'La fusion des institutions des Communautés européennes', Rev. Marché Commun. (1966), pp 834-56

NOEL, Emile, La Fusion des institutions et la fusion des Communautés européennes (Nancy: Imprimerie Idoux, 1966)

WEIL, Gordon, 'The merger of the institutions of the European Communities', Am. J. Int. Law (1967), pp 57-65

13.24.3.12.6.3 PARLIAMENT

BIRKE, Wolfgang, European Elections by Direct Suffrage: a Comparative Study of the Electoral Systems used in Western Europe and their Utility for the Direct Election of a European Parliament (Leiden: Sijthoff, 1971)

13.24.3.12.6.4 OTHER INSTITUTIONS

NOEL, Emile, Le Comité des représentants permanents- Publications de l'Institut d'Etudes Européennes de l'Université Libre de Bruxelles, 1968, no 1: Institutions communautaires et institutions nationales dans le développement des Communautés, pp 4-48

NOEL, Emile, 'The Committee of Permanent Representatives', J. Common Market Stud. (1966/7), pp 219-51

13.24.3.12.6.5 COURT OF JUSTICE

The work by VALENTINE is a basic textbook on the Court. The articles by LAGRANGE, Avocat General of the Court, are most interesting.

ANTOINE, A, 'La Cour de justice de la CECA et la CIJ. Etude critique de la Cour de justice de la CECA', Rev. Gén. Droit Int. Public, vol 57 (1953), pp 210-61

BAECHLE, H M, Die Rechtsstellung der Richter am Gerichtshof der europäischen Gemeinschaften (Berlin, 1961). 149 pp.

BEBR, G, Judicial Control of the European Communities (London: Stevens, 1962). 268 pp.

BREITNER, F, Der Gerichtshof der Montangemeinschaft und seine Anrufung bei fehlerhaften Organakten (Hamburg, 1952) 130 pp.

BRIETNER, F, Der Gerichtshof der Montangemeinschaft und seine Anrufung bei fehlerhaften Organakten 2nd edition (Hamburg, 1954). 97 pp.

BRICMONT, G, 'Résumé des règles de compétence et de procédure de la Cour de Justice des Communautés européennes', Journal des tribunaux (17 May 1959), pp 329

CAHIER, Philippe, 'Le recours en constatation de manquements des états membres devant la Cour des Communautés européennes', Cah. Droit Eur. (1967), pp 123-62

CARRILLO SALCEDO, J A, La recepción del recurso contencios-oadministrativo en la Comunidad europea del carbón y del acero (Sevilla, 1958). 216 pp.

CATALANO, N, Manuel de droit des communautés européennes (Paris, 1962). 456 pp.

COLIN, Jean-Pierre, Le Gouvernement des juges dans les Communautés européennes (Nancy: Faculté de Droit et des Sciences Economiques, Université de Nancy, 1963). 2 vols. Vol 1 'Les fonctions de la

Cour de justice des Communautés européennes';
vol 2 'La politique jurisprudentielle de la Cour de
justice des Communautés européennes'
DELVAUX, Louis, Le Cour de justice de la
Communauté européenne du charbon et de l'Acier.
Exposé sommaire des principes (Paris: Librairie
général de droit et de jurisprudence, 1956)
DELVAUX, Louis, 'Le contrôle de la Cour de Justice
de la CECA sur les faits et sur les circonstances',
Annales de droit et de science politique (1956)
ERADES, L, & MATHIJSEN, P S R F, 'De verhouding
van de rechtspraak van het Hof der Europese
gemeenschappen tot die van de nationale rechters in
de lidstaten'. Preadviezen voor de Nederlandse
vereniging voor internationaal recht, no 49,(February
1964), 43 pp.
EYNARD, Sergio F, 'L'article 169 du traité de Rome:
douze ans d'application de la procédure d'infraction a
l'égard des états membres de la CEE', Revue du
droit européen (1970), pp 99-125
FELD, W, 'The Court of Justice of the European
Communities: Emerging political power? An examination of selected decisions of the Court's 1961-1962
term', Tulane Law Review, vol 38, no 1 (December
1963), pp 53-80
FERRIERE, Georges, 'Le contrôle de la légalité des
actes étatiques par la Cour de justice des
Communautés européennes', Rev. Gén. Droit Int.
Public (1967), pp 879-1008
FROMONT, Michel, "L'influence du droit français et
du droit allemand sur les conditions de recévabilité
du recours en annulation devant la Cour de justice
des Communautés européennes', Rev. Trimest.
Droit Eur. (1966), pp 47-65
HAY, P, 'Federal jurisdiction of the Common Market
Court', Am. J. Comp. Law, vol 12 (1963), pp 21-40

HOUTTE, A van, 'De bevoegdheid van het Hof van
 Justitie der EGKS, de Gemeenschappelijke markt en
 van Euratom', Rechtskundig Weekblad, vol 21, no 37
 (8 June 1958), pp 1995-2008
HOUTTE, A van, 'La Cour de justice de la CECA', Ann.
 Eur. (1954), pp 183
HEUT, P, 'La Commission de recours de l'OECE',
 J. Droit Int., vol 80 (1953), pp 256-85. In French
 and English
KNAUB, Gilbert, 'La procédure devant la Cour de
 justice des Communautés européennes', Rev.
 Trimest. Droit Eur. (1967), p 269
KNOPFLE, R, 'Das Klagerecht Privater vor dem
 Gerichtshof der europäischen Gemeinschaften',
 Neue juristische Wochenschrift, vol 12, no 13 (26
 March 1959), pp 553-6
KRYLOV, S B, Mezdhunarodnyi soud Organizatsii
 obiedinennykh natsii. (Voprtossy mezhdunarodnovo
 prave i protsessa v evo praktike za desiat let - 1947-
 1957) (Moscow, 1958). 167 pp.
LAGRANGE, M, 'La Cour de justice de la CECA', Rev.
 Droit Public & Sci.Polit. (1954), pp 417-37
LAGRANGE, M, 'L'ordre juridique de la CECA vu à
 travers la jurisprudence de sa Cour de justice',
 Rev. Droit Public & Sci. Polit. (1958), pp 841-65
LUDOVICY, J, 'La jurisprudence de la Cour de
 justice de la CECA', Rev. Gén. Droit Int. Public,
 vol 60 (1956), pp 111-30
MATTHIES, H, 'Zur Nachprüfungsbefungnis des
 Gerichtshofs der Montanunion', Z. Ausl. Öff. Recht
 & Völkerrecht, vol 16, nos 3-4 (March, 1956)
McMAHON, J, 'The Court of the European Communities,
 Judicial interpretation and international
 organization', Br. Yearb. Int. Law (1961), pp 385-
 406
MERTENS DE WILMERS, J, & VEROUGSTRAET,
 'Proceedings against member states for failure to

fulfil their obligations', Common Market Law Rev.,
  vol 5 (1970), pp 385-406
MIGLIAZZA, A, La Corte di giustizia delle Comunità
  europee (Milano, 1961). 459 pp.
MOSER, B, Die überstaatliche Gerichtsbarkeit der
  Montanunion (Wien, 1959). 79 pp.
NERI, S, 'Il ricorso dei privati davanti alla Corte di
  giustizia della CECA', Rivista di studi politici
  internazionali, vol 23, no 3 (July-September 1956),
  pp 362-98
NERI, Sergio, 'Le recours en annulation dans les
  Communautés européennes: rôle et limites', Rev.
  Marché Commun (1967), pp 452-65
REEPINGHEN & ORIANNE, La Procédure devant la
  Cour de justice des Communautés européennes
  (Bruxelles: Larcier/Paris: Dalloz, 1961)
REUTER, E, 'Le recours en carence de l'article 175
  du traité de la CEE dans la jurisprudence de la Cour
  de justice des Communautés européennes', Cah.
  Droit Eur. (1972), p 159
RICHEMONT, Jean de, Communauté européenne du
  charbon et de l'acier. La Cour de justice. Code
  annoté (Paris: Librairie du Journal des Notaires et
  des Avocats, 1954)
RIPHAGEN, W, 'The case law of the European Coal and
  Steel Community Court of Justice', Ned. Tijdschr.
  Int. Recht, vol 2 (1955), pp 384-408
ROEMR, K, 'Die Kostenordnung des Gerichtshofes der
  EGKS', Neue juristische Wochenschrift, vol 8, no 17
  (29 April 1955), pp 617-18
ROTH, G, 'Die Klagebefugnis im Verwaltungsprozess
  der EGKS', Thesis. Mainz, 1956, 92 pp.
SOLDATOS, Panayotis, 'L'introuvable recours en
  carence devant la Cour de justice des Communautés
  europeennes', Cah. Droit Eur. (1969), pp 313-34
STEIN, E, 'The Court of Justice of the European Coal
  and Steel Community: 1954-1957', Am. J. Int. Law,
  vol 51 (1957), pp 821-9

ULE, R, 'Der Gerichtshof der europäischen Gemeinschaft für Kohle und Stahl als europäischer Verwaltungsgericht', Deutsches Verwaltungsblatt (1952)
VALENTINE, D G, The Court of Justice of the European Coal and Steel Community (Den Haag: Nijhoff, 1955)
VALENTINE, D G, 'The competence of the Court of Justice of the European Coal and Steel Community', in Symbolae Verzijl (Den Haag: Nijhoff, 1958), pp 387-402
VALENTINE, D G, 'Jurisdiction of the Court of Justice of the European Communities to annul executive action', Br. Yearb. Int. Law, vol 35 (1960), pp 174-222
VALENTINE, D G, The Court of Justice of the European Communities (London: Stevens, 1965). 2 vols.
VANDERSANDEN, Georges, 'Le recours en intervention devant la Cour de Justice des Communautés européennes', Rev. Trimest. Droit Eur. (1969), pp 1-27
VIGNES, D, 'I ricorsi giurisdizionali delle imprese private contro le decisioni nell'Alta Autorità del Piano Schuman', Rivista di studi politici internazionali, vol 19, no 4, (October-December 1952), pp 657-70
VIGNES, D, Les Recours juridictionnels des entreprises privées contre les décisions de la Haute Autorité du Plan Schuman (Paris, 1952). 4 pp.
WAELBROECK, Michel, 'La notion d'acte susceptible de recours dans la jurisprudence de la Cour de justice des Communautés européennes', Cah. Droit Eur. (1965), pp 225-36
WALL, Edward H, The Court of Justice of the European Communities. Jurisdiction and Procedure (London: Butterworths, 1966)

WEBER, Yves, 'La preuve du détournement de pouvoir devant la Cour de Justice des Communautés Européennes', Rev. Trimest. Droit Eur. (1967), pp 507-52

WEINARD, G, 'Wesen und Aufgaben des Gerichtshofes der Montanunion', Thesis. Mainz, 1956, 98 pp.

YOUNG, R, 'The Court of the European Coal and Steel Community', American Bar Association Journal, vol 39 (1953), pp 922-3

13.24.3.12.6.5.1 JUDICIAL CONTROL OF THE COMMUNITIES

BEBR, G, Judicial Control of the European Communities (London: Stevens, 1962)

BREITNER, F, 'Supranationaler Rechtsschutz. Sein Umfang und seine Organisation innerhalb der Europäischen Gemeinschaft', Europa-Archiv, vol 9 (1954), pp 6263-72

BRINKHORST, L J, & SCHERMERS, H G, Judicial Remedies in the European Communities, A Case Book (London: Stevens/Deventer: Kluwer, 1969). Supplement 1972

CASSONI, G, 'I principi generali comuni agli ordinamento degli stati membri quele fonte sussidaria del diritto applicato dalla Corte di giustizia delle Comunità europee', Diritto Internazionale, vol 13 (1959), pp 428-63

13.24.3.12.6.5.2 RIGHT OF PETITION OF INDIVIDUALS

ANGULO, Manuel P, & DAWSON, Frank G, 'Access by natural and legal persons to the Court of Justice of the European Communities', Common Market Law Rev., vol 5 (1967), pp 583-649

BEBR, G, 'Judicial remedy of private parties against normative acts of the European Communities: the role of the exception of illegality', Common Market Law Rev., vol 4 (1966), pp 7-31

CATALANO, Nicola, 'Les voies de recours ouvertes aux personnes physiques ou morales contre les actes non réglementaires de la Commission CEE', Sociaal Economische Wetgeving (1965), pp 526-66

DAIG, Hans Wolfram, 'Zum Klagerecht von Privatpersonen nach Art 173 Abs 2 EWG-, 146 Abs. 2 EAG-Vertrag', in Festschrift für Otto Riese (Karlsruhe: Verlag C F Muller, 1964), pp 187-219

JEANTET, F C, 'Les intérêts privés devant la Cour de justice de la CECA', Rev. Droit Public & Sci. Polit. (1954), pp 684-713

KOVAR, Robert, 'Le droit des personnes privées à obtenir devant la Cour des Communautés le respect du droit communautaire par les états membres', Annu. Fr. Droit Int. (1966), pp 509-43

13.24.3.12.6.5.3 PREJUDICIAL QUESTIONS

ALEXANDER, Willy, 'Questions préjudicielles: l'application récente de l'article 177 CEE par la Cour de justice et par les juridictions nationales', Cah. Droit Eur. (1965), pp 47-58

ALEXANDER, Willy, Questions et réponses préjudicielles dans la procédure de la Cour de justice des Communautés européennes (Bruxelles: Institut d'Etudes Européennes, 1964). Publications de l'Institut d'Etudes Européennes, no 8

DUMON, F, Le Renvoi préjudiciel (Bruges: de Tempel, 1965)

HEUVEL, H van den, Prejudiciele vragen en bevoegdheidsproblemen in het Europees recht (Deventer/Antwerpen, 1962). 85 pp. With summaries in English, French and German

LAGRANGE, M, 'The European Court of Justice and
National Courts. The Theory of the Acte Claire: a
bone of contention or a source of unity?' Common
Market Law Rev., vol 8 (1971), pp 313-24

LECOURT, Robert, Le Juge devant le marché commun
(Genève: Institut Universitaire de Hautes Etudes
Internationales, 1970). (Etudes et Travaux no 10)

MARSHAW, J L, 'Ensuring the observance of the law in
the interpretation and application of the EEC Treaty:
The role and functioning of the renvoi d'interpretation
under Article 177', Common Market Law Rev., vol
7 (1970), pp 258-85

PEPY, Andre, 'Le rôle des juridictions nationales dans
l'application de l'article 177 et la jurisprudence de
la Cour de Justice', Cah. Droit Eur. (1966), pp 21-39

RICHEMONT, J de, 'Le rôle de la Cour de justice
des Communautés économiques dans l'application de
l'article 177 du Traité de Rome', Cah. Droit Eur.
(1966), pp 459-89

13.24.3.12.7 LAW-MAKING IN THE
COMMUNITIES

See also above DETTER, under law-making by organizations in general, Section 13.16.

BERTRAM, C, 'Decision-making in the EEC: the
management committee procedure', Common Market
Law Rev., vol 5 (1967/8), pp 246-64

BOERNER, Bodo, Die Entscheidungen der Hohen Behörde
(Tübingen: Mohr (Paul Siebeck), 1965)

La Décision dans les Communautés européennes.
Grands Colloques Européens, No 2: Publications de
l'Institut d'Etudes Européennes de l'Université Libre
de Bruxelles

DUMON, F, 'La formation de la règle de droit dans
les Communautés européennes', Rev. Int. Droit
Comp. (1960), pp 75-107

ECONOMIDES, Constantin P, Le Pouvoir de décision des organisations internationales européennes (Leiden: Sijthoff, 1964). Aspects Européens - Série E: Droit - No 3

LAGRANGE, Maurice, 'Le pouvoir de décision dans les Communautés européennes: théorie et réalité', Rev. Trimest. Droit Eur. (1967), pp 1-29

LAGRANGE, Maurice, Le Processus d'élaboration des décisions dans les Communautés Européennes: théorie et réalité (Deventer: Kluwer, 1968). Europese Monographieen, no 10: Besluitvorming in de europese Gemeenschappen, pp 11-42

LOUIS, J V, Les Règlements de la Communauté économique européenne (Bruxelles: Presses Universitaires de Bruxelles, 1969). Publications de l'Institut d'Etudes Europeennes de l'Université Libre de Bruxelles - thèses et travaux juridiques no 3

MORAND, C A, La Législation dans les communautés européennes (Paris: Librairie générale de droit et de jurisprudence, 1968)

MORAND, C A, 'Les recommendations, les résolutions et les avis du droit communautaire', Cah. Droit Eur. (1970), p 623

OPHUELS, C F, 'Les règlements et les directives dans les traités de Rome', Cah. Droit Eur. (1966), pp 3-20

PESCATORE, P, 'Remarques sur la nature juridique des décisions des représentants des états membres réunis au sein du conseil', Sociaal-Economische Wetgeving (1966), p 579

PINAY, P, 'L'exercice du pouvoir réglementaire dans la Communauté economiqué européenne à propos de l'élimination des discriminations en matière de transport', Annu. Fr. Droit Int. (1960)

SCHERMERS, H G, 'Besluiten van de vertegenwoordigers der lid-staten; Gemeenschapsrecht', Sociaal-Economische Wetgeving (1966), pp 545-79

WOHLFAHRT, H, 'Von der Befugnis der Organe der europäischen Wirtschaftsgemeinschaft zur Rechtsetzung', Jahrb. Int. Recht (1960)

13.24.3.12.8 VOTING IN THE COMMUNITIES

LJUBISAVLJEVIC, B, Les Problèmes de la pondération dans les institutions européennes (Leiden: Sijthoff, 1959). 199 pp.
OPHUELS, C F, 'Die Mehrheitsbeschlüsse der Räte in den europäischen Gemeinschaften', Europa (1966), 193-586

13.24.3.12.9 EUROPEAN CIVIL SERVANTS

BLOCH, Roger, & LEFEVRE, Jacqueline, La Fonction publique internationale et européenne (Paris: Librairie générale de droit et de jurisprudence, 1963). Collection Economie et Legislation Européennes, no 1
CLEMENS, Adrian, Der Europäische Beamte und sein Disziplinarrecht (Leiden: Sijthoff, 1962). Europaische Aspekte, Reihe E: Recht No 1
EULER, August Martin, Europäisches Beamtenstatut: Kommentar zum Beamtenstatut der EWG und EAG (Köln: Carl Heymanns Verlag, 1966)
HOLTZ, Theodor, Handbuch des Europäischen Dienstrechts (Baden-Baden: Verlag August Lutzeyer, 1964). With supplements.
KORDT, A, Der Europäische Beamte (München/Berlin, 1955)
TEKUELVE, Ewald, 'Das Beamtenrecht der Europaischen Gemeinschaften', Bayerische Beamtenzeitung (1968), no 10, pp 146-8; no 11, pp 172-3, no 12, pp 184-5, (1969), no 1, pp 8-12

13.24.3.12.10   EXECUTION OF ACTS

See also Section 13.24.3.12.6.5.1 on judicial control.
KOVAR, R, LAGARDE, P, & TALLON, D,
   'L'exécution des directives de la CEE en France',
   Cah. Droit Eur. (1970), pp 274-302
OSTERHELD, H, Die Vollstreckung von Entscheidungen
   der Europäischen Gemeinschaft für Kohle und Stahl
   in der Bundesrepublik Deutschland (Frankfurt, 1954)
RAMBOW, Gerhard, 'L'exécution des directives de la
   Communauté économique européenne en République
   Fédérale d'Allemagne', Cah. Droit Eur. (1970), pp
   379-411

13.24.3.12.11   ACTS TAKEN BY
                MEMBER STATES

Although member states may, through their representatives be united in the Council of the Communities, they do, occasionally, act, as it were, in their own right and take decisions imputable to them and not to the organizations. On this highly interesting issue see:
BEBR, Gerhard, 'Acts of representatives of the
   governments of the member states taken within the
   Council of Ministers of the European Communities',
   Sociaal-Economische Wetgeving (1966), pp 529-45
FOIS, Paola, Gli accordi degli Stati membri delle
   Communità Europee (Milano: Giuffré, 1968)
KAISER, Joseph H, 'Die im Rat vereinigten Vertreter
   der Regierungen der Mitgliedstaaten', in Zur
   Integration Europas (Karlsruhe: Verlag C F Muller,
   1965)

13.24.3.12.12 COMMON MARKET

13.24.3.12.12.1 CIRCULATION OF GOODS, WORKERS AND CAPITAL

EHLE, & MEIER, EWG Warenverkehr. Aussenhandel-Zöllen-Subventionen (Köln: Schmidt, 1971)
MAESTRIPIERE, C, La Libre Circulation des personnes et des services dans la CEE (Heule: UGA, 1972)
MENAIS, G P, Le Marché européen des capitaux (Paris: Les Editions de l'Epargne, 1969)

13.24.3.12.12.2 RIGHT OF ESTABLISHMENT

EVERLING, Ulrich, Das Niederlassungsrecht im Gemeinsamen Markt (Berlin/Frankfurt: Verlag Franz Vahlen, 1963). English text: The Right of Establishment in the Common Market (New York/Chicago/Washington: CCH, 1964)
KISS, Alexandre Charles, 'Entrée en vigueur de la Convention Européenne d'Etablissement et de la Charte Sociale Européenne', Annu. Fr. Droit Int. (1965), pp 686-91
MAZZEOTTI, Manlio, et al, La Liberté d'établissement et la libre prestation des services dans les Pays de la CEE (Milano: Giuffré, 1970)
PLATZ, Klaus Wilhelm, 'EWG-Niederlassungsrecht und individuelle Rechtspositionen', Beiträge zum ausländischen öffentlichen Recht und Völkerrecht, vol 45 (Köln: Carl Heymanns Verlag, 1966)

13.24.3.12.12.3 COMPETITION

ALEXANDER, W, Brêvets d'invention et règles de concurrence du Traité CEE (Bruxelles: Bruylant, 1971)
BRAUN, Antoine, GLEISS, Alfred, & HIRSCH, Martin, Droit des ententes de la Communauté européenne

(Bruxelles: Larcier/Paris: Dalloz, 1967)
CEREXHE, E, 'L'interprétation de l'article 86 du traité de Rome et les premiers décisions de la Commission', Cah. Droit Eur. (1972), p 272
CONSTANTINESCO, Leontin, 'Les positions dominantes: aspects juridiques', in Les Ententes à l'échelle européenne (Paris: Dunod, 1967), pp 79-100
DERINGER, A, Competition Law of the EEC (Chicago: CCH, 1968)
DUBOIS, Jean-Pierre, La Position dominante et son abus dans l'article 86 du Traité de la CEE (Paris: Librairies Techniques, 1968)
GERVEN, Walter van, Principles du droit des ententes de la Communauté économique européenne (Bruxelles: Bruylant, 1966)
GIDE-LOYRETTE-NOUEL, Le Droit de la concurrence des Communautés européennes. Traité pratique - Recueil de textes (Paris: Joly, 1969)
GRAUPNER, R, The Rules of Competition in the European Economic Community (Den Haag: Nijhoff, 1965)
HONIG, Frederick, BROWN, William J, GLEISS, Alfred, & HIRSCH, Martin, Cartel Law of the European Economic Community (London: Butterworth, 1963)
McCLACHLAN, D L, & SWANN, D, Competition Policy in the European Community (London/New York/Toronto: Oxford University Press, 1967)
MOK, M R, 'The cartel policy of the EEC Commission, 1962-1967', Common Market Law Rev. (1968), pp 67-103
OBERDORFER, C W, GLEISS, Alfred, & HIRSCH, Martin, Common Market Cartel Law 2nd edition (Chicago: CCH, 1971). 302 pp.
PLAISANT, R, FRANCESCHELLI, R, & LASSIER, J, Droit européen de la concurrence, articles 85 a 89 du Traité CEE (Paris: Delmas, 1966)

13.24.3.12.12.4 TRANSPORT

DESPICHT, Nigel S, Policies for Transport in the
   Common Market (Sidcup, Kent: Lambarde Press,
   1964)
DESPICHT, Nigel, The Transport Policy of the
   European Communities (London: PEP, 1969). European Series, no 12
FERRON, Olivier de, Le Problème des transports et le
   Marché Commun (Genève: Droz, 1965). Etudes
   d'histoire économique, politique et sociale, vol 48
FISCHER, A, L'Organisation des transports dans le
   cadre de l'Europe des Six (Leiden, Sijthoff, 1968)
On ECSC:
KLAER, Werner, Der Verkehr im Gemeinsamen Markt
   für Kohle und Stahl. Beiträge zur europaischen
   Verkehrspolitik (Baden/Bonn: Lutzeyer, 1961)

13.24.3.12.12.5 HARMONIZATION OF LEGISLATION

GROEBEN, Hans van der, La Politique de la
   Commission européenne dans le domaine du
   rapprochement des législations (Bruxelles: Service
   des publications des Communautés européennes, 1969)
L'Harmonisation dans les Communautés (Bruxelles:
   Editions de l'Institut de Sociologie, 1968). Publications
   de l'Institut d'Etudes des Européennes de l'Université
   Libre de Bruxelles - Enseignement complementaire -
   Nouvelle série, no 2, 288 pp.
SEMINI, A, La CEE Harmonisation des législations
   (Paris: Delmas, 1971)
SCHWARTZ, I E, 'Zur Konzeption der Rechtsangleichung
   in der Europäischen Wirtschaftsgemeinschaft', in
   Probleme des europäischen Rechts, Festschrift für
   Walter Hallstein (Frankfurt, 1966), pp 474-514

STEIN, E, Harmonisation of European Company Laws -
National Reform and Transitional Coordination
(New York: Bobbs-Merrill, 1971)

13.24.3.12.12.6 EEC COMMERCIAL POLICY

See also international relations in Section 13.24.3.12.
15 and treaty-making power in Section 13.2.4.3.12.14.
EVERLING, Ulrich, 'Legal problems of the common
  commercial policy in the European Economic
  Community', Common Market Law Rev., vol 4
  (1966), pp 141-65
KIM, Cae-One, 'The common commercial policy of the
  EEC', Journal of World Trade Law (1970), p 20
KIM, Cae-One, 'Developments in the commercial
  policy of the European Economic Community', Common
  Market Law Rev., vol 7 (1970), pp 148-67
KOVAR, Robert, 'La mise en place d'une politique
  commerciale commune et les compétences des
  états membres de la Communauté économique
  européenne en matière de relations internationales
  et de conclusion des traités', Annu. Fr. Droit. Int.
  (1971), p 783
LE TALLEC, Georges, 'The common commercial
  policy of the EEC', Int. & Comp. Law Q. (1971),
  p 732

13.24.3.12.13 INTERNATIONAL RELATIONS
              OF THE COMMUNITIES

BETTE, A G, 'Les relations extérieures de
  l'Euratom', in Aspects du droit de l'énergie
  atomique (Paris: Centre français de droit comparé,
  1967), vol 2, pp 459-74
Colloque sur les relations entre la Communauté
  économique européenne et les pays en voie de
  développement (Renouvellement de la Convention de

Yaoundé) Berlin. September/October 1968 (Paris: Ediafric, La documentation africaine, 1970)

DIJK, P van, 'Het optreden van de EEG als rechtspersoon op het terrein der buitenlandse betrekkingen', Ars Aequi, vol 15, no 7 (1966), pp 217-31

EVERTS, Philip P, (ed), The European Community in the World: the External Relations of the Enlarged European Community (Rotterdam: University Press, 1972)

FELD, Werner, 'The competences of the European Communities for the conduct of external relations', Texas Law Review (1965), pp 891-926

FELD, Werner, The European Common Market and the World (Englewood Cliffs, NJ: Prentice-Hall, 1967)

GANSHOF Van der MEERSCH, W J, 'Les relations extérieures de la CEE dans le domaine des politiques communes et l'ârret de la Cour de justice du 31 mars 1971', Cah. Droit Eur. (1972), p 129

GARRETSON, Albert H, 'Some aspects of the foreign relations power of the European Communities', Washington Law Review (1966), pp 411-22

HEINRICHS, A, Die auswärtigen Beziehungen der europäischen Gemeinschaft für Kohle und Stahl, insbesondere ihr Verhältnis zur OEEC, (Bonn, 1961)

KIM, Cae-One, La Communauté européenne dans les relations commerciales internationales. Institut d'Etudes Européennes de l'Université Libre de Bruxelles (Bruxelles: Presses Universitaires de Bruxelles, 1971)

MONACO, R, 'Les relations extérieures de la CECA', Annu. Eur. (1956), pp 75-95

PESCATORE, P, 'Les relations extérieures des communautés européennes. Contribution à la doctrine de la personnalité des organisations internationales', Acad. Droit Int. Recl. Cours, vol 103 (1961), pp 1-244

PRIEUR, R, Les Relations internes et externes de la Communauté européenne du charbon et de l'acier (Paris, 1958)

RAUX, Jean, Les Relations extérieures de la Communauté économique européenne (Paris: Editions Cujas, 1966)

RAUX, Jean, 'La Cour de justice des Communautés et les relations extérieures de la CEE', Rev. Gén. Droit Int. Public (1972), p 36

REICHLING, Charles, Le Droit de légation des Communautés européennes (Heule: editions UGA, 1964). Centre international d'études et de recherches européennes - cours.

Les relations extérieures de la Communauté européenne unifiée. Institut d'études juridiques européennes de la faculté de droit de l'université de Liège, 1969

SOCINI, R, Le organizzazioni internazionali a carattere europeo considerate nei loro rapporti reciproci (Padova, 1957)

SOTO, J de, 'Les relations internationales de la Communauté européenne du charbon et de l'acier', Acad. Droit Int. Recl. Cours, vol 90 (1956), pp 29-116

WAELBROECK, Michel, 'L'arrêt AETR et les compétences externes de la Communauté économique européenne', Integration (1971), pp 78-89

13.24.3.12.14 TREATY-MAKING POWER OF THE COMMUNITIES

BOGAERT, E R C van, Overzicht van het verdragsrecht der Europese organisaties (Gent, 1966)

COSTONIS, John J, 'The treaty-making power of the European Economic Community: the perspectives of a decade', Common Market Law Rev., vol 5 (1968), pp 421-57

GLAESNER, H J, 'Treaty making power and legislation of the European Community', Assoc. Auditeurs & Anc. Auditeurs Acad. Droit Int. La Haye Annu, vol 31 (1961), pp 147-59

HALLIER, H J, 'Die Vertragschliessungsbefugnis der europäische Gemeinschaft für Kohle und Stahl', Z. Ausl. Öff. Recht. & Völkerrecht, vol 17 (1957), 428-47

LORCHER, G, Der Abschluss völkerrechtlicher Verträge nach dem Recht der drei europäischen Gemainschaften. (EGKS, EWG und EAG). Ein Beitrag zur Rechtsstellung organisierter Staaten Verbindungen (Bonn, 1965)

MEGRET, J, 'Le pouvoir de la Communauté économique européenne de conclure des accords internationaux', Rev. Marché Commun, no 75 (December 1964), pp 529-36

MELCHIOR, Michel, 'La procédure de conclusion des accords externes de la Communauté économique européenne', Rev. Belg. Droit Int. (1966), pp 187-215

RAUX, J, 'La procédure de conclusion des accords externes de la Communauté européenne de l'énergie atomique', Rev. Gén. Droit Int. Public, vol 69 (1965), pp 1019-50

SOCINI, R, 'Considerazioni sullo 'jus tractatum' delle organizzazioni europee', Riv. Diritto Eur., vol 2 (1962), pp 123-30

TESTA, Gaetano, 'L'intervention des etats membres dans la procédure de conclusion des accords d'association de la Communauté économique européenne', Cah. Droit Eur. (1966), pp 492-513

13.24.3.12.15   THE COMMUNITIES
AND THIRD STATES

See also Sections 13.15 on international relations,
13.24.3.12.17 on association agreements and
13.24.3.12.12.6 on commercial policy.
GIARDINA, A, Comunità europee e stati terzi (Napoli, 1964)
HAGEMANN, M, Die europäische Wirtschafts integration und die Neutrlität und Souveranität der Schweiz (Basel, 1957)
PESCATORE, P, Les Communautés européennes et les pays tiers (Roma, 1964)
REY, J, 'Die EWG und ihre Beziehungen zur Drittländern', vol 15 (1960), pp 433-41
SIMMONDS, K R, 'The Community and the neutral states', Common Market Law Rev., vol 2 (1964), pp 5-20
TOMUSCHAT, Christian, 'EWG und DDR. Völkerrechtliche Überlegungen zum Sonder-status des Aussenseiters einer Wirtschaftsunion', Europa (1969), pp 298-332
WOHLFAHRT, E, Fondements juridiques des relations entre les Communautés européennes et les étatstiers (Bruxelles: Institut d'Etudes Européennes, 1964). Publications de l'institut d'études européennes, no 6
WENGLER, W, 'La communauté, les pays tiers et les organisations internationales'. Congrès int. d'études sur la Ceca. Stresa, 1957

13.24.3.12.16   THE RELATIONSHIP BETWEEN
THE COMMUNITIES AND GATT

See also the nature of the Communities in Section 13.24.3.12.2.
JAEGER, Franz, GATT, EWG and EFTA. Die

Vereinbarkeit von EWG- und EFTA-Recht mit dem
GAAT-Statut (Bern: Verlag Stämpfli & Cie, 1970).
Schweizerische Beiträge zum Europarecht, no 4
PANHUYS, H F van, 'Conflicts between the law of the
European Communities and other rules of international law', Common Market Law Rev., vol 3
(1965/6). pp 420-49

13.24.3.12.17 ASSOCIATION OF THE COMMUNITIES WITH STATES

See also international relations in Section 13.15, treaty-making power in Section 13.24.3.12.14 and relationship to third states in Section 13.24.3.12.15. Some of the association agreements are designed to pave the way for full membership. On the association of developing countries in Africa see also, DELUPIS, Ingrid, The East African Community and Common Market, listed in Section 13.24.3.14.

L'Association a la Communauté Economique
  Européenne: Aspects juridiques (Bruxelles: Presses
  universitaires de Bruxelles, 1970)
ALEXANDER, W, 'L'association entre la Communauté
  économique et la Grèce', Rev. Hell. Droit Int., vol
  15 (1962), pp 10-50
ANANIADES, L C, L'Association aux Communautés
  européennes (Paris: Pichon & Durand Auzias, 1967).
  352 pp.
COUSTE, P B, L'Association des pays d'outre mer à
  la Communauté économique européenne (Paris, 1959)
DRAETTA, U, 'L'associazione alla CEE nel diritto
  internazionale', Annuario di diritto internazionale,
  vol 1 (1965), pp 198-203
EHRHARDT, C A, 'Die Assozierung von Übersee-
  Ländern mit der EWG', Aussenpolitik, vol 14 (1963)
  pp 381-92

ELIAS, T O, 'The association agreement between the European Economic Community and the Federal Republic of Nigeria', Journal of World Trade Law, vol 2 (1968), pp 189-208

EVERLING, U, 'Die Neuregelung des Assoziationsverhältnisses zwischen der Europäische Wirtschaftsgemeinschaft und den afrikanischen Staaten und Madagaskar sowie den überseeischen Ländern und Hoheitsgebieten', Z. Ausl. Öff Recht & Völkerrecht, vol 24 (1964), pp 472-574

FERRANDI, J, L'Intervention de la CEE dans les pays associés (Bruxelles, 1962)

FURLER, H, 'Die Neugestaltung der Assoziation zwischen der EWG und den afrikanischen Staaten und Madagaskar', E A, vol 17 (1962), pp 133-8

HOUBEN, P H J M, De associatie van Suriname en de Nederlandse Antillen met de Europese economische Gemeenschap (Leiden, 1965)

MONACO, R, 'L'accordo di associazione tra la comunità economica europea e la Grecia', Riv. Diritto. Eur., vol 2 (1962), pp 227-40

NEHRING, A, Die Assozierung überseeischer Länder mit dem gemeinsamen Markt (Göttingen, 1963)

OPPERMANN, Th, 'Die Assozierung Griechenlands mit der Europäischen Wirtschaftsgemeinschaft', Z. Ausl. Öff. Recht & Völkerrecht, vol 22 (1962), pp 486-508

PLESSOW, U, Neutralität und Assoziation mit der EWG Dargestelt am Beispiel der Schweiz, Schwedens und Österreichs (Köln: Carl Heymann, 1967)

POULANTZAS, N M, Aspects juridiques de l'association prévue par l'article 238 du traité de la Communauté économique (Paris, 1959)

REY, J, 'L'association de la Grèce et de la Turquie à la CEE', Annu. Eur., vol 11 (1963), pp 50-62

ULRICH, H, 'Der zeitliche Geltungsbereich der Assoziation der assozierten afrikanischen Staaten

und Madagaskars and die Europäische
Wirtschaftsgemeinschaft', Zeitschrift für das
gesammte Handels- und Wirtschaftsrecht, vol 130
(1968), pp 298-350

SEIDL-HOHENVELDERN, I, 'Die Assoziation der
neutralen Staaten mit der EWG im Lichte des
Völkerrechts', Östereichisches Zeitschrift für
Aussenpolitik, vol 5 (1965), pp 164-77

TELCHINI, I, 'L'assoziazione in diritto, internazionale
con particolare riguardo all'accordo Grecia-Comunità
Economica Europea', Diritto Internazionale, vol 15
(1961), pp 318-33

VEDOVATO, G, 'L'associazione alla CEE degli stati
africani e malgascio. Rivista di studi politici internazionali', vol 31 (1963), pp 42-118

WOLFRAM, D, Die Assozierung überseeischer Gebiete
an die EWG. Eine Untersuchung der völkerrechtlichen Problematik (Köln, 1964)

13.24.3.12.18 THE RELATIONSHIP BETWEEN THE LAW OF THE EUROPEAN COMMUNITIES AND THE LAW OF THE MEMBER STATES

On this controversial problem see also the
relationship between international law and internal law
in general in Section 3, relationship between treaties
and internal law in Section 7.13.13.2, constitutionality
of treaties in Section 7.13.13.4. See the work by
RIPHAGEN listed under Section 13.24.3.12.1. See
also the prejudicial procedure of the Court in Section
13.24.3.12.6.5.3 for the distribution of power between
national courts and the Community Court.

AGO, R, 'International organisations and their functions
in the field of internal activities of states', Nord.
Tidsskr. Int. Ret., vol 27 (1957), pp 1-18

BALLADORE PALLIERI, G, 'Les pouvoirs des organisations économiques européennes a l'interieur des états membres', Z. Ausl. Öff. Recht & Völkerrecht, vol 23 (1963), pp 473-84

BEBR, G, 'The relation of the ECSC law to the law of the member states: a peculiar legal symbiosis', Columbia Law Review (June 1958), pp 767-97

BEBR, Gerhard, 'Law of the European Communities and municipal law', Modern Law Review, vol 33 (1971), p 481

BRINKHORST, L J, 'Het europees parlement en de voorrang van het gemeenschapsrecht', Sociaal-Economische Wetgeving, vol 13 (1965), pp 633-44

CONSTANTINIDES-MEGRET, Colette, Le Droit de la Communauté économique européenne et l'ordre juridique des états membres (Paris: Librairie général de droit et de jurisprudence, 1967)

DEHOUSSE, F, 'De voorrang van het Gemeenschapsrecht boven het recht der lid-staten', Tijdschrift voor Bestuurswetenschappen en Publiek Recht, vol 20 (1965), pp 353-83

DONNER, André, 'Les rapports entre la compétence de la Cour de Justice des Communautés Européennes et les tribunaux internes', Acad. Droit Int. Recl. Cours, vol 115 (1965), pp 5-58

DUMON, F, 'Conflits entre les normes résultant des traités ayant institué les Communautés européennes et celles des droits nationaux des états membres. Application des articles 85 et 86 du traité CEE par les tribunaux nationaux', Rev. Int. Droit Comp., vol 17 (1965), pp 55-72

FROWEIN, J, 'Zum Verhältnis zwischen dem EWG-Recht und nationalem Recht aus der Sicht des Gerichtshofes des Europäischen Gemeinschaften', A B B, vol 10, no 8 (30 August 1964), pp 233-8

GAUDET, M, 'Incidences des communautés européennes sur le droit interne des états membres', Annu. Fr. Droit Int., vol 8 (1963), pp 5-26

'Gemeinschaftsrecht und nationale Rechte', (Köln: Carl Heymann, 1971)
IPSEN, H P, 'The relationship between the law of the European communities and national law', Common Market Law Rev., vol 2 (1965), pp 379-402
JAENICKE, G, 'Das Verhältnis zwischen Gemeinschaftsrecht und nationale Recht in der Agrarmarktorganisation der Europäischen Wirtschaftsgemeinschaft', Z. Ausl. Öff. Recht & Völkerrecht, vol 23 (1963), pp 485-535
Le Juge national et le droit communautaire (Leiden: Sijthoff/Bruxelles: Larcier, 1966)
MARCUS-HELMONS, S, 'Le droit communautaire et les droits nationaux des états membres', Annales de droit sociale politique, vol 24 (1964), pp 149-69
MATTHIES, H, 'Artikel 65 des EGKS-Verträges und der nationale Richter', Zeitschrift für das gesamte Handelsrecht, und Wirtschaftsrecht, vol 128 (1965), pp 99-113
MATTHIES, H, 'L'article 65 du traité CECA et le juge national', Annales de droit sociale politique, vol 24 (1964), pp 123-36
MÜNCH, F, 'Die Abgrenzung des Rechtsbereiches der supranationalen Gemeinschaft gegenüber dem innerstaatlichen Recht', B d G V (1958) pp 73-93. With discussion on pp 116-38
MONACO, R, 'Norme comunitarie e diritto statuale interno', Riv. Diritto Eur., vol 2 (1962), pp 3-17
MOSCONI, F, 'Orientamenti giurisprudenziali sull/ adattamento del diritto statale ai trattati comunitari', Diritto Internazionale, vol 19 (1965), pp 135-59
PANHUYS, H F van, 'Conflicts between the law of the European communities and other rules of international law', Common Market Law Rev., vol 3 (1966), pp 420-49
PIOLA-CASELLI, C, 'Verhältnis des EWG-Vertrages zum nationalen Recht', ABB, vol 10, no 7 (30 July 1964), pp 219-21

RIGAUX, F, 'L'application du droit communautaire par les juridictions belges (1961-1964)', A D, vol 25, no 3 (1965), pp 277-92

RIPHAGEN, W, 'Iets over de betekenis der structuur van verdragen en besluiten van internationale instellingen voor de internationale en de interne rechtsorde', in Opstellen aangeboden aan Prof. mr. dr. van den Bergh ter gelegenheid van zijn aftreden als hoogleraar in het nederlandse staatsrecht aan de Universiteit van Amsterdam (1960), pp 192-210

ROUCOUNAS, E J, 'L'autorité, en droit interne de l'accord d'association de la Grèce a la Communauté économique européenne', Rev. Hell. Droit Int., vol 15 (1962), pp 367-74

SALMON, A, 'L'application en France des directives de la CEE', Rev. Marché Commun, no 79 (April 1965), pp 165-8

SCHLOCHAUER, H J, 'Das Verhältnis des Rechts der Europäischen Wirtschaftsgemeinschaft zu den nationalen Rechtsordnungen der Mitgliedstaaten', Arch. Völkerrechts, vol 11 (1963), pp 1-34

TALLON, D, & KOVAR, R, 'The application of Community law in France', Common Market Law Rev., vol 4 (1966), pp 64-77

TELCHINI, I, 'L'interpretazione di norme comunitarie e le giurisdizione nazionali', Diritto Internazionale, vol 17 (1963), pp 247-58

WAELBROECK, M, 'Le juge belge devant le droit international et le droit communautaire', Rev. Belg. Droit Int. (1965), pp 348-68

ZULEEG, Manfred, 'Das Recht der Europäischen Gemeinschaften im innerstatlichen Bereich', (Koln: Carl Heymann, 1969)

13.24.3.12.19 DIRECT APPLICATION OF COMMUNITY LAW

BEBR, Gerhard, 'Directly applicable provisions of Community law: the development of a Community concept', Int. & Comp. Law Q. (1970), p 257

CONSTANTINESCO, Léontin-Jean, Die unmittelbare Anwendbarkeit von Gemeinschaftsnormen und der Rechtsschutz von Einzelpersonen im Recht der EWG (Baden-Baden: Nomos Verlagsgesellschaft, 1969). Schriftenreihe zum Handbuch für Europäische Wirtschaft, vol 40

DUMON, F, 'La notion de "disposition directement applicable" en droit européen', Cah. Droit Eur. (1968), p 369

GELDEREN, M van, 'Le problème de l'applicabilité directe des règles de concurrence dans la Communauté économique européenne', Ned. Tijdschr. Int. Recht, vol 5 (1958), pp 366-76

LOUIS, J V, 'Applicabilité directe du règlement', Cah. Droit Eur. (1972), p 325

MERTENS DE WILMERS, Josse, 'De directe werking van het europese recht', Sociaal-Economische Wetgeving, no 2 (1969), pp 62-81

PRASCH, Gerhard, Die unmittelbare Wirkung des EWG-Vertrages auf die Wirtschaftsunternehmen (Baden-Baden: Nemos Verlag, 1967)

13.24.3.13 THE ARAB LEAGUE

ANABTAWI, Munzer F, Arab Unity in Terms of Law (Groningen 1962). 263 pp.

BIEGEL, L C, De Arabische Liga; een belangrijke phase in de strijd om de politieke eenheid van de Arabische wereld (Amsterdam: C P J van der Peet, 1954). xi + 212 pp. Politieke en Sociale Facetten, no 1

BOUTROS-GHALI, B Y, 'The Arab League', Int. Conciliation, no 498 (1954)
MACDONALD, Robert, The League of Arab States (Princeton, NJ: Princeton University Press, 1965). 407 pp.
LAISSY, Michel, Du Panarabisme à la Ligue Arabe (Paris: G I Maisonneuve, 1948). 248 pp.
YESSADE, Pierre B, La Ligue Arabe (Paris, 1968). 261 pp.

13.24.3.14 EAST AFRICAN COMMUNITY (EAC)

DELUPIS, I, (née Detter), The East African Community and Common Market (London: Longmans/Stockholm: Norstedt, 1970). 185 pp.

13.24.3.15 ORGANIZATION FOR AFRICAN UNITY (OAU)

CERVENKA, Zdenek, The Qrganisation of African Unity and its Charter 2nd edition (London: C Hurst & Co, 1969). xii + 253 pp.

13.24.3.16 CENTRAL AMERICAN COMMON MARKET (CACM)

COCHRANE, James D, The Politics of Regional Integration: The Central American Case (Den Haag: Nijhoff, 1969). 225 pp.
SIMMONDS, K R, 'The Central American Common Market', Int. & Comp. Law Q., vol 16 (1967), pp 911-55 (text included). See also Simmonds in Int. & Comp Law Q., vol 19 (1970), pp 376-81

13.24.3.17 LATIN AMERICAN FREE TRADE ASSOCIATION (LAFTA)

DELL, Sidney, A Latin American Common Market? (London: Oxford University Press, 1966). 336 pp.

13.24.3.18 ORGANIZATION OF AMERICAN STATES (OAS) AND THE PAN AMERICAN MOVEMENT

ACCIOLY, Hildebrando Pompeo Pinto, Raizes ou causas historicas do panamericanismo (Rio de Janeiro: Ministerio das Relações Exteriores, Servico de Publicações, 1953). 77 pp.
ALVAREZ, A, Le panaméricanisme et la 6me conférence panaméricaine (Havana/Paris: Editions internationales, 1928). 190 pp.
BALL, M M, 'The Organization of American States and the Council of Europe. A comparative study', Br. Yearb. Int. Law, vol 26 (1949), pp 150-76
BALL, M Margaret, The OAS in Transition (Durham, NC: Duke University Press, 1969)
CAICEDO CASTILLA, J J, 'Organización de los estados Americanos', Escuela de funcionarios int. (1955-6), pp 147-209
CAICEDO CASTILLA, J J, The Work of the Inter-American Juridical Committee (Washington, 1964)
CANCINO; F C, 'El problema de las relaciones entre un organismo regional y mundial. Practica en el caso de la OEA', Anuario juridico interamericano, vol 4 (1952-4), pp 26-43
CUEVAS CANCINO, F, 'Practica en las relaciones entre la organización de los Estados Americanos y las Naciones Unidas', Revista de la Escuela nac. de jurisprudencia, vol 4, no 13 (1954), pp 63-77
DE CONDE, A, 'The Organization of American States: Peace and power politics', World Affairs Interpreter, vol 22, no 4 (Winter 1952), pp 402-14

DUPUY, R J, 'L'évolution du panaméricanisme vers le fédéralisme', Thesis. Paris, 1948
DUPUY, R J, Le nouveau panaméricanisme. L'évolution du système inter-américain vers le fédéralisme (Paris, 1956). 256 pp.
ERMARTH, F, Die panamerikanische Union und ihre Rechtsnatur im Völker- und Landesrecht (Berlin/ Grünewald, 1934)
FENWICK, Ch G, 'L'Organisation des Etats américains, ses principes et ses buts', Bulletin interparlementaire, vol 38 (1958), pp 36-43
FENWICK, C G, 'The charter of the Organization of American States as the "law of the land"', Am. J. Int. Law, vol 47 (1953), pp 281-4
FENWICK, C G, 'The competence of the Council of the Organisation of American states', Annuario juridico interamericano (1949), pp 21-39
FENWICK, C G, 'The revision of the pact of Bogota', Am. J. Int. Law, vol 48 (1954), pp 123-6
FENWICK, C G, The Organization of American States: the transition from an unwritten to a written constitution', Am. J. Int. Law, vol 59 (1965), pp 315-20
FENWICK, Charles G, The OAS (Washington, 1963)
FREEMAN, A V, 'The political powers of the OAS council', in Law and Politics in the World Community (1953), pp 252-78
GOMEZ ROBLEDO, A, 'Las instituciones juridicas en las relaciones interamericanas', Cursos monográficos (1956), pp 117-84
JIMENEZ DE ARACHAGA, E, 'La coordination des systèmes de l'ONU et de l'Organisation des états américains pour le règlement pacifique des différends et la sécurité collective', Acad. Droit Int. Recl. Cours, vol 111 (1964), pp 419-526
KUNZ, J L, 'The Bogotá charter of the Organization of American States', Am. J. Int. Law, vol 42 (1948), pp 568-89

KUTZNER, Gerhard, Die Organisation der Amerikanischen Staaten (Hamburg 1970). 399 pp.

LANGROD, G, 'Les problèmes administratifs du régionalisme international. (Histoire et réalisations de panaméricanisme)', Rev. Hell. Droit Int., vol 10 (1957), pp 132-230

MORGAN, G G, 'The Organization of American States: a problem of administrative reorganization', Revue internationale des sciences administratives, vol 18 (1952), pp 501-29

NASCIMENTO E SILVA, G E do, 'Estrutura e funcionamento da Organização des estados Americanos', Boletim da Sociedade brasileire d. dir. int., vol 12, nos 23-4 (1956), pp 38-61

PENFIELD, W S, 'The legal status of the Pan American Union', Am. J. Int. Law, vol 20 (1926), pp 257-62

ROBERTSON, A H, 'Revision of the Charter of the Organization of American States', Int. & Comp. Law Q., vol 17 (1968), pp 346-67

SOLA CANIZURES, F de, 'Les conférences et les conventions panaméricains. Sources légales et bibliographiques du droit international américain', Rev. Gén. Droit Int. Public, vol 53 (1949), pp 89-128

STOETZER, O Carlos, The Organization of American States: An Introduction (New York: Praeger, 1965)

THOMAS, Ann V, & THOMAS, A J, Jr, The organization of American States (Dallas, Tex: Southern Methodist University Press, 1963)

VOOGD, L C de, La OEA y las Naciones Unidas. Contribución de la Organización de los estados americanos al afianzamento de las Naciones Unidas (Buenos Aires, 1956)

YEPES, J M, 'La conference panaméricaine de Bogotá et le droit international américain', Rev. Gén. Droit Int. Public, vol 53 (1949), pp 17-88

YEPES, J M, & PEREIRA DA SILVA, F C, Commentaire theorique et pratique du pacte de la Societé des

Nations et des Statuts de l'Union panamericaine (Paris, 1934-9). 3 vols
YEPES, J M, Philosophie du Panaméricanisme et organisation de la paix. Le Droit panaméricain (Neuchâtel, 1945)
YEPEZ, Jesus Maria, From the Congress of Panama to the Conference in Caracas, 1826-1954 (Caracas, 1955)
On privileges and immunities of the OAS see:
FERRER VIEYARA, E, Notas sobre privilegios e immunidades en organismos internacionales y en especial en la Organización de los estados americanos (Córdoba, Argentina, 1950)

14 International Economic Law

14.1 PERMANENT SOVEREIGNTY OVER RESOURCES

On this controversial subject see the works listed below and, also, DELUPIS, Finance and Protection, listed in Section 14.5.

GESS, K N, 'Permanent sovereignty over natural resources, an analytical review of the UN declaration and its genesis', Int. & Comp. Law Q., vol 13 (1964), p 398

MUGHRABY, M A, Permanent Sovereignty over Oil Resources: A Study of Middle East Oil Concessions and Legal Change (Beirut, 1966)

14.2 INTERNATIONAL ECONOMIC LAW IN GENERAL

'Aspects du droit international économique, élaboration, contrôle, sanction', Actes du 5 Colloque de la Société française pour le droit international (Paris, 1972)

SCHWARZENBERGER, G, The Principles and Standards of International Economic Law (Leiden, 1966) and Acad. Droit Int. Recl. Cours, vol 117 (1966)

SCHWARZENBERGER, Georg, Economic World Order.

A Basic Problem of International Economic Law
(Manchester: Manchester University Press, 1970).
xii + 159 pp.

14.3 MULTINATIONAL COMPANIES

ANGELO, H G, 'Multinational corporate enterprises',
   Acad. Droit Int. Recl. Cours, vol 125 (1968), p 447
GOLOMAN, B, 'The law of international companies',
   J. Droit Int., vol 90 (1963), pp 321-89

14.4 STATE TRADING IN GENERAL

See also Section 7.10.1 on state immunity.
BEHRMANN, J H, 'State trading by undeveloped
   countries', Law and Contemporary Problems, vol 24
   (1959)
COHEN, S, 'Problems of state trading and jurisdictional
   immunity in English and American courts', New
   York Law Forum (1962)
DOMKE, M, 'Arbitration of state trading relations',
   Law and Contemporary Problems, vol 24 (1959),
   p 317
FAWCETT, J E S, 'Legal aspects of state trading', Br.
   Yearb. Int. Law, vol 25 (1948), pp 34-8
FRIEDMANN, S, 'Changing social arrangements in
   statetrading states and their effect on international
   law', Law and Contemporary Problems, vol 24
   (1959), p 350
FRIEDMANN, S, 'State trading in history and theory',
   Law and Contemporary Problems, vol 24 (1959), p
   243
HAZARD, J N, 'Soviet government corporations',
   Michigan Law Review (1943), p 850
MESTMÄCKER, E J, 'Die Abgrenzung von öffentlich-
   rechtlichem und privatrechtlichem Handeln im
   Wettbewerbsrecht', Neue juristische Wochenschrift
   (1969), p 1

MIKESELL, R F, & WELLS, D A, 'State trading in the Sino-Soviet bloc', Law & Contemporary Problems (1959), p 435
QUIN, M, 'State trading in Western Europe', Law & Contemporary Problems, vol 24 (1959), p 398
SHEPARD, P, Sovereignty and State-Owned Commercial Entities (New York, 1951)
SEIDL-HOHENVELDERN, I, 'The impact of state-trading on classical international law', Yearb. World Aff. (1962), p 159
SUCHARITKUL, S, State Immunities and Trading Activities in International Law (London, 1959)
SZEKANDI, P, 'Contracts between a state and a foreign private company - reflection of the effectiveness of the arbitration process', East African Law Journal, vol 2 (1966), p 281
ZOUREK, J, 'Some comments on the difficulties encountered in the judicial settlement of disputes arising from trade between countries with different economic and social structures', J. Droit Int., vol 86 (1959), pp 639-85

14.5 PROTECTION OF PROPERTY AND FOREIGN INVESTMENTS

On this subject the work by NWOGUGU is of outstanding merit. My own book listed below gives an up-to-date account of available insurance schemes.

AMMANN, U, Der Schutz ausländischer Privatinvestitionen in Entwicklungsländern aus völkerrechtlicher, völkswirtschaftlicher und betriebswirtschaftlicher Sicht (Zürich/St Gallen, 1967)
BAADE, H W, 'Gesetzgebung zur Förderung ausländischer Kapitalanlagen', vol 26 of Dokumente, edited by Forschungstelle für Völkerrecht und ausländisches öffentliches Recht der Universität Hamburg (Frankfurt a M/Berlin 1957)

BENTER, H, Deutsches Vermögen im neutralen Ausland (Göttingen, 1964)
BINDSCHEDLER, R, 'La protection de la propriété privée en droit international public', Acad. Droit Int. Recl. Cours, vol 2 (1956), p 179
BÖCKSTIEGEL, K H, Der gegenwärtige Schutz der Ausländsinvestitionen im allgemeinen Völkerrecht (Teile I und II) DB 1964, 1471 ff und 1507 ff
BÖCKSTIEGEL, K H, Der Schutz des Privateigentums im Ausland, Monatsschrift VDA,(1964). 123 pp.
BÖCKSTIEGEL, K H, Neue Entwicklungen zum Schutz von Investitionen in Entwicklungsländern (AWD, 1967). 41 pp.
CAVARE, L, La protection des droits contractuels reconnus par les états à des étrangers à l'exception des emprunts (Valladolid, 1956)
CHARPENTIER, J, 'De la non-discrimination dans les investissements', Annu. Fr. Droit Int. (1963), p 35
COBOS, E, 'The international protection of small investment', World Peace through Law Center, 65,660 ff.
COLLINS, L A, & ETRA, A, 'Policy, politics, international law and the United States investment guaranty program', Columbia Journal of Transnational Law, vol 4 (1966), p 240
DELUPIS, Ingrid (née Detter), Finance and Protection of Investments in Developing Countries (London: Gower Press, 1973)
DOMKE, M, (ed), Internationaler Schutz von Anleihegläubigern (Mainz, 1934)
EBB, L F, Regulation and Protection of International Business: Cases, Comments and Materials (St. Paul, Minn: 1964)
FATOUROS, A A, 'Obstacles to private foreign investment in underdeveloped countries', Current Law and Social Problems, vol 2 (1961), p 194

FATOUROS, A A, Government Guarantees to Foreign Investors (New York: Columbia University Press, 1962)
FISHER-WILLIAMS, 'International law and the property of aliens', Br. Yearb. Int. Law (1926), p 1
GIESEKE, Industrieinvestitionen in Entwicklungslandern, Risiken und Chancen (Hamburg, 1963)
GUGGENHEIM, 'Der völkerrechtliche Schutz von Investitionem in Ausland', Annu. Suisse Droit Int. (1956), p 57
HORNSEY, G, 'Foreign investment and international law', Int. Law Q. (1950), p 552
HUANG, T F, 'Some international and legal aspects of the Suez Canal question', Am. J. Int. Law, vol 51 (1957), p 277
KOJANEC, Giovanni, Investimenti all'estero. Regime Giuridico e Garanzie Internazionali (Padova: Cedam, 1970). vi + 194 pp.
KRONFOL, Zouhair A, Protection of Foreign Investment. A Study in International Law (Leiden: Sijthoff, 1972). 176 pp.
LILLICH, R B, The Protection of Foreign Investment: Six Procedural Studies (Syracuse, NY: Syracuse University Press, 1965)
LATTRE, J M, de, La Mise en valeur de l'ensemble euroafricain français et la participation de capitaux étrangers, (sociétés à participation étrangère compagnies à charte) (Paris, 1954)
MAWALLA, J R, 'Law rules to encourage international investments', World Peace through Law Center Conference Report (1963), p 292
McDANIELS, J F (ed), International Financing and Investment (Dobbs Ferry, NY: Oceana, 1964)
NARITOMI, N, 'Transnational trade and investment', World Peace through Law Center Conference Report (1965), p 281

NEUMANN WHITMAN, M von, Government Risk-Sharing in Foreign Investment (Princeton, NJ: Princeton University Press, 1965)
NWOGUGU, E I, The Legal Problems of Foreign Investment in Developing Countries (Manchester: Manchester University Press, 1965)
PFUHL, E, 'Gewährleistung und Garantie im zwischenstaatlichen Au enhandel des Ostbloks', Recht in Ost und West, vol 2 (1958), p 1
PUGH, J, Legal Aspects of Foreign Investment (London, 1959)
RAY, G W Jr, 'The development and maintenance of an oil operation in the Middle East,' in Legal Problems in International Trade and Investment (World Community Association, Yale Law School, 1962)
RAY, G W Jr, 'Transnational trade and investments-guarantees of foreign investments', World Peace through Law Center Conference Report (1965), p 266
RHYNE, Ch S, 'Weltrecht zum schutz der Weltinvestitionen', Gesellschaft zur Förderung des schutzes von Auslandsinvestitionen, no 3, p 67 Übersetzung einer Rede vor der American Bankers Association in New York 1958
RUBIN, S J, Private Foreign Investment (Baltimore, Md: Johns Hopkins Press, 1956)
RICCI, D de, Investissements en Amérique Latine, Aspect juridique et fiscal (Paris, 1955). Supplement published in 1957
SCHACHTER, O, 'Private foreign investment and international organisation', Cornell Law Quarterly (1959/60), p 171
SCHWARZENBERGER, G, 'The protection of British property abroad', Current Legal Problems, vol 5 (1952), p 295
SCHWARZENBERGER, G, 'The principles and standards of international economic law', Acad. Droit Int. Recl. Cours, vol 117 (1966), p 1

SCHWARZENBERGER, G, 'Decolonisation and the protection of foreign investments', Current Legal Problems, vol 20 (1967), p 213

SCHWARZENBERGER, G, Foreign Investments and International Law (London: Stevens, 1969)

SCHWEBEL, S M, 'International protection on contractual arrangements', Am. Soc. Int. Law Proc. (1959), p 266

SEIDL-HOHENVELDERN, I, 'Eigentumsschutz durch Resolutionen internationaler Organisation', in Der Schutz des privaten Eigentums, Festschrift für Hermann Janssen (1958), p 193

SEIDL-HOHENVELDERN, I, 'Judicial protection of foreign investments', in Mélanges à la Mémoire de S Séfériades (Athens, 1961), vol 1, p 251

SEIDL-HOHENVELDERN, I, 'Investitionen en Entwicklungsländern und das Völkerrecht', Annales Universitates Saraviensis, vol 1 (1963)

SHAWCROSS, Lord, 'The problems of foreign investments in international law', Acad. Droit Int. Recl. Cours, vol 1 (1961), p 335

SIMANTIRAS, C J, 'Principles concerning legal protection of international investment', World Peace through Law Center Conference Report (1965), p 769

VEITH, W, & BÖCKSTIEGEL, K H, Der Schutz von ausländischen Vermögen im Völkerrecht (Baden-Baden, 1962)

VERDROSS, A v, 'Protection of private property under Quasi International Agreements', in François-Festschrift (Varia iuris gentium. Liber amicorum J P A François (Leiden, 1959), p 355

WELLS, E J M, 'Guarantees in international economic law', Int. & Comp Law Q., vol 6 (1955), p 426

WITENBERG, J C, 'La protection de la propriété immobilière des étrangers', J. Droit Int., vol 55 (1928), p 579

14.6 TREATIES ON TRADE AND MONETARY MATTERS

HAWKINS, H C, Commercial Treaties and Agreements: Principles and Practice (New York, 1951)
NOLDE, B, 'Droit et technique des traités de commerce', Acad. Droit Int. Recl. Cours, vol 2 (1924), p 295
NUSSBAUM, A, 'International monetary agreements', Am. J. Int. Law, vol 38 (1944), p 242
SAYRE, F B, 'How trade agreements are made', Foreign Affairs, vol 16 (1938), p 417
SCHEUNER, Ulrich, 'Zweiseitige Handelsverträge und multilaterale Handelsverbindungen', Die Friedens-Warte, vol 52 (1954), p 97
WILSON, R R, 'A decade of new commercial treaties', Am. J. Int. Law, vol 50 (1956), p 927
WILSON, R R, 'Postwar commercial treaties of the United States', Am. J. Int. Law, vol 43 (1949), p 262

14.7 TREATIES FOR PROTECTION OF PROPERTY AND INVESTMENTS

See also SCHWARZENBERGER's foreign investment listed in Section 14.5.
ADAM, H, 'Le droit de propriété dans la convention européenne des droit de l'homme', Rev. Droit Public & Sci. Polit. (1953), p 332
ALENFELD, J, 'Die Investitionsförderungsverträge der Bundesrepublik Deutschland', Dissertation. Köln, 1968
BÄULKE, K E, 'Die materiellen Eigentumsschutzbestimmungen in den Verträgen der Bundesrepublik Deutschland zur Förderung und zum Schutz von Kapitalanlagen im Ausland und die allgemeinen Grundsätze des Völkerrechts über die Beachtung ausländischer, wohlerworbener Vermögensrechte', Dissertation. Würzburg, 1965

BRANDENBURG, J, 'Verträge der Bundesrepublik Deutschland über die Förderung und den gegenseitigen Schutz von Kapitalanlagen in Lateinamerika', Dissertation. Köln, 1968

CONNELL, H P, 'United States protection of private foreign investment through treaties of friendship, commerce and navigation', Arch. Völkerrechts, vol 9 (1961/2), p 256

HOFMANNSTHAL, 'Eine Konvention für die Behandlung Konfiszierten Eigentums', AWD (1959), p 145

HYDE, J N, 'Economic development agreements', Acad. Droit Int. Recl. Cours, vol 1 (1962), p 271

KERN, E, 'Die Investitionsförderungsverträge der Bundesrepublik und die deutsche Entwicklungshilfe', Beilage zu BAnz, no 82 (3 May 1964)

METZGER, S D, 'The Abs-Shawcross convention: comments on the round table', Journal of Public Law (1961), p 110

PREISWERK, R, La Protection des investissements privés dans les traités bilatéraux (Zürich, 1963)

SCHWARZENBERG, R G, 'The Abs-Shawcross draft convention on investment abroad: a critical commentary', Journal of Public Law (1960), p 147. Longer version in Current Legal Problems (1961), p 213

SEIDL-HOHENVELDERN, I, 'The Abs-Shawcross draft convention to protect private foreign investment: comments on the round table', Journal of Public Law (1961), p 100

VIGUER, C, 'L'accord franco-algérien du 26 juin 1963 en matière d'arbitrage pétrolier pour le respect des droit acquis au Sahara', Annu. Fr. Droit Int. Public (1964), p 383

WALKER, H, Jr, 'Treaties for the encouragement and protection of foreign investment: present United States practice', Am. J. Comp. Law, vol 5 (1956)

WILSON, R R, '"Treaty-merchant" clauses in commercial treaties of the United States', Am. J. Int. Law, vol 44 (1950), p 145

WILSON, R R, 'Property protection provisions in
United States commercial treaties', Am. J. Int.
Law, vol 45 (1951), p 83
WILSON, R R, 'Natural-resources provisions in
United States commercial treaties', Am. J. Int.
Law, vol 48 (1954), p 355
WILSON, R R, ' "Treaty-investor" clauses in
commercial treaties of the United States', editorial
comment Am. J. Int. Law, vol 49 (1955), p 366

14.8 STATE CONTRACTS

See also Sections 14.9 on concessions and 14.10 on
state loans, 7.13.5.7 on agreements with other than
states.

BÖCKSTIEGEL, K-H, Der Staat als Vertragspartner
 ausländischer Privatunternehmen, (Frankfurt:
 Athenäum 1971)
JENNINGS, R Y, 'State contracts in international law',
 Br. Yearb. Int. Law, vol 37 (1961), p 156
LALIVE, J F, 'Contracts between state or a state
 agency and a foreign company', Int. & Comp. Law Q.,
 vol 13 (1964), p 987
MANN, F A, 'The law governing state contracts',
 Br. Yearb. Int. Law, vol 21 (1944), p 11
MANN, F A, 'State contracts and state responsibility',
 Am. J. Int. Law, vol 54 (1960), p 572
MANN, F A, 'State contracts and international
 arbitration', Br. Yearb. Int. Law, vol 42 (1967),
 pp 1-2
MANN, F A, 'The proper law of contracts concluded
 by international persons', Br. Yearb. Int. Law
 (1959), p 34
SACERDOTI, G, I Contratti tra Stati e Stranieri nel
 Diritto Internazionale (Milano: Giuffré, 1972). 406 pp.
VERDROSS, A, 'Quasi-international agreements and
 international economic transactions', Yearb. World
 Aff., vol 18 (1964), p 230

VERDROSS, A, 'Protection of private property under quasi-international agreements', Ned. Tijdschr. Int. Recht (July 1959), pp 355-62
WADMOND, L, 'The sanctity of contract between a sovereign and a foreign national', Address at the London Meeting of the ABA, 1957

14.9 CONCESSIONS AND ECONOMIC DEVELOPMENT AGREEMENTS

Cf. Section 7.13.5.8
CARLSTON, K S, 'International role of concession agreements', Northwestern University Law Review (1957), p 618
CARLSTON, K S, 'Concession agreements and nationalization', Am. J. Int. Law, vol 52 (1958), p 260
CALVERTH, H G, 'The law applicable to concessions', University of Malaya Law Review (1959), p 265
CATTAN, H, The Law of Oil Concessions in the Middle East and in North Africa (Dobbs Ferry, NY: Oceana, 1967)
CATTAN, H, The Evolution of Oil Concessions in the Middle East and North Africa (Dobbs Ferry, NY: Oceana, 1967)
DEVELLE, P, La Concession en droit international (Paris, 1936). 235 pp.
GEIGER, R, 'The unilateral change of economic development agreements', Int. & Comp. Law Q. (1974), pp 73-104
GULDBERG, T, 'International concessions: a problem of international economic law', Acta scandinavica juris gentium (1944), p 47
HENDRYX, F, 'A sovereign nation's legal ability to make and abide by a petroleum concession contract', Paper delivered to the Arab Oil Congress held in Cairo 16-23.4.1959, printed in: Platt's Oilgram

News Service (NY ed), vol 28, no 4 (1959), pp 2-3
HYDE, J N, 'Economic development agreements',
   Acad. Droit Int. Recl. Cours, vol 105 (1962), p 271
KALTENBACH, A, 'Die Erdölkonzessionen im
   Mittleren Osten', Information der Internationalen
   Treuhand AG Basel 1957, no 11, p 16
LALIVE, J F, 'Abrogation or alternation of an
   economic development agreement between state and a
   private foreign party', Business Lawyer, vol 17
   (1962), p 434
MIKDASHI, Z, A Financial Analysis of Middle Eastern
   Oil Concessions: 1901-1965 (New York: Praeger,
   1966)
MOSLER, H, Wirtschaftskonzessionen bei
   Änderungen der Staatshoheit. Eine völkerrechtliche
   Studie zum Hoheitswechsel und zur Hoheitsausübung
   auf fremdem Staatsgebiet (Stuttgart, 1948)
O'CONNELL, D P, 'Economic concessions in the law
   of state succession', Br. Yearb. Int. Law, vol 27
   (1950), p 93
RAY, G W T, 'Economic development agreements',
   World Peace through Law Center Conference Report
   (1963)
QUACK, K, 'Die Beendigung von Strom-Konzessions-
   verträgen', Archiv des Öffentlichen Rechts, vol 91
   (1966), p 355
SIKSEK, S G, The Legal Framework of Oil Concessions
   in the Arab World (Beirut, 1960)
SIERN, R, 'Zur Problematic des energiewirtschaft-
   lichen Konzessionsvertrages', Archiv des
   Öffentlichen Rechts, vol 84 (1959), p 137; 273
TORIGUIAN, S, Legal Aspects of Oil Concessions in
   the Middle East (Beirut: Hamaskaine Press, 1972).
   317 pp.

14.10 STATE LOANS

See also BROCHES under World Bank, Section 13.24.2.24.7

ADAM, H T, 'Les accords de prêt de la Banque Internationale pour la Reconstruction et le Développement', Rev. Gén. Droit Int. Public, vol 55 (1951), p 41

BORCHARD, E M, 'International loans and international law', Am. Soc. Int. Law Proc. (1932), p 135

DELAUME, G R, 'Jurisdiction of courts and international loans', Am. J. Comp. Law, vol 6 (1957), p 189

Delaume, G R, 'The proper law of loans concluded by international persons: a restatement and a forecast', Am. J. Int. Law, vol 56 (1962), p 63

DELAUME, G R, Legal Aspects of International Lending and Economic Development Financing (Dobbs Ferry, NY: Oceana, 1967)

DELAUME, G R, 'Des stipulations de droit applicable dans les accords de prêt et de développement économique et de leur rôle', Rev. Belg. Droit Int. (1968), p 336

DRAGO, L M, 'Les emprunts d'état et leurs rapports avec la politique internationale', Rev. Gén. Droit Int. Public (1907), p 251

ERLER, G, 'Schwäche und Stärke ausländischer Geldforderungen als völkerrechtliches Problem', in Festschrift für Hans Niedermeyer (Göttingen, 1953), p 77

JEZE, G, La Garantie des emprunts publics d'état (Paris, 1924)

O'CONNELL, D P, 'Secured and unsecured debts in the law of state succession', Br. Yearb. Int. Law, vol 28 (1951), p 204

POLITIS, N E, Les Emprunts d'état en droit international (Paris, 1894)

SACK, A N, Les Effets des transformations des
états sur leur dettes publiques et autres obligations
financières (Paris, 1927)
VAN HECKE, G, 'Problemes juridiques des Emprunts
internationaux', Dissertation. Leiden, 1955
WYNNE, W H, State Insolvency and Foreign Bond-
holders, vol 2 'Selected cases histories of
governmental foreign bond defaults and debt
readjustments' (New Haven, 1951)

14.11 NATIONALIZATION

There is a vast number of books on nationalization
of property and investments of aliens and those below
are but a selection of the most important ones and
those which still today retain some interest.
Particularly valuable works are those by KATZAROV
and WORTLEY and SEIDL-HOHENVELDERN. See also
for recent nationalizations and their compensation,
my own Finance and Protection, listed in Section 14.5.
For the question of evaluation of assets, see the work
edited by Lillich, listed below.

ADRIAANSE, P, Confiscation in Private International
  Law (Den Haag, 1956)
AGUAYO, Leopoldo Gonzáles, La Nacionalización de
  bienes extranjeros en América Latina. I & II
  (Mexico: Universidad Nacional Autónoma de México,
  1969). vi + 412 pp, (Book 1); 295 pp, (book 2)
BINDSCHEDLER, R L, Verstaatlichungsmassnahmen
  und Entschädigungspflicht nach Völkerrecht unter
  besonder Berücksichtigung der schweizerischen
  Praxis über den Schutz schweizerischer
  Vermögenswerte im Ausland (Zürich, 1950)
BIRKE, W, Die Konfiskation ausländischen
  Privatvermögens im Hoheitsbereich des
  konfiszierenden Staates nach Friedensvölkerrecht
  (Hamburg, 1959)

BÖCKSTIEGEL, K H, Die allgemeinen Grundsätze des Völkerrechts uber Eigentumsentziehung - Eine Untersuchung zu Art 1 des Zusatzprotokolls der Europäischen Menschenrechtskonvention (Berlin, 1963)

BÖCKSTIEGEL, K H, 'Neue Entwicklungen im internationalen Enteignungsrecht' A W D (1963), p 361

BRÜEL, E, 'Die völkerrechtliche Stellung des Suezkanals und die Nationalisierung der Kanalgesellschaft', Arch. Völkerrechts (1958/9), p 24

CHRISTIE, G C, 'What constitutes a taking of property under international law?' Br. Yearb. Int. Law, vol 38 (1962)

DAWSON, F G, & WESTON, B H, '"Prompt, adequate and effective": a universal standard of compensation', Fordham Law Review, vol 30 (1962)

DELSON, R, 'Whether a taking of an alien's property without compensation, or in derogation of the terms of contract, is in violation of public international law', Proceedings and Committee Reports of the American Branch of the International Law Association (1959/60), p 33

DELSON, R, 'Nationalization of the Suez Canal Company: issues of public and private international law', Columbia Law Review, vol 57 (1957), p 755

DOMKE, M, 'Foreign nationalizations: some aspects of contemporary international law', Am. J. Int. Law, vol 55 (1961), p 585

FACHIRI, A P, 'Expropriation and international law', Br. Yearb. Int. Law, vol 6 (1925)

FAWCETT, J E S, 'Some foreign effects of nationalisation of property', Br. Yearb. Int. Law, vol 27 (1950)

FOIGHEL, I, Nationalisering af Fremmed Ejendom (Copenhagen, 1961)

FOUILLOUX, G, La Nationalisation et le droit international public (Paris, 1962)

FRIEDMANN, S, Expropriation in International Law (Paris, 1953)

FRIEDRICH, R, Verstaatlichung von Elektrizitätswerken mit internationaler Konzession (Aarau, 1948)

GREGORY, C N, 'Expropriation by international arbitration', International Law Association Conference Report (1907), p 29

HERZ, J H, 'Expropriation of foreign property', Am. J. Int. Law, vol 35 (1941), p 243

HJERNER, L A E, The General Approach to Foreign Confiscations. Scandinavian Studies in Law, no 2 (1958

HYDE, C C, 'Confiscatory expropriations', Am. J. Int. Law, vol 32 (1938)

HYDE, C C, 'Compensation for expropriations', Am. J. Int. Law, vol 33 (1939)

JACQUIGNON, L, Le Régime des biens des entreprises nationales: contribution au droit des nationalisations (Paris, 1956)

JESSUP, Ph C, 'Confiscation', Am. Soc. Int. Law Proc. (1927)

JÈZE, G, 'De la responsabilité pécuniaire de l'Etat italien enverses nationaux et les étrangers à raison de l'établissement d'un monopole public des assurances sur la vie', Revue de la science politique française (1912), p 433

KATZAROV, K, Théorie de la Nationalisation (Neuchâtel, 1960)

KATZAROV, K, The Theory of Nationalization (Den Haag, 1964)

KEGEL, G, Probleme des internationalen Enteignungs-und Währungsrechts (Köln/Opladen, (1956)

KÜFFMANN, G, 'Der Schutz des Privateigen- Ausländern nach Völkergewohnheitsrecht im Frieden unter besonderer Berücksichtigung der Entschadingungspflicht bei Enteignungen', Dissertation. Würzburg, 1966

LILLICH, R B, 'The jurisprudence of the foreign compensation commission', Int. & Comp. Law Q., vol 13 (1964), p 899

LILLICH, R B, (ed), The Valuation of Nationalized Property in International Law (Charlottesville, Va; University Press of Virginia, 1972-3). 2 vols.

MÜNCH, F, 'Les effects d'une nationalisation à l'étranger', Acad. Droit Int. Recl. Cours, vol 98 (1959), p 415

NOVA, R de, 'L'esproprio in diritto internazionale', Il Politico, vol 16 (1951)

OLMSTEAD, C J, 'Nationalization of foreign property interests, particularly those subject to agreements with the state', New York University Law Review, vol 32 (1957), p 1122

PETREN, S, 'La confiscation des biens étrangers et les relations internationales auxquelles elle peut donner lieu', Acad. Droit Recl. Cours, vol 109 (1963), p 491

RE, E D, Foreign Confiscations in Anglo-American Law: A Study of the 'Rule of Decision' Principle (New York, 1951)

RUBIN, S J, 'Nationalisation and compensation - a comparative approach', University of Chicago Law Review, vol 17 (1950)

SCHNEIDER, H, Die Liquidation deutschen Auslandsvermögens und ihre vertragliche Hinnahme durch die Bundesrepublik: Ein Rechtsgutachten zur verfassungsrechtlichen Problematik der deutsch-niederländischen Abkommen von 1960 und 1962 (Heidelberg, 1964)

SEIDL-HOHENVELDERN, I, Internationales Konfiskations- und Enteignungsrecht (Tübingen, 1952)

SEIDL-HOHENVELDERN, J, 'Communist theories of confiscation and expropriation: critical comments', Am. J. Comp. Law, vol 7 (1958), p 541

SEIDL-HOHENVELDERN, I, 'Zur Theorie der Verstaatlichung', Osteuropa-Recht, vol 7 (1961)
SEIDL-HOHENVELDERN, I, 'Title to confiscated property and public international law', Am. J Int. Law, vol 56 (1962)
SEIDL-HOHENVELDERN, I, 'Reprisals and the taking of property', Nord. Tidsskr, Int. Ret (1962), p 470
SEIDL-HOHENVELDERN, I, 'Zur Konfiskation von Aktionärsrechten', ZAIPR, vol 28 (1964)
SEIDL-HOHENVELDERN, I, 'Entschädigungsleistungen des Heimatstaates an durch politische Ereignisse im Ausland geschädigte Staatsangehörige', Schriftenr. Dtsch. Gruppe Assoc. Auditeurs & Anc. Auditeurs Acad. Droit Int. La Haye, 3 (1969), p 75
TROLLER, A, Internationale Zwangsverwertung und Expropriation von Immaterialgütern (Basel, 1955)
VEDEL, G U A, Le Droit à indemnisation des français d'Algérie atteints par des mesures de dépossession (Paris, 1965)
VERDROSS, Alfred von, 'Die Konfiskation ausländischen Privatergentums nach Friedensvölkerrecht', Z. Öff. Recht (1925), p 321
VITTA, E, 'Espropriazione e nazionalizzazione nel diritto internazionale', Riv. Diritto Int. (1953), p 1201
WHITE, G, Nationalization of Foreign Property (London: Stevens, 1962)
WORTLEY, B A, Expropriation in Public International Law (London: Cambridge University Press, 1959)

14.12 ACQUIRED RIGHTS

Some, like myself, would deny that acquired rights exist in public international law. (See Finance and Protection listed under 14.5). However, I may refer to the following works for supporters of the theory of acquired rights.

ABS, H J, Der Schutz wohlerworbener Rechte im
internationalen Verkehr als europäische Aufgabe
(Heidelberg, 1956)
SCHÜCKING, W, 'Der Schutz der wohlerworbenen
Rechte im Völkerrecht', in Festgabe für Max
Huber (Zürich, 1934), p 198

14.13 PARTICULAR INVESTMENT DISPUTES

See also case studies in my book on finance and
protection listed under 14.5.
BAADE, H W, 'Indonesian nationalisation measures
before foreign courts: a reply', Am. J. Int. Law,
vol 54 (1960), p 801
BASTID, S, 'Le droit international public dans la
sentence de l'Aramco', Annu. Fr. Droit Int. (1961),
p 300
BISHOP, W W, Jr, 'The Anglo-Iranian Oil Company case',
Am. J. Int. Law, vol 45 (1951), p 749
BÜLCK, H, 'Tinoco-Konzessions-Fall', in Wörterbuch
des Völkerrechts, edited by K Strupp & H J
Schlochauer (Berlin: de Gruyter, 1960-2), vol 3, p
445
CHENG, B, 'The Anglo-Iranian Oil dispute', World
Affairs (1951), p 387
DOMKE, M, 'The Israeli-Soviet Oil Arbitration',
Am. J. Int. Law, vol 53 (1959), p 787
FENWICK, C G, 'The order of the International Court
of Justice in the Anglo-Iranian Oil Company case',
Am. J. Int. Law, vol 45 (1951), p 723
FORD, A W, The Anglo-Iranian Oil Dispute of 1951-
1952: A Study of the Role of Law in the Relations of
States (Berkeley/Los Angeles, 1954)
FRIEDE, W, 'Der neue Mexikanische Erdölstreit', Z.
Ausl. Öff. Recht. & Völkerrecht, vol 9 (1939/40),
p 31

FARMANFARMA, A, 'The oil agreement between Iran and the international oil consortium: the law controlling', Texas Law Review, vol 34 (1955), p 259

FARTACHE, M, 'De la compétence de la Cour internationale de justice dans l'affaire de l'Anglo-Iranian Oil Co', Rev. Gén. Droit Int. Public (1953), p 584

HOVEYDA, F, 'Les aspects juridiques de la nationalisation des industries pétrolières en Iran', Revue de droit international pour le Moyen-Orient, vol 1 (1951/2), p 127

GHOSH, S K, The Anglo-Iranian Oil Dispute: A Study of Problems of Nationalization of Foreign Investment and Their Impact on International Law (Calcutta, 1960)

LALIVE, J F, 'Un récent arbitrage Suisse entre un organisme d'état et une société privée étrangère (Sapphire International Petroleums Limited c. National Iranian Oil Company)', Schweiz. Jahrb. Int. Recht, vol 19 (1962), p 273

LIANG YUEN-LI, & KWEN CHEN, 'The question of domestic jurisdiction in the Anglo-Iranian Oil dispute before the Security Council', Am. J. Int. Law, vol 46 (1952), p 272

LUNZ, L A, 'Die Nationalizierung der Suez-Kanal-Gesellschaft ist ein souveränes Recht Ägyptens', Rechtswiss. Informationsdienst (Soviet Zone) (1958) p 247

KISSAM, L T & LEACH, E K, 'Sovereign expropriation of property and abrogation of concession contract', Fordham Law Review (1959/60), p 177

KOROVIN, E, 'The Suez Canal and international law', News A Soviet Review of World Events, no 22 (1956), p 2

LA PRADELLE, R de G de, 'L'Egypte, a-t-elle violé le droit international en nationalisant la compagnie universelle du canal maritime de Suez?' Int. Recht & Dipl. (1958), p 20

LISSITZYN, O J, 'Iranian oil, foreign investment and the law', Foreign Affairs Reports, vol 2 (1953), p 17
MENZEL, C, 'Das deutsche Vorkriegsvermögen in Rußland und der deutsche Entschädigungsvorbehalt' (Berlin/Leipzig, 1931)
MOSCONI, F, 'La giurisprudenza italiana de dopequerra in terma di espropriazione estere', Diritto Internazionale (1960), p 170
NUSSBAUM, A, 'The arbitration between the Lena Goldfields Ltd, and the Soviet government', Cornell Law Quarterly, vol 36 (1950), p 31
O'CONNELL, D P, 'A Critique of Iranian oil litigation', Int. & Comp. Law Q., vol 4 (1955), p 267
PINTO, R, 'L'Affaire de Suez: problèmes juridiques', Annu. Fr. Droit Int. (1956), p 20
RAUSCHNING, D, 'Der Streit um den Suezkanal. Analyse - Materialien - Bibliographie', no 27 of Hektographierte Veröffentlichungen der Forschungsstelle für Völkerrecht und ausländisches öffentliches Recht der Universität Hamburg, Hamburg 1956
RAUSCHNING, D, 'Rechtsprobleme der Suez-Kanal-Krise', Jahrb. Int. Recht (1956/7), p 257
RAUSCHNING, D, 'Die Abwicklung des Suezkanalkonfliktes', Jahrb. Int. Recht (1957/8)
RASCHHOFER, H, Die Vermögenskonfiskationen der Ostblockstaaten. Zur völkerrechtlichen Natur der ostdeutschen und völksdeutschen Vermögensverluste (Frankfurt/Berlin, 1956)
SASSOON, D M, 'The Soviet-Israel oil arbitration', Journal of Business Law (1959), p 132
SABLIER, E, 'La signification de l'affaire du pétrole iranien', Politique étràngere (1953), p 17
SCELLE, G, 'La nationalisation du Canal de Suez et le droit international', Annu. Fr. Droit Int. (1956), p 3
SEIDL-HOHENVELDERN, I, & IPSEN, P, Entschädigungspflicht der Bundesrepublik für

reparationsentzogenes Auslandsvermögen
(Heidelberg, 1962). Part 1 'Völkerrechtliche
Aspekte' (Seidl-H); Part 2 'Verfassungsrechtliche
Begründung' (Ipsen)

VISSCHER, P de, 'Les aspects juridiques fondamentaux
de la question de Suez', Rev. Gén. Droit Int. Public
(1958), p 400

WIEBRINGHAUS, H, 'Zu einigen völkerrechtlichen
Problemen innerhalb des englisch-iranischen
Ölkonflikts', Juristische Rundschau (1951), p 673

WIEDENSOHLER, G, Der Schutz deutscher Privatinvestitionen in Libyen (Hamburg, 1965)

WOOLSEY, L H, 'The expropriation of oil
properties by Mexico', Am. J. Int. Law, vol 32
(1938), p 519

WORTLEY, B A, 'The Mexican oil dispute 1938-1946',
Grotius Soc. Trans., vol 43 (1957), p 15

WORTLEY, B A, 'Indonesian nationalisation measures:
an intervention', Am. J. Int. Law (1961), pp 680-3

Index of Authors

Abendroth, W. 277
Abi-Saab, G. 127, 361
Abranches, Dunshee de 172
Abs, H. J. 581
Abt, G. 452
Accioly, H. 26, 160, 285, 286, 292, 428, 559
Ackerman, E. D. 139
Acrement, Albert 338
Adair, E. R. 201
Adam, H. 500, 516, 570, 575
Adamkiewicz, W. 271
Adriaanse, P. 576
Aga Khan, Sadruddin 257
Agarwala, C. B. 96
Ago, R. 26, 82, 91, 263, 395, 455, 471, 553
Agoro, I. O. 163
Agrawala, S. K. 81, 439
Aguayo, Leopoldo Gonzales 576
Aguilar Navarro 26
Akehurst, M. 26, 423
Åkermalm, Gunnar 508
Akzin, B. 472, 473
Al-Baharna, H. 116
Albertini, R. von 129
Albrecht, D. 425
Alcala-Zamora Y Castillo, N. 240
Al Chalabi, Hassan Abdel Hadi 390

Alciator, Maurizio 231
Alcock, Anthony 503
Alekseyev, A. 415
Alenfeld, J. 570
Alessi, 495
Alexander, L. 141, 147, 152
Alexander, Sidney S. 517
Alexander, W. 538, 543, 551
Alexandrowicz, C. H. 51, 80, 140, 455, 468
Alfaro, R. J. 114, 386
Alfin Y Delgardo, F. 160
Alker, Hayward R. 483
Allen, E. W. 152
Allen, F. E. 265
Alstyne, W. W. van 164
Altea, Conde de 286
Altheim, F. 491
Aluwalia, K. 464
Alvarado, G. T. 141, 157
Alvarez, A. 26, 36, 60, 65, 67, 82, 83, 141, 381, 407, 559
Amachree, T. 221
Amado, Gilberto 386
Amberg, R. 316
Amelin, A. B. 418
Amerasinghe, C. F. 26
Ammann, U. 565
Anabtawi, Munzar F. 557
Anand, R. P. 63, 127, 336, 351, 359
Ananiades, L. C. 551
Anderson, C. F. 186
Anderson, C. P. 153, 320
Anderson, D. R. 292
Anderson, S. V. 281, 518
Andrassy J. 26, 135, 162, 336, 351, 473, 484
Andreae, J. P. Fockema 348
Angelo, H. G. 564

Angulo, Manuel P. 537
Antalovsky, Eugen 257
Antoine, A. 532
Antonopoulos, H. 228
Anzilotti, D. 26, 67, 123, 186, 428
Appleman, John F. 443
Aramburu y Menchaca, A. A. 157
Arangio-Ruiz, G. 59, 431, 455
Aréchaga, E. J. de 328, 476, 486 (See Jimenez)
Ares, R. 455
Arevalo y Carreno, C. 289
Argentier, Claude 503
Arias, L. G. 440
Arminjon, P. 83
Armstrong, Cole A. 172, 497
Arnold, R. 273
Arnold-Forster, W. 390
Aron, Raymond 369
Aron, T. M. 337
Aroneanu, E. 216, 381, 386
Arons, D. M. 174, 175
Aronstein, G. 366
Arzinger, R. 112, 127
Asamoah, O. 484
Asbeck, F. M. van 207, 228, 376
Atassy, A. 312
Atienza, G. 381
Attia, Gamal el Din 498
Aubert, J. F. 320
Aubert, L. M. B. 148
Aubrey, Henry G. 517
Auburn, F. M. 138
Auby, J. M. 148
Audinet, Eugène 251
Audry, Léon 339
Auer, P. de 306
Aufricht, H. 106, 130, 308, 328, 508

Auger, R. 172
Auguste, B. 157
Avramov, S. 80
Axline, W. A. 528
Aycinena Salazar, L. 344
Azcarate, P. de 218
Azcarraga y Bustamente, J. L. 141, 157, 481
Azuni, D. 141
Azzam, T. 153

Baade, H. 123, 443, 491, 565, 581
Baak, J. C. 83, 386
Babinski, L. 273
Bacalu, J. 225
Bachmann, Hans 507
Badawi, A. H. 165
Badiali, G. 489
Baechle, H. M. 532
Baenziger, Jakob 393
Baffrey, M. 222
Bagley, T. H. 219
Bahramy, A. 257
Bailas, Demetrios 273
Bailey, Sir K. 141
Bailey, K. H. 505
Bailey, S. D. 397, 415, 483, 486, 488
Baker, James C. 508
Baker, P. J. Noel 114
Balasko, A. 339
Balcells, M. 455
Balch, T. W. 138
Baldoni, C. 151, 257, 292
Baldwin, G. B. 196
Balicki, Jan 386
Ball, M. M. 559

Balladore-Pallieri, G. 27, 67, 94, 96, 241, 273, 292, 381, 397, 404, 461, 554
Ballis, William 397
Ballreich, H. 328
Balogh, Elemer 251
Bar, C. L. von 245
Bar, L. von 347
Barabolya, 142
Barbier, Robert L. 201
Barclay, Sir Thomas 336
Bardeleben, Herbert von 378
Barents, 455
Bares, Charles 395
Barile, G. 67
Barkun, M. 59
Barnes, George Nicoll 503
Barnes, William 190
Barnett, S. W. 480
Barraine, R. 476
Barrett, R. W. 418
Bartolomei, D. M. 207
Barton, G. P. 196
Bartos, M. 200
Bar-Yaacov, Nissim 247
Basak, Adam 362
Basch, Antonin 507
Basdevant, Jean 123
Basdevant, Jules 15, 27, 245, 273, 303, 425
Basdevant, S. 462
Baskin, I. I. 27
Bassiouni, M. C. 436
Bastid, P. 52, 207, 387
Bastid, S. 27, 83, 135, 305, 336, 351, 364, 456, 462, 498, 521, 581
Basu, K. K. 443
Bathurst, M. E. 196
Batstone, K. K. 164

Battifol, H. 303
Baty, T. 27, 120, 148, 381, 397
Bauer, Elmar F. 216
Bäulke, K. E. 570
Baumgarten, F. 347
Bauza, Araujo 172
Baxter, R. R. 84, 165, 196, 358, 370, 397, 432, 434
Bayer, F. 97, 303, 339
Bayet, A. 206
Bayitch, S. A. 153
Beales, A. C. F. 369, 370
Beaton, L. 370
Beaufort, D. 398
Beaumont, K. M. 171
Bebr, G. 227, 532, 537, 538, 542, 554, 557
Beck, J. S. H. 151
Beckel, Graham 500
Beckett, Sir Eric W. 196, 521
Beckett, W. E. 137
Beddard, 233
Bedjaoui, M. 119, 364
Beer, Francis A. 521
Beesley, J. A. 142
Beggs, S. W. 135
Behrmann, J. H. 564
Belaunde Moreyra, A. 67, 293
Belli, Pierino 49
Belman, M. J. 186
Bender, F. 510
Benes, E. 207
Benoist, J. 268, 303, 321
Benter, H. 566
Benton, W. E. 425, 444, 498
Bentwich, N. 99, 196, 207, 251, 475, 479
Bentz, J. 102
Berber, F. 27, 164
Berber, G. 515

Berenstein, A. 280, 286, 505
Beresford, Spencer M. 182
Berezowski, G. 107
Bergbohm, K. 96
Bergendal, Ragnar 257
Berger, P. 310
Berile, G. 68
Berkner, Lloyd V. 172
Berkov, Robert 511
Berlia, G. 296, 336, 344
Bernal, J. D. 370
Bernard, Montague 381
Bernardini, A. 222, 510
Bernes, A. 2
Bernhardt, R. 117, 270, 271, 273, 278, 301
Berthoud, P. 376
Bertram, C. 539
Besly, E. F. W. 368
Besterman, Theodore 511
Bettanini, A. M. 262
Bette, A. G. 546
Beus, J. G. de 84
Bhutto, Z. A. 496
Bial, L. G. 321
Bianchi, R. L. 165
Bibier, M. 456
Bidart Campos, G. J. 68
Biegel, L. C. 557
Bierzanek, R. 160
Bilfinger, C. 387, 407, 456
Binder, L. 285
Bindschedler, Robert Denise 33
Bindschedler, 413, 420, 476, 516, 566, 576
Bioux, J. 321
Bipoun-Woum, Joseph-Marie 66
Birke, W. 576
Birke, Wolfgang 531

Birkenhead, Frederick Edwin Smith, 1st Earl of 27
Birkett, Sir William Norman 444
Birnbaum, Karl E. 488
Bishop, W. 6, 27, 186, 293, 581
Biscottini, G. 27, 77, 100, 123, 245, 249
Bissell, T. S. G. 454
Bissonette, P. A. 434
Bittner, Ludwig 263
Blackett, Patrick Maynard Stuart 416
Blagoev, B. 505
Blair, P. W. 116
Blamont, 244
Blanks, H. J. 1
Blau, G. 501
Blayac, Raoul 501
Blix, H. 130, 273, 286, 306, 387
Bloch, Joachim-Dieter 281
Bloch, Roger 541
Blom-Cooper, L. J. 197
Blondel, A. 98
Bloomfield, Lincoln P. 370
Blühdorn, R. 304
Blum, Rolf 404
Blum, Y. Z. 137
Bluntschli, J. C. 27, 113
Bobbio, N. 94, 207
Bobrov, R. L. 476
Böckstiegel, K. H. 566, 569, 572, 577
Bodda, G. 468
Bodin, J. 49
Bodmer, H. 456
Bodson, Nicole 197
Boeck, Charles-Jean-Barthelemy 245
Boeckh, Hans von 528
Bogaert, E. van 287, 310, 548
Bogdanov, O. V. 375, 494
Boguslavskij, M. M. 186

Bohan, Richard T. 425
Bohme, Eckart 432
Böhme, W. 172
Boissier, L. 419
Bokor-Szego, Hanna 127
Bolesta- Koziebrodzki, Leopold 257
Bölger, B. 286
Bonger, H. 207
Bonhoeffer, Klaus 330
Bonnevie, C. 207
Boratynski, S. 456
Borchard, E. 91, 201, 201, 268, 398, 407, 575
Borcier, Paul 520
Borel, Eugene 339
Borsi, Umberto 392
Bos, M. 342
Bosco, G. 27
Bose, H. v. 151
Böse, P.O.R. 27
Bose, Robert 370
Boskey, S. 289, 291
Bot, B.R. 130
Bothe, M. 415
Bouchez, L.J. 157, 166
Boudet, F. 289, 461
Boulding, Kenneth 370
Bourely, M.G. 172
Bourgeois, L. 52, 387, 473
Bourne, C.B. 164
Bourquin, J. 216
Bourquin, M. 27, 110, 140, 370, 442, 476
Boushehri, M. 483
Bouthoul, G. 398
Boutros-Ghali, B. 515, 558
Bouve, A. 245
Bowdett, D.W. 103, 142, 378, 390, 391, 456, 498
Boyd, Andrew 486, 521

Boye, T. 407, 420
Braatøy, B. 387
Brach, 441
Bracht, H. W. 207, 296, 310
Bradley, M. 179
Brandner, K. 312
Brandon, M. 189, 191, 264, 273, 289, 316, 493
Brandweiner, H. 190, 419
Braun, Antoine 543
Braun, U. 419
Brehme, G. 127
Breitner, F. 532, 537
Brennan, G. A. 6
Bretton, P. 376, 398
Bricker, John W. 197
Bricmont, G. 532
Briere, R. P. Y. 387, 404
Brierly, J. L. 28, 55, 84, 310, 343, 379, 407, 479
Briggs, H. W. 6, 84, 130, 202, 208, 310, 313, 352, 360, 492, 494
Brinkhorst, L. J. 537, 554
Brinton, J. Y. 186, 197
Broches, A. 507
Brockers, A. 289, 291
Broms, B. 112, 387
Brook, D. 496
Brookfield, S. H. 191
Brooks, Eugene 185
Brouckere, Jans de 398
Brown, D. J. Latham 28
Brown, E. D. 142
Brown, Peter Campbell 191
Brown, P. M. 84, 130, 296, 407
Brown, William Adam Jr. 514
Brown, W. J. 544
Brownlie, I. 18, 28, 379
Brüel, E. 102, 277

Brügel, 230
Brugiere, P. 483
Brühl, E. 166
Brunet, R. 208, 226
Bruns, J. 395
Bruns, V. 13, 55, 349, 358
Buchan, Alastair 398
Buchanan, Sir G. S. 511
Buchmann, J. 127
Buell, R. L. 315
Buenos Aires, 507
Buergenthal, Thomas 239, 512
Buerstedde, Sigismund 530
Buil, O. 498
Bülck, H. 216, 581
Bull, Hedley 375
Bünger, K. 1, 123
Burckhardt, W. 310
Bürgenthal, Th. 233
Burke, W. T. 142, 149, 161, 162, 163
Burnett, Philip Mason 434
Burns, A. L. 371, 498
Burton, J. W. 375
Burton, M. E. 473
Bustamente Y Sirven, A. S. de 28, 99, 148, 164, 349
Butler, Sir Geoffrey 28
Butler, Harold 370
Butler, W. 142, 148, 157
Buza, L. 379
Buzzati, G. C. 391
Bynkershoek, C. Van 49, 50
Byrd, E. M. 268, 282

Cabaleiro Martinez, E. 287
Cabranes, J. A. 222

Cadoux, C. J. 398
Caflisch, L. 123, 352
Cahier, P. 462, 464, 532
Cahn, H. J. 120
Caicedo Castilla, J. J. 148, 559
Caldwell, W. E. 370
Calegorypoulos, S. S. 287, 391, 398, 404, 407
Calhoun, L. J. 505
Caloyanni, M. 344
Calverth, H. G. 573
Calvez, J. Y. 79
Calvo, C. 24, 28, 381
Calvocoressi, Peter 370
Camara, J. S. 287
Camargo, P. P. 208
Campbell, Alan 523, 528
Campbell, E. 153
Campbell, N. J. 153
Camuzet, Luce 434
Cancino, F. C. 559
Cansacchi, G. 101, 117
Cantril, H. 398
Canyes, M. S. 84, 290
Capitant, R. 327
Capotarti, F. 225, 226, 308, 468, 489, 523
Cappelli, Fiorella 251
Carbone, S. M. 102
Cardozo, M. H. 191, 260
Carey, J. 226, 227, 521
Carlebach, A. 428
Carlston, K. S. 339, 573
Carmoy, Guy de 456
Carneiro, L. 285
Carr, Edward Hallett 370
Carre de Malberg, R. 113
Carreau, D. 508, 509
Carrillo Salcedo, J. A. 110, 532

Carro, V. D. 208
Carroz, J. 461, 482
Carter, P. B. 186
Cartou, Louis 516, 523
Cassese, A. 216, 222, 238, 251, 377
Cassin, R. 208, 228, 241
Cassoni, G. 537
Castagne, Andre 521
Castaneda, J. 127, 484
Castaños, S. 28, 237, 389
Castberg, F. 28, 29, 336, 391
Castel, J. G. 29, 65, 316
Castrén, E. 29, 84, 119, 257, 398, 417, 481
Catala-Franjou, Nicole 183
Catalano, G. 269
Catalano, N. 528, 532, 538
Cattan, H. 573
Catudal, H. M. 282, 331
Caty, Gilbert 115
Cavaglieri, A. 29, 94, 102, 106, 314, 381, 382, 392
Cavare, Louis 29, 131, 186, 339, 411, 495, 496, 566
Cecchetto, R. 360
Cercler, R. 509
Cerexhe, E. 544
Cervenka, Zdenck 558
Chafee, Z. 231
Chailley, P. 265
Chakravarti, R. 227
Chalmers, George 15
Chalufour, Aline 197
Chandrasekhara Rao, P. 298
Chapal, P. 339, 358
Chapman, W. M. 153
Chappell, D. 142
Chappez, Jean 343
Charlier, R. E. 142
Charpentier, J. 131, 566

Charteris, A. H. 153
Chaudet, J. P. 376
Chaudri, M. A. 515
Chaumont, C. 172, 371, 387, 457, 462, 476, 498
Chayes, A. 183, 396
Chayet, C. 268
Chen, Ti-Chiang 131, 213
Cheng, B. 84, 98, 99, 168, 170, 172, 173, 352, 362, 364, 366, 439, 581
Cheprov, Ivan 173
Chiavario, A. 233
Chiesa, F. 364
Chiu, Hung Dah 66, 465
Chklaver, G. 7, 18
Chowdhuri, R. N. 398, 489
Christie, G. C. 577
Christol, C. Q. 173, 347, 396
Churchill, R. 145
Chu Tze-Fen, 483
Ciasullo, A. L. 208
Clarke, E. 260
Clark, G. 29, 398
Clark, Roger Stenson 227
Claude, I. L. Jr. 219, 496
Cleef-Greenberg, E. V. 423
Clemens, Adrian 541
Clifford, Happa Belle 508
Clute, R. 123, 331
Cobban, A. 112
Cobbett, P. H. 5
Cobos, E. 566
Cocatre-Zilgien, A. 344, 522
Cocca, A. A. 173, 183
Cochrane, James D. 558
Codding, G. A. Jr. 501, 502, 511
Cohen, B. V. 477, 495
Cohen, Dean Maxwell 173

Cohen, J. A. 66
Cohen, M. 191
Cohen, S. 564
Cohn, E. J. 131, 186
Cohn, G. 408, 428
Colbert, Evelyn Speyer 394
Colegrove, K. W. 285
Colin, Jean-Piere, 532
Colino, Richard E. 173
Colliard, C. A. 6, 18, 159, 164, 173, 457, 464
Collins, E. 6
Collins, L. A. 566
Colombos, C. J. 142, 408
Comba, A. 364
Comte, A. 233
Conac, Gerard 168
Conforti, B. 461
Connell, H. P. 571
Constantinesco, L. 544, 557
Constantinides-Megret, Collette 554
Constantinoff, J. 84
Constantopoulos, D. S. 55, 76
Coombes, David 530
Cooper, J. C. 168, 170, 173, 174, 182, 185
Corail, J. L. de 277
Corbett, P. 29, 91, 202, 473
Coret, Alain 115
Corsini, V. 457
Cory, Helen 339
Cosentini, F. 29, 208
Costadoat, Pasini 168
Costonis, John J. 548
Cot, J. P. 334
Cottrell, Alvin 522
Courster, B. H. 208
Coussirat-Coustere, V. 9, 352
Couste, P. B. 551

Coutant, Pierre 197
Couticov, A. 101
Cowan, Margaret 201
Cox, W. W. 293
Crandall, S. B. 273
Crane, Robert D. 174
Crayen, A. D. von 293
Crichton, G. H. 161
Crocker, H. G. 84
Csabafi, I. A. 174
Csarada, Janos 29
Cuadra, H. 208
Cuevas Cancino, F. 457, 559
Curti Gialdino, A. 317
Curtis, George Ticknor 391
Cussy, Ferd de 14
Cutler, J. Ward 245
Cybichowski, Z. 412
Czabafi, Imre 185

Daggett, A. P. 153
Dahl, Karl Nandrup 503
Dahm, G. 29, 107
Dai, P. 513
Dale, T. 498
Dalloz, 202
Dalmau y De Olivart, 2
Dalpen, C. H. 184
Dam, Kenneth W. 514
Damalas, B. V. 476
D'Amato, A. 94, 431
Darby, W. E. 336
Darwin, H. G. 174
Dascovici, N. 29
David, G. 303

Davies, David 371
Davis, C. R. 396
Davis, Harriet Eager 473
Davis, M. 153
Dawson, F. G. 245, 537, 577
Dawton, Robert MacGregor 114
Day, B. 222
Day, G. 486
Deak, F. 191
Dean, A. H. 142, 143, 282
Debbasch, C. 352
Debbash, Odile 412
Decenciere-Ferandiere, A. 68
De Clercq, A. 15
Decleva, M. 265, 466, 472
De Conde, R. 559
Decoufle, A. 275
Deener, David R. 191
Degan, V. 99, 296, 305
Degras, Jane 17
Dehaussy, J. 76, 101, 191, 265, 291, 319, 365, 496
Dehousse, F. 98, 287, 554
Dehousse, Maurice 290
Delaume, G. R. 282, 575
Delbez, L. 30, 336, 398, 488
Delcoigne, G. 416
Delessert, Charles 245
Deletre, Yves 245
Delivanis, J. 391
Dell, Sidney 559
Del Russo, A. L. 208, 209
Delson, R. 577
Delupis, I. (née Detter) 30, 139, 166, 457, 558, 566
Delvaux, L. 525, 533
Dembling, P. 174, 175
Dennemark, Sigurd 313
Dennis, W. C. 317

Depiereux, Stegan 432
Deringer, A. 544
Derwent, G. H. Johnstone 222
Deschanps, E. E. F. 398
Deschamps, E. 12, 13, 14, 453
De Schutter, B. 3
De Smith, S. 116
Despagnet, F. 30, 123
Despicht, N. 545
Despres, J. P. 505
Desrioux, J. 342
D'Estefano, M. A. 396
Detter, I. 263, 315, 465, 468, 519 (See also Delupis)
Deutsch, Karl W. 30
Devaux, J. 30, 268
Develle, P. 573
Deveze, A. 398
Dhokalia, R. P. 84
Diamandesco, Jean 387
Dickinson, E. D. 6, 74, 113, 442
Dickschat, D. A. 297
Diebold, William Jr. 526
Diedreks, 175
Diefenbacher, 463
Diena, G. 30, 68
Dietze, C. 209
Diez de Valasco, M. 233, 291
Dijk, P. van 528, 547
Dimitrijevie, Vogin 257
Dinh, Nguyen Quoc 76, 153, 391
Dinstein, Yoram 191, 196
Dinu, Madeline C. 168
Diplock, W. J. K. 249
Djuvara, M. 55
Doehring, K. 202, 245, 257
Doeker, G. 284
Doering, W. 123

Döll, B. 472
Dold, G. 328
Dölle, H. 129, 297
Dolleman, J. 361
Dollot, R. 138
Domke, M. 331, 564, 566, 577, 581
Donati, A. 104
Donnediue de Vabres, H. 76, 387, 444
Donner, Andre, 554
Dor, Laris 451
Dordevic, J. 80
Douence, J. C. 153
Dougherty, James E. 522
Dourdienevsky, V. 30
Douroselle, J. B. 53
Doyle, S. 183
Draetta, U. 551
Dragic, D. 419
Drago, L. M. 575
Dreyer, J. P. 85
Dreyfus, S. 366
Drost, Heinrich 30, 120
Drost, Pieter N. 209, 436, 442
Dubisson, M. 352
Dubois, Jean-Pierre 544
Ducrocq, Louis 394
Dugard, C. 127, 216
Duguit, L. 55
Dull, P. S. 444
Dulles, J. F. 282
Dumas, J. 209, 346
Dumbauld, E. 344
Dumon, F. 538, 539, 554, 557
Dumont, Jean 14
Dunbar, N. C. H. 187
Duncan Hall, H. 489
Dunn, Frederick Sherwood 202

Duparc, P. 15
Du Plooy, R. A. 276
Dupuis, C. 30, 52
Dupuis R. J. 110, 143, 159, 239, 382, 457, 466, 560
Durante, F. 202, 347, 492
Durdenevskii, V. N. 376
Durieux, A. 121
Durieux, J. 279
Duroselle, J. B. 127
Duynstee, F. J. F. M. 279
Dyke, Vernon van 432

Eagleton, C. 30, 112, 291, 387, 399, 429, 432, 479
Ebb, L. F. 566
Echterhölter, R. 233
Eckert, H. 107
Economides, Constantin P. 540
Edmunds, Sterling E. 30
Edwards, J. L. J. 121
Eek, H. 30, 68, 131, 143, 168, 245, 281, 488
Eekelaar, J. M. 131
Efron, R. 525
Ehler, S. Z. 269
Ehrhardt, C. A. 551
Ehrhardt, D. 116
Ehrlich, L. 352
Ehryn, G. 233
Eibe, J. von 306
Eichhorn, K. 143
Eisemann, P. 9, 352
Eisenberg, A. 391
Eka, B. U. 99
El-Ayouty, Y. 129
Elbe, Joachim von 405
Elena, L. 245

Eles, G. T. 473
Eliaerts, C. 3
Elian, George 352
Elias, T. O. 313, 552
Elkin, A. 517
Ellert, 197
El-Naggar, S. 492
Ely, N. 157, 161
Ely, R. B. III 282
Engel, S. 31, 298, 306, 352, 481
Enriques, G. 329, 349, 351, 399
Entezami, M. F. 510
Enzweiler, J. A. 293
Eppstein, John 55
Erades, L. 74, 317, 319, 326, 533
Erber, P. 382
Erich, R. 85, 131, 408
Erler, G. 575
Erler, J. 512
Ermacora, F. 110, 209, 227
Ermarth, F. 560
Errera, J. E. Symon 529
Escher, R. H. von 306
Esmein, 382
Esperson, O. 498
Essen, J. L. F. van 187, 352
Estep, Raymond 183
Estep, Samuel D. 184
Etienne, B. 119
Etra, A. 566
Etremott, 335
Euler, August Martin 541
Eustathiades, C. Th. 209, 234, 290, 429
Evans, A. E. 326
Evatt, Herbert Vere 477
Evensen, J. 159, 441, 502
Everling, W. 529, 543, 546, 552
Everts, Philip P. 547

Evgenev, V. V. 435
Evrigenis, D. J. 353
Ewell, M. 227
Eymess, V. 168
Eynard, Sergio F. 533
Eysinga, W. J. M. van 164, 525
Ezejiofor, G. 209

Faatz, Adolf 392
Fabela, Isidro 382
Fabozzi, C. 78, 222, 321
Fabri, 496
Fachiri, A. P. 296, 349, 360, 577
Fairman, C. 187, 197, 273, 296, 310
Fakher, Hossein 477
Falcke, Horst P. 395
Falco, Mario 116
Falk, A. 337
Falk, R. A. 59, 371, 417, 425, 484
Faluhelyi, Ferenc 31
Farer, T. 419
Farmanfarma, A. 353, 582
Farr, Warren F. 446
Farran, C. D'O. 107
Fartache, M. 353, 582
Fasan, F. 175
Fasching, H. W. 337
Fasihpour, H. 511
Fatou, Raymond 245
Fatouros, A. A. 366, 566, 567
Fattal, Antoine 152
Fauchille, P. 31, 168, 395
Favilli, V. 81, 457
Favre, A. 97, 299
Fawcett, J. E. S. 31, 81, 114, 175, 183, 234, 265, 276,
            343, 430, 457, 508, 564, 577

Feblowicz, S. 246
Fedozzi, P. 31, 123, 161, 382
Fehlmann, P. R. 280
Feilchenfeld, E. 121, 412
Feinberg, N. 219, 310, 347, 349, 405, 472, 474
Feld, W. 533, 547
Felder, J. F. 113
Feldman, D. I. 27
Feldman, George J. 184
Feliciano, Florentino P. 379, 400
Feller, A. 11, 192, 202, 349, 368
Fenn, P. T. 148
Fensterwald, B. Jr. 189
Fenwick, C. G. 5, 31, 168, 222, 264, 293, 382, 396, 560, 581
Feraud-Giraud, L. J. D. 417
Ferguson, C. G. 230
Ferrandi, J. 552
Ferrari Bravo, L. 68
Ferrer, Manuel Augusto 185
Ferrer Vieyara, E. 562
Ferriere, Georges 533
Ferron, O. de 143, 545
Feuer, G. 490
Fiedorowicz, G. 117
Fields, Harold 251
Fifield, Russell H. 376
Filipucci Giustiniani, G. 64
Finch, G. A. 92, 283, 412, 522
Finer, Herman 488
Finkelstein, Maurice 337
Finlay, L. W. 154
Fiore, M. 78
Fiore, Pasquale 31
Fischel, Wesley R. 202
Fischer, A. 123, 219, 545
Fischer, G. 349, 416, 503, 511, 513

Fischer, G. 349, 416, 503, 511, 513
Fischer, P. H. 526
Fisher, Adrian S. 375
Fisher-Williams, 567
Fitzgerald, G. F. 432, 439
Fitzmaurice, Sir Gerald 31, 92, 138, 143, 187, 287, 293, 296, 353
Fiumel, H. de 517
Fleischer, C. A. 154
Fleischmann, Max 14
Fleming, D. F. 353
Fleming, J. Marcus 508
Fleury, L. 347
Flockher, Adolph von 382
Florio, F. 457
Flory, M. 119, 190, 197, 251, 486, 496, 498
Flory, T. 514
Focsaneau, L. 143, 489, 492
Fodere, Pradier, 202
Foignet, René 31
Foighel, I. 43, 577
Fois, P. 231, 519, 542
Folchi, M. O. 439
Follows, John W. 503
Ford, A. W. 581
Ford, W. J. 419
Forster, Kent 369
Fortuin, H. 88, 164
Fortuin, U. R. H. 52
Foster, W. F. 353
Fouilloux, G. 119, 577
Foulcke, G. 31
Fouques-Duparc, J. 219
Foures, R. 474
Fowler, J. E. 284
Fox, H. 340
Franceschelli, R. 544

Francioni, F. 204
Franck, T. 284, 441
François, J. P. A. 31, 32, 85, 250
Frangulis, A. F. 209, 263
Franz, F. 246, 251, 257
Frankenstein, 499
Franklin, C. M. 143
Fraser, C. F. 246
Frazier, R. H. 209
Freeman, Alwyn 433
Freeman, A. V. 432, 560
Freeman, Harrop A. 379
Frei, P. H. 379
Frenzke, D. 131, 315
Freymond, P. 287, 517
Freytagh-Loringhoven, A. von 268
Fridman Lutzkaya, J. 162
Fried, J. 267, 501
Friede, W. 581
Friedmann, L. 399
Friedmann, S. 564, 578
Friedmann, W. 6, 32, 60, 97, 158, 162, 344, 366
Friedrich, J. 209
Friedrich, R. 578
Friesenhahn, 228
Frings, Paul 252
Frisch, W. 246
Fromont, Michel 533
Frowein, J. 123, 554
Frutkin, A. W. 175
Frye, W. R. 499
Fulton, T. W. 161
Furet, M. F. 375, 431
Furler, H. 552
Furniss, E. S. Jr. 522
Furrer, H. P. 9
Furrier, 93

Fusinato, G. 452

Gabus, Eric 405
Gadolin, Carl Axel Johan von 210
Gàl, G. 175
Galbe, J. L. 436
Galina, A. 421
Gallina, G. 210
Gallois, Pierre M. 371
Galloway, Eilene, 175
Gamillscheg, F. 367
Ganju, M. 210
Gannini, A. 144
Ganshof van der Meersch, W. J. 516, 523, 528, 547
Garaicoa, J. 32
Garchon, C. 463
García Álvarez, M. 32
Garcia Amador, F. V. 32, 143, 162, 429
Garcia-Arias, L. 382, 405, 457
Garcia Bauer, C. 210, 227, 344
Garcia, E. A. 225
Garcia-Mora, Manuel R. 257
García Pérez, A. 32
Carcía Robles, A. 143. 148, 375
García Sayan, E. 148
Gardner, R. 184, 225, 487
Gardot, André, 52
Gargas, S. 249
Garner, J. W. 32, 101, 131, 189, 308, 310, 423, 425, 408
Garretson, A. H. 164, 547
Gascard, J. 2
Gastrén, Erik J. S. 119
Gaudet, M. 554
Geck, W. K. 290, 313

Geffcken, Friedrich Heinrich   382
Geiger, R.   573
Gelberg, L.   523
Gelderen, M. van   557
Gellermann, K. P.   329
Gellhorn, Walter   210
Gellner, C. R.   519
Gemma, S.   131, 262
Genet, L.   32
Genèt, R.   137, 310
Gentile, F. C.   486
Gentili, A.   50
Georgesco, V. A.   68
Georiades, E.   168
Georgopoulos, C.   287
Gerould, James Thayer   408
Gerven, Walter van   544
Gess, K. N.   563
Ghillany, F. G.   14
Ghillany, F. W.   14
Chirardini, G.   383
Ghobashy, O. Z.   310, 314
Ghosh, R. C.   275
Chosh, S. K.   582
Gianni, G.   94
Giannini, A.   85
Giardina, A.   329, 550
Gibson, W. M.   81, 246
Gide, Loyrette J.   528
Gidel, G.   114, 121, 144, 157, 158, 161
Gide-Loyrette-Novel,   544
Gieseke,   567
Gigoj, S.   431
Gihl, T.   32, 92, 148, 187, 265, 399, 436
Gilmour, D. R.   383
Ginsburg, G.   321
Ginther, K.   124

Giraud, E. 60, 111, 305, 308, 365, 391, 419, 422, 481
Giuliano, M. 16, 32, 192, 455
Gjelsvik, Nikolaus 32
Glaesner, H. J. 468, 529, 531, 550
Glahn, G. V. 33, 142
Glaser, 210, 227, 436, 444
Glazer, J. Henry 502
Gledhill, A. 222
Gleiss, Alfred 543, 544
Glueck, Sheldon 444
Goebel, J. 113, 138
Goedhuis, D. 175
Goellner, A. 313
Goerdeler, R. 121
Goes van Naters, M. van der 306, 470, 524
Goethem, F. v. 457
Gohler, Hans 399
Golay, P. W. 476
Gold, J. 509
Goldberg, 210
Goldie, L. F. E. 154, 158
Goldschmidt, H. W. 358
Goldschmidt, R. 210, 339
Goloman, B. 564
Golsong, H. 210, 232, 234, 241, 519
Golubev, N. N. 33
Gomez Orbaneja, A. 510
Gomez Robledo, A. 293, 560
Gonsiorowski, Miroslas 408
Goodhart, Arthur L. 197
Goodrich, Leland M. 350, 477, 479, 496, 499
Goossens, Ch. 327
Gopalakrishnan, R. 293
Gordenker, Leon 488
Gordon, E. 298, 302, 379
Gordon, F. 494
Gordon, J. C. 192

612

Gordon, W. C. 326
Gore, Albert 175
Gormley, 244, 249, 347
Gorter, W. 514
Goslinga, W. J. 210
Gottlieb, A. E. 154, 184, 219, 375
Gottschalk, Egon 425
Goubine, V. F. 293
Gouet, Ivon 94
Gould, Wesley L. 33, 59, 74
Goule, P. 18
Goy, Raymond 252, 464
Goyard, C. 440
Grabar, V. 30
Graham, M. W. 128, 131
Graber, D. A. 412
Grabski, S. 136
Grahl, Madsen A. 252, 258
Granfelt, H. 311, 387
Grassetti, C. 75
Grassi, M. 108
Graupner, R. 122, 544
Graven, Jean 444
Grayson, C. T. 124
Green, B. C. 187
Green, J. F. 227
Green, L. C. 5, 10, 108, 154, 158, 216, 234, 258, 260,
    391, 425, 440, 442, 445, 496, 526
Greenberg, J. 234
Greenspan, Morris, 399, 401
Gregg, Robert W. 491
Gregory, C. N. 578
Greig, D. W. 33, 132, 362
Grenon, J. Y. 284
Grevtsova, T. P. 321
Grewe, W. G. 115, 445
Grieve, 421

Grieves, Forest L. 337
Griffin, W. L. 164
Grimal, H. 129
Grimm, F. 317
Grimm, G. 444
Grisel, E. 158, 361
Grob, F. 369, 399
Groeben, Hans von der 528, 545
Gross, A. 18, 162
Gros Espiell, Hector, 148
Gross, E. A. 477, 487, 493, 496
Gross, G. S. 278
Gross, Herbert, 517
Gross, L. 301, 353, 354, 363, 445, 479, 487, 489
Grossen, J. M. 202, 341
Grotius, H. 50
Grottanelli de Santi, G. 329
Grützner, Heinrich 258
Grzybowski, A. 518
Grzybowski, K. 64, 144
Guckel, P. 337
Guépin, Claude 184
Guermanoff, Dimitri 339
Guerreau, Maurice 503
Guerrero, J. G. 85, 343, 358, 383
Guetzevitch, B. M. 210
Guggenheim, P. 33, 52, 68, 78, 91, 94, 113, 119, 210, 234, 280, 313, 319, 334, 354, 388, 421, 567
Guidi, 246
Guilleminet, Raymond 252
Gukwurah, A. O. 135
Guldberg, T. 573
Gündisch, H. J. 97
Guradze, H. 210, 235
Gurke, H. 33
Gutierrez, Alberto Ostria 132

Gutmann, F. 154
Gutt, C. 507
Gutteridge, J. 192, 414, 477, 479
Gutzwiller, M. 85, 106
Gutzwiller, M. 211
Guyomar, G. 224, 339, 346, 354

Ha Vinh Phuong, 286
Haake, E. 108
Haas, D. 278
Haas, E. 60
Haas, R. 167
Haastert, H. F. W. M. van 510
Habicht, M. 345, 371
Hackworth, G. H. 6, 33, 85, 354
Haemmerle, A. 94
Haesler, T. 343
Häfliger, Hans, 258
Hagedan, H. 383
Hagemann, M. 550
Hagerup, Francis, 33
Hagras, Kamal M. 492
Hahn, H. J. 472, 517, 524, 530
Hainka, F. 218
Halderman, John W. 477, 499
Hale, R. W. 148
Haley, A. G. 175, 176, 433
Hall, 197
Hall, R. Cargill 176
Hall, William Edward 33
Hallbronner, K. 433
Halleck, H. W. 33
Hallier, W. J. 347
Hallier, H. J. 550
Hambidge, Gove 510

Hambro, E. 9, 78, 79, 97, 246, 252, 258, 260, 261, 302, 337, 346, 354, 358, 362, 363, 479
Hamburger, E. 211
Hamburger, L. 504
Hammarskjöld, A. 337, 421
Hammerbacher, G. 124
Hambrell, Sven 252
Hamzeh, F. S. 335
Hannover, Prince Heinrich von 176
Hansson, Michael 252
Haraszti, G. 263, 299
Hardy, J. 297, 337
Hardy, M. J. L. 431
Hardy, S. 529
Harhammer, Allen 316
Harle, E. 97, 98
Harriman, E. A. 408
Harris, D. J. 6, 116, 216
Hartingh, F. de 144
Hassmann, Heinz 408
Hatch, V. 283
Hatschek, J. 33, 34
Hauchmann-Tcherniak, T. 306
Haupt, G. 169
Hauri, Kurt 327
Hautefeuille, Laurent Basile 383
Hawkins, H. C. 570
Hay, P. 516, 533
Hayoit de Termicourt, R. 321
Hayton, R. D. 138, 169
Hazan, Edouard Tawfik 392
Hazard, J. N. 85, 331, 375, 564
Head, J. L. 169, 245
Healy, T. H. 246
Heathcote, 498
Hecker, Gottfried 249
Hedemann, J. W. 97

Heere, W. Y. 3
Heffter, A. W. 34, 63
Hegel, F. 34
Heggstad, O. 34
Heirman, J. H. 176
Heilborn, P. 34, 92
Heinrich, W. 176
Heinrichs, A. 547
Heintz, Frank Joseph 515
Heinze, Kurt 445
Heinzen, B. G. 149
Hekhuis, Dale J. 371
Heldrich, Andreas 337
Heller, Karl 383
Hemleben, Sylvester John 371
Hendry, J. M. 275
Hendryx, F. 573
Henkin, L. 162, 211, 293, 354
Henrichs, Wilhelm 258
Heraud, G. 521, 528
Herbig, G. 119
Berbst, L. 121
Herczegh, G. 34, 97
Hermoso, A. 197
Herrera Pellerano, H. 294
Hershey, A. S. 34, 151, 192, 383
Hertel, A. 392
Herter, Ch. A. 283
Hertslet, Lewis 15
Hertz, W. 388, 392
Herz, H. 117
Hertz, J. H. 578
Herzog, B. 287
Herzog, R. 235
Hettlage, Karl M. 383
Heuron, A. de 321
Heut, P. 534

Heuvel, H. van den 538
Heuven-Goedhart, G. J. van 252
Hexner, E. P. 298, 299, 507, 509
Heydte, F. A. von der 34, 106, 137
Heyman, F. J. 364
Heymann, E. 187
Higgins, A. P. 34, 360, 399
Higgins, R. 371, 389, 457, 477, 490, 496
Hiitonen, Ensio 504
Hill, Chesney 132, 192
Hill, D. J. 463
Hill, Martin 192, 474
Hilleke, Heinrich 399
Hindmarsh, A. E. 379, 393
Hingorani, C. R. 176
Hinsley, F. H. 371
Hirsch, A. M. 164
Hirsch, Martin 543, 544
Hjerner, L. A. E. 578
Hjertonsson, Karin (nee Oldfeldt) 144
Höbert-Petersen, B. 470
Hoch, F. 433
Hochepied, J. P. 202
Hodges, H. G. A. M. 383
Hofbauer, R. 308
Hoffmann, G. 108
Hoffmann S. 30, 275, 283, 457, 499
Hofmannsthal, 571
Hogan, Albert Edmond 395
Hogan, J. C. 176
Hogan, W. N. 358, 478
Hogg, J. F. 302, 354
Högtun, G. 321
Hohenwart, G. 345
Hoijer, O. 263
Holborn, L. W. 252, 513
Holcombe, A. N. 211

Holder, W. E. 6
Hold-Ferneck, A. 34
Holland, D. C. 192
Holland, Sir Thomas Erskine 34, 399
Hollenweger, P. 466
Holloway, K. 277, 294
Holmbäck, Å. 315
Holmes, 499
Holtz, Theodor 541
Holtzendorff, Franz Joachim Wilhelm Philipp von, 34, 35
Holzer, E. 124
Hombourg, R. 170
Homburg, R. 176
Honing, F. 85, 261, 366, 544
Hoog, V. G. 144
Hooker, W. S. Jr.
Hopkins, 235
Horak, J. N. J. B 275
Horie, Shigeo 509
Hornsey, G. 567
Horsford, C. E. S. 433
Horvath, B. 241
Horwitz, Solis 445
Hoskins, H. L. 522
Houben, P. H. J. M. 530, 531, 552
Houlard, M. 266
Houtte, A. van 534
Hoveyda, F. 582
Howard-Ellis, Charles 477
Hoyt, E. C. 306
Hsu, Fu-yung 252
Hsuan-Tsui Liu, 295
Hsueh, S. S. 495
Hsu Mo, 378
Huang, T. F. 567
Huber, J. 274

Huber, M. 35, 113, 119, 211, 337
Hudson, M. O. 6, 8, 13, 85, 202, 222, 290, 294, 297 302, 337, 349, 354, 355, 362, 408, 425, 426 450
Huet, P. 365
Hugelman, K. G. 124
Hula, E. 211
Hull, R. H. 423
Humber, P. O. 362, 494
Hummell, R. 229
Hur, P. 9, 352
Hurst, Sir Cecil 35, 86, 159, 192, 317
Hussey, Luther N. 192
Huxley, Julian 510
Hyde, C. C. 35, 302, 304, 321, 336, 383, 408, 413, 578
Hyde, J. N. 571, 574,
Hyde, O. N. 128

Iaccarino, U. 337
Iankov, A. 361
Idem, 296
Imbert, Armand 521
Ipsen, P. 555, 583
Irani, P. 322
Ireland, G. 136, 154
Isay, H. 35, 246
Isenburg, M. 496
Ismay, Lord 522
Ivrakis, S. 485

Jackson, John H. 514
Jackson, Robert Houghwout, 445

Jacobini, H. B. 65
Jacovides, 57
Jacque, R. P. 101
Jacquignon, L. 578
Jaeger, Franz 550
Jaeger, W. 7
Jaenicke, G. 92, 457, 525, 526, 555
Jägerskiöld, Stig 69, 400
Jahn, Eberhard 253
Jahnke, L. G. 331
Jahrreiss, H. 433
Jakovljevic, B. 419
Janeczek, E. 445
Janos, A. C. 417
Janousek, Jeseph O. 192
Janowsky, N. 211
Janssen-Pevtschin, J. Velu 211
Jasentuliyana, 503
Jaspar, E. J. E. M. H. 468
Jeannel, J. 440
Jeantet, F. C. 538
Jellinek, G. 55, 114
Jemolo, A. C. 246
Jenks, C. W. 35, 121, 176, 187, 211, 217, 166, 274,
  298, 306, 328, 337, 338, 355, 363, 458,
  461, 464, 467, 504, 506
Jennings, R. Y. 35, 86, 92, 137, 170, 153, 361, 412,
  572
Jeschek, Hans-Heinrich 433
Jessup, P. 35, 60, 144, 149, 154, 162, 176, 263,
  355, 360, 388, 408, 421, 423, 458, 579
Jeze, G. 287, 575, 578
Jimenez de Arechaga, 35, 69, 229, 329, 348, 355,
  429, 477, 560
Jitta, D. Josephus 55
Jobst, III V. 294, 308, 506
Johnson, Bo. 144

Johnson, D. H. N. 132, 137, 144, 145, 149, 154, 169, 339, 408, 439, 440, 484, 485, 499, 513
Johnson, D. M. 154
Johnson, G. A. 504
Johnson, R. W. 154, 164
Jokl, M. 296
Joksimovic, Ilija 253
Jones, E. B. 162, 184
Jones, F. L. 306
Jones, H. H. 306
Jones, J. M. 121, 151, 193, 265, 288, 355
Jones, J. Walter 52
Jones, Stephen B. 136
Joseph, C. 203
Jouhaux, Leon 504
Jully, L. 294, 355
Jumeau, A. 190
Junckerstorff, H. K. 219
Jurt, J. 57
Juvigny, P. 244
Kaasik, N. 335, 377
Kaeckenbeeck, L. G. 124, 164
Kafka, G. E. 412
Kahn, Herman 399
Kahng, Tae Jin 486
Kaiser, J. 322, 542
Kalshoven, F. 197, 394, 400, 417
Kaltenbach, A. 574
Kamanda, A. M. 258
Kamarovsky, L. 36
Kane, W. E. 417
Kaplan, L. S. 522
Kaplan, M. A. 36
Kappeler, D. 294
Kappelmann, 463
Kappus, Georg 400
Kapteyn, P. J. G. 524, 528

Karaosmanoglu, A. L. 496
Karbach, 220
Karelle, Jacques, 519
Kaser, Michael 518
Kasme, Badr. 482
Katz, M. 338
Katzarov, C. 494, 495, 578
Katzenbach, N. de B. 36, 177, 184
Kaufmann, E. 36, 55, 124, 317, 322
Kaufmann, Wilhelm 453
Kaul, F. K. 445
Kazansky, P. 36
Kazwak, M. K. 81
Kebedgy, Michel S. 383
Keeley, J. R. 317
Keen, F. N. 409
Keenan, Joseph B. 437
Keeton, G. W. 36
Kegel, G. 317, 578
Kehden, M. I. 155
Keith, A. B. 193, 271
Keith, K. J. 121, 362
Keller, Arthur, S. 137
Keller, Ludwig 394
Kelsen, H. 36, 55, 69, 94, 111, 114, 124, 132, 263,
    329, 338, 372, 388, 391, 412, 429, 437,
    441, 445, 477, 522
Kemmeter, Fritz de 519
Kennedy, E. M. 454
Kent, H. S. K. 149
Kenworthy, W. 164
Kerley, E. L. 193, 486
Kern, E. 571
Kerno, I. 86, 294, 363
Kerr, Philip 400
Kertesz, S. D. 226
Kewenig, W. 235

Keydel, Hans 400
Keynes, J. M. 372
Khadduri, Majid 400
Khadjenouri, M. 294
Khan, R. 417, 423, 482, 496
Khoshkish, Anoushiravan 151
Kiernik, S. 290
Kierse, Amelia L. 184
Kilmuir, Viscount (Sir David Maxwell Fyfe) 445
Kim, Cae-One 546
Kimminich, O. 190, 253, 258
King, A. 197, 198
King, J. J. 506
King, J. K. 193, 365
Kirk, Grayson 372
Kirsten, J. 119
Kish, J. 138
Kisker, G. W. 372
Kislov, A. 169
Kiss, A. C. 7, 76, 101, 173, 291, 430, 519, 520, 543
Kissam, L. T. 582
Klaer, Werner 545
Kleen, Richard 36
Kleffens, A. van 327
Klein, C. B. 149
Klein, F. 124, 255, 318
Kleyntjens, J. 270
Kleut, P. 417
Klineberg, Otto 511
Klinghoffer, H. 124, 412
Klüber, J. L. 36
Klug, U. 235
Knaub, Gilbert 534
Kniefiem, August von 446
Knitel, H. G. 454
Knopfle, R. 534
Knudson, John Immanuel 474

Kobarg, W. 246
Kocot, K. 480
Koers, A.W. 155, 162
Kohler, J. 36, 393
Kojanec, G. 329, 567
Kojevnikov, F. 30
Kolasa, J. 483
Kolodkin, A. 149, 163, 396
Komarnicki, T. 383, 421
Komarnicki, Waclaw 388
Konishi, M. 481
Koo, Wellington Jr. 463
Kooijmans, P.H. 113
Kopal, V. 176, 481
Kopelmanas, L. 92, 94, 322, 327, 377, 388, 477
Korbel, J. 423
Korbonski, Andrzej 518, 523
Kordt, A. 541
Korovin, E. 37, 375, 409, 582
Korowicz, M. St. 37, 108, 114, 219
Kotani, T.S. 81
Kotzsche, Lothar 400
Kouzbari, 488
Kovar, R. 538, 542, 546, 556
Ko-Wang Mei 418
Kozhevnikov, F.I. 37
Kranzbühler, Otto 446
Kraske, Erich 203
Krasner, Stephen D. 509
Kraus, H. 100, 217, 266, 278, 384
Krenz, F.E. 139, 253
Kreyssig, G. 526
Krezdorn, F.J. 268, 515
Krilov, S. 169
Krispi, I. 338
Krivitchkova, E.S. 499
Kroeli, J. 170, 177

Kronfol, Zouhair A. 567
Kruger, H. 329, 377
Kruger-Sprengel, E. 522
Krülle, Siegrid 136
Kruse, H. 471
Kruse-Jensen, C. 400
Krylov, S. 30, 37, 355, 534
Kucera, B. 86
Kucherov, S. 177
Kuei, Tsung Yao 400
Küffman, G. 578
Kugelmeier, A. M. 318
Kuhfeld, A. M. 177
Kuhn, A. K. 250, 299
Kühne, W. 160
Kvlski, W. W. 372
Külz, H. R. V. 165
Kung, E. 331, 514
Kunz, J. L. 37, 56, 60, 69, 86, 94, 116, 117, 124, 132, 158, 219, 271, 378, 391, 400, 405, 409, 458, 464, 560, 525
Kuratowski, 198
Kuster, Otto 445
Kutner, L. 211, 217, 227
Kutzner, Gerhard 561
Kuwahara, T. 156
Kwen Chen 582
Kym, Chong Soo 405
Kyriacopoulos, E. 79, 235, 282

Labeyrie-Menahem, C. 501
La Brière, Y. de 270, 394
Lachance, 212
Lacharriere, G. de 331, 499
Lachaze, Marcel 253

Lachs, M. 177, 266, 299, 442, 458, 465
Lacombe, J.-Saporta 170
Lacour, J. T. 171
Lacruz Berdejo, J. L. 235
Ladame, Paul A. 246, 483
Lador-Lederer, J. J. 155, 212, 384, 458
Lafitte, F. 253
La Fontaine, H. 11, 453
Lagarde, E. 132
Lagarde, P. 542
Lagrange, M. 426, 534, 539, 540
Laharmy, 258
Laing, Lionel H. 80
Laissy, Michel 558
Lakhtine, W. 138
Lalive, J. F. 187, 241, 421, 572, 574, 582
Lalive P. A. 212, 224
Lamberti Zanardi, P. 391
Lambiris, J. 290
Lambrinidis, John S. 519
Lammasch, H. 261
Lamour, Philippe, 246
Lanares, P. 217
Lande, Adolph 458
Lande, G. R. 485
Landy, E. A. 506
Lanfranchi, F. 16
Lang, J. 158
Lang, Y. 483
Lange, Christian L. 372
Lange, Gunnar 519
Langenhove, Fernand van 219, 497
Langer, R. 132, 137
Langner, A. von George 320
Langrod, G. 253, 366, 367, 462, 488, 518, 561
Lanning, 219
Lanschot, W. van 88

Lapenna, Ernesto 247
La Pergola, A. 69
Lapenna, Ivo 64
Lapidoth, R. 282, 322
La Tradelle, A. de 11, 26, 108, 149, 318, 346, 409
La Pradelle, P. de 37, 136, 169, 177, 318, 414, 423 433, 439, 512
La Pradelle, R. de G. de 582
Larnaude, F. 132, 433
Larson, A. 111, 338
La Ruche, Francis 421
Lasok, 446
Lassalle, C. 525
Lasserson, 220
Lassier, J. 544
Lasswell, H. D. 178, 213
Lattre, J. M. de 567
Laun, Rudolf 167, 392
Lauria, F. 166
Lautenschläger, K. 223
Lauterpacht, E. 75, 239, 384, 471, 499, 520
Lauterpacht, Sir Hersch 37, 38, 52, 75, 86, 104, 106 111, 132, 133, 156, 161, 187, 212, 227, 228 229, 241, 294, 296, 297, 300, 301, 328, 342 346, 349, 355, 360, 361, 384, 405, 409, 423 442
Lavergne, B. 521
Laves, W. H. C. 511
Law, Castor ,H. P. 343
Lawrence, Sir Geoffrey (Lord Oaksey) 446
Lawrence, T. J. 38
Lawrence, W. Ph. D. 501
Lawrence-Winfield 38
Lawson, R. C. 19, 355
Lay, S. Houston 145, 177
Laylin, J. G. 165
Layton, R. 318

Lazarett, S. 198
Lazarev, M. 190, 376
Lazovsky, S. 24
Lazovsky, S. 47
Leach, E. K. 582
Leanza, U. 318
Leca, J. 306
Leclercq, C. 499
Lecourt, Robert 539
Lederer, Z. J. 388
Lee, L. T. 205
Lefebure, M. 75
Lefevre, Jacqueline 541
Le Fur, L. 7, 18, 38, 55, 212, 271, 388, 423
Leganano, Gioranni da 50
Le Goff, Marcel 170
Legros, 437
Leibholz, G. 253
Leibnitz, G. G. 14
Leifer, M. 166, 232
Leigh, G. I. F. 203
Leive, David M. 441
Lemkin, R. 217
Lemoine, G. X. 474
Lemoine, M. 171
Leng, Shao-Chuan 66
Leonard, L. L. 155
Leonard, Raymond 516
Lerche, Peter 259
Leriche, A. 267, 316
Lerner, N. 231
Leroy, P. 489
Lesser, S. T. 318
Lessing, Hans 250
Le Tallec, Georges 546
Level, P. 320
Leventhal, Harold 446

Levi, Sandri 217
Levie, H. S. 198
Levin, D. B. 38
Levine, D. B. 429
Levitt, A. 283
Levy, G. 155
Levy, J. P. 2
Lewis, Malcolm M. 276
L'Huillier, J. 38, 165
Li, Kuo-Lee 177
Liacouras, P. J. 302, 355
Liais, M. 86
Liang, Yuel-Li 86, 87, 275, 288, 294, 306, 423, 482, 483, 494, 582
Lillich, R. B. 429, 567, 579
Limburg, J. 212
Limburg, Stirum 384
Linares Fleytas, A. 87
Lincoln, G. 60
Lindstedt, A. L. 274
Lindt, August R. 253
Lingelbach, William Ezra 384
Linze, 446
Lipartiti, C. 56, 69, 70, 94, 311
Lipsky, George A. 38, 372
Lipson, Leon 177, 179
Lipstein, K. 528
Lisovskij, V. J. 38
Lissitzyn, O. J. 6, 38, 87, 107, 137, 169, 177, 309, 311, 355, 458, 583
Liszt, Franz von 38
Litvine, Max 171
Ljubisavljevic, B. 541
Lloyd, Georgia 374
Lloyd, W. B. Jr. 377
Løchen, Einar 235
Lockwood, B. B. J. 441

Lodigiani, A. 239
Lodrup, P. 171
Loewenfeld, E. 187
Loewenstein, K. 111
Loher, A. 331
Loive, David M. 502
London, K. 128
Looper, R. B. 275, 280, 285
Lopez Villamil, H. 158
Lörcher, G. 465, 550
Louis, J. V. 531, 532, 540, 557
Lourie, 499
Löwegren, Gunnar H. 508
Luard, E. 136, 212, 372, 417
Lu-Chun-Kai, 388
Lucien-Brun, J. 270
Ludovicy, J. 534
Lukashuk, I. I. 38, 267, 274, 465
Lume, R. D. 433
Lunz, L. A. 582
Lusena, C. 246
Lüst, R. 177
Lycklama à Nijholt, J. F. 169
Lyon-Caen, Gérard 376
Lyons, A. B. 193
Lyons, F. S. L. 373
Lysen, A. 409

MacBride, R. L. 283, 322
MacChesney, B. 145, 231, 283, 395
McClachlan, D. L. 544
McClure, W. 283
Maccoby, Simon 28, 394
McConaughty, J. B. 1
MacCorkle, Stuart Alexander 133

McCuen, J. J. 417
McDaniels, J. F. 567
MacDonald, R. St. J. 155, 360, 558
McDougal, M. S. 38, 70, 145, 149, 161, 163, 178, 179, 213, 227, 299, 379, 395, 396, 400, 416, 431, 487
McEwan, A. C. 136
McFee, W. 145
McGibbon, I. C. 102, 103, 133
McGlintock, Charles, G. 371
Mach, N. von 520
Machado, Hugo de Chunha 178
Machowski, J. 464
Macic, R. 213
McIntyre, S. H. 318
MacKay, R. A. 161
Mackenzie, Norman 80
McLaughlin, J. 188
Maclean, Donald A. 99
McMahon, J. 179, 305, 534
McMahon, Matthew M. 413
McNair, A. D. (Lord McNair) 7, 38, 88, 97, 111, 133, 171, 263, 266, 304, 309, 318, 322, 329, 338, 350, 373, 401, 412, 424
McNulty, 235
McVitty, Marion H. 416
McWhinney, E. 39, 128, 140, 179, 376, 439
Madhavtirtha, S. 223
Maenecke, R. 276
Maestripiere, C. 543
Magarasevic, A. 429
Magee, James S. 491
Magyary, Geza 349
Mahadevan, T. M. P. 271
Mahaim, Ernest 504
Mahmassani, S. 63
Maier, Reimer, H. 217

Makarov, A. N. 124, 247, 248, 253, 297, 423
Makowski, Julien 409
Malavialle, A. M. 173
Malberg, R. Carre de 39
Maldestam, A. 212
Maldestam, 219
Malik, A. M. 506
Malintoppi, A. 468, 485, 501
Malkin, H. W. 294, 395
Mallardo, V. 524Mallison, W. T. Jr. 396
Malloy, 16
Mance, Sir Henry Osborn 136
Mancini, 87
Mandelsloh, A. 409, 423
Mandelstam, A. 212, 213, 219, 388, 423
Mangoldt, H. von 66
Mangone, G. J. 160, 451
Manin, A. 512
Manin, Philippe, 497
Mankiewicz, Rene H. 178
Manley, R. H. 145
Mann, F. A. 39, 118, 122, 137, 572
Mapelli, Lopez Enrique 171
Marak, 93
Marburg, Theodore 474
Marcovitch, L. 266, 485
Marcus-Melmons, S. 268, 555
Marcy, C. 288
Marek, K. 9, 57, 70, 118
Maresca, A. 205, 263
Maresch, A. 87
Margiotta Broglio, G. 217
Margolis, E. 80, 416
Maridakis, Georges 446
Marin López, A. 70
Markov, M. G. 178, 185
Marotta Rangel, V. 328

Marotta Rangel, V. 328
Marseillan, L. 510
Marshaw, J. L. 539
Marston, G. 138, 489
Martens, Ch. de 5, 14
Martens, Fedor Fedorovich 39
Martens, G. F. de, 13, 39
Martens, H. L. 151
Marti de Veses Puig, M. del C. 367
Martin, A. 9, 93, 226, 375, 479
Martin, C. E. 400
Martin, W. 474
Martinez Baez, A. 322
Martinez-Useros, J. 468
Martini, Alexis 247
Martini, R. de 413
Marz, R. 87
Maryan Green, N. A. 39
Mason, Henry, L. 526
Masquelin, J. 279, 322
Massarek, Eduard, 446
Massfeller, Franz 248
Massin, J. 151
Masters, R. D. 75
Masterson, William E. 152
Mateesco, C. 94
Mateesco, Mircea, 171, 178
Mateesco, Nicolas 39
Mathieu, M. 474
Mathijsen, P. 526, 529, 530, 533
Matte, N. M. 169, 178
Matte, Nicholas Mateesco 178
Mattern, J. 111
Mattern, Karl Heinz, 190
Matthies, H. 241, 526, 534, 555
Maugham, Viscount 446
Maull, H. 249

Maurach, R. 64
Maurice, Sir John Frederick 400
Maus, B. 361
Mawalla, J.R. 567
Maxwell, Fyffe, D. 368
May, M.A. 373
Mayda, J. 271
Mazzeotti, Manlio 543
Medina Ortega, M. 149
Meeker, L. 396
Megerle, K. 125
Megret, J. 465, 529, 550
Meier, B. 248
Meier, Gert 471, 543
Meissner, B. 64, 93, 125, 523
Meissner, H.O. 278
Melander, Goram 253
Melchior, Michel 550
Menais, G.P. 543
Mendelssohn - Bartholdy, A. 304
Mendizabal, A. 213
Mendlovitz, Saul H. 371
Menesez Pallares, A. 480
Mengelle, F. de Marosy 443
Mengozzi, P. 160
Menon, M.A.K. 502
Mensbrugghe, Y van der 166
Menschaar, C.L. 356
Menter, Martin 179
Menzel, C. 583
Menzel, E. 39, 70, 75, 278, 323
Mercier, Andre 261
Mercier, J. 367
Merignhac, A. 340
Merillat, H.C.L. 128
Merkl, A. 118
Merle, M. 235, 468

Meron, Theodor 198, 344
Merryman, J.H. 139
Mertens, P. 420, 466, 511
Mertens de Wilmers, J. 534, 557
Messineo, A. 219
Mestmäcker, E.J. 564
Mestre, A. 323
Metall, R.A. 31, 263, 297
Metson, William 521
Mettgenberg, 259
Metzger, S.D. 299, 571
Meurer, Ch., 348
Meyer, A. 179
Meyer, C.V. 149
Meyer, Heinrich, 259
Meyer-Cording, U. 491
Meyer-Lindenberg, H. 145
Meyriat, J. 127
Meyrowitz, H. 401, 418, 424
Miaja de la Muela, A. 39, 101
Michaels, David B. 188
Michal, V. 356
Michelwaite, Claude B. 198
Middlebush, Frederick Arnold 133
Mieck, A. 76
Miehsler, H. 76
Miele, Alberto 421
Miele, M. 39, 78, 421
Migliazza, A. 356, 459, 535
Mikdashi, Z. 574
Mikesell, R.F. 509, 565
Mikhailov, V.S. 155
Miller, David Hunter 409
Miller, H. 88
Miller, Schachter 499
Millette, Anne Marie Jacony 323
Mills, W. 401

Minear, Richard H. 446
Miner, Dwight Carroll 166
Mir Eskandari, A. N. 502
Mirkine-Guetzévitch, B. 40, 66, 213, 228, 229, 273, 405
Mironov, N. V. 323
Misra, K. P. 133
Mochi Onory, A. G. 121
Modéen, T. 220, 290
Modelski, G. 418
Moderow, W. 307
Modinos, P. 213, 224, 235, 239
Modžorjan, L. A. 106
Mok, M. R. 544
Molen, J. 161, 217, 309
Møller, Axel 40
Molodstov, S. 145
Moltmann, G. 323
Monaco, R. 40, 70, 78, 279, 294, 305, 309, 318, 323, 327, 395, 455, 458, 467, 468, 525, 529, 547, 552, 555
Monconduit, F. 239
Mondroe, D. C. 194
Monzani, M. 247
Moore, J. B. 7, 11, 261
Moore, John Norton 424, 426
Moran Wiecki, W. 388, 459
Morelli, G. 40, 57, 70, 334, 338, 368
Moreno Quintana, L. 40, 259, 459
Morgan, G. G. 561
Morgan, S. H. 397
Morgenstern, F. 70, 204, 205, 259
Morgenstern, P. 2
Morin, J. Y. 155
Morley, Felix 474
Morozou, G. I. 481
Morozov, 493

Morris, C. 338
Morrison, C. C. 232, 300, 405
Mosconi, F. 327, 556, 583
Moser, B. 535
Moskowitz, M. 213, 228
Mosler, H. 57, 71, 77, 109, 213, 242, 384, 459, 472, 527, 574
Moulin, H. A. 384
Moura, 224
Mourgeon, 226
Mouskhely, M. 100, 114, 323
Moussa, F. 203
Mouton, M. 158
Movtchane, A. P. 88
Moye, M. 40
Moynier, G. 453
Mrazek, I. 307
Mrazek, I. 481
Meuller, G. O. W. 437
Muench, F. 278
Mughraby, M. A. 563
Mukherjee, S. K. 40
Müller, A. 104, 440
Müller, Edward J. 254
Munch, F. 71, 77, 145, 188, 556, 579
Munro, H. 345
Muracciole, L. 323
Muralt, R. W. G. de 121
Murchison, J. T. 169
Murphy, C. F. Jr. 198, 430
Murray, John J. 194
Mushkat, M. 480
Muther, Jeannette E. 476, 480
Myers, D. P. 240, 265, 314, 410, 453, 474
Myrdal, Gunnar 491

Nagel, H. 71, 469, 518
Nagy, K. 300
Nahlik, S. E. 201
Nakamura, K. 223
Nanda, V. P. 436
Nanes, A. S. 525
Nantwi, E. K. 346
Narayana Rao, K. 320
Naritomi, N. 567
Nascimento E. Silva, G. E. 203, 205, 561
Nathan, Otto 373
Nathan-Chapotot, Roger 254
Nathanson, L. 231
Naurois, L. de 304
Nava, S. 262
Nawaz, M. 125, 267, 373
Neal, M. 228
Nedjati, Z. M. 213
Nehring, A. 552
Neidle, 375
Nelson, L. D. M. 136, 155, 166
Nemours, A. 480
Neree tot Babberich, M. F. F. A. de 527
Neri, S. 288, 297, 535
Nettl, J. P. 275
Neumann, Inge S. 3
Neumann Whitman, M. von 568
Newman, R. A. 100, 230
Nguyen-Huu-Try, 125
Niboyet, J. P. 18, 88
Nicholas, H. G. 477
Nichols, A. 421
Nicoloff, A. M. 307
Nicolopoulos, G. 288
Nield, R. R. 145
Niemeyer, Gerhart 40
Niemeyer, Th. 40, 88

Nieto, Sale 235
Nijholt, Lycklama, 169
Nikolaev, A. N. 149
Ninčić, D. 392
Nippold, Orfried 40
Nisot, J. 266, 271, 320, 474
Noel, Emile 531
Nolde, B. 331, 570
Nonnenmacher, G. G. 236
Norden, Heinz 373
Nordquist, M. 145
Nørgaard, Carl Aage 108
Nostitz-Wallwitz, Oswalt von 424
Nouel, P. H. 528
Nova, R. de 220, 422, 579
Novogrod, J. C. 423
Nozari, F. 179, 315
Numelin, Ragnar 201
Nussbaum, A. 52, 405, 570, 583
Nwogugo, E. I. 155, 568
Nys, E. 40, 52, 405

Oberdorfer, C. W. 544
Oberthür, K. 203
Obieta, Joseph A. 166
O'Brien, C. C. 499
O'Brien, W. 7, 128
O'Connell, D. P. 40, 80, 106, 115, 119, 120, 121, 149, 150, 158, 276, 299, 574, 575, 583
Oda, S. 141, 145, 150, 152, 155, 158, 163
Oddini, M. 151
Odishaw, Hugh 179
Offnutt, Milton 150
Ogawa, Y. 294
Ogdon, Montell 194
Oglesby, R. R. 417

Ohira, Z. 155, 156
Okoye, F. C. 128
Oldenhage, G. 473
Oliver, C. T. 262, 264
Olivi, Augusto 401
Olivi, G. 102
Olmstead, C. J. 164, 579
Ophuels, C. F. 540, 541
Oppenheim, H. F. 331
Oppenheim, L. 41, 95, 475
Oppenheimer, F. W. 190
Opperman, Th. 552
Orcasitas Llorente, L. 367
Orent, B. 139
Orfield Lester D. 7, 199
Orianne, 535
Oritz, 138
Orve Y Arregui, Jose Ramon de 515
Örvik, T. 422
Osnitskaya, G. A. 179
Osterheld, H. 542
Ostrorog, L. 220
Otlet, Paul 401, 451, 475
Ottawa-Rene, F. 291
Ottenwalder, P. 52
Ottolenghi, G. 41
Oudendijk, J. K. 141, 155
Oulianova, N. N. 291
Oxman, B. H. 146

Pachter, H. M. 396
Padelford, N. 60, 133, 424, 515
Padirac, R. 113, 213, 236, 242
Paddoux, G. 271
Padwa, D. J. 156, 513

Pahr, W. P. 329
Pal, R. 389, 437, 446
Palazzoli, C. 140
Pallieri, C. B. 274
Pålsson, L. 529
Panebianco, M. 485
Panhuys, H. F. van 77, 194, 199, 218, 248, 261, 280, 551, 555
Pannwitz, Rudolf 373
Papacostas, Alkis-Basile N. 179, 323
Papacostas, B. G. 271
Papadatos, P. A. 446
Papalambrou, A. 323
Papandréou, A. 161
Papas, C. N. 332
Paradisi, B. 56
Pardos Perez, J. L. 213, 238, 242
Paredes, A. M. 41
Paret, P. 418
Park, C. S. 283
Park, T. S. 295
Parry, A. 529
Parry C. 7, 93, 203, 213, 248, 274, 395, 437, 482, 490
Partsch, J. 71, 236
Pastor Ridruejo, J. A. 323, 329, 356
Pastuhov, V. D. 450
Paszkowski, M. 482
Patel, Satyaurata, R. 41, 133
Patey, J. 145
Patrnogic, J. 419, 420
Patterson, G. 522
Paul, 57
Pauw, F. de 501
Payot, F. 75
Pazarci, H. 433
Paz, Soldan, C. E. 512

Peaslee, A. 19
Pechota, V. 335
Pella, V. V. 437, 443
Pelloux, R. 236
Pelzer, Norbert 431
Penfield, W. S. 561
Peng, M. M. 169
Pennisi, 384
Pepin, E. 179, 184
Pepy, Andre 539
Perassi, T. 41, 79, 259, 351
Pereira, André Conçalves 41
Pereira da Silva, F. C. 475, 561
Pergent, J. 180
Pergler, C. 81, 304
Perkins, Dexter 384
Perrin, G. 356
Personnaz, J. 435
Pescatore, P. 232, 281, 324, 332, 525, 526, 528 540, 547, 550
Petrascu, Nicolas N. 379
Petreen, G. 242
Petren, S. 579
Peyner, Henri 517
Pfeifenberger, W. 478
Pfeiffer, C. 248
Pfeifer, G. 236
Pfeifer, H. 125
Pfloeschner, F. 76
Pfluger, H. 101
Pfuhl, E. 568
Phelan, Edward Joseph 504
Philipse, A. 350
Phillimore, Sir Robert Joseph 41
Phillimore, Sir Walter (Lord Phillimore) 114, 437
Phillipps, Eduardo 41
Phillips, G. G. 277

Phillips, L. H. 470
Phillipson, C. 41, 52, 401
Picciotto, Cyril H. 75
Pictet, J. 414
Piggott, Francis, 205
Pignochet, A. 180
Pigorsch, W. 77
Piip, A. 88
Pilidis, 466
Pillet, Antoine 52
Pilling, J. 236
Pilotti, M. 348
Pilloud, C. 295
Pinay, P. 540
Pino Diaz, Rosa 218
Pinto, R. 118, 199, 225, 277, 418, 420, 459, 524, 583
Piola-Caselli, C. 555
Piotrowski, G. 389, 485
Piper, Don Courtney 167
Piradov, A. S. 384
Pisani, G. 259
Piterskii, Nikolai 373
Plaisant, R. 544
Planitz, H. 206
Plantey, A. 199
Platon, C. G. 156
Platz, Flaus Wilhelm 543
Plessow, U. 552
Plischke, E. 118, 203, 318
Poblete Troncoso, M. 228, 459
Poch de Caviedes, A. 311
Podesta Costa, L. A. 41, 295
Poelje, G. A. van 365
Poirier, P. 499
Polach, J. G. 530
Polak, C. H. F. 229
Polents, O. E. 288

Poliakov, L. 446
Politis, N. 11, 41, 56, 300, 335, 336, 338, 394, 422, 430, 575
Polledri, M. 524
'Pollux', 480
Polvêche, I. 159
Polyanskii, N. N. 356, 447
Pomerance, M. 362
Pompe, C. A. 165, 330, 443
Pontanus, J. I. 50
Pordea, G. A. 220, 268, 389
Pot, C. W. van der 88
Potter, P. B. 42, 161, 311, 384, 424, 450, 499
Poulantzas, Nicholas 151, 180, 348, 466, 552
Poulin, G. 254
Poulouse, T. T. 115
Praag, L. van 188
Pradier-Fodere, P. L. E. 42
Prasch, Gerhard 557
Pratap, D. 362
Preiswerk, R. 571
Preuss, L. 76, 77, 194, 283, 324, 326, 362, 430
Price, Harry Bayard 517
Price, Peter 373
Prieur, R. 527, 548
Prins, W. F. 223
Probst, R. 180
Probst, Y. 461, 482
Prosperetti, G. 218
Proudfoot, Malcolm Jarvis 254
Przewoznik, B. 461
Pufendorf, Samuel 50
Pugh, J. 568
Pugh, R. C. 6, 188
Puig, J. C. 65, 158
Puissochet, J. P. 524
Pye, Kenneth A. 200

Quack, K. 574
Quadri, R. 42, 56, 93, 102, 180, 248, 529
Qual, Lino Di 485
Quaritsch, H. 111
Queneudec, J. P. 146, 433
Quin, M. 565
Quintano-Ripolles, A. 225, 438

Raafat, Waheed, 373
Raalte, E. van 527
Rabbath, Edmond 424
Rabin, Edward H. 432
Rabl, K. 112, 125
Radbruch, Gustav 99
Radojkovic, M. 389
Radojvic, 88
Raeder, A. 52
Raestad, A. 95, 11, 118, 151, 194, 203, 250, 259, 410, 433
Raeymaeker, O. de 459
Raggi, C. G. 125
Raginskii, M. Y. 447
Raja, C. K. N. 311
Rajan, M. S. 487
Raju, G. S. 298
Ralston, J. H. 340, 341
Ramaswamy, M. 223
Rambert, Georges 410
Rambow, Gerhard 542
Ramo, Simon 180
Ramundo, Bernard A. 376
Rangel, V. M. 285
Rank, R. 318
Rao, H. S. Gururaj 424
Raoux, M. 512

Rapisardi-Mirabelli, A. 71, 262, 265, 393, 401, 453
Rappaport, M. J. 447
Rappard, W. E. 223, 373
Raschhofer, H. 583
Rasting, Carl 42
Ratcliffe, J. A. 180
Rauchberg, H. 88
Rauchhaupt, F. W. von 42, 88, 180
Rauschning, D. 583
Raux, J. 465, 548, 549
Ray, G. W. Jr. 568, 574
Ray, J. 262, 475
Razi, M. 483
Re, E. D. 7, 199, 579
Read, J. E. 264
Read, J. M. 254
Real, J. 401
Reale, E. 249, 259
Rechid, A. 63
Recht, 259
Redlich, M. D. 42, 203
Redslob, R. 42, 53, 56, 373
Reepinghen, 535
Reeves, J. S. 89, 150, 194, 261
Réglade, M. 267
Regout, Robert 405
Rehm, G. W. 180
Reibstein, E. 53
Reichert-Facilides, F. 129
Reichhelm, Konrad 389
Reichling, Charles 548
Reid, H. D. 139
Reiff, H. 146, 194, 274, 320, 324, 453
Reinsch, P. 139
Reisman, W. Michael 346
Reith, Charles 401
Reitzer, L. 291, 435

Remeg, P. P. 108
Renault, L. 12, 13, 14, 42
Rencki, G. 520
Renouvin, 53
Renouz, Y. 24
Rentier, Jeannine, 520
Reuter, E. 535
Reuter, P. 18, 42, 99, 264, 334, 348, 459, 464, 524, 527
Reuterskiöld, C. A. 42
Reut-Nicolussi, E. 118, 254, 438
Revel, G. 335
Reves, E. 373
Revon, Michel 340
Rey, J. 550, 552
Rhyne, Ch. S. 568
Riad, A. 500
Riad, Fouad A. M. 188
Ribi, Rolf C. 518
Ricci, D. de 568
Rice, W. G. 271, 280, 324
Richardson, J. E. 180
Richardson, Lewis F. 373
Richemont J. de 527, 535, 539
Riches, Cromwell Adams 463
Rideau, J. 377
Ridder, Helmut 401
Riese, O. 171
Riesenfeld, S. A. 58, 156
Rigaux, F. 324, 556
Rikhye, General 500
Rill, H. P. 78
Ripert, G. 97
Riphagen, W. 324, 467, 527, 535, 556
Ristelhueber, Rene, 513
Ritter, G. 206
Ritter, W. 394

Rivier, A. 42
Riza Gullu, A. 71
Riz A Porta, G. G. 330
Roberts, L. M. 4
Robertson, A. H. 213, 214, 232, 236, 242, 516, 520, 524, 561
Robertson, W. S. 156
Robin, Raymond 412
Robinson, J. 2, 220, 478
Robinson, N. 229, 250
Rochette, J. 108
Rode-Verschoor, I. H. Ph. de 170
Rodgers, R. S. 514
Rodick, Burleigh Cushing 393
Rodiere, R. 528
Roemr, K. 535
Roesner, P. 332
Rogge, Heinrich 254
Rohn, P. 459, 520
Rohnfelder, G. 307
Rolin, Albéric, Baron 261
Rolin, H. 43, 88, 236, 237, 240, 242, 362, 424
Röling, B. V. A. 43, 242, 389, 443, 447
Rolland, L. 401
Rom, A. von 512
Romano, S. 43, 125
Rommen, H. 214
Ronning, C. Neale 205
Ronzitti, Natalino 120
Röper, Erich 125
Rörig, F. 150
Ros, E. J. 311
Roseman, D. M. 146
Rosenne, S. 89, 133, 264, 291, 301, 356, 359, 363, 364, 482
Rosenow, B. J. 156
Rosner, Gabriella 499, 500

Ross, A. 7, 43, 93, 413, 478, 480
Rossello, P. 453
Rossillion, C. 332
Rosting, H. 220
Roth, Andreas Hans 247
Roth, G. 535
Roth, P. 125
Rothmann, G. 102
Rouard de Card, Edgard 340
Roucounas, E. 330, 556
Rougier, Antoine 418
Rouse, 199
Rousseau, C. 43, 112, 150, 159, 262, 277, 288, 309, 320, 384, 425, 441
Rousset, 14
Roussos, G. 268
Router-Hameray, Bernard 471
Rovine, Arthur W. 488
Roxburgh, R. F. 330
Roy, Nirmal Kumar 401
Roy, S. N. G. 434
Rozakis, C. L. 442
Rozmaryn, S. 324
Rubin, A. P. 56
Rubin, S. J. 568, 579
Rubinstein, G. 416
Ruck, Erwin 43
Ruda, J. M. 295
Rudolf, W. 77
Rudstein, Simon 350
Rudzinski, A. 487
Ruegger, P. 340
Ruhland, C. 89
Ruhland, Kurt 13
Ruiz Moreno, Isidoro 43
Rumpf, Helmut 401
Rundstein, Szymon 406

Rupp, Hans Heinrich 232
Rusis, 214
Russel, R.B. 476, 480, 500
Russett, Alan de 460
Russett, Bruce M. 483
Russo, A.L. del 232, 237
Rutenberg, Gregory 410
Rutgers, V.H. 406, 410
Ruyssen, T. 93
Ruzie, D. 365
Ruze, Robert 270

Saa, Parez 170
Saavedra Lamas, Carlos, 410
Saba, H. 274, 469, 515
Sabelli, dei 220
Sablier, E. 583
Sacchetti, Vgo 507
Sacerdoti, G. 572
Sack, A.N. 121, 122, 576
Sahovic, M. 89
Saint-Girons, B. 116
Salander, G.A. 206
Saldaña, Quintiliano 438
Salgado, P. 214
Salmon, A. 493, 556
Salmon, Jean J.A. 133
Salomon, J. 270
Salomon, R. 254
Salvadori, M. 522
Salvin, M. 522
Salvioli, Gabriele 43, 71, 108, 311, 324, 340, 341, 350, 402, 430
Salvioli, Guiseppe 402
Sand, Peter 171
Sander, F. 118

Sanders, W. 295
Sandifer, D. V. 214, 223
Sandiford, R. 146
Santa Pinter, J. J. 324
Santucci, J. C. 119
Saporta, M. 512
Sarailieff, Georges V. 425
Sarraute, R. 254
Sarup, Amrit 140
Sarup, R. K. P. 81
Sassoon, D. M. 583
Sathyamurthy, Tennalur V. I. 511
Satow, Sir Ernest 203
Sauer, E. 43, 44, 111
Sauer, W. 44
Sauser-Hall, G. 165, 413
Savarit, R. 283, 325
Savasten, D. H. 419
Savelberg, M. M. L. 65
Sayre, F. B. 490, 570
Sayre, P. 478
Scelle, G. 44, 56, 93, 125, 133, 159, 250, 259, 307, 319, 327, 392, 402, 406, 426, 450, 504, 583
Scerni, G. 248, 385, 395
Scerni, M. 99, 350, 469
Schachor-Landau, C. 357
Schachter, O. 103, 134, 180, 267, 373, 478, 480, 486, 488, 500, 568
Schaeffer, Rolf 259
Schafer, M. 443
Schapiro, L. B. 150
Schätzel, D. 247
Schätzel, W. 214, 248, 254, 402, 414
Schaumann, Wilfred 113
Schechter, A. 301, 305, 365
Schechtman, J. B. 220, 254
Scheftel, J. 250

Scheidtmann, U. 295
Scheingold, S. A. 527
Schelling, T. C. 373
Scheman, L. D. 214
Scheman, L. R. 243
Schenkman, J. 512
Schermers, H. G. 295, 460, 501, 519, 537, 540
Scheuffler, H. 288, 502
Scheuner, U. 58, 71, 345, 469, 478, 570
Schiavone, Guiseppe 332
Schick, F. B. 447, 448
Schiffer, W. 71, 475
Schilling, K. 125, 445
Schindler, D. 218, 319, 402, 422
Schirmer, Gregor 389
Schläfereit, H. 469
Schlei, M. S. 416
Schlei, N. A. 431
Schlesinger, R. B. 97
Schlochauer, H. J. 341, 350, 356, 373, 430, 462, 556
Schlögel, A. 414
Schluter, Bernhard 472
Schmid, E. 220
Schmitthoff, C. M. 189
Schneckebier, Laurence Frederick 453
Schneider, H. 579
Schneider, J. 385, 466
Schnyder, Felix 254
Schöcking, W. 389
Schön, Paul 393
Schönborn, W. 120, 135, 393
Schönherr, K. H. 283
Schou, August 209
Schrans, Guy 529
Schreiber, Anna P. 244
Schröter, Carl 502

Schuck, E. G. 199
Schucking, W. 335, 345, 409, 475, 581
Schüle, A. 438
Schule, D. 348
Schüler, Alfred 254
Schumann, Erich 394
Schuster, Ernest J. 413
Schwartz, I. E. 545
Schwartz, L. E. 180
Schwarz, Leo W. 255
Schwartz-Liebermann, Wahlendorff v. 463
Schwartz, Mortimer D. 176, 432
Schwartz, Murray, L. 199
Schwarzenberg, R. G. 571
Schwarzenberger, G. 7, 36, 44, 58, 195, 214, 223, 301, 325, 332, 341, 357, 374, 392, 402, 406, 413, 416, 439, 448, 475, 479, 568, 569
Schwebel, S. M. 377, 570
Schweisfurth, T. 64
Schweitzer, M. 58
Schwelb, E. 58, 194, 199, 214, 218, 223, 226, 229, 231, 237, 307, 309, 357, 470
Schwenk, Edmund H. 199
Scott, J. B. 11, 53, 63, 89, 113, 229, 315
Scrimali, A. 330
Secretan, J. 506
Séfériadès, Stelio 44, 95, 348, 394
Seida Gomez, Vila 218
Seidl-Hohenveldern, I. 44, 71, 78, 98, 99, 125, 129, 189, 226, 230, 255, 363, 368, 420, 438, 460, 461, 467, 470, 471, 553, 565, 569, 571, 579, 580, 583
Sela Y Sampil, Aniceto, 44
Selak, C. B. 150, 156, 167
Seligman, Eustace 497
Semini, A. 545

Sen, B. 118
Sen, B. 203
Sepulveda, C. 325
Sereni, A. P. 44, 63, 98, 128, 221, 332, 341, 341, 426, 430, 460
Serra, Enrico 389
Sestier, J. M. 440
Seton-Watson, Hugh 374
Setser, V. G. 189
Shah, Nasim Hasan 385
Seyersted, F. 365, 461, 462, 500
Shalit, Anthony R. 234
Shalowitz, A. 146
Shamma, S. 340
Shapiro, Leonard 17
Sharma, S. P. 301
Sharp, R. H. 134
Sharp, W. S. 488, 501
Shatzky, B. 295, 313, 325
Shaw, C. M. 459
Shawcross, C. N. 171
Shawcross, Lord 569
Shearer, I. A. 261
Shedal, G. 138
Shepard, P. 565
Shepherd, Vincent 65
Shihata, I. F. I. 357
Shinobu, Jumpei 426
Shotwell, J. T. 402, 504
Shou-Sheng-Hsueh 494
Shubber, S. 439
Shurshalov, V. M. 271, 272
Shuster, George N. 511
Shy, J. W. 418
Sibert, M. 44, 264, 272, 374
Sibley, J. 259
Sidenbladh, Karl 325

Sidjanski, D. 232, 237, 272, 389
Siern, R. 574
Siksek, S. G. 574
Simantiras, C. J. 569
Simberg, J. W. F. 439
Simeonoff, I. 288
Simeonoff, I. 311
Simmonds, K. R. 195, 550, 558
Simmonds, R. R. 146
Sinha, S. Prakash 128
Simon, M. 226, 232
Simons, Anne Patricia 479, 496
Simons, W. 53, 345
Simpson, John Hope 255
Simpson, J. L. 340, 359
Sinclair, I. M. 188, 304
Singer, J. David 493
Singh, B. 418
Singh, M. Nagendra, 416
Singh, N. 81, 472
Sinha, Bhek Pati 309
Sinha, S. Prakhesh 128, 259
Siorat, L. 104
Siordet, F. 420
Siotis, J. 418, 491
Siotto Pintor, M. 107
Skubiszewski, K. 380, 469
Slatin, L. 195
Sloan, F. B. 214, 228, 363
Slonim, S. 490
Slouka, Z. J. 159
Slusser, R. M. 96, 264, 288
Sly, John F. 502
Small, J. M. 255
Smets, P. F. 466, 511
Smirnoff, Michael S. V. 180
Smith, C. 72, 342

Smith, Ernest H. 195
Smith, H. A. 44, 75, 99, 146, 165, 402
Smyrniadis, G. 214
Snijder, R. C. 332
Sobaghan, Joseph R. 183
Söder, J. 494, 495
Soderquist, Nils 395
Sofronie, G. 72, 402
Sohn, L. B. 7, 18, 29, 45, 230, 340, 341, 345, 357, 358, 389, 434, 472, 497, 500
Sola Canizures, F. de 561
Soldatos, Panayotis 535
Sommer, 493
Sørensen, M. 45, 93, 146, 242, 307, 441, 460, 520, 518
Soto, J. de 320, 527, 548
Sottile, A. 410, 448
Soubeyrol, J. 341
Sountausta, 112
Spaight, J. M. 170, 402
Spatafora, 497
Spencer, J. H. 301
Sperduti, G. 56, 72, 95, 108, 215, 230, 237, 274, 393, 494
Spiropoulos, J. 45, 89, 108, 134, 410, 426, 448
Sprung, Rudolf 529
Stadtmüller, G. 53
Stambuk, George 200
Stanger, R. J. 200, 337
Stanley, Timothy W. 523
Starace, V. 357
Starke, J. G. 45, 72, 96, 357, 374
Starushenko, G. B. 384
Stassinopoulos, M. 304
Staudacher, Hermann 395
Stawell, F. Melian 376
Stedingk, Yvonne von 255

Steed, W. 308
Steffan, B. A. 295
Steger, F. S. E. 393
Stein, E. 416, 516, 535, 546
Steinbach, Peter A. 247
Steiner, G. 422
Steiniger, P. A. 89
Steinlein, Wilhelm, 389
Sterky, Hakan 503
Stevenson, J. R. 146
Stewart, R. R. 276, 506
Stichele, M. van der 325
Stillmunkers, P. 359
Stilz, Richard 393
Stimson, H. 410, 448
Stinson, J. W. 272
Stirling, Patrick 195
Stoerk, F. 247
Stoessinger, J. B. 493
Stoetzer, O. Carlos 561
Stokvis, H. J. 507
Stoll, J. A. 341
Stone, J. 221, 300, 342, 374, 390, 438
Stone, O. 159, 195
Stosic, B. D. 454
Stowell, Ellery C. 45, 195, 385
Strachey, A. 403
Strange, Susan 527
Strisower, Leo 403
Strohl, Mitchell P. 167
Strömberg, H. 45, 188
Strupp, K. 2, 14, 45, 53, 89, 345, 385, 438
Stuart, Graham H. 117, 203, 204
Stryckmans, F. 240
Sturzo, Luigi 406
Stuyt, A. M. 12, 99, 274
Suarez, Francisco 50
Sucharitkul, S. 189, 565

Sucharitkul, S. 189, 565
Suh, I. R. 359
Sulkowski, J. 505
Sultan, H. 300
Summers, L. M. 340
Summers, Robert Edward 460
Sundberg, Halvar G. F. 45
Sundberg, J. W. F. 171
Sundbom, I. 332
Sureda, A. R. 112
Surrency, E. C. 284
Sursalov, V. M. 264, 313
Süsterhenn, 237
Suy, E. 101, 188, 242, 270, 357
Svarlein, O. 45
Svarlien, O. 215
Swan, C. 146
Swann, D. 544
Swanton, J. R. 403
Swift, R. N. 53
Syatauw, J. 9, 128, 357
Sydow, G. de 267
Symonides, J. 377
Szablowski, G. J. 284
Szasz, Paul C. 514
Szekandi, P. 565
Szokoloczy-Syllaba, Adrienne 519
Sztucki, J. 160

Taborsky, E. 125
Tachi, S. 396
Tager, P. 254
Tager, Thomas E. 181
Takano, Yuichi 285
Talaat, Al Ghunaimi 63

Talalaev, A. N. 313
Tallon, D. 542, 556
Tambaro, G. 403
Tammes, A. J. P. 103, 237, 460, 469
Tandon, Mahash Prasad 46
Tandon, Rajesh 46
Tandon, Y. 497
Tao Cheng 146
Taraconzio, T. A. 64
Tarazi, Salah el Dine 325
Tardu, M. 243
Tashin, H. 104
Taube, M. de 53, 272
Taubenfeld, H. J. 176, 177, 181, 374, 403, 422
Taulbee, J. L. 418
Tayler, W. L. 276
Taylor, Alastair M. 126
Taylor, J. T. 195
Taylor, Paul B. 325
Taylor, Telford 448
Tchernoff, N. 204
Teclaff, L. A. 165
Tchirkovitch, S. 221
Teissedre, Jean 517
Teitelboim, Sergio 150
Tekuelve, Ewald 541
Telchini, I. 553, 556
Telders, B. M. 274
Tempesta, Adalberto 181
Tenekides, G. 126, 215, 311
Tennant, J. S. 304
Terrou, F. 181
Testa, Gaetano, 549
Teubaum, H. 385
Teuben, H. N. 218
Teyssaire, J. 396
Textor, Johann Wolfgang 50

Thayer, Charles W. 204
Theiler, E. 90
Thery, Rene 390
Thierry, Hubert 140
Thirlway, H. W. A. 90, 95, 237
Thirring, Hans 390
Thomas, A. J. 244, 264, 385, 390, 415, 561
Thomas, A. V. W. 264, 385, 390, 415, 561
Thomas, D. D. 184
Thomas, W. Bryn 374
Thomashevsky, Joseph M. 255
Thommen, T. K. 189
Thompson, Virginia 221
Thomson, G. A. 511
Thönnes, August 315
Thornely, P. W. 195
Thorneycroft, E. 430
Thullen, George 490
Tiedemann, K. 232
Timberg, S. 337
Timmerman, J. Aeg. 506
Tobay, Borgoni, 259
Tobiassen, Lief Kr. 495
Tobin, H. J. 308, 309
Tokareva, P. A. 460
Toll, Baron Benno von 454
Toman, J. 402, 414
Tommasi Di Vignano, A. 102
Tomsič, I. 314
Tomuschat, Christian 550
Toriguian, S. 574
Tornaritis, Criton G. 108
Torres Bernardez, S. 204
Tosti, G. 204
Toussaint, C. E. 490
Trabucchi, Alberto 529
Trachtenberg, B. 250

Trampler, K. 126
Trelles, C. Barcia 54
Trémeaud, H. 255
Treves, A. 448
Treves, G. 528
Treves, T. 16
Triepel, Heinrich 72
Trifu, S. 430
Trinkler, B. 280
Tripp, B. M. H. 511
Triska, J. F. 96, 224, 233, 264, 288
Troller, A. 580
Trolliet, Pierre 385
Trubel, H. 218
Truyol, A. 56
Tseng, Yu-Hao 315
Tucker, R. W. 36, 403, 406
Tung, W. L. 61
Tunkin, G. 36, 46, 64, 95, 98, 195, 376
Turack, Daniel C. 249
Turlington, E. 276
Turpin, Jean 259

Ubertazzi, G. M. 463
Udina, M. 90, 122, 126, 259, 260, 269, 478, 505, 527
Udokang, Okon 122
Ueria, J. 205
Uhler, O. M. 413
Ule, R. 536
Ulloa, A. 46
Ullmann, E. von 46
Ulrich, H. 552
Umozurike, U. O. 454
Undén, O. 188, 522, 443

Unemura, M. T. 444
Unger, A. 218
Urbanek, H. 342
Urrutia, F. J. 65, 90
Ustor, E. 518

Vaissière, R. 159
Valentine, D. G. 536
Váli, F. A. 139
Valindas, P. G. 93
Valki, L. 466
Valladão, H. 63, 72, 181
Vallat, Sir Francis 46, 159, 160, 215, 478, 484, 487
Vallee, C. 159
Valindas, P. 98
Valloton, G. 249
Valticos, N. 79, 225, 244, 506
Valverde, Antonio L. 385
Vandenbosch, Amry 478
Vandenbrande, L. 72
Van der Meulen J. 529
Van der Molen, G. H. J. 54
Vanderpol, A. 403
Vandersanden, Georges 536
Van der Vlugt, W. 54
Vandy, Francois 410
Van Hecke, G. 576
Vanwelkenhuyzen, A. 211
Vasak, K. 224, 225, 237, 241, 326
Vasilenko, V. A. 38
Vasquez, M. S. 46, 181
Vattel, E. de 51, 147
Vaucher, M. 343
Veblen, T. 374
Vedel, G. 348, 580

Vedovato, G. 262, 490, 553
Veicopoulos, N. 115, 269
Veiter, Theodor, 254, 255, 260
Veith, W. 569
Velasco, Manuel Diez de 292
Velasco, R. 332
Vellas, P. 18, 47, 516
Velu, J. 218, 237
Venezia, Jean-Caude 394
Venturini, G. 101, 115, 126, 134
Verbaet, Ch. 325Verdoodt, A. 230
Verdross, A. V. 47, 56, 57, 58, 72, 73, 95, 98, 99, 118, 122, 204, 237, 243, 247, 272, 314, 328, 330, 340, 411, 422, 438, 478, 485, 569, 572, 573, 580
Vergez, Henriquez Homero 478
Verloren Van Themaat, P. 524, 528
Vernaeve, L. 529
Vernant, Jacques 255
Vernon, Raymond 515
Verosta, S. 73, 126
Verougstraert, 534
Verplaetse, J.G. 181, 312
Verri, P. 414
Verschoor, 175
Verzijl, J. 9, 54, 147, 206, 221, 312, 314, 357, 358, 360, 367, 403
Veuthey, M. 420
Vichinsky, A. 24, 47
Vichniak, 220
Viefhaus, E. 221
Vignano, A. T. de 340
Vignes, C. H. 367
Vignes, D. 200, 325, 332, 368, 529, 536
Vignol, René 390
Viguer, C. 571
Villacres, J. 200

Villamin, M. L. 440,
Vincke, C. 188
Vinogradoff, P. 54
Virally, M. 58, 73, 126, 469, 478, 489, 500
Vis, L. 238
Visscher, C. de 47, 58, 90, 93, 95, 136, 215, 224, 297, 298, 299, 300, 342, 357, 380, 392, 392, 426, 430, 440
Visscher, F. de 166, 315
Visscher, P. de 66, 166, 204, 274, 279, 326, 478, 527, 584
Visser, L. E. 333
Visser, 'T Hooft, H. Ph. 147, 163
Viswanatha, S. W. 54
Vitoria, Francisco de 51
Vitta, E. 238, 264, 295, 314, 580
Vlasic, I. A. 161, 178, 182
Vliebergh, H. 279
Voelckel, M. 200
Voicu, I. 300
Voight, A. 206
Volchkov, A. F. 443
Vollenhoven, C. van 54, 200
Vom Frieden 403
Vom Krieg 403
Voncken, J. 308, 512
Voogd, L. C. de 561
Voss, H. 523
Vossburgh, J. 3
Vosskamp, H. W. 377
Vulcan, C. 335, 360, 364

Wachter, Alfred von 385
Wackernagel, J. 47
Wade, E. C. S. 277

Wadmond, L. 573
Waelbroeck, M. 304, 529, 536, 548, 556
Waelder, Robert 374
Waeldoeck, M. 103
Wagner, W. 171
Waldkirch, E. V. 47
Waldkirch, G. 422
Waldock, C. H. M. 134, 139, 238, 343, 359, 360
Waldock, Sir Humphrey 47, 215, 380
Walker, A. 385
Walker, H. Jr. 571
Walker, W. L. 134, 150
Wall, Edward H. 536
Walsh, Thomas J. 267
Walter, H. 238
Walters, Francis P. 475
Waltz, K. N. 403
Walz, G. A. 57, 73, 173
Wang, Ming 170
Warne, J. D. 523
Wartburg, W. v. 363
Wasmund, Gunther 411
Wassenberg, H. A. 171, 182
Waters, Maurice 204
Watkins, R. D. 188
Watts, A. D. 200, 367, 401
Weaver, G. L. P. 244
Weaver, James H. 508
Weber, H. 426
Weber, Paul 411
Weber, W. 215, 278
Weber, Yves 537
Weberhorst, J. 146
Wedderburn, K. W. 189
Wefelmeier, H. J. 358
Wegmann, Friedrich 289
Wegner, A. 54, 108, 460

Wehberg, H. 60, 134, 249, 272, 307, 335, 358, 374, 375, 380, 403, 406, 411, 413, 418, 448, 451, 475
Weiden, Paul 393
Weidenmann, H. U. 510
Weldner, R. 315
Weil, G. L. 238, 240, 531
Weinard, G. 537
Weinschel, Herbert 113
Weinstein, J. L. 263
Weiss, C. 243
Weiss, M. 238
Weissberg, Guenter 479
Weiss, P. 189, 248, 251, 255, 256, 260
Wells, D. A. 565
Wells, E. J. M. 569
Welwood, W. 51
Wengler, W. 47, 90, 106, 129, 218, 269, 320, 454, 466, 467, 550
Wenk, Edward 163
Wenner, G. 315
Wenzel, I. 73
Werner, A. R. 147
Werner, H. 256
Wessner, H. P. M. 215, 243
Westlake, J. 47, 394, 396, 414
Weston, B. H. 577
Wheaton, Henry 47
Wheeler-Bennett, J. W. 411
Whitaker, Urban G. Jr. 48
White, G. 342, 580
White, I. 3
White, T. R. 377
Whiteman, M. M. 7, 435
Whitton, J. B. 200, 272, 284
Whiting, A. 60
Widmer, Hans 380

Wiebringhaus, H. 73, 239, 240, 243, 584
Wiedensohler, G. 584
Wiesler, L. 243
Wightman, D. 491
Wijmen, P. C. E. van 326
Wilcox, Clair 515
Wilcox, F. 289, 360, 385
Wild, P. S. Jr. 272
Wildbolz, H. 503
Wildhaber, L. 374
Wilhelm, A. 415
Wilhelm, René-Jean 380
Wilkinson 120
Williams, G. L. 151
Williams, Sir John Fischer 46, 134, 312, 251, 358, 375, 411, 475
Williams, W. L. 374
Willoughby, Westel Woodbridge 426
Willrich, Mason 416
Wilson, C. E. 3, 195
Wilson, G. G. 46, 309, 312
Wilson, R. 302, 331, 341, 570, 571, 572
Winiarski, B. 165, 346, 359
Winkler, C. H. 330
Winkler, G. 326
Winton, Harry N. M. 1
Wise, E. M. 437
Wise, R. L. 487
Witenberg, J. C. 12, 342, 569
Wodie, F. 126
Woetzel, R. K. 438, 449
Wohlfahrt, H. 529, 541, 550
Wold, 224
Wolf, F. 368, 505
Wolff, Christian von 51
Wolff, E. 319
Wolfram, D. 553

Wolfrom, M. 165
Wolgast, E. 46
Wood, H. McKinnon 109
Woodliffe, J. C. 156, 441
Woolsey, J. M. 446
Woolsey, L. H. 136, 284, 309, 316, 426, 484, 584
Worley, F. 284
Wortley, B. A. 440, 529, 580, 584
Wright, Christopher 182
Wright, H. 126, 414
Wright, Philip Quincey 434
Wright, Q. 73, 134, 135, 215, 266, 284, 297, 303, 309, 312, 314, 327, 328, 333, 385, 390, 396, 404, 406, 407, 411, 422, 427, 443, 449, 479, 481, 500
Wright, R. 170
Wright, Sir Robert Alderson (Lord Wright) 449
Wunschik, J. 330Wynne, W. H. 576
Wynner, Edith 374
Wyss, Georg 422

Yakemtchouk, R. 66, 308, 523
Yanguas Messia, J. Ma. 216
Yankov, A. 361
Yates, J. 24
Yates, P. L. 510
Ydit, M. 117
Yeltekin, N. 216
Yemin, Edward 469
Yepes, E. 150
Yepès, J. M. 65, 147, 264, 427, 475, 562, 561
Yessade, Pierre B. 558
Yi-Ting-Chang 304
Yntema, H. E. 435
Yokota, K. 135, 443

Yotis, Ch. 345
You, P. 300
Young, E. 195, 204
Young, R. 156, 159, 160, 195, 537
Yuen-Li Liang, 295

Zachariade, Z. 454
Zacklin, R. 147, 470
Zakharov, N. A. 48
Zanardi, P. L. 392
Zanden, J. W. van der 280
Zanghi, C. 244, 377
Zannini, W. 289, 385
Zarges, A. N. 170
Zeileissen, C. 196
Zellweger, H. 434
Zemanek, K. 73, 120, 263, 462, 466
Zhukov, G. P. 182, 185
Ziccardi, P. 48, 95, 497
Zorgbibe, C. 420
Zorn, Albert 48
Zotiades, G. B. 58, 275
Zouche, Richard, 51
Zourek, J. 205, 390, 449, 565
Zuleeg, Manfred 556
Zumstein, H. 280
Zvenko, R. Rode 249
Zwanenberg, Anna van 151
Zweigert, K. 99, 129, 528
Zylicz, M. 182
Zypthen-Adeler, H. 256

Ref
Z
6461
D63
1975

OCT 14 1976